FROMMER'S
WONDERFUL WEEKENDS
FROM NEW YORK CITY

F R O M M E R ' S

WONDERFUL WEEKENDS
FROM NEW YORK CITY

BY MARILYN WOOD

Macmillan • USA

MACMILLAN TRAVEL
A Simon & Schuster Macmillan Company
1633 Broadway
New York, NY 10019

Find us online at **http://www.mgr.com/travel** or
on America Online at Keyword: **Frommer's.**

Library of Congress Cataloging-in-Publication Data

Wood, Marilyn, 1948–
Wonderful Weekends from New York City

"A Frommer book."
Includes index.
1. Middle Atlantic States—Description and travel—
Guidebooks. 2. New England—Description and travel—
1981–   —Guidebooks. 3. New York Region—
Description and travel—Guidebooks. I. Title. II.
Title: Wonderful Weekends from New York City (form-
erly Marilyn Wood's Wonderful Weekends).
F106.W795 1996   917.4'0443   87-6991
ISBN: 0-02-860929-8

Editor: Ron Boudreau
Production Editor: Trudy Brown
Design by Amy Peppler Adams—designLab, Seattle
Digital Cartography by Raffaele Degennaro and Ortelius Design
Maps copyright © by Simon & Schuster, Inc.

Special Sales
Bulk purchases (10+ copies) of Frommer's Travel Guides are available
to corporations at special discounts. The Special Sales Department
can produce custom editions to be used as premiums and/or for sales
promotion to suit individual needs. Existing editions can be produced
with custom cover imprints such as corporate logos. For more information write to: Special Sales, Simon & Schuster, 1633 Broadway,
New York, NY 10019.

Manufactured in the United States of America.

CONTENTS

VERMONT & NEW HAMPSHIRE
◄○►

MAPS

About the Author

Marilyn Wood came to the United States from England to study journalism at Columbia University. The former editorial director of Macmillan Travel, she has also worked as a reporter, ranch hand, press officer, and book reviewer. In addition, Marilyn is the author of *Frommer's London from $55 a Day* and *Frommer's Toronto,* a co-author of *Frommer's Canada,* and a contributor to *Frommer's Europe from $50 a Day.* Currently she's at work on *Wonderful Weekends* guides from San Francisco, Boston, and Washington, D.C.

Invitation to the Reader

In researching this book, I discovered many wonderful places—inns, restaurants, shops, and more. I'm sure you'll find others. Please tell me about them, so I can share the information with your fellow travelers in upcoming editions. If you were disappointed with one of my recommendations, I'd love to know that, too. Please write to:

Marilyn Wood
Frommer's Wonderful Weekends from New York City
℅ Macmillan Travel
1633 Broadway
New York, NY 10019

A Disclaimer

Please be advised that travel information is subject to change at any time—and this is especially true of prices. We therefore suggest that you write or call ahead for information when making your travel plans. The authors, editors, and publisher cannot be held responsible for the experiences of readers while traveling. Your safety is important to us, however, so we encourage you to stay alert and be aware of your surroundings. Keep a close eye on cameras, purses, and wallets, all favorite targets of thieves and pickpockets.

SIX IMPORTANT TOPICS

Prices & Hours: Although I've made every effort to obtain correct and current prices and hours for establishments and attractions, these can change swiftly and dramatically. Changes in ownership, changes in policy, and inflation can all affect this information. For prices beyond 1996, add about 10% to 15% to the given rates per year.

Reservations: These are a must on weekends. For accommodations they should be made well in advance, in some cases as much as three months ahead and in exceptional circumstances as much as a year (at Saratoga, for example, during the racing meet). Dinner reservations, especially for Friday and Saturday, should be made ahead of time.

Minimum Stays: Most places demand minimum stays of two or three nights on weekends and four nights on holiday weekends during high season, sometimes year round. This information hasn't always been included, so check ahead.

Deposits: These are often nonrefundable since they're the innkeeper's only defense against those folks who don't show up, especially when the weather is inclement. Always clarify this when you book.

Taxes: I haven't included these in the quoted rates. Percentages vary from state to state.

A Note on the Dining Listings: Since this book is designed for people taking weekend breaks, where possible I've listed the restaurants under headings that reflect this fact. That is, "Dinner Only" means that the restaurants under this heading aren't open for lunch on Saturday or Sunday. It does not mean that they don't serve lunch at all—they may well do so on weekdays, but they're not open for lunch to weekenders.

Getting In & Out of New York City

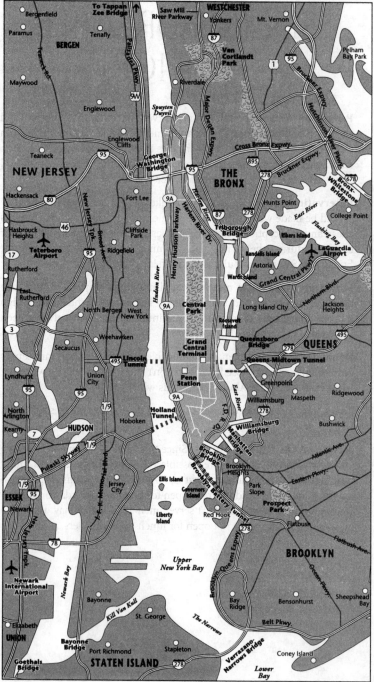

Introduction

By Thursday, most of us harried urban or suburban dwellers are looking forward to the weekend, eagerly anticipating a break from our busy work routine and the chance to get away from the tarmac—to relax, calm our jangled nerves, and rediscover who we really are. And that's what this book is all about: two- or three-day breaks among the lakes, or in the mountains, or in the forests, or down along the shore, or even in another exciting but refreshingly new metropolis—and all within two to four hours' driving time of the city of New York.

So often we forget that the city is surrounded by many alluring yet serene hideaways and head off either for far-flung destinations or to a summer house to which we retreat every weekend for two or three months, rain or shine, to meet the same faces and the same vistas. Why not take a risk and explore what's around you in your own backyard, meet new faces and new friends, and explore new places every weekend? In short, why not come weekending?

There are country markets and fairs, horse shows, music, theater, apple and oyster festivals, flower shows, antique car markets, horse races, and a myriad of other festive celebrations and events to attend. There are all kinds of unique museums and art galleries; historic homes filled with the drama and personalities of those who've lived there; whole villages that seem to exist as tranquilly today as they did 200 years ago; fascinating communities of Shakers, mystics, and Amish; artists' and writers' studios; ostentatious and lavish mansions by the sea where outrageous events were staged; fantastic buildings created by personalities like Frederic E. Church and Henry Chapman Mercer; and camping, fishing, skiing, sailing, swimming, or doing whatever you relish and enjoy. Or you can simply opt for a rocking chair and a cup of tea or a cocktail on a broad veranda overlooking a verdant garden or vista.

And while you're enjoying all this, you can stay in 17th-century riverside inns; old sea captains' homes; luxurious hotels that once welcomed Paganini; Italianate, Greek Revival, and castlelike mansions that once belonged to robber barons; bracketed and gingerbread Victorian fantasies with turrets and lacy trimmings; farms where you'll be awakened by the crowing of the cockerel; old mills; and even a caboose surrounded by quiet fields. Your choices are endless, and so are the delights of the table— juicy sweet lobsters from New England's waters, continental cuisine served in elegant hotel dining rooms or old-world taverns, hearty farm meals, and picnics savored at music festivals or by the ocean.

To arrange your weekend in a way that suits your particular needs and personality requires a certain amount of planning. When you have only two days, you need to know where you want to stay and can't waste precious moments trekking to a well-regarded restaurant at Saturday noon only to find it closed or in circling around looking for a perfect picnicking spot.

This guide has been researched and written to forestall such problems and deliver you, the weekender, from any such headaches, leaving you free to concentrate on roaming and fully enjoying your weekend your way. It's designed to help you step by step in the planning process. Each destination opens with a section that lists details about getting there by car or public transportation and estimated driving times, plus a box on ultra-special seasonal events you may want to plan your weekend around (or plan to avoid, depending on your attitude toward crowds). Getting out of the city on a Friday afternoon or evening can be a real hassle and you may well want to choose public transport over driving. If you do decide to rent a car, book well in advance. Unfortunately, detailed road maps are really beyond the scope of this book, but you can get some by calling the Automobile Association of America, if you're a member, at 212/757-2000.

After these opening sections, there follows a brief general introduction to the history and highlights of the place, then a detailed description of what your weekend is really all about: what to see, what to do, and what to explore. Inevitably, it's a very personal choice. When it comes to museums, you may feel like Louis Kahn, who commented (though he designed several), "I get tired immediately upon entering a museum," or, conversely, like Thomas Hoving, who described a museum as a "place for people to battle against the blows of technology and the misery of life." You may regard the ocean in the words of Wallace Stevens as "dirty, wobbly, and wet," or you may relish sailing on it as much as Sir Francis Chichester obviously did. You may relegate sports and those who practice them to the "Toy Department," or you may enjoy the challenge of rigorous exercise.

Therefore I've described the many choices available and offered some guidance about how to organize your two or three days and highlighted what I consider the real finds of each destination. You, of course, will pursue your own interests, whether they're architecture, historic houses, antiques, graveyards, gardens, art galleries, museums, theater, birdwatching, fruit picking, or more active pursuits from windsurfing to skiing, swimming, golf, horseback riding, and so on. These last I've covered in a section on special and recreational activities at the end of each chapter (except in certain cases where it made more sense to place them at the end of each section in the chapter). In this section I've located public sports facilities wherever possible, but I make no claims as to their quality and standards of service.

I tackle the problem of lodging next, and while I'm on the subject, I can't urge you strongly enough to make reservations—in peak summer and fall seasons, as much as five or six months in advance, *especially on weekends*. I've selected what I consider especially appealing places—an Italian palazzo, a working Mennonite farm, a converted grist mill—including a great number of inns and bed-and-breakfasts wherever they exist, grand and sometimes funky downtown hotels that often offer alluring weekend packages, and, on rare occasions, your typical motel chain for those who desire that kind of accommodation or where there simply is no other alternative. In each case, I've endeavored to convey the atmosphere and type of lodging and treatment you can expect to receive. I've listed the rates, but I urge you always to check on them when you make reservations because undoubtedly prices will have changed by the time this book reaches your hands. And do keep in mind that many inns have two- or sometimes three-night minimums on weekends and that weekend packages are offered on a space-available basis. Though this doesn't pretend to be a camper's guide, I've included some camping ideas, usually state parks and other wilderness areas. Commercial campgrounds and trailer parks aren't listed here.

Next I cover the problem of meals. I know an Englishwoman who built a successful restaurant around the honest, nutritious breakfast she served, one that's so difficult to find unless you know where to go—freshly squeezed juices, farm eggs, fine Canadian bacon, good spicy sausage, homemade bread and muffins. If your lodging doesn't provide breakfast, you, too, will have to search for a breakfast or brunch spot, unless you're willing to settle for the easily found Howard Johnson's, McDonald's, or Denny's. Wherever possible, I've tried to help you out, though it hasn't always been easy—and in some cases I've given up. Similarly, Saturday lunch can prove elusive—many restaurants close for lunch on Saturday—and so I've tried to find the best of those available. Often, though, on a balmy Saturday you'll want to take a picnic somewhere overlooking the ocean or a river. Sadly, I've discovered that unlike in France or England, where you can pull into a field and stretch out among the poppies with a fine bottle of wine, some garlic sausage, and a baguette, it's a little harder and more formal in the United States. So I've tried to direct you to state parks and other idyllic settings for your leisurely meal *en plein air* and also to the suppliers of your picnic fare.

For dinner I've described a selection of restaurants serving a diversity of cuisines for you to choose from. And in each destination I've included unique local favorites. In all cases I've relied on a mixture of my own judgment and experience as well as local recommendations. Hours and prices are all included to help your planning.

And finally, though many of the country destinations that appear in this book lack any rousing nightlife (which is precisely why you've chosen to go there, isn't it?), I've tried to include some nightlife options, if only in a cozy convivial bar.

T. H. White wrote, "The Victorians had not been anxious to go away for the weekend. The Edwardians, on the contrary, were nomadic." Let's be positively nomadic. And one final thing—if you feel like it, you can always rewrap this volume in a brown paper cover and rename it "Marvelous Midweek Breaks from New York City" if your working routine affords you such blissful luxury.

Either way, happy traveling!

CONNECTICUT

The Litchfield Hills, Norwalk & the Danbury-Ridgefield Area

Distance in Miles: Norwalk, 45; Westport, 47; Danbury, 66; Woodbury or Litchfield, 99; Sharon, 111; Winsted, 117

Estimated Driving Time: 1 hour to Westport, 2 hours to Litchfield, 2 hours to Winsted

◄○►◄○►◄○►◄○►◄○►

Driving: Take the Henry Hudson Parkway north to the Sawmill River Parkway, take Rte. 684 north to Brewster, and then get on I-84 east to Danbury (Exit 7). Take Rte. 7 north to New Milford and then Rte. 202 east to Litchfield.

For the Salisbury area, take the Taconic Parkway to Rte. 44 all the way into Salisbury, or take I-684 to Rte. 22 north and then to Rte. 44.

For Winsted, take I-84 to the Waterbury exit and pick up Rte. 8 north.

Bus: Bonanza (tel. 800/556-3815) travels to New Milford, Kent, Southbury, Gaylordsville, Sheffield, Danbury, and Waterbury.

Train: The closest destinations by train are Brewster, Danbury, and Waterbury East (via Metro North's Harlem line), and South Norwalk, Westport, Southport, and Fairfield (via Metro North's New Haven line). Call 212/532-4900.

Further Information: For more about the area's events and festivals and about Connecticut in general, call or write **Connecticut State Tourism,** 865 Brook St., Rocky Hill, CT 06067 (tel. 860/258-4335, or 800/282-6863).

For specific information about the Litchfield area, contact the **Litchfield Hills Travel Council,** P.O. Box 968, Litchfield, CT 06759 (tel. 860/567-4506); and about Danbury, Bethel, and Ridgefield, contact the **Housatonic Valley Travel Commission,** 46 Main St. (P.O. Box 406), Danbury, CT 06813 (tel. 203/743-0546).

For more on Norwalk and Westport, contact **Coastal Fairfield County Visitor Information,** 297 West Ave., Norwalk, CT 06850 (tel. 800/866-7925).

One weekend or several spent exploring the northwest corner of Connecticut, the so-called Litchfield Hills, will take you along roads bordered by hedgerows dotted with colorful wildflowers, past sagging old russet barns, through forests and fields and over rolling hills to the classic New England town of Litchfield and the lesser-known but picturesque hamlets of Cornwall, Sharon, and Salisbury. All are perfect in their quiet unassuming way, hence their appeal to their many wealthy residents, like Henry Kissinger, Tom Brokaw, Oscar de la Renta, and Philip Roth. In Salisbury you're only 4 miles from the Massachusetts border, 12 miles from the southern Berkshire town of South Egremont, and well within striking distance of Tanglewood and Lenox.

The prime reason, though, for visiting this pretty part of Connecticut is to unwind in the countryside—by cycling along backroads, stopping at roadside inns, enjoying historic villages where gracious houses stand under stately old trees surrounded by perfectly manicured lawns, browsing in the many antiques stores, seeking out craft and country fairs, hiking through the forests, boating on the lakes, canoeing on and fishing in the rivers, and generally refreshing and resuscitating the tarnished urban spirit.

You can travel in one long loop from New Milford, hugging the banks of the Housatonic River along Rte. 7, to Bull's Bridge and Kent. Continue along Rte. 7 and you'll come to the villages of Cornwall Bridge, West Cornwall, and Cornwall. At West Cornwall you can either continue farther north on Rte. 7 to Falls Village, the center of canoeing on the Housatonic, or detour west to Sharon, the auto-racing track at Lime Rock, Salisbury, and Lakeville before rejoining Rte. 7 and then turning off east along Rte. 44 to Norfolk. From Norfolk it's only 10 miles or so to Riverton, home of the Hitchcock chair factory, and Winsted, site of a renowned spring mountain laurel festival. Another 10 miles brings you to Torrington, only a stone's throw along Rte. 202 from Litchfield. From Litchfield you can take Rte. 202 past Bantam and New Preston, with a detour to Lake Waramaug, and return eventually to New Milford. You can drive a shorter loop by starting in Southbury and taking Rte. 67 to Roxbury, then Rte. 199 to Washington and Washington Depot, before returning along Rte. 47 to Southbury via Woodbury. This makes for a particularly fine antiquing weekend.

Another weekend can be enjoyed exploring the revitalized Historic District of South Norwalk and afterward driving north to Wilton and Cannons Crossing, then into Ridgefield and nearby Bethel and Danbury. Each has something to offer the visitor, as you'll discover farther on.

Events & Festivals to Plan Your Trip Around

May: Dogwood Festival, Greenfield Hill, Fairfield (usually the first and second weekends).

Sports-car racing, Lime Rock (begins Memorial Day weekend and continues on major holidays until mid-October). Call 860/435-2571.

June: Winsted Mountain Laurel Festival, with a parade, a waterskiing exhibition, and other entertainments. Contact the mayor's office (tel. 860/379-2713).

Falls Village Music Mountain Chamber concerts, with the Manhattan String Quartet and others (through mid-September). Call 860/824-7126 for information and reservations.

Yale's Norfolk Chamber Music Festival, with the Tokyo String Quartet and others, at the Ellen Battell Stoeckel Estate, Norfolk (through July). Call 860/436-3690 for information or 860/542-3000 for the box office.

July: Round Hill Scottish Games, Norwalk (July 4).

Open house tour, Litchfield (usually the Saturday after July 4).

Sharon Audubon Festival, with lectures and nature walks led by top authorities (late July).

August: SONO Arts Celebration, Washington and South Main streets (usually the first weekend).

Art of Northeast USA, at the Silvermine Guild Center for the Arts, 1037 Silvermine Rd., Norwalk. Call 203/966-5617.

September: Goshen County Fair (usually Labor Day weekend).

Norwalk Oyster Festival, with arts, crafts, a boat parade, fireworks, folk dancing, and, of course, oysters (usually the weekend after Labor Day). Contact the Norwalk Seaport Association, 81 Washington St., South Norwalk, CT 06854 (tel. 203/838-9444).

Chrysanthemum Festival, Bristol (last week of September, first of October). Contact the Bristol Chamber of Commerce, 55 N. Main St., Bristol, CT 06010 (tel. 860/584-4718).

October: Riverton Fair (usually the second weekend).

Salisbury Antiques Fair and Fall Festival (usually the second weekend). Contact the Salisbury Town Hall (tel. 860/435-9511).

THE LITCHFIELD HILLS &
HOUSATONIC RIVER

ALONG THE HOUSATONIC FROM NEW MILFORD
TO THE CORNWALLS

Area Attractions

If you appreciate arts, crafts, and cuisine, you'll want to stop in New Milford at the **Silo** on Upland Road, off Rte. 202 (tel. 860/355-0300), which is owned by Ruth and Skitch Henderson of Boston Pops fame. Here in a wonderful old barn you'll find a first-rate gallery featuring some fine local arts and crafts; a store selling kitchenware, china, and gourmet foodstuffs; and a cooking school where you can take weekend classes.

Hours: Daily 10am–5pm.

Return to New Milford and take Rte. 7 north through Gaylordsville to **Bull's Bridge,** which dates back to the Revolution and is one of two covered bridges in the state open to automobile traffic. From here it's only 3 miles to Kent, where there are several fine antiques shops, boutiques, and several art galleries. For example, the **Kent Antiques Center,** in Kent Station Square on Main Street (tel. 860/927-3313), has 12 dealers. The **Paris–New York–Kent Gallery,** also in Kent Station Square (tel. 860/927-3357), has a solid reputation as a fine-arts gallery. On Rte. 7, a mile north of Kent, is the **Sloane Stanley Museum** (tel. 860/927-3849), which has an extensive collection of Early American tools amassed by the late artist/writer Eric Sloane to commemorate "the early American's ingenuity, craftsmanship, and reverence for wood." Lathes, chisels, scythes, and axes are displayed to emphasize their many versatile uses. Sloane's cluttered studio has also been faithfully re-created and some of his paintings are on view in a special gallery.

Hours: Late May–Oct, Wed–Sun 10am–4pm. **Admission:** $3 adults, $1.50 seniors and children 6–17.

Slightly farther north, **Kent Falls State Park** is well known for its 200-foot waterfall, which is especially lovely in spring. Take the short steep trail to the head of the falls.

About 10 miles north of Kent you'll reach Cornwall Bridge, home of the famous **Cornwall Bridge Pottery** (tel. 860/672-6545), renowned for stoneware. Continue north, passing by Housatonic Meadows State Park, into the village of West Cornwall. Before your reach the village, if you're interested you can sign up for a canoeing adventure with **Clarke Outdoors** (see "The Litchfield Hills Area: Special & Recreational Activities," below). West Cornwall is well known for its fine craftspeople, but best known for its **covered bridge,** built in 1837 of native oak; it's on Rte. 128 (off Rte. 7 north, 5 miles north of Cornwall Bridge). This is a scenic spot, the bridge spanning the rapids below.

West Cornwall has two excellent craft stores worth browsing: **Cornwall Bridge Pottery Store** (tel. 860/672-6545) and **Ian Ingersoll Cabinetmakers** (tel. 860/672-6334), which specializes in reproduction furniture in the Shaker tradition. Continue north along Rte. 7 into Falls Village, but before you reach the town, detour along Rte. 112 to the car-racing track at Lime Rock. The stretch of the river around Falls Village was at one time heavily industrialized, and the mills and factories (most significantly the Ames Iron Works) turned Falls Village into a boomtown in the early 1800s. The Falls Village hydroelectric plant still functions today. From Falls Village take Rte. 126 north to Rte. 44 and continue on Rte. 44 until it links with Rte. 7. From here Rte. 7 crosses the border into Massachusetts to Sheffield and Great Barrington (see the Berkshires chapter).

At Cornwall Bridge, you can turn off along Rtes. 4 and 41 to Sharon, a charming old town noted for its gracious large homes. From Sharon, pick up Rte. 41 north through Lakeville, home of the **Hotchkiss School,** to Salisbury. This picturesque village is the site of a busy flea market in late September and also of a large antiques fair in the fall, when the foliage is at its peak. From Salisbury take Rte. 44 back to Rte. 7.

New Milford Lodging

The mid-18th-century **Homestead Inn,** 5 Elm St., New Milford, CT 06776 (tel. 860/354-4080), is at the center of town facing the Village Green. The main building's eight rooms are traditionally furnished with chintz wallpapers, dried flower wreaths, and other country touches. Another six rooms, clean and comfortable, are in a motel-style building. Guests may use the living room and front porches to relax.

Rates (including continental breakfast buffet): $88–$100 double in the main house, $75–$83 double in the motel building.

Bull's Bridge & Kent Lodging & Dining

The British and the American flag fly outside the white clapboard house with green shutters named the **Chaucer House,** 88 N. Mountain St., Kent, CT 06757 (tel. 860/927-4858). It's conveniently located on the main street, a short stroll from the Kent galleries and stores. British owners Alan and Brenda Hodgson welcome guests warmly into their home, where they offer four rooms (two with bath). A full breakfast is served.

Rates (including breakfast): $79–$89 double.

Litchfield Hills

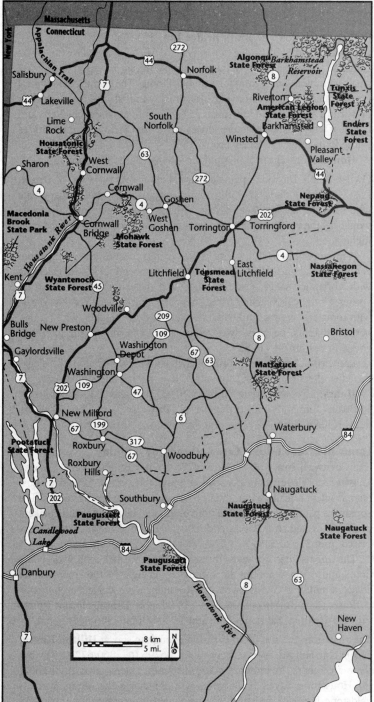

Named after Jacob and Mary Bull, who established the first inn here during the Revolution, the **Bull's Bridge Inn,** 333 Kent Rd., on Rte. 7 between Kent and Bull's Bridge (tel. 860/927-1617), is a local favorite. Folks gather at the bar separating the two simple dining rooms, and there's a small patio with an awning for summer dining. The menu offers typical continental/American dishes like blackened swordfish or salmon, chicken or shrimp fajita with fruit salsa, grilled maple-mustard chicken, and meatloaf with mashed potatoes. Prices range from $9 to $16. Bull's Bridge is also known for its Sunday brunch.

Hours: Mon–Thurs 5–9:30pm, Fri–Sat 5–10pm, Sun noon–9pm.

Owner Dolph Traymon's piano artistry alone makes the **Fife 'n' Drum,** Rte. 7, Kent (tel. 860/927-3509), worth a trip. Dolph, a Juilliard graduate who used to play for Peggy Lee and Frank Sinatra, plays nightly. Some would say the very popular tap room is also worth the trip. The food rates highly too.

A mixture of barn siding, bricks, and country scenes, the dining room is quite formal and a few of the dishes are flambéed tableside. Duckling with a brandied sauce, steak au poivre, and chateaubriand are classic favorites, along with veal and fish dishes. The herb-crusted chicken breast with tomatoes, capers, and balsamic sauce and the chicken with juniper berries, shallots, peppers, sweet chili, garlic, and gin set the tastebuds going. Prices run $15 to $23.

Luncheon changes daily. Brunch changes weekly and along with eggs Benedict offers roast leg of lamb, chicken au poivre, and similar fare.

Hours: Mon and Wed–Thurs 11:30am–3pm and 5:30–9:30pm, Fri 11:30am–3pm and 5:30–10pm, Sat 11:30am–3pm and 5:30–10:30pm, Sun 11:30am–9pm.

Cornwall Bridge & West Cornwall Lodging & Dining

The **Cornwall Inn,** Rte. 7, Cornwall Bridge (tel. 860/672-6884), is well known to locals for its hearty food at reasonable prices. A roadside hostelry, it offers a really warm, homey welcome in two dining rooms. The cooking is plain—steaks, grilled trout or salmon, honey-mustard chicken, prime rib, baked stuffed sole, and fettuccine with clam sauce or Alfredo, priced from $10 to $19.

The inn also has five guest rooms (three with bath), with wide-plank floors and country antique furnishings, plus eight plainer rooms in an adjacent building. Guests have access to a sitting room and an outdoor pool.

Rates (including breakfast): $80–$115 double. **Dining Hours:** Thurs–Fri 5:30–8:30pm, Sat noon–2pm and 5:30–8:30pm, Sun noon–7pm.

The view from the sun room is reason enough to stay at **Hilltop Haven,** 175 Dibble Hill Rd., West Cornwall, CT 06796 (tel. 860/672-6871), but there are others, including the 63 surrounding acres on a bluff above the Housatonic River. Book lovers will appreciate the library with its fieldstone fireplace and walls, soaring cathedral ceiling, Oriental rugs, floor-to-ceiling glass bookcases, and Victorian furnishings. There are also a homey sitting room and a wraparound veranda. Grand Marnier French toast is one of the likely breakfast items. Only two rooms have a bath, a phone, and air conditioning, making them a veritable hideaway.

Rates (including breakfast): $115 double.

West Cornwall Dining

The **Brookside Bistro,** on Rte. 128 in West Cornwall (tel. 860/672-6601), has a serene location overlooking a fast-flowing brook. In summer the deck is the preferred dining area; at other times diners sit on burgundy or dusty-pink banquettes at butcher-block tables in a light, modern room. The menu changes frequently but always features French classics. For example, there might be full-flavored coq au vin, ribeye steak with béarnaise sauce, and mussels poached in a broth of white wine and shallots and served with garlic mayonnaise. Prices range from $15 to $16. Appetizers might include brie en croûte with leek sauce, pâté maison, or eggplant tart layered with spinach, tomatoes, onions, and basil. Similar classics are offered at lunch—beef bourguignon and seafood gratin (scallops and shrimp baked in a casserole) and several charcuterie salads.

Hours: Thurs–Mon noon–2pm and 6–9pm. **Closed:** Three weeks in Mar.

Sharon Lodging

The 1890 **Colonial Bed & Breakfast,** Rte. 41 (P.O. Box 25), Sharon, CT 06069 (tel. 860/364-0436), is an elegant center-hall colonial home set on 5 acres. The innkeeper was formerly a Pan Am flight attendant and the comfortable living room is filled with objets d'art she acquired all over the world—Japanese screens, Indian Buddhas, Etruscan pieces, and so on. The three guest rooms (all with bath) are spacious and eclectically furnished with a mixture of pieces. One has a private entrance and offers a kitchenette with a hotplate, sink, and microwave. The suite with twin beds and a sitting room is pleasant too.

Rates (including breakfast): Summer, $119 double weekends, $95 double weekdays. The rest of the year, $105 double weekends, $85 double weekdays.

Lodging & Dining in Dover Plains, N.Y.

Across the state border, the **Old Drovers Inn,** on East Duncan Road, 3 miles south of Dover Plains off Rte. 22 (tel. 914/832-9311), is loaded with atmosphere acquired over the last 250 years. The stairs leading to the four guest rooms creak, as do the floors, and the ceilings are low. The upstairs library offers three walls of books for reading in the comfy chairs in front of the wood-molded fireplace. Two other sitting rooms are available, both with fireplaces—one formally furnished in Empire style with a striking bull's-eye mirror. The guest rooms (three with a wood-burning fireplace) are variously furnished. One has a sleigh bed; another contains cannonball beds, wing chairs for fireside dozing, candlestand tables, and wainscoting. The Meeting Room has a unique barrel-shaped ceiling and is furnished with two antique beds, a fireplace, a desk, and wing chairs.

The Tap Room, with its crackling fire, heavy wood beams, stone walls, and attractive old banquettes, is one of the region's most appealing dining rooms. Pewter and china adorn the space; copper pans, scoops, and strainers grace the brick fireplace. The tables are set with candles, pewter, and burgundy cloths. The bill of fare is written on a chalkboard, and although it changes daily, it's likely to offer the following for dinner: browned turkey hash with mustard sauce, broiled double-cut rack of lamb chops, roast monkfish filet with yellow-pepper vinaigrette, and saddle of venison with wild mushrooms and lingonberries. Appetizers might include lobster-and-corn chowder, vegetable terrine with tomato vinaigrette, and cheddar-cheese soup, an Old Drovers specialty. Dinner prices run $17 to $35; luncheon fare is similar but priced from $11.75 to $18.75. The outdoor patio is lovely in summer.

Rates: $140–$200 double weekdays, $300–$375 double weekends.
Dining Hours: Mon noon–2:30pm (dinner by reservation only, with last booking at 7pm), Thurs noon–2:30pm and 5:30–8:30pm, Fri noon–2:30pm and 5:30–9:30pm, Sat noon–9pm, Sun 1–8:30pm.

An Exceptional Retreat & a Special Dining Experience in Amenia, N.Y.

For a truly inspirational weekend retreat, head to **Troutbeck,** Leedsville Road, Amenia, NY 12501 (tel. 914/373-9681). Acres of flower- and shrub-filled gardens spread around this lovely ivy-covered Tudoresque country house, which once belonged to Myron B. Benton, a poet/naturalist friend of John Burroughs, Emerson, and Thoreau; it was a gathering place for 1920s literati and liberals. A brook courses through the gardens (you cross a small humpbacked stone bridge to reach the slate-roofed portico) and along its banks daffodils, blue grape hyacinth, and crimson, gold, and purple tulips blossom in spring. Lilacs and apple blossoms add their fragrant scent and colors. Wooden seats dot the lawns—ideal perches for quiet contemplation. Beyond the gardens are over 400 wooded acres.

During the week the property is used for conferences, but on weekends it's open as a country resort. Thirty-six accommodations are in the main house or in nearby buildings (13 in the main house, 18 in the farmhouse, 5 in the Garden House); 31 have baths and 8 have fireplaces. Many have porches and feature canopied beds. Each is decorated uniquely with antique reproductions. Some are furnished in Early American; in the main house the style is more European.

The house is filled with gorgeous authentic antiques. The entrance-parlor floors are covered with Oriental runners and rugs; Chinese porcelain lamps harmonize with a handsome French partner's desk, while richly upholstered French chairs, Queen Anne chairs, and a carved sideboard all blend perfectly. Beamed ceilings, leaded windows, and fresh flowers underline the very English atmosphere. For quiet conversation there's a luxurious sitting room with a grand player-piano and fireplace, plus an adjacent bar with another sitting area and fireplace.

The dining rooms overlook a pond populated with white ducks. The menu changes weekly, but a weekend menu might begin with steamed mussels provençal or a strudel of rock shrimp, chèvre, roasted shallots, and mushrooms with red-pepper coulis. The entrees might consist of nine or so dishes—grilled swordfish with a pineapple-and-cilantro salsa, seared duck with a sauce of cassis, oranges, and port wine, or chicken breast stuffed with sun-dried tomatoes, artichoke hearts, spinach, and smoked mozzarella. Among the desserts might be a chocolate ganache torte or black-bottom lemon cheesecake. An open bar is included for inn guests, and wine is served during meals. In good weather, lunches are served poolside.

There are also tennis courts, indoor and outdoor pools, 13,000 books, and videotapes.

Rates: Fri 5pm–Sun 2pm, $650–$875 per couple (including six meals with drinks). One night only, $360–$485 per couple (including three meals with drinks).

The **Cascade Mountain Winery & Restaurant,** Flint Hill Rd. (tel. 914/ 373-9021), is a leading Hudson Valley winery making a good seyval blanc as well as beaujolais-style reds and late-harvest dessert wine. You can enjoy a visit to the winery, which provides complimentary tours and tastings, and enjoy a luncheon enhanced by the wines. The lunch menu offers a good balance between salads and light and heavier dishes. There might be a fine smoked-trout plate as well as pork medallions in apple-cider sauce; chimichangas stuffed with black beans, goat cheese, and roasted red peppers; and a cheese plate featuring Coach Farms and Hollow Road cheeses. The potato pancake filled with smoked salmon and crème fraîche is a luxurious beginning. To finish, select the thick and rich frozen sabayon with blackberries or fresh apple crisp, also enhanced by sabayon. Prices are $8.50 at lunch and $15 to $20 at dinner.

Hours: Winery tours, daily 10am–6pm; dining, Sun–Fri noon–3pm, Sat noon–3pm and 6–9pm.

Lakeville Lodging & Dining

Although the exterior of the **Interlaken Inn,** 74 Interlaken Rd. (west of Rte. 41 on Rte. 112), Lakeville, CT 06039 (tel. 860/435-9878), screams "modern convention complex," the rooms will win you over with their plush comforts, especially the seven duplex town-house suites at the back of the property, each with a full kitchen, a living room with fireplace, a sleeping loft containing two double beds, two baths, and a tree-shaded deck. The Victorian House's 11 old-world rooms have brass beds and antiques, while the 55 deluxe rooms have a pleasant contemporary look.

And 6 rooms, with Queen Anne reproductions, are in a fine English Tudor–style house.

The Interlaken is set on 26 beautifully kept acres. You can lounge by the heated outdoor pool or on the shore of Lake Wononscopumic, where canoes, paddleboats, and rowboats are available. Two tennis courts, a nine-hole golf course plus pitch-and-putt facility, and a fitness center with racquetball courts complete the facilities.

The Vineyard is for dining in a contemporary atmosphere—grilled tuna with roasted red-pepper beurre blanc, veal chasseur, medallions of pork served with fruit chutney, and a clambake for two. Crab cakes, soups, and tomato slices with mozzarella and basil and are among the appetizers. Save room for the chocolate decadence, a rich chocolate-mousse cake layered with raspberry confit and chocolate cream and served with raspberry sauce, or the laken torte, a walnut-and-maple cake soaked in rum and served with crème Chantilly. Main-course prices range from $16 to $22. There's also a deck for summer dining. Brunch ($16 per person) is buffet style, offering prime rib, ham, smoked salmon, salads, canapés, and much more. The Circuit Lounge, overlooking the pool and cocktail lounge, doubles as a luncheon spot; it's filled with "auto art," which should appeal to Lime Rock visitors. On weekend nights bands entertain here; at Sunday brunch there's usually a folk singer or two.

Rates: Deluxe rooms and Victorian House, $115 double weekends, $99 double weekdays; town-house suite, $275 for two. Rates reduced about 20% in winter. **Dining Hours:** Mon–Thurs 7–10am, 11:30am–2:30pm, and 5:30–9pm; Fri 7–10am, 11:30am–2:30pm, and 5:30–10pm; Sat 7–10:30am, 11:30am–2:30pm, and 5:30–10pm; Sun 7:30–10am, 11am–2pm, and 5:30–9pm.

Lakeville Dining

The **Woodland Restaurant,** Rte. 41 (tel. 860/435-0578), is an airy plant-filled restaurant. In one of the six large booths you can dine at lunchtime on a Woodlands specialty of a muffin with mushrooms, onions, and tomatoes or more substantially at dinner on such items as chicken breast sautéed with leeks and wild mushrooms, salmon crusted with pistachio nuts and served with lemon-champagne beurre blanc, and balsamic-glazed pork chops with grilled eggplant and risotto cakes, priced from $14 to $19.

Hours: Tues–Thurs 11:30am–2:30pm and 5:30–9pm, Fri 11:30am–2:30pm and 5:30–10pm, Sat 11:30am–2pm and 5:30–10pm, Sun 5:30–8:30pm. **Closed:** Two weeks right after Labor Day and two weeks in Mar.

Salisbury Lodging & Dining

The **Ragamont Inn,** Main Street, Salisbury, CT 06068 (tel. 860/435-2372), has offered solace and sustenance to the passing traveler for the last 180 years; today people are still sitting happily under the green-and-white-striped awning shielded from the main street by a hedge or cozily ensconced in the dining room with wide-plank floors warmed by a blazing fire.

The 12 guest rooms are unique and very fairly priced—a suite with a fireplace and low-beamed ceiling rents for only $110. Room 6 is particularly attractive, thanks to the cast-iron stove, pine floor, shield-back chairs, and old desk that give it character.

The dining room is known for the many Swiss-inspired dishes of chef/owner Rolf Schenkel—sauerbraten, wienerschnitzel, and jaegerschnitzel (with white wine and mushrooms), along with fine fresh scrod, salmon, swordfish, and other seafood. Main courses range from $14 to $20. The Linzer torte and peach-custard pie are dessert favorites, while at brunch raclette and beef burgundy add some interest to the usual eggs Benedict and waffles menu.

Rates: May–Nov 1, $85–$115 double. **Dining Hours:** Wed–Thurs 5:30–9pm, Fri–Sat 6–10pm, Sun 11:30am–2pm (brunch) and 5–9pm.

Under Mountain Inn, 482 Under Mountain Rd. (Rte. 41), Salisbury, CT 06068 (tel. 860/435-0242), is 5 miles out of Salisbury in a secluded 1732 white clapboard farmhouse on 3 acres. Here Peter and Marged Higginson offer seven rooms (all with bath) that provide a serene home away from home. They'll most likely contain a large canopied or four-poster bed, a couple of Williamsburg blue wing chairs, and a fine cherry highboy placed on wide-plank floors that are softened by hook rugs. Early American wallpapers add character. The downstairs parlors are comfortable, and among the Early American furnishings you'll find an antique Welsh cupboard that Marged's grandfather made.

In the three intimate dining rooms with fireplaces a limited menu featuring seafood, game (in season), roast goose, chicken tarragon, and similar fare is offered. For British expatriates or Anglophiles there's steak-and-kidney pie and bangers and mash, and Marged provides a "proper" cup of tea out of a pot with a cozy. For dessert there's authentic sherry trifle and home-baked pies. Main courses are priced from $12 to $18. The Union Jack flies outside and the *Manchester Guardian* is available, along with a number of books about Britain.

Rates: $180–$220 (MAP) room for two. **Dining Hours:** Fri–Sat 6–9:30pm.

At the center of Salisbury, the lovely **White Hart Inn,** on the Green, Salisbury, CT 06068 (tel. 860/435-0030), is more than 200 years old. Its 26 rooms are prettily decorated in chintz with antique reproductions (all have a bath, a TV, a phone, and air-conditioning). The inn is famous for the well-prepared and beautifully presented cuisine served in Julie's New American Sea Grill, a comfortable dining room that has a glamorous glow in the evening. Start with the grilled medallions of lobster tail with hoisin vinaigrette or house-smoked sea scallops with asparagus tips and grape-fruit. Among the main courses might be grilled red snapper with fresh nectarines, confit of rosemary and vidalia onions, pan-seared chicken breast with porcini duxelle stuffing and Oloroso sherry, or grilled filet mignon with caraway-herb rub and beet-infused demiglaze. Prices range from $16 to $26. The tavern with a double fireplace is also a popular spot. The front porch is the quintessential place to catch the quiet stirring of a New England village.

Rates: May–Oct, $100–$200 double; Nov–Apr, $85–$160 double.

Dining Hours: Mon–Tues 7:30–10am and noon–2:30pm; Wed–Thurs 7:30–10am, noon–2:30pm, and 5:30–9pm; Fri 7:30–10am, noon–2:30pm, and 5:30–10pm; Sat noon–2:30pm and 5:30–10pm; Sun noon–2pm (buffet) and 5–9pm.

EAST TO NORFOLK, RIVERTON & WINSTED

Area Attractions

From Salisbury, you can take Rte. 44 all the way to Norfolk, which in mid-June and July hosts **Yale's Norfolk Chamber Music Festival** (tel. 860/542-3000), featuring, among others, the Tokyo String Quartet at the Ellen Battell Stoeckel Estate.

To get a sense of this quintessential New England village, walk around the **Green,** noting the Eldridge Fountain, designed by Stanford White; the tall-steepled Church of Christ (ca. 1814), next to the White House (home of the Yale Summer School of Music and Art); the Richardson-style library (ca. 1888); and the Historical Society Museum, featuring a small collection of Connecticut clocks and other local historic artifacts.

Norfolk also has some offbeat attractions. For example, you might like to call ahead and arrange a visit to **harpsichord maker** Carl Dudash's studio (tel. 860/542-5753). At **Hillside Gardens,** Litchfield Road, Norfolk (tel. 860/542-5345), you can purchase some herbaceous perennials and view the gardens of Mary Ann and Frederick McGourty, who are well known in horticultural circles. The **Horse and Carriage Livery** (tel. 860/542-6085) is another interesting stop, where you can sign up for a horse-drawn ride in winter or summer.

Norfolk also boasts three state parks for hiking and picnicking: **Haystack Mountain** (from Norfolk, follow Rte. 44 west and take Rte. 272 north for a mile to the entrance), **Campbell Falls State Park** (another 6 miles along Rte. 272), and **Dennis Hill State Park** (take Rte. 272 south). Haystack and Dennis Hill have at their summits stone monuments affording grand views.

Back on Rte. 44, either you can proceed into Winsted, the self-proclaimed mountain laurel capital, then double back on Rte. 20 to Riverton, or you can drive directly to Riverton by cutting off on one of the backroads.

Riverton was once called Hitchcocksville after the famous **Hitchcock chairs,** still manufactured in the factory (tel. 860/379-4826) where Lambert Hitchcock made his first chair (in 1826) on the bank of the Farmington River, down the street from the Old Riverton Inn.

Hours: Mon–Sat 10am–5pm, Sun noon–5pm.

The **Hitchcock Museum** (tel. 860/738-4950), housed in an old church, displays original furniture stenciled by Hitchcock and his contemporaries.

Hours: Apr to mid-Dec, Thurs–Sun noon–4pm.

Nearby, **People's State Forest,** Rte. 44, Barkhamsted, is a must during fall, as is the area around Winsted in spring, when this town throws a big **Mountain Laurel Festival.** The best place to view the blossoms is at Indian Lookout, off Rte. 4 in Torrington, halfway to Litchfield.

Norfolk Lodging & Dining

The **Mountain View Inn,** Rte. 272, Norfolk, CT 06058 (tel. 860/542-6991), occupies a restored 1875 Victorian. The oak staircase leads to seven rooms (six with bath), some with brass, others with wicker, and still others with heavier Victorian pieces. Guests are served a full American breakfast. On Friday and Saturday the inn is open for dinner; among the specialties offered are steaks, catch of the day, Dijon chicken, and eggplant parmigiana, priced from $15 to $30. Guests can relax on the porch overlooking a corner of the 5-acre grounds and walk to the chamber-music concerts at the Yale Summer School. There's swimming in nearby Toby Lake-Pond.

Rates (including breakfast): $75–$85 double without bath, $95–$145 double with bath.

The **Blackberry River Inn,** Rte. 44, Norfolk, CT 06058 (tel. 860/542-5100), contains 20 rooms (3 with fireplaces), furnished with chintz and maple pieces in a country style. The rooms in the main inn have a fireplace and the suites have either a fireplace or a Jacuzzi. Double fireplaces warm the public areas in the lounge/parlors, and guests can use the cherry-paneled library. There are 27 acres to enjoy, particularly in winter on cross-country skis. An outdoor pool and a tennis court complete the facilities.

Rates (including breakfast): $75–$210 double. **Closed:** Mar. **Dining Hours:** Fri 6–9pm, Sat 6–9:30pm, Sun 5–8pm.

Manor House, the Inn at Norfolk, Maple Avenue (P.O. Box 701), Norfolk, CT 06058 (tel. 860/542-5690), is indeed as grand as it sounds. A late Victorian with tall Elizabethan chimneys and lattice windows, it was built in 1898 by architect Charles Spofford, who helped design, of all things, the London Underground. He was the son of Ainsworth Rand Spofford, a Cincinnati publisher who served in Abe Lincoln's administration. Charles was friendly with Louis Comfort Tiffany, who gave the windows that adorn the library and living room as a housewarming gift. Fine architectural details can be found throughout the house—a classical stucco frieze in the living room depicting Day being led by Night across the Sky, an Italianate green-tile fireplace in the dining room, a cherry-paneled staircase, and geometric patterns everywhere.

Mannequins dressed in antique costumes are scattered about, reflecting the inspiration of Diane Tremblay, who runs the place with her husband, Henry. Both love catering to guests, providing information about the area, and preparing breakfast, which is served in a formal dining room at a large table surrounded by shield-back chairs. A sideboard and silver service add to the gracious atmosphere. Orange waffles, scrambled eggs with chives, blueberry pancakes, and poached eggs with lemon butter and chive sauce might be breakfast choices; these are accompanied by homemade breads, honey from beehives on the property, or raspberries from their own raspberry canes.

Eight uniquely decorated rooms, two with fireplaces, are available. The large Spofford Room has a carved-wood fireplace, a private balcony, and a variety of furnishings—canopied bed, rocker, chest of drawers, dressing table, and cane-backed sofa. The Lincoln Room also has a fireplace; a sleigh bed with a half canopy and a Récamier sofa are two of the pieces rich in character. La Chambre is a small but charming room furnished with a brass-and-iron bed and lilac wing chairs. The English Room features a two-person whirlpool. Additional amenities include games (board games, Trivial Pursuit) in an airy conservatory-style room and chairs and tables for outdoor relaxing.

Rates (including breakfast): $100–$200 double.

Deanne Raymond and George Schumaker have created luxurious surroundings at **Greenwoods Gate,** 105 Greenwoods Rd. East, Norfolk, CT 06058 (tel. 860/542-5439). The parlor of this 1797 center-hall colonial home is richly furnished with Oriental carpeting, pale-lemon wing chairs, a drop-leaf cherry table, a needlepointed French-style chair, and a grand piano; the focal point is the fireplace. The breakfast room contains a round table and, among other fine objects, a breakfront and Deanne's teapot collection. The coziest room is undoubtedly the wood-paneled country-style kitchen, decorated with wicker baskets and a cookie-cutter collection. Here Deanne prepares breakfasts of fresh juice and fruit compote, featuring such dishes as omelets with cream cheese and strawberries, Grand Marnier French toast, and an open-face frittata with spinach, onions, and feta cheese. A deck off the kitchen furnished with white wicker makes an ideal breakfast spot.

All the guest rooms have fresh flowers, starched and ironed bedsheets, and fragrance and other amenities in the baths. The E. J. Truscott Suite, off the kitchen, is very romantic: A Belgian lace coverlet and pillows grace the brass-and-iron bed, while an Empire chest, porcelain lamps, a marble bedside table, and a dollhouse filled with charming miniatures are set against China blue wallpaper. The Lucy Phelps Room is small but prettily turned out in green and rose. The Levi Thompson Suite is the most spectacular and private accommodation. Here you'll find a Jacuzzi bath and a split of champagne. A small foyer leads into a bilevel pink-and-blue room, the lower half serving as a sitting room. Upstairs, the cherrywood bed sits under a brilliant stained-glass window. It's like being in your own dollhouse.

Rates (including breakfast): $80 (Lucy Phelps Room) to $225 (Levi Thompson Suite) for two.

Riverton Lodging & Dining

The **Old Riverton Inn,** Rte. 20 (P.O. Box 6), Riverton, CT 06065 (tel. 860/379-8678), has been quenching the thirsty, feeding the hungry, and soothing the tired since 1796—the uneven floors and small doorways testify to its age. The 12 homey rooms are all uniquely decorated. Room 3, for instance, has a chenille bedspread, a chest, a chair, and an adjustable wooden floor lamp, while its bath has a clawfoot tub/shower. Another room contains wicker chairs and a spinning wheel. A couple of rooms have spindle four-poster beds with a canopy.

Traditional fare is served in the low-beamed dining room—good seafood and steaks, plus such specialties as veal marsala (with mushrooms and Marsala wine) and chicken with black cherry sauce, from $15 to $20.

Rates (including breakfast): $85—$175 double. **Dining Hours:** Wed–Fri noon–2:30pm and 5–8:30pm, Sat noon–2:30pm and 5–9pm, Sun noon–8pm.

LITCHFIELD

Litchfield Attractions

Graceful tree-lined streets, 18th-century residences, and the much-photographed Congregational church at the east end of the Village Green make Litchfield a fine example of a Colonial Revival village. Although many of the homes were built in the late 18th century, a lot have been drastically altered from their original appearance. In fact, many were "colonialized" during the late 19th and early 20th century. Begin your explorations by picking up a map at the historical society (below) or at the information booth at the west end of the Green (summer only).

Try to spend some time at the **Litchfield Historical Society, Library, and Museum,** on the corner of South Street and the Green (tel. 860/567-4501), viewing the permanent display of portraits by Ralph Earl, including one of Mariann Wolcott, whose father, Oliver, was a town luminary and a signer of the Declaration of Independence. A lady of great determination, if her portrait is anything to go by, she undoubtedly helped mold the bullets cast from the statue of George III that had been dragged from New York to her very own backyard during the Revolution. Other exhibits explore the town's history through local furniture, decorative arts, textiles, and photographs.

Hours: Mid-Apr to mid-Nov, Tues–Sat 11am–5pm, Sun 1–5pm. **Admission** (including Tapping Reeve House and Law School, below): $3, free for children 15 and under.

Note: Once a year, Litchfield's **historic homes** are opened to the public, usually during the second weekend in July. Confirm the dates with the historical society or the Litchfield Hills Travel Council.

From the historical society, a walk down South Street will bring you to the **Samuel Seymour House** (third down on the right), now the Episcopal rectory but once John C. Calhoun's lodging place while he attended **Tapping Reeve's Law School** (tel. 860/567-4501), located in the two buildings next door.

Tapping Reeve was a Princeton graduate who moved to Litchfield in 1773, bringing his frail wife, Sally, sister of Aaron Burr, who became Reeve's first law student. On the tour of the house you can see the parlor Reeve used initially as a classroom and several rooms filled with the usual period antiques. What's most interesting is the wonderfully detailed inventory of his 1824 estate, which lists, among other things, "60 pounds of butter (not good) @ 10¢—$6; 160 pounds of ham and shoulders @ 6¢ a pound—$9.60," and "dwelling house and homestead . . . $3,600."

In the law school building next door, to which he later moved, you can view portraits of the many famous men who were trained at this first law school, including two vice presidents, Aaron Burr and John C. Calhoun; three Supreme Court justices; six cabinet members; artist George Catlin; and more than 100 congressmen. The school's curriculum and rules and the personal lives of Judge Reeve and his partner, Judge Gould, also make for interesting reading.

Hours: Mid-May to mid-Oct, Tues–Sat 11am–5pm, Sun 1–5pm.

Across from the law school you can see **Oliver Wolcott's house,** to which the equestrian statue of George III was dragged all the way from Bowling Green after it had been pulled down by New York's Sons of Liberty. Here it was melted down into bullets by the redoubtable ladies of Litchfield. Mr. Wolcott was, of course, a signer of the Declaration of Independence, a member of the Continental Congress, and governor of Connecticut from 1796. During his lifetime he entertained George Washington, the Marquis de Lafayette, and Alexander Hamilton at this house, which is still in the Wolcott family.

If you continue south to where the road divides and take the right fork, you'll come to another famous son's house, that of **Ethan Allen,** the Revolutionary War hero who captured Fort Ticonderoga with his Green Mountain Boys.

Heading in the other direction up North Street from the Green will bring you to the **home of Benjamin Talmadge** (1775), George Washington's aide, past the site of **Miss Pierce's School,** the first

American institution of higher education for women, founded in 1792. Young women from the school continued to take their daily walks under the elms to the tune of a flute and flageolet until 1855. Just beyond Prospect Street, on the left side, is the site of the **Beecher homestead,** where Henry Ward Beecher and his sister, Harriet Beecher Stowe, were born. Ahead, in the middle of the fork, stands the **house of Alexander Catlin,** uncle to the more famous George, and a member of the Wolcott, Talmadge group that formed the Litchfield China trading company. You can also browse through the shops clustered along **West Street** facing the Green and along **Cobble Court** at South and East streets.

Within a few miles of the village are several interesting spots: The **White Memorial Foundation,** west of Litchfield on Rte. 202 (tel. 860/567-0857), established in 1913, is a lovely place to stroll, whatever the season. Within this 4,000-acre wildlife sanctuary are 35 miles of hiking, cross-country skiing, and horseback-riding trails; several picnic areas; and a museum (tel. 860/567-0015; open Tues–Sat 9am–5pm, Sun 11am–5pm) dedicated to conservation and ecology. This museum includes various exhibits of interest to children and adults, like a working beehive, fish, and stuffed birds. The Holbrook Bird Observatory overlooks an area specially landscaped to attract a variety of birds in all seasons. Field trips are offered on Saturday. And there's camping at three campgrounds.

Two miles east of Litchfield, the **Haight Vineyard,** 29 Chestnut Hill Rd. (tel. 860/567-4045), off Rte. 118, offers walks through the vineyards, fermentation and aging areas, and the usual tastings. It was established in 1978.

Hours: Mon–Sat 10:30am–5pm, Sun noon–5pm.

White Flower Farm (tel. 860/567-8789), just south of Litchfield, is a 200-acre retail and mail-order plant nursery you might enjoy, either for shopping or for just viewing the colorful displays in the 8-acre garden and the greenhouse (especially beautiful in July, when the begonias bloom).

Lourdes Shrine, off Rte. 118, has a grotto and is a quiet place for contemplation.

Out at Lake Waramaug, the **Hopkins Vineyard** (tel. 860/868-7954) occupies a 19th-century barn in an idyllic spot overlooking the lake and offers self-guided tours and some fine wines for tasting. The vineyard shop is stocked with gourmet foods and home, garden, and wine accessories.

Hours: May–Dec, Mon–Sat 10am–5pm, Sun 11am–5pm (weekends only in winter).

Litchfield Lodging & Dining

Litchfield itself has no truly special places to stay, except for the **Tollgate Hill Inn,** P.O. Box 39, Litchfield, CT 06759 (tel. 860/567-4545), 3 miles north of the Village Green. Innkeepers Fritz and Anne Zivic have meticulously restored this fine 225-year-old Colonial, retaining those small details—like the original iron latches and hinges and the salmon milk-paint in the bar—that give the place a special feel.

They've furnished their 15 rooms and 5 suites with locally made reproductions of antique cherry candlestands, Shaker tables, quilt stands, and a butler's bar and added extra-special elements like goose-down comforters and choice Hinson wallpapers. The two front rooms have a fireplace and four-poster canopied bed. The suites have a fireplace, VCR, bar/refrigerator, and canopied bed. Each unique room (with a bath, air-conditioning, a TV, and a phone) is known by its predominating color: peach, red, green, brown, lavender, or blue. Guests enjoy breakfast—freshly squeezed fruit juice, croissants, banana or blueberry bread with sweet butter—in their rooms, served on fine china arranged on a wicker tray.

The dining rooms consist of a small formal room with an arched corner cupboard and an Oriental carpet, a low-ceilinged tavern room, and a very large "Ballroom" overlooked by a real fiddler's loft. Each has a welcoming fire in winter. The seasonal menus offer primarily American dishes, with a touch of the European—shellfish pie (shrimp, scallops, lobster, and crab in cream sauce), fresh fish, roast prime rib (on weekends), thick veal chop with coriander-tomato jus, duck with honey-balsamic glaze, and always a pasta of the day. Prices range from $16 to $24.

Rates (including breakfast): Mid-May to Jan 1 and all weekends, $120–$150 double; from $185 suite. The rest of the year, $100–$125 double; $160 suite. **Dining Hours:** Mon–Fri noon–3pm and 5:30–9pm, Sat–Sun noon–3pm (Sun brunch) and 5:30–10pm. **Closed:** Tues Nov–May and the first two weeks of Mar.

Litchfield Dining

The best dining is to be found at the Tollgate Hill Inn (above) and the restaurants around Lake Waramaug, most notably the Hopkins and Boulders Inns (below).

In Litchfield itself, though, is the outstanding **West Street Grill,** West Street, On the Green (tel. 860/567-3885), a study in black. Black-and-white-striped banquettes, black-framed mirrors, and black Windsor chairs create the sleek ambience. The food is rated as some of the best in the state. The menu changes seasonally, but there's always a broad range of tempting appetizers. The steamed Prince Edward Island mussels are subtly enhanced with tomatoes, roasted fennel, garlic, and pastis broth. The pan-seared polenta with sautéed mushrooms and parmesan melts in the mouth. Vegetarians will love the roasted red and yellow peppers with an eggplant mousse and shaved fennel. Among the main courses are several pastas—like fettuccine with a trio of mushrooms, shallots, fresh thyme, and olive oil—plus salmon with roasted corn, braised leeks, and plum tomatoes or grilled marinated leg of lamb with white beans, mint, roasted tomato stew, date chutney, and Swiss chard.

Hours: Mon–Thurs 11:30am–2:30pm and 5:30–9:30pm, Fri 11:30am–2:30pm and 5:30–10:30pm, Sat 11:30am–3:30pm and 5:30–10:30pm, Sun 11:30am–3:30pm.

Opposite the Green, **Spinell's Litchfield Food Company,** West Street (tel. 860/567-3113), prepares spectacular box lunches and picnics. You can select from their 20 or so sandwiches and dozens of breads, cheeses, pâtés, and salads (pasta, rice, marinated vegetables, you name it). You might then walk out with a hamper containing smoked salmon, marinated portobello mushrooms, chicken breast stuffed with cheese and herbs, artichoke hearts in vinaigrette, a baguette or two, chocolate-mousse balls rolled in hazelnuts, and fresh seasonal fruit. A box lunch for one costs $7 to $15.

Hours: Mon–Sat 8am–7pm, Sun 8am–6pm.

Area Lodging & Dining

Lake Waramaug Lodging

Choice accommodations lie about a 15-minute drive west of Litchfield around Lake Waramaug, a summer resort area settled in the 1890s. Each of the four accommodations here will appeal to a different type of personality.

The largest is a mini-resort-like property, the **Inn at Lake Waramaug,** New Preston, CT 06777 (tel. 860/868-0563, or 800/LAKE-INN), run by the delightful and extremely hospitable John and Karen Koiter. To describe it as a resort probably gives the wrong impression, for it has more of the atmosphere of an old country inn, set on a hill overlooking the lake, with acres of lawns shaded by grand sugar maples. The core of the main building was built as a home around 1795, and it's here that people gather around the parlor fire for long conversations or curl up privately with one of the many available books. In the large dining room, with a lovely porch for outside morning or evening dining, fires blaze at night or on chilly mornings. The "resort" label stems from the many facilities—an indoor pool, table tennis, a billiard and games room, a clay tennis court, rental bicycles, and a full complement of lakeside offerings, including rental canoes and sailboats, free rowboats, and a showboat steamer that plies the lake on summer afternoons. Winter activities include ice skating on the lake, cross-country skiing, horse-drawn-sleigh rides, sledding, and tobogganing.

Breakfast is served inside or on the terrace with a view of the lake and the lovely trees and shrubs. Cereal, fresh fruits of all sorts, and breads are spread out, while the main dishes are cooked to order. Lunch is taken lakeside (in summer) if you wish, and dinner is served in the dining room, with a special Saturday candlelight buffet. Among the specialties might be pork loin with apple-ginger salsa or Calvados sauce, horseradish-crusted salmon, or the pasta of the day, priced from $16 to $22.

There are five rooms in the original inn, each with a bath and queen-size canopied bed (no phone). The other 18 are in motel-style buildings, where rooms are tastefully decorated, several featuring queen-size canopied beds and fireplaces. Rooms 30 to 35 offer prime views of the lake. All are air-conditioned.

Rates (including breakfast and dinner): May–Oct, $218–$239 double weekends, $184–$204 double weekdays. Nov–Apr, $184–$204 double weekends, $148–$166 double weekdays. *Note:* On holiday weekends a three-night minimum stay is required; there's a two-night minimum on weekends at other times. **Dining Hours:** Mon–Sat 6–9pm, Sun 11:30am–2:30pm (winter only) and 5–8pm.

The **Boulders Inn,** Rte. 45, New Preston, CT 06777 (tel. 860/868-7918), is smaller and seems quieter than the Inn at Lake Waramaug, but it offers a private beach for swimming, canoes, Sunfish, bicycles, a tennis court, and hiking trails up Pinnacle Mountain. As the name suggests, the main 1895 building is of fieldstone, with shingles, and it contains six individually decorated rooms (all with bath). Several have sunny windowseats overlooking the lake and all are furnished with antiques—sleigh beds, candlestand side tables, blanket chests, and the like. The comfortable living room furnished with sofas, wing chairs, and well-stocked bookcases gives lake views. Four contemporary cottages, housing eight rooms, are nicely tucked away on the wooded hillside for ample privacy. Each has a porch, woodstove, and picture window facing the lake; some have a Jacuzzi. There are also three rooms in the carriage house, all with a wood-burning fireplace.

The inn's stone-walled dining room has a good reputation for serving such delights as steamed lobster in tarragon-tomato broth; honey-and-cumin roasted duck with sweet onions, sage, and shiitake mushrooms; or prime aged sirloin with portobello mushroom sauce. Prices range from $18 to $25. A full breakfast of eggs, pancakes, or omelets and afternoon tea also are served. Guests must take breakfast and dinner during summer, and whenever meals are being served MAP rates apply.

Rates (including breakfast and dinner): May–Nov 1 and weekends year round, $275–$325 double. Winter rates $50 less. $225–$275 for bed and breakfast only. **Dining Hours:** Summer, daily 6–8:30pm.

The **Hopkins Inn,** 22 Hopkins Rd., New Preston, CT 06777 (tel. 860/868-7295), is known primarily for serving the area's best food (April to December only). When you dine here under the spreading chestnut tree, on a terrace overlooking the lake, watching the sun go down and the sky fill with stars, waited on by young women dressed in colorful dirndls, you'll swear you're dining by the Danube. The Swiss and many Austrian favorites on the menu will only help to confirm the impression—backhendl with lingonberries, wienerschnitzel, and rahmschnitzel. The desserts are classics like pear belle Hélène and crème caramel. Figure $30 per person for dinner. Make sure you have dining reservations, especially on Friday and Saturday. The back tavern room is remarkable for its folk-painted bar and huge, rough-hewn beams.

The lemon-yellow house, built in 1847 as a summer home, offers nine rooms and a two-room apartment available late March to December. The apartment and seven of the rooms have private bath or shower. None contains a TV or phone; the furnishings are adequate in their homey old-fashioned way. If you're lucky, you'll get a room with a brass bed or an Eastlake-style sofa.

Rates: $72 double with bath and lake view, $67 double with bath only, $62 double with lake view only; $80 per night apartment, weekly or monthly. **Dining Hours:** Apr–Oct, Tues–Fri noon–2pm and 6–9pm, Sat noon–2pm and 5:30–9:30pm; Nov–Dec, Tues–Fri 6–9pm, Sat 5:30–9:30pm, Sun 12:30–8:30pm. **Afternoon Snacks:** June–Aug, Tues–Sat 2–3:30pm.

New Preston Dining
Le Bon Coin, Rte. 202 (tel. 860/868-7763), is a typical French restaurant located in a small house occupying quite an isolated spot. The decor is simple—country paneling, lace curtains, and paintings of typical French scenes—but the food is good and there's always a variety of enticing specials. Start with the assortment of smoked fish or the pork-and-duckling pâté flavored with cognac and port. Choose from among steak au poivre; shrimp sautéed with tomatoes, parsley, and garlic; lamb sautéed with egg-plant, peppers, tomatoes, and fresh herbs; or chicken breast with wild mushrooms. Crêpes Suzette or crème caramel makes a perfect conclusion. Prices run $13 to $23.

Hours: Mon and Thurs–Sat noon–2pm and 6–9pm, Sun 5–9pm.

SOUTHBURY, WOODBURY, WASHINGTON & ROXBURY

Area Attractions
Start in Southbury, at the junction of Rte. 6 and I-84, and follow Rte. 6 east, passing Southbury Plaza. Take your first left at the set of lights to Heritage Village, a condominium complex that also shelters the **"Bazaar,"** with 25 specialty shops, two art galleries, three restaurants, and a resort—all under one roof.

Retrace your route and continue on Rte. 6 east toward Woodbury, driving along the **"Grand Army Highway of the Republic,"** so named because of its rich history as a major thoroughfare, used by George Washington, Lafayette, and Rochambeau during the Revolution. For a side trip you can take Rte. 64 east off Rte. 6 to the **Whittemore Sanctuary,** especially recommended for birdwatchers, and to **Lake Quassapaug** in Middlebury, a large natural lake open to the public for swimming and boating. A family amusement park, **Quassy,** is also on the shoreline.

Going back on Rte. 6 east, you'll come to Woodbury, dubbed the antiques capital of Connecticut. There are close to 40 really fine **specialist antiques shops** to browse and shop—featuring everything from Early

American furniture and paintings to country French, 18th-century English, Oriental and Navajo rugs, and art deco. Write for the "Woodbury Antique Buyer's Guide," obtainable from the Litchfield Hills Travel Council, P.O. Box 968, Litchfield, CT 06759 (tel. 860/567-4506).

The two most historic points of interest in Woodbury are the Herd House and the Glebe House, within 1,500 yards of each other on Hollow Road (off Rte. 6 in the center of town). The **Herd House** is in fact two houses that've been joined (one ca. 1680, the other ca. 1720). It's furnished with period pieces and features a well-stocked herb garden. The **Glebe House** (tel. 860/263-2855) dates from the 1700s and was owned by the town's first Episcopal priest, John Rutgers Marshall, who managed to survive the turmoil and oppression suffered by many New England Anglicans, who were often presumed to be Loyalists—whether or not they were. Weeks after American independence was secured, a group of clergy met secretly here to elect Samuel Seabury the first American bishop of the Episcopal church, an action that effectively assumed the separation of church and state and thereby helped establish religious tolerance in the new nation. Today the house contains period furniture and displays documents tracing the development of the Episcopal church.

Hours: Apr–Nov, Wed–Sun 1–4pm. **Admission:** $4.

From Woodbury, continue on Rte. 6 north to the junction of Rte. 61, taking it to **Bethlehem.** The best time to visit is at Christmas, when a special celebration features holiday arts and crafts, hayrides, festive music, a minifestival of lights, and, of course, a post office where thousands of letters get the "Bethlehem" Christmas stamp. In August a horse show is held at the Bethlehem Fairgrounds, followed by a country fair in September.

At the junction of Rtes. 61 and 132, take Rte. 132 west and travel through pastoral scenery. At the junction of Rtes. 132 and 47, take Rte. 47 north to **Washington,** a picturesque town much of whose charm derives from its setting on top of a hill. The heart of town lies on the Green around the Congregational church, built on the site of the original 1742 meetinghouse. Facing the Green are lovely 18th-century residences and a small post office housed in a white-clapboard Colonial building that it shares with the country drugstore. The **Museum of the Gunn Memorial Library,** in a 1781 Colonial house on the Green, exhibits 18th- and 19th-century furniture, china, dolls, and dollhouses.

Farther along Rte. 47 lies Washington Depot, with an assortment of stores. The **Hickory Stick Bookshop** (tel. 860/868-0525) is worth stopping at for new and secondhand books; it's a civilized place that even provides wing chairs for leisurely browsing.

Retrace your route along Rte. 47 to its junction with Rte. 199 and turn right. Follow 199 for about 1¼ miles and turn right at the sign for the **Institute for American Indian Studies,** in Washington (tel. 860/ 868-0518), which traces local Native American history through displays of their artifacts. Cases contain exhibits taken from a local paleo-Indian site—bone harpoons, adzes and net sinkers, semilunar knives, and soapstone vessels. Artifacts from the Woodland period include luminescent turtle-shell bowls, copper and shell beads, and hand-thrown decorated pots. Kaolin pipes, beaded moccasins, and metal axes represent the later contact period, from 1550 to 1700. Probably the most interesting display, particularly for children, is the reconstruction of a longhouse made by Onondaga Indians and filled with everyday utensils and artifacts. The immense 12,000-year-old mastodon skeleton found at the Pope Estate in Farmington in 1913 will also impress the kids—the beast stood 9 feet tall at the shoulder, had a 13-foot-long tail, and weighed 10 tons. You can also walk a 20-minute trail along which trees and plants are marked, tracing the evolution of the natural habitat from 12,000 years ago to today, and then view a simulated archeological site and a replicated Algonkian Village.

Hours: Mon–Sat 10am–5pm, Sun noon—5pm. **Closed:** Major holidays. **Admission:** $4 adults, $3.50 seniors, $2 children 6–16.

Continue on Rte. 199 into the quiet, scenic village of Roxbury, which celebrates **Old Roxbury Days** on the last weekend in July with a fiddlin' contest, a chicken barbecue, an antique car display, arts and crafts, and more. From Roxbury, Rte. 317 leads to Rte. 67, which takes you back to Rte. 6 and into Southbury.

A Southbury Resort

The **Heritage Inn,** Heritage Village, on the Village Green, Southbury, CT 06488 (tel. 860/264-8200), makes an ideal base for exploring the Woodbury/Washington/Roxbury area. It's not a small inn; rather, it's a 163-room property with a large games room equipped with five pool tables, dartboards, table tennis, and card tables; a bar that throbs on weekends; and rooms containing stereo/tapedeck radio and a full supply of audiocassettes (from Beethoven to Boy George) for rent. Yet the place still has a rustic feel.

The rooms look past silver birches over a green golf course to wooded hills beyond. They've been decorated with a New England flair, including Ethan Allen–style beds, wing backs, and iron floor lamps; dried country floral wreaths are used as wall accents. TVs, phones, and baths with full amenities are standard.

Timbers on the Green restaurant occupies a large high-ceilinged room. Service when I was there was a little erratic but the hostess/maître d's humor could save any situation. The prime rib is excellent, and the rest of the primarily American menu is also fine. Art deco–style Splash features more casual fare.

Besides the facilities I've already mentioned, there's an outdoor pool, 9- and 18-hole golf courses, three outdoor tennis courts, two racquetball courts, a fitness room equipped with Universal machines, cross-country ski trails, saunas, a whirlpool, and massage therapy. For shopping, the

Heritage Village Bazaar is next door. Mountain bikes and trout fishing equipment are available. And all this is only an hour from Manhattan.

Rates: May–Oct, $139–$149 double. The rest of the year, $119–$129 double. Weekend packages are offered throughout the year.

Woodbury Lodging & Dining

The **Curtis House,** Main Street (U.S. 6), Woodbury, CT 06798 (tel. 860/263-2101), claims to be the state's oldest inn, opened by Anthony Stoddard in 1754. The venerable clapboard Federal house with black shutters and 12-on-12 windows is crowned by tall brick chimneys. An elegant portico surmounted by a balcony leads into the center hall. Past the grandfather clock, a creaking staircase leads to 14 air-conditioned guest rooms (8 with bath and canopied bed); in the carriage house are 4 more air-conditioned rooms with bath. In Room 22 in the main house you'll find beds with white canopies and coverlets, standing on painted floorboards; a chest of drawers, a side chair, and a metal closet complete the furnishings. Other rooms are similar. Some rooms have a TV; none has a phone.

The ground-floor public rooms boast great character. The ceilings and door frames are low, the floors uneven, and the furnishings comfortably old. The ticking of the wall clock adds to the homey feel. In the parlor you can curl up in a wing chair or on a sofa and watch TV or read the magazines scattered on a table. The dining room, decorated in colonial cranberry, has a similar air. The fare is typical New England—roast stuffed turkey, broiled bluefish, Yankee pot roast, and roast leg of lamb (weekends only), priced from $14 to $20.

Rates: $35–$45 double without bath, $50–$65 double with bath. **Dining Hours:** Mon 5–8:30pm, Tues–Thurs noon–2pm and 5–8:30pm, Fri–Sat noon–2pm and 5–9pm, Sun noon–8pm. **Closed:** Christmas.

Merryvale Bed & Breakfast, 1204 Main St. South, Woodbury, CT 06798 (tel. 860/266-0800), stands on 4 wooded acres along Rte. 6. It was built in 1789 on what was then the well-traveled road between Boston and Washington. It has retained many of its appealing architectural features—a large covered side porch, wide-plank floors, and fireplaces. There are five guest rooms and suites, each individually decorated with antiques and period-design wallpaper. The Miriam Tangier Smith Room features a canopied bed and Laura Ashley decor and boasts a clawfoot tub in the bath. My favorite is the Hannah Phoenix Bull Smith Room, with a brass bed, a walnut armoire, and—best of all—its own covered porch. The third-floor suite with its dormer windows and painted floorboards is a country charmer. Guests are served a full breakfast. In the evenings the well-furnished living room is ideal for relaxing in front of the fire or watching TV. There's also an extensive library of books available.

Rates (including breakfast): $109–$125 double. 10% discount Jan–Feb.

Woodbury Dining

Phillips Country Kitchen, in Woodbury's Middle Quarter shopping complex (tel. 860/263-2545), on Rte. 6 south of Woodbury, is famous for muffins, chicken pies, and good breakfasts. You'll probably have to join the line, unless you're willing to sit at the counter instead of in the booths.

Hours: Mon–Tues 6:30am–2pm, Wed–Sat 6:30am–7pm, Sun 7:30am–7pm.

Fritz's Restaurant, 10 Sherman Hill Rd., Rte. 6 (tel. 860/263-3036), offers a menu mixing Austrian and Italian specialties. Among the main courses you'll always find wienerschnitzel and zwiebel roastbraten, a New York strip steak in red-wine onion sauce. You might also find chicken Venezia with prosciutto and mozzarella or a simple duck with orange sauce. Start your meal with the pâté maison or herring in mustard sauce and finish with an apple strudel or any of the inspired pastries.

Hours: Daily 11:30am–2:30pm and 5–10pm.

Washington & Washington Depot Lodging & Dining

Such a pretty and venerable town as Washington warrants an old-fashioned luxury inn like the **Mayflower Inn,** 118 Woodbury Rd. (Rte. 47), Washington, CT 06793 (tel. 860/868-9466). Cross the bridge by the pond inhabited by two swans and take the winding tree-lined drive that leads to the house on the crest of the hill. It's set on 28 acres graced with splendid rhododendrons and maple trees and landscaped with rose gardens, wildflower cutting gardens, and knot gardens of boxwood and red barberry. Originally the Ridge School (1894), it was converted into an inn in 1920. Current owners Adriana and Robert Mnuchin, who exhibit fine taste and a superb eye for color and decoration, have spent millions reconstructing the property and have successfully turned it into a captivating five-star Relais & Châteaux. Of the 17 rooms and 8 suites, 15 are in the clapboard Mayflower Building, with a striking gambrel roof. Each has been individually decorated with the very best—luxurious fabrics, Frette linens and bathrobes, positively plush upholstery, and exquisite antiques and 18th- and 19th-century art. All have spacious marble baths with brass-and-Limoges fittings. Other features include fireplaces, stocked minibars, TVs in cabinets, down comforters, four-poster canopied beds, and walls papered in Regency stripes or Empire petit fleur.

The public areas are certainly as lavish, if not more so. The parlor is very inviting with its swag curtains, gilt-framed landscapes, and fine English antiques. The sumptuously paneled library is extraordinary and offers a large book collection that can be read sitting in the leather armchairs or on the cushioned windowseat. The porch is beguiling too, with its white wicker rockers overlooking the south lawn and Shakespeare garden where a bust of the playwright is surrounded by flowers and shrubs that bear markers carrying lines from the Bard. To reach the other accommodations in the Speedwell and Standish buildings you'll pass the well-tended Terrace Gardens. Facilities include a state-of-the-art fitness club open daily, offering facials, shiatsu, aromatherapy, reflexology, and massages; an attractively landscaped heated outdoor pool with pool house; a tennis court; hiking trails; and a games room.

The cuisine in the dining room is also stellar, emphasizing fresh local ingredients. Start with the house game sausage or house-smoked salmon accompanied by lahvash (Middle Eastern bread) that's baked on the premises. The specialties are creative American: The crab cakes are enriched by a delicate scallop mousse, the cattle bean soup is enhanced by shoulder hocks smoked over applewood, and the meatloaf is bound with oatmeal instead of bread. At dinner you'll find about six entrees, ranging from $16.50 to $30. The fish could be seared yellowfin tuna with eggplant-cilantro relish; there might also be a simple roast natural chicken brimming with flavor and accompanied by plum ketchup and a grilled sirloin with cucumber-caper relish. Desserts range from ice creams and sorbets to warm chocolate tart with espresso sauce and coffee ice cream. The tables are set with Limoges china, crystal, and silver. The room's centerpiece is a magnificent floral and produce display. Orchids are everywhere, not only here but throughout the house. The adjoining piano bar is a convivial place for cocktails and late-night conversation.

Rates: $250–$375 double; $415–$515 suite. **Dining Hours:** Mon–Sat 7:30–10am, noon–2pm, and 6–9pm; Sun 7:30–10am, noon–2pm, and 5–8pm.

For lunch, many people head to Washington Depot, to **The Pantry,** Titus Square (tel. 860/868-0258). It serves some of the best soups, salads, and sandwiches around, plus you can browse through all the gourmet foods, gifts, and culinary accessories. The chalkboard menu might offer a broccoli-leek or chicken-corn chowder, which can be followed by kedgeree or a more traditional Reuben sandwich. The desserts are excellent—like Linzer torte and lemon cake. Afternoon tea is also served.

Hours: Tues–Sat 10am–6pm.

The Litchfield Hills Area
Special & Recreational Activities

Antiquing: Stores abound in Kent, Litchfield, New Preston, Salisbury, and Woodbury (which has the greatest number). If you cross the border into Massachusetts on Rtes. 7 and 7A around Sheffield and Ashley Falls, you'll discover another good hunting ground.

Auto Racing: Lime Rock Park, Rtes. 7 and 112, hosts some of the largest spectator events in the Northeast and is home to the Skip Barber Racing and Driving Schools.

Bicycling: For rentals, go to the Cycle Loft, 25 Litchfield Commons, Litchfield (tel. 860/567-1713). It also sponsors group rides.

Boating: O'Hara's Landing Marina, 254 Twin Lakes Rd., Salisbury (tel. 860/824-7583), offers boats for rent.

Camping: White Memorial Foundation, on Rte. 202 west of Litchfield (tel. 860/567-0089), has several camping areas, open mid-May to October; the most popular is at Point Folly, a peninsula extending into Bantam Lake that's convenient for swimming and fishing.

Lake Waramaug State Park, New Preston, CT 06777 (tel. 860/868-0220), has 78 sites, open from mid-May to October 1.

Macedonia Brook State Park, Kent, CT 06757 (tel. 860/927-3238, or 927-4100 for camping), offers 84 sites near a brook in the Appalachian Trail area.

Housatonic Meadows State Park, Cornwall Bridge, CT 06754 (tel. 860/672-6772), has 104 sites near the river.

Hemlock Hill Resort Campground, Hemlock Hill Rd.(P.O. Box 828), Litchfield, CT 06759 (tel. 860/567-2267), offers 100 wooded sites, two outdoor pools, and other facilities. Open until mid-October.

Canoeing: Riverrunning Ltd., 85 Main St., Falls Village, CT 06031 (tel. 860/824-5579), offers canoeing, rafting, and kayaking trips and rentals. In spring and early summer there are even some white-water trips on the Housatonic. Rental prices range from $30 to $50 per day; also available are weekend packages including overnights at a bed-and-breakfast.

Clarke Outdoors, Rte. 7 (P.O. Box 163), West Cornwall, CT 06796 (tel. 860/672-6365), has canoes, kayaks, and rafts for rent and provides shuttle service back to your starting point on the Housatonic River. The approximate charge per day is $40 to $45.

Country Fairs: Contact Connecticut State Tourism, 865 Brook St., Rocky Hill, CT 06067 (tel. 860/258-4335, or 800/282-6863), for information on these fun-filled celebrations with contests, auctions, entertainments, and demonstrations.

Fishing: *Barkhamsted:* West Hill Pond, off Rte. 44. *Cornwall:* Housatonic Meadows State Park, Rte. 7, Cornwall Bridge. *Litchfield:* Lake Waramaug State Park, Rte. 45; Mount Tom State Park, Rte. 202. *Salisbury:* East Twin Lake, off Rte. 44. *Sharon:* Mudge Pond, off Rte. 4.

Those who wish to learn fly fishing should contact Housatonic Anglers, 484 Rte. 7 (P.O. Box 282), West Cornwall, CT 06796 (tel. 860/672-4457), which offers three-day schools for novices and half- and full-day guided trips.

Fruit Picking: *Sharon:* Ellsworth Hill Farm and Orchard, Rte. 4 (tel. 860/364-0249), for raspberries and apples. *Washington*

Depot: Hallock Orchards, Calhoun St. (tel. 860/868-2863), for apples, peaches, and more.

Golf: *Litchfield:* Stonybrook Golf Club, Milton Road (tel. 860/567-9977), with nine holes.

Hiking: *Cornwall:* Mohawk Mountain, from Rte. 4. *Kent:* Kent Falls State Park, Rte. 7. *Litchfield:* White Memorial Foundation, Rte. 202; Mount Tom State Park, a few miles west of Bantam on Rte. 202. *Norfolk:* Haystack Mountain State Park on Rte. 272 north and Dennis Hill State Park on Rte. 272 south are both spectacular. *Salisbury:* Bear Mountain, from Rte. 41.

For detailed hiking trail information, write to the Connecticut Forest and Park Trail Association, 16 Meriden Rd., Rock Fall, CT 06481 (tel. 860/346-2372), or the Office of State Parks, 79 Elm St., Hartford, CT 06106-5127 (tel. 860/424-3200). The Appalachian Trail cuts through the region.

Horseback Riding: *Bantam:* Sunny Ray Farm, Rte. 202 (tel. 860/567-0522), will rent you a horse and let you ride it in the rink. *Litchfield:* Lee's Riding Stable, Inc., 57 E. Litchfield Rd. (off Rte. 118) offers trail riding (tel. 860/567-0785).

Ice Skating: On Lake Waramaug or at Mount Tom State Park.

Mountain Laurel Viewing: From mid- to late June at Indian Lookout, Torrington.

Picnicking: You can always dine on the Green in Litchfield. More secluded spots are to be found at the White Memorial Foundation, Lake Waramaug State Park, Kent Falls State Park, or Mount Tom. Pick up supplies at Spinel's Litchfield Food Company, a gourmet take-out just off the Green.

Skiing: *Cornwall:* Mohawk Mountain, 46 Great Hollow Rd. (off Rte. 4), Cornwall, CT 06753 (tel. 860/672-6100), has a vertical drop of 640 feet, five lifts, and a 95% snowmaking capacity. There are 14 trails, five chair lifts (including a triple), and a rope tow. Lift rates are $25 per day.

Cross-country skiing can be enjoyed at *Kent:* Macedonia Brook State Park, off Rte. 341. *Litchfield:* White Memorial Foundation and Mount Tom State Park, on Rte. 202 just west of Bantam. *New Preston:* Around Lake Waramaug. *Woodbury:* Woodbury Ski Area, Rte. 47 (tel. 860/263-2203), has 20km (12½ miles) of groomed trails that are made with manmade snow and lit at night.

The Wilderness Shop, Rte. 202, 85 West St., Litchfield (tel. 860/567-5905), rents cross-country skis.

State Parks: *Barkhamsted:* People's State Forest, Rte. 44, has hiking trails, picnicking, fishing, and cross-country skiing. *Cornwall:* Mohawk Mountain State Park, off Rte. 4, Cornwall-Goshen-Litchfield, offers picnicking and downhill and cross-country skiing. *Cornwall Bridge:* Housatonic Meadows State Park, on

Rte. 7 a mile north of town, has camping, fishing, picnicking, and hiking on the Appalachian Trail. *Kent:* Kent Falls State Park, Rte. 7, is picturesque for picnicking; Macedonia Brook State Park, off Rte. 341, has excellent hiking, fishing, picnicking, and cross-country skiing. *Norfolk:* Haystack Mountain State Park, on Rte. 272 north, and Dennis Hill State Park, on Rte. 272 south, have hiking and picnicking. *Washington:* Mount Tom State Park, Rte. 202, Morris-Washington-Litchfield, offers hiking, picnicking, stocked fishing, swimming, and cross-country skiing; Lake Waramaug, on Rte. 475, 5 miles north of New Preston, has swimming, camping, fishing, and picnicking facilities. For information, write the Office of State Parks, 79 Elm St., Hartford, CT 06106-5127 (tel. 860/424-3200).

Swimming: *Kent:* Macedonia Brook State Park, off Rte. 341. *Litchfield-Bantam:* Mount Tom State Park, off Rte. 202. *New Preston:* Lake Waramaug State Park.

FROM NORWALK & WESTPORT TO RIDGEFIELD

◄◦►

About half an hour's drive from New Preston is the Ridgefield-Danbury area, which you can also use as a base (there are three inns) to explore Litchfield to the north, Candlewood Lake, Bethel, and adjacent areas. From Ridgefield it's only a short drive to the coastal towns of Westport and Norwalk.

Area Attractions

Norwalk

Not exactly on everyone's "A" list for a weekend retreat, Norwalk actually will surprise you. There's plenty to see and do—a fantastic mansion; the famous oyster festival; a South Norwalk street lined with galleries, interior design stores, and restaurants (though not nearly as pristine and appealing as it once was); and the biggest attraction, the **Maritime Center** (tel. 203/852-0700), an aquarium housing more than 120 species of marine life native to Long Island Sound, plus a maritime museum and an IMAX theater. The museum offers a variety of exhibits, like the recent one dedicated to jellyfish, which introduced visitors to the lion's mane, a jellyfish with 800 tentacles that can sting even after it's dead, and the moon jellies that look like floating flying saucers. Kids especially enjoy the Touch Tank (where they can hold snails, clams, and other tidal sea creatures), the feeding time at the seal pool, and the boat-building shop. Some may also enjoy safely watching the sharks in the 110,000-gallon tank. An exciting adventure can be enjoyed on the three-hour marine life study cruises aboard the research vessel *Oceanic*. Marine life is collected at several depths. An onboard video microscope allows you to examine tiny plankton caught at the surface, and everyone helps pull up the trawl net to examine its contents. Reservations are recommended for the cruises, which cost $15.

Hours: Summer, daily 10am–6pm; winter, daily 10am–5pm. **Admission:** $7.50 adults, $6.50 seniors and children 2–12; $6 and 4.50, respectively, to IMAX.

Once a thriving industrial center, Norwalk has a concentration of fine 19th-century buildings, many located in the **Historic District along Washington Street.** The majority of these Italianate buildings were constructed between 1870 and 1920 and feature cast-iron trim, delicately detailed facades, and corbeled brickwork. Many have been refurbished and now house galleries and eye-catching stores and restaurants.

And the **harbor** is experiencing a maritime renaissance. Once a major schooner and steamboat port, it became an oystering center between 1885 and 1910. Then pollution and a major hurricane that damaged the beds virtually destroyed the industry. Recently, though, it has been revived into a $3- to $4-million industry and is the excuse for one of Norwalk's largest festivals. The whole waterfront is still being developed and linked to the Historic District. The lynchpin of all this is the $22-million Maritime Center (above).

The **Lockwood Mathews Mansion Museum,** 295 West Ave. (tel. 203/838-1434), is Norwalk's best-kept secret. This magnificent French Renaissance Revival mansion, still being restored, was built in 1863 for LeGrand Lockwood of Lockwood and Co., a banking and brokerage firm that had invested successfully in railroads. Although LeGrand spent $1.5 million to construct this home, he lived in it for only four years—in 1869, when the gold market was manipulated, he was forced to mortgage it and died shortly thereafter. The Mathews family purchased the mansion and lived in it for the next 60 years, which probably accounts for the minimal number of changes that've been made to the structure. From the outside it doesn't look very splendid, but the interiors are magnificent. Much of the work was completed by European stonecutters and woodcarvers, who were hired at $1 and 50¢ per day, respectively. Today their skills would be priceless. From the entrance portico, 3-inch-thick mahogany doors lead into the central hall, supported by smooth gray-and-white marble pillars. The library has a coffered ceiling, and the floors are inlaid with eight woods; the room is lit by a chandelier with a fringe. The music room's coffered ceiling is embellished with paintings of musical instruments. Bird's-eye maple doors and a marble fireplace surmounted by delicate etched-glass panels add even more luxury. The drawing room contains the only furniture original to the house—a circular ottoman and a carved Victorian sofa, its medallions matching those that crown the door frames. In the tiny turreted games room a Waterford chandelier lights the painted walls and ceiling, which are being restored to their former luster. The dining room has incredible carving on view and a richly decorated gold-leaf ceiling.

From the 42-foot-high rotunda, topped by a skylight, a grand staircase with carved inlaid banisters leads to the bedrooms, two of which are used for semipermanent special exhibitions. When I was there they were occupied by a display of musical boxes of all sorts, including a musical clock picture, a grand player piano, and a domed musical tableau with a flitting bird, a clock, and a waterfall. The Italian marble baths, English ceramic bowls, and bathtubs enclosed in solid oak with etched glass, are also worth noting. The tour of this exquisite testimony to fine craftsmanship lasts about an hour.

Hours: Mar to mid-Dec, Tues–Fri 11am–3pm, Sun 1–4pm (tours given hourly). **Closed:** Major holidays. **Admission:** $5 adults, $3 seniors and students, free for children 11 and under.

You may not think visiting a supermarket is a prime weekend activity, but **Stew Leonard's,** 100 Westport Ave. (tel. 203/847-7213), is somewhat of a phenomenon. A sign on the oven here boasts that 1,080 dinner rolls, 480 filled croissants, 450 hard rolls, 450 butter croissants, 360 grinders, and 120 Italian loafs can all be baked on one rack! A few paces away in the dairy-processing plant, cartons of milk are filled and move around like massed soldiers on a conveyor belt—10 million quarts of milk sold in a year. In the juice plant, 151 million oranges are used to produce 29 million quarts of juice.

Stew Leonard managed to build a rip-roaring business because his store serves the customer in the full sense. First, it's fun. Life-size musical puppets perform country music in the canned-goods area; a human dairy cow trots down the aisles greeting customers; outside, the little farm—complete with a water mill and live crowing cocks and geese—attracts the kids. And then there are those personal touches: a suggestion box, a whole wall of photographs of happy customers pictured proudly carrying their Stew Leonard shopping bags all over the world, and a photo gallery of "neighbors and customers"—Lowell Weicker, Phil Donahue and Marlo Thomas, and Henry Kissinger among them. Photographs of the managers and personnel also smile down from the walls. Fish, meat, lobsters, caramel corn—the foods are all here in this emporium where Rule 1, boldly displayed at the entrance, states: "The customer is always right!" It's followed by Rule 2: "If the customer is ever wrong, reread Rule 1." This place is a veritable attraction in itself and one that other supermarkets might emulate.

Hours: Daily 7am–11pm.

South Norwalk's Washington Street

Galleries, shops, restaurants, and boutiques line this street leading down to the waterfront. Starting at the junction of Washington and North Main, here are several stores of note: **Primo** sells up-to-the-minute lighting fixtures; **& Co** sells household accessories, china, gifts, and soaps; and **Sono General Store** specializes in gourmet items, porcini and cèpe mushrooms, all kinds of oils and vinegars, coffees, and teas. You can also obtain salads and sandwiches, along with dishes like veal with basil sauce, and eat at one of the four tables. **Sassafras** features folk art.

On the opposite side of the street, starting at the river end, doll fanciers will love the collection of dollhouses and furniture at **Molly Brody Miniatures.** Just up the street, **Earth Stuff** sells toys and tools for the environment, while **Miller Fine Art** is the major gallery on the street.

Silvermine, Wilton, Cannon Crossing, Ridgefield & Danbury

In nearby New Canaan, you can call at the **Silvermine Guild Arts Center,** 1037 Silvermine Rd. (tel. 203/966-5617 or 966-5618), a complex of galleries and school of art well known for the annual Art of the Northeast competition and the biennial National Print Show. Founded in 1922 by the Silvermine Guild of Artists, the center also features a summer chamber-music series and a variety of workshops and lectures.

Hours: Wed–Sat 11am–5pm, Sun 1–5pm.

From New Canaan, Rte. 106 will bring you to Wilton; from Norwalk, take Rte. 7.

The **Wilton Heritage Museum,** Wilton Historical Society, 249 Danbury Rd., Wilton (tel. 203/762-7257), is housed in a handsome 1756 central-chimneyed Colonial. It offers you the opportunity to view a series of authentically furnished and decorated period rooms: an early 18th-century kitchen with a kas of Norwalk redware (once common cookware, but now more treasured than fine European china because of its rarity); an 18th-century parlor with boxed-in beams, containing a treasured Ralph Earl portrait and a corner cupboard of 18th-century English ceramics; and an 1835 early Empire formal dining room with a painted canvas floor cloth. Upstairs, the 1825–29 late Federal bedroom contains a fluted pencil four-poster and exquisite samplers, silhouettes, and "mourning pictures," while the Doll and Toy Room charms with figures like a penny wooden doll and an apple doll and dollhouses dating back to 1870. The museum also has an extensive costume collection and examples are displayed on mannequins. Two ground-floor rooms are used for temporary exhibitions (when I visited, a textile display of patterns and designs, showing the processes by which they were made). A nice time to visit is during Christmas season, when the house is decorated for a Victorian Christmas and candlelight tours are given.

Hours: Tues–Thurs 10am–4pm (occasionally Sun 2–4pm).

Cannon Crossing, at the Cannondale Railroad Station, in Wilton (tel. 203/762-2233), reminds me for some reason of Brigadoon. It's a small village, dreamed of and assembled here by actress June Havoc. In fact, she rescued and restored it, investing her life's savings from stage, screen, and TV appearances. Years ago, June's husband found a derelict mill here and they used to come by and picnic. Close to 20 years ago they bought the 8 acres on both sides of the river, restored the mill, and set about saving other local landmarks. Though June moved on, the stores thrive and form a mini design center of sorts. Part of the still-functioning station operates as the Depot, run by Benedictines who sell capes from Guatemala; crafts and fabrics from Turkey, China, and other nations; and religious and philosophical books and tapes.

The schoolhouse serves as the delightful Old Schoolhouse Cafe. Here you can sit on the flagstone patio under the sycamore and maple, listening to the flowing river while you sample an omelet, a salad niçoise, a broccoli-and-ham quiche, a pasta salad, or similar offerings for $8 to $11 (open Tues–Sun 11am–5pm). Other shops are in the Cow Barn and Keeping Barn, including Penny Ha'Penny, which specializes in English foodstuffs—jams, jellies, Heinz salad creams, crackers, and sweets—as well as gifts and crafts. Green Willow Antiques operates out of the original farmhouse. Other stores worth exploring vend quilts, pillows, and other country items; the tinsmith Jim sells his hand-wrought items styled after Early American patterns; Annabelle Green assembles her own beautifully fetching flower arrangements; Designer Consigner offers creative home-decorating items; and the Cannon Dale Gallery features works by local artists.

Hours: Tues–Sun 11am–5pm.

Continue north on Rte. 7 to the junction of Rte. 102, turn left, and follow the signs into Ridgefield.

Here, begin at the **Keeler Tavern Museum** (1733), 132 Main St. tel. 203/438-5485). From 1772, when it became an inn, this old building was a regular stop on the stagecoach run between New York and Boston. It was also a Revolutionary meeting place, no doubt the reason why the British lobbed a cannonball—which is lodged there to this day—at it in 1777 during the Battle of Ridgefield. For over 130 years it remained in the Keeler family; in 1907 architect Cass Gilbert purchased the property as his summer home, adding some interior embellishments. Tour the tap room, ladies' parlor, dining rooms, sleeping rooms, and well-equipped kitchen. The gardens provide a peaceful oasis.

Hours: Wed and Sat–Sun 1–4pm. **Closed:** Jan. **Admission:** $3 adults, $1 children 11 and under.

The **Aldrich Museum,** 258 Main St. (tel. 203/438-4519), housed in a 1783 building, displays contemporary art and offers a quiet sculpture garden with changing modern pieces.

Hours: Tues–Sun 1–5pm. **Admission:** $3 adults, $2 seniors; free for children 11 and under.

From Ridgefield, take Rte. 35 north to join Rte. 7, which will take you into Danbury. Composer Charles Ives was born here, and you can visit this Pulitzer Prize winner's birthplace at 5 Mountainville Rd. (tel. 203/743-5200; open Wed–Sun 2–5pm). He's also commemorated by the **Charles Ives Center for the Arts,** Mill Plain Road (tel. 203/837-9226), an outdoor performance facility with a pagoda-style bandshell extending out over a pond in a woodland setting. In summer it offers a schedule of all kinds of classical, pop, jazz, and folk artists, many of them playing the kinds of music that so inspired Ives. Local lore claims that there's one native frog that croaks in time with the music. Picnics here are a must.

The **Scott Fanton Museum,** 43 Main St., Danbury (tel. 203/743-5200), features textiles, woodworking tools, and Revolutionary War memorabilia and includes the Dodd Hat Shop, which interprets the history of the hat-making industry. The museum also maintains Charles Ives's birthplace, which contains many of his original furnishings, including his piano.

Hours: Wed–Sun 2–5pm.

From Danbury it's just a hop to **Candlewood Lake,** an attractive summer romping ground great for picnicking, boating, swimming, and fishing. Or just east of Danbury lies **Bethel,** a town with attractive 18th-century homes along South Main Street. Note the 1750 House, the Opera House, and Dicksons. The town is conveniently located for exploring **Putnam Memorial State Park,** a haven for picnicking, cross-country skiing, and hiking.

If you prefer the shore to wandering the backroads of southwestern Connecticut, then it's only a short drive from Norwalk into **Westport.** Dubbed Beverly Hills East, this well-kept town flanks the Saugatuck River. Along the river's west bank, stone and other benches are set on the ground under the willows and other trees, making for a tranquil resting spot. On Main Street in town (as befits its celebrity status) you'll find branches of Barney's, Anne Taylor, Portico (on the opposite side of the river), and other top-of-the-line stores. Farther east on the Boston Post Road are plenty of nationally known emporiums. You can watch Westporters shopping at the **Hay Day Country Farm Market,** an upscale supermarket where everything is displayed in picture-perfect fashion in wooden crates or gleaming display cabinets—from the fish to the meats to the produce and the flowers. Drop in at the café and enjoy an espresso. (Note that the magazine racks here don't hold *People* and the *Enquirer.* They're strictly reserved for *Martha Stewart's Living, Cook's Illustrated, Food & Wine,* and similar.) In Westport, beach access is a problem because a sticker is required—you'll have to stay at the Inn at Longshore or at one of the other bed-and-breakfasts that provide beach tags or you'll have to head for **Sherwood Island State Park** (tel. 203/226-6983). Here, there's a 1½-mile beach with a bathhouse, but it gets very crowded after Memorial Day. Parking is $8 on weekends.

Norwalk Area Lodging & Dining

An appealing place to stay is the **Silvermine Tavern,** Silvermine and Perry avenues, Norwalk, CT 06850 (tel. 203/847-4558). There are six rooms in the lovely old inn, which overlooks the mill pond, and four over the country store across the street. They're simple and unremarkable, each with white chenille spreads on pine beds, lace curtains, a desk, two chairs, and a dresser. The public areas are furnished far more lavishly, with antiques, and there are two parlors with fireplaces, one with a TV. The tavern is a pleasant quaffing spot: Old farm implements and folk art decorate the walls, while a female figure stands beside the bar as a reminder of the not-so-long-ago state law that banned women from coming within a foot of the bar. A dining patio overlooks the mill pond with its resident swans. The menu selections run from classic New England favorites like lobster pie and prime rib to veal saltimbocca and roast duckling with mulled-cider sauce, costing $15 to $23. A 20-dish buffet brunch is served Sunday.

Rates: $90–$110 double. **Dining Hours:** Mon and Wed–Thurs noon–3pm and 6–9pm, Fri–Sat noon–3pm and 6–10pm, Sun 11am–2:30pm (brunch).

Norwalk Dining

The scene along Washington Street changes frequently, but here are some of the more stable establishments. **Pasta Nostra,** 116 Washington St. (tel. 203/854-9700), catches the eye with its black-and-white mosaic-tile floor, track lighting, and combination of banquettes, bentwood chairs, and oak tables.

The aromas coming from the kitchen stimulate the appetite. The menu changes weekly, but among the exceptional hors d'oeuvres might be pâté of chicken livers and mushrooms or a mozzarella-and-prosciutto roll with sun-dried tomatoes. The pastas are made on the premises: Try the unique cappellacci con zucca (Emiglian squash–filled tortellone served with cheese, prosciutto, and toasted hazelnuts) or the spicy red linguine with an asparagus sauce with butter and parmesan. You'll also find a couple of local fresh fish dishes, like pan-fried gray sole or Peconic Bay scallops. Prices range from $14 to $23. Chocolate almond-rum cake and an extra-special pineapple-strawberry tiramisù round out the menu.

Hours: Wed–Sat 5:30pm–closing.

Donovan's, 138 Washington St. (tel. 203/838-3430), was here long before the street became (newly) fashionable, having been established in 1889. It's a simple beer-and-hamburger joint with blue gingham tablecloths and prize-fighter portraits looking down at the wooden tables and booths.

Hours: Mon–Sat noon–3pm and 5–10pm, Sun noon–6pm.

At the corner of Washington and South Main, **Rattlesnake,** 2–4 S. Main St. (tel. 203/852-1716), a high-ceilinged bright space, attracts a good crowd for southwestern cuisine. The bar is—guess what?—shaped like a rattlesnake.

Hours: Mon–Tues 11:30am–9pm, Wed–Thurs 11:30am–10pm, Fri–Sat 11:30am–11pm, Sun noon–9pm.

Meson Galicia, 10 Wall St. (tel. 203/866-8800), also known as Rte. 1, has earned a reputation locally for fine food. It's an attractive bilevel restaurant: The upper tier is a gallery of booths fashioned from church pews and separated by lace curtains; the lower, a skylit dining room with Windsor chairs. It serves authentic Spanish food to the accompaniment of Spanish music. Besides the daily specials—halibut in green sauce, roast chicken with Tío Pepe sherry sauce—the menu features dishes like duckling with figs and sherry sauce and braised chicken with rioja red-wine sauce, priced from $18 to $23. You could make a meal out of the 10 or so tapas offered—like Galician crêpes stuffed with marinated salmon and eggplant confit, Catalán tomato bread with serrano ham and manchego cheese, and duck tenderloin with sautéed artichokes and sweet-and-sour cherry sauce. My choice for dessert is either the orange-chocolate mousse or the Galician-style rice pudding.

Hours: Tues–Fri noon–3pm and 6–9pm, Sat–Sun 6–9pm.

A traditional local favorite, the **Lighthouse Restaurant,** 2 Wilton Ave. (tel. 203/847-7500), thrives especially on weekends when happy diners feast on a variety of seafood—swordfish, sautéed crabmeat, poached salmon, cioppino, broiled fish, Alaskan king crab legs, and broiled or deep-fried scallops, priced from $12 to $30. Among the appetizers you'll find oysters casino or Rockefeller, scungilli salad, or clams from the raw bar, plus stuffed mushrooms and shell macaroni stuffed with crab, shrimp, and scallops in a cheese sauce with wine. Italian specialties are available too—veal parmesan, francese, and so on—for non–fish eaters. The atmosphere is typical of a fish restaurant: tanks in which brilliantly colored tropical fish glide around, portholelike stained-glass windows, and plain wooden booths.

Hours: Mon–Thurs noon–3pm and 5:30–10pm, Fri noon–3pm and 5:30–11pm, Sat 5:30–11pm, Sun 5:30–10pm.

Trimmed lawns and flowering borders suggest that the **Silver Star,** 210 Connecticut Ave. (tel. 203/852-0023), is no ordinary diner. And indeed it's not. It's 750 square feet complete with a large semicircular bar with lots of chrome and Mylar and a hefty dash of extra pizzazz. It's also the best breakfast place around here—36 omelets alone to choose from! And you'll be dining in a formal room off tables set with cloths under glass, seated on cushy Breuer-style chairs. Or you can choose the more typical diner quarters. The dinner menu is extensive, featuring seafood, chicken, beef, and veal—everything from shrimp teriyaki to liver anglaise and veal marsala—ranging from $8 to $15. And if you can't find anywhere else open, the Silver Star's lights will be blazing and the folks noshing.

Hours: Sun–Thurs 6am–2am, Fri–Sat 24 hours.

South & East Norwalk Dining

South Norwalk has a good restaurant right down on the Norwalk river-front: The outdoor dining deck at **Sono Seaport,** 100 Water St. (tel. 203/854-9483), is very popular. Fresh fish and shellfish are the specialty, from $7 to $15.

Hours: Daily 11am–10pm.

In East Norwalk, just a few blocks away, **Skipper's,** Beach Road, Cove Marina (tel. 203/838-2211), offers waterfront dining year round. Lobsters from the tank and fresh seafood are the specialties, along with steak, chops, and chicken.

Hours: Tues–Sun 11:30am–10pm.

Ridgefield Area Lodging & Dining

The **Elms Inn,** 500 Main St., Ridgefield, CT 06877 (tel. 203/438-2541), has been thriving as an inn since 1799, so you can expect the comforts of a room like no. 42, with a large inviting four-poster canopied bed, or no. 32 with a similar four-poster, French needlepointed chairs, an oak dresser, and a rocker. There are 4 rooms in the main house and 16 in the annex, all beautifully contemporary with a smattering of antiques. A TV, a phone, and air conditioning are included.

The meals are exquisitely served, in either the Colonial-style low-beamed tavern or a series of intimate dining rooms. The luncheon menu includes an expertly prepared steak tartare, really first class; dinner often brings game—venison, pheasant, and partridge—along with the more usual, although finely prepared, rack of lamb with rosemary sauce, pork chops Normandy (with apples, brandy, cider, and cream), and salmon with lemon-dill sauce. Entrees range from $16 to $30.

Rates (including continental breakfast): $109–$120 double. **Dining Hours:** Mon–Tues and Thurs–Sat noon–2:30pm and 6–9:30pm, Sun 11:30am–2pm (brunch) and 5–8:30pm.

The **West Lane Inn,** 22 West Lane, Ridgefield, CT 06877 (tel. 203/438-7323), occupies a handsome two-story mansion on a broad lawn, framed by a stand of majestic old maples. The front porch is set into a center semicircular bay that adds infinite interest to the facade and the interior spaces. A gracious staircase crowned with a rare spindlework screen leads to 14 unusually large rooms, some with a fireplace, two queen-size beds, chintz-covered wing chairs, and a bamboo desk and bed headboard. All rooms have a bath, a color TV, a radio, and a phone.

Rates (including breakfast): $150 double.

Adjacent to the West Lane, but under separate management, is the **Inn at Ridgefield** (tel. 203/438-8282), serving French fare in elegant surround-ings. You'll find such classics as Dover sole meunière, chateaubriand, duck with sweet-and-sour raspberry sauce, and wienerschnitzel, priced from

$21 to $32. The most extravagant appetizer choices are the Beluga Malossol caviar and the lobster cocktail. There's also a $48 five-course table d'hôte offering a choice of at least six entrees.

Hours: Mon–Fri noon–2pm and 6–9pm, Sat noon–2pm and 6–10pm, Sun noon–2pm and 3–8pm.

Stonehenge, Rte. 7 (P.O. Box 667), Ridgefield, CT 06877 (tel. 203/ 438-6511), is the area's most appealing inn. Outside of town, it's set on 19 acres, surrounded by trees, with a rambling English-style garden in front and a pond charmingly inhabited by ducks, swans, and Canadian geese in back. In the parlor are fine antiques, books, and some very special Mathew Brady portraits, each explicated by a text about the subject's life. There are 16 rooms in three buildings on the property; all have a bath, air-conditioning, a TV, and a phone. They're well furnished, often with four-posters and other reproductions, but not spectacular. Breakfast can be delivered to your room.

The dining room overlooking the pond offers a first-class cuisine, including specialties like Swiss-style veal with wild mushrooms, shallots, and brandy over cabernet-flavored mashed potatoes; roast free-range poussin with sun-dried cranberry sauce; and sautéed Dover sole with lemon and capers in brown butter with toasted almonds—all for $15 to $28. Salmon-colored tablecloths and old prints make for a romantic setting in the outer porch dining room, while the pine-paneled Druid piano bar/ parlor, warmed by a fire in winter, makes for a cozy dining nook. In summer guests can use the in-ground pool; there are also hiking trails at the edge of the property.

Rates (including continental breakfast): $130–$170 double. **Dining Hours:** Mon–Sat 6–9pm, Sun 11:30am–2:30pm (brunch) and 6–9pm.

Nearby, across the New York border in North Salem, **Auberge Maxime,** Ridegefield Rd., North Salem (tel. 914/669-5450), at the junction of Rtes. 121 and 116, will excite duck lovers. The chef prepares duck in at least five ways—from traditional, with orange sauce, to less traditional, with wild mushrooms and garlic or with wild blueberries. The rest of the seasonal menu may feature such classics as grilled salmon with mustard vinaigrette, grilled chicken breast with morelles, and rack of lamb provençal. Treat yourself to a soufflé for dessert. The tables are decorated with carved wooden decoys; the dining room is country elegant, its tables set with fine china and silver candelabra. In summer, it's pleasant to sit out on the patio and have a cocktail.

Hours: Thurs–Tues noon–3pm and 6pm–closing.

Bethel Lodging

The **Best Western Stony Hill Inn,** U.S. 6, Bethel, CT 06801 (tel. 203/ 743-5533), has been operated and well maintained by the same family for more than 50 years. The motel-style rooms are spotless, and even the telephone mouthpieces are turned over to show they've been cleaned and sanitized. The furniture is modern, consisting of a table, two chairs, a dresser, a bed, and a color TV. The property is set back from the road behind a well-treed grassy slope and pond with resident swans. An outdoor fenced-in pool and play area with swings and a slide will keep the kids happy. In the main building people gather for cocktails in a comfortable room with a large fireplace. In the dining room, looking out onto the pond, a typical Italian-American menu is offered. While you're here, see the wooden replica of Washington Crossing the Delaware, one of the few artifacts saved from the famous, now-mourned Danbury Fair. Facilities include a golf driving range.

Rates: $60 double with one bed, $66 double with two beds.

Bethel Dining
San Miguel, 8 P. T. Barnum Sq. (tel. 203/748-2396), is popular for a full variety of Mexican cuisine—burritos, enchiladas, chimichangas, chiles rellenos—and daily specials like paella and filet mignon con queso. Prices range from $8 to $15.

Hours: Tues–Thurs 5–9pm, Fri–Sat 5–10pm, Sun 5–9pm.

Danbury Dining
Tuxedo Junction, 2 Ives St., Danbury (tel. 203/748-2561), is a good-time nostalgic kind of place. People elbow one another at the long bar alongside scenes from Marilyn Monroe's classics, *The Little Rascals, The Honeymooners,* and other old popular favorites. The murals on the other side of the room were painted by local Jack Barrows, caricaturing everyone from Elvis Presley to W. C. Fields. Entertainment is provided on Sunday, Monday, and Tuesday. In summer, dine out under the colorful awning.

Hours: Daily 11:30am–11pm.

Westport Lodging & Dining
Behind the red-brick Italianate exterior of the **Inn at National Hall,** 2 Post Rd. West, Westport, CT 06880 (tel. 203/221-1351), along the Saugatuck River, visitors will discover a voluptuous and sometimes-whimsical decor (like the trompe-l'oeil library-elevator). The 15 guest rooms are lavish: The Indian Room is extraordinary, with a hand-painted Indian pageant mural, a 20-foot coffered ceiling, and expansive river views. In the Turkistan Suite a curved staircase leads to a bedroom with a canopied king-size bed. A four-poster draped with yards of tasselled gold fabric awaits in the Squirrel Room, lit by a gilded oak chandelier. Each suite's sitting area is made comfortable with plush sofas, handsome Chippendale and similar 17th- and 18th-century English antiques, and fine decoratively molded bookcases. The floor-to-ceiling windows are draped in fine style. All rooms have a bath, a cable TV, a VCR, a phone, and a refrigerator; extra amenities include safes, padded hangers in the closets, shaving mirrors, heated towel racks, and bathrobes. Each room also has

individual stenciling created by a team of artists supervised by a master from England: For example, the Melon Room has a melon mural and blue cloud-filled ceiling; the Tree of Life Room features gold and ocher stenciled vines. Coffee and a newspaper will be set outside your door on a hassock, then you can trot down to sample the continental breakfast buffet or enjoy a full breakfast in your room (you must order the night before).

The inn's **Restaurant Zanghi** (tel. 203/221-7572) drips with atmosphere, established largely by the lighting design, the muted colors of the room, and the curvaceous bar and Corinthian columns at the entrance. Even here trompe-l'oeil is in evidence, for a tassel is designed into the backs of the chairs. A window behind the bar affords views of the kitchen; large windows also provide river views. Expect a well-orchestrated experience. The menu changes seasonally but will likely offer 10 to 12 entrees—like filet mignon whose flavor is brought out by the Stilton, veined Cheddar, and fried vidalia onions; grilled glazed salmon with tomato-lemon-shallot salsa; pan-roasted rack of veal with wild mushrooms and toasted couscous with marsala-scented sauce; or my favorite, pistachio-crumbed calf's liver with rosemary/lavender-infused burnt-honey sauce. Prices range from $13 for a vegetarian dish to $27, with most around $20. Among the appetizers, I'd single out the oysters with tomato-horseradish sauce and seared tuna sashimi on greens with tomato-ginger vinaigrette. The culmination of the meal will be dessert—tiramisù with slightly bitter chocolate sorbet and espresso-bean sauce, a "burnt" banana on shortbread with sweet ginger ice cream and freshly made sorbets and ice creams. Guests may relax in front of the fire in the parlor and enjoy the open bar at cocktail hour.

Rates (including breakfast): $205 double; from $315 suite. **Dining Hours:** Mon–Sat noon–2:15pm and 6–9pm (a little later Fri–Sat), Sun 6–9pm.

The **Cotswold Inn,** 76 Myrtle Ave., Westport, CT 06880 (tel. 203/226-3766), doesn't pretend to be old and seasoned. Instead, it aims to provide a modern version of colonial New England. The rooms are furnished with reproductions—Chippendale and Queen Anne wing chairs, highboys, four-posters, butler's tray tables, and the like—and feature appropriate appointments like brass candlesticks, lamps, and sconces. Two rooms have canopied beds and one has a fireplace; all have a cable TV, a phone, and air conditioning. The most handsome is the Wheeler Suite, decked out in apricot and white, with a canopied bed matched with a highboy and Queen Anne loveseat and armchairs. A continental breakfast of fruit, yogurt, and baked goods is served; wine and snacks are available in the early evening.

Rates (including breakfast): $185–$210 double; $235 suite.

The **Inn at Long Shore,** 260 Compo Rd. South, Westport, CT 06880 (tel. 203/226-3316), offers 14 rooms in a prime location overlooking Long Island Sound. The biggest attractions here are the access to the town's golf course, eight clay tennis courts, and pool and beach facilities. The inn's restaurant, **Splash** (tel. 203/454-7798), offers Pacific Rim cuisine and takes full advantage of the view. Among the appetizers is spicy grilled shrimp, which can be followed by a piquant mahi mahi with ginger, garlic, and chiles or spicy stir-fried scallops. Prices are $18 to $24.

    Rates: $135 double. **Dining Hours:** Tues–Thurs 11:30am–2:30pm and 6–10pm, Fri–Sat 11:30am–2:30pm and 6–11pm, Sun 11am–4pm.

Westport Dining
As in any upscale fashionable town, the restaurants here tend to come and go but some stalwarts remain. The current star is **Restaurant Zanghi** at the Inn at National Hall (above).

One of my favorites is the tiny **Da Pietro's,** in town at 36 Riverside Ave. (tel. 203/454-1213). There's only a handful of tables, but the atmosphere is romantically rustic. The high ceilings are supported by small semicircular beams and the cream walls accented with European tapestries. Brass lanterns cast a warm glow over the room at night. Ladderback rush-seated chairs with cushions pull up to tables set with crisp white cloths and candles. The cuisine is classic northern Italian with a touch of southern French. The most popular dish is the rack of lamb with garlic, rosemary, and white wine. The pastas and risottos excite too, combining such ingredients as lobster, wild mushrooms, and artichokes or whatever is freshest in the market. My favorite is a risotto with Maine lobster, vidalia onions, and white wine finished with a touch of cream, parsley, and fresh tomatoes. Other outstanding dishes include roasted duck with black cherries and kirsch and grilled salmon finished with balsamic vinegar, olive oil, and fresh mint. Among the desserts are classics like crème brûlée and profiteroles and a sublime chocolate velvet cake. Prices range from $16 to $26.

    Hours: Mon–Sat 5–10pm.

Other famous Westport locales are the **Cafe Christina** in the Old Library at the center of town at 1 Main St. (tel. 203/221-7950), and several places out along the Boston Post Road, such as the **Pompano Grill,** at no. 1460 (tel. 203/259-1160); the **Meeting Street Grill,** at no. 1563 (tel. 203/256-3309); **Pane e Vino,** at no. 1431 (tel. 203/255-1153), for sophisticated Italian cuisine; and **Sakura,** at no. 680 (tel. 222-0802), for sushi and traditional hibachi cuisine.

Weston Dining
The **Cobbs Mill Inn,** on Rte. 57 north in Weston (tel. 203/227-7221), offers pretty dining on a terrace under the falls at the former grist mill. Veal Cordon Bleu, filet mignon béarnaise, venison, wienerschnitzel, duck, and chicken, at prices from $18, are the order of the day.

    Hours: Mon–Thurs 11:30am–2:30pm and 5pm–closing, Fri–Sat 11:30am–2:30pm and 6pm–closing, Sun 11am–3pm (brunch) and 5pm–closing.

The Ridgefield Area
Special & Recreational Activities

Antiquing: Rte. 7 is known as Antiques Way and around Wilton is a good place to begin. There are about half a dozen shops in Bethel; in Ridgefield, Southport is another great center, where a number are clustered along Pequot Avenue.

Bicycling: For rentals, go to the Better Bicycle Center, 181 Main St., Norwalk (tel. 203/847-0848), open Monday to Saturday.

Boating: At Candlewood Lake boats can be rented.

Canoeing/Kayaking: From April to October, Norwalk Islands Sea Kayaker Tours, 160 Water St., South Norwalk (tel. 203/866-6771) offers two-hour, half-day, full-day, and overnight tours for people at all skill levels. Rentals are also available. There are some winter trips too.

The Outdoor Sports Center, 80 Danbury Rd., Wilton (tel. 203/762-8324), rents canoes and kayaks.

Fishing: Try Candlewood Lake (Squantz Cove), New Fairfield, off Rte. 39 (tel. 203/797-4165), or Lattins Cove, Danbury, off Rte. 7, north of I-84.

Fruit Picking: Blue Jay Orchard in Bethel (tel. 203/748-0119) has apples, peaches, pears, and strawberries.

Golf: *Danbury:* Richter Park Golf Course, Aunt Hack Road (tel. 203/792-2552). *Fairfield:* H. Smith Richardson Golf Club, Hoydens Lane (tel. 203/255-7300). *New Milford:* Candlewood Valley Country Club, Rte. 7 (tel. 203/354-9359). *Norwalk:* Oak Hills Municipal, 165 Fillow Ave. (tel. 203/838-0303). *Ridgefield:* Ridgefield Golf Club, Ridgebury Road (tel. 203/748-7008).

Hiking: Devil's Den Preserve, 33 Pent Rd., Weston (tel. 203/226-4991), has more than 20 miles of trails and offers interpretive nature programs. Putnam Memorial State Park offers opportunities for hiking too.

Horseback Riding: Most of the area's stables specialize in dressage and other equestrian skills. Stonyside Farms, 121 Kensett Dr., Wilton (tel. 203/762-7984), offers one-hour trail rides by reservation.

Sailing: The Norwalk Sailing School, Calf Pasture Beach, Norwalk (tel. 203/852-1857), offers adult weekend classes and rents sailboats and sea kayaks June to August. The Longshore Sailing School, 260 South Compo Rd., Westport (tel. 203/226-4646), offers classes and rents rowboats, canoes, and windsurfers as well as sailboats from June to August.

In South Norwalk, the Sound Sailing Center, 160 Water St. (tel. 203/838-1110), operates a half-day intro to sailing and full-day instructed sailing. Rentals are available. Open May to November.

Skiing: Cross-country skiing is available in Putnam Memorial State Park.

Windsurfing: At Calf Pasture Beach in Norwalk from June to Labor Day, Gone with the Wind Surfing Lessons (tel. 203/852-1857) teaches all ages and levels. Rentals are available.

Essex, the Connecticut River Valley & Hartford

Distance in Miles: Middletown, 101; Essex, 110; Hartford, 113; Old Saybrook, 113

Estimated Driving Time: About 2 hours

<hr />

Driving: Take I-95 north to Rte. 9 going to Essex. For Middletown, take the Merritt Parkway to I-91, then pick up Rte. 66 east.

Bus: Peter Pan (tel. 800/343-9999) travels to Middletown and Hartford.

Train: Amtrak travels to Old Saybrook and Hartford. For information call 800/872-7245.

Further Information: For more about the area's events and festivals and about Connecticut in general, call or write **Connecticut State Tourism,** 865 Brook St., Rocky Hill, CT 06067 (tel. 860/258-4335, or 800/282-6863).

For specific information about the area (except Essex and Old Lyme), contact the **Connecticut River Valley and Shoreline Visitors Council,** 393 Main St., Middletown CT 06457 (tel. 860/347-6924).

For Hartford, contact the **Greater Hartford Convention & Visitors Bureau,** One Civic Center Plaza, Hartford, CT 06103 (tel. 860/728-6789). For information about Farmington, contact the **Farmington Valley/West Hartford Chamber of Commerce** (tel. 860/527-9258).

<hr />

Today you can stand at the lower reaches of the Connecticut River and survey a scene that has changed little since Adrian Block first sailed up the river in 1614, for the banks have remained largely unscarred by the industrial mills and manufacturing plants that marred so many other New England river towns. The towns you'll encounter—Old Lyme, Hadlyme, and East Haddam on the east bank and Old Saybrook, Essex, Deep River, Chester, Haddam, and Middletown on the west—are all (except perhaps Middletown) entrancing old towns that have retained their 18th- and 19th-century serenity. Lacking any waterfalls and therefore waterpower, they avoided the destiny that created such industrial towns as Holyoke and Springfield.

No wonder the Native Americans called this river the Quinnehtukqut ("long tidal river")—its waters, abundant with salmon and shad, flow 400 miles from the Québec–New Hampshire border all the way south to Long Island Sound. At one time salmon was so plentiful it was given to servants, and shad was reserved for the animals. Although the Dutch discovered the river, it was John Winthrop, Jr., who came from the Massachusetts Bay Colony to found another colony at the behest of certain English Puritans and Cromwellian followers. This colony flourished largely because of the river's gifts and the trade that the waterway encouraged. Ivoryton, for example, was so named because it was the final destination for shiploads and cartloads of ivory brought from the East to this small town, where the Pratt Read factory continues to turn out piano and organ keys (albeit no longer ivory ones). Essex grew into a major shipbuilding town where the first U.S. Navy boat, the 24-gun *Oliver Cromwell*, was constructed during the American Revolution, a fact that the British never forgot. They took vengeance during the War of 1812, when they bribed a local youth to help them navigate the treacherous sandbars at the river's narrow neck and proceeded to shell the town and destroy 28 ships, or $160,000 worth of American shipping. Today anchored in that same harbor are all shapes and sizes of yachts and pleasure craft. Their bronzed crews, sporting Topsiders and crewnecks, can be found winding down after a day's sail over a pint of ale or a drink in the old tap room at the area's finest hostelry, the Griswold Inn (below).

Farther upriver, East Haddam was a great shipbuilding town that turned out many of the great schooners that sailed downriver and then to points all around the world. One of the shipbuilders, William Goodspeed, was a hotel owner and theater lover who wanted to attract people to the area. So he built his very own Goodspeed Theater, a six-story gingerbread extravaganza in East Haddam (the theater is on the top floor and his offices and a general store are below). For years people traveling upriver stopped to attend a show. Sometimes whole Broadway shows were transported here to Goodspeed's theater, which thrived from 1876 until the 1920s, when river travel was eclipsed by the railroad and, more important, by the automobile. Goodspeed's opera house then became a state garage and warehouse. Threatened with demolition in the 1950s, it was narrowly rescued from the wrecker's ball by a dedicated group. Now audiences can enjoy entertaining evenings in this Victorian gem, currently dedicated to preserving the legacy of American musical theater.

Close by, on the southernmost hill of the so-called Seven Hills, William Gillette was so moved by the beauty of the wooded bluffs and the river that one evening, on a return journey from Long Island, he cancelled his

Events & Festivals to Plan Your Trip Around

May: Essex Shad Festival.

June: Rose Festival, Hartford.

July: River Festival, Hartford—music, boat races, fireworks (July 4).

Niantic Lions Lobster Festival, East Lyme—seafood, arts and crafts (July 4).

The Deep River Muster of Fife and Drum. Contact Deep River Town Hall at 860/526-6024 (usually the third weekend).

September: Berlin Fair, about 10 miles south of Wethersfield. It has all kinds of arts and crafts, bakery, photo, needlework, livestock, and other exhibits, along with country events like horse and oxen draws, frog jumps, nail driving contests, and corn husking bees (usually the last weekend).

The Durham Fair, largest in the state. Call 860/349-3625 (usually the last weekend).

Chrysanthemum Festival, Bristol (last week of September and first in October).

October: Apple Harvest, Southington, about 14 miles from Hartford—a parade, arts and crafts, and apple-related fare (early October). Contact the Southington Chamber of Commerce (tel. 860/628-8036).

Head of the Connecticut Regatta, Middletown (usually Columbus Day weekend).

November: Wesleyan Potters Exhibit and Sale, Middletown (through December).

December: Festival of Lights, Hartford, when Constitution Plaza is ablaze with 250,000 Christmas lights (the day after Thanksgiving to New Year's Day).

Torchlight Parade, muster, and carol sing, Old Saybrook (usually the second Saturday).

plans for constructing a summer mansion at Greenport and built his idiosyncratic castle here.

During the late 19th century it was common to see a huge sidewheeler churning up the river from New York City to Hartford on a 140-mile journey that, with luck, might take 18 hours. Such steamer passenger service continued until 1931, when it finally succumbed to the motor car and the railroad, which had come to the valley in 1871. Today you can take a nostalgic ride aboard one of the old-style locomotives that

Connecticut

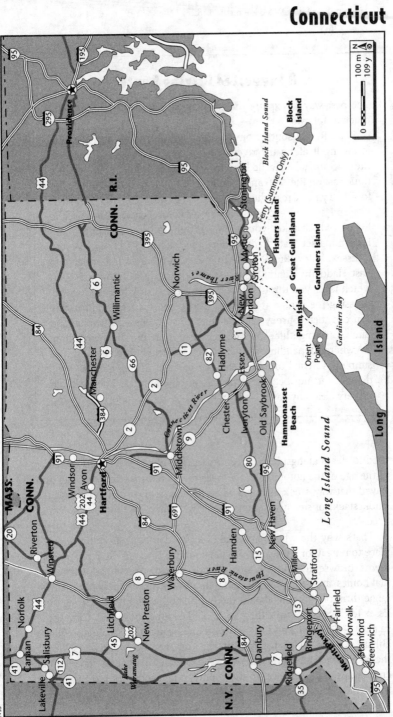

A Suggested Driving Route

The best way to explore the whole area is to drive a loop pretty much as follows:

Take Rte. 9 south from Middletown and turn onto Rte. 9A, following it along the river to Chester. At Chester turn east on Rte. 148 and take the old ferry to Hadlyme and Gillette Castle. Continue east on Rte. 148 and then Rte. 82 and turn south on Rte. 156 to Old Lyme. Cross the river by bridge on I-95 south and take Rte. 154, looping around to Saybrook Point, Fenwick, and back to Rte. 1, which takes you to Westbrook and out to Clinton and Hammonasset State Park. From here take Rte. 153 via Ivoryton to Essex, follow Rte. 9 north to Rte. 82, and cross the bridge into East Haddam. Continue on Rte. 82 to the junction of Rte. 151, which leads you through Moodus and eventually links to Rte. 66. Crossing the bridge at Portland brings you back to Middletown. You can then journey into Hartford to view the state capital and catch some nightlife. You can, of course, start and finish your loop anywhere, depending on where you overnight. To make things simple, I've tried to follow this particular itinerary, because logic demands it, not because it reflects my preferences. Those should be very clear anyway.

used to steam alongside the river. As the age of sail and steam gave way to the age of the automobile, the river towns returned to a slumber and stayed that way, stuck in an era when the tall masts of schooners and the smokestacks of steamers jammed the river, when life flowed at a gentler pace.

That's why the whole area makes a wonderfully refreshing, magical place to retreat for a weekend. You can ramble through these pristine old towns, browse in antiques stores, wander down streets lined with Colonial homes, and stop in at comfortable country inns. Experience the nostalgic thrill of climbing aboard the big steam locomotive that runs from Essex to Chester or cruise the river aboard all kinds of vessels, passing the same wooded bluffs and seeing the same beauty that inspired William Gillette. Canoe, swim, fish, go fruit picking, cross-country ski, skate on the lakes, enjoy an evening at the Goodspeed, stop in at art galleries and craft shops, and just revel in the countryside, shoreline, and riverbanks that Childe Hassam loved to paint. You'll return home totally rejuvenated—if you return at all.

MIDDLETOWN, CHESTER & DEEP RIVER

Area Attractions

Home to **Wesleyan University**'s appealing campus, **Middletown** offers varied cultural events—concerts, theater, and art shows, many staged at the university's Center for the Arts; call 860/347-9411, ext. 2807, for a schedule. The **Wesleyan Potters Craft Center**, 350 S. Main St. (tel. 860/347-5925), is also here. The best time to visit is during the annual sale from Thanksgiving to mid-December, when all kinds of crafts are on display. Wander around the old campus and note what's going on at the riverside **Harbor Park**, the location for many special events, including the culmination of the **Head of Connecticut Regatta** on Columbus Day weekend. Both 1-hour and 2½-hour cruises operate daily from Harbor Park from early June to Labor Day (weekends only in October). In fall, special 4-hour cruises travel the river to Gillette Castle from early June to Labor Day and on weekends in fall for leaf viewing. On Friday you can take the Jambalaya cruise departing at 7:30pm from Hartford. Cruise prices range from $6 to $12. For information, contact Deep River Navigation Company, P.O. Box 382, Deep River, CT 06417 (tel. 860/526-4954).

To the west of Middletown is the small town of **Durham,** an old farming community that has changed little since the 19th century; here you can recapture the era at the annual **Durham Fair,** the largest and one of the most popular in the state.

Southwest of Middletown, **Middlefield** offers the **Powder Ridge Skiing Area** (tel. 860/349-3454) and **Lyman Orchards,** at the junction of Rtes. 147 and 157 (tel. 860/349-1793), a real treat at apple-blossom time or at fall harvest. The orchard's 25,000 trees (60% apples) are spread over 300 acres, and you can pick apples, strawberries, raspberries, pumpkins, and peaches. The farm, owned by the Lyman family since 1741, possesses a fascinating history and occupies some of the most scenic land in the valley. The farm store, Greenfield's, has all kinds of goodies: raw honey; pies, breads, and cookies taken from ovens right on the premises; varieties of squash and melon I'd never seen—in other words, a mass of farm-fresh produce all at very good prices. Events are often scheduled during summer and fall weekends. The store is open daily from 8am to 6pm. The golf course here, part of the farm and quite spectacularly designed by Robert Trent Jones, has eight water holes on the front nine.

From Middletown you can head south for **Chester,** a pretty village worth strolling around and browsing in its antiques, book, and craft stores, before heading for the ferry (in operation since 1769, April to November only) that'll take you across the river to Hadlyme and Gillette Castle.

Cromwell Lodging

Just west of Middletown you can find modern accommodations and an array of facilities at the **Radisson Hotel & Conference Center,** 100 Berlin Rd. (Rte. 72), Cromwell, CT 06416 (tel. 860/635-2000). A domed indoor pool surrounded by tropical plants, a lush garden dining room, and a multilevel lounge with a skylit bar and dancing keep the place hopping. The 217 rooms, some with cathedral ceilings, are all nicely furnished and fully appointed with a color TV, a phone, and climate control.

   Rates: $90 double.

Middletown Dining

Harbor Park, 80 Harbor Dr. (tel. 860/347-9999), is designed to make you feel as though you're aboard ship, with its sailcloth-canvas partitions attached to the staircase railings and neon-lighted mast at the center of the multilevel restaurant/lounge. On the ground floor is a large lounge that gives astounding views of the river, as do the two dining levels above. Specialties include a lobster pot—their version of a clambake consisting of a 1-pound lobster, a pound each of steamers and mussels, and an ear of corn served in a pewter pot—plus steaks, chicken teriyaki, fresh seafood (scrod, broiled sole, paupiettes of sole with shrimp mousse, scampi primavera), and more. The prices, from $10 to $19, include salad, bread, and vegetable. Sunday offers a 25-item buffet brunch and made-to-order omelets and waffles.

   Hours: Sun–Thurs 11:30am–2:30pm and 5–9pm, Fri–Sat 11:30am–2:30pm and 5–11pm.

Chester Lodging & Dining

A truly idyllic retreat on 12 acres surrounded by state forest, the **Inn at Chester,** 318 W. Main St., Chester, CT 06412 (tel. 860/526-9541), was created by building onto a Colonial farmhouse. In the process, the old and the new have been harmoniously combined to create a hospitable, gracious, but modern inn. Owner Deborah L. Moore is a remarkable, energetic woman who pays attention to every little detail and really cares about making her guests comfortable. Get her talking on her previous career.

   The 42 spacious rooms are decorated elegantly with Eldred Wheeler reproductions: The most formal have a Chippendale-style chest and desk; the less formal have more country-style pieces—hoopback Windsor chairs, clubfoot tables, and porcelain or brass lamps. In all rooms (except three in the main house) the TV is tucked in a cabinet; a phone and air-conditioning complete the appointments. Extra touches include fresh flowers and the services of a masseuse.

   The old barn that was moved here houses the delightful **Post and Beam** restaurant, which offers excellent New American cuisine. Start with the flavorful wild-mushroom strudel with a truffle vinaigrette, the spicy shrimp with a salsa of black beans and mango, or one of the extra-special soups, like red-pepper bisque served with a polenta croûton. Among the eight or so main courses ($19 to $24) might be salmon filet enhanced by a passionfruit vin blanc; rack of lamb with Provençal sauce; or cinnamon-cured and -smoked duck with port-wine sauce. For a perfect end select the orange crème brûlée or the crushed-chocolate soufflé with cappuccino mousse.

Guests may retire downstairs to either the well-equipped fitness room or the pool room and library (some wonderful volumes too) warmed by a fire on winter nights. From spring to early fall the grounds resemble an English garden redolent with lilacs, roses, hollyhocks, and many other flowering plants and shrubs. For outdoor exercise there's a tennis court, bikes, and miles of nature trails in the adjacent state forest. Nearby Cedar Lake is good for swimming or ice skating.

Rates: $100–$160 double. **Dining Hours:** Mon–Sat 11:30am–2:30pm and 5:30–9pm, Sun 11:30am–2:30pm and 3:30–7:30pm.

Chester Dining

As close as you'll get to a French country bistro, the **Restaurant du Village**, 59 Main St. (tel. 860/526-5301), is always gaily bedecked with plants and flowers placed in window boxes and along the small alley that leads to the entrance. Inside, you'll find two small rooms: one a cozy lounge/dining area with a terra-cotta bar; the other, an intimate dining room made a little more formal by the gilt-framed paintings gracing the walls. The menu changes frequently, but the cuisine is always imaginative. At the time of my visit, appetizers included a house veal-and-pork terrine studded with pistachios and served with cranberry chutney; snails sautéed with shiitake mushrooms in a garlic-and-parsley sauce flavored with Pernod and stuffed into a puff pastry shell; or an inspired gâteau aubergine—thinly sliced eggplant grilled and combined with layers of sautéed spinach and roasted red peppers, served with a chunky tomato sauce. There were about six main dishes, among them duck with sun-dried cherries and cranberries in a ginger-scented sauce and medallions of filet mignon served with a cognac sauce and topped with carmelized shallots and garlic. Game is often featured and there's always fresh fish, like the delicious roast monkfish with bacon and roast garlic cloves served with crème fraîche and Spanish sherry-wine vinegar sauce. Prices range from $23 to $26. For dessert, you'll be lucky if the special gâteau is featured—a chocolate genoise filled with orange liqueur–scented chocolate mousse and raspberry jam, covered in Belgian chocolate ganache.

Hours: Memorial Day–Columbus Day, Tues–Sun 5:30–10pm (seatings at 5:30 and 8:15pm); the rest of the year, Wed–Sun 5:30–10pm. Jan–Mar, usually open weekends only.

A covered bridge over the Pattaconk Creek leads to the **Chart House**, Rte. 9, Exit 6 (tel. 860/526-9898); located in a restored brush factory, it offers cozy dining and a pleasant lounge with oak furnishings and plush sofas. The menu features steaks, chicken, and seafood.

Hours: Mon–Fri 5:30–9pm, Sat 5–10pm, Sun 4–9pm.

Fiddler's Seafood, 4 Water St. (tel. 860/526-3210), is a plain and simple restaurant room decked out in Wedgwood blue and furnished with bentwood chairs set at tables spread with white tablecloths. Nautical lithographs decorate the walls. A variety of fish is offered, depending on availability—swordfish, baked or stuffed sole, clams, shrimp casino, lobster, and bouillabaisse. Prices range from $12 to $20.

Hours: Tues–Thurs 11:30am–2pm and 5:30–9pm, Fri–Sat 11:30am–2pm and 5:30–10pm, Sun 4–9pm.

Next door to Fiddler's (above), the **Wheat Market** (tel. 860/526-9347), is a great take-out spot that also has a few tables with wrought-iron chairs if you want to rest a while.

Hours: Mon–Sat 9am–6pm.

The Mad Hatter, Main Street (tel. 860/526-2156), is so named because the baker who prepares the cuisine here loves to wear hats. Among her major accomplishments are the eight or so kinds of bread she bakes—sour dough, double raisin, and a wonderful bittersweet Belgian chocolate, for example. Light lunches are also available. Start with a soup like carrot-ginger and follow with Tuscan white-bean salad or chicken-and-almond salad on any of the wonderful breads.

Hours: Wed–Thurs 8am–8pm, Fri–Sun 8:30am–9pm.

Deep River Lodging

An obvious love of life and an incredible amount of energy are reflected in **Riverwind,** Main Street, Deep River, CT 06417 (tel. 860/526-2014). The proud owner of this engaging bed-and-breakfast is Barbara Barlow, who hails from Smithfield, Va., where she taught learning-disabled children for many years. Her current life evolved from her part-time work as a restoration specialist. When she was asked to restore a house in Connecticut, she fell in love with the area, opened an antiques store, and then set about renovating this 1850 beige clapboard house. And a wonderful job she's done, filling it with curious personal collectibles and furnishings. As her father was a hog farmer, Barbara has a definite fondness for pigs, so all kinds of references appear throughout—tiny wooden toys, weathervanes, and other "pig" art, not to mention Smithfield hams hanging in the kitchen. Bird's nests also appear tucked away in different places.

In the parlor and breakfast room antiques abound—decoys, a sleigh, a collection of arrowheads Barbara personally unearthed from Virginia soil, a basket filled with large cones, an old quilt draped over a wooden field rake and tacked above the fireplace, a blanket chest serving as a coffee table. A filling breakfast is served at a harvest table in front of the fire in winter.

The eight guest rooms are up the stairs (each step prettified by dried flower arrangements). Each room is unique but all feature colorful old quilts and floor stenciling. The Smithfield Room's centerpiece is a maple rope bed (converted, of course), covered with a red, white, and blue quilt that inspires the decor. Personal accents include a miniature doll's chest that belonged to Barbara's grandmother and the *Oxford Book of English Verse* tucked into the bedside table. In Zelda's green room, with a high carved oak bed and rope rug, the bath is most entertaining (check out the 1862 wall plaque). This room also contains an old Virginia hotel washstand and Barbara's grandmother's oak hall tree. The Havlow Room is named after her family farm and features pine furnishings and charming cornhusk dolls representing the travelers on the Yellow Brick Road. The most spectacular is the Champagne and Rose Room, featuring a mahogany pencil-post canopied bed and rose-colored wingbacks as well as a Japanese steeping tub in the bath and a private balcony.

For guests' leisure there are four common rooms (two with fireplaces), including the games room with board games and a porch furnished with wicker. For breakfast you can expect—what else?—Smithfield ham and pig-shaped biscuits, coffee cake, fruit compote, and fresh fruit. In the back yard are hibachis for guests' use; feel free to pour yourself a welcome glass of sherry from the decanter in the living room.

Rates (including breakfast): $92–$150 double.

HADLYME & GILLETTE CASTLE

Just off Rte. 82 rise the towers of a 24-room Rhenish fantasy called **Gillette Castle** (tel. 860/424-3200), where actor William Gillette and his 15 cats lived from 1919 to 1937. Constructed of granite and hand-hewn timbers, the house will amaze you with the eccentric mechanical devices Gillette invented—huge cantilevered wooden locks on the massive entrance doors, wooden light switches, a dining table and desk chair that slide on metal runners, a cocktail cabinet rigged with several locks, and mirrors placed strategically to view who was into the liquor or was at the front door (so he could decide whether he was home). Here he entertained his friends—most notably with his outdoor railroad that ran down from "Grand Central Terminal," along the river's bluffs, and across a fragile bridge strung between two massive outcroppings of rock.

In the upstairs rooms, among Gillette's personal memorabilia are photographs depicting this stunningly handsome man as he appeared in *Dream Maker*, *Secret Service*, and *Private Secretary*, and in his most famous role as Sherlock Holmes. Fascinating to peruse are his scrapbooks, theater reviews, letters, notes that he wrote to neighboring children, anecdotes, watercolors and oils, and an incredible number of cutesy cat artifacts. The whole place is capped by a magnificent view from the terrace and the tower, which you can climb only if you visit off-season.

So attached was he to his idiosyncratic creation that in his will he stated that "this 122-acre property should not pass to any blithering saphead who has no conception of where he is or with what surrounded." After his death, it became a state park in 1944 and now encompasses more than 200 acres.

Hours: Memorial Day–Columbus Day, daily 10am–5pm; Columbus Day to the last weekend before Christmas, Sat–Sun 10am–4pm. **Admission:** $4 adults, $2 children 6–11.

OLD LYME

Area Attractions

Miss Florence Griswold was the mentor, patron, and friend of many of America's great turn-of-the-century painters—Childe Hassam, Henry Ward Ranger, Willard Metcalf, Charles Ebert, Carleton and Guy Wiggins—who painted the surrounding landscapes when they spent their summers boarding at her Georgian mansion in Old Lyme between 1900 and 1915. Her home is now appropriately the **Florence Griswold Museum,** at 96 Lyme St. (tel. 860/434-5542). The artists painted the house's door panels and overmantels with Connecticut scenes as a gift to their landlady, and today these treasured examples of the American impressionist movement are displayed on the lower floor. Also on view is the Chadwick studio, a turn-of-the-century artist's studio on the grounds.

Hours: June–Dec, Tues–Sat 10am–5pm, Sun 1–5pm; Jan–May, Wed–Sun 1–5pm. **Admission:** $4 adults, $3 seniors, free for children 11 and under.

Across the street these same artists built a museum/gallery for their summer exhibits that's still a prestigious summer gallery; now it's also home to the **Lyme Art Association,** 70 Lyme St. (tel. 860/434-7802), which sponsors several shows a year.

Hours: May to mid-Oct, Tues–Sat noon–5pm, Sun 1–5pm. **Admission:** Donation requested.

Elizabeth Tashjian is an attraction in herself (she's been on the *Tonight Show* and several other talk shows) at her very own **Nut Museum,** 303 Ferry Rd. (tel. 860/434-7636). In her 19th-century mansion, so nutty is she about nuts, she has gathered and displays all kinds of paintings, sculptures, nutcrackers, and "nutty" artifacts.

Hours: May–Oct, Wed and Sat–Sun 1–5pm. **Admission:** $3 and one nut of any variety.

Old Lyme Lodging & Dining

Canopied beds, lace curtains, and colorful quilts add charm and elegance to most of the rooms at the **Bee and Thistle Inn,** 100 Lyme St., Old Lyme, CT 06371 (tel. 860/434-1667), an attractive 1756 residence set back from the road on 5 acres of tree-shaded gardens along the Lieutenant River (where you can sit peacefully in the garden watching the river flow). The 11 guest rooms (9 with bath) include a twin with pine furnishings and Oriental rugs and a large two-room family suite—one room containing a double bed, a single, and a couch-bed; the other, a single—renting for only $75. Fires light up the parlors in winter, making the wing chairs and comfy sofas all the more inviting.

Breakfast, lunch, and dinner are served either by the fireside in the pretty dining room or on the two adjacent terra-cotta–tile terraces. Freshly squeezed juices, fresh fruits, omelets or strawberry crêpes, kippers, and homemade muffins make for a satisfying breakfast delivered to your room or served on the sun porches or in front of the fire. The dining room's menus change seasonally, with the food far from the traditional boring New England fare, for it's sophisticated and finely prepared. At dinner you might find crab ravioli poached in a ginger broth with shiitake mushrooms, baby corn, scallions, and haricots verts; grilled venison on a roasted onion jus with caramelized onions; or ragoût of chicken with roasted shallots and crimini mushrooms. There's always a vegetarian dish too. Prices range from $19 to $27. Try the house specialty dessert called a pecan diamond, swathed in caramel sauce. The luncheon is also very appealing.

Rates: $75–$130 double. **Dining Hours:** Mon and Wed–Sat 8–10am, 11:30am–2pm, and 6–10pm; Tues 8–10am; Sun 8–10am, 11am–2pm (brunch), and 6–10pm.

Across the street, a different ambience prevails at the **Old Lyme Inn,** 85 Lyme St. (P.O. Box 787), Old Lyme, CT 06371 (tel. 860/434-2600), an impressive 1850s farmhouse/mansion with a tree-shaded lawn and a porch. Large tapestries cover the walls of the high-ceilinged Empire-style dining room, handsomely decorated in royal blue. Polished silver and fine stemware are placed on white-clothed tables along with a single salmon-colored rose. Well known for its cuisine, the inn's restaurant was thrice awarded three stars by the *New York Times*. A few of its tempting dishes are lobster thermidor, ballotine of Connecticut pheasant stuffed with dried fruits and nuts and served with a sauce of green peppercorns and port, and chicken roulade filled with spinach, mushrooms, and garlic sausage and served with tomato sauce. Prices range from $20 to $28. For appetizers there are close to a dozen seafood, shellfish, and meat dishes to choose from, as well as a couple of soups. If the raspberry cheesecake japonaise is featured, order it: layers of meringue and chocolate topped with fresh raspberries—who could possibly resist?

A lighter and less expensive menu is served in the handsome Victorian Grill Room, where there's also jazz guitar on Friday and Saturday evenings. In the front hall, note the paintings and stenciling done by Gigi Horr-Liverant depicting local scenes, as well as the many paintings and watercolors found throughout. All were collected by innkeeper Diana Atwood, who carries on the local tradition in her appreciation of art and artists.

The antique curly maple staircase leads to 13 guest rooms (all with bath), each furnished uniquely with ornate mirrors, old chests, and cannonball or canopied beds covered with candlewick spreads. All have air conditioning, TVs, radios, and phones, and you'll also find some extra touches, like witch hazel made in nearby Essex and mints on your pillow.

Rates (including continental breakfast): $105–$160 double. **Closed:** The first two weeks of Jan and Christmas Eve. **Dining Hours:** Mon–Sat noon–2:30pm and 6–9:30pm, Sun 11am–3pm and 4–9pm.

OLD SAYBROOK

Area Attractions

From Old Lyme drive down to Old Saybrook and then head out along Rte. 154 to **Saybrook Point,** marked by two lighthouses—the inner one more often photographed than the outer. Loop around from Saybrook Point across South Cove, past the select community of **Fenwick,** which counts Katharine Hepburn among its residents, and through **Westbrook,** a typical beachfront community with shingled homes (here Frankie's serves dependable shore dinners; Bill's Seafood accepts the bathing-suit crowd), all the way out to **Hammonasset State Park.** By the way, if you can see across the Sound to Long Island as you go, they say it's going to rain within 72 hours.

Old Saybrook Lodging

The **Saybrook Point Inn & Spa,** 2 Bridge St., Old Saybrook, CT 06475 (tel. 860/395-2000), is a stylish modern complex at the mouth of the Connecticut River overlooking Long Island Sound. The 62 rooms and seven suites, most with water views, are comfortably furnished with antique Chippendale and Queen Anne reproductions and reveal the extra attention to detail that makes the difference in any accommodation—an Italian tile bath with a hairdryer and pool towels, a desk with a phone with dataports for computers and fax, a sitting area and a fireplace, a refrigerator and wet bar. Each suite features a living/dining area, a Jacuzzi tub, a separate shower, and bathrobes.

The facilities are extensive—an indoor and outdoor pool with attractive deck, a fully equipped fitness center, and a spa offering facials,

Swedish body treatment, aromatherapy, acupressure, and more. Bicycles are available for rent and the marina offers 120 slips. There's a patio from which guests can contemplate the boats bobbing at the docks. The Terra Mar Grille looks out on the water, and here guests can enjoy some excellent northern Italian and modern American cuisine. For example, you might start with blackened sea scallops with Créole rémoulade and salsa cruda, then follow with either lobster-and-scallop lasagne with roasted vegetables and tomato-basil coulis or herb-roasted chicken breast with sautéed wild mushrooms. The comfortable lounge is furnished with upholstered bamboo chairs.

Rates: Memorial Day–Oct, $180–$255 double; $305 suite.

A fieldstone mansion, the **Castle Inn at Cornfield Point,** Hartland Drive, Old Saybrook, CT 06475 (tel. 860/388-4681), is blessed with a spectacular location atop the cliffs overlooking Long Island Sound, with a distant view of Saybrook Point. It was built around 1906 as a summer cottage for Hartford Insurance's George Watson Beach, and the interior has retained such lavish decorative features as the stained-glass panels gracing the entrance and the doors leading into the dining room. Sadly, though the 21 rooms are large and many have inviting windowseats and glorious views, the furnishings tend to faded Scandinavian modern; Room 119 with its wicker furnishings is an exception. No phones or TVs are provided here. An outdoor pool and access to a private beach are distinct pluses. To get here, take I-95 to Exit 67. Bearing right, go to the third light and turn left onto Main Street. Go two more lights and turn right onto Maple Avenue. Bear left at the stop sign, taking the first right onto Hartland Drive.

Rates (including continental breakfast): $100–$130 double. **Dining Hours:** Mon–Fri noon–2:30pm and 5–9:30pm, Sat noon–2:30pm and 5–10:30pm, Sun 11:30am–2:30pm (brunch) and 4–9pm.

The **Sandpiper Motor Inn,** 1750 Boston Post Rd. (U.S. 1), Old Saybrook, CT 06475 (tel. 860/399-7973), is a modern accommodation offering fully equipped rooms (phone, color TV) decked out in pastels, with floral quilts on the bed and light-oak furnishings. There's a fenced-in outdoor pool. Local beach passes are provided to guests.

Rates: $90–$125 (the higher price for rooms with couch and wet bar). Prices reduced in winter.

Old Saybrook Dining

The **Dock,** at Saybrook Point (tel. 860/388-4665), takes full advantage of its water view and vista across the mouth of the Connecticut River to Great Island. Watch the barges and other craft slipping by or the anchored yachts bobbing dockside while you dine on exceptionally well prepared seafood—haddock, swordfish, scampi, scallops, sole, and lobster (one of the prime attractions), all cooked in a variety of ways—along with the usual steak, veal parmigiana, and chicken for the unconvinced or uninitiated fish diner. Prices run $12 to $28. You'll find the place bursting on weekend nights, with sometimes a two-hour wait in store. In that case, repair to the bar and listen to the entertainment—a piano-and-drums combo the night I stopped by. In winter a fire in the fieldstone fireplace will warm your very cockles. Start with a sampler of the chowders or choice morsels from the raw bar, then move on to the seafood. If the halibut special in dill sauce is available, I highly recommend it.

Sunday brunch is served buffet style, although the omelets and waffles are cooked to order. The nightly entertainment varies from jazz to a pianist/vocalist.

Hours: Mon–Thurs 11am–9pm, Fri–Sun 11am–10pm (Sun brunch 11am–2pm). **Closed:** Mon–Tues in winter.

A 1950s drive-in on Rte. 1, **Johnny Ads,** 910 Boston Post Rd. (tel. 860/388-4032), is famous for its foot-long hot dogs enjoyed by the bathing-suit crowd. Some of the local dignitaries also enjoy them too, as did the late Gov. Ella Grasso, who popped in when she summered in East Lyme. For casual dining, try the popular **Saybrook Fish House,** 99 Essex Rd. (tel. 860/388-4836), where among the nautical regalia of nets and lanterns you can obtain a variety of fresh fish broiled in white wine and butter sauce and a wide choice of shellfish—from shrimp, lobster, and scampi to scungili and little necks. No reservations are taken and the wait on Saturday nights could be long (maximum of about two hours). There are always some appetizers at the bar if you're really famished. Complete dinners are priced from $14 to $21.

Hours: Mon–Thurs noon–4pm and 4:30–9:30pm, Fri noon–4pm and 4:30–10pm, Sat noon–3:30pm and 4–10pm, Sun 1–9pm.

For a change of cuisine, there's also **Luigi's,** 670 Boston Post Rd. (tel. 860/3889190), an informal spot that offers pizza and sandwiches along with more substantial fare like scampi, mussels marinara, veal parmigiana, spaghetti with clam sauce, and one or two steaks.

Hours: Tues–Thurs and Sun 11am–9pm, Fri–Sat noon–10pm. **Closed:** Usually two weeks in Jan.

Westbrook Lodging & Dining

Lee and Vern Mattin fell in love with their **Captain Stannard House,** 138 S. Main St., Westbrook, CT 06498 (tel. 860/399-4634). It's quite understandable, for the house is a beauty with its peaked gables, central cupola, and fan window over the entrance. The original building dates back to about 1860, when it was built by sea captain Stannard, who owned and commanded several ships that sailed mostly to the Orient. He also owned the legendary *Savannah*, which was used in the Mexican War. The house has served various purposes during its lifetime, from a dance studio and an upholstery shop to a boys' school and a roominghouse.

The six air-conditioned rooms have nice touches like fresh flowers, a clock radio, and books and magazines, as well as liquid soap and air freshener in the bath. Each room is unique: For example, the Captain's Quarters has a four-poster whose canopy with a pretty pale-blue lacy trim; the walls have stenciled borders, and a chair and a rocker offer comfortable seating. Breakfast is served in the bright dining room complete with a fireplace and baby grand.

Lee and Vern have traveled a lot during their careers and are mindful of business travelers' needs, so they offer an office with a phone available and will fulfill any special requests. Downstairs is a fridge for your use. Beach passes are available for the local strand, only an eight-minute walk away. In summer you can use the bicycles; play croquet, darts, or billiards; or simply relax on the back deck and lawn. Breakfast consists of homemade muffins, juice, and coffee.

Rates (including continental breakfast): From $110 double.

The **Water's Edge Inn & Resort,** 1525 Boston Post Rd., Westbrook, CT 06498 (tel. 860/399-5901), stands on a bluff overlooking the Sound. In this large modern condo/resort complex, accommodations are in 68 villa blocks surrounding a central cobblestone building. These contain two-bedroom units, with those on the second floor featuring balconies. The rooms are typically modern, with a TV, a phone, and unremarkable reproduction furnishings. The dining room, which looks out on the water, has an excellent reputation; it serves a wide range of dishes—from seafood paella and vegetable lasagne to medallions of veal with maple-mustard cream and filet mignon with truffle sauce. Prices range from $15 to $24. The brunch is renowned—including breads, fruit, cheese, salads, a raw bar, and desserts, plus three hot entrees and several stations serving omelets, roasts, and pasta. Dining on the terrace in summer is particularly pleasant. Facilities include an indoor pool, a well-equipped fitness center with a spa for massage and facials, and two tennis courts. Paddleboats, sailboats, and windsurfers are available at the beach.

Rates: $105–$165 standard double, $120–$215 waterfront double; from $120 suite.

Aleia's, 1353 Boston Post Rd., Westbrook (tel. 860/399-5050), is small enough so the kitchen staff can pay close attention to each dish as it's prepared. All the 10 or so appetizers are so varied and appealing that it's hard to choose among them. For example, there's a fine seared yellowfin tuna dressed with orange-and-wasabe soy sauce or luscious portobello mushrooms combined with marinated goat cheese and roasted red peppers and served with peppered bread sticks. You can follow with any of the six pastas—from the simple cappellini seasoned in an oven-roasted tomato-basil sauce to the rich capellini in a lobster-and-shellfish bouilla-baisse with saffron and fresh vegetables—or any one of the entrees, which might be a heart-warming roast chicken with aromatic herbs and a garlic sauce or an ultra-flavorsome seared veal chop with a wild-mushroom sauce accompanied by artichoke, caramelized onion, and potato ragoût. Prices range from $16 to $24.

Hours: Tues–Thurs 11:30am–2:30pm and 5:30–9pm, Fri 11:30am–2:30pm and 5:30–10pm, Sat 5:30–10pm, Sun 5:30–9pm.

Interested in local color, lots of people, and food at reasonable prices? Then a table at **Bill's Seafood,** 548 Boston Post Rd. (Rte. 1), Westbrook (tel. 860/399-7224), will suit you just fine. Sit out on the deck and watch the craft maneuver under the bridge into the marina while you feast on crab-and-lobster rolls, clams, fish, or whatever is scrawled on the chalkboard. The fried clams are the proclaimed popular favorite. Inside, the dining room is strictly Formica-topped tables in a bar room. Real seafarers flock here.

Hours: Sun–Thurs 11am–9pm, Fri–Sat 11am–10pm.

You'll cross over an old wisteria-covered footbridge to reach the **Captain Dibbell House,** 21 Commerce St., Clinton, CT 06413 (tel. 860/669-1646), an 1866 Victorian. Four rooms are offered here, all furnished with antiques and country accents like the quilts on the beds. The Garden Room's wicker bed sports a ring quilt and walls stenciled with flowers. In the Captain's Room the brass bed is swagged with fabric and dotted with cushions. Furnishings include a handsome blanket chest and a sitting area. A breakfast of muffins, coffee cake, or sweet rolls is served in the dining room, in the garden gazebo, or in your room. Throughout the house owners Ellis and Helen display the local art they've collected as well as articles they've hand-woven themselves. Fresh flowers and bathrobes in the rooms are nice extras, and so is the chocolate on the pillow in the evening. Guests have the added conveniences of a refrigerator stocked with beverages; bicycles; beach chairs, umbrellas, and beach towels; and transfer from the airport, stations, or marina.

Rates: $80–$100 double (slightly lower Nov to mid-May).

A Beachfront Lodging in Madison

The **Madison Beach Hotel,** 94 W. Wharf Rd., Madison, CT 06443 (tel. 203/245-1404), is a real seaside place, with a certain Victorian flavor. From the parking lot, climb the few steps into the weathered-gray balconied building and the dunes and the Sound spread before you, dotted with rocky outcroppings and a brilliant windsurfer's sail. Turn into the lobby and sink into a cushioned wicker rocker or step out onto the veranda and really breathe the shore air.

The 35 rooms have individual heating and air-conditioning, a TV, and a phone. Second- and third-floor rooms have balconies; they're simply furnished with hardy seaside furniture. The baths feature pine floors. These are simple seaside accommodations.

The Wharf Dining Room is attached to the hotel and shares the marvelous view of the Sound on two sides. Fresh flowers grace the bar. Pink napkins and tablecloths, rattan furniture, and silk flower arrangements give a tropical air to the room. Dinner-menu prices range from $12 for deep-fried clams to $22 for king crab legs. There's always a chicken du jour, along with filet mignon and prime rib. Salads, sandwiches, and burgers make up the lunch menu. Upstairs, the Crow's Nest sports nautical rigging and decor, a central bar from which to view the ocean scene or, even better, from an outside balcony table. Before you leave, check out the guest register dating from 1920—you might recognize some of the names.

Rates: Mid-May to Sept, $110–$125 double; from $160 suite. The rest of the year, rates are less. **Closed:** Jan 2–Feb. **Dining Hours:** Daily 11:30am–2:30pm and 5:30pm–closing.

ESSEX

Essex Attractions

The town of Essex itself is an attraction, with its quiet tree-lined streets bordered by fine old **colonial houses,** many of them shipbuilders' and sea captains' homes that've survived from the days when Essex was a great shipbuilding town. Take some time to walk the streets, browse in the stores, pop into the Griswold Inn (below), and explore the harbor area at the foot of Main Street, where the 1878 **steamboat dock** has been restored. It now houses the **Connecticut River Museum** (tel. 860/767-8269), displaying models, tools, paintings, and instruments relating to the river's history and that era when a 230-ton sidewheeler was a common sight en route from Hartford to New York City. The museum also includes a replica of the first U.S. submarine, the 1775 *Turtle.*

Hours: Tues–Sun 10am–5pm. **Admission:** $4 adults, $3 seniors, $2 children 9–12.

The **Valley Railroad** came to the valley in 1871, and today you can take a nostalgic trip courtesy of the Valley Railroad, Railroad Avenue (tel. 860/767-0103), aboard an old steam locomotive from Essex to Chester. The trip can be combined with a cruise up the river, past Gillette Castle (above) and the Goodspeed Opera House (below), so you can hear the lore and tales of the river and even picnic aboard.

People cluster along the station's platform, anticipating the roar of the train coming down the tracks, smoke hissing and billowing and whistle blasting its arrival. The engineer stokes the roaring orange-red fire in the firebox before slowly pulling out at the "All Aboard" signal. You can ride either in the 1915 passenger cars or in the 1927 Pullman parlor car, seated on plush ruby-red swivel armchairs while you listen to the old radio's background music from the 1920s and 1930s. The train uses 3 tons of coal and 3,000 gallons of water on its rhythmic journey past the tidal wetlands, where wild rice and bull reeds sway, and along the riverbank to Chester and back to Deep River. Here those taking the riverboat cruise debark. The whole trip (rail and river combined) takes about two hours. Although it's beautiful at any time of year, summer and fall are particularly spectacular; so is December, when Santa Claus boards the train on weekends.

Hours: Different schedules prevail in spring, summer, and fall, and there's a special Santa schedule. **Admission:** Train only, $8.50 adults, $4.25 children 3–11; train and cruise, $14 and $7, respectively; $3 extra to ride in the parlor car.

Essex Lodging & Dining

Affectionately known as "the Gris," the **Griswold Inn**, 36 E. Main St., Essex, CT 06426 (tel. 860/767-1776), is the kind of place that inspires genuine love and loyalty from visitors and residents alike. In this lovely 1776 inn the food is good and fairly priced, and the atmosphere is extremely congenial and unpretentious. People enjoy themselves here, and you're likely to engage the people at the next table in conversation. The tavern is always festive, as is the crowd that frequents it—a mixture of locals and sailors and yachting crew in summer. An old popcorn machine dispenses in the corner, a cast-iron stove warms the place, and a small Christmas tree sparkles year round. There's entertainment and impromptu dancing every night. Especially popular are Friday night's banjo entertainment and Monday night's sea chanteys. The dining rooms behind and off the tavern display museum-quality collections of marine art—Currier and Ives shipping prints, many related to the days when Essex turned out the fastest clippers on the ocean; marine oils by Antonio Jacobsen; and artifacts from the steamboat era. The largest dining room is, in fact, a covered bridge. Fires blaze in each dining room in winter.

A traditional treat is the Gris's Sunday Hunt Breakfast (a modest $13), when you can help yourself to unlimited servings of eggs, bacon, ham, sausage, grits, fried potatoes, kippers, chicken, lamb kidneys, creamed chipped beef, smelts, and whatever other dishes are offered. At dinner the menu offers a goodly number of fine fresh fish dishes and traditional items like Yankee pot roast and prime rib, priced from $13 to $20. Save some room for the mud-slide pie for dessert.

The accommodations are found up the creaky stairs, along the low uneven corridors, where the rooms are quaint and old-fashioned, with exposed beams, hooked rugs, old armoires, and a marble-topped vanity or similar in the corner. All have baths and air conditioning; some even have water views. House guests help themselves to fresh fruit and toasted muffins served with fine jams and marmalades in the library in the morning. In summer you must reserve several months in advance, especially on weekends.

Rates (including continental breakfast): $100–$115 double; from $145 suite. **Dining Hours:** Mon–Thurs 11:45am–3pm and 5:30–9pm, Fri 11:45am–3pm and 5:30–10pm, Sat 11:30am–3pm and 5–10pm, Sun 11am–2:30pm (Hunt Breakfast) and 4:30–9pm.

Essex Dining

The Black Seal, 29 Main St. (tel. 860/767-0233), is a cozy, casual, convivial bar/restaurant with a distinctly nautical flavor. In the Sail Loft bar oars stretch from one end of the ceiling to the other; the dining room sports an upturned scull, ships' lanterns and models, and even a rack of navigational charts. Pretty floral cloths cover the tables. Though famous for its seal's delight—steamed mussels, clams, shrimp, scallops, and calamari in a red clam sauce over pasta—the Black Seal also features a broad variety of items, from salads and sandwiches and burgers to pizza, steaks, and stir-fry dishes. Prices range from $7 to $17.

Hours: Mon–Thurs 11:30am–3:30pm and 5–9:30pm, Fri 11:30am–3:30pm and 5–10pm, Sat 11:30am–4pm and 5–10pm, Sun 11:30am–4pm and 5–9pm.

Oliver's Taverne, Plains Road, Rte. 153 (tel. 860/767-2633), offers good-value burgers and sandwiches, all under $9. A good place for luncheon, it's also a popular nighttime spot and is great for beer lovers, since it stocks beers from all over the world.

Hours: Daily 11:30am–10pm.

IVORYTON

Ivoryton Lodging & Dining

The **Copper Beech Inn,** 46 Main St., Ivoryton, CT 06442 (tel. 860/767-0330), has been voted the most popular restaurant in the state for a decade or more. A formal dinner with silver service is served in three lovely rooms, each furnished in a different period style. The wood paneling, Oriental porcelain collection, and other fine accents provide an elegant atmosphere. The menu usually contains about a dozen items, such as breast of pheasant served with glazed shallots and a brown pheasant glaze; steamed fresh lobster with a sauce of shallots, fresh sorrel, and cream; and a loin of venison roasted and served with a sauce of game stock, wildflower honey, pecans, and crushed black pepper. Prices range from $21 to $26. Two favorite appetizers are the terrine of smoked Scottish salmon, salmon mousse, black truffles, and chives (served with a chilled herb-cream sauce, garnished with osetra and flying-fish caviars) and the savory tart of fresh chard, scallion, apples, and raisins dusted with parmesan and served with a warm tomato-cream sauce.

The desserts are worth sampling too. Among them might be freshly made sweetened ravioli with poppyseed-and-almond filling served with a warm lemon sauce or a bombe glacé au nougat et au chocolat made with macadamia-almond nougat and cinnamon-chocolate ice creams and served with a warm chocolate sauce. If you wish to dine here, you'll need to reserve well in advance, especially for a weekend. Just off the inn's front parlor is a plant-filled conservatory overlooking the gardens and the venerable tree that gives the inn its name. Here you can enjoy a quiet drink.

There are also 13 elegantly decorated accommodations, 4 in the main house and 9 in the carriage house, all with bath and air-conditioning. The carriage-house rooms have Jacuzzi tubs, TVs, and French doors leading onto decks.

Rates (including buffet breakfast): $115–$175 double. **Dining Hours:** Tues–Sat 5:30–9pm, Sun 1–9pm.

Centerbrook Dining

In neighboring Centerbrook, **Steve's Centerbrook Cafe,** 78 Main St. (tel. 860/767-1277), has a reputation for being "brilliant but inconsistent." Under the control of young French-inspired chef Steven Wilkinson, the restaurant turns out fine classic French cuisine priced à la carte from $13 to $18.50. To start, the lobster-and-corn chowder is richly flavored, while the Oriental barbecued duck with plum-sauce glaze with sour-cherry relish and hot mustard stimulates the appetite. Follow with a pasta dish like wild-mushroom ravioli with haricots verts and prosciutto with a light cream sauce; a grilled dish like marinated and grilled pork loin with carmelized onions, thyme jus, and peach chutney; or a classic like veal medallions with sweet vermouth, sage, and prosciutto.

During the day people stop by the Fine Bouche pâtisserie for desserts like Sachertorte and blueberry cheesecake. But the pièce de résistance, for which Wilkinson is famous, is a marjolaine, an almond-hazelnut torte layered with crème fraîche and bittersweet Belgian chocolate (which you can enjoy as dessert after dinner). An extensive fine wine list is available.

The ambience varies from room to room. The front porch room is airy and Oriental in flavor, having been furnished with rattan chairs. In the two other rooms, chintz wallpapers, a Federal-style fireplace, and chair rails impart a more formal atmosphere.

Hours: Tues–Sun 5:30–9pm.

HADDAM, EAST HADDAM & MOODUS

Area Attractions

East Haddam is the home of the gorgeously intricate Victorian **Goodspeed Opera House,** 1 Goodspeed Plaza (tel. 860/873-8668). Built in 1876 by wealthy entrepreneur/shipbuilder William Goodspeed, it thrived as a theater until the 1920s, when traffic and life passed it by. The theater, atop the six-floor building, has been beautifully restored and dedicated to the preservation of the American musical. Around it a small village of antiques, craft (especially good), and gift stores has grown up.

Tours: June to mid-Oct, Mon and Sat 11am–1:30pm. **Admission:** $2 adults, $1 children 11 and under.

Just across the river you can see the **cruise boats** that sail from Haddam and across the Sound to the ports of Sag Harbor and Greenport, where you have three hours to explore before returning. On some cruises there's Dixieland entertainment. For more information, contact the New England Steamboat Lines, Marine Park, Haddam, CT 06438 (tel. 860/345-4507).

Sailings: Usually late June to Labor Day, daily.

Along the way, just outside East Haddam on Rte. 82, you may want to stop at the **Christmas Shoppe** (tel. 860/873-9352), where 'tis the season year round.

Hours: Memorial Day–Dec 24, daily 10am–5pm.

East Haddam Lodging & Dining

At night the 1826 Victorian mansion known as the **Inn at Goodspeed's Landing–Gelston House,** 8 Main St. (P.O. Box 262), East Haddam, CT 06423 (tel. 860/873-1411), across from the Goodspeed Opera House, takes on a particular romance with its riverside setting, luminous interior, and summer garden strung with twinkling lights. The dining room's pink tablecloths, green napkins, and low lighting make it positively romantic; especially when it's filled with pretheater diners the atmosphere is charged with a certain anticipation.

Your meal might begin with mushrooms stuffed with crabmeat, cheese, and herbs or grilled marinated shrimp served chilled with red-pepper/avocado sauce. Among the main courses, choices run to breast of duck with plum chutney, lobster ravioli with a cognac-cream sauce and fennel, and veal stir-fry with lemon and capers. There's a pretheater prix-fixe menu for $24.50 and a prime rib buffet dinner on Sunday night. If you have to wait for a table, there's an elegant mirrored bar lit by gilt sconces and emerald-green Waterford crystal chandeliers.

Upstairs are six extremely large guest rooms: three doubles and three suites. Some have river views through floor-to-ceiling Palladian windows (Room 21, for instance). Drop-leaf side tables, colored engravings of landscapes hanging above a sleigh bed, an Empire-style table nestled against two period side chairs, a secretary complete with a set of Kipling and other books, ceramic table lamps, and beige wall-to-wall carpeting bestow a special quality on the rooms. Gilchrist & Soames soaps, talc, shoeshine, and shampoo in the bath add to one's sense of well-being. The beer garden is open daily.

Rates: $110–$135 double; $250 suite. **Dining Hours:** Summer, Wed–Sat 11:30am–2:30pm and 5–9pm, Sun 11am–2:30pm and 4–7pm. Call for winter hours.

Only a few hundred yards from the Goodspeed Opera House, the **Bishopsgate Inn,** Goodspeed Landing, East Haddam, CT 06423 (tel. 860/873-1677), is run by Molly and Dan Swartz, who have created a cozy but elegant atmosphere with a certain theatrical flavor. Both are transplanted New Yorkers and have long associations with the theater—Dan as director of the Brooklyn Center at Brooklyn College and Molly as a buyer for several costume houses. In this 1818 home are six guest rooms (four with bath and fireplace), all furnished with Empire-style and pine country pieces and other antiques. The suite features a huge bath with a double sink and sauna. A continental breakfast of home-baked items like apple-crisp bread is served in the country kitchen.

Rates (including breakfast): $85–$110 double.

A Moodus Resort

In the quiet countryside just east of East Haddam are several resorts, if that's your style. The most famous is the **Sunrise Resort,** P.O. Box 415, Moodus, CT 06469 (tel. 860/873-8681), a 56-acre property set on 500 acres run by the Johnson family.

This won't be everyone's idea of a weekend retreat, but it's great fun for families. In season there's round-the-clock entertainment. Facilities include a large outdoor pool, miniature golf, scuba lessons, art lessons, tennis courts, an exercise room, a sauna, a whirlpool, canoes, and more, all designed to keep the whole family occupied. After-dark entertainments are provided too—movies, magicians, poolside bands, and saloon-style piano playing. Several theme weekends are offered, like Traditional Jazz and Bluegrass.

The 160 guest rooms are in fairly modern two-floor motel units, older cabins back in the woods, or refurbished cabins at the river's edge. On the Salmon River, a tributary of the Connecticut River, besides the boats and canoes for use by guests you'll find a quiet oasis where an early-morning breakfast is served every Tuesday as the sun rises behind the trees. There's no bar, but set-ups are provided for those interested and wine or champagne is served at special events or celebrations.

Rates (AP): $80–$100 double.

After Dark

Theater

The **Goodspeed Opera House,** 1 Goodspeed Plaza, East Haddam (tel. 860/873-8668), is dedicated to preserving the works of America's musical greats—Irving Berlin, Jerome Kern, Cole Porter—and introducing new works of the musical theater. It was, for example, the birthplace of such Broadway successes as *Annie* and *Man of La Mancha.* Tickets are $20 to $35. The season runs from mid-April to early December.

The **Ivoryton Playhouse,** Main Street, Ivoryton (tel. 860/767-8348), offers summer stock and community-oriented events.

The **National Theater of the Deaf,** a professional ensemble of deaf and hearing actors, spends most of its time touring internationally but presents a summer Storytelling Series on the grounds of its home at The Meeting House, Goose Hill Road, Chester (tel. 860/526-4971). The free performances are held every Sunday in June.

Evening Cruises
Evening cruises are operated on the river from June to Labor Day. For information, contact the New England Steamboat Lines, Marine Park, Haddam, CT 06438 (tel. 860/345-4507). Sunset cruises are operated by the Deep River Navigation Company, River Street, Deep River, CT 06417 (tel. 860/526-4954).

Other Entertainment
The **Griswold Inn,** Main Street, Essex (tel. 860/767-1776), always has some good musical entertainment on hand—Dixieland, sea chanteys, banjo, and the like—and people dance on Friday and Saturday nights. **Oliver's Taverne** (above) is a popular drinking spot. For quieter entertainment, just take a stroll around Essex or Chester or down by the water by the light of the moon or setting sun.

The Connecticut River Valley
Special & Recreational Activities

Antiquing: There are four or five interesting stores for browsing in Essex and one or two in Chester, including a store that specializes in making lamps of all kinds patterned after the old designs. Other shops are dotted around the area.

Bicycling: Rentals are available at Sew 'n' So, 21 Main St., in Essex (tel. 860/767-8188), for $16 per day.

Camping: The area possesses several choice spots, including some special camping reserved for canoeists where the only access is by canoe—making for a genuine camping experience. These campsites are available by reservation only between May 1 and September 30. Write to: Manager, Gillette Castle State Park, East Haddam, CT 06423 (tel. 860/526-2336), at least three weeks in advance of your chosen dates. Such camping exists at Hurd State Park, East Hampton; Gillette Castle State Park, Hadlyme; and Selden Neck State Park, Lyme.

Camping with shore access can be found at either Hammonasset State Park, P.O. Box 271, Madison, CT 06443 (tel. 203/245-1817), where 560 sites are available near the 2-mile sandy beach; or at Rocky Neck State Park, P.O. Box 676, Niantic, CT 06357 (tel. 860/739-5471), with 169 sites.

For wilderness camping try Devil's Hopyard State Park, East Haddam, CT 06423 (tel. 860/873-8566), so called because, the story goes, the Devil lived there, presumably brewing beer if you want to be literal about it.

For detailed information on state parks, call 860/566-2304.

Canoeing: North American Canoe Tours, 65 Black Point Rd., Niantic, CT 06357 (tel. 860/739-0791), rents canoes on the banks of the Connecticut River below Gillette Castle in Haddam. Reserve ahead. The cost is $30 per day.

Fishing: Bashan Lake, off Rte. 82 in East Haddam; Moodus Reservoir, with access 2 miles east of Moodus and a mile southeast of Rte. 149.

Fruit Picking: *East Haddam:* Founders School Farm, River Road (tel. 860/873-1489), for sweet corn, squash, beans, pumpkins. *Middlefield:* Lyman Orchards, at the junction of Rtes. 147 and 157 (tel. 860/349-1566), for apples, raspberries, sweet corn, tomatoes, squash, pumpkins.

Golf: Lyman Meadow Golf Club, Rte. 157 (tel. 860/349-8055); Cedar Ridge Golf Course, Drabik Road, East Lyme (tel. 860/739-7395), 18 holes, par 54.

Hiking: Plenty of area state parks have trails—Hurd, Gillette Castle, Selden Neck, Chatfield Hollow. For detailed information, contact the Connecticut Forest and Park Association, 16 Meriden Rd., Rockfall, CT 06481 (tel. 860/346-2372).

Horseback Riding: Cricklewood Farm, off Rte. 82 between Salem and Colchester (tel. 860/859-2124), offers lessons only.

Picnicking: The river affords plenty of picnicking opportunities. At Hurd State Park you'll have to climb down to the river. Pick up supplies in Middletown or East Haddam. Farther south, Gillette State Park makes a beautiful picnic setting. Pick up supplies in Chester and take the ferry across the river to the park. Haddam Meadows State Park offers picnicking beside the river in a largely unwooded area filled with goldenrod and wildflowers. Stop in East Haddam for supplies.

For shore picnics, head for Rocky Neck or Hammonnasset State Park. Pick up supplies in Old Lyme and Clinton, respectively.

Skiing: Downhill at Powder Ridge, Middlefield, CT 06455 (tel. 860/349-3454), off Rte. 147, provides five slopes, four chair lifts, and 21 trails.

State Parks: For information, contact the Department of Environmental Protection, State Parks Division, 79 Elm St., Hartford, CT 06106-5127 (tel. 860/566-2305).

Swimming: Shore swimming at Rocky Neck State Park, East Lyme (tel. 860/739-5471), with a boardwalk and so on ($12 weekend parking); also at Harvey's Beach, Old Saybrook; in Chester at Cedar

Lake. Some of the resorts in Moodus open their facilities for the day for a moderate fee: for example, Sunrise (tel. 860/ 873-8681).

Tennis: Check with the local chamber of commerce for high school locations.

HARTFORD

If you were to continue up the Connecticut River by boat from Middletown you'd soon reach Hartford. On land it's only a short drive up Rte. 9 and I-91 into this city, which—believe it or not—has several American cultural gems. State capital and world-famous insurance center, Hartford certainly isn't a bucolic dream weekend destination, but you may be pleasantly surprised, for the city and its environs offer a lot to the visitor.

For me the most thrilling experience is a visit to Mark Twain's bulky, convoluted mansion and the smaller, simpler home of Harriet Beecher Stowe that stands only 100 yards away from Twain's. They were two of the many notable residents of Nook Farm, a brilliant intellectual community that thrived here in the mid- to late 1800s. Just around the corner in West Hartford, you can visit the home of the indefatigable compiler of the American dictionary, Noah Webster. Downtown Hartford boasts the first public art museum established in the United States, the very fine Wadsworth Atheneum, and some first-rate architecture, including buildings by Henry Hobson Richardson. Here you'll also find Charles Bulfinch's first commission, the Old State House, where the Hartford Convention met from 1814 to 1815 to discuss the possible secession of New England from the Union. And you can seek out the plaque commemorating the Hartford Charter Oak, in which the Connecticut charter was safely hidden from Sir Edmund Andros, James II's governor-general of New England, who'd demanded its surrender. At the center of the city is the 41-acre Bushnell Park, complete with a nostalgic working carousel. Nearby, in the lovely village of Farmington, you can view a collection of Manet and other impressionist artists, hanging in an antiques-furnished home. From here it's only 15 minutes north to historic Simsbury, and a little farther on is the old prison in East Granby and the New England Air Museum. Only a 10-minute drive south of Hartford is the historic village of Wethersfield. In short, there's plenty to keep you amused.

Hartford Attractions

The **Hartford Convention and Visitors Bureau** (tel. 860/728-6789) has developed a walking tour of the city, and you can pick up the brochure at the Visitors Information Center in the Old State House (see below).

Highlights on the tour route include the following:

The Old State House

Charles Bulfinch's first commission, at 800 Main St. (tel. 860/522-6766), in the center of Hartford, is beautiful in its simplicity and rich in the historical events it has witnessed: the 1814–15 Hartford Convention to discuss the possibility of New England's secession from the Union; an 1868 visit by Charles Dickens, who complimented the conduct of the court; and in 1839 the dramatic first trial of the *Amistad* prisoners, slaves who'd mutinied and seized the vessel on which they were being transported from the Spanish West Indies. It also served as the state capitol from 1796 to 1878. Today it functions as an arts and cultural center, but you can tour the graceful symmetrical rooms that served variously as the court, senate, and house chambers and view Gilbert Stuart's only full-length portrait of General Washington. Check out the fine crafts shop downstairs.

Note: The building is closed for renovations as we go to press but will reopen in spring 1996.

Hours: Mon–Sat 10am–5pm, Sun 2–5pm. Hours may change when the building reopens.

Walking south along Prospect Street, you'll come to:

The Travelers Tower

From the tower at 700 Main St. (tel. 860/277-4208), 527 feet above the street, you can enjoy a real bird's-eye view of the city. Both an elevator and stairs are used to reach the top.

This is also the home office of the Travelers Insurance Companies, whose first customer had his life insured for $5,000 for a four-block trip from the post office, where he worked, to his home. Total premium: 2¢. The tower occupies the site of the old Sanford Tavern, where Sir Edmund Andros demanded the charter and from which the charter was taken and squirreled away in an oak tree. The original tree succumbed to a storm in 1856, but its grandchild supposedly stands on the grounds of the Center Church and is commemorated by a plaque as the Hartford Charter Oak. From the top of the tower you can look down upon Constitution Plaza, Hartford's example of urban renewal.

Tours: May–Oct, but call for an appointment. **Admission:** Free.

Continue south along Main Street and you'll come to the:

Wadsworth Atheneum

At 600 Main St. (tel. 860/247-9111), across from Carl André's controversial *Stone Field* (36 boulders, seemingly thrown down haphazardly, commissioned in 1975 for $87,000), the Wadsworth is a delight. It's a perfect size for the museumgoer, housed in five buildings around a sculpture court and filled with an impressive selection of art—Monets, Renoirs, a couple of Boudins, a group of interesting American primitives, including a lovely Asa Ames polychromed wood statue of a child with a lamb,

Hartford

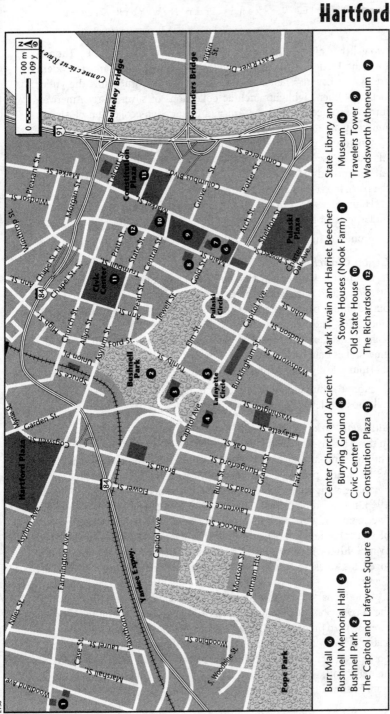

Burr Mall **6**
Bushnell Memorial Hall **5**
Bushnell Park **2**
The Capitol and Lafayette Square **3**

Center Church and Ancient
Burying Ground **8**
Civic Center **11**
Constitution Plaza **13**

Mark Twain and Harriet Beecher
Stowe Houses (Nook Farm) **1**
Old State House **10**
The Richardson **12**

State Library and
Museum **4**
Travelers Tower **9**
Wadsworth Atheneum **7**

2136

73

two galleries of large 19th-century Hudson River landscapes by Thomas Cole and Frederic Church, and several works by Henry Tanner. Modern art by Sol Lewitt, Duane Hanson, and Joseph Cornell fills the Hilles Gallery. Other highlights include collections of silver, Early American furniture, porcelain, and the Amistad Foundation's collection of African American art.

On your way out, don't miss Alexander Calder's *Stegosaurus*, tucked (if you can use such a word of this massive sculpture) away between the Atheneum and the adjacent Municipal Building in Burr Mall. This is also the place to eat in the city at the Museum Cafe.

Hours: Tues–Sun 11am–5pm. **Admission:** $5, free for children 12 and under; free for everyone Thurs.

From the Atheneum, backtrack and cross Main Street to the:

Center Church

Its first pastor was Thomas Hooker, who left Cambridge, Mass., in 1635–36 and walked to Newtown or, as we call it, Hartford. He's believed to be buried under or near a corner of the present church, which has stood since 1807 and contains several Louis Comfort Tiffany windows. Take some time to explore the adjacent **Ancient Burying Ground**, where the gravestones date back to 1640.

Hours: Daily noon–3pm. **Admission:** Free.

From the burial ground and church, take Gold Street west, down the hill, crossing Jewell Street into:

Bushnell Park

In this 41-acre park shaded by some 500 trees you can relax a while, but children and antiques or art lovers should see the **carousel** with its 48 brilliantly painted hand-carved horses and ornate lovers' chariots, complete with a calliope and automatic drums and cymbals. Built in 1914, it was brought from Canton, Ohio, and operates daily in summer (weekends only in spring and fall). For only 25¢ you can recapture part of your childhood and try to grab the brass ring. Note also the **Civil War Soldiers Memorial** that arches over Trinity Street. The architect loved his work so much that he and his wife are buried in the East Tower.

Exit the park via Trinity Street and walk south to Capitol Avenue. On the corner, pop into **Bushnell Memorial Hall** for a look at the art deco interior, then proceed up Capitol Avenue (going west), past the equestrian statue of Lafayette with a turtle placed near the horse's left rear hoof (supposedly the sculptor's wry comment on the 10-year delay that preceded his payment!). On the south side of Capitol Avenue, diagonally across from Bushnell Hall, you'll find the:

Special Highlights for Architecture Buffs

Besides the buildings already mentioned, you'll most likely want to see Henry Hobson Richardson's 1877 Cheney Building, now called simply the **Richardson,** 942 Main St. Restaurants and specialty shops occupy the lower floors; luxury apartments, the upper floors. It's on Main Street north of the Old State House.

The **Butler-McCook Homestead,** at 396 Main St. (tel. 860/ 522-1806), is Hartford's oldest home and remained in a single family until the 20th century. Its interior reflects a full range of stylistic changes from 1782 to the turn of this century.

Hours: May 15–Oct 15, Tues–Thurs and Sun noon–4pm. **Admission:** $2 adults, 50¢ children.

Contact the **Antiquarian and Landmarks Society,** 394 Main St. (tel. 860/247-8996), for details about other houses of interest— like Coventry's Nathan Hale Homestead or Hartford's Victorian Italianate Isham-Terry house.

State Library, Supreme Court & Baldwin Museum of Connecticut History

The library, the court, and the museum are at 231 Capitol Ave. (tel. 860/ 566-3056), where the original Royal Charter and the Colt firearms collection are displayed, along with documents, portraits, and artifacts relating to Connecticut history.

Hours: Mon–Fri 9:30am–4pm. **Admission:** Free.

And, finally, head toward Richard Upjohn's:

State Capitol

The capitol is Hartford's most impressive building, easily identified by its shimmering golden dome, topped by a spire. A tour will acquaint you with its many eclectic details, murals, statues, and furnishings, all reflecting the state's history.

Tours: Mon–Fri hourly 9:15am–1:15pm; also, Apr–Oct, Sat hourly 10:15am–2:15pm.

Nearby Attractions

Nook Farm

An important cultural-intellectual community, Nook Farm, 77 Forest St., off Farmington Avenue (take Exit 46 off I-84), West Hartford, was settled in the last half of the 19th century by interrelated families and friends. Among them were such celebrities as Isabella Beecher Hooker, women's rights leader; Charles Dudley Warner, author and editor of the *Hartford Courant*; William Gillette, playwright and actor famous for his portrayal of Sherlock Holmes; and Mark Twain and Harriet Beecher Stowe.

Painted his favorite turkey red, **Mark Twain's house** (tel. 860/493-6411) is large, grand, and rather ungainly compared to the smaller Beecher house across the way. Once inside, you'll discover more quirks incorporated into the house by the ornery eccentric humorist. For example, the telephone, which he abhorred, is located in a closet, and the etched windows in the top-floor study, where he wrote *Tom Sawyer, Huckleberry Finn*, and several other volumes, depict the activities Twain considered most important in life—smoking, drinking, and billiards. In the bedroom he placed the pillows at the foot of his bed so he could gaze at the ornately carved Venetian headboard, for which he'd paid a princely sum. Twain lived here with his wife, three daughters, and 11 cats from 1874 to 1881, when his debts (he'd lost $750,000 in two capital investment ventures) forced him to sell the house and flee to Europe on a lecture tour. A visit to the house is particularly rewarding because it reflects Twain's whimsical personality and because you're able to enter the rooms instead of having to peer in from outside.

The **Beecher house** (tel. 860/525-9317), built in 1871, is far more ordinary. Harriet moved here in 1873 and stayed until her death in 1896. The house still has many pieces of Mrs. Stowe's furniture, paintings by her, and also the kitchen designed to her specifications as outlined in *The American Woman's Home*, which she co-authored with her sister. They were first to recommend that plants, instead of curtains, be hung in windows! Whereas Twain's house contains a specific writing room, albeit filled with a full-size billiard table, the Beecher house has no such room, only a tiny desk where she supposedly wrote many of her 33 (yes, that's right) books. One gets the impression that she probably wrote on the run, wherever and whenever she could grab the time between her daily tasks.

Hours: Twain house, Memorial Day–Columbus Day, Mon–Sat 9:30am–4pm, Sun noon–4pm; other months, closed Tues. Stowe house, Mon–Sat 9:30am–4pm, Sun noon–4pm; other months, closed Mon. **Admission:** Twain house, $7.50 adults, $7 seniors, $3.50 children 6–12; Stowe house, $6.50 adults, $6 seniors, $2.75 children 6–12.

From Nook Farm you can take Farmington Avenue west to West Hartford's Main Street, turning left down Main Street to the:

Noah Webster House / Historical Society of West Hartford

At 227 S. Main St. (tel. 860/521-5362), you can tour the 18th-century farmhouse and birthplace of the author of the *Blue Backed Speller* (1783) and the *American Dictionary* (1828). The home and museum contain period furnishings, Webster memorabilia, and varied changing exhibits. **Hours:** June 15–Aug, Mon–Tues and Thurs–Fri 10am–4pm, Sat–Sun 1–4pm; Sept–June 14, Thurs–Tues 1–4pm. **Admission:** $5 adults, $4 seniors, $1 children 6–12.

By the way, if you're interested in other Hartford literary landmarks, *New Yorker* editor Brendan Gill grew up in a rambling turn-of-the-century home at 735 Prospect St., while Wallace Stevens lived a few blocks away at 118 Westerly Terrace. In West Hartford, Sinclair Lewis resided briefly at 27 Belknap Rd.

Science Museum of Connecticut
Here in West Hartford, you'll also find the Science Museum, 950 Trout Brook Dr. (tel. 860/231-2824), with a small aquarium, a mini-zoo, a planetarium, and lots of "hands-on" activities the kids will love. **Hours:** Mon–Sat 10am–5pm, Sun noon–5pm. **Closed:** Major holidays. **Admission:** $5 adults, $4 children 3–18.

Get back onto Farmington Avenue and follow it to Farmington's attractions.

Hill-Stead Museum
Located at 35 Mountain Rd., Farmington (tel. 860/677-9064 or 677-4787), this was once the home of self-made millionaire/steel magnate Alfred Atmore Pope, a pioneer collector of impressionist art. After his death his daughter, Theodate Pope, preserved his collection in its original setting at the family home, which she had helped design for him at the age of 16. She eventually became the wife of John Wallace Riddle, former ambassador to Russia and Argentina, and one of the first women in this country to become an architect. A number of notable personages visited her at Hill-Stead: Painter Mary Cassatt loved to walk through these rooms; Henry James described the house in *The American Scene* as "apparently conceived—and with great felicity—on the lines of a magnificent Mount Vernon"; Isadora Duncan danced in the gardens; and poet John Masefield contemplated the surrounding pastoral meadows. The Monets, Whistlers, and Manets are hung as if the house were still occupied, in rooms filled with netsuke, majolica, Bari bronzes, Chinese porcelain, clocks, rugs, and fine antiques—an American bull's-eye mirror here, a Chippendale secretary there. Hill-Stead still covers 150 acres of fields and woodlands. The grounds feature a reconstruction of the original Sunken Gardens designed by prominent landscape gardener Beatrix Farrand. **Hours:** Apr–Oct, Tues–Sun 10am–5pm; Nov–Mar, Tues–Sun 11am–4pm. By guided tour only; last tour given an hour before closing. **Admission:** $6 adults, $5 seniors, $3 children 6–12.

Other Farmington Attractions

These include the **Stanley Whitman House,** 37 High St. (tel. 860/677-9222), built by Deacon John Stanley in 1720. A fine example of early New England architecture constructed around a massive central chimney, it features an overhanging second story and a lean-to added across the back, giving it the traditional saltbox shape. The house is furnished in the same way it was in the 18th century, when the Stanley, Smith, and Whitman families lived here. The colonial dooryard garden features the culinary, medicinal, and herbal plants that were used at the time for such purposes.

Hours: May–Oct, Wed–Sun noon–4pm; Mar–Apr and Nov–Dec, Sun noon–4pm. **Admission:** $3 adults, $2 seniors and children.

And while you're in Farmington, drive past the **stately homes** lining Main Street (many built before 1835), noticing also the unmarked but renowned **Miss Porter's School,** one of the oldest and finest boarding schools for girls in the country, founded in 1844 when tuition was $200 for 42 weeks of instruction and board. Jackie Kennedy Onassis was one of the school's more famous pupils.

Only a 20-minute drive south of Farmington, the **New Britain Museum of Art,** 56 Lexington St. (tel. 860/229-0257), has a fine collection of American art, including works by Gilbert Stuart, William Jennys, Frederic Church, Albert Bierstadt, John Singer Sargent, Childe Hassam, and Charles Burchfield. They're displayed in a fine old residence. More modern works can be found in the new wing.

Hours: Tues–Sun 1–5pm. **Admission:** Donation requested.

Massacoh Plantation

After Mystic Seaport (below), Massacoh Plantation, 800 Hopmeadow St., in historic Simsbury (tel. 860/658-2500), is Connecticut's largest historical complex, representing Farmington Valley history from 1670, when Simsbury was first settled by about 12 families from Windsor. The Phelps House (1771) is the cornerstone. It has been decorated the way it would've been from 1827 to 1849, when it operated as the Canal Hotel, a stop on the 24-hour route from Northampton, Mass., to New Haven, Conn. The house remained in the Phelps family until 1962, and consequently its history is known and the house itself has been well preserved.

Among the more intriguing interior features are the original canvas ceiling, the witches' crosses flanking the fireplace in the tavern, and the coffin door (so called because it was wide enough to get a coffin through, and the door that all inhabitants went through last). In the kitchen you'll learn how those early cooks determined the temperature of the beehive ovens and see the cooking utensils and staples they used—horsehair sifters, stick whisks, and sugar cones. Upstairs the splendid ballroom was used for special family and other social occasions. Don't miss viewing the very rare Higley copper, minted in 1737, which states "Value Me as You Please" on it. This coin was first struck in 1737 by Dr. Samuel Higley.

Also on the grounds stands a replica of a 1683 meetinghouse; an ice house; a white barn filled with old sleighs and carriages, including an authentic tin peddler's cart used until 1925; a schoolhouse built in 1740 and refurbished in 1825; and the fuse building from the local Ensign Bickford Company, which houses original fuse and primer cord equipment. There's also McDaniel's Art Gallery.

Hours: May–Oct, Sun–Fri 1–4pm; winter, Phelps House only, Sun–Fri 1–4pm. **Admission:** $5 adults, $4 seniors, $2.50 children.

On the way out to Simsbury you'll be able to view in the distance the **Heublein Tower** (tel. 860/677-0662), standing atop the mountain ridge 1,000 feet above the Farmington River in Talcott Mountain State Park. This 165-foot-high folly was built in 1914 as a summer home for Gilbert Heublein. It can be visited to enjoy the panoramic views from late April to November 2 on Saturday and Sunday only. Access is from Rte. 185.

New England Air Museum

Only 10 miles north of Hartford off I-91 on Rte. 75, this museum at the Bradley Airport, Windsor Locks (tel. 860/623-3305), will give you a telescoped view of aviation history. Here are over 80 aircraft, ranging from romantic biplanes and boxlike steel kites strung together with straps, to World War II fighters and modern jets and helicopters (Igor Sikorsky emigrated from Kiev to Connecticut), all meticulously restored. Movies are shown daily. The museum even has parts of a gas balloon used by Silas Brookes—a Malcolm Forbes of the 1880s.

Hours: Daily 10am–5pm. **Closed:** Major winter holidays. **Admission:** $6.50 adults, $3.50 children 6–11.

Old Newgate Prison & Copper Mine

Just off Rte. 20 west of the airport in East Granby lies the Old Newgate Prison and Copper Mine (tel. 860/653-3563), where you can tour the dungeonlike chambers of this first chartered copper mine, which became Connecticut's first state prison and housed British sympathizers during the American Revolution.

Hours: Mid-May to Oct, Wed–Sun 10am–4pm. **Admission:** $3 adults, $1.50 seniors and children 6–17.

Old Wethersfield

About 8 miles south of Hartford, Old Wethersfield, the onion-raising capital of the colonies in the 18th century, is now a fascinating historic district where over 150 pre-1850 structures have been preserved. Barns, warehouses, and carriage houses have been transformed into shops selling everything from crafts and antiques to toys and gardening supplies.

If shopping is not your favorite pastime, two historic sites are worth visiting. The **Buttolph Williams House** (1692), at Broad and Marsh streets (tel. 860/529-0460), shelters an outstanding collection of pewter, Delft, fabrics, and furniture and displays a fine 17th-century kitchen filled with wooden plates and salvers, wrought-iron utensils, and a rare semicircular settle.

The **Webb-Deane-Stevens Museum**, 211 Main St. (tel. 860/529-0612), consists of three 18th-century homes that were used for Washington's conference with Rochambeau to plot the strategy that led to the defeat of the British at Yorktown. Each house reflects the individual lifestyle of its owner: merchant, diplomat, and tradesman. The decorative arts collections span the period from 1640 to 1840.

Hours: May–Oct, Wed–Mon 10am–4pm; Nov–Apr, Sat–Sun 10am–4pm (last tours at 3pm). **Admission** (for three-house tour): $6 adults, $5 seniors, $2.50 students 12–18, $1 children 6–11.

For more information on other local historic houses, call the **Wethersfield Historical Society** at 860/529-7656.

A Family Amusement Park

Lake Compounce, America's oldest amusement park, reopened in 1986 after a multi-million-dollar renovation turned it into **Hershey Lake Compounce,** Lake Avenue (I-84, Exit 31), Bristol (tel. 860/583-3631). It has retained its Victorian charm. The carousel still spins to the calliope's song, but now there's more: a thrilling Wildcat roller coaster, a mountain flume, and other water rides. Performers of all sorts entertain on the main stage. Turn-of-the-century shops, arcades, and dining places also draw the crowds to this attractively located amusement park where the lake still sparkles at the foot of the mountain. Open summer only. Call for schedule and admissions.

Hartford Lodging

Sad to say, Hartford has no really outstanding lodgings choices, but the major hotels do offer weekend packages. The nicest accommodations can be found at the **Goodwin Hotel,** 1 Hayne's St. (tel. 860/246-7500), an apartment building that's been converted into a full-service hotel. The 124 extra-large rooms are handsomely decorated with modern sleigh beds and other reproductions. Other amenities include a phone with computer jack, a well-lit desk, and a phone and hairdryer in the bath. The restaurant, Pierpont's, which is very popular locally, occupies a lovely room of glazed mahogany and mirrors. There's also a piano bar/lounge.

Rates: $161 double weekdays, $87 double weekends.

For budget accommodations, try the **Ramada Inn–Capitol Hill,** 440 Asylum St., Hartford, CT 06103 (tel. 860/246-6591), next to the Amtrak station and only four blocks from the Old State House.

Rates: $62 double weekends.

Far more fetching accommodations can be found at the **Babcock Tavern and B&B,** 484 Mile Hill Rd. (at Cedar Swamp), in Tolland (tel. 860/875-1239), where the innkeepers have been collecting antiques for more than 40 years. The public areas (like the tap room, with an open hearth and exposed beams, and sitting room) are furnished with interesting pieces—a spinning wheel, a steeple clock, Shaker boxes, baskets, and much more. Breakfast is served by candlelight to the strains of Mozart or the like at pine tables. There are three guest rooms: The East Room features a brass bed and Shaker settle among its furnishings. The Ballroom, the largest, is the most appealing; it contains a canopied bed, a rocker, and such decorative pieces as a cradle and wash stand. To get here, take I-84 to Exit 67. Then make a right onto Rte. 31.

Rates (including breakfast): $70–$90 double.

The **Tolland Inn,** On the Green, Tolland (tel. 860/872-0800), has nine rooms (all with bath) furnished variously with maple or brass beds, Mission-style rockers, and other pieces (some even crafted by the owner). The most expensive room has a fireplace and spa tub for two.

Rates (including breakfast): $65–$125 double.

For additional B&Bs, contact **Nutmeg Bed and Breakfast,** 222 Girard Ave., Hartford, CT 06105 (tel. 860/236-6698), which will guide you to B&Bs throughout the state. Call for a directory. Rates for these B&Bs range from $60 to $150 double.

Hartford Dining

For light casual fare, there are many choices in the modern **Civic Center,** where the Promenade houses a collection of bright, cafeteria-style fast-food outlets, all sharing dining areas. Another area to head for is around Union Station.

For a serene unique setting, the **Museum Cafe,** 600 Main St. (tel. 860/728-5989), is at the Wadsworth Atheneum. The interior has a minimalist black-and-gray look accented by one or two large Chinese urns and other porcelain pieces, but in summer the restaurant moves out into the courtyard. The menu is small and select. Among the dinner entrees are smoked duck breast with wild mushroom ragoût, grilled venison with port sauce, and grilled spiced tuna with Moroccan eggplant, tomatoes, niçois olives, raisins, and spices. Some of the great unusual appetizers include the jicama, roasted chicken and peppers with arugula, snow peas, and tangerine vinaigrette, and the duck confit with endives, smoked potatoes, and pickled vidalia onions. Prices range from $8 to $9.50. Save room for the tempting desserts—my favorite is lemon mousse in raspberry purée.

Hours: Tues–Thurs 11:30am–2pm, Fri–Sat 11:30am–2pm and 5:30–9:30pm, Sun 11:30am–2:30pm (brunch).

Brown Thomson, 942 Main St. (tel. 860/525-1600), has been around for years. It's in the Richardson building and has a warm convivial atmosphere partially created by the huge Richardsonian arches supporting the ceiling. Stained glass, moose and elk trophies, and other artifacts complete the decor, but it's not overdone to the point of being tacky. The long menu offers everything from sandwiches and burgers to barbecued chicken, steaks, and pasta, priced from $7 to $15.

Hours: Sun–Thurs 11:30am–10pm, Fri–Sat 11:30am–midnight.

At the popular **Peppercorn's,** 357 Main St. (tel. 860/547-1714), the art on the walls is for sale. This restaurant offers a range of pastas, risottos, and pizzas as well as a limited number of main courses. Two winning appetizers are the lobster- and scallop-filled ravioli with lobster-cream sauce and the ravioli filled with ricotta, spinach, and orange rind in a sauce of fresh orange, sage, butter, and parmigiano reggiano. For an entree I recommend such fish dishes as the oven-roasted fish of the day or the sea bass with orange/black-pepper aïoli. The ossobuco is flavorsome too, braised with white wine, herbs, garlic, and lemon rind. Prices range from $11 to $21.

Hours: Mon–Tues 11:30am–2:30pm and 5–10pm, Wed 11:30am–2:30pm and 5–10:30pm, Thurs 11:30am–2:30pm, Fri 11:30am–2:30pm and 5–11:30pm, Sat 5–11:30pm.

Crowds jam the tables and bar on weekends at **Bourbon Street North,** 70 Union Place (tel. 860/525-1014), an outpost serving Cajun and Créole cuisine. You can start with a selection from the raw bar or the Cajun popcorn shimp served with a honey-mustard sauce. Mo's gumbo is a thick brew of sausage, shrimp, and okra. All the traditional favorites are available to follow—étouffée, jambalaya, catfish Créole, and red beans and rice.

Hours: Mon–Wed 11:30am–2:30pm, Thurs 11:30am–8:30pm, Fri 11:30am–10pm, Sat 7–10pm.

Once a typical cozy Italian bistro, **Carbone's,** 588 Franklin Ave. (tel. 860/296-9646), has been redecorated in a plush but rather nondescript style, featuring upholstered beige booths and classical Italian prints. A no-smoking area sports modern wicker Breuers. The food is well prepared and there's plenty of it. The menu offers a full range of pastas, seafood, and meat dishes, for $13 to $23. Among the pastas are paglie e fieno in Gorgonzola sauce, which you can follow with such items as beef filets in cognac and mustard, chicken inglese (marinated with lemon, olive oil, and sherry, then broiled with mustard sauce), or veal zingarelli (sautéed with spinach, veal sausage, artichokes, and mushrooms, then baked with Italian sharp cheese).

Hours: Mon–Fri 11:30am–2:30pm and 5–10pm, Sat 5–10pm.

Trucs, 735 Wethersfield Ave. (tel. 860/296-2818), serves the best Asian cuisine in Hartford. Among the favorite entrees are bo huc lac (or shaking beef), cubes of filet mignon marinated in a special sauce, then sautéed in garlic and served with vinaigrette sauce on a bed of watercress. Or try vit quay, lacquered duck marinated in five spices and garlic sauce, then roasted with crisp skin and served with orange; or the equally popular barh xeo ("happy pancake"), a rice-batter pancake stuffed with shrimp, pork, chicken, fresh mushrooms, onions, and bean sprouts, served in Vietnamese sauce. Prices range from $9 to $15. Two appetizers are worth noting: ha noi soup, containing sliced beef and rice sticks; and the special shrimp roll (kha gro Truc dac biet), a triangular roll stuffed with crabmeat, pork, and vegetables around a large shrimp and then wrapped in crisp rice paper and served with sauce. America inspires the desserts, which range from lemon, chocolate, or apricot mousse to a very special binh chocolate, with almond paste spread between cake and mousse (chocolate-mousse cake). The atmosphere is pleasing. The front part of the restaurant is given over to a tiled solarium, while the rear offers a long light-oak bar, comfortable bamboo chairs, and tables covered with forest-green cloths and glass.

Hours: Mon–Sat 11am–2pm and 5–10pm, Sun 5–10pm.

Costa del Sol, 901 Wethersfield Ave. (tel. 860/296-1714), has a warm atmosphere. Guitar music plays in the background and soft sconces light the stucco walls. The cuisine is also fine. To start, opt for the garlic shrimp or Spanish sausage; if you're a true Mediterranean, order the octopus Galicia. Follow with a classic like paella mariscara or seafood casserole with green sauce. For those who prefer beef, the tenderloin with brandy sauce is a perfect marriage. Prices range from $13 to $22.

Hours: Tues–Fri 11:30am–2pm and 5:30–10pm, Sat 5–10pm, Sun 4–9pm.

Area Dining & Lodging

Avon Dining

The Forge Room at the 1757 **Avon Old Farms Inn**, 1 Nod St. (tel. 860/677-2818), is especially inviting, particularly in winter, when a blazing fire casts a warm glow over the stone floors and the blacksmith's tools adorning the walls. The tables have been artfully arranged, leaving the actual horse stalls intact. You can also opt to dine in the two small rooms off the entrance that are the inn's oldest or in the two other large, modern, and, to me, less appealing sections.

Come in July or August on Friday night and you can partake of their clambake; otherwise choose from a primarily American menu—roast rib of beef au jus served with a popover, shrimp filled with walnut stuffing, and their own veal sentino (veal medallions broiled with asparagus, mushrooms, and a mild imported Danish cheese). Prices range from $17 to $25. The brunch draws crowds for a huge $15 buffet spread.

Hours: Mon noon–2:30pm, Tues–Thurs noon–2:30pm and 5:30–9:30pm, Fri noon–2:30pm and 5:30–10pm, Sat noon–2:30pm and 5:30–10:30pm, Sun 10am–2:30pm (brunch) and 5:30–8:30pm.

Farmington Dining

In **Apricots**, 1593 Farmington Ave. (tel. 860/673-5903), crowds gather downstairs in the pub with piano entertainment. Upstairs are two dining rooms, one with a river view. The menu changes weekly, but here are some recent offerings: rack of lamb with a mustard hollandaise or sauce provençal; grilled swordfish with orange and green onions in a walnut-butter sauce; wood-smoked duckling with green-peppercorn sauce and cranberry chutney; and sautéed shrimp, cucumbers, and tomatoes in a rose-mary, basil, and white-wine butter. Among the appetizers are poached shrimp with a champagne-chive beurre blanc, pâté with a Cumberland sauce, and escargots en vol au vent with garlic cream. Entree prices run $15 to $28.50. A lighter pub menu is also available. Brunch includes traditional egg dishes with items like fish or a pasta du jour and a seafood crêpe.

Hours: Mon–Sat 11:30am–2:30pm and 6–10pm, Sun 11:30am–3pm (brunch) and 5:30–9pm.

Simsbury Lodging & Dining

Simsbury 1820 House, 731 Hopmeadow St. (Rte. 10), Simsbury, CT 06070 (tel. 860/658-7658), is a restored red-brick Georgian home, built in 1820 by Elisha Phelps, son of Noah Phelps, an American patriot. From the gracious entrance with leaded windows, a scrolled staircase leads to the 34 prettily decorated rooms, all with phones and air-conditioning, most with antique reproductions and color schemes derived from the co-lonial period—Wedgwood blue and cranberry. The bedspreads are French chintz, the lamps are porcelain, and in some rooms a Federal-style club-foot desk serves as a bedside table. The two leather or pastel-colored wing chairs are comfortable, and the large armoire and chest of drawers with brass handles serve well for storage. The baths are tiled, the towels are fluffy, and the amenities include shampoo, body lotion, emery boards, hair conditioner, and a sewing kit. Some rooms have balconies; some also have four-poster beds without canopies, and some are tucked away under the sloping ceilings of the roof.

On the ground floor, the parlor with its Federal-style fireplace is invit-ing—a comfortable sofa, wing chairs, and a collection of newspapers and magazines. A small service-only bar is furnished with Chippendale chairs and card tables.

The dining room downstairs is has a good reputation for its food. Besides the regular menu, which changes seasonally, daily specials might offer venison in a sauce of red wine and truffles; tuna with a pommery-mustard butter; or halibut with basil and tomatoes, served in a lobster-and-cream sauce. Other choices are filet of sole baked with fresh herbs, mussels, and vermouth or sweet butter; grilled Cornish hen with California white zinfandel sauce; sirloin grilled and served with a sauce of shallots and red wine; and duckling studded with peppercorns and served with port sauce and cranberry relish. The Kahlúa crème brûlée and phyllo with strawberries and raspberry sauce make a perfect ending to a first-class meal. Brunch consists of classic egg dishes.

Rates: $105–$140 double. **Dining Hours:** Mon–Fri 11am–2:30pm and 5:30–9pm, Sat 5:30–9pm, Sun 11am–3pm (brunch) and 5:30–9pm.

Additional Simsbury Dining

The **Chart House,** 4 Hartford Ave. (tel. 860/658-1118), in a pleasant clapboard house bordered by pretty flower gardens, offers a series of small dining rooms as well as an enclosed sun porch set with white wicker furniture and splashes of greenery. The food is traditional American— seafood and steak from $14 to $25.

Hours: Mon–Thurs 5–10pm, Fri–Sat 5–11pm, Sun 4–9pm.

After Dark

For current events, check the *Hartford Courant* listings. The city offers some good theater at the **Hartford Stage,** 50 Church St. (tel. 860/ 527-5151).

The **Hartford Ballet** (tel. 860/525-9396), the **Hartford Symphony** (tel. 860/246-8742), and the **Connecticut Opera** all perform at Bushnell Memorial Hall, 166 Capitol Ave. (tel. 860/527-0713), which also hosts Broadway musicals and shows.

The **Civic Center** (tel. 860/727-8080) presents concerts, ice shows, and other similar popular events.

Sports fans can attend the games of the **Hartford Whalers** (tel. 860/ 728-3366) from October to May at the Civic Center. For tickets to games, call 800/WHALERS.

Bars/Music

The **Russian Lady Cafe,** 191 Ann St. (tel. 860/525-3003), is filled with artifacts rescued from buildings doomed to demolition (even the statue adorning the exterior was rescued from the old Rossia Insurance building). Live rock bands perform.

For cocktails, there's **Brown Thomson & Co.,** 942 Main St. (tel. 860/ 525-1600), a convivivial bar. Sports fans hang out at **South Beach,** 201 Ann St. (tel. 860/522-4685), a sports bar.

Hartford
Special & Recreational Activities

Antiquing: The greatest selection of antiques stores can be found in nearby Coventry and west of Hartford in Farmington, along Rte. 44 in Avon, Canton, and farther west.

Golf: *Avon:* Bel Compo Golf Club, Rte. 44 (tel. 860/678-1358).
   Farmington: Tunxis Plantation Country Club, Town Farm Road

(tel. 860/677-1367); *Simsbury:* Simsbury Farms Golf Club, Old Farms Road (tel. 860/658-6246).

Ice Skating: On the pond in Elizabeth Park, Prospect Avenue and Asylum Street.

Picnicking: The city's own Elizabeth Park and Rose Garden, at Prospect Avenue and Asylum Street, makes a lovely setting for a picnic among the 900 varieties of roses that bloom there in summer. Or you can head for the banks of the Connecticut River, taking the first exit east of Hartford on I-91. Pick up supplies downtown at the Civic Center.

Tennis: Public courts are available at Elizabeth Park and at various public high schools. Call the Convention and Visitors Bureau for details (tel. 860/728-6789).

Mystic & the Connecticut Shoreline

Distance in Miles: New London, 121; Mystic, 130; Norwich, 138; Westerly, R.I., 147

Estimated Driving Time: 2 to 3 hours

◄o►◄o►◄o►◄o►◄o►

Driving: Take the FDR Drive to the New England Thruway (I-95).

Bus: Greyhound (tel. 800/231-2222) travels to New London. Peter Pan (tel. 800/343-9999) travels to Ledyard.

Train: Amtrak travels to New London, Mystic, and Westerly. For information, call 800/872-7245.

Further Information: For more about the area's events and festivals and about Connecticut in general, call or write **Connecticut State Tourism, 865 Brook St., Rocky Hill, CT 06067** (tel. 860/258-4335, or 800/282-6863).

For specific information about the area, contact **Connecticut's Mystic and More,** 27 Masonic St. (P.O. Box 89), New London, CT 06320 (tel. 860/444-2206); the **Mystic Chamber of Commerce,** 16 Cottrell St. (P.O. Box 143), Mystic, CT 06355 (tel. 860/572-9578); the **Mystic and Shoreline Visitor Information Center,** Olde Mistick Village, CT 06355 (tel. 860/536-1641); or the **Eastern Connecticut Chamber of Commerce,** 35 Main St., Norwich, CT 06360 (tel. 860/887-1647).

◄o►◄o►◄o►◄o►◄o►

If you've ever felt the call of the sea or the desire for messing around in boats, then you'll be strongly attracted to Mystic and the Connecticut shoreline, which put you in direct touch with the sea and the lives of seafarers who went out from these whaling and shipbuilding towns to risk their lives on the world's oceans.

In Mystic, besides the two prime attractions—the seaport and the aquarium—you can experience the life on the river that cuts through downtown Mystic. You can even spend one or both of your weekend days sailing out of Mystic harbor aboard a replica of the tall-masted schooners

Events & Festivals to Plan Your Trip Around

May: Sea Music Festival, Mystic Seaport (usually mid-May).

June: Rose/Arts Festival, Norwich—featuring entertainment, arts and crafts, and the Big Rose Parade (usually mid- to late June).

Yale-Harvard Regatta, New London (usually the second Saturday). Contact Connecticut's Mystic and More, 27 Masonic St. (P.O. Box 89), New London, CT 06320 (tel. 860/444-2206).

Windjammer Weekend, Mystic Seaport—when schooners and sail-training vessels gather before the race to Newport (mid-June).

July: Blessing of the Fleet, Stonington Harbor—a mass, procession, and blessing in the Portuguese tradition (usually the second Sunday).

Antique and Classic Boat Rendezvous, Mystic Seaport, complete with flotilla (usually late July).

Coast Guard Day, New London and Mystic Seaport (usually the last Saturday).

August: Mystic Outdoor Art Festival (second weekend).

December: Lantern Light/Yuletide Tours, Mystic Seaport (throughout the month).

that used to sail from here around the world. Across the harbor, in Stonington, an unspoiled old whaling town that still maintains a fishing fleet, the streets are lined with clapboard sea captains' homes, many now owned by celebrities. Stonington is also the place to go for some fine romantic dining. North of Mystic and Stonington, you can take trips along the backroads to a cider mill, a vineyard, or the historic Denison Homestead, where you can wander along the trails in the scenic nature reserve. And for those who've caught the gambling disease, there's the largest-grossing casino on the East Coast operated by the Native Americans at Ledyard. At Groton, you can tour the first nuclear submarine, the *Nautilus,* and the World War II submarine, the U.S.S. *Croaker,* a sober reminder of how far and how fast technology has come since the 1940s.

Various boat trips leave from here, including interesting oceanographic expeditions. Across the other side of the Thames River's mouth, New London holds some surprises. If you drove through you'd think it was just another rather ugly industrial town, but it possesses one of the East Coast's finest arboretums, a fine small museum, a special dollhouse and doll museum, the impressive Coast Guard Academy, and the summer home of one of America's greatest playwrights, Eugene O'Neill. Only 30 minutes up the Thames from New London lies Norwich, an old town that has a fascinating art and sculpture museum, the Slater Memorial, a lovely

Sightseeing Suggestions

I suggest that first-time visitors spend the first half day at the seaport and the second half at the aquarium, then the next day exploring New London and Groton's attractions. Those familiar with the seaport may want to skip it altogether and explore the coastline—Harkness State Park and New London/Groton—on their first day and then drive east to Stonington, Misquamicut, and Watch Hill on the next. Or you can strike inland and wander along the backroads to Norwich.

recently restored lodging place with full spa treatments, and an Indian museum nearby.

Besides all these attractions, the area affords wonderful opportunities for fishing, sailing, windsurfing, hiking, and swimming. And you can explore a coastline dotted with state parks, like Harkness and Bluff Point, and lined with fine beaches, from New London's Ocean Beach (with a boardwalk and an amusement park) to the more rugged and natural beaches of Rhode Island.

MYSTIC & STONINGTON

Area Attractions

Mystic Seaport

There's always something happening at this 17-acre replica of a 19th-century seafaring village on Rte. 27 (tel. 860/572-0711). Mystic Seaport is the largest marine museum in the United States, built appropriately enough on the site of the George Greenman and Company shipyard, which constructed such vessels as the *David Crockett* (its average speed on 25 voyages around Cape Horn to San Francisco was never equaled).

For today's seafarers, the coal-fired steamboat *Sabino* (1908) chugs out from the dock every hour, daily from May to mid-October, for a 30-minute trip down the Mystic River; at Christmas lantern-light tours and caroling add to the holiday festivities of a 19th-century village; sea chantey and other music festivals are put on in summer; and as you stroll through the village you'll hear the clanking and hammering of the many craftspeople and artisans still demonstrating and practicing nautical trades—barrel making, sail making, figurehead carving, and ship smithing. In the stores alongside them you can view the products that would've been on sale and have whatever you wish explained to you. In the clockmaker's store, for instance, you may even learn how to work an astrolabe. Hearth-cooking demonstrations go on in Buckingham House, while the many special demonstrations of seafaring skills range from sail setting and furling aboard the square-rigged *Joseph Conrad* (1882) to whaleboat rowing.

By the way, the whaling film is extremely informative and will give you some idea of how hair-raising a "Nantucket sleigh ride" can be and just how short-lived but vital the whale industry was in the mid-1800s. Another informative show (a small fee is charged), given at the Planetarium, concerns celestial navigation.

To get a fix on the context of it all, you may want to begin in the Stillman Building, which contains an exhibit tracing the history of the last wooden whaler afloat, the *Charles W. Morgan,* and illuminating New England's fishing and shipping history. Don't miss the beautiful and moving (when you think about under what emotional and physical conditions this art was practiced) scrimshaw that's displayed on the upper floor or the dramatic (and sometimes alarming or even amusing) figure-heads in the Wendell Building across the way.

Although the museum actually owns about 480 craft—smacks, sloops, sandbaggers, and even something called a New Haven sharpie—there are three main ships to go aboard: the last survivor of America's once-vast fleet of wooden whalers, the *Charles W. Morgan* (whose 37 voyages between 1841 and 1921 yielded 54,483 barrels of oil and 152,934 pounds of whalebone); the 1921 *L. A. Dunton* (a fishing schooner that went regularly to the Grand Banks and whose lower deck and hold give you a good idea of the arduous task a fisherman faced living in such cramped quarters for so long at sea); and the square-rigged *Joseph Conrad* (1882).

The museum suggests that you spend at least four hours here, but you could easily spend a full day, dreaming deep about the myths and mysteries of the sea and those that sail upon it. In summer you'll find many crowds, so get there early; the nicest time to visit (as usual) is in spring or fall, when everything seems less frantic. Fast food is available at the Galley; full-service meals at the Seamen's Inne, whose tavern section is the coziest and most appealing, but where only good luck and timing will ensure a seat.

Hours: Exhibit buildings and ships, daily 9am–5pm (Nov–Apr, exhibits only, daily 9am–4pm); grounds, daily 9am–6pm (to 7pm July–Aug). **Admission:** $15 adults, $7.50 children.

Mystic Marinelife Aquarium
This magnificent facility at 55 Coogan Blvd., Exit 90 off I-95 (tel. 860/572-5955), houses 3,500 marinelife specimens in 40 exhibits. On your visit, try to attend one of the hourly training sessions given in the Marine Theater, where the natural talents of dolphins, sea lions, and whales never cease to amaze and delight audiences. Dolphins leap 20 feet in the air,

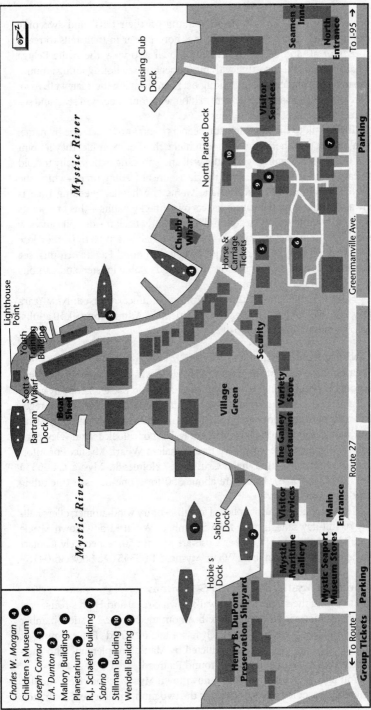

Mystic Seaport

Charles W. Morgan **4**
Children's Museum **5**
Joseph Conrad **3**
L.A. Dunton **2**
Mallory Buildings **8**
Planetarium **6**
R.J. Schaefer Building **7**
Sabino **1**
Stillman Building **10**
Wendell Building **9**

2137

Mystic River

Lighthouse Point

Youth Training Building

Scott's Wharf

Bartram Dock

Boat Shed

Cruising Club Dock

Chubb's Wharf

North Parade Dock

Horse & Carriage Tickets

Visitor Services

Seamen's Inne

North Entrance

To I-95 →

Parking

Security

Village Green

The Galley Restaurant

Variety Store

Greenmanville Ave.

Route 27

Visitor Services

Main Entrance

Sabino Dock

Hobie's Dock

Mystic Maritime Gallery

Mystic Seaport Museum Stores

Henry B. DuPont Preservation Shipyard

← To Route 1

Parking

Group Tickets

performing triple spirals, even "walking on their tails" and sweeping through the water, propelled by the 8 horsepower in their tails to reach speeds of 50 and 60 miles per hour. You'll also view the white Beluga whale kissing and cavorting with his trainer and sea lions goofing around, tossing and balancing balls, talking back, and waving their farewell. Also, don't miss Seal Island, a 2½ -acre exhibit with four species of seals and sea lions, including Steller's sea lions.

If you talk to their enthusiastic keepers, who know each one by name, you'll learn that there's quite a social hierarchy. For example, they'll point out the old seal leaning against the wall and snoozing, who's really too old to care or do anything except struggle ashore at feeding time—which she prefers to attend last because she wants "no hassle." Feeding time is always fun, and each creature has its own finicky habits—this one wants only tails, another only heads, and so on. Cute. Back inside you can view sand tiger sharks close enough to examine their sharp teeth (if they lose one, they replace it immediately), a giant 25-pound Pacific octopus, sea horses, peculiar fish that burrow in the sand, a blue lobster, and exhibits dealing with particular habitats.

Hours: Daily 9am–4:30pm (to 7pm in summer). **Closed:** New Year's Day, last week of Jan, Thanksgiving, Christmas. **Admission:** $9.50 adults, $8.50 seniors, $6 children 5–12.

Cruising from Mystic

Recapture the aura of the days when Mystic was filled with whalers and schooners lying cheek by jowl against smacks and packet sloops by cruising aboard the *Mystic Whaler, a* windjammer schooner that sails on regular three-hour and one-, two-, three-, or five-day voyages on Long Island and Block Island sounds; it calls at Sag Harbor, Block Island, Newport, and other ports. The sails leave from Whaler's Wharf, Mystic. For information, contact **Mystic Whaler Cruises** at 7 Holmes St., Mystic, CT 06355 (tel. 860/536-4218). Prices are about $60 for a one-day sail (including lunch) on weekends.

The schooner *Argia*, a replica of a 19th-century windjammer, offers half-day or full-day sails, leaving from Steamboat Wharf in downtown Mystic from May to the end of October. Costs are $31 or $60, respectively. Contact **Voyager Cruises**, Steamboat Wharf, Mystic, CT 06355 (tel. 860/536-0416).

Downtown Mystic, Old Mystic & Environs

After visiting the seaport, take a walk down Gravel and High streets, past the many **historic houses** that've been outlined in the Mystic Chamber of Commerce's walking tour. Each has a tale attached. For example, at 27 Gravel St., seances were conducted by Matilda Appleman, who sheltered slaves traveling the Underground Railroad.

You may also want to explore downtown Mystic at the river's mouth, where the bascule **drawbridge** joins the two municipalities of Stonington and Groton. Actually, there's no such political entity as Mystic. This downtown area was developed when shipbuilding became big business in the mid- to late 1800s. Drop in and browse the crafts, fashion, book, gift, and antiques stores here, including **Factory Square.**

Up the river, Old Mystic slumbers quietly along with its post office, general store, and few residences. You may want to visit **Olde Mistick Village,** at the junction of I-95 and Rte. 27 (tel. 860/536-4941), a quaint shopping complex designed to look like a New England village of around 1720; the shops are usually open Monday to Saturday from 10am to 6pm and Sunday from noon to 5pm.

From here you can drive out to **Clyde's Cider Mill** on North Stonington Road, Old Mystic (tel. 860/536-3354), which operates from the last weekend in September to Thanksgiving. Or drive east to visit **Stonington Vineyards,** on Taugwonk Road (tel. 860/535-1222), one of the few wineries that've located in this area. It produces annually more than 7,000 cases of wine that are distributed locally.

Tours: Daily at 2pm; in winter call ahead to confirm.

Looping back toward Stonington, you can stop at the **Denison Homestead and Nature Center,** Pequotsepos Road, Mystic (tel. 860/536-9248). Since 1722 the homestead has belonged to five generations of Denisons, one of Connecticut's first families, and it's interesting because each room has been furnished to reflect the five different periods. Trails crisscross the 125-acre sanctuary (tel. 860/536-1216).

Hours: May 20–Oct 15, Wed–Mon 1–5pm. **Admission:** $3 adults, $1 children 2–16.

Stonington Village & Watch Hill

In the dining section I'll describe several restaurants where you might want to dine, but before you do, take some time to discover this old whaling village, where Stephen Vincent Benet and James MacNeill Whistler both had residences, where Edgar Allan Poe loved to visit, and where today many a celebrity chooses to hide away as did the late James Merrill. Narrow streets lined with old sea captains' homes and Victorian residences cluster on a peninsula running between Stonington Harbor on one side and the Pawcatuck River and Fisher's Island Sound on the other. Stroll down Water Street to the 1840 **Stonington Light** (tel. 860/535-1440), which now houses a collection of whaling and fishing artifacts, toys, Stonington firearms, and stoneware.

Hours: May–Oct, Tues–Sun 11am–5pm. **Admission:** $3 adults, $1 children 6–12.

From Stonington, it's only a short drive to **Watch Hill,** a quiet gracious shore enclave that possesses a number of rambling Victorian shore hotels, like the Ocean House, which have seen better days. The town is not too crowded, and while you're here stroll down to the carousel; stop at the Book & Tackle Shop, stacked with piles of old and new books and a good selection of historic postcards; have an ice cream across the street or a cup of coffee and a snack; walk to the Watch Hill Lighthouse; or just sit out on the Harbour House's deck and watch the scene. For a casual meal head for the **Olympia Tea Room** on Bay Street (tel. 860/348-8211), a good old-fashioned soda fountain/café serving some updated dishes like sautéed shrimp with feta cheese, chicken fajitas, and lots of seafood.

Mystic Lodging & Dining

The Inn at Mystic, Rte. 1, Mystic, CT 06355 (tel. 860/536-9604), was formerly called the Mystic Motor Inn, and it still looks very much like a classy motor inn. However, it now also offers accommodations in the "Inn and Gatehouse," an imposing Colonial Revival mansion, with a classical pediment supported by Corinthian columns, that stands on a hill at the back of the property. The mansion's ground-floor formal dining room and parlor, with exquisite 17th-century pine paneling and carved mantel decorated with Delft tiles, are open to guests and used for weddings and parties, while upstairs the 10 guest rooms are lavishly furnished with canopied beds, antique sofas, and porcelain lamps; 4 rooms even have whirlpool baths that you can stand in and still look out over the harbor.

Besides the new inn, the place has some other outstanding attributes: the view of the harbor, 13 acres of landscaped grounds sloping down to the river, and some very comfortable rooms, many prettily furnished with antique reproductions of Federal-style mirrors and desks, brass lamps, and full- or half-canopied beds. TVs are tucked away in cabinets. The East Wing rooms, built in 1978, are even more luxurious, with fireplaces, wing chairs, handsome highboys, baths with Jacuzzi tubs and bidets, and sliding doors that lead to a balcony.

The inn's **Flood Tide Restaurant** has a good reputation. Here in a pretty country dining room such classics as beef Wellington, chateaubriand, rack of lamb, and whole roast pheasant are nicely presented along with more spicy dishes like the pineapple-ginger shrimp. The tasty array of appetizers includes smoked salmon rosettes with a Dijon sauce and escargots with mushroom and garlic baked in a ramekin, with a flaky pastry crust. Prices run $15 to $28. Other dishes include roast duckling with peach glaze, broiled filet mignon wrapped in bacon and served with mushroom caps and sauce Foyot, and venison chasseur. Special dessert treats are the bananas Foster and chocolate fondue, though there are plenty of other delectable choices. The restaurant is open year round, and so are the wine bar and piano lounge. Additional facilities include a heated outdoor pool, tennis courts, and canoes and sailboats for rent.

Rates: Summer, $170–$240 double in the motor inn, $165–$245 double in the Inn and Gatehouse. Winter, $165–$210 double in the motor inn, $135–$235 double in the Inn and Gatehouse. Special packages are available during winter and spring, usually including two nights' accommodations, sometimes including dinner. **Dining Hours:** Mon–Thurs

7–10:30am, 11:30am–2:30pm, and 5:30–9:30pm; Fri 7–10:30am, 11:30am–2:30pm, and 5:30–10pm; Sat 7–10:30am and 5:30–10pm; Sun 7–10:30am, 11am–3pm (brunch), and 5:30–9:30pm.

The **Steamboat Inn,** 73 Steamboat Wharf, Mystic, CT 06355 (tel. 860/ 536-8300), is down on the riverfront so you can look out your window and see the sailboats. There are 10 delightfully decorated rooms, all with whirlpool bath, TV, phone, and air conditioning; 6 have wood-burning fireplaces. The Ariadne room features a canopied bed made up with beige and peach linens and has the additional luxury of a fireplace and a loveseat for lounging. The Summer Girl is decorated in pine and pastels. The Mystic has great water views from two windows. A continental breakfast is served in a sunny room with black-and-white flooring and glass-topped tables.

Rates (including breakfast): Summer and fall weekends, $175–$245 double (slightly less other seasons).

The **Whalers Inn,** 20 E. Main St., Mystic, CT 06355 (tel. 860/536-1506), occupies a super-convenient downtown location. In the older section of this 40-room establishment designed around a motor court, the rooms tend to be small, with one double bed, but they're attractively furnished with four-posters and wingback chairs and sport rich color schemes like Chinese red and forest green. The eight rooms in the 1865 House are more floral/pastel. All have a bath, TV, and phone. There are several dining choices: Bravo Bravo for fine dining, Cafe Bravo for alfresco dining, and a bagel shop. At the first you'll find a variety of pasta dishes available as well as such items as grilled chicken breast with a three-mustard sauce and roast duck with peach-and-peppercorn sauce, priced from $12 to $18. For those traveling by train, the inn is only four blocks from the railroad station.

Rates: Summer weekends, $100–$130 double.

The **Mystic Hilton,** 20 Coogan Blvd., Mystic, CT 06355 (tel. 860/ 572-0731), has 187 rooms, an indoor/outdoor pool, a restaurant, and a lounge. It's full-service all the way.

Rates: $175 double weekends.

Other Mystic accommodations run to the typical modern chains: **Days Inn,** Rte. 27 (P.O. Box 88), Mystic, CT 06355 (tel. 860/572-0574); **Howard Johnson,** Rte. 27, Mystic, CT 06355 (tel. 860/536-2654); and **Ramada Inn,** Rte. 27 (P.O. Box 427), Mystic, CT 06355 (tel. 860/536-4281).

Rates: Summer, $62 double (Days), $75 double (Howard Johnson), and $75 double (Ramada).

Mystic Dining

Breakfast & Lunch

BeeBees, 33 W. Main St. (tel. 860/536-4577), is a favorite breakfast spot. **2 Sisters Deli,** 4 Pearl St. (tel. 860/536-1244), is good for sandwiches and other luncheon fare.

Picnics & Other Food to Go

In West Mystic, **Grossman's** fish and cheese market, 401 Noank Rd. (tel. 860/536-1674), is open Tuesday to Saturday from 9am to 6pm and Sunday from 10am to 5pm. And **Mystic Market,** 375 Noank Rd. (tel. 860/536-1500), is a deli/bakery that makes picnics to go.

Lunch & Dinner

The **Captain Daniel Packer Inne,** 32 Water St. (tel. 860/536-3555), has a very attractive ambience, especially in the downstairs low-beamed tavern, made even cozier by the fire. The upstairs dining room is traditional—Windsor chairs and polished wood tables, lit by hurricane lamps. The food is also traditional. Start with little necks, escargots, or stuffed mushrooms before moving on to rack of lamb dijonnais or four-peppercorn chicken, from $13 to $19. At lunch, burgers and sandwiches, quiche, and such dishes as baked stuffed sole are available for $6 to $9.

Hours: Daily 11am–3pm and 5–10pm.

In Olde Misticke Village, the well-liked **Steak Loft** (tel. 860/536-2661), set in a pretty barnlike building decorated with plenty of farm gadgets, purveys (surprise) steaks—sirloin, teriyaki, tenderloin—for $12 to $23. Seafood and chicken are also on the menu.

Hours: Daily 11:30am–2:30pm and 4:30–9:30pm; lounge, daily 11:30am–11pm.

The **S & P Oyster House,** 1 Holmes St. (tel. 860/536-2674), occupies a great vantage point from which to view the life of the river and the boats passing under the rare bascule bridge right in downtown Mystic. The menu offers an assortment of steaks and seafood, including steak teriyaki, shrimp kebabs, fish and chips, stuffed sole, and a variety of oysters. Prices range from $11 to $22. At lunch, burgers and sandwiches are the primary fare.

Hours: Mon–Fri 11:30am–3pm and 5–9pm, Sat 11:30am–3pm and 5–10pm, Sun noon–9pm.

Dinner Only

J. P. Daniels, Rte. 184, Old Mystic (tel. 860/572-9564), is a favorite romantic dining spot housed in a comfortably rustic historic barn whose raftered ceiling is high enough to hang a sleigh and a carriage from it. The place is warmly lit at night. Among the appetizers you might choose are stuffed mushrooms, clams casino, chicken teriyaki, or tomato-and-mozzarella salad. On the menu will be about seven pasta dishes, like fettuccine primavera or St. Michelle (prosciutto, shrimp, peas, and Alfredo sauce). The entrees might be grilled sweet-and-sour shrimp, veal Oscar, coq au vin, steaks, and the house specialty duck, stuffed with seasonal fresh fruits and topped with a special duck sauce finished with apricot brandy. Prices run $11 to $19. The desserts are classics like peach Melba and chocolate mousse.

Hours: Mon–Thurs 5–9pm, Fri–Sat 5–9:30pm, Sun 11am–2pm.

Old Mystic Lodging & Dining

In Old Mystic, 2 miles from the coast, Ruth Keyes is the innkeeper of two lovingly restored buildings: the Crary Homestead, a 1770 Colonial farmhouse, and the atmospheric Haley Tavern (1740). They've been transformed into a secluded retreat named the **Red Brook Inn,** 10 Welles Rd. (P.O. Box 237), Old Mystic, CT 06372 (tel. 860/572-0349).

Throughout the houses Ruth has stenciled the wide-plank floors and furnished the rooms with authentic colonial antiques and fabrics. There are 11 rooms available, 7 with working fireplaces. The favorites are in the atmospheric Tavern building with its low doors, creaking floors, original latches and windows, and authentic tap room. The Ross Haley Chamber features a 1790 high four-poster mahogany canopied bed embellished with fabric made in 1815. The crocheted canopy in the Mary Virginia Chamber is also over 100 years old. The solid-walnut cannonball bed in the Henry Haley Room sports a States quilt crafted in Michigan depicting all the state flowers. The rooms in the homestead are less formal and have more of a country feel, with four-posters, quilts, old blanket chests, antique rockers, and cherry side tables. In the West Room there's an unusual so-called Mammy bench rocker, an ingenious early timesaver.

Down in the parlor guests can gather around the fire for a game of chess or backgammon and admire Ruth's glass collection, which includes many whale-oil lamps. The keeping room, however, is her real pride and joy, containing a wide colonial hearth, with all the accoutrements for hearthside cooking. Ruth has mastered this art, and on winter weekends from November to March she serves special colonial hearthside dinners consisting of spit-roasted meats and vegetables cooked over the fire. It's lit only by candlelight or natural light and the breakfast is served on fine china at Early American wood tables. Most likely it'll be apple, zucchini, or banana-nut bread; fresh peaches, grapefruit, or other seasonal fruit; muffins; walnut waffles or blueberry pancakes; and some unusual corn sticks. The 7 acres of grounds ensure tranquillity and are ideal for picnicking area or playing croquet.

Rates: $125–$200 double. Special two-night packages (with dinner) from $400.

Foxwoods Casino & Ledyard Lodging

Foxwoods Resort & Casino, Rte. 2 (P.O. Box 410), Ledyard, CT 06339 (tel. 860/885-3000), is the largest casino in the nation and has generated a great deal of controversy. The original bingo hall opened in 1986 and was followed by the casino in February 1992. In three short years it has grown into a major complex with two hotels, 16 restaurants and food courts, 40 retail outlets, a spa/fitness center, and an entertainment complex that attracts 16 million people per year—that's 45,000 per day. Today the casino rooms hold 3,900 slot machines and more than 230 table games, including a room devoted to poker.

The Resort Hotel provides 312 typical modern-style rooms above the casino. Services include 24-hour room service and concierge; facilities include two gourmet restaurants, an indoor pool, and a health club/spa. The Two Trees Inn is a three-story building in Mashantucket, across from the casino. It has 280 rooms, casual dining, and an indoor pool and exercise facility. There's a 24-hour complimentary casino shuttle. A museum and research center is scheduled to open in 1997, but until it does visitors can gain a little information about the tribe and its history and culture in the display area below the lobby.

Dining facilities range from Cedars Steakhouse, Al Dente (serving northern and southern Italian cuisine), and Han Garden (for Chinese) to the Festival Buffet, pizza outlets, and other lounges with casual fare. Among the entertainment facilities are several special-effects theaters: Turbo Ride has seats that move in sync with the onscreen action; Cinedrome 360 features a 360° screen and converts at night into a dance club; the Fox Giant Screen Theatre is precisely that; while Cinetropolis offers the ultimate in virtual reality, allowing groups of six to take command of different ships and journey beneath the ocean to save the eggs of the Loch Ness monster. And there's also headline entertainment that has included Donna Summer, Aretha Franklin, and Kenny Rogers, plus boxing events. The biggest event of the year is Schemitzun, the Feast of Green Corn and Dance, which brings thousands of Native Americans to Foxwood to compete for cash prizes in dance and drum competitions and to entertain and sell and demonstrate crafts and culture. It's usually held for four days in mid-September.

Rates: Resort Hotel, $145–$210 double, depending on season. Two Trees Inn, $110–$160 double.

In sharp contrast, the **Applewood Farms Inn,** 528 Colonel Ledyard Hwy., Ledyard, CT 06339 (tel. 860/536-2022), is away from the hubbub in an 1826 center-chimney farmhouse on 33 acres. Fronted by stone walls and fences and still affording peaceful vistas, it offers six guest rooms full of character, four with fireplace. The Lillian Room contains a canopied bed and Laura Ashley decor. Stenciling enhances the Benadam Room, with an antique bed covered with white eyelet linens. There are three common rooms, two with fireplaces where guests can relax. A full breakfast is served.

Rates (including breakfast): $125–$260 double.

Stonington & North Stonington Lodging & Dining

Just east of Mystic lies the charming unspoiled whaling town of Stonington, which offers one simple accommodation. At **Lasbury's Guesthouse,** 24 Orchard St., Stonington, CT 06378 (tel. 860/535-2681), the owners rent three rooms: one with bath and two in a separate cottage sharing a bath.

Rates: Summer, $90 double.

North Stonington stretches inland and here you'll find a unique experience at the following hostelry and tap room.

Randall's Ordinary, Rte. 2 (P.O. Box 243), North Stonington, CT 06359 (tel. 860/599-4540), delivers an authentic and fun colonial dining experience in an atmospheric 18th-century home. Set on 27 acres, it consists of a complex of buildings that include a magnificent huge barn that was moved from New York State and attached to a silo and is now used for accommodations. The rooms in the barn are large and feature plank floors and high ceilings supported by strong beams. They're furnished with hoop canopied beds, pine furnishings, Hitchcock rockers, and modern amenities like a TV and phone. The decorative accessories are appropriate, like iron latches on the doors and tin sconces and iron toilet paper holder in the bath. The most extraordinary room is the suite in the silo, with a Jacuzzi loft, a skylit sitting area, a gas-fired fireplace, and an Adirondack-style bed.

The rooms in Randall's Ordinary—a National Landmark built in 1685—all have fireplaces and are more colonial in scale. They lack a TV and phone but are authentically decorated in teal or similar milk paint and comfortably furnished with wingbacks and other antiques. Meals are served here by staff dressed in period attire. At dinner ($30 per person) you can watch the meal being cooked over the fire in huge pots, on the spit, or in the oven. A la carte menus are offered at breakfast and lunch. Try the homemade sausages or the huge "ordinary" breakfast of griddle cakes, scrambled eggs, bacon, sausage, and fried apples and potatoes. Lunch brings assorted regional favorites—cod cakes, Nantucket scallops, and grilled venison sausage skewered with peppers, onions, and mushrooms. The property has recently been purchased by the tribe that operates Foxwoods. Expect a major investment and substantial changes in the near future.

Rates: $125 double; $205 silo suite. **Dining Hours:** Sun–Fri 7–11am, noon–3pm, and one dinner seating at 7pm; Sat 7–11am, noon–3pm, and dinner seatings at 5 and 7:30pm.

Stonington Dining

From Mystic, you may well prefer, as many locals do, to pop over to Stonington, where you have two fine choices. For romantic dining there's the **Harborview,** 60 Water St. (tel. 860/535-2720), where the front tap room is always, in summer at least, filled to the rafters with seafaring and other convivial sorts, all crammed into the small atmospheric bar (in which you can also obtain a fine lunch or dinner). In the low-lit dining room patrons are entertained by a harpist and, looking out over the harbor, dine on such dishes as bouillabaisse, grilled mussels, and assorted veal dishes, priced from $15 to $22. Ham, shrimp cocktail, turkey, vegetables, potato au gratin, fettuccine, eggs Benedict, fruits, and pastries make up the big Sunday buffet brunch.

Hours: Daily 11:30am–10pm (Sun brunch 11am–2pm).

Just up the street, **Noah's,** 115 Water St. (tel. 860/535-3925), is unpretentious and comfortable, yet still pretty at night. It's frequented by a local crowd that enjoys the moderately priced ($8 to $17) limited menu, which features grilled chicken breast, steaks, and such fresh seafood as cod Portuguese and broiled flounder. Perhaps start with chicken-liver pâté with sherry and pistachios.

Hours: Tues–Thurs 7–11am, 11:30am–2:30pm, and 6–9pm; Fri–Sat 7–11am, 11:30am–2:30pm, and 6–9:30pm; Sun 7am–noon, 12:15–2:30pm, and 6–9pm.

Behind Harborview, down at the water's edge, **Skipper's Dock** (tel. 860/535-2000) offers a plain setting for about 8 to 10 fresh fishes that can be prepared with scallion-ginger sauce, honey-mustard sauce, or other combinations. There's also fish chowder and fisherman's stew Portuguese and lobsters and a clambake, of course. Prices run $12 to $20.

Hours: Summer, daily 11:30am–10pm; fall and off-season, Mon 5–9pm, Thurs–Fri 5–10pm, Sat 11:30am–10pm, Sun 11:30am–9pm. **Closed:** Jan–Mar.

Noank Lodging

Noank is on a small peninsula about 2 miles from Mystic. The **Palmer Inn,** 25 Church St., Noank, CT 06340 (tel. 860/572-9000), is a 16-room mansion built in 1907 for a member of the famous Palmer shipbuilding family. Its exterior is impressive, with a semicircular 30-foot-high columned portico; equally impressive is the interior, with its high ceilings supported by wood columns, among other architectural details. I especially like the sunrise-sunset stained-glass fan windows that change colors throughout the day.

Patricia White has restored the place, furnishing the six rooms (all with bath, one with fireplace) in a Victorian manner. One room possesses a king-size wicker bed, a couch, a chair, and a side table, all of wicker. A favorite room is the dusky-rose master suite (with fireplace), where the walls are covered in French turn-of-the-century-design wallpapers, the windows have lace curtains, and the furnishings are oak. The satin eider adds a luxurious touch. One room has access to the semicircular balcony above the portico, offering a view past the church steeple to the water. Among the furnishings in the brass room are a brass bed and an oak dresser; the bath retains the old clawfoot tub and pedestal sink. The oak suite contains Eastlake oak pieces and has a little balcony and stained-glass windows. All rooms boast amenities like designer linens, plush towels, Crabtree & Evelyn soap, shampoo, and hairdryers. The guests gather in the large parlor around the fireplace or at the table at breakfast. In the smaller parlor, a comfortable sofa, wing chairs, and board games are the attractions.

At breakfast you'll find fresh fruits, home-baked items, and entertaining conversation, helped along by Pat, a former clinical psychologist who thrives on meeting and chatting with guests and seems to have hotelkeeping in her blood. She'll even show you, on those long winter nights, how to make a pomander.

Rates (including breakfast): $130–$215 double.

Noank Dining

For summer luncheon or an early-evening dinner, you can't beat **Abbot's Lobster in the Rough,** 117 Pearl St. (tel. 860/536-7719), at the western tip of Mystic harbor in Noank, also formerly a whaling town, but a far less opulent one than Stonington on the opposite side of the harbor. Stonington residents were ship captains and ship owners; Noank's were whalers, plain and simple.

Here at the water's edge the view only adds to the succulent flavor of the lobster. Wait while your order of lobster, crab, or lobster roll ($7 to $9.50), mussels, clams, or steamers is cooked in the large steamers behind the counter, then take it outside to the colorful picnic tables where you can observe the river craft and the gulls circling overhead, breathe the salty air, and listen to the halyards clinking against the masts and summoning you to the sea. Prices are very reasonable—$14 for a 1¼-pound lobster served with coleslaw, drawn butter, and chips; $33 for a 2- to 3-pounder. Other items are priced from $5. Before you leave, tour the holding facility, where they keep up to 22,000 pounds of these delicious crustaceans. Bring your own wine or beer. To get here, take Rte. 1 to Rte. 215 into Noank and turn down Pearl Street.

Hours: May–Labor Day, daily noon–9pm (weekends only until Columbus Day).

At the **Sea Horse Restaurant,** 65 Marsh Rd. (tel. 860/536-1670), a simple local tavern-style spot, you can obtain really fresh fish at reasonable prices—broiled flounder; fisherman's platter of fried clams, shrimp, scallops, and fish; and surf and turf—from $8 to $17. At luncheon there's fish and chips and sandwiches for under $8.

Hours: Sun–Thurs 11am–9pm, Fri–Sat 11am–10pm.

The Fisherman, 937 Groton Long Point Rd. (tel. 860/536-1717), also serves good fresh seafood even in winter, when a fire warms the hearth and a pianist entertains. The wide choice of fresh seafood—scrod, sole amandine, swordfish, stuffed shrimp—is supplemented by steaks, chicken français, beef Wellington, and (weekends only) prime rib. Prices run $13 to $21.

Hours: Mon–Thurs 11:30am–3pm and 4:30–9:30pm, Fri–Sat 11:30am–3pm and 4:30–10pm, Sun 11:30am–9pm. **Closed:** Mon off-season.

Shelter Harbor, R.I., Lodging

From Mystic-Stonington, if you take Rte. 1 or the more scenic Rte. 1A, which rejoins Rte. 1 beyond Westerly, you'll reach Shelter Harbor, a tiny community originally laid out as a musician's retreat, where the streets are named after composers like Bach and Verdi.

You can stay at the **Shelter Harbor Inn,** 10 Wagner Rd. (off Rte. 1), Westerly, RI 02891 (tel. 401/322-8883), a restored 18th-century farmhouse whose sun porch/bar is a popular gathering place on weekend nights. The two small parlors offer the comforts of leather armchairs, a braided rug, a stove, and plenty of reading material. In the dining room, where floral wallpaper, pine cabinets, and wainscoting impart a country air, the menu might offer grilled swordfish with pineapple salsa, sautéed veal with double tomato relish, and grilled sirloin along with daily specials. Entrees run $13 to $20. Breakfast (7:30 to 10:30am) offers create-your-own omelets, banana-walnut French toast, granola, and other items. Prices average $5 or $6.

There are 9 guest rooms in the house, 3 with fireplaces, each comfortably furnished, and 10 recently decorated rooms in the barn. In the Coach House are 4 additional rooms with fireplaces. Some rooms have private decks, and all have access to a third-floor deck with panoramic views and a hot tub.

While you're here, try your hand at paddle tennis on the two lighted courts. The inn also provides access to a 2-mile stretch of beach a short drive away in Weekapaug.

Rates (including breakfast): July–Aug, $98–$132 double. May–June and Sept–Oct, $98–$132 double Fri–Sat, $77–$111 double Sun–Thurs. Nov–Apr, $87–$111 double Fri–Sat, $77–$102 double Sun–Thurs. **Dining Hours:** Mon–Sat 11:30am–3pm and 5–10pm, Sun 11:30am–3pm and 4–9pm.

GROTON & NEW LONDON

Groton Attractions

Shipbuilding continues to this day in Groton, where the nation's largest submarine producer, the General Dynamics Corporation, is located. Here the six-story-high Trident submarines are being built, each costing $1 billion and taking four to five years to construct.

The highlight of any visit, especially for men and boys, is a tour of the $7.9-million **Nautilus Memorial Museum,** off Rte. 12 at the Naval Submarine Base (tel. 860/449-3174 or 449-3290); take Exit 86 off I-95. The displays in the museum building relate the history of submarine development, from the legend of Alexander the Great's descending in a glass barrel, as depicted in a medieval manuscript, to Sir Edmund Halley's 1690 "diving tub," and one version that might've worked—William Bourne's boat described in *Inventions and Devices* (1578) consisting of a flexible inner hull of leather acting as one wall of a ballast tank against a rigid wooden outer hull. On one wall there's a 50-foot-long scale model of a fleet boat showing everything detailed to one inch. The Nautilus Room traces the history of the subs bearing the name, from the first launched in 1954 that sent out the message "under nuclear power." Video stations show films of loading missiles, a day in the life of a submariner, and so on. In earlier models, like the U.S.S. *Gate,* the men can be seen running around in shorts because of the heat (this was before air-conditioning). En route to the boat a whole wall of models shows all classes of submarines ever built, from the *Holland* to the *Nautilus,* clearly depicting a steady process of streamlining. You can also use the periscopes to sight trucks speeding along I-95.

The tour of the "boat" itself is most fascinating. Only 60 people are allowed aboard at one time, so get there early or be prepared to wait, often on a windy footbridge/gangplank. The *Nautilus* was the first nuclear-powered submarine. It broke records by cruising deeper (400 feet), faster (20 knots), and for longer periods (287 hours, covering 4,039 miles in one stretch) than any other. It carries 111 sailors and officers in highly confined quarters where every space-saving device is used—fold-away sinks, narrow bunks that double as storage boxes. While on board you'll carry an electronic wand that activates commentaries about each area—navigation center, radar room, sonar room, attack center, radio room, and the 10-foot-long by 2-foot-wide galley. The 1950s pinups were donated by the original crew.

Hours: Mid-Apr to mid-Oct, Tues 1–5pm, Wed–Mon 9am–5pm; winter, Wed–Mon 9am–4pm. **Closed:** New Year's Day, one week in May and Dec, Thanksgiving, Christmas. **Admission:** Free.

Head up the hill to **Fort Griswold,** Monument Street (tel. 860/445-1729), which was attacked by a British force led by Benedict Arnold on September 6, 1781. When the American officer surrendered and handed over his sword, it was turned against him and he fell to his death. A massacre followed. Today the park provides glorious views of the Thames River and Fisher's Island and stays open from 8am to sunset daily. A museum tells the story.

Hours: Memorial Day–Labor Day, daily 10am–5pm; Labor Day–Columbus Day, weekends 10am–5pm.

Cruises from Groton

Project Oceanography, Avery Point, Groton, sponsors enormously interesting two-hour trips led by expert guides aboard an Enviro-Lab. You'll learn how to use oceanographic instruments, pull in a trawl net filled with fish, and how lobsters are caught. For information, call 860/445-9007, or 800/364-8472. The boat departs from the Avery Point Campus of the University of Connecticut.

Admission: $16 adults, $12 children.

New London Attractions

The **U.S. Coast Guard Academy,** Mohegan Avenue and Rte. 32 (tel. 860/444-8270), has made its home here since 1910. At the visitor's pavilion you can view a slide program that'll introduce you to cadet life and visit the museum to see the nautical models, paintings, and memorabilia. Dress parades are held in spring and fall (usually on Friday; call for dates), and you can also go aboard the 295-foot square-rigged training barque *Eagle* on Sunday in spring and fall from 1 to 4pm. On this cutter cadets receive under-sail training handling more than 20,000 square feet of sail and over 20 miles of rigging. More than 200 ropes must be coordinated during a major ship maneuver and the cadets must learn the name and function of each.

Hours: Visitor's pavilion, May–October, daily 10am–5pm.

Two other attractions are almost next door to each other. The **Connecticut Arboretum,** Williams Street (tel. 860/439-5020), on the Connecticut College campus, is one of the East's finest small (415 acres) preserves with many miles of self-guided trails. The **Lyman Allyn Art Museum,** 625 Williams St. (tel. 860/443-2545), is a richly rewarding small museum. The period furniture collection on the ground floor is especially well diagrammed and described so that, in effect, any visitor can trace the hallmarks of each period from Jacobean through Queen Anne, Chippendale, Hepplewhite, and Empire to early Victorian. The glass collection includes Tiffany, art glass, Art Nouveau, and Stiegel. China and clocks are also on display, along with a rare and lovely collection of English silver pocket nutmeg graters.

Downstairs has special appeal to children, for it contains an outstanding collection of dollhouses, doll furniture, toys, and dolls. Among them are French bisque heads, wood-peg-jointed dolls, all-wood American dolls, auto peripatetikos (walking dolls), and china and wax and papier-mâché heads. Upstairs, a series of small galleries displays Greek terra-cottas; Egyptian, Roman, ancient Near Eastern, pre-Columbian, African, Indian, and Japanese art and artifacts; and 19th-century impressionist paintings. The Chinese galleries are especially strong.

Hours: Museum, Tues, Thurs–Fri, and Sun 1–5pm; Wed 1–9pm; Sat 11am–5pm. **Admission:** $3 adults, $2 seniors and students, free for children 11 and under.

New London was a great whaling port, second only to New Bedford in its heyday. To get a sense of its history, pick up a map at the **New London Chamber of Commerce,** 1 Whale Oil Row (tel. 860/443-8332), and walk around. Explore Huntington Street, Captain's Walk, and Whale Oil Row. Continue on Whale Oil Row to Washington Street, then take the first right onto Starr—a whole street lined with 21 restored 19th-century homes once belonging to whaling folk.

Take a left onto O'Neill Drive and right onto Pearl Street to view the **New London Custom House** (1833) on Bank Street (tel. 860/442-7848). It was customary for the Customs officer to climb up into the attic and onto the roof to scan the harbor and check that no whaling ships had avoided paying duty. Inside, maritime artifacts are displayed.

Hours: By appointment only.

Shaw's Mansion, 305 Bank St. (tel. 860/443-1209), is named after Nathaniel Shaw, who was appointed naval agent for the colonies by the Continental Congress.

Hours: Wed–Fri 1–4pm, Sat 10am–4pm. **Admission:** $3 adults, $2 seniors, $1 children 12 and under.

Eugene O'Neill spent much of his boyhood in New London at the **Monte Cristo Cottage,** 325 Pequot Ave. (tel. 860/443-0051), a gray-and-white frame house in which his family summered from 1884 to 1921. It was named after the play that paid his father $50,000 a year. When the family came here the area was a popular summer resort on the Thames. From here, O'Neill went to sea, returning in 1924 to work as a cub reporter on the *New London Telegraph*. This was the setting for his tragic *Long Day's Journey into Night* (a Pulitzer Prize winner) and his comic *Ah, Wilderness!*, and no doubt its oceanside setting inspired this young lad to sail the seas and write about the life he experienced there.

For O'Neill fans, and for anyone who empathizes with the tragedy of his family, this house has tremendous emotional impact. Especially evocative is the eerie Long Day's Journey into Night Room, containing the playwright's desk, the table from the original Broadway production, and James O'Neill's rum jug; here you can observe the small changes O'Neill slipped into his stage setting.

The 15-minute introductory film is one of the best of its kind that I've ever seen, professionally filmed and dramatically portraying the family: dashing matinee idol father James, whose good looks and golden voice made him one of the most promising U.S. actors but who sacrificed his talent for money; mother Mary Ellen Quinlan from Indiana, who gave up her dream of becoming a concert pianist when she married James and whose morphine addiction began when she sought relief from the pain of childbirth; son Jamie, who died of alcoholism; and son Eugene, born in a Broadway hotel in October 1888, whose life was dogged by a secret shame and a need to escape from reality.

Hours: Memorial Day–Labor Day, Mon–Fri 1–4pm; other times, by appointment. **Admission:** $4.

Nearby, the **Eugene O'Neill Theater Center,** 305 Great Neck Rd., Waterford (tel. 860/443-5378), has been established on grounds that sweep down to the Sound. This is a must for any theater lover, especially during the Playwrights' Conference from early July to early August, when a dozen or so plays selected from nearly 2,000 are developed in staged readings. Some may go on to Broadway success, as did *Agnes of God* and *Nine*. In August musical theater and cabaret are featured in a similar fashion. At other times you may catch a workshop in session, as I did when students were practicing their fencing for those swashbuckling period roles.

Groton Lodging

Best Western's **Olympic Inn,** 360 Rte. 12, Groton, CT 06340 (tel. 860/445-8000), has 104 rooms, each furnished with a desk, a sofa, dressers, and modern amenities. An exercise room, saunas, a lounge, and a restaurant complete the facilities.

Rates: Summer, $95–$130 double (less in winter).

Following the coastline west from Mystic will bring you to Groton Long Point, where the houses cluster along the shore. The only accommodation to be found among the many residences is the **Shore Inn,** 54 E. Shore Rd., Groton Long Point, CT 06340 (tel. 860/536-1180), facing out across the Sound to Fisher's Island. The seven accommodations are pleasant.

Rates (including continental breakfast): Apr–Nov, $90 double.

New London Lodging & Dining

A grand fountain plays in front of the entrance to the **Lighthouse Inn,** 6 Guthrie Place, New London, CT 06320 (tel. 860/443-8411), a rambling old refurbished resort hotel. The ground-floor public rooms filled with Eastlake and other Victoriana are elegant with their 15-foot-high ceilings. Swagged curtains cover the windows, and the cocktail lounge with a fireplace even has a chintz ceiling. The dining room looks out onto the Sound.

The house was built in 1902 as a summer residence for the Guthries of Pittsburgh. The 27 rooms in the main building all have a bath. Some are huge, especially those with bay windows. Each room has been decorated with different chintz wallpaper and cream swag drapes. One room retains Mr. Guthrie's built-in shirt-and-sock closet complete with stepladder. The third-floor rooms, with sloping ceilings, are particularly appealing. There are 24 more accommodations, in the carriage house and other buildings on the estate. Some have canopied beds.

On Saturday there's dining and dancing to a four-piece orchestra. The dining room offers typical continental/American cuisine—lobster thermidor, bouillabaisse, poached salmon, beef Wellington, and rack of lamb dijonnaise—priced from $16 to $29.

Rates: $150–$265 double in the main house, $110–$150 double in the carriage house (highest price is for the waterfront suite with a whirlpool bath).

The **Queen Anne Inn,** 265 Williams St., New London, CT 06320 (tel. 860/447-2600), is a downtown bed-and-breakfast set in an intricately decorated Victorian with a witch's cap tower and an ornate frieze on its peaked gable. Two parlors, both with fireplace, are comfortably furnished for guests' use, and in summer the rockers on the porch are favorite lounging places.

The 10 air-conditioned rooms (8 with bath) are variously and quite beautifully furnished. The Captain's Room has a working oak fireplace and a brass bed among its comforts. There's also a lovely bridal suite featuring a private balcony and fireplace and furnished with a brass canopied bed and deep-blue swag drapes.

Rates (including breakfast and afternoon tea): $80–$160 double.

At the waterfront, there's also a Radisson.

NORWICH

From Groton and New London, the River Thames flows northward to Norwich, about a 30-minute drive away.

Norwich Attractions

The outstanding discovery in Norwich, besides the handsome Victorian homes (for me at least), was the **Slater Memorial Museum,** Norwich Free Academy, 108 Crescent St. (tel. 860/887-2506). Stephen Earle's romanesque building is a magnificent treasure in itself; the main galleries, filled with plaster casts of famous Greek and Renaissance sculptures, are amazing for their beauty, their number, and their rarity, for they'd be impossible to secure today; and the other collections are also very fine. There are wonderful temple carvings in the Oriental collection; exquisite ceramics, baskets, beadwork, and masks among the Indian artifacts; some choice American primitives and some entrancing watercolors by George Henry Clements (1854–1935) in the art collections. And these are just the highlights.

Hours: June–Aug, Tues–Sun 1–4pm; Sept–May, Mon–Fri 9am–4pm, Sat–Sun 1–4pm. **Closed:** Holidays. **Admission:** $2 adults, $1 seniors and students, free for children 11 and under.

Representative of the time when Norwich was the 12th-largest city in the colonies, the **Leffingwell House,** 348 Washington St. (tel. 860/889-9440), is a fine example of a 1675 Colonial that opened as a public house in 1701 and served as an important stage stop between Boston and New London. The rooms are full of interest, and the commentary is always lively.

Hours: Summer, Tues–Sun 1–4pm; winter, Sat–Sun by appointment only. Admission: $3 adults, $1 children.

While you're in Norwich, take a drive around the village and explore the **Norwichtown Historic District,** an area around the Green where over 50 pre-1800 homes are concentrated, one of them the home of a signer of the Declaration of Independence, Samuel Huntington. Visit also **Yantic Falls,** off Sachem Street, off Rte. 2, known locally as Indian Leap because of the legend that during the last great battle between the Narragansetts and Mohegans in 1643, one band of Narragansetts were forced to plunge into the falls and were killed. The **Indian Burial Grounds** on Sachem Street is the resting place of Uncas, Mohegan chief who gave the land for settlement.

Another highlight is the 350-acre **Mohegan Park,** Mohegan Avenue, off Rtes. 2 and 32, which offers swimming and picnicking, a zoo (tel. 860/887-0062), and a beautiful rose garden where 2,500 bushes bloom from May to November. The best time to visit is late June.

Downtown Norwich also possesses many historic buildings of architectural interest. Pick up a walking tour map at the Norwich Tourism Office, 69 Main St. (tel. 860/886-4683), and explore.

A Nearby Native American Museum

A visit to the **Tantaquidgeon Indian Museum,** Rte. 32, Uncasville (tel. 860/848-9145), is a unique experience. It's a very personal collection begun in 1931 by the late John Tantaquidgeon and his son, Harold, direct descendants of Uncas, chief of the Mohegan Nation. It's housed in a stone building behind the home of Harold and Gladys Tantaquidgeon.

The 86-year-old Gladys will relate the history of the local Native Americans; the artifacts also tell their own story. Photographs capture all the Mohegan descendants of Occum, who were born in 1723 in a wigwam. He attended school locally and traveled to England soliciting funds, greatly impressing the earl of Dartmouth, whose donations helped found Dartmouth College. Among the artifacts are roach or crest-type headdresses of deer hair, food bowls made only of sugar maple or applewood, Ralph Sturges sculptures, a birchbark Penobscot canoe, corncob dolls, snowshoes, warclubs fashioned from roots, birch buckets, exquisitely crafted straw baskets (including Makawisaug, tiny baskets that were used to put out a little cornbread or meat for the Little People in the forest), stone axes (including one whose blade took seven hours to fashion), and wampum beads made from clam and conch shells. There are also models showing the Green Corn Festival (last celebrated here in 1938), when brush arbors are built and thanks given for the corn harvest, and depicting village scenes in which inhabitants are spearfishing, deer hunting, gathering corn, and tanning skins.

Another room, devoted to Plains and West Coast Indians, is filled with Navajo, Seminole, Hopi, and Tlingit artifacts, including a dramatic wolf Kachina doll and a majestic Cree headdress.

Hours: May–Oct, Tues–Sun 10am–3pm. **Admission:** Donation requested.

Norwich Lodging

The **Norwich Inn,** Rte. 32, Norwich, CT 06360 (tel. 860/886-2401, or 800/892-5692), is a particularly appealing landmark that has been restored to its former elegance, with a dash of tropical and plantation-style largesse. Built in 1929, the inn originally drew such celebrities as George Bernard Shaw, Charles Laughton, and Frank Sinatra before it fell into decay. Now the place exudes elegance and romance, especially at night, when a faint breeze stirs the potted palms and ferns and floodlights around the central courtyard pool cast dancing shadows on the walls of the gallery that leads into the dining room. The 75 guest rooms are all designed in warm shades of cinnamon, sand, and Nantucket blue and have such added touches as ruffled curtains, pretty linens, botanical prints, dried-flower wreaths, quaint step stools for the four-poster beds, and ceiling fans. Chintz-covered armchairs and sofas, country-print wall-papers, pine armoires, and brass fittings and old tubs in the baths create a comfortable country air. They also contain TVs, pushbutton phones, and Gilchrist & Soames soaps and toiletries.

In summer you can sip a frosty mint julep in the peach-colored sun room, or on a snowy evening you can relax by the fire in the Prince of Wales bar. For dining you have a choice of the outdoor deck overlooking the Norwich golf course or the elegant Prince of Wales dining room that offers fine cuisine along with great spa cuisine. Although the menu changes daily, you may find swordfish marinated in citrus and soy, filet of beef in five-spice hoisin marinade, or roast chicken basted with natural juices. Prices range from $18 to $26. On the spa menu (which lists calories in each dish and is monitored for percentages of fat, protein, and carbohydrates) you may enjoy a tasty vegetable pot pie or a pork loin with pear-peppercorn sauce that's terrific and only 360 calories. The spa desserts concentrate on fruit flavors in contrast to the regular menu, which features bread pudding with vanilla sauce or bourbon-pecan torte. There's a good brunch served too.

The spa is designed around a central indoor pool and features glass-enclosed exercise rooms, soundproof treatment rooms for massage, hydrotherapy, loofah scrubs, and deep-cleansing facials. The treatment is carefully designed to each individual's needs and goals for a revitalization of both mind and body. Among the spa facilities are rowing machines, NordicTrack machines, fitness bicycles, weight-training equipment, a mini-trampoline, and free weights, along with fitness classes that range from aerobics to yoga, stress management, and weight training. Body treatments—massage, cellulite massage, herbal wrap, and hydrotherapy—and beauty treatments are also offered. In addition, golf and tennis are available. The inn has recently been purchased by the tribe that operates Foxwoods. So expect some major changes.

Rates: May–Oct, $160–$255 double weekends, $140–$235 double weekdays; winter, $145–$240 double weekends, $125–$220 double weekdays. Standard spa package (room, three meals per day, full spa treatments), from $335 per person per night based on double occupancy. **Dining Hours:** Mon–Thurs 7–10am, noon–2pm, and 6–9pm; Fri 7–10am, noon–2pm, and 6–10:30pm; Sat 7–10:30am, noon–3pm, and 6–10:30pm; Sun 7–10:30am and noon–3pm.

Less expensive accommodations can be found at the **Ramada Norwich**, One Sheraton Plaza, Norwich, CT 06360 (tel. 860/889-5201), which offers such extras as an indoor pool.
Rates: $65–$95 double Mon–Fri, $100–160 double Sat–Sun.

The **Norwich Motel,** 181 W. Town St., Norwich, CT 06360 (tel. 860/ 889-2671), offers above-average motel accommodations with a nice outdoor pool.

Rates: $60–$64 double.

Norwich Dining

Besides the Norwich Inn, Norwich possesses an interesting historic place for luncheon or dinner: **Chelsea Landing,** Water Street (tel. 860/889-9932), located in a building that has been standing since 1761 and was variously a distillery, a hotel, and a grocery store. It's a cozy and simple place, with gingham cloths on the tables. The seafood is invariably good and is supplemented by a menu featuring Yankee pot roast, sandwiches, and omelets, all at incredibly low prices—$5.25 tops at lunch, $9 to $17 at dinner.

Hours: Mon–Thurs 11am–2pm and 5–10pm, Fri 11am–2pm and 5–11pm, Sat 5–11pm, Sun 5–10pm.

The Mystic Area
Special & Recreational Activities

Antiquing: Several stores are worth visiting in Stonington; also one or two in downtown Mystic.

Beaches: Ocean Beach, Ocean Ave., New London (tel. 860/447-3031), offers a sandy beach complete with boardwalk, concessions, and an amusement park that features a fun triple water slide and an outdoor pool. This is New London's most crowded playground.

Most people head east toward the beach at Watch Hill, R.I., if they prefer quiet and dignity, or to Misquamicut, the honkytonk of Rhode Island beaches that appeals to the younger crowd.

Harkness State Park and Bluff Point State Park both possess quieter ways to enjoy the shoreline.

Bicycling: Mystic Cycle Center, 42 Williams Ave., Rte. 1 (tel. 860/ 572-7433), rents 10-speeds, mountain bikes, and tandems. Rates start at $15 per day.

Boating: Shaffer's Boat Livery, Mason's Island Road, Mystic (tel. 860/ 536-8713), has cruising boats for rent. In Noank, Coastline Atlantic (tel. 860/536-2689) rents sailboats; Wild Bill's Tackle Shop (tel. 860/536-6648) rents fishing craft. Spicer's Marina in Groton (tel. 860/445-9729) rents small fishing boats with 9-hp engines for $60 a day.

Fishing: *Groton:* The largest party-fishing boat, the *HelCat II,* sails from the HelCat dock, 181 Thames St. (tel. 860/535-2066 or 445-5991), charging about $28 per person per day for regular fishing trips. *Mystic:* Shaffer's Boat Livery, Mason's Island Road (tel. 860/536-8713), rents 16-foot skiffs with 6-hp engines for

$60 per day. *New London:* The party boat *Captain Bob II* sails from New London's City Dock (tel. 860/442-1777). *Waterford:* Try Captain John's Sport Fishing Center, 15 First St. (tel. 860/ 443-7259), which charges $25. *Noank:* Mijoy, 12 River St. (tel. 860/443-0663), sails year round from the Noank Shipyard in Noank or Marster's Dock in New London; prices start at $25.

　　Several lakes in North Stonington also offer good fishing: try Billings Lake (north from Rte. 2 on Cossaduck Road) or Wyassup Lake (off Rte. 2 about 4 miles north of North Stonington).

Fruit Picking: *East Lyme:* The Yankee Farmer, 441 Old Post Rd. (tel. 860/739-5209), for apples, blueberries, raspberries, strawberries, and tomatoes. *Norwich:* Malerba Brothers, 634 New London Turnpike (tel. 860/887-2913), for strawberries.

Gaming: See "Foxwoods Casino and Ledyard Lodging," above.

Golf: *Groton:* Shennecossett Municipal, Plant Street (tel. 860/445-0262); Trumble Golf Course, High Rock Road (tel. 860/445-7991). *Norwich:* Norwich Municipal, 685 New London Turnpike (tel. 860/ 889-6973). *Stonington:* Pequot Golf Club, Wheeler Road (tel. 860/ 535-1898); Elmridge-Pawcatuck Golf Club (tel. 860/599-2248).

Hiking: Ideal spots for walking are the Connecticut Arboretum, Williams Street, New London (tel. 860/447-1911); Bluff Point State Park, in Groton; and also the coastline from Watch Hill out to Napatree Point.

Picnicking: For shore picnicking, my first choice would be Harkness State Park, where you can spread your feast out and dine looking across the Sound before going down to explore the beach (no swimming). Take Rte. 1 out of New London to Rte. 213. There's an adjacent special facility for the disabled with wooden ramps that run out onto and along the beach. Rocky Neck State Park is similar. Fort Griswold makes an ideal spot overlooking the Thames River and Fisher's Island. Or you might head for Bluff Point and Coastal Reserve, Groton, a 100-acre nature reserve. In Norwich, Mohegan Park is the place.

State Parks: *Groton:* Bluff Point Coastal Reserve, Depot Road, for great hiking, fishing, and picnicking; Haley Farms State Park, Rte. 215, Brook Street, has nature trails, hiking, and biking paths. *Waterford:* Harkness Memorial State Park, Rte. 213 (tel. 860/ 443-5725), has picnicking and fishing, plus a shoreline for walking (no bathing).

Swimming: See "Beaches," above.

Tennis: *East Lyme:* Lyme Racquet Club, 22 Colton St. (tel. 860/ 739-6281), charges $30 per hour plus a $5 guest fee. *Mystic:* For local high school courts, call the Mystic Visitor Information Bureau (tel. 860/536-1641). The Inn at Mystic also has a court.

MASSACHUSETTS

The Central Berkshires & the Pioneer Valley

Distance in Miles: Egremont, 120; Great Barrington, 125; Springfield, 153; Pittsfield, 168; Williamstown, 176; Deerfield, 178

Estimated Driving Time: Egremont, 2½ hours; Deerfield and Williamstown, 3½ hours

◄◦►─◄◦►─◄◦►─◄◦►─◄◦►

Driving: For the southern Berkshires (Great Barrington, Lenox, Lee, the Egremonts), take the Taconic Parkway to Rte. 23 (Hillsdale exit) to Great Barrington and then Rte. 7 north for Stockbridge, Lenox, and Lee. Pick up Rte. 20 to Pittsfield and then Rte. 2 for Williamstown. For Williamstown, you can also take the New York State Thruway (I-87) to Albany, picking up I-787 to Troy to Rte. 2 east.

For Deerfield, take I-95 north to I-91 north to Exit 24. Historic Deerfield is just off Rtes. 5 and 10.

Bus: Greyhound/Trailways (tel. 800/231-2222) travels to Lenox, Lee, and Pittsfield. The stop closest to Deerfield is Greenfield, from which Deerfield is a 5-mile taxi ride. Bonanza (tel. 800/556-3815) goes to Great Barrington, Stockbridge, Lee, Lenox, Pittsfield, and Williamstown. Peter Pan Bus Lines (tel. 800/343-9999) services Amherst, Northampton, Holyoke, and Springfield.

Train: Amtrak (tel. 800/872-7245) stops at Springfield.

Further Information: For more about the area's events and festivals and about Massachusetts in general, call or write the **Massachusetts Office of Travel & Tourism,** 100 Cambridge St., Boston, MA 02202 (tel. 617/727-3201, or 800/447-6277).

For specific information about the area, contact the **Berkshire Visitors Bureau,** Berkshire Common Plaza Level, Dept. MA, Pittsfield, MA 01201 (tel. 413/443-9186); the **Stockbridge Chamber of Commerce,** P.O. Box 224, Stockbridge, MA 01262 (tel. 413/298-5200); the **Lenox Chamber of Commerce,** P.O. Box 646, Lenox, MA 01240 (tel. 413/637-3646); or the **Southern Berkshire Chamber of Commerce,** 362 Main St., Great Barrington, MA 01230 (tel. 413/528-1510).

Events & Festivals to Plan Your Trip Around

Summer Festivals: End of June to Labor Day—Jacob's Pillow Dance Festival (tel. 413/243-0745); Williamstown Theatre Festival (tel. 413/458-8145); Berkshire Theatre Festival (tel. 413/298-5576 after June 1); Tanglewood (tel. 413/637-1666), or contact the Boston Symphony Orchestra, Symphony Hall, Boston, MA 02115 (tel. 617/266-1492).

June: American Craft Enterprises Craft Fair, West Springfield (formerly held in Rhinebeck, N.Y.).

July: Aston Magna Festival, Great Barrington (tel. 413/528-3595)—featuring 17th- and 18th-century works performed on original instruments at various locations on weekends.

August–September: South Mountain Chamber Concerts, South Mountain, P.O. Box 23, Pittsfield, MA 01201 (tel. 413/442-2106).

September: Josh Billings Race combines a 26-mile cycle trip from Great Barrington to the Stockbridge Bowl, two laps by canoe around the lake, and a 6-mile run to Tanglewood (usually mid-September). That same weekend the town returns to an earlier tradition with the Lenox Tub Parade, when horse-drawn carriages ("tubs") decorated with the harvest of the season parade through the streets, the way the "cottagers" used to do saying their good-byes before they headed back to the city.

The Big E, a 12-day fair held at the Eastern States Exposition Grounds, West Springfield (usually the weekend after Labor Day). Call 413/737-2443.

October: Harvest festival at the Berkshire Botanical Garden, Stockbridge (tel. 413/298-3926).

December: The Annual Holiday House Tour gives visitors the opportunity to view historic properties (private homes, churches, inns, and so on) that aren't necessarily open to the public.

For Deerfield area information, contact the **Pioneer Valley Convention & Visitors Bureau,** 56 Dwight St., Springfield, MA 01103 (tel. 413/787-1548); or the **Mohawk Trail Association,** P.O. Box 7, Dept. MA, North Adams, MA 01347 (tel. 413/664-6256).

For specific information about these towns, contact the **Amherst Area Chamber of Commerce,** 11 Spring St., Amherst, MA 01002-2392 (tel. 413/253-0700); or the **Greater Northampton Chamber of Commerce,** 62 State St., Northampton, MA 01060 (tel. 413/584-1900).

Suggested Driving Routes

You'll probably want to visit several times during summer, once to attend one or more of the cultural events, again to visit all the attractions clustered around Stockbridge or farther north in Hancock and Williamstown, and still again to experience the mountains and lakes by hiking, fishing, or canoeing. Therefore I haven't arranged this chapter around a single typical weekend, but rather have tried to outline all the possibilities that each town and area offers. It's up to you to choose. To guide you a little, though, here are a few suggested drives through the Berkshires that'll help you in planning your explorations.

The Central Berkshires

From Pittsfield, drive along Rte. 20 (about 5 miles) to Hancock Shaker Village, and from there go down to Tanglewood, via Rte. 41, and West Stockbridge. On Rte. 183, directly across from the Tanglewood entrance, a country road leads to the Pleasant Valley Wildlife Sanctuary. From here head east and pick up Rte. 7 into Lenox, before heading south again on Rte. 7 to the Mount, Edith Wharton's mansion. Return to Rte. 20 and take it south to Lee, en route to the Jacob's Pillow Dance Festival set off the road. Take Rte. 20 to Rte. 8, which leads you, via Washington and Hinsdale, into Dalton for a tour of the Crane Museum (weekdays only), then wind up at Arrowhead just south of Pittsfield.

From Pittsfield, go northeast along Rte. 8 to Adams, birthplace of Susan B. Anthony. Pick up Rte. 116 to Savoy going through town. Just outside, take a right on River Road, which leads you to Windsor

It would require many weekends to "do" the Berkshires, because the events and attractions are so many and so varied. First, of course, there are the outstanding cultural events—Tanglewood, the Williamstown Theatre Festival, South Mountain chamber-music concerts, Jacob's Pillow Dance Festival—that bring people flocking to this scenic area of lakes and wooded hills. There's the history that yields all kinds of attractions, some of a literary or artistic kind (like the homes of Herman Melville, Edith Wharton, Nathaniel Hawthorne, William Cullen Bryant, Daniel Chester French, and Norman Rockwell), and others of a more worldly kind (like the sumptuous mansions lining the streets and dotting the countryside around Lenox and Stockbridge, namely Blantyre, Bellefontaine, Wheatleigh, and Naumkeag). And last but far from least is the landscape—Mounts Greylock,

Jambs in the Windsor State Forest and eventually into Cummington, where a detour along Rte. 9 brings you to William Cullen Bryant's birthplace. Backtrack along Rte. 9 past Notchview into Dalton and finally Pittsfield.

The Southern Berkshires

Starting from Great Barrington, proceed east along Rte. 23 through Monterey before turning north to Tyringham, past sculptor Sir Henry Hudson Kitson's fantasy gingerbread house. From there loop round along Rte. 102, through South Lee into Stockbridge, to explore all of that village's highlights.

Starting in Sheffield, take Rte. 7 north to Great Barrington, stopping at Searles Castle and dropping into the Albert Schweitzer Center, if it interests you. From here, get onto Rte. 23 to South Egremont. En route you can turn off at the junction of Rte. 41 to explore Mount Everett and BashBish Falls. Then double back to South Egremont and take Rte. 41 south to Sheffield, turning right off Rte. 7 at the Bushnell-Sage Library in Ashley Falls, from which you can reach Bartholomew's Cobble and the Ashley House.

The Northern Berkshires

Drive from Williamstown along the Mohawk Trail all the way to Whitcomb Summit, where you can choose to continue along the trail to Shelburne Falls, turn back, or turn into the Savoy Mountain State Forest, visiting Tannery Falls and following a new loop back into North Adams for the return to Williamstown.

Devote a good part or a whole day to exploring Mount Greylock's slopes from Lanesborough.

Everett, and Monument—and the forests that surround them, granting all kinds of opportunities for hiking, skiing, blueberrying, birdwatching, picnicking, and just plain basking in the beauty of it all. In short, this is a rich area to mine for weekends or longer stays.

The first settlers of the Berkshires were the Mahkeenac Indians, who, driven by the Iroquois from the Hudson Valley, found the lush streams, lakes, and wooded hills around Stockbridge and Great Barrington abundant hunting and fishing grounds. As the pioneers traveled west from the Massachusetts Bay Colony, they moved into the area as well, establishing thriving farming and trading communities—the first at Sheffield in 1733 and the second at Stockbridge in 1735. Some settlers attempted to convert the Native Americans to Christianity, as did the Rev. John Sergeant, whose Mission House can be seen today in Stockbridge. During the Revolutionary War, Berkshire County supported the patriots' cause, and indeed, as early as 1774 the townsfolk of Great Barrington showed their resistance by refusing to allow royal judges to sit in court. The Revolution's domestic turmoil was also experienced here when Daniel Shay led his famous farmers' rebellion against the Articles of Confederation in 1787, an event recalled by a marker on Rte. 23 in South Egremont, where he supposedly surrendered to Col. John Ashley of Sheffield. Soon after the Revolution the Shakers arrived. This community of pacifist celibates who dedicated their lives to hard work established their City of Peace in 1790 at Hancock, and it's a fascinating place to visit today.

Less simple folk soon followed, turning the area into a playground for the wealthy. First to arrive was Boston financier Samuel Gray Ward, who persuaded his friends, the Higginsons, to join him. Such figures as Nathaniel Hawthorne, Herman Melville, Oliver Wendell Holmes, Henry Wadsworth Longfellow, and James Russell Lowell came soon after, but these early comers were people of modest means compared to those that followed. Largely attracted by the stories about the Berkshires written by these authors, the wealthy built ever-more-ostentatious mansions and mock palaces in their efforts to imitate European aristocracy. These people represented the great fortunes that had been made from steel, milling, railroads, and other industries in the 19th century, and they looked for places to vacation and display their money. Those who enjoyed the ocean summered at such resorts as Newport, Cape May, and Bar Harbor, while those who preferred the mountains discovered the Berkshires and Saratoga Springs. Edith Wharton, tired of Newport and marriage, built her $40,000 mansion here in 1901 and used to drive the dusty roads in her large automobile, with her frequent visitor, Henry James, often at her side. Harley Procter of Procter & Gamble also built a cottage in Lenox, and industrialists like George Westinghouse, the Vanderbilts, and Andrew Carnegie established great estates in the area. From about 1880 to 1900 the Berkshires experienced their heyday; thereafter, their popularity declined with the advent, among other things, of the automobile and later of the airplane, both of which afforded increased mobility to all. The mansions stood empty and useless, and most were sold off and converted into schools, camps, and guesthouses. Bellefontaine, for example, which had been copied from the Petit Trianon at Versailles and reputedly cost $1 million to build in 1899, sold for a mere $70,000 in 1946.

Despite the wealthy influx, the Berkshires always retained its image as a creative artistic colony. Nathaniel Hawthorne wrote his *Tanglewood Tales* looking out over Lake Mahkeenac (the Stockbridge Bowl). In 1850 he met Herman Melville at a Monument Mountain picnic, and they visited each other often. Melville even dedicated *Moby-Dick* to Hawthorne. William Cullen Bryant, editor of the *New York Post*; Oliver Wendell Holmes; Henry Wadsworth Longfellow; and James Russell Lowell are just a few of the writers associated with the Berkshires. Artist Daniel Chester French built his Chesterwood in 1898, and much later Norman Rockwell, chronicler of America's small-town life, came to the Berkshires. The artistic tradition of the area was further entrenched with the establishment of major cultural events like the Berkshire Music Festival, founded in 1936 when Serge Koussevitsky conducted the first concert at Tanglewood; the Jacobs Pillow Dance Festival, established by Ted Shawn five years later; and the Berkshire Theatre Festival, which had already been stirring audiences for many years and helped establish the careers of legendary figures like James Cagney, Ethel Barrymore, and Katharine Hepburn.

These summer events still draw enormous crowds, but no matter what time of year you choose to visit the Berkshires, they will always delight. In winter they present the idyllic winter captured in Norman Rockwell's famous seasonal illustration of Stockbridge. There's skiing at Catamount, Jiminy Peak, Brodie, Berkshire East, and Butternut; cross-country skiing everywhere; skating on the lakes; and sledding. Then to help you recover from your outside exertions you'll find hot toddies and blazing fires waiting for you in quaint old-fashioned inns. Whether you come to ski or nod by the fireside in winter, to wander amid the mountain laurel in spring, to view the fantastic palette of the trees in fall, or to spread out your blanket and picnic under the stars at Tanglewood to the sounds of Beethoven or Mozart, you'll experience a deep thrill and contentment that'll leave you wanting to return time and time again.

THE BERKSHIRES

◄◊►

LENOX

Lenox Attractions

Today, you can stay in many of the **old mansions** that were once the summer retreats for such industrial magnates as Harley Procter, George Westinghouse, and Andrew Carnegie, who were drawn to the Berkshires' unspoiled beauty, particularly to the tidy farms and streets of Lenox.

Besides these wonderful mansions, the main attraction is, of course, the Berkshire Music Festival of Tanglewood, just outside Lenox; it overlooks the lovely Stockbridge Bowl, which inspired Nathaniel Hawthorne to write his *Tanglewood Tales*. Although the festival may have lost some of its original musical seriousness and serenity, it still attracts dedicated listeners to its shaded lawns and large music shed and is a very pleasant way to spend some of your time in the Berkshires. (For details, see "Cultural Events in the Berkshires," below.)

A walk around the village past the rambling old clapboard houses is always a pleasure. On your way, at the corner of Walker and Main streets you'll pass the old **Curtis Hotel,** a noted 19th-century stage stop that welcomed such illustrious guests as Chester Arthur, Franklin Roosevelt, Dwight Eisenhower, Jenny Lind, and Serge Koussevitzky. Today it has been remodeled into a home for the retired.

From here walk to the top of the hill on Main Street to see the **"Church on the Hill,"** a fine New England Congregational church erected in 1805.

At the junction of Rtes. 7 and 7A, you can tour **The Mount** (tel. 413/637-1899), an impressive mansion with a dramatic widow's walk, an octagonal tower, and a balustraded terrace with Greek urns. Here Edith Wharton lived while she wrote her novel *Ethan Frome* (1911), which is set in the Berkshire countryside.

Tours: May–Oct, Mon at 2 and 3pm, Tues–Sun 9am–2pm. Later, Shakespeare takes over the grounds.

For a change of pace, the **Pleasant Valley Wildlife Sanctuary,** West Mountain Road (tel. 413/637-0320), maintained by the Audubon Society, offers miles of nature trails. It's just off Rte. 7 north of Lenox.

Admission: $3 adults, $2 children 3–16.

Lenox Lodging & Dining

Although there are plenty of wonderful accommodations within a 30-minute drive of Tanglewood, which I'll describe later, Lenox is the closest place to stay and the village is full of notable hostelries. You'll have to book well in advance, pay ahead, and probably stay a minimum of two or three nights.

The true connoisseur stays house-party–style at **Blantyre,** 16 Blantyre Rd., Lenox, MA 01240 (tel. 413/637-3556 after May 1, 413/298-3806 off-season); it was built in 1902 for Robert Paterson, the president of W. J. Sloane, the director of a Manhattan bank, and a friend of Carnegie. Modeled after his wife's Scottish ancestral home and costing $135,000 ($300,000 with furnishings), it was the most expensive and lavish villa in the Berkshires (The Mount cost only $40,000).

In its heyday, when the summer set walked to and from one another's houses attended by maids with lanterns, Blantyre was the scene of tea parties, games, charades, and formal balls and dinners. Thereafter it experienced a checkered but nevertheless fascinating history. In 1925 it, along with 250 acres, was sold to a Howard Cole for a mere $25,000; it served briefly as a country club before being bought by filmmaker D. W. Griffith, who dreamed of turning it into an East Coast studio but died before he could do so. Various owners tried to make something of it until finally Senator and Mrs. Fitzpatrick, the inspiration behind the Red Lion in Stockbridge, bought it and created this luxurious accommodation.

So magnificent, and veritably museum quality, are the furnishings that the proprietors have had to close the house to uninvited visitors because

The Berkshires

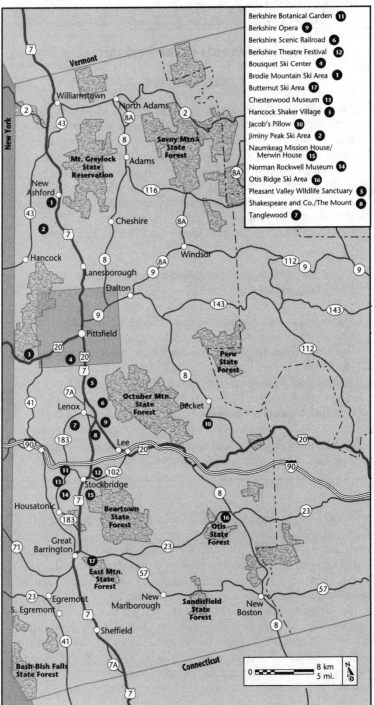

Berkshire Botanical Garden **11**
Berkshire Opera **9**
Berkshire Scenic Railroad **6**
Berkshire Theatre Festival **12**
Bousquet Ski Center **4**
Brodie Mountain Ski Area **1**
Butternut Ski Area **17**
Chesterwood Museum **13**
Hancock Shaker Village **3**
Jacob's Pillow **10**
Jiminy Peak Ski Area **2**
Naumkeag Mission House/
Merwin House **15**
Norman Rockwell Museum **14**
Otis Ridge Ski Area **16**
Pleasant Valley Wildlife Sanctuary **5**
Shakespeare and Co./The Mount **8**
Tanglewood **7**

1792

Cultural Events in the Berkshires

Dance

Jacob's Pillow, P.O. Box 287J, Lee, MA 01238 (tel. 413/243-0745), is the superb 10-week dance festival founded by Ted Shawn when modern American dance, especially by males, was considered rather out of the ordinary. Over the years it has featured such greats as the Paul Taylor Dance Company, Cynthia Gregory, the Mark Morris Dance Group, and the Trisha Brown Company. There are picnic grounds and bar and café facilities. Tickets cost $10 to $35. The festival runs from the end of June to Labor Day. Jacob's Pillow is located off Rte. 20 on George Carter Road in Becket, east of Lee.

Music

Spread your blanket and your picnic on the lawn at the 210-acre site of **Tanglewood,** West Street (Rte. 183), Lenox, MA 01240 (tel. 413/637-1600), overlooking the lovely Stockbridge Bowl. Fuchsias and begonias make the scene even lovelier in summer, when the festival runs for nine weeks from early July to late August. Get there two hours before the performance if you want space near the Music Shed. Performances are on Friday at 7 and 9pm and Saturday at 8:30pm, with matinees on Sunday. For information before June 15, call Symphony Hall in Boston (tel. 617/266-1492).

    South Mountain Concerts, P.O. Box 23, Pittsfield, MA 01202 (tel. 413/442-2106), features such chamber music greats as the Beaux Arts Trio and the Tokyo and Guarneri string quartets. Schedules vary, but concerts are usually held on Sunday afternoons from late

too many were coming to gawk at the splendor. In the main hall, lit by shimmering chandeliers, Elizabethan and Jacobean pieces and Oriental vases are arrayed before the ornately carved fireplace. The similarly furnished music room features a priceless Coromandel screen and a grand piano. There are 4 guest rooms and 4 suites in the main house and 14 beautifully appointed rooms in the carriage house, by the open-air pool.

    The suites are spectacular. The Cranwell has a dramatic four-poster bed and various furnishings, all beautiful genuine antiques—ormolu mirrors, inlaid tables, porcelain lamps, and couches and chairs covered with fine fabrics. The ceilings are at least 14 feet high, with elegant moldings. A pink marble fireplace, gilt-framed portraits, a pencil-poster bed with a dusky-rose eider, a silver brush set on a mahogany desk, and

August to mid-October, approximately every two weeks. Tickets run $18 to $20. Performances are given in a concert hall built in 1918 by the concert's founder, Elizabeth Sprague Coolidge.

Theater
The **Williamstown Theatre Festival** undoubtedly represents the cream of the theatrical crop in the Berkshires. For information, call 413/597-3400 or write P.O. Box 517, Williamstown, MA 01267.

The **MacHaydn Theater,** Rte. 203, Chatham, NY 12037 (tel. 518/392-9292), is where some of the best authentic summer stock can be found—refreshing, enthusiastic productions of *My Fair Lady, Sweet Charity, Oklahoma!,* and the like.

The **Berkshire Theatre Festival,** Main Street, Stockbridge, MA 01262 (tel. 413/298-5536, or 413/298-5576 after June 1 for the box office), offers a four-play season from late June to late August in a Stanford White–designed building constructed in 1886 as a casino. Such figures as Katharine Hepburn and James Cagney started their careers here.

Bring a picnic to enjoy before the outdoor performance at the dramatic mansion setting of **Shakespeare & Company,** The Mount, Plunkett Street (off Rte. 7), Lenox, MA 01240 (tel. 413/637-1197, or 413/637-3353 after June 17 for the box office). The season runs from July to late August.

The **Music Theater Group,** at the Lenox Art Center, off Rte. 183 (P.O. Box 544), Stockbridge, MA (tel. 413/298-9463), performs avant-garde musical theater works during July and August, Wednesday to Sunday.

even a bathroom with crystal light fixtures and a marble sink are just a few of the highlights of the Laurel Suite. All baths contain shampoo, conditioner, lotions, bath salts, and Crabtree & Evelyn soaps.

Because of the limited number of rooms you may well not be able to secure a room unless you reserve at least one year ahead. Please don't harass the staff—this is simply a fact that's beyond their control.

In the paneled dining room, hung with rich tapestries, guests sit at a long Tudor refectory table bearing a lace cloth and impressive table settings of crystal and fine china. At $65 per person, the three-course dinner is probably the best bargain in Lenox for distinguished cuisine. Among the five entrees you might find seared yellowfin tuna with shiitake mushrooms and lemon-ginger emulsion or medallions of veal on sweetcorn pancakes, wild blueberries, spring onions, and maple-vinegar jus. For breakfast the conservatory makes a beautifully bright setting. Other facilities include the aforementioned pool and four tennis courts.

Rates: Main house, $275 double without fireplace, $400 double with fireplace; from $425 suite. Carriage house, $250–$320 double. Two-day minimum stay required weekends and July–Aug and Oct.

Canyon Ranch, 165 Kemble St., Lenox, MA 01240 (tel. 413/637-4100), is the outpost of the famous Tucson establishment of the same name. It's the place to go to restore your health and well-being, learn ways to relieve stress, change old unhealthy habits, and lead a more healthful life. The setting will certainly help to restore some lost vitality, for it occupies a marble-and-brick mansion, Bellefontaine, surrounded by 120 acres of woodland. It consists of the Mansion, the Spa, and the 120-room inn, connected by covered glass walkways. The Mansion houses an elegant dining room; medical and behavioral consultation areas; and a beautiful library featuring an ornately carved marble fireplace, Palladian windows, a carved ceiling, and filled floor-to-ceiling bookcases. The Spa offers every conceivable form of exercise and body therapy—like exercise rooms, indoor and outdoor tennis, racquetball and squash, indoor and outdoor pools, suspended indoor running track. There are 30 fitness classes each day. Treatments include mud and salt, herbal and aroma wraps, a variety of massages and facials, and other salon services. On hand is a professional staff to assist you in developing a healthful diet and regimen with the help of techniques ranging from biofeedback to hypnotherapy. In the dining room the menu lists nutritional information; besides eating healthfully here, guests can learn how to continue the habit outside.

Rates: $440 per person per night; summer, three-night weekend packages (including a series of health services packages) start at $1,470.

Overlooking a lake, **Wheatleigh,** Hawthorne Road (P.O. Box 824), Lenox, MA 01240 (tel. 413/637-0610), the magnificent former home of the Countess de Heredia, has 22 acres of lawn and gardens. Modeled after a 16th-century Italian palazzo, it was built on the site of the tavern of Gideon Smith, a Tory who was hanged for his folly. The gravel driveway ends in a circular courtyard with a central marble fountain standing in front of the canopy of wrought iron and glass. The most striking features of the great entry hall are the huge white marble fireplace, sculpted with cupids and flowers, and the grand staircase, also of marble.

Upstairs are 11 spacious rooms and 4 smaller accommodations, each possessing its own flavor and mood. They all have extremely high ceilings, a marble fireplace, air-conditioning, a phone, and a large old-fashioned bath. Some have a canopied bed, while the furnishings are a combination of English and French antiques. The rooms in the rear have lovely views of the lake. The house also has a unique accommodation in the former aviary—a duplex where Leonard Bernstein always stayed when he was conducting at Tanglewood.

The restaurant at Wheatleigh is also a gem, with swag curtains, Chippendale chairs, fine table settings, and unique Dalton wall plaques. The $72 prix-fixe menu is supplemented by low-fat and vegetarian menus and a *menu dégustation*. On the first, you'll find two main dishes, like sautéed halibut with fresh saltwater shrimp and loin of lamb with garlic flan and rosemary-infused jus. Breakfast offers an interesting array of egg dishes, including poached eggs with mornay sauce served on an English muffin.

On the 22-acre grounds landscaped by Frederick Law Olmsted are a serene rock garden, a pool surrounded by fragrant pines and conifers, and a tennis court. In winter the grounds are good for cross-country skiing.

Rates: $155–$350 double. **Dining Hours:** Mon 8–10:30am, Tues–Sun 8–10:30am and 6–9pm.

The beautiful residence now known as the **Gateways Inn,** 71 Walker St., Lenox, MA 01240 (tel. 413/637-2532), was once the mansion of Harley Procter (of Procter & Gamble). Wrought-iron gates mark the entrance to the drive that leads to the classical white-columned portico; a balustrade runs along the top of the front facade. Inside, a sweeping staircase leads to nine large elegant accommodations, three with fireplaces, all furnished differently with large Victorian pieces, most often of mahogany. All rooms have a bath (many featuring an old-fashioned pedestal sink), a phone, and air-conditioning.

The Gateways is known for its excellent cuisine, served in elegant surroundings. On the seasonal menu you might find such entrees as a delicately flavored rack of lamb provençal, penne alla arrabbiata (one of a dozen pastas), veal marsala, or salmon continentale (topped with shrimp and lobster and finished with a dill-champagne sauce). The restaurant is especially noted for its desserts: apfelstrudel, luscious Black Forest torte, and strawberries Gateways (fresh strawberries with kirschwasser, whipped cream, and Melba sauce, blended into a super treat).

Note: If you stay at the Gateways, you can use the pool, bicycles, and tennis court at the Haus Andreas, nearby in Lee, under the same management.

Rates (including continental breakfast): Mid-June to Oct, $180–$205 double Thurs–Sun, $115–$150 double Mon–Wed. Nov to mid-June, $135–$160 double Thurs–Sun, $95–$115 double Mon–Wed. **Dining Hours:** Summer, daily 5–9pm; winter, Mon–Sat 5–9pm.

Idyllically situated across from the west entrance to Tanglewood, the **Apple Tree Inn,** 334 West St. (P.O. Box 699), Lenox, MA 01240 (tel. 413/637-1477), stands on 22 acres in the midst of a fragrant apple orchard, bordering the 750-acre Pleasant Valley bird sanctuary. The rooms in the 110-year-old house, with dormers and a classical portico, offer spectacular views over the Stockbridge Bowl and daisy-dappled fields to the hills beyond. Eleven rooms and two suites are in the main house. Room 4 has eyelet lace pillowcases on the bed, attractive Schumacher flower-and-bird wallpaper, ruffled curtains, and an inviting windowseat, along with an armchair and a braided rug. Room 2, the Blue Room, affords a large pineapple bed with a step stool, two armchairs, a small ormolu mirror placed over a chest, and lace-curtained French doors leading to a private terrace with a magnificent view. Room 1 is decorated in forest green, its brass bed sporting an apple-green/pink eider and frilly linens; the floors have a rag rug, and pine furnishings and two chairs and a table are planted firmly in the bay. Room 3 is where Leontyne Price used to stay in a pretty country room of celery and pink hues; a brass bed, marble-topped side tables, a fireplace, and a dresser complete the decor. Rooms 5 and 6 have skylights, while the suite (no. 8) has books and records as well as a fireplace, a TV, and other amenities. The third-floor rooms come in odd, interesting shapes. A newer guest lodge has 20 motel-style rooms that are still pleasant, clean, and tasteful, and some people prefer them because they're closer to the pool. All rooms are air-conditioned and have a bath.

The pool is spectacularly located. An arbor walk under climbing roses and clematis leads to it, and it's surrounded by flagstones and borders of roses, poppies, tulips, stocks, and other flowers. From here you have a marvelous view over the valley to distant hills. There's also a clay tennis court for tennis enthusiasts, plus cross-country ski trails and miles of hiking.

For guests' comfort there's a parlor decorated with plush couches and armchairs, small chess and backgammon tables, and a piano where you might be lucky enough to find one of the featured Tanglewood artists "rehearsing."

There are two dining rooms. The former billiard room (known as the Tavern), with a large brick fireplace and oak beams and paneling, serves late-night snacks in summer and full meals in winter. The circular Gazebo is lighter in ambience, furnished in dusky rose with white bentwood chairs. The tented ceiling is strung with tiny lights. In summer you can dine to the symphonic melodies wafted here on the breezes from Tanglewood. There's also a deck for outdoor dining brightened by colored umbrellas and by some of the 350 rose varieties the innkeeper has cultivated. The food is continental/American: medallions of veal with a roasted-garlic sauce, broiled salmon with lemon butter, and filet mignon béarnaise. Several pasta dishes are available, like fettuccine with smoked scallops, shiitake mushrooms, and scallions. Desserts include profiteroles, pie of the day, and seasonal fruits. Brunch varies. Dinner prices range from $15 to $25. You can retire here after the concert for a late-night dessert and coffee.

Rates: End of June to Labor Day and weekends Oct 1–24, main house, $150 double without bath, $180–$270 double with bath; $325–$425 suite. Guest lodge, $150–$160 double. Rates drop about 20% in spring and fall and about 30% in winter, with $50–$65 for guest-lodge rooms. Weekday rates are lower too. **Closed:** Jan 2 to late Apr. **Dining Hours:** Thurs–Sat 5:30–9pm, Sun 10:30am–2pm (brunch) and 5:30–9pm.

The **Birchwood Inn,** 7 Hubbard St., Lenox, MA 01240 (tel. 413/ 637-2600), is tastefully decorated and impeccably run. Set halfway up the hill, across from the "Church on the Hill," it was built in the late 1700s for the Dana family. Later it became a veterans' home before being converted into a stunning inn. The 12 guest rooms (all with phone, 6 with bath) are individually and distinctively decorated, with antique reproductions and beautiful wallpapers; 4 have four-poster canopied beds. Downstairs, the sunken living room is especially charming, with inviting windowseats, gilt mirrors, and bookcases filled with interesting volumes; a smaller den makes a cozy stopping place for late-night conversation before retiring. One-bedroom efficiency apartments are located in the carriage house.

Rates (including continental breakfast): July–Aug, $100–$210 double. Oct, $70–$160 double. Winter, $80–$145 double.

Across from the Birchwood Inn, **Whistler's Inn,** 5 Greenwood St., Lenox, MA 01240 (tel. 413/637-0975), is named after the second owner of the house, Whistler's nephew. There's a charming air about this 1820 French/ English Tudor mansion with its mansard roof and lattice windows, approached via a lovely lych gate. The ground-floor music room has a grand piano and a marvelous library complete with comfortable wing chairs and a marble fireplace to read beside; the formal dining room has a large table and Chippendale chairs seating eight. Upstairs are 11 rooms (all with bath, most with air conditioning). Six have dormer windows and sloping ceilings, and painted chests among the furnishings: There are two doubles with brass beds and three with cannonball or pineapple bedsteads. The two master bedrooms, with fireplaces and couches, are particularly welcoming. On sunny days you can take a light breakfast of muffins and coffee or tea on the back veranda overlooking the 7 acres of grounds.

Rates (including breakfast): June 16–Oct, $100–$210 double weekends, $90–$190 double weekdays. Nov–June 15, $90–$170 double weekends, $80–$150 double weekdays.

Garden Gables, 141 Main St. (P.O. Box 52), Lenox, MA 01240 (tel. 413/ 637-0193), is a delightful accommodation surrounded by 5 acres of beautiful gardens. The original house was built in 1780 but extensions were added in 1909. The Canadian owners are extremely relaxed and friendly. The 14 rooms are all different and comfortably furnished in an unpretentious manner, with chintz or floral wallpapers and assorted furnishings. You might discover a maple bed, a maple dresser combined with a brass bed, or (as in Room 15, which has a brick fireplace) a Shaker pencil four-poster and wing chairs. Room 15 also has a 72-foot-long bath and a small porch. Room 9 is a favorite with a rose quilt and solid carved four-poster; it has a deck furnished with wicker and a Jacuzzi tub and separate shower. There are two tastefully decorated large sitting rooms for guests. One features a copper-hooded fireplace and is furnished with a Steinway grand, comfortable slipcovered chairs and couches, plenty of books, and some fine art on the walls. Fresh flowers are found through-out—a romantic touch. Fine crystal, candles, and Sheraton-style chairs set the scene in the dining room, where a full buffet breakfast is served: croissants, muffins, bagels, fruit, yogurt, cereal, and a hot dish like smoked salmon quiche.

Rates (including breakfast): Summer weekends, $130–$220 double. The rest of the year, rates slightly less.

Peggy and Richard Houdek, who migrated from California, where he was an arts administrator and music critic and she was the managing editor of *Performing Arts* magazine, naturally sought a culturally rich area in which to relocate as innkeepers. They found an 1804 landmark building, **Walker House,** 64 Walker St., Lenox, MA 01240 (tel. 413/637-1271), minutes from Tanglewood. Being music lovers, they've decorated each of their eight spacious rooms (all with bath, five with fireplaces) in honor of a particular composer. In the somber-colored ground-floor Beethoven room, which has a fireplace, are portraits and a bust of the genius. Upstairs there's a lighter, sunnier Chopin room; a brilliant-blue Tchaikovsky room; a summery green-and-white Verdi room; rooms named after Handel, Puccini, and Mozart; and an intimate room honoring Debussy. Downstairs is a large comfortable parlor with a grand piano, a cozy hearth, plenty of fine reading material, and some atrociously healthy plants. Similarly healthy-looking specimens share the long wide veranda with comfortable wicker furniture. Breakfast conversation flows easily at the tables, and fast friendships are made, solemn promises delivered, and cards and addresses exchanged over a repast of fresh juice or baked fruit, Peggy's home-baked muffins, cereal, hard-boiled eggs, and plenty of piping-hot freshly ground coffee.

Of course, the special delight of a stay here is the sound of glorious classical music that usually fills the house throughout the day. On cold winter nights the 7-foot projection TV on which films, operas, and sports are shown is much appreciated. There are also 2 acres of wooded grounds for guests to explore. This is a no-smoking inn.

Rates: July–Aug, $110–$190 double weekends, $90–$110 double week-days. Most of June and Sept, $90–$110 double weekends, $70–$100 weekdays. Oct, $110–$150 double weekends, $90–$130 double weekdays. Nov to mid-June, $90–$110 double weekends, $70–$90 double weekdays.

Seven Hills, Country Inn and Resort, 40 Plunkett St., Lenox, MA 01240 (tel. 413/637-0060), is a lavish, gracious resort that has much to recommend it. The public rooms are extravagantly furnished; the 27 acres include two tennis courts, a large pool, and well-kept landscaped gardens. The personnel are selected from the major music schools—Juilliard, Mannes, Manhattan, and Peabody—and when they're not waiting tables they perform. The nightclub is most elegant, with a softly lit mauve-pink tented ceiling and low plush sofas, and on weekends it features Broadway and jazz artists like Natalie Lamb and Ed Linderman; Monday to Wednesday local artists perform.

The whole place is built on a grand scale. The so-called living room is more like a baronial hall, with floor-to-ceiling gilt mirrors, intricately carved and needlepointed Charles II chairs, and a central double fireplace of carved wood on one side and wedding-cake stucco on the other, ornamented with cherubs and gryphons. Other features include another grand piano, handsome large carved sideboards, and dragon-decorated chairs. Windowseats look out over the wide flagstone terrace set with umbrellaed tables and marble benches; its balustrade supports a series of sculpted marble lions. Gravel paths lead between carved pillars and vine arbors down to the pool. The gardens are filled with peonies, shrubs, and trees.

In the Music Room every Wednesday and Sunday the wait staff performs, and though the management doesn't like to publicize particular names, many famous artists have performed here. Folk and square dancing is also enjoyed once a week during summer.

The 55 varied guest rooms are located in the main building or motel-style units. A carved paneled staircase decorated with two compelling landscapes leads to what, to me, are the nicest rooms. Room 1 has a fireplace, a large mahogany bed and chest, a Williamsburg cane eagle chair, a side chair, and a dresser, all set on a slate-blue carpet against similarly colored paper, ball fringe curtains, and eyelet lace linens. Room 3 has a fireplace and a small balcony. Room 7 boasts a fireplace, a high Victorian burled maple bed, and a marble-topped dresser coupled with bold floral-and-bird wallpaper.

A light supper menu is served in the Nightspot, where there's a $5 cover charge. Owner Jim Eder and his wife, Patricia, have opened a 100-seat restaurant and offer contemporary continental cuisine (like roasted salmon with roasted yellow-pepper coulis or chicken breast with a sauce of portobello mushrooms and port wine, priced from $20 to $27). The carved walnut Italian chairs, the Oriental-style Van Luit wallpaper, and the bronze-and-porcelain chandelier make an elegant setting. For additional entertainment there's a library with a TV and a small lounge with a grand piano and a wood fireplace.

Seven Hills is definitely an experience. It's a chance to taste the opulent way of life that used to exist in the Berkshires but with a refreshing lack of excessive pretense.

Rates: Summer–fall, $104–$250 double. Off-season, $84–$150 double. MAP offered.

The **Cliffwood Inn,** 25 Cliffwood St., Lenox, MA 01240 (tel. 413/637-3330), occupies a large mansion set back from the road only two blocks from the center of Lenox. It's now filled with the antiques and antique reproductions collected by owners Joy and Scottie Farrelly, who are also dealers in Eldred Wheeler's colonial reproductions. Floor-to-ceiling gilded mirrors and a handsome marble fireplace add to the living room's grand atmosphere. French doors lead to a wide back porch where begonias hang and rockers overlook the pool and gazebo. The oval dining room features a magnificent 400-year-old sideboard and is lit by a Venetian chandelier. Here a continental breakfast of fresh fruit, muffins, and breads is served.

An impressive semicircular drive leads to the oval portico supported by classical Ionic columns. The detailing of this building—carved shell and urn moldings above the windows, some of which are oval—is quite fine and certainly worthy to be the summer home of the U.S. ambassador to France, for whom it was built in 1889. In the entry hall, 18th-century marble French tables support majolica and other exquisite porcelain. To the right is a favorite little corner anchored by a fireplace with windowseats.

There are seven guest rooms (all with bath and air conditioning, six with fireplaces), each named after a Farrelly ancestor. The Jacob Gross, Jr., room has a four-poster canopied bed, easy chairs in front of the fireplace, and a balcony. The owners also offer some distinct advantages to guests— a computerized up-to-date calendar of cultural events, access to Tanglewood just down the street by a less heavily trafficked entrance, and a knowledge of French, Spanish, and Italian.

Rates (including breakfast): July–Aug and foliage season, $110–$210 double. Nov to mid-May, $80–$145 double.

The **Village Inn,** 16 Church St. (P.O. Box 1810), Lenox, MA 01240 (tel. 413/637-0020), is the one place where you can stop for a formal English Devonshire cream tea, complete with tiny crustless sandwiches, homemade scones and preserves, and a pot of fine tea of your choice. It's served in the dining room daily from 3 to 4:30pm. At this friendly, comfortable place, run by Clifford Rudisill and Ray Wilson, the public areas are, in my opinion, more charming than the rooms. The reception desk, which doubles as a bar, faces the small parlor where comfortable armchairs near the hearth are ideal for chatting over a glass of sherry or for settling down to a good read. Across the hall is a larger parlor with a grand piano and plenty of comfortable antique furnishings, plus there's a separate TV room.

The 32 rooms (all with bath and phone) are eclectically furnished in a homey, old-fashioned way; some have canopied beds. The Dining Room has an excellent reputation for value. Menu selections might include pork tenderloin with pears, Calvados, and cider; grilled venison with lingonberry sauce; or scampi sautéed in garlic, shallots, white wine, tomatoes, and marsala, garnished with golden raisins and pine nuts, priced from $16 to $22. There's also a downstairs tavern for after-concert snacks.

Rates: Nov–June, $65–$160 double. July–Oct, $80–$210 double. Year round (except July–Oct) there's a 30% discount Mon–Wed. Two-night minimum on weekends. **Dining Hours:** Tues–Sat 5:30–9pm; breakfast and tea served daily in summer, weekends only in other seasons.

At the **Candlelight Inn,** 35 Walker St., Lenox, MA 01240 (tel. 413/637-1555), handsome breakfronts, copper kitchenware, chintz curtains, and a beamed ceiling contribute to the French Provincial air of these candlelit dining rooms, warmed by a fire in winter. Ample portions of modern continental/American fare are served—cold poached salmon with chive rémoulade, grilled shrimp with tomato salsa and cayenne pepper, grilled quail with roasted garlic sauce, and beef tenderloin with green-peppercorn sauce—all priced from $14 to $21. Upstairs, eight guest rooms (all with bath) are available.

Rates: $75–$165 double, depending on season. July–Aug, three-night minimum required on weekends. **Dining Hours:** Summer, Sun–Thurs noon–3pm and 6–9pm, Fri–Sat noon–3pm and 5:30–9pm; winter, Mon–Thurs 6–9pm, Fri 5:30–9pm, Sat noon–3pm and 5:30–9pm, Sun noon–3pm and 6–9pm.

The **Brook Farm Inn,** 15 Hawthorne St., Lenox, MA 01240 (tel. 413/637-3013), just down the hill from Lenox center, occupies a century-old house. What makes this place special is the keen pleasure innkeepers Anne and Joe Miller take in literature and music. One wall of the living room is devoted to books, many of them poetry, and the strains of all kinds of music—Mozart, light opera, or Broadway musicals—waft through the house. A poem of the day begins each morning and Joe reads poetry during Saturday-afternoon tea. There are 12 rooms (all with bath, 6 with fireplaces). Room 2 features a canopied bed, wing chairs, and the romance of a fireplace and small balcony. The coziest if not the grandest rooms are tucked under the eaves. One is decked out in deep purple and mauve lit by a skylight. Furnishings might include a brass bed, a Hitchcock rocker, a cottage dresser, and similar country pieces. Outback, guests can relax in the hammock or enjoy the in-ground pool. A full breakfast is served buffet style and on Sunday morning breakfast is accompanied by a quartet from the Tanglewood Institute.

Rates (including breakfast): Summer and winter weekends, $115–$180 double. Weekdays and spring and fall, lower rates.

If you prefer modern accommodations with all the razzmatazz of TVs, phones, bars, and lounges, there are plenty around, like the **Berkshire Quality Inn,** 390 Pittsfield/Lenox Rd. (Rte. 7), Lenox, MA 01240 (tel. 413/637-4244), which has an outdoor pool and tennis courts; or the **Susse Chalet,** Rtes. 7 and 20, Lenox, MA 01240 (tel. 413/637-3560), which also has a pool.

Rates: $65–$70 double.

The **Yankee Motor Lodge,** Rtes. 7 and 20, Lenox, MA 01240 (tel. 413/499-3700), has made some gesture toward achieving a New England atmosphere by installing fireplaces in some of its 60 rooms. There's also a pool here.

Rates: Summer weekends, $140–$180 double. Winter weekends, $70–$110 double.

Tanglewood operates an **accommodations hotline** providing rooms in local homes. Call the festival number: 413/637-1600.

Lenox Dining

Besides the outstanding restaurants at the establishments I've covered under "Lenox Lodging & Dining," above, there are several more fine dining options.

Lenox 218, 218 Main St., Rte. 7A (tel. 413/637-4218), is spanking modern. The upfront bar is boldly decorated with black and white tile and the bar has a purple scaffoldlike sculpture above. The two dining rooms are dramatically designed in black, featuring Milan-style chairs, walls accented with Japanese prints, and tables set with gray cloths and black napkins. The cuisine ranges from oven-roasted natural chicken to roast duck with raspberry-Chambord sauce and rack of lamb. There are also half a dozen pasta dishes, such as linguine with clam sauce and penne with marinara sauce topped with mozzarella, plus daily specials. Prices range from $13 to $22. For an appetizer I recommend the polenta with tomato-and-basil sauce. The shrimp cocktail is extra-tangy with its horse-radish-and-chili-sauce accompaniment. The desserts tend to be popular favorites like pies and shortcakes and hot-fudge sundaes. Light snacks are available in the bar.

Hours: Daily 11:30am–2:30pm and 5–10pm.

The Pillars Carriage House, Rte. 20, New Lebanon, NY (tel. 518/794-8007), has two dining rooms. One is modestly decorated with tables set with forest-green cloths and captain's chairs; the other is slightly more formal. There's also a bar area warmed in winter by a fire. The cuisine leans to traditional continental and Italian. All the staid classics are available—veal Oscar, chateaubriand, filet of sole Nantua, duck flambéed with cherries and Grand Marnier. Prices range from $15 to $23.

Hours: Tues–Sat 5–10pm, Sun 4–9pm. **Closed:** From Dec 31 for six weeks.

Antonio's Restaurant, 15 Franklin St. (tel. 413/637-9894), is a comfortable, casual California-style place that sports a miscellaneous collection of postcards, banknotes, business cards, and buttons covering one entire wall in the front. Here you can tuck into oversize portions of Italian specialties—paglia e fieno (with peas and proscuitto); linguine with clam sauce; steak pizzaiola; the house veal made with mushrooms, scallions, and tomatoes in a sour-mash bourbon sauce; or chicken bianco sautéed in white wine with garlic, pimentos, scallions, and capers in a brown sauce. Prices range from $12 to $20.

Hours: Mon–Sat 4–10pm (may close a bit earlier off-season).

The **Church Street Cafe,** 69 Church St. (tel. 413/637-2745), is a local favorite for soups, salads, burgers, and pasta dishes, all priced under $7 and served in a pleasant atmosphere of light wood and plants. The menu changes seasonally, but at dinner expect an eclectic array of dishes, from a vegetable platter to grilled pork tenderloin with caramelized onions and apples or chicken stew in red-wine and wild-mushroom sauce. Seafood and pasta dishes include cannelloni stuffed with herbed sausage and parmigiano reggiano or salmon with roasted shallots. Prices range from $14 to $17. Don't overlook the delicious appetizers—like the black-bean ravioli with spicy smoked chile-and-tomato broth or wild-mushroom tart with fresh thyme and white truffle oil.

Hours: Summer, daily 11:30am–2pm and 5:30–9pm; spring and fall, Mon 5:30–8:30pm, Tues–Thurs 11:30am–2pm and 5:30–8:30pm, Fri–Sat 11:30am–2pm and 5:30–9pm.

Across the street, **Cafe Lucia,** 90 Church St. (tel. 413/637-2640), is a fine dinner choice for a variety of Italian dishes. Start with the carpaccio or the roasted peppers and follow with any of the pasta dishes, like the linguine with clam sauce, or more substantial dishes, including an ossobuco, veal milanese, and always a fish of the day. Prices range from $12 to $23. In summer the patio under the awning is a pleasant spot from which to survey the Lenox town scene.

Hours: Summer, daily 5:30–9:30pm; winter, Tues–Sat 5:30–9pm.

Cheesecake Charlie's, 60 Main St. (tel. 413/637-3411), serves breakfast from 8 to 11am, but the prime attractions are the 13 flavors of cheesecake and the daily specials. If you order in advance you can choose from 50-plus flavors.

Picnic Suppliers

Obviously you'd expect to find many picnic suppliers in Lenox for all those bountiful Tanglewood spreads. Here are two:

Crosby's, 62 Church St. (tel. 413/637-3396), offers gourmet food to go. There are two picnics a week to choose from and a full range of deli and salad items.

Hours: Summer, Sun–Wed 10am–6pm, Thurs–Sat 10am–8pm; winter, Thurs–Sat 11am–5pm, Sun 11am–3pm.

Special desserts can be found at **Suchele Bakers,** 27 Housatonic St. (tel. 413/637-0939).

Hours: July–Aug, Mon–Sat 7am–6pm, Sun 7am–12:30pm; Sept–June, Tues–Sat 7am–6pm, Sun 7am–12:30pm.

LEE

Though Lee has lived largely in the shadow of Lenox and achieved a reputation for being lively and more modern, but careless of its beauty, recently the town has shown greater interest in preserving its past. You'll see this from the descriptions of the accommodations that follow. Still, the main attraction is the superb Jacob's Pillow Dance Festival just east of Lee in Becket.

Lee & South Lee Lodging & Dining

The **Haus Andreas,** 85 Stockbridge Rd. (R.R. 1, Box 605B), Lee, MA 01238 (tel. 413/243-3298), is a 200-year-old mansion with a pastoral view. Originally built by a Revolutionary War soldier, it was modernized by George Westinghouse, Jr., and was briefly, in 1942, the residence of Queen Wilhelmina of the Netherlands, her daughter, Princess Juliana, and her granddaughters, Beatrix (now the queen) and Irene. The public areas include a large comfortable living room, a good reading area with a fireplace, and a TV room. Although all the 10 rooms (4 with fireplace) are furnished differently, you might find an intricately carved mahogany bedstead or a marble-topped chest. It's a lovely, quiet place (no TVs or phones in the rooms) and has a pool, bicycles for guest use, and a tennis court.

Rates (including continental breakfast): Summer, $110–$190 double weekdays, $160–$260 double weekends. Winter, $70–$160 double weekdays, $110–$190 double weekends The lower prices are for rooms without bath. July–Aug, a minimum three-night stay is required.

At the **Federal House Inn,** Main Street (Rte. 102), South Lee, MA 01260 (tel. 413/243-1824), a classically proportioned restored home, the decor and antique furnishings in the public areas lead you to expect more of the 10 rooms upstairs. They're pleasant enough, to be sure, with a bath, air conditioning, chintz wallpapers, white candlewick spreads, and plank floors, but they're not as distinguished as one might've hoped. The dining rooms, however, have been a smash hit on the Tanglewood scene for years. Two elegant rooms, each with only about seven tables, are the setting for some classic continental cuisine—crabmeat cakes with corn-and-red-pepper relish, house smoked trout, and pheasant-and-sausage pâté served with fresh horseradish sauce, pear chutney, and Dijon mustard sauce. You can follow with such possibilities as pork medallions with wild mushrooms and duckling with a seasonal fruit sauce. Prices run $15 to $22.50.

Rates: $165 double weekends, $95–$165 double weekdays. **Dining Hours:** July–Aug, daily 5:30pm–closing; winter, Thurs–Sun 5:30pm–closing.

If you stay at the **Historic Merrell Inn,** Main Street (Rte. 102), South Lee, MA 01260 (tel. 413/243-1794), you'll be overnighting in a truly historic hostelry. Among its authentic features is the original 1817 circular birdcage bar (no longer in use). Now listed in the National Register of Historic Places, this brick Federal building (1794) with double balcony was bought in 1980 by Faith and Charles Reynolds, two ex-teachers who have carefully restored it according to architectural and historical records. It looks as much like a stagecoach stop as it ever did, from the small entry hall featuring a tall case clock, a Federal mirror, and candlesticks, to the old tavern room with a fireplace, pewter, and appropriate period furniture. The original iron latches have been retained throughout the house. The nine rooms upstairs (all with bath, air-conditioning, and phone) have been exquisitely decorated with colonial period furnishings, most with canopied beds. Guests have use of a TV rooom, but best of all is the gazebo down by the river for relaxing on a summer afternoon. *Note:* Swimming is available at Benedict Pond in Beartown Mountain State Park, only a 10-minute drive away.

Rates (including full breakfast): Mid-June to Oct, $125–$165 double weekends, $90–$120 double weekdays. Nov to mid-June, $90–$140 double weekends, $80–$120 double weekdays.

The **Chambery Inn,** 199 Main St., Lee, MA 01238 (tel. 800/537-4321), is an unusual accommodation because it occupies a former school. The people who converted it had the wit to retain the chalkboards, which provide a wonderful outlet for a variety of commentary. As you can imagine, the six guest rooms (all with a TV, phone, and whirlpool bath) are extra-large and have very high ceilings. Each is a suite possessing a sitting area with a fireplace and a king-size canopied or queen-size bed. The furnishings are comfortable, the floors are covered with thick pile carpets, and the windows are draped with lace. You might find an elegant peer mirror in your room. Chippendale-style tables and desks and sofas complete the picture. The largest room, Le Lycée, has five huge windows looking out onto the street; the bed is covered in a Ralph Lauren Indian design coverlet, and there's a glass table with a capital as its base among the furnishings. L'Aubusson is decorated as you'd expect, with tapestries, and contains a handsome rolltop desk. There's also a well-equipped room for the disabled.

Rates: Summer–fall, $205 double. The rest of the year, $155 double.

The **Morgan House Inn,** 33 Main St., Lee, MA 01238 (tel. 413/243-0181), is not a well-seasoned rural New England inn for the well-heeled traveler; it's a historic coaching inn on the the main street of Lee. Built in 1817 as a private residence, it was converted into a stagecoach inn in 1853 and received such renowned visitors as Ulysses S. Grant and George Bernard Shaw, whose carefully preserved signatures can be seen on the wall by the reception desk. The 13 guest rooms are furnished in a country style. The inn's tavern bar is frequented by a mix of locals and travelers, and its low-ceilinged tavern dining room is unpretentious and warm and comfortable, with polished wood tables and paneling. It offers traditional dishes like Yankee cranberry pot roast and roast duck with cinnamon-spiced orange sauce as well as shrimps, scallops, and lobster with herbs and chardonnay sauce. For an appetizer, try the goat cheese bundles with sun-dried tomatoes and basil. Prices range from $15 to $20. It's also a convenient, popular spot for lunch, when the prices and quality are hard to beat for such dishes as chicken and mushrooms in a popover and pasta primavera, plus salads and sandwiches priced from $5 to $11. The paintings gracing the walls are works of owner Lenora Bowen.

Rates: July–Oct, $75–$100 double weekdays, $95–$155 double weekends. Nov–June, $55–$70 double weekdays, $65–$90 double weekends.
Dining Hours: Mon–Thurs 11:30am–2:30pm and 5–9pm, Fri–Sat 11:30am–2:30pm and 5–9:30pm, Sun noon–9pm (brunch 10:30am–2:30pm).

The Best Western **Black Swan Inn,** on Laurel Lake, Rte. 20W, Lee, MA 01238 (tel. 413/243-2700), is a modern accommodation with a fine situation on the lake. All 52 rooms have a bath, air-conditioning, a pushbutton phone, a TV, a chest, two armchairs, and a table, plus celery-and-rose quilts on the beds; lakeside rooms have decks, and some rooms also have Jacuzzi tubs and gas-operated fireplaces. A pool abuts the lake for sunning. An exercise room, a steamroom, a sauna, a games room, and boats complete the facilities. There's also a lounge with a central fireplace and a chintz country dining room offering continental cuisine.
Rates: Summer, $90–$205 double. Fall, $85–$160 double. Winter, $70–$110 double.

The **Oak n' Spruce,** 190 Meadow St., South Lee, MA 01260 (tel. 413/243-3500), is a comfortable unpretentious resort where the 150 rooms are modern and the public areas homey. One- and two-bedroom condo units have fully equipped kitchens; some have Jacuzzi tubs as well. The facilities include tennis courts, horseback riding, indoor and outdoor pools, a nine-hole par-3 golf course across the road, easy downhill skiing, and a fitness center. There's a lounge and a restaurant too.
Rates: $90–$140 double; around $200 condo. Special packages and seasonal discounts available.

Lee Dining
Celebrity seekers should know about **Joe's Diner** in Lee (tel. 413/243-9756), one of the few places that stays open late and serves good solid food that's well appreciated by the performers at the local theater and musical centers. You can fortify yourself with a full pork dinner for a mere $5.50.
Hours: Mon–Fri till midnight, Sat till 6pm.

Sullivan Station, Railroad Street, Lee (tel. 413/243-2082), housed in a converted railway station, is a good Saturday lunch spot and is convenient at the beginning or end of the scenic ride that leaves from here. The menu features pastas and such main courses as veal with spinach and Swiss cheese, rack of lamb, and baked Boston scrod for $11 to $15. There's also a light menu available.
Hours: May 2–Oct, daily 11:30am–9:30pm (Sun brunch 11am–3pm); Nov–May 1, Wed–Sun 11:30am–9:30pm (Sun brunch 11am–3pm).

A Nearby Becket Bed-and-Breakfast
Canterbury Farm, Fred Snow Road, Becket, MA 01223 (tel. 413/623-8765), is really secluded, on a dirt road off Rte. 8 about 1½ miles

south of Becket. It's popular with ski tourists. The three upstairs rooms share a bath and are decorated in plain country style with colorful quilts, braided rugs, and country dressers on wide-board floors. One ground-floor room has a full bath and shower. Canterbury Farm is a genuine old 1780 farmhouse with sloping door frames and a lived-in look, run by a young couple with two young boys. A breakfast of eggs and muffins is served. There are 11 miles of ski trails to traverse; skis are available for rent and lessons are given.

Rates (including breakfast): $65–$110 double.

STOCKBRIDGE

Stockbridge Attractions

The name most often associated with Stockbridge is that of Norman Rockwell. His pictures and magazine covers captured the essence of life in an earlier, more innocent America. Born in New York City in 1894, Rockwell moved to Stockbridge in 1953, and he remained here, working in his studio over Nejaime's Market, until he died in 1978. He's buried in Stockbridge cemetery. In his life he painted 4,000 pictures, many of them covers for the *Saturday Evening Post* and *McCall's*, and at the **Norman Rockwell Museum,** Rte. 183 (tel. 413/298-4100), you can see a good many of them. You can see his first *Saturday Evening Post* cover (it appeared in 1916) of the schoolboy pushing a baby carriage, or, one of my favorites, a family seen heading off for a day trip or vacation, children hanging out the window in their excitement, grandma sitting under her hat like a solemn stooge, and the same family returning, children down-cast and grandma still stolid, stern, and unmoved. Rockwell's studio is open also from May to October.

Hours: May–Oct, daily 10am–5pm; Nov–Apr, Mon–Fri 11am–4pm, Sat–Sun 10am–5pm. **Closed:** Major winter holidays. **Admission:** $8 adults, $2 children 6–18.

On Main Street at Sergeant Street, stop in at the **Mission House** (tel. 413/298-3239), built in 1739 as the home of the Rev. John Sergeant, first missionary to the Stockbridge Indians. The house has a fine collection of furnishings, and the garden is interesting, displaying plants only from that period.

Hours: Memorial Day–Columbus Day, Tues–Sat 10am–4:30pm, Sun and holidays 11am–3:30pm. **Admission:** $3 adults, $1 children 15 and under.

Across the street from the Red Lion (below), **St. Paul's Episcopal Church** has some famous associations—Charles McKim (of the renowned firm McKim, Mead and White) was the architect, the baptistery was created by Augustus Saint Gaudens, one of the nave windows is by Louis Comfort Tiffany, and the chancel window is by LaFarge.

Farther along Main Street you'll come to the **Children's Chimes,** erected on the site of the original mission church by David Dudley Field, as a memorial to his grandchildren. The chimes are played every evening at sunset from "apple blossom time until frost."

The modest cottage where Hawthorne wrote *Tanglewood Tales* can be seen on Hawthorne Street near Tanglewood. Of the view (still unchanged) across the Stockbridge Bowl, he wrote: "I cannot write in the presence of that view."

The marvelous house on Prospect Hill, **Naumkeag** (tel. 413/298-3239), was designed by Stanford White in 1886 for Joseph H. Choate, President McKinley's ambassador to the Court of St. James's. The 26 sumptuous rooms and formal gardens with fountains and Chinese pagodas give a good insight into the opulent lifestyle of the time.

Hours: Memorial Day–Columbus Day, Tues–Sun 10am–5pm. **Admission:** House and garden, $6.50; garden only, $5; $2.50 children 6–12.

A must in Stockbridge is a visit to the **Berkshire Botanical Garden,** Rtes. 102 and 183 (tel. 413/298-3926), a glorious place in any season. From spring to early fall the spectacular 15 acres of flowering shrubs display primrose, delphiniums, clematis, roses of all hues, brilliant azaleas, rhododendrons, a variety of annuals and perennials, and (in spring) apple blossom and dogwood. In the herb garden, every fragrant plant is labeled. The gift shop has some interesting items.

Hours: May–Oct, daily 10am–5pm. **Admission:** $5 adults, $4 seniors, free for children 11 and under.

Daniel Chester French referred to his summer home, **Chesterwood,** off Rte. 183 (tel. 413/298-3579), as heaven, and certainly the view of Monument Mountain, from both the house and his radiant 23-foot-high studio, does warrant such a description. The skylit studio, where he worked from 1898 to 1931, is most remarkable for the floor-to-ceiling double doors through which he rolled his sculptures on a small railroad trestle out into the daylight to examine them. One can also imagine his taking a break to entertain guests in the adjoining reception area furnished with a fireplace, a library, and a piano: The studio contains sketches, plaster casts, and bronze models of his sculptures, including the seated Lincoln and the Minuteman statue at Concord North Bridge. From the house and studio, you can wander through the gardens. In the barn are sketches and working models of many of his other famous works—*Brooklyn* and *Manhattan,* formerly at the entrance to the Manhattan Bridge, and *Alma Mater,* at Columbia University, for example.

Chesterwood is about 2 miles west of Stockbridge. Take Rte. 102 west to Rte. 183; turn left and drive for about a mile and follow the signs.

Hours: May–Oct, daily 10am–5pm. **Admission:** $6.50 adults, $3.50 children 13–18, $1.50 children 6–12.

Stockbridge Lodging & Dining

The Red Lion, Main Street, Stockbridge, MA 01262 (tel. 413/298-5545), a large country inn whose porch faces the main street, has become a symbol of hospitality in Stockbridge and the Berkshires. Many vacationers come expressly to visit it, flocking into the front parlor, where the fires blaze, and overflowing into the snug tavern or downstairs into the larger Victorian pub, the "Lion's Den," with nightly entertainment. The original structure, which served as a small tavern on the Albany–Hartford–Boston stage route in 1773, was destroyed by fire in 1896. A string of celebrities has bedded down here, among them Presidents McKinley, Teddy and Franklin Roosevelt, and Coolidge, as well as William Cullen Bryant and Henry Wadsworth Longfellow.

Today there are 109 air-conditioned, individually decorated rooms. In summer the courtyard, colorfully decorated with flowers, makes a lovely dining spot. A pool completes the facilities.

The Red Lion's dining room specializes in New England favorites—scrod, prime rib, and turkey—ranging from $15 to $25. Two remarkable features here are the friendly personnel and the quality of the food, which are sustained even when 1,200 people are served per day (200 at breakfast, 500 at lunch, and 500 at night). At a recent meal the swordfish was moist and served with delicious roasted potatoes and peas, garnished with lemon neatly covered with cheesecloth; my dining partner's prime rib was juicy and certainly prime. Celery, carrots, squash, and onion in vinegar dressing preceded dinner, along with hot rolls. The salads were fine as well.

Crystal chandeliers, large gilt mirrors, willow-pattern china, damask tablecloths, and a posy of fresh flowers on each table set the elegant tone. Teapots lining the lintel of the partition add interest. At the Red Lion you'll be living amid the charm of Staffordshire china, colonial pewter, and 18th-century furniture. Jacket and tie for men are required at dinner; no jeans are permitted.

Rates: Nov–May 22, $90 double with bath weekdays, $125 double with bath weekends. May 23–Oct, $140 double with bath weekdays, $165 double with bath weekends. Year round, $90 double without bath. July–Aug, a minimum two-night stay required on weekends. **Dining Hours:** Mon–Thurs 7–10am, noon–2:30pm, and 6–9pm; Fri 7–10am, noon–2:30pm, and 6–9:30pm; Sat 8–10am, noon–2:30pm, and 6–9:30pm; Sun 8–10am and noon–9pm.

A discreet wooden sign hangs in front of the **Inn at Stockbridge,** Rte. 7 (P.O. Box 2033), Stockbridge, MA 01262 (tel. 413/298-3337). Step onto the classical portico and into the plushly furnished parlor/hall graced with a grand piano and comfortable wing chairs set around the hearth. Although the eight guest rooms (all with bath, air conditioning, and phone) are not as lavishly decorated with antiques, they're all very prettily furnished with antique reproductions—two-posters, highboys, wing chairs, and more. The Chinese Room has Oriental accents in the wallpaper and accessories while the Rose Room sports cabbage-rose wallpaper and an antique English armoire. The Terrace Room has a private terrace and whirlpool tub under a skylight. At the back of the house, the garden's lilacs and other flowering shrubs provide a welcome retreat. So does the pool.

Hosts Alice and Len Schiller serve a full breakfast on fine china. Alice turns out some extraordinary fare—fresh fruit cup, cheese-and-ham soufflé, cinnamon coffee cake, and a very special brew. Sunday breakfasts are extra-special, consisting of a mimosa followed by eggs Benedict and banana bread.

Rates: July–Oct, $205–$245 double weekends, $185–$205 double weekdays. Nov–June, $170–$200 double weekends, $140–$160 double weekdays.

Set on a quiet backroad not far from Stockbridge, the **Williamsville Inn,** Rte. 41, West Stockbridge, MA 01266 (tel. 413/274-6118), boasts all the pleasures of an English country inn. It has the physical makings of a delightful accommodation, a small and cozy 1797 farmhouse with wide-plank floors, fireplaces throughout the public areas, comfortable wing chairs, and antiques. There are 16 guest rooms, 2 with fireplaces, some with four-posters, country furniture, and private baths. There's also a pool and a tennis court. The four dining rooms serve American cuisine—like venison, roast duck, filet of beef, and chicken. Entrees range from $16 to $22. For dessert, try the chocolate-mousse cake, Williamsville mocha, or the varied parfaits.

Rates: July–Oct, $150–$200 double. Nov–June, $140–$180 double. Three-night minimum required on summer weekends. **Dining Hours:** July–Sept, daily 5–10pm; Oct–June, Thurs–Sun 6–9pm.

The **Roeder House,** Rte. 183, Stockbridge, MA (tel. 413/298-4015), is a lovely Federal-Colonial–style house built in 1856, surrounded by 4 acres of well-tended gardens. Throughout the house owners Diane and Vernon Reuss have hung numerous Audubon prints. All six guest rooms have a bath and are furnished with antiques in fine taste and fetching colors. The Red Bird Room sports Lambeth wallpaper with a peafowl design and a luxurious silk fabric on the wingback chairs, and the bed is covered with a handmade log cabin quilt. Ben's Room contains a four-poster with a crocheted canopy. On the ground floor is a room boasting a hoop canopy with Laura Ashley linens, a Chinese rug, and wingbacks with iron floor lamps well placed for comfortable reading. A bell will summon you to a breakfast table set with crystal and fine English china and lit by candles. The fare may include blueberry coffeecake, fruit compote, a frittata, peach juice, and hazelnut coffee. Guests may use the well-designed and well-landscaped pool and enjoy the screened-in porch and trellissed gardens.

Rates: Summer weekends, $205–$215 double; spring and fall weekends, $185–$205 double. Winter rates slightly less.

Picnicking Supplies in Stockbridge

Choices include the **Main Street Market Cafe,** on Main Street (tel. 413/ 298-0220), which serves a great breakfast, a wide variety of lunch items— soups, salads, sandwiches, burgers, grilled vegetables, hummus, and tahina—and pretty much whatever you want to select in the market. The café is comfortable and cheery.

Hours: Daily 7:30am–7pm (later Thurs–Fri, when dinner is by reservation only).

WEST STOCKBRIDGE

Though West Stockbridge has been touted as the au courant place in the Berkshires, unless you like wandering around artificially old shops and boutiques, there's really little else here, except for two restaurants, one of which has a deeply moving story attached to it.

West Stockbridge Dining

Luy Nguyen and his wife, Trai Thi Duong, escaped from Vietnam and went first to Hartford, before being invited to West Stockbridge to open the **Truc Orient Express,** Harris Street (tel. 413/232-4204). Their photograph album, which is proudly displayed, tells the story of their family and their reunion with their young son, separated from them for six years until Sen. Ted Kennedy came to their assistance. Try the crab- and-asparagus soup, then choose among such main dishes as shrimp with straw mushroom, sweet-and-sour chicken, or a delicious Vietnamese-style Mongolian hotpot, all priced from $9 to $17. The atmosphere is extremely pleasant, with bamboo chairs and wicker-based glass-topped Parsons tables set on tile floors in light and airy space.

Hours: Sun–Thurs 11:30am–3pm and 5–9pm, Fri–Sat 11:30am–3pm and 5–10pm. **Closed:** Mon in winter.

La Bruschetta, West Stockbridge (tel. 413/232-7141), offers a fresh approach to the ingredients in its up-to-the-minute Italian cuisine. It's hard to choose among the appetizers, most of which lean to vegetarian tastes. The braised escarole is enhanced with white beans, mushrooms, tomatoes, garlic, and pecorino while the roasted peppers are ingeniously combined with salsa verde, anchovies, local chèvre, cerignola olives, and grilled garlic bread. These can be followed by one of three or so pastas (like spinach linguine with sautéed shrimp, clams, and crimini mushrooms with a spicy tomato-saffron sauce) or one of the secondi piatti (like roast lamb shank braised with tomatoes, white wine, onions, garlic, and black olives and served with Gorgonzola polenta and butternut squash or the grilled salmon with grilled mushrooms, sautéed spinach, and an Italian parsley sauce). Prices range from $14 to $17.

Hours: Thurs–Tues 6–9pm.

After Dark

At the **Shaker Mill Tavern,** on Albany Road (Rtes. 102 and 41) in West Stockbridge (tel. 413/232-4369), the many international beers offered attract a young crowd. A deck café is open in summer, and jazz, Latin, and comedy entertainment are offered Thursday to Sunday nights.

THE EGREMONT AREA

South Egremont is a lovely, quiet village worth stopping in to browse through the several antiques stores, the bookshops, and the old-fashioned general store. On Rte. 23, it's surrounded by some dramatic scenery and provides access to Mount Everett and BashBish Falls. Other great antiques hunting grounds are nearby in Ashley Falls and Sheffield along Rtes. 7 and 7A. If you continue west along Rte. 23 you'll come to Catamount, crossing the border into New York, where there are a couple of renowned restaurants.

South Egremont Lodging & Dining

The **Egremont Inn,** Old Sheffield Road (P.O. Box 418), South Egremont, MA 01258 (tel. 413/528-2111), is a charming place built in 1780 with a wraparound veranda. The tavern is especially alluring with its curved brick fireplace, low ceilings, and colonial-style furnishings. The dining room offers new American cuisine, and prices range from $13.50 for vegetable ragoût over capellini to $22.50 for grilled lamb chops garnished with herb butter. Other appealing dishes might be game hen with caramelized apples and sweet onion, salmon steak with tomato-caper salsa, and breast of duck with apricot chutney. The tavern menu offers burgers, pasta, and salads. Facilities include a pool and two tennis courts. None of the 23 guest rooms has a phone or TV. Live jazz or similar is presented in the tavern on Saturday.

Rates: Spring–summer, $105–$145 double weekends, $90–$120 double weekdays. Winter, $105–$145 double weekends, $90–$120 double weekdays. Special packages available. **Dining Hours:** Wed–Sun 5:30–9:30pm.

At the **Weathervane Inn,** Rte. 23 (P.O. Box 388), South Egremont, MA 01258 (tel. 413/528-9580), seasonal potted flowers bloom on the side porch of this attractive white clapboard house with black shutters, into which you'll be welcomed by the Murphy family. There are 10 rooms, all with private bath. Room 6 is tucked over the kitchen under the eaves, which gives it an interesting shape and feel. It's large enough to accommodate two brass beds, a marble-topped dresser adorned with a dried-flower arrangement, a maple side table, and a desk and armchair. The bathrooms contain lavender or other liquid soap. All rooms have electric blankets and air conditioning, and at night you'll find a miniature nightcap— amaretto perhaps.

Breakfast is served in a skylit room decorated with Hitchcock chairs and tables set with red-and-white tablecloths. It overlooks the back lawn. The meal is well cooked and you'll most likely tuck into Irish soda bread, fresh squeezed juice, eggs of your choice with home-fries, sausage or bacon, and toast.

The dining room is inviting, decked out in country style in Williamsburg blue, with tables set with white tablecloths, swag chintz curtains, and a hutch filled with decoys. The menu changes daily but there might be Cornish hen with kiwi sauce, duck with black cherries, or pork tenderloin with apple and Calvados and always a couple of fresh fish dishes. Among the appetizers, try the chicken-liver pâté or escargots in puff pastry.

Adjacent to the dining room is a sitting area with couch and chairs arranged in front of the large hearth. A small service bar is in the corner. There's also a lounge with TV, books, and games, eclectically furnished with simple country pieces. The outdoor pool has a good deck for sunning, or you can rock on the painted blue rockers that beckon on the porch.

Rates: $185–$195 double weekends (MAP), $105–$145 double weekdays (B&B). **Dining Hours:** July–Oct, Thurs–Mon 6–9pm; Nov–June, Fri–Sat 6–9pm, except on special holidays.

A large white clapboard house, where you can sit on the porch and look over toward the lush greens of the Egremont Country Club, the **Windflower Inn,** Rte. 23 (Egremont Star Rte., Box 25), Great Barrington, MA 01230 (tel. 413/528-2720), offers warm hospitality in antique-style surroundings. There are 13 rooms, all with a bath, some with fireplaces. The dining room serves a $30 prix fixe that might feature three or four entrees like veal marsala, duck with plum sauce, or salmon with sorrel sauce. There's an outdoor pool. Golf and tennis facilities are conveniently located across the road.

Rates: $180–$230 double (MAP). Three-night minimum required on summer weekends. **Dining Hours:** Daily 6–8:30pm (by reservation only).

South Egremont Area Dining

For breakfast and an experience that'll probably recall your childhood if you're over 25, head for the **Gaslight Store** (tel. 413/528-0870) in South Egremont. Here a few tables have been placed in the center of an old-fashioned general store that sells everything from aspirin to salami, newspapers to candy, complete with real wooden counters, scratched and burnished from use.

The Old Mill, Rte. 23, South Egremont (tel. 413/528-1421), is famed for its picturesque setting overlooking a small brook and has an excellent local reputation for consistently fine meals. The ambience is romantically country, the room lit by a Shaker-style chandelier and little copper table lanterns that make the white linens and wide-board floors glow. The walls are adorned with Early American tools—adzes and planes. The menu offers a diverse range of dishes: There'll likely be several pastas (like penne with sweet fennel sausage, broccoli rabe, and tomatoes) and seafood dishes that have some flair (like pan-seared salmon with cumin or cioppino with saffron aïoli and garlic croûtons). Recommendable are the roast duck with prunes, caramelized onions, and port sauce and the rack of lamb with garlic, herbs, and sherry-vinegar demiglace. To start I'd select either the oven-roasted clams with sweet peppers and bacon or the smoked trout with horseradish crème fraîche and cucumber-dill salad.

The daily specials might include onion soup with Swiss cheese and a tart with goat cheese and sun-dried tomatoes among the appetizers, and broiled swordfish with garlic-herb butter or prime rib as entrees. A tasty country pâté is served with celery rémoulade and garnished with lettuce and tomatoes. Portions are large (at least by my standards). A house salad contains lettuce, tomatoes, and mushrooms. Among the desserts, my favorites are the profiteroles, but you might prefer crème brûlée, apple-walnut tart, or peach Melba.

Hours: Sun–Thurs 5–9:30pm, Fri–Sat 5–10:30pm. **Closed:** Mar and Mon Nov–May.

Farther along Rte. 23 you'll come to **John Andrew's,** South Egremont (tel. 413/528-3469), a refreshing change from the traditional New England–style restaurants that abound in the Berkshires. White tablecloths, the original black chairs from New York's Copacabana, and track spot-lighting provide a comfortable art deco ambience. Among the appealing appetizers are grilled shrimp with black-bean cakes, sweetcorn, chipotle, and cilantro; whole roasted garlic with peasant bread, goat cheese, sun-dried tomatoes, and black olives; and grilled barbecued quail. The main courses are made with the freshest of ingredients and free-range poultry. You might find grilled yellowfin tuna with white-bean salad, candied lemon zest, and basil oil; roast pork loin with sage, juniper berries, and leeks; or grilled leg of lamb with cumin and chiles and a papaya salsa. Prices range from $14 to $19. Desserts change daily. Cocktails or meals can be taken on the pleasant deck out back.

Hours: Summer, daily 5:30pm–closing; winter, Mon and Thurs–Sat from 5:30pm, Sun 11:30am–2:30pm (brunch) and from 5:30pm.

North Egremont Lodging & Dining

Some locals recommended the dining room at the **Elm Court Inn,** Rte. 71, North Egremont, MA 01252 (tel. 413/528-0325), more highly than any other in the area. Choices might include grilled swordfish with wasabi soy sauce, roast duck with orange-ginger sauce, and rack of lamb provençal. The chef trained in Zurich and certain dishes (like veal à la Suisse) are accompanied by those delicious rösti potatoes. Prices range from $18 to $24. Floral curtains, a fireplace, and polished wood tables with placemats and a sprig of fresh flowers complete the decor. There's also a small cozy bar with a brick hearth.

The three simply furnished guest rooms (one with bath) feature chenille bedspreads, chintz curtains, painted chests, and braided rugs. Room 4 is the nicest, with its corner cupboard, dresser, small captain's desk, couch, blue-and-white braided rug, and burgundy curtains. The sink has a marble surround.

Rates: $70–$75 double. **Dining Hours:** Wed–Sat 5–9pm, Sun 4–8:30pm.

Hillsdale, N.Y., Lodging & Dining

Across the state border, **Swiss Hutte,** Rte. 23, Hillsdale, NY 12529 (tel. 518/325-3333), a beautifully kept accommodation at the base of Catamount, offers some of the finest cuisine in the area. The expertly groomed grounds include a pool; gardens containing herbaceous borders, roses, and a pond; and two tennis courts. In the restaurant, aglow with red lanterns, specialties include wienerschnitzel and continental fare like duck à l'orange or rack of lamb, plus delicious desserts like hazelnut torte and raspberry cream pie. Prices run $15 to $25, including dessert and beverage. The rooms are simply furnished motel-style units.

Rates: Summer (MAP), $95 per person double (three-night stay required weekends). Winter (MAP), $90 per person double (two-night minimum stay required holiday weekends). **Dining Hours:** Summer, daily noon–2pm and 5:30–9pm; winter, Wed–Sun noon–2pm and 5:30–9pm.

At **Aubergine,** on Rtes. 23 and 22 (P.O. Box 387), Hillsdale, NY 12529 (tel. 518/325-3412), chef/owner David Lawson and his wife have furnished this 1783 brick Dutch Colonial home with many of their own antique heirlooms. Interesting features of the inn include three splendid Palladian windows, a corner cupboard of museum quality, and eight fireplaces, all but one with the original mantelpiece.

The inn's ground floor consists of a handsome center hall; four dining rooms, each with a fireplace; and a bilevel Victorian bar/lounge (ca. 1850) with an unusual curving stairway leading to the gallery level. Chef Lawson was former executive chef at Blantyre (see "Lenox Lodging & Dining" in the Lenox section, above), and his cuisine has won wide acclaim, so people go out of their way to dine here. The menu, which changes monthly, is limited in keeping with the chef's desire to use only the freshest ingredients. It might offer a pavé of salmon au poivre accompanied by a fondue of leeks and rich red-wine sauce; pan-fried sirloin steak with port-braised shallots and sauce béarnaise; or fettuccine with wild mushrooms, crème fraîche, garden herbs, and white-truffle butter. Among the appetizers might be a terrine of eggplant, roasted peppers, and chèvre and Maine scallop cakes with shiitake mushrooms, scallions, and bean sprouts with a warm ponzu vinaigrette. The house-smoked quail with apple chutney shows off the local Hudson Valley delicacy well. For dessert try the Grand Marnier soufflé or the chocolate-hazelnut cake with pistachio sauce. The wine cellar concentrates on fine French and American wines, but you can also sample such local wines as the Millbrook chardonnay. Prices run $15 to $23.

There are four guest rooms, each decorated in a particular color scheme. Those on the second floor share a bath; the third-floor Lavender and Coral rooms have private baths. The furnishings are antique reproductions—candlestands, pine chests, and Windsor rocking chairs.

Rates: $80–$100 double. **Dining Hours:** Wed–Sun 5:30pm–closing.

GREAT BARRINGTON & SHEFFIELD

Great Barrington Attractions

Great Barrington is the largest town in the southern Berkshires, a major crossroads and commercial center. Just outside town, you may want to explore the **Albert Schweitzer Center,** 50 Hurlburt Rd. (tel. 413/528-3124), where you'll find this quotation to ponder while you wander along Philosopher's Walk, by the brook, or in the universal children's garden: "The meaning of maturity which we should develop in ourselves is that we should strive always to become simpler, kinder, more honest, more truthful, more peace-loving, more gentle, and more compassionate." Lecture and concert series are given through the summer at this special haven.

Hours (Grounds): June–Aug, Tues–Sat 10am–4pm, Sun noon–4pm; Mar–May and Sept–Nov, Thurs–Sat 10am–4pm; Dec–Feb, by appointment only.

Inveterate shoppers and browsers will probably want to stop at **Jenifer House,** on Stockbridge Road, about a mile north of Rte. 23 on Rte. 7 (tel. 413/528-1500), a series of clapboard buildings each specializing in different merchandise—fine furniture, country clothes, and more.

Hours: Mon–Sat 9am–5:30pm, Sun 10am–5pm.

Great Barrington Lodging

Little John Manor, One Newsboy Monument Lane, Great Barrington, MA 01230 (tel. 413/528-2882), is certainly one of the town's most secluded bed-and-breakfasts; I missed it several times. It's on Rte. 23 but tucked away on a quiet loop, behind the *Newspaper Boy* statue, a gift presented to Great Barrington by Col. William L. Brown, publisher of the *New York Daily News* in 1895.

Owners Paul DuFour and Herb Littlejohn have run resorts before and their experience shows. They offer four rooms (sharing two baths), immaculately kept and pleasingly decorated in harmonious colors. For example, the twin has rose carpeting, Wedgwood-blue curtains, and a colorful floral bedspread. Fresh flowers stand on a chest and tissues are available. A small double features a bed with eyelet pillowcases and dust ruffle and a white eiderdown, set off by an oak dresser, a bishop's chair, and Japanese prints. The living room is comfortably cluttered with a number of Toby jugs, among other things. Couches, rockers, and other chairs cluster around the white brick fireplace and the TV.

The dining-room table extends to seat eight. A full English breakfast is served. Tea and coffee and juice are placed on the sideboard and piping-hot scrambled or fried eggs, ham, English sausage, mushrooms, broiled tomatoes, and potatoes in jackets emerge from the kitchen. English muffins or crumpets are served with homemade jams and marmalade. An afternoon tea of scones, Scottish oatcakes, banana bread, and fruit butters is either served in the lounge or taken out to the benches scattered through the garden or to the porch.

A hutch in the dining room is filled with oils and vinegars Paul makes from the 55 to 60 varieties of herbs he cultivates in the garden. Each is clearly marked and you'll smell and see everything from marjoram and horseradish to Egyptian onion. In summer the borders bloom with peonies, lilies, roses, and other flowers. You can sit and contemplate the fields and wooded hills in the distance.

Rates (including breakfast): Memorial Day–Oct, $80–$100 double (higher rate for room with fireplace); Nov–Memorial Day, $70–$85 double (higher rate for room with fireplace).

At **Green Meadows,** 117 Division St., Great Barrington, MA 01230 (tel. 413/528-3897), owners Frank Gioia and Susie Kaufman have created a self-contained B&B wing by converting four rooms at the back of this 1880 Victorian farmhouse, which stands on 6 acres looking out over fields. All rooms have a bath and air conditioning and are prettily decorated and sparkling. The ground-floor room contains a brass bed with a navy-blue floral comforter, an oak dresser, and a side table, set against pink walls. The rooms upstairs are similar, with wide pine floors but decorated in different colors—rose and celery primarily. Breakfast is satisfying, likely beginning with berries or melon followed by an omelet or French toast with local maple syrup.

Rates (including breakfast): $80–$95 double.

Irv and Jamie Yost, owners of the **Turning Point Inn,** Rte. 23 at Lake Buel Road (R.D. 2, Box 140), Great Barrington, MA 01230 (tel. 413/528-4777), bring the personal touch to their business by sending guests handwritten notes with their brochures. They've restored an old stagecoach stop right near Butternut (east of Great Barrington) and offer six guest rooms, two with shared bath. There are a couple of parlors to relax in, and the whole place has a distinct home-away-from-home feeling. There's also a two-bedroom housekeeping cottage available. The full breakfast consists of eggs, cereal, breads, and fruit.

Rates (including breakfast): $85–$105 double; $210 cottage.

Seekonk Pines, 142 Seekonk Cross Rd., Rte. 23, Great Barrington, MA 01230 (tel. 413/528-4192), a little farther west along Rte. 43, represents great value in this area. Innkeepers Linda and Chris Best bring their own personalities and talents to bear on this very homey accommodation. Throughout the house hang watercolors painted by Linda and quilts restored by her. Linda and Chris are singers, and, given an accompanist at the piano, if you're lucky they'll perform for guests. The house was built between 1830 and 1832 as a farmhouse and remained in the same family for three generations. One of the previous owners was a friend of Thomas Edison, and Edison's portrait hangs among those of the previous owners in the entrance hall.

Each of the six guest rooms has a bath and is named after a previous owner. In the largest, the Harry G. Treadwell, the bed is covered by a quilt made by Linda's great-grandmother, Chinese paintings adorn the walls, and a chest of drawers, side tables, blanket chest, and two comfortable chairs complete the furnishings. The other rooms are also comfortably furnished, and the shared bath contains a little cushioned pew and marble sink top. Quilts are found in every room, and stenciling appears in many.

The dining-room table supported a vase of purple Canterbury bells when I last visited. A breakfast of fresh fruit and homemade muffins is served, along with juice and coffee or tea. The garden is quite lovely— filled with foxgloves, lupines, sweet williams, and pansies. There's an outdoor pool secluded by a private hedge and fence, and for indoor entertainment a TV/VCR, books, and chess and other games are available in the living room. Bikes are also available.

Rates (including breakfast): Memorial Day–Oct, $85–$115 double; Nov–Memorial Day, $75–$90 double.

Great Barrington Dining

The **Castle Street Cafe,** 10 Castle St. (tel. 413/528-5244), occupies a large high-ceilinged storefront where the brick walls are accented with large pieces of art portraying food ingredients in all their wondrous colors and shapes. There's a small bar, and jazz usually plays quietly in the background. The cuisine is carefully prepared. The flavor of the grilled chicken breast is set off with a black trumpet mushroom sauce; the black-currant sauce doesn't overwhelm the duck. For the less hungry there's even a simple burger served with straw potatoes and pastas too. The chocolate-mousse cake rates high.

Hours: Sun–Mon and Wed–Thurs 5–9pm, Fri–Sat 5–10pm.

The **Boiler Room Cafe,** 405 Stockbridge Rd. (tel. 413/528-4280), occupies an old farmhouse in which there are several intimate dining rooms. The cuisine is contemporary American with a distinct leaning toward the Mediterranean. Among the appetizers is a marvelous Mediterranean plate for two comprised of grilled shrimp tapenade, lentils with parsley vinaigrette, grilled baby leeks, and lamb sausage with almond sauce, marinated chèvre, peppers, and olives. Pastas and pizzas—like the cornmeal pizza with fontina, grilled red onions, potatoes, and raisins—can be ordered as main dishes or you can choose one of the fine wood-grilled dishes, including marinated duck breast with tart caramel sauce. Among the more traditional items are roast rack of lamb marinated with mustard and thyme and salmon filet with a red wine, balsamic, and caper sauce that's full of flavor. Prices range from $8 to $21.

Hours: Tues–Sat 5pm–closing.

Martin's, 49 Railroad St. (tel. 413/528-5455), offers good healthful cuisine. You'll find such items as veggie burgers, scrambled tofu that really does substitute for eggs, apple pancakes, and omelets made with the likes of salsa, hot peppers, and cheese. The tables are plain wood and the nice thing is that they serve breakfast all day.

Hours: Daily 6am–3pm.

La Tomate, 293 Main St. (tel. 413/528-3003), will introduce you to Provençal cuisine that's lighter than traditional French and uses olive oil rather than butter as the cooking medium. The limited menu, emphasizing fish and shellfish, assures well-prepared dishes. There might be a wonderful salmon served on cream choucroute and bacon with vinegar sauce; sautéed lobster with morel-brandy sauce; or a simpler variety of fish, shrimp, and scallops grilled with ginger-lemon-wine sauce. On the meat side, the cuisine exhibits more Spanish/southwestern flair with sautéed chicken breast with jalapeños, tomatoes, and melted asiago cheese and veal with mushrooms, spinach, and espagnole sauce. There are also several delicious pasta dishes, the most characteristic being the pasta basilic and tomatoes, with black olives, basil, capers, herbs, cheese, and olive oil. To start, there's a classic onion tart; roasted goat cheese with mushrooms, thyme, and garlic; and mussels in tomato, white wine, and garlic. Prices range from $18 to $22. Finish with any of the delicious tarts.

Hours: Tues–Thurs and Sun noon–2pm and 5–9pm, Fri–Sat noon–2pm and 5–10:30pm.

20 Railroad Street, whose name describes its address (tel. 413/528-9345), is a classic tavern/restaurant with a 28-foot-long Victorian carved mahogany bar and oak booths. The menu is broad, ranging from Philly cheese steaks and tuna melts and burgers to a hot turkey platter, pasta with seafood and sun-dried tomatoes, and grilled sirloin, priced from $5 to $13. The brunch menu provides good value and offers cooked-to-order choices like omelets, French toast, quiche, and other egg dishes, plus selections from the regular menu.

Hours: Daily 11:30am–10pm.

Across the street, **Daily Bread Bakery,** 17 Railroad St. (tel. 413/528-9610), has tempting breads, cookies, and pies made of seasonal fresh fruits. They're delicious and fun and "contain no refined sugar unless marked."

Sheffield Lodging

From the minute you see the **Ivanhoe Country House,** Rte. 41, Under Mountain Road, Sheffield, MA 01257 (tel. 413/229-2143), you know it's nicely kept. The white clapboard house with black shutters is neat and trim, and so are the lawns and flowers. The oldest part of the house dates to 1780.

Dick and Carole Maghery have nine rooms, all with bath and furnished differently. Two are on the first floor: One large room has a fireplace and a large porch that accommodates a private Ping-Pong table along with wicker furnishings; the room itself contains a bed with a white eiderdown, two chests, an armoire, armchair, and a bath with a clawfoot tub. Rag rugs made by a local lady are found throughout. The Sunrise Room, which shares a bath, has a painted country bed, a sidetable, a chest, a dresser, and rust-and-blue chintz wallpaper. The Lakeview Room, which does indeed have a view, is decorated in dusky rose. The Willow Room has a sleigh bed, a Windsor rocker, and other appealing pieces. There's also a two-bedroom unit with a kitchenette and porch that's very private—ideal for families or two couples. Both bedrooms have a fireplace and brass bed.

The living room is comfortably large and welcoming, with Victorian sofas, chestnut paneling, a brick fireplace, wing chairs, a TV, and plenty of books and magazines spread out on top of an early piano. French doors lead onto a brick terrace with umbrellaed tables where you can sit and contemplate the lake or look across the lawn over a rockery to a stand of pine trees. Begonias and other flowers brighten the gardens. You'll probably meet the four golden retrievers (Dick and Carole used to raise them). The pool is beautifully located on the crest of a hill, where chaise longues are lined up for sunworshipers. From the grounds there's a serene view of Berkshire Lake. The continental breakfast can be delivered to your room.

Rates (including breakfast): May–Oct, $109–$115 double weekends, 90–$100 double weekdays; $185 two-bedroom unit. Nov–Apr, $60–$80 double; $135 two-bedroom unit.

Staveleigh House, South Main Street, Sheffield, MA 01257 (tel. 413/229-2129), is a private home set back from Rte. 7; it's operated by widows Dorothy Marosy and Marion Whitman. Throughout the house feminine touches are evident. Many of the quilts on the beds or walls, including the large one on the staircase wall, were crafted by Marion, while the rugs were hooked by Dorothy. Plants brighten the rooms, and the landing is inhabited by teddy bears. There are five rooms (three upstairs and two down), two with bath. The most charming features a dresser (with mirror), a rocker, and a chaise longue, all made of wicker, and plank wood floors; a quilt hangs over the bed rail. In the bath the floor has been decorated with sponge painting. Another favorite, on the ground floor, has a private entrance at the back; it's radiantly decorated in yellow and white with maple furnishings.

In the living room the name Staveleigh is carved above the grate, though neither owner knows the exact provenance. The center hall's walls have been opened so the living room flows into the dining room, where the table is spread with a lace cloth. Here a full breakfast is served—juice, fresh fruit, a hot dish like puffed oven pancakes, and homemade muffins and jams. The room is personalized by a cobalt-blue glass collection and a display case containing a salt cellar collection.

Rates (including breakfast): $85 double without bath, $100 double with bath.

When Ronald and Judith Timm had the task of furnishing **Centuryhurst,** Main Street (Rte. 7), Sheffield, MA 01257 (tel. 413/229-8131), they had the distinct advantage of owning and operating the antiques store located in the barn behind the main house. It's no surprise, then, that the four rooms sharing two baths are furnished with early 19th-century American pieces, many also featuring clocks collected by Ron. For example, you'll find tiger maple cannonball beds, grain-painted dressers and blanket chests, mirrors with reverse painted glass, and many other decorative pieces. The house was built in 1800 and still has its original hardware, unique keystone archways, and an unusually large fireplace with beehive oven. There are two large sitting rooms, both with fireplaces. Guests can also use the in-ground pool on the 3 acres of landscaped grounds or relax in the old New England porch rockers. Clock mavens will love the store, which also specializes in Wedgwood and offers two floors of American country furniture.

Rates (including breakfast): $56–$76 double.

The **Stagecoach Hill Inn,** Rte. 41, Sheffield, MA 01257 (tel. 413/229-8585), exudes history. It's a rambling 1794 brick building set on 160 acres. By 1802 there was a barn on the property; it's now the dark, beamed MacDougall's tavern, where the bar is decorated with car badges and other auto insignia. The tavern is frequented by many Lime Rock drivers and fans and is made cozy by the double-brick hearth tiled on one side with Delft and by the oil lamps hanging from the beams. There's even a comfortable raised section with couches and a TV. The brick building was constructed in 1820 and the smaller building in back was erected in the mid-1800s as a poorhouse. The place has since functioned variously as a summer house, a guesthouse, and (since 1946) an inn.

The previous owners were English and certain traces of their influence remain. A sign invites lords, ladies, and gentlemen to follow the pointer past the tavern into the dining rooms. Here an innovative menu is offered at dinner—for example, the grilled chicken and portobello pot pie with roasted garlic mashed-potato crust, game hen with cabernet-braised vegetables, and pork medallions with raspberry-horseradish glaze. Prices range from $11 to $22. To start, try the grilled rosemary polenta with green-chile sauce and parmigiano-reggiano or the smoked chicken and jalapeño pâté with pepperoncini, griddled dark bread, and Dijon mustard. Pub fare is available in the tavern Thursday to Tuesday.

The 11 rooms (most with bath, all with air conditioning and phone) are in the main house and cottage annex. They're furnished with an eclectic mix of antiques and antique reproductions. The nicest rooms, to my mind, are in the addition out back. Room 5, for instance, has a rope four-poster covered with an old red-and-blue quilt, a sidetable draped with a floor-length tablecloth, wing chairs, a dresser, and a chest; the floor is covered with an area rug. Room 4 is even brighter, thanks to the fantail light. Facilities also include an outdoor pool.

Rates: July–Oct, $95–$135 double. Nov–June, $95–$120 double.
Dining Hours: Sun–Tues and Thurs 5:30–9:30pm, Fri–Sat 5:30–10:30pm.

The **Ramblewood Inn,** Under Mountain Road (P.O. Box 729), Sheffield, MA 01257 (tel. 413/229-3363), is located in an unusually spacious log house tucked away in the pine woods. All the guest rooms have a tiled bath and are attractively furnished with pine beds, polished pine-wood floors, ruffled curtains, and gray wall-to-wall carpeting with a pinkish hue. The ground-floor room has a cathedral-style ceiling and light-filled atrium. One room has a private deck adorned with flower-filled tubs. The upstairs rooms are also prettily and variously decorated, with one wall sporting chintz wallpaper, cream-and-rust curtains at the windows, a Hitchcock rocker, and other furnishings. Quiche, blueberry pancakes, omelets, and sausage and eggs are likely breakfast dishes, along with home-baked items. Guests may use the canoe on the lake across the road.

Rates (including breakfast): $90–$125 double.

Orchard Shade, Maple Avenue (P.O. Box 669), Sheffield, MA 02157 (tel. 413/229-8463), is the name given to this beautiful 1840 house standing on 10 acres with well-tended gardens and a pool. The seven guest rooms share three baths, and all are furnished tastefully with antiques. In one you might find an Empire-style chest and bull's-eye mirror, along with a camelback sofa and wicker chair. Another might have painted cottage-style furniture. The parlors with fireplaces are comfortable and decorated with rugs, interesting objects, family portraits, and a good selection of books, art, and sculpture. A breakfast of breads and pastries is served.

Rates (including breakfast): $75–$185 double.

Hartsville Dining

The **Hillside Restaurant** is a few miles southeast of Great Barrington on Rte. 57 (off Rte. 23) in Hartsville (tel. 413/528-3123). In an old farmhouse set on the crest of a hill with a beautiful Berkshire Valley view, this restaurant serves continental/Italian specialties (from $14 to $19) like veal francese or marsala, steak au poivre, and similar dishes. Staffordshire china is used for service; the two dining rooms are warmed by fires in winter, while in summer there's a porch that takes full advantage of the view.

Hours: Summer, daily noon–2pm and 5–9pm; winter, Wed–Sun 5–9pm.

New Marlborough & Sandisfield Lodging & Dining

At the **Old Inn on the Green & Gedney Farm,** Rte. 57, New Marlborough, MA 01230 (tel. 413/229-3131), the Old Inn is indeed set back behind a green in an 18th-century building with a classic double-porched facade. There are five rooms here (one with bath, the other four sharing two baths), each eclectically furnished in very country style. For example, the room might contain an iron-and-brass bed, a desk, an armoire, a wing chair, and a white-painted table and chair. Some rooms have access to the long front balcony. Gedney Farm is a short distance down the road, and the 12 accommodations here (all with bath) are in a magnificent turn-of-the-century Normandy-style barn; the interior decoration is refreshingly different from that of the traditional New England inn, with rooms painted in brilliant southwestern colors. Some have granite fireplaces and tiled whirlpool baths.

The Old Inn's four colonial-style dining rooms have fireplaces and are lit entirely by candles. Here a prix-fixe dinner is served on Saturday. Dinner specialties vary from week to week, but the menu might begin with smoked salmon roulade with niçois olive tapenade and roasted pepper oil, followed by Grenoble-style Dover sole with braised-leek tart and orange/basil/red onion relish or sesame-crusted wild boar chops with celery-root flan, wild-mushroom fettuccine, and spicy plum sauce. The finale might bring Key lime tart with candied citrus or raspberry sorbet in white-chocolate cups with blackberries. A fine repast indeed and well worth the $48 price tag. During the week an à la carte menu is served in the dining rooms or on the canopied terrace by candlelight. Prices range from $17 to $20, and you'll always find a fish of the day and a less expensive pasta of the day, as well as such dishes as grilled sea scallops with saffron/roasted-pepper sauce and loin of pork with shallot-gooseberry jus and a salad of roasted corn and pinto beans. The wine list is extensive. Breakfast is served in the room with a refectory table. The Courtyard Cafe at Gedney Farm is open for lunch on summer weekends. The Gallery at Gedney Farm features a variety of art shows during the year, including an outdoor sculpture part in summer and fall.

Rates (including breakfast): Old Inn, $110–$155 double. Gedney Farm, $170–$185 double; from $215 suite.

The oldest section of the **New Boston Inn,** 101 N. Main St., Rtes. 8 and 57 (Village of New Boston), Sandisfield, MA 01255 (tel. 413/258-4477), dates back to 1735. Today it serves as the tap room of this zesty country inn with eight rooms (all with bath). The floors are bleached wood; the decor is soft florals. Room 4 is stenciled with a Tree of Life done by a local artist. The inn also offers a cottage-style Victorian suite with a striking turkey-red rush-seat chair and desk. The cove-ceilinged ballroom now serves as a place where guests gather to talk or play billiards. According to local legend, Pearl Buck wrote *The Good Earth* here, Vladimir Horowitz played in the ballroom, and Anne Morrow Lindbergh wrote *Gift from the Sea* here. A full breakfast of bacon, sausage, and French toast is served.

Rates (including breakfast): $105 double.

PITTSFIELD, DALTON & THE NORTHWESTERN CORNER OF THE BERKSHIRES

Area Attractions

Pittsfield and Dalton, the industrial heart of the Berkshires, present a very different face from the picturesque villages I've covered thus far. Neither one is pretty, but they do possess some attractions that are of interest. Indeed, you may wish to begin at the **Berkshire Museum,** 39 South St. (tel. 413/443-7171), in the center of Pittsfield, where some of the displays will help you come to grips with the area's history. Here you'll find some fine paintings from the Hudson River School and exhibits concentrating on ancient civilizations and nature.

Hours: July–Aug, daily Mon–Sat 10am–5pm, Sun 1–5pm; Sept–June, Tues–Sat 10am–5pm, Sun 1–5pm. **Admission:** $3 adults, $2 seniors, $1 children 12–18; free Wed and Sat 10am–noon.

Just south of Pittsfield lies **Arrowhead,** at 780 Holmes Rd. (tel. 413/442-1793), where Herman Melville lived from 1850 to 1863. As you stand in the room where he wrote *Moby-Dick*, *Pierre*, *The Confidence Man*, and the *Piazza Tales* (including "Bartleby the Scrivener"), you can imagine how often he must've contemplated the grim visage of Mount Greylock with despair, for his novels and stories were failures and he was dogged by debt. Even sadder, after he died his wife threw out his books because she thought they were all worthless. Three rooms are devoted to his life and works and other memorabilia. The house is also the headquarters of the Berkshire County Historical Society.

Hours: Memorial Day–Labor Day, daily 10am–5pm; Labor Day–Oct, Fri–Mon 10am–5pm; Nov–May, by appointment only. **Admission:** $4 adults, $3 children 6–16.

From Pittsfield you have access (5 miles along Rte. 20) to a really fascinating attraction, one that's best visited when the weather is clement, for you'll have to do a lot of outdoor walking. This is the **Hancock Shaker Village,** Rte. 20 (P.O. Box 898), Pittsfield, MA 01202 (tel. 413/443-0188). There's still plenty to see indoors, so just don your boots and slickers on rainy days.

Allow at least three hours to tour this fascinating living museum dedicated to the Shakers, a communal religious sect that in 1790 established

Hancock, the City of Peace, as the third of 18 Shaker communities settled in the United States.

Founded by Mother Ann Lee, the Shakers were dedicated to celibacy, simplicity, and equality. They were known for their excellence in agriculture and industry and their lively dance-worship, which gave the sect its name. Celibates, they took children and orphans into their community; the children were free to leave if they wanted and many did. You can see the dorms where the men and women slept separately, their separate staircases, and the corridors where two narrow strips of carpet were placed—one for the women to walk on, the other for the men.

They rose at 4:30am in summer, at 5am in winter, to begin their daily round of farming, crafts making, and cooking. You can tour 20 original Shaker buildings, and along the way you can watch the old crafts being performed—cooking appropriate to the period, following Shaker recipes; furniture making; box making; weaving; and so on. There's also a Discovery Room where you can try your hand at spinning and weaving or slip on Shaker-style clothing. The village also has a working farm with historic breeds of livestock and vegetable and herb gardens. In the museum shop fine crafts can be purchased—their famous wool cloaks, tables, chairs, candleholders, boxes, vinegars, and herbs. A delightful outing.

Note: Don't go to Hancock Village itself. The Shaker Village is separated by a mountain barrier. Coming from the north, take Rte. 7 south to Rte. 20 west. From the south, take Rte. 22 to Rte. 295 and then east to Rte. 41 north.

Hours: Apr–Nov, daily 9:30am–5pm. **Admission:** $10.

The **South Mountain Chamber Concerts** are given about a mile south of Pittsfield.

Due east of Pittsfield lies the other industrial town of Dalton, where you can explore part of its heritage at the **Crane Museum,** South Street (tel. 413/684-2600), off Rte. 9, by viewing the exhibits documenting the art of fine paper making since 1801. Unfortunately, you'll have to come here on a weekday.

Hours: June to mid-Oct, Mon–Fri 2–5pm.

Pittsfield & Dalton Lodging

For those who prefer a modern, lively hotel, Pittsfield offers the **Berkshire Hilton Inn,** Pittsfield, MA 01201 (tel. 413/499-2000), with 175 air-conditioned rooms, an indoor pool, three lounges, and a restaurant.

Rates: Summer, $155–$195 double. The rest of the year, $120–$160 double.

The **White Horse Inn,** 378 South St. (Rtes. 7 and 20), Pittsfield, MA 01201 (tel. 413/442-2512), is a beige clapboard home with cream shutters and an elegant portico supported by classical pillars. All eight rooms (with bath) are neat and clean, furnished with oak desks, beds, dressers, or similar. The breakfast room, with flowers adorning the glass-topped tables, overlooks the lawn and trees in back. An ample continental breakfast of fruit, cereal, and homemade muffins and quiche is served.

Rates (including breakfast): July–Labor Day, $100–$140 double. May–June and Labor Day–Nov, $70–$90 double.

The **Dalton House,** 955 Main St., Dalton, MA 01226 (tel. 413/684-3854), always has seasonal flowers—geraniums, marigolds, fuchsia—displayed on the long front porch, for owners Gary and Bernice Turetsky also happen to run the adjacent florist (where over 2,500 geraniums and other plants are raised). In the main house, built by a Hessian soldier in 1810, are nine rooms and two suites, all with bath and air-conditioning. The six rooms in the carriage house out back are especially nicely decorated to achieve a country look that mingles the contemporary and the old-fashioned. The public areas in the house itself are warm and cozy, made so by the large fireplace in the sitting room, which also contains a piano; some people like to retire to the loft area for cards or TV or some other form of relaxation, especially after a day's skiing (this is a popular spot for ski groups). Breakfast is served buffet style in the skylit Shaker-style dining room. In summer, loungers and tables are placed out on the deck, and guests can enjoy the large pool.

Rates (including breakfast): July–Aug, $90–$120 double. Sept–June, $60–$80 double.

Pittsfield Dining

An entrance surrounded by chianti bottles welcomes you to the homey **Giovanni's,** on Rte. 7 just south of Pontoosuc Lake (tel. 413/443-2441). Tiffany-style lamps and a few hanging plants and unframed pictures of Venice set the scene for tasty Italian dishes. Typical appetizers—gnocchi and calamari fritti—are priced from $5. Pastas run from $9 for plain spaghetti with sausage or meatballs to $13 for spaghetti with shrimp and clam sauce. Main courses encompass everything from veal and peppers and chicken cacciatore for a mere $11 to Giovanni's combination—a strip sirloin served with fried shrimp or scallops or crab legs, for $18. Filet mignon, veal marsala, broiled swordfish, and scrod are other menu choices.

Hours: Sun–Thurs 4:30–9pm, Fri–Sat 4:30–10pm.

Lodging & Dining over the New York Border

The **Inn at Shaker Mill,** Cherry Lane (off Rte. 22), Canaan, NY 12029 (tel. 518/794-9345), is idyllically situated by a flowing brook and waterfall. This lovely 1824 stone grist mill affords peace and quiet, for here you can sit in the living room and actually listen to the water running over the rocks. The couches are modern and so are the wood stoves; Shaker stools serve as coffee tables; books are plentiful. Ingram Paperny, who has lived here for 28 years, restored the mill, handcrafting most of the built-in furniture himself. Some people may find the 20 rooms a bit too austere, the Shaker inspiration too strong. Furnishings consist of a wood sidetable, a chest, wide-board floors, and beams. The most appealing accommodation is a top-floor skylit apartment with wicker furnishings and a kitchen. There's a TV in the living room. The best pastimes, though, are sitting out by the brook and looking across the fields dotted with cows or taking a stroll through the countryside. Meals are obligatory on summer weekends (bring your own wine). The prime reason for visiting the inn is the warm welcome given by Ingram, who relishes conversation and obviously has warm interest and affection for his guests.

Rates: Summer, $185 per person, MAP, for full weekend; $60–$65 daily B&B on weekends. The rest of the year, $160 per person.

The **Sedgwick Inn,** Rte. 22, Berlin, NY 12022 (tel. 518/658-2334), is an exquisite home filled with antiques collected by Robert and Edith Evans, who restored and opened this inn as "a retirement project" after long careers in psychology. They offer four rooms (with bath) and a two-room suite, plus six motel-style units. The room I viewed contained two brass beds and a bird's-eye maple dresser; if the others reflect the quality of the public areas, they ought to be beautiful.

The place is very comfortable and full of interesting artifacts. In the living room is a case filled with ivory pieces, figureheads, toby jugs, other small appealing collectibles, and a number of stone sculptures, the work of Faith Evans. A sofa, wing chairs, an Oriental rug, and a fireplace ensure comfort. A Will Moses, given to the Evans by the artist; a fan fetchingly framed; and other objects grace the walls. A marvelous etched-glass door depicting peacocks—a great find—leads to the porch breakfast room, which has a view of the garden and is furnished with white metal chairs and tables on a brick floor. The library offers magazines, books, and comfortable chairs; in the corner, the cupboard is filled with jewelry and small antique items for sale. A gift shop and gallery are behind the inn. Wicker chairs line the front porch.

Burgundy placemats on polished wood tables are found in the Coach Room Tavern, a popular restaurant for which you'll need a reservation on weekends. The kitchen is supervised by Edith and the chef turns out many soups, such as mushroom and hazelnut or lentil and ham. The menu changes weekly but will feature five entrees and a vegetarian choice. There might be Thai garlic-and-limte chicken; poached red snapper with sesame and crystal-ginger beurre blanc; roast loin of pork with garlic, rosemary, and sage; and always a Black Angus filet mignon. Edith is Viennese and desserts are her specialty—Belgian dark-chocolate ganache with kona crème fraîche and chocolate Frangelico cream trifle are two choices. A pianist plays on Friday and Saturday evenings.

Rates (including breakfast): $105 superior double, $80 motel-type double; $125 suite. **Dining Hours:** Wed–Sat 11:30am–2pm and 5–9pm, Sun 11:30am–2pm (brunch) and 1–8pm.

It's not surprising that the **Mill House Inn** (P.O. Box 1079, Hancock, MA 01237), on Rte. 43 in New York's Stephentown (tel. 518/733-5606), really does look like a Central European mountain chalet, for one of the owners, Romana Tallet, wife of Frank, hails from the former Yugoslavia. The Tallets will welcome you into their truly cozy living room with its large arched stucco fireplace that throws out much-needed heat on winter days. There's a small games room and a small pool in back, and croquet is available; the Tallets go to great lengths to ensure that everyone is content. They're also well versed and forthcoming about the area's attractions. All their rooms have air-conditioning and a bath with continental-style shower; they're eclectically furnished, some with pine. In summer, breakfast is served on the terrace. The inn is only 10 minutes from Mount Greylock.

Rates (including breakfast): $90–$100 double; $110–$150 suite. Three-night minimum July–Aug and holiday weekends.

For a change from standard American cuisine, there's a Japanese restaurant, **Shujis,** in New Lebanon (tel. 518/794-8383), just across the New York–Massachusetts border on Rte. 22 south at Rte. 20, occupying what used to be Governor Tilden's stone mansion, complete with turrets. Inside, a little bridge takes you over the Japanese rock garden studded with pagodas into the dining rooms, where you can sample a sushi or sashimi dinner, chicken teriyaki, or sukiyaki priced from $12 to $24 (higher for items like king crab).

Hours: Summer, Sun–Thurs 6–8:30pm, Fri–Sat 5–9pm; winter, Wed–Fri 6–8:30pm, Sat–Sun 5–8:30pm. **Closed:** Mid-Nov to late Apr.

Master chef Jean Petit has been attracting patrons to his secluded **Les Pyrénées,** off Rte. 295, in Canaan, N.Y. (tel. 518/781-4451), for 30 years. A stone stairway covered by a red, white, and blue awning leads to the restaurant; flowers bloom on either side. The front room is a low-lit bar, and the dining room behind glows. Gilt portraits, many of family and friends, adorn the Chinese pink-lacquered walls. The atmosphere is relaxed. The dishes are primarily French classics—chicken in burgundy, poached halibut in a sauce of white wine and cream, poulet au champagne, or frogs' legs, priced from $12 to $32, the higher price for pheasant with pâté de foie gras and truffles. Among the desserts, the crème brûlée is extra-special. Cash or personal check only.

Hours: Summer, Tues–Sat 5–10pm, Sun 5–9pm; winter and spring, Fri–Sat 5–10pm, Sun 4–9pm.

Hancock & Jiminy Peak Lodging & Dining

The **Hancock Inn,** Rte. 43, Hancock, MA 01237 (tel. 413/738-5873, or 800/882-8859), is an expression of Ellen and Chester Gorski. A small concrete path lined with irises and marigolds leads to the small porch/ foyer filled with ferns and cane rockers. Opening the door, you'll discover a very Victorian hallway. Old stern Victorian portraits stare down from the walls; a Victorian-style couch and sideboard stand by imperiously. To the right, a doorway surmounted by a semicircular stained-glass window leads into the dining room, where the tables are set with white cloths and napkins, a sprig of fresh flowers, and glass candleholders. A large wall clock ticks away. Grapevine wreaths and cream ball-fringe curtains add a country touch. In winter it's warmed by the wood-burning stove.

The food has been highly rated by the *Albany Times Union* critic. The menu is limited, featuring eight or so dishes like duckling braised in port wine with figs; filet mignon with shallots, red wine, and cognac; fish of the day; and chicken breast sautéed in a light apricot sauce. Prices run $14 to $20. Desserts are created by Ellen—homemade ice creams, white-chocolate–mousse cheesecake, crème brûlée with strawberries. They'll be served on fine Depression glass of a harmonious color: cobalt blue, green, or burgundy.

The eight guest rooms (with bath) are very idiosyncratically styled, not in a lushly decorated perfect way. Room 1 has stenciled walls, a country pine dresser and bed, a sidetable, a wardrobe, a desk with a handful of old books, and a costumed doll in the corner. Other rooms might have an old country teardrop dresser, a bird's-eye maple or Jenny Lind bed, a comfortable chair like an old carpet chair rocker, or a rare Larkin desk. The place has great charm and Ellen is a warm, entertaining hostess.

Rates (including breakfast): $80 double weekends, $60 double weekdays. Extra person $12. **Dining Hours:** Fri–Sun 5–10pm.

The **Jiminy Peak Inn and Mountain Resort,** Corey Road, Hancock, MA 01237 (tel. 413/738-5500), is a well-designed, very attractive complex at the base of the mountain of the same name. All the accommodations are suites; each is modern, containing a kitchen with a dishwasher, a stove, a fridge, a toaster, a kettle, and so on, plus a living room with a couch that makes up into a queen-size bed, a TV hidden in a cabinet, comfortable seating, and a service bar. A bath with two sinks (a vanity outside) and a bedroom with a brass bed and pine furnishings complete the layout. The six-on-six and eight-on-eight windows give each an old-fashioned air.

The dining room, the **Founders Grill,** has a full view of the mountain, while the bar area has a stone fireplace and comfy wing chairs and a couch in which to rest those ski-sore limbs. The food is typical American/ continental fare—chicken parmigiana, chicken and seafood kebabs, prime rib, and baked scallops, priced from $10 to $20. It's also good for breakfast.

The list of additional facilities is long. There are six tennis courts and an outdoor pool from which you can see tree-covered mountains. Facing the mountain is another outdoor heated pool that's used year round and is great for sunning. Just off this pool area is a Jacuzzi, an exercise room with Universal equipment, a sauna, and a resident masseuse. The lower-level games room furnished with video games is only one area the kids enjoy. Bicycles are available for rent, and the Alpine slide is thrilling fun in summer ($4 a ride, $13 for a five-ride book, or 1½ hours' worth for $9.75). There's also horseback riding and laser trap shooting available. The miniature golf here is unique: Beautifully landscaped, each hole is a scale reproduction of a famous hole. Hazards include water, shrubs, and small firs, and little stone walls, waterfalls, and petunias are part of the landscaping. Trout fishing is offered at the stocked pond. Patio and picnic tables stand outside the round house, which is the tavern in winter, a sandwich place in summer. The grounds are well kept. Colorful window boxes and fences with rambling roses betray that extra attention to detail that has made Jiminy Peak the prime skiing and summer resort in the Berkshires.

Rates: One-bedroom suite, $90 weekdays, $105 weekends ($45 for a third night to a weekend); two-bedroom suite, $120 weekdays, $140 weekends ($60 for a third night); three-bedroom suite, $170 weekdays, $190 weekends ($85 for a third night). A two-night minimum stay is required. **Dining Hours:** Summer, Sun–Thurs 5–9:30pm, Fri–Sat 6–9pm; winter, Thurs–Sun 6–9pm. Breakfast depends on season.

WILLIAMSTOWN

Williamstown Attractions

Established in 1753 as a plantation called West Hoosuck, Williamstown was renamed after Col. Ephraim Williams in 1755, when he left an estate for founding a free school with the proviso that the township's name be changed. And that's why **Williams College,** whose buildings are scattered along Main Street against a mountain backdrop, is in this pretty town of rolling hills and dales. You can tour the college by going to the Admissions Office in Hopkins Hall. The college's museum of art, in Lawrence Hall on Main Street (tel. 413/597-2429), and the Hopkins Observatory are also worth visiting. But the outstanding attractions are really the Clark Institute and the Williamstown Festival.

The **Sterling and Francine Clark Art Institute,** 225 South St. (tel. 413/458-9545), houses a distinguished personal art collection purchased between 1912 and 1955. Most famous for a room of Renoirs and paintings by Monet, Degas, Pissarro, and other 19th-century French artists, the collection also contains other fine works—Cassatt pastels; Venetian scenes by Sargent; several Homers, including *Undertow* (1886), a luminous picture of lifeguards pulling two girls from the waves; a Remington bronze; some glorious Corots; Turner's *Rockets and Blue*

Lights; and two Morisots, along with representatives from many other schools and periods.

What makes the collection so remarkable is that Clark bought only what he liked, and his taste was impeccable. His favorite work was Renoir's *Onions,* because he especially appreciated the artistry that could transform a mundane onion into a shimmering object of beauty. Part of the museum is set aside for special exhibits.

Hours: Tues—Sun 10am—5pm. **Closed:** New Year's Day, Thanksgiving, Christmas. **Admission:** Free.

The Adams Memorial Theatre (tel. 413/597-3400) is home to the **Williamstown Theatre Festival,** under the direction of Peter Hunt; it has established itself over the last 40 years as the premier summer theater in the Berkshires. The festival's stars have included Richard Chamberlain, Blythe Danner, Christopher Walken, Richard Dreyfuss, Roberta Maxwell, Christopher Reeve, and Maria Tucci; they've performed on the Main Stage in classics by Williams, Brecht, Chekhov, Shaw, Ibsen, and others, and on the Other Stage in new works by Beth Henley, A. R. Gurney, Jr., Derek Walcott, and Jane Anderson. For information, write to P.O. Box 517, Williamstown, MA 01267.

Williamstown Lodging & Dining

Williamstown at last has a tasteful, if modern, accommodation, **The Orchards,** Rte. 2 East, Williamstown, MA 01267 (tel. 413/458-9611, or 800/225-1517). While the exterior may not look that inviting, the interior is extremely pleasing and, best of all, the layout centers on a large triangular garden with a rockery and pond. Here you can relax on the deck with its umbrellaed tables and enjoy cocktails or an after-theater supper. The focal point of your arrival will be the large living room whose floors are covered in Oriental jade-and-rose rugs. The fireplace mantel comes from England, the marble from Vermont. Bookshelves span each side of the mantel, and the elegance is further underlined by the grand piano, large crystal chandelier, antique furnishings, and what will certainly be a bounteous bouquet of flowers. A personal touch is revealed in the glass cases containing the owner's collections of antique silver teapots and of model soldiers ranging from a French Algerian cavalryman to a Norman knight.

The 49 extra-large guest rooms (15 with fireplaces) have been carefully designed and handsomely decorated in smoky blues and dusty pinks with wallpaper panel moldings. The marble-floored baths are fully tiled and have the added convenience of double sinks; a separate tub and shower; and many extras, like Crabtree & Evelyn soap, a scallop-shell soap dish, shampoo, and a sewing kit. Each room features solid-wood closet doors, a TV in an armoire, a nightlight, bathrobes, a refrigerator, a bar with a basket of fruit and bottles of Perrier, and plenty of working and seating space at the desk, armchairs, and table. The so-called smaller rooms (hardly small) lack the separate tub and shower and the refrigerator. The

Tennessee Williams Suite is huge, decked out in Wedgwood blue with a pencil four-poster without canopy.

Plush dark-green walls, pastel-patterned banquettes, Queen Anne chairs, dusty-rose napkins and tablecloths, fresh flowers in stem vases, and fine china provide the appropriate backdrop for wonderful food in the dining room. Start with the crab cakes with basil-mustard sauce or the feuilleté of smoked salmon on greens with quail eggs, crème fraîche, and caviar. There'll be about eight main courses—like salmon medallions wrapped in leeks with scallion compote or free-range chicken with ancho chili sauce, shallot confit, and roasted mushrooms. The roast lamb loin on ratatouille is enhanced by a rich barolo sauce. Prices range from $20 to $28. The desserts are carefully prepared and so good it's hard to select just one, but the opera torte with mocha sauce, Grand Marnier, cream, and shaved chocolate is certainly up there.

Facilities include an exercise room with stationary bikes, a sauna/whirlpool, and (most intriguing) an environmental chamber that provides suntan, rain, whirlpool, sauna, and steambath in one. When I visited, a small outdoor pool was under construction. The lounge draws a crowd and is particularly attractive in winter, when a fire roars in the large stone fireplace. It's well equipped with board and other games for those long, dark evenings and, of course, with comfortable lounge chairs.

Rates: Memorial Day to mid-Nov, $165–$230 double. The rest of the year, $135–$185 double. Special packages available. **Dining Hours:** Daily 7–10am, noon–2pm, and; Sun–Thurs 7–10am, noon–2pm, and 5:30-8:30pm; Fri-Sat 7–10am, noon–2pm, and 5:30–9pm.

River Bend Farm, 643 Simmonds Rd. (Rte. 7), Williamstown, MA 01267 (tel. 413/458-3121), rewards guests with an authentic historic experience and a warm hospitable stay. The house was built in 1770, and when you stand in the tap room it's as if time had stood still. The wood paneling, iron door latches, cupboard filled with pewter, and grandfather clock all make it real. So does the paneled keeping room with its great hearth, numerous hutches, copper sink, and herbs hung up to dry. Here a breakfast of granola, breads, and fruit is served. There are five rooms, each furnished with appropriate antiques and accents like wrought iron or Shaker-style tin lamps. The ground-floor room features Williamsburg blue paneling and is furnished with a double bed, blanket chest, wingback chair, and maple chest. An Oriental rug embellishes the plank floors. The smallest room is furnished with a corkscrew bed and a simple bench; wood pegs serve as a closet. What makes the room glow is the pumpkin pine paneling. The grounds are entrancing too.

Rates (including breakfast): $105 double.

Field Farm House, 554 Sloan Rd., Williamstown, MA 01267 (tel. 413/458-3135), is a refreshing surprise. It was once the home of Lawrence Bloedel, an art collector and Williams College librarian, and some of his collection can still be seen on the grounds and in the house, including a striking sculpture called *Sandy in Defined Space* by Richard McDermott Miller. The house and the interior design is 1940s modern. The original architect was Frank Lloyd Wright, but another architect finished it. The rooms have a minimum of furnishings because most pieces are built into the space—dressers, drawers, closets. Other pieces are Danish modern, like the glass-topped tables and chairs in the North Room. This room also features a fireplace with brilliant tiles painted with butterfly designs and a small deck. The seamless carpet is original to the house and the pinch-pleat track curtains are designed to shut out all light. The Master Bedroom is a study in serenity: A cream-white carpet, a teak dresser, and a fireplace with tiles depicting bluebirds are the crucial elements along with a huge deck commanding mountain views. The living room's woodwork is stunning and the cork parquet floor is quiet and certainly unique. Books and sculptures add interest to the room, and there are great views of the mountains, the beaver pond, and the grounds—all 254 acres. In summer guests may use the lovely kidney-shaped pool or tennis court and hike the marked trails, which can be used for cross-country skiing in winter. This eye opener certainly made me see Danish modern in a new light. To reach the property, take Rte. 7 south to Rte. 43. Sloan Road is off to the right.

Rates: $95 double.

On Rte. 7 you'll find the comfortable **Northside Motel,** 45 North St., Williamstown, MA 01267 (tel. 413/458-8107), run by Isabell and Alex Nagy. The motel has an unusually homey atmosphere and a cozy breakfast room.

Rates (including breakfast): Summer, $65 double. Winter, $50 double.

Williamstown Area Dining

Simple food, a glowing fireplace in winter, and classical music playing in the background make **Savories,** 123 Water St., Rte. 43 (tel. 413/458-4820), a fine relaxing place for a tasty dinner. Choices include steak, turkey, seafood, and eggplant marinara or parmigiana, all priced from $10 to $20.

Hours: Wed–Sun 5–10pm.

Two miles south of Williamstown on Rtes. 2 and 7, **Le Jardin** (tel. 413/458-8032) serves excellent food in elegant surroundings. You may begin with caviar or, less extravagantly, with a fine homemade soup, then follow with one of the daily specials on the chalkboard menu. Among the favorites are duckling with a Bing cherry sauce, poached salmon with a dijonnais sauce, veal marsala, and a fine rack of lamb. Prices range from $15 to $22. There are also six rooms (four with fireplaces) available in this lovely country-house atmosphere.

Rates: $80–$100 double. **Dining Hours:** Sun–Mon and Wed–Fri 5–9pm, Sat 5–10pm. **Closed:** Nov–Mar.

The **Mill on the Floss,** Rte. 7, New Ashford (tel. 413/458-9123), has country charm and serves some fine, if traditional, French cuisine. The limited menu offers such classics as coq au vin, duck à l'orange, poached salmon hollandaise, and rack of lamb, priced from $18.50 to $26. Start with the escargots with garlic butter or crab cake with a piquant Dijon sauce.

Hours: Tues–Sun 5pm–closing.

The **Springs Restaurant,** Rte. 7, New Ashford (tel. 413/458-3465), between Pittsfield and Williamstown, is a rather typical roadside restaurant. It's not exactly romantic or overly decorated, but the food is good and wholesome, and there's plenty of it. The menu is vast and any main dish (veal Oscar, Boston scrod moutarde, chicken breast rollatini) will be accompanied by a baked clam and relishes, salad, vegetables, and soup. Prices range from $10 to $20.

Hours: Mon–Sat 11:30am–9:30pm, Sun 11:30am–9pm.

MOUNT GREYLOCK

While you're in the Berkshires, climb or drive to the summit of Mount Greylock and then ascend the spiral stairway to the top of the tower. From here you have a 360° vista looking out over 50 miles to the Catskills and over 100 miles to the Adirondacks.

You can even sojourn here at **Bascom Lodge,** P.O. Box 1800, Lanesboro, MA 01237 (tel. 413/1743-1591), built in the 1930s to accommodate hikers. Lodgings are in four bunkrooms sleeping six to eight or in four private rooms (all share corridor baths). A family-style breakfast and dinner ($10) are served daily. Snacks and sandwiches are available from a counter and can be eaten at the refectory tables.

Rates: Aug and Sat year round, bunk room, $35 nonmembers, $28 members; private room, $80 nonmembers, $65 members. At other times, bunk room, $30 nonmembers, $25 members; private room, $70 nonmembers, $60 members. Rates discounted for Appalachian Mountain Club members. **Closed:** Late Oct to mid-May.

NORTH ADAMS & ADAMS

Area Attractions

From Williamstown it's only a short drive to North Adams, gateway town to the Mohawk Trail. The trail leads out to Whitcomb Summit, where you can stop for a breakfast or a meal before traveling on through Florida and Charlemont, all the way to Shelburne Falls and eventually into the Pioneer Valley.

North Adams and Adams, a few miles to the south, were famous in the 19th century as manufacturing towns producing paper, textiles, and leather goods. You may want to stop at some of the **mill outlets** that offer discounted prices on clothing. Adams is also famous for being the birthplace of Susan B. Anthony, whose home at 67 East Rd. is a private residence that's not open to the public.

The Heritage State Park in North Adams gives further insight into the town's history. Two other state parks are accessible from North Adams: Mount Greylock (above) and a much smaller park featuring a natural marble bridge.

At the western gateway to **Heritage State Park,** Furnace Street in North Adams (tel. 413/663-8059), start at the visitor center, where displays relate the story of how the remarkable 4¾-mile, $14-million tunnel was blasted and built through the mountains in 1875. Some 195 men were killed or injured during the 25 years it took to build. It was quite a feat because at that time no one knew how to make sure that the two tunnels from each side of the mountain would meet in the middle. When the final blast was made, the total error in alignment was a mere 9/16 inch! The story is told in movies, displays, and photographs. The tunnel helped fuel the town's growth, and the most fascinating photo exhibits reveal the course of this growth and the community's daily life. In 1898, unlike today, North Adams was a thriving community of 25,000 that supported 500 businesses, including 58 grocery stores, 19 saloons, 17 barbers, 16 shoe stores, 11 cigar factories, 9 blacksmiths, 11 bicycle dealers, 8 hotels, 7 photographers, 5 florists, 5 undertakers, and 2 daily and 3 weekly newspapers. From the displays you'll learn what the average wage was, how much staples cost, and much, much more lively history. Afterward, browse in the many stores—a country bakery, a country gift store, an ice-cream parlor—housed in restored 19th-century structures set around a cobbled courtyard.

Hours: Daily 10am–5pm. **Closed:** New Year's Day, Jan 15–18, Easter, Thanksgiving, Christmas.

Just outside the center of North Adams on Rte. 8 north is a natural phenomenon worth visiting, the **Natural Bridge State Park** (tel. 413/663-6392). Rangers will point out and explain the park's outstanding features. Among these are "glacial erratics," great striated glacial stones; a narrow, deep gorge (50 feet from ceiling to floor) cut at the rate of ¹/₁₆ of an inch per year by the stream; botanically rare species like maidenhair ferns and horsetails; and a marble dam and a marble stack that still stands because the quarry workers needed it to retreat behind after they set their charges. The natural bridge was formed during the last glacial period 13,000 years ago, although technically it's a 550-million-year-old marble formation created from shells that existed in the prehistoric ocean. Over millions of years, sand, silt, and mud were changed into limestone and eventually into marble. From the 1800s to 1940 a marble quarry was operated, until the mill in which the marble was ground to make lime burned down. Yes, it's true. Make sure you go down to the platform that gives the best view of the bridge. Stairways crisscross the huge rocks, making it easy for you. Such steps were not there for the intrepid youths who carved their names on the rocks. See if you can find the Williams College fraternity sign or the signature of J. S. Barnforth, dated 1740. It's said that Nathaniel Hawthorne carved his name, but it's never been found. He did mention the bridge in his *Visitations*.

Hours: Memorial Day–Columbus Day, daily 10am–6pm. On weekends, guided tours and talks approximately every 45 minutes. **Admission:** $2.

North Adams Dining

The **Freight Yard Pub** in Heritage State Park, North Adams (tel. 413/663-6547), is popular for reasonably priced meals. Specials are written on a chalkboard and may include a dinner for two consisting of chicken Cordon Bleu and fried clams or top sirloin and scallops. The regular menu offers fish and chips, sandwiches, and burgers, priced from $6 to $12. The decor is typical modern pub—wood tables, a brick fireplace, a pine bar, and a popcorn machine. On weekends a DJ spins the music.

Hours: Daily 11:30am–1am.

The Berkshires
Special & Recreational Activities

Antiquing: South Egremont is an excellent hunting ground, and so is Rte. 7 around Sheffield and Rte. 7A through Ashley Falls. Other stores are dotted throughout the Berkshires.

Boating: *Lee:* Laurel Lake, on Rte. 20. *Pittsfield:* At Pontoosuc Lake water-sports equipment is available for rent by the hour—motorboats ($12.50 with a 10-hp engine, $21 for 50 hp, and $29 for 75 hp), waterskis ($5), canoes ($7), rowboats ($6), and paddleboats ($7); wave runners rent for $30 per 20 minutes, and sailboats are available. For information, contact U-Drive Boat Rentals, 123 Burke Ave., Pittsfield, MA 01201, or 1551 North St. (Rte. 7), Pontoosuc Lake (tel. 413/442-7020). The Ponterril YMCA, in Pittsfield (tel. 413/499-0647), also has boats for rent at its Pontoosuc Lake facility (open Memorial Day to Sept 1): canoes rent for $8 per hour, Sunfish for $15 per hour, and a sailboat with a mainsail and jib for $20 per hour. Call the marina at 413/499-0694.

Camping: *Lenox area:* Woodland Hills Family Campground, Austerlitz, NY 12017 (tel. 518/392-3557), offers camping convenient to Tanglewood at 160 sites with water, electric, and sewer hookups, plus a full range of facilities. Open May 1 to Columbus Day. It charges $15 to $18.

North Egremont: Try Prospect Lake Park, Prospect Lake Road, North Egremont, MA 01252 (tel. 413/528-4158), only 6 miles from Great Barrington. Ideal for families because of the great number of facilities—boat rentals (Sunfishes, paddleboats, canoes), tennis, lake fishing, and two swimming beaches. Open mid-May to October. From $20.

Pittsfield-Dalton area: Pittsfield State Forest, Cascade Street (tel. 413/442-8992), has 31 sites at various locations through-out the park. In Windsor State Forest, River Road, Windsor (tel. 413/684-9760), there's camping in the scenic Windsor Jambs area.

Canoeing: The Connecticut, Battenkill, Hoosic, and Upper Housatonic rivers provide easy paddling. The more experienced may want to try the Westfield or Deerfield River after a good rain. For information, rentals, and sales, contact Berkshire Outfitters Canoe and Kayak Center, Rte. 8, Cheshire Harbor, Adams, MA 01220 (tel. 413/743-5900); or Riverrun/North, Rte. 7, Sheffield, MA 01257 (tel. 413/528-1100).

Fishing: *Lee:* Laurel Lake, ramp off Rte. 20. *Pittsfield:* Pontoosuc Lake, ramp off Hancock Road near Rte. 7. Onota Lake is known for trophy-size bass and lake trout. *Stockbridge:* Stockbridge Bowl, ramp off Rte. 183.

Golf: *Great Barrington:* Egremont Country Club, Rte. 23 (tel. 413/528-4222), with 18 holes; *Lenox:* Cranwell Golf Course, 55 Lee Rd. (tel. 413/637-0441), with 18 holes, par 71. *Pittsfield:* Pontoosuc Lake Country Club, Ridge Avenue (tel. 413/445-4217), with 18 holes, par 70. *South Lee:* Oak 'n' Spruce Resort (tel. 413/243-3500). *Williamstown:* Taconic Golf Course, Meacham Street (tel. 413/458-3997), with 18 holes, par 71; Waubeeka Golf Links, Rtes. 7 and 43 (tel. 413/458-5869), with 18 holes, par 72.

Hiking: In this area you'll find plenty of mountain terrain. *Lanesboro:* This is the gateway to Mount Greylock. A visitor center is located on Rockwell Road, just off Rte. 7, although the most scenic route up the mountain is probably via Notch Road from North Adams. *Lenox:* The Pleasant Valley Wildlife Sanctuary, off Rte. 7 between Lenox and Pittsfield (tel. 413/637-0320), offers 7 miles of hiking trails. It's owned by the Massachusetts Audubon Society, which also operates a nature museum. *Pittsfield:* Berry Mountain in the Pittsfield State Forest is great for blueberrying, viewing the azalea fields, picnicking, and camping, as well as just plain walking. *South Egremont:* Walk the path to the summit of 2,626-foot Mount Everett for fine views of New York, Massachusetts, Vermont, and Connecticut. Access is from Rte. 23 or 41 via South Egremont or from Rte. 22 via Copake Falls. *Sheffield:* Just south of Sheffield and west of Rte. 7, Bartholomew's Cobble gives prime views of the Housatonic. *Stockbridge:* Hike to the summit of Monument Mountain (1,642 feet), on Rte. 7 between Great Barrington and Stockbridge. *Williamstown:* The Hopkins Memorial Forest, Bulkey Road off Rte. 7, has 25,000 acres on the slopes of the Taconic Mountains, plus miles of trails, including self-guided nature trails. There's a museum also. *Windsor:* Notchview has 15 miles of hiking trails.

For information about the Appalachian Trail, contact Pittsfield State Forest, Cascade Street, Pittsfield, MA 01201 (tel. 413/442-8992).

Horseback Riding: *Lenox:* Under Mountain Farm (tel. 413/637-3365) offers one-hour trail rides with an instructor for $45.

Picnicking: See the Lenox and Stockbridge dining sections for picnic suppliers. Tanglewood is not the only spot for picnicking; other places abound—Berry Mountain (in the Pittsfield State Forest), Mount Everett (reached from Rtes. 23 or 41 via South Egremont), at the bottom of Monument Mountain, or Mount Greylock, and at Windsor Jambs in the Windsor State Forest (tel. 413/684-0948).

Skiing: The Berkshires offers five skiing areas. The tallest and toughest is Berkshire East, P.O. Box S, Charlemont, MA 01339 (tel. 413/339-6617); see "The Pioneer Valley & Mohawk Trail: Special & Recreational Activities," at the end of this chapter. *Great Barrington:* Butternut, Rte. 23, Great Barrington, MA 01230 (tel. 413/528-2000), has a vertical drop of 1,000 feet, 22 trails with dramatic views, one poma and six chair lifts (one quad, one triple, four double) that can accommodate 10,000 skiers per hour, 98% snowmaking capacity, and a base lodge. The terrain is about 20% beginner and advanced and 60% intermediate. Cost is about $40 per day. There's also about 6 miles of cross-country. *Hancock:* Jiminy Peak, Corey Road (off Rte. 7 or 43), Hancock, MA 01237 (tel. 413/738-5500), offers day and night skiing on 26 trails accessed by four chair lifts and one tow. Also, a summer slide. *Hillsdale, N.Y.:* Catamount, Hillsdale, NY 12529 (tel. 518/325-3200 or 413/528-1262), offers fine skiing for beginners, intermediates, and experts on over 24 trails serviced by four double chairs and one J-bar. The steepest trail, dropping 500 feet over a 1,700-foot distance, is the Flipper Dipper. The mountain offers a 1,000-foot vertical drop and 95% snowmaking capacity. There's a modernized base lodge with cafeteria and cocktail lounge and picture windows looking out onto the mountain. Also offers a mountain coaster in summer. *Lenox:* Cross-country skiing in Kennedy Park. *New Ashford:* Brodie Mountain, Rte. 7, New Ashford, MA 01237 (tel. 413/443-4752), has 28 trails approached via four chair lifts and two tows. *Windsor:* Cross-country at Notchview.

State Parks & Forests: *Great Barrington:* East Mountain State Reservation, Rte. 7 (tel. 413/528-2000), for hiking and skiing at Butternut. *Lanesboro:* Mount Greylock State Reservation, Rockwell Road (tel. 413/499-4263 or 4262), for bicycling, camping, fishing, hiking, horseback riding, picnicking, cross-country skiing, and snowmobiling. *Lee:* October Mountain State Forest, Woodland Road (tel. 413/243-1778 or 243-9726), for bicycling, camping, fishing, hiking, horseback riding, cross-country skiing, and snowmobiling. *Monterey:* Beartown State Forest, Blue Hill Road (tel. 413/528-0904), for bicycling, boating, camping, fishing, hiking, horseback riding, picnicking, skiing, snowmobiling, and swimming. *Mount Washington:* Mount Washington State Park and Mount Everett, East Street (tel. 413/528-0330), which also offers BashBish Falls along with 15 wilderness camping sites, hiking, horseback riding, and snowmobiling. *Otis:* Toland State Forest, Rte. 23 (tel. 413/269-6002), for boating, fishing, hiking, horseback riding, cross-country skiing, and snowmobiling. *Pittsfield:* Pittsfield State Forest, Cascade Street (tel. 413/442-8992), for bicycling, boating, camping, fishing, hiking, horseback riding, picnicking, cross-country skiing, snowmobiling, and swimming. *Williamstown:* Taconic Trail State Park (tel. 413/499-4263), for hiking, horseback riding, and cross-country skiing. *Windsor:* Windsor State Forest, River Road (tel. 413/684-9760), for bicycling, camping, fishing, hiking, picnicking, cross-country skiing, swimming, and snowmobiling.

Swimming: *Great Barrington:* The Egremont Country Club (tel. 413/528-4222) has an outdoor pool. *Pittsfield:* Pittsfield State Forest (tel. 413/442-8992) has a beach with lifeguards; Pontoosuc Lake has a free supervised beach. *South Lee:* The Oak 'n' Spruce Resort (tel. 413/243-3500) has outdoor and indoor pools; no children under 16. *Stockbridge:* At the Stockbridge Bowl off West Street. *Williamstown:* Sand Springs, off Rte. 7 near the Vermont line, has a 50- by 70-foot mineral pool with a year-round temperature of 74°. *Windsor:* Windsor Jambs.

Tennis: *Lee:* The Greenock Country Club, West Park Street (tel. 413/243-3323), has two clay courts available. Reservations needed. *North Egremont:* Prospect Lake Park, Prospect Lake,

3 miles west off Rte. 71, has two courts. *Pittsfield:* The Berkshire West Athletic Club, Tamarack Road (tel. 413/499-4600), has eight outdoor and six indoor courts. *South Egremont:* The Egremont Country Club (tel. 413/528-4222) has four courts; the Jug End Resort (tel. 413/528-0434) has five outdoor courts. *South Lee:* The Oak 'n' Spruce Resort (tel. 413/243-3500) has two clay courts. *Williamstown:* Williams College (tel. 413/597-3151) has 12 clay and 12 hard courts.

THE PIONEER VALLEY

The region derives its name from the early settlers who arrived here during the 17th century, lured to what was then a frontier by its physical beauty, fertile soil, and abundant water supply. Extending from the New Hampshire and Vermont borders in the north to the Connecticut border in the south, it's contiguous to the Berkshires on the west and Worcester County and Old Sturbridge Village on the east. The area's major draws are Historic Deerfield and the many attractions in Amherst, Springfield, Holyoke, Northampton, and their surrounding areas.

HISTORIC DEERFIELD

Deerfield Attractions

To escape the harried, trying times of this century there's one place to hide: Deerfield, a village that has managed to retain its 18th-century serenity, grace, and civility, thereby providing a real weekend haven to refresh and restore rushed and troubled 20th-century spirits.

When the Rev. William Bentley of Salem, Mass., rode on horseback into Deerfield in the spring of 1782, he said, "The Street is one measured mile, running North and South. . . . there is a gate at each end of the Street and about 60 houses in the Street in better style, than in any of the Towns I saw." Some 25 of the handsome houses on which Bentley remarked still stand on "The Street" in Deerfield.

When I last visited, it was fall. Golden, red, and orange leaves hung on the trees, squirrels were gathering nuts, and Deerfield boys walked to and fro with a confident (almost swaggering) air, rustling the golden leaves strewn on the ground. Dried corn hung below gleaming brass door knockers, brilliant-orange pumpkins lay in the adjacent fields, and staked

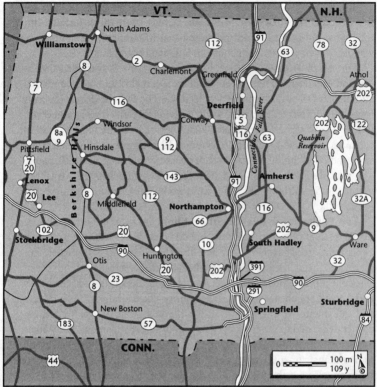

yellow mums and dahlias even stood in front of the gas station on Rte. 5, a sure sign that I was in New England, where beauty, especially flowers, still matters very much in daily life. It was timeless.

But let's return to **"The Street,"** with its rows of lovely 18th-century houses, an inn, and a church. The focal point of the village has remained the **church,** originally the parish of Sam Mather and John Shelburne, the latter killed by French and Indians in 1704. Walk by the church and you can see the rocks bearing memorial plaques in remembrance of the massacre and destruction of this fragile and then westernmost outpost of colonial settlement. The inn, of course, was and is another focal point of the village (I'll discuss it later).

Thirteen museum houses dating from about 1720 to 1850 display more than 20,000 objects made or used in America from 1600 to 1900. These houses have indeed been preserved, but not in an artificial way. They're unadulterated by cute costumed guides spouting canned commentaries. Instead the guides are real, their lives and their roots are right here, and the history they tell us is in their bones, their blood, and their hearts. To see the key houses requires at least one day; a whole weekend would be preferable just to immerse yourself in the 18th-century atmosphere. Head first for the **Hall Tavern Museum,** across from the Deerfield Inn, for maps, information, and an audiovisual introduction. For first-time visitors, the curator recommends the following highlights:

The **Allen House** (1720) is for real collectors. It was the home of Mr. and Mrs. Henry Flynt, founders of the Deerfield Heritage Foundation, and displays their distinguished collections. The **Fabric House** is a must for anyone interested in needlework, weaving, and the history and evolution of fabric design techniques. Examples of work include Marseilles, calamaricco, wood-block-printed fabrics, 19th-century appliquéed quilts, and candlewicking, all of top museum quality. In addition, about 20 mannequins display 17th-, 18th-, and 19th-century costumes of various fabrics, including Spitalfields silk and hand-embroidered and hand-painted French silk.

The **Parker and Russell Silver Shop,** in an adjacent farmhouse, displays silver objects made from melted coins before 1800. A guide will explain the art of silversmithing and how the artisan uses a series of hammers (first metal, then wood and leather) to achieve a really smooth sheen. The collection includes Paul Revere spoons, plus tankards, braziers, bowls, and Apostle spoons by various silversmiths—like Dummer, Coney, Myers, and deLamerie. In the middle of it all, you'll come across a charming corner dedicated to the cross-eyed hero of British democracy, John Wilkes, a passion apparently of Mr. Flynt's. In the workshop you can see all the tools and instruments used to chase silver; the pewter collection and work room are also worth a visit.

The **Wells-Thorn House** is the oldest, having been built in 1717, only 13 years after the massacre, which no doubt explains why the wooden walls were built so thickly with no, or very small, windows, a form of construction that contributes to a distinct barricaded feeling. Here in this house, though, you can almost enjoy a mini-course in furniture and design by stepping from the Colonial through the Federal and Queen Anne periods to the Georgian section of the house, which was added 34 years later. The **Asa Stebbins House** was Deerfield's first brick house. Built in 1799, it's a typical home for a rich farmer who sat in the state legislature, containing some beautiful work by cabinetmaker Daniel Clay, Willard clocks, and a magnificent staircase enhanced by stunning hand-painted French wallpaper.

At **Frary House** (1740) you'll have several interesting things pointed out to you—for example, the tea caddy that has a lock on it (not surprising, when tea was $50 a pound), a straw doll with a face like a death mask (originally made because the daughter had left to live with the Indians), and a demonstration of "Pop Goes the Weasel." This house and the adjacent Barnard Tavern were bought and restored by a fascinating woman, Alice Baker, "to rescue it and provide for mother and for dancing." She restored it in 1892 and annually held a costume ball in the upstairs ballroom with its fiddlers balcony. In the tavern you can see mud shoes for horses as well as clay pipes, which were rented to those who frequented the place. By the way, watch your p's and q's (pints and quarts).

And finally, there's the **Jonathan Ashley House,** which from 1732 to 1780 belonged to the parish minister, who was a stubborn Tory. The parishioners denied him firewood and even locked him out of his pulpit.

Hours for Houses: Mon–Sat 9:30am–4:30pm, Sun 11am–4:30pm. **Admission:** $5 for one house, $10 for a ticket that's good for a week. **Closed:** Major winter holidays. For information call 413/774-5581 or write Historic Deerfield, P.O. Box 321, Deerfield, MA 01342.

The **Memorial Hall Museum** (tel. 413/774-6476) is appropriately named, for the collection displayed constitutes both the Indian and Puritan heritage of the inhabitants of the Pocumtuck Valley. You can see the tomahawk-gashed doors from the Sheldon homestead, an eerie reminder of the 1704 massacre when Deerfield was an isolated frontier outpost. The photographs taken by the Allen sisters, two early glassplate camerawomen who took up photography after they went deaf and could no longer teach, provide a fascinating, sometimes sentimental, sometimes very stylized, record of village life. Here also are displays of Society of Blue and White needlework—part of the turn-of-the-century craft movement—plus locally made furniture, kitchenware, and musical instruments.

Hours: May–Oct, Mon–Fri 10am–4:30pm, Sat–Sun 12:30–4:30pm; Apr and Nov, by appointment. **Admission:** $2.

Deerfield Lodging & Dining

The **Deerfield Inn,** The Street, Deerfield, MA 01342 (tel. 413/774-5587), features a dining room where brass chandeliers and lanterns cast a warm glow over the polished Georgian-style tables and Queen Anne chairs. The dinner menu changes monthly but might feature such dishes as tuna with a Szechuan black-bean butter sauce and pork ribeye with a Kentucky bourbon/peppercorn sauce. Prices range from $17 to $25. There are 23 guest rooms—11 in the main house (1884) and 12 in the south wing, reached by a covered walkway; all are furnished with reproductions and antiques. The common rooms are convivial and furnished with exquisite antiques and fabrics that reproduce patterns culled from the examples in the town's decorative arts collection. Along the main house's halls you may find an elegant writing desk tucked into a little nook or a bookcase filled with books of plays and a variety of classics.

Rates (including breakfast): $135 double. **Dining Hours:** Daily 7:30–9am, noon–2pm, and 6–9pm.

For cheaper accommodations, there's a **Motel 6** at Rtes. 5 and 10, South Deerfield, MA 01373 (tel. 413/665-7161).

Rates: From $38 single; from $44 double.

SPRINGFIELD

If you don't want to spend both weekend days exploring Deerfield, then you have several options. Many visitors choose to drive over to Amherst-Northampton and Springfield or to follow the Mohawk Trail north to Williamstown. Let's begin at the southern end of the valley in Springfield.

Springfield Attractions

Downtown Springfield has been spruced up, and you may want to visit **Court Square** to get a sense of the town's history. The square's original bounds have been extended by a brick plaza. At the corner stands the enormous gray stone crenellated courthouse, complete with a bell tower, designed by H. H. Richardson. Across from it, the Old First Church, established in 1637, is in fact the fourth building on the site, having been erected in 1819 by a Northampton man, Isaac Damon. The copper rooster weathervane crowning the spire was crafted in London and brought to America in 1750. Built of wood, including the columns supporting the classical pediment, it's a splendid piece of architecture, boasting a soaring tower with an outside ambulatory, 12-on-12 windows, and black shutters.

The park in front of the church is pleasantly well kept. The lawns are neatly trimmed, the gazebos decorated with hanging baskets of flowers, and the antebellum fountain and ornamental trees and shrubs attractive. From the benches in the park you can view the campanile, a copy of the one in Venice's piazza San Marco; unfortunately, you can no longer climb to the top. On the same side of the square as the courthouse, take a closer look also at a six-story Renaissance Revival building, the historic Springfield Buyer's block. A series of fluted pillars frame the shopfronts on the ground floor, two sets of verdigrised window treatments are accented with classical decoration, and at one end the building is topped by a copper-based tower punctured by a series of Palladian latticework windows all topped by more glass panes and a witch's cap turret.

Opposite this highly rhythmic building across the park are the impressive Symphony Hall and City Hall. The whole area is a testament to the confident 19th-century mercantile spirit.

Springfield's Museums

These museums are very impressive and very conveniently located together around a tree-shaded quadrangle off Chestnut Street. The entrance is marked by Augustus Saint-Gaudens' statue of *The Puritan*.

The oldest building on the quad, the **George Walter Vincent Smith Art Museum,** 222 State St. (tel. 413/733-4214), is an 1895 Renaissance Revival villa housing the vast collections of its namesake and his wife, Belle Townsley Smith. Avid collectors, the couple acquired an exotic array of Japanese arms and armor, screens, Noh masks, lacquers, textiles, and ceramics. Note the large wheel shrine (late 18th and early 19th century) made of keyaki wood and carved beautifully—each animal or natural element symbolizing an abstract characteristic like power or longevity. The Japan Decorative Arts Gallery displays exquisite objects—netsukes, imari and other porcelains, glistening shun uri lacquer objects, okimono ivory figures, inro, tea ceremony implements, and a fantastic 19th-century hand-carved vase by Kyozo Ishiguro, depicting Buddha and his 500 disciples.

One of the largest collections of cloisonné in the Western world is displayed upstairs. The six processes of production are clearly illustrated and explained, and a variety of objects—vases, incense burners, ewers, bowls, birds, and animals—on view. Most spectacular is an 18th-century covered vessel in the form of a temple drum that's decorated with the flowers of the four seasons—lotus, plum, peony, and chrysanthemum.

The museum's collection of 19th-century American art is quite strong, containing works by Albert Bierstadt, Samuel Colman, George Inness, Frederic Church, and the largest number of paintings by J. G. Brown in a public museum. I particularly enjoyed the watercolors by Alfred Thompson Bricher. Other galleries of note are the Sculpture Hall, housing plaster casts of classical and Renaissance sculptures, and a couple of rooms containing exquisite kilims and rugs from Anatolia and the Caucasus.

Hours: Thurs–Sun noon–4pm. **Admission** (to all four museums): $4 adults, $1 children 6–18.

The **Museum of Fine Arts,** 49 Chestnut St. (tel. 413/732-6092), is itself a fine example of art deco architecture. Inside, the visitor is immediately struck by Erastus Salisbury Field's huge canvas *Historical Monument of the American Republic, 1867,* which dominates the ground-floor gallery. Other American works of note are Winslow Homer's watercolor *New Novel,* Fredric Church's *New England Scenery,* and significant works by Copley, Remington, and Sargent. The upstairs galleries exhibit such notable European artists as Chardin, Boucher, Corot, Eugene Boudin, Courbet, Millet, Rouault, and other impressionists. Among the less-frequently viewed paintings are Gauguin's *Seascape in Britanny* and John Singer Sargent's *Glacier Streams—the Simplon*. The 20th-century gallery displays works by Bellows, Sheeler, O'Keeffe, and Lyonel Feininger. Modern sculptors are also represented—Alexander Calder, Richard Stankiewicz, and George Sugarman. In short, there's much to enjoy here.

Hours: Thurs–Sun noon–4pm. **Closed:** Major holidays. **Admission** (to all four museums): $4 adults, $1 children 6–18.

The **Connecticut Valley Historical Museum,** 194 State St. (tel. 413/732-3080), preserves the history and traditions of the Connecticut River Valley. The artifacts and documents on display tell the story of the region from 1636 to the present. The exhibits provide an overview of Springfield's growth from a town with only 11,300 inhabitants in 1850 to one with 150,000 in 1930 only 80 years later. This rapid growth was fueled by the manufacture of all kinds of products—armaments during the Civil War, beer, soda, carriages, cigars, corsets, saddles, saws, and all other manner of goods. A whole gallery is in fact devoted to Springfield's famous firearms industry. The story of the lives of Springfield's residents is told through photographs, correspondence, objects, advertisements, and portraits done by itinerant artists. The Genealogy and Local History Library contains the Ellis Island passenger records and more than 1.3 million archival documents which attract researchers and family historians from around the country.

Hours: Thurs–Sun noon–4pm. **Admission** (to all four museums): $4 adults, $1 children 6–18.

The **Springfield Science Museum,** 236 State St. (tel. 413/733-1194), contains 10 galleries, a planetarium, an aquarium, and an observatory. Kids will love the dinosaur hall, the Transparent Anatomical Mannekin (a life-size transparent woman that describes her physical systems and how they function), the hands-on exhibits in the Exploration Center, and the programs on the Native Americans, Africa, etc.

Hours: Thurs–Sun noon–4pm. Planetarium programs given Sat–Sun; observatory open one evening per month. Call for exact times. **Admission** (to all four museums): $4 adults, $1 children 6–18.

Springfield's Other Attractions

Springfield was the home of the first American-made automobile— Thomas Blanchard's steam carriage. The city is also credited with the invention of the first gasoline pump and the production of everything from jewelry to paint, from shoes to the famous Springfield rifle. The city still possesses a number of **factory outlets and mill stores** stocking everything from fabrics and fashions to batteries and paper goods.

At the **Springfield Armory,** 1 Armory Sq. (tel. 413/734-8551), a large museum housed in the original 1850 Main Arsenal, many examples of the kind of weaponry manufactured here from 1794 to 1968 are on display. Enter either from Federal Street or from the junction of Byer and State streets.

Hours: Summer, daily 10am–5pm; winter, Tues–Sun 10am–5pm. **Closed:** Major winter holidays. **Admission:** Free.

The **Basketball Hall of Fame,** 1150 W. Columbus Ave., off I-91 (tel. 413/781-6500), is a fitting attraction since the game was invented in 1891 by Dr. James Naismith at Springfield College. It includes action films and exhibits on great teams and players.

Hours: Sept–June, daily 9am–5pm; summer, daily 9am–6pm. **Admission:** $8 adults, $5 seniors and children 7–15.

Stagewest, One Columbus Center (tel. 413/781-2340), features plays and musicals from September to May.

Springfield Lodging & Dining

At the **Holiday Inn,** 711 Dwight St., Springfield, MA 01104 (tel. 413/781-0900), the rooms are spacious and well equipped, each with a VCR, a TV tucked into a cabinet, a desk, a couch, and a full-length mirror. There's an Italian restaurant on the 12th floor, plus an indoor pool and a fitness room.

Rates: $90 double.

A traditional favorite, the **Student Prince and Fort,** Fort Street off Main (tel. 413/734-7475), ladles out hearty German fare and 1-liter "boots" of beer from its bar festooned with an incredible collection of steins. In my opinion, dining in the bar area is the most fun, tucked away on high-backed settles. There's also a dining room that's warmed in winter by a fire in its large brick hearth. The menu is extensive—jaegerschnitzel (and several other schnitzels) with noodles, sauerbraten with potato dumplings and spiced red cabbage, zwiebelfleisch (an onion-gravy pot roast), broiled scrod, bratwurst with sauerkraut and potatoes, and filet mignon Rossini. Prices run $9 to $17. *Ein prositt* to this fine local spot.

Hours: Mon–Sat 11am–11pm, Sun noon–10pm.

HOLYOKE

Area Attractions

The prime attraction of this industrial town is the **Holyoke Heritage State Park,** 221 Appleton St. (tel. 413/534-1723 for information), 8 acres of parkland bordering one of the canals. The park, which celebrates the city's role as one of the first planned industrial centers in the nation, overlooks old brick mills once used for the manufacture of paper and thread. The visitor center displays exhibits depicting the history of its industrial development and the lives of its early residents. An antique rail car takes people on a 20-mile round-trip to Westfield. There's also a children's hands-on museum and an antique carousel. To get here, take Exit 4 from I-90 onto I-91 north. From I-91, take Exit 17A and continue straight to the fork, where you bear right, continuing through three sets of traffic lights. The park is 100 yards on the left.

Hours: Tues–Wed and Fri–Sun 9am–4:30pm, Thurs 9am–9pm. **Admission:** Free.

Further insights can be gained at the **Wistariahurst Museum,** 238 Cabot St. (tel. 413/534-2216), once the home of industrialist William Skinner, who founded the Skinner Silk Mills. Classical period furniture and decorative arts reveal the lifestyle of an early industrial magnate.

Hours: Wed and Sat–Sun 1–5pm.

In the area but near the city, **Mount Tom** offers skiing in winter and an alpine and water slide in summer.

Holyoke Lodging & Dining

Even though the **Yankee Pedlar,** 1866 Northampton St., Holyoke, MA 01040 (tel. 413/532-9494), is at the junction of well-traveled Rtes. 55 and 202, the old clapboard buildings, the country rooms, and the garden and gazebo in back create a country atmosphere. In the evening it's a lively place: The bar is in full swing to the rhythm of the piano player, the popcorn machine fills the bar with a good nutty aroma, and the dining rooms are crowded.

The 47 guest rooms are located in five buildings. Some are in the main inn, but many are in clapboard buildings across the tarmac. All are comfortable and contain a TV, a phone, air-conditioning, and an alarm clock. Rooms in the 1850 House have four-posters minus canopies, Marseilles bedspreads, bold floral curtains and equally striking stenciling, a clubfoot desk, and a comb-back Windsor chair, all set on ruby-red carpeting. The fanciest rooms are in the Captain Holyoke House and the Carriage House, where the four-posters sport straight chintz canopies or fish-net canopies. Carriage House rooms have the added impact of a cathedral ceiling and chandelier. Either a continental or a full breakfast is served in the bar for an extra charge.

In the post-and-beam tavern dining room the fare combines typical New England items with more inventive American and Italian dishes. Served by waitresses in colonial costume, relishes—bean, beet, and cottage cheese—begin the meal. As an appetizer, try the prosciutto-wrapped shrimp cocktail dressed in a scallion/lemon/pepper vinaigrette or wild-mushroom ravioli in a port-wine reduction with roasted red peppers and fresh sage. Among the specialties are Boston bay seafood navarine, a hearty combination of shrimp, scallops, clams, mussels, and lobster simmered with vegetables and potatoes in a rich seafood navarine sauce; prime rib; and Italian dishes like veal sautéed with roasted peppers, capers, and fresh orange served in a beurre blanc flavored with lemon and white wine. At night the wood tables and low light from the Shaker sconces and modified oil lamps give the room a warm romantic glow.

In the Herb Garden restaurant a different atmosphere prevails—pots of rosemary, dill, and tarragon grace the tables and wrought-iron shell-motif chairs face the tables set with Port Meirion. Afternoon tea and dinner are served here under the glass dome at tables set with green placemats and pink napkins.

Rates: $70–$100 double. **Dining Hours:** Mon–Sat 11:30am–2pm and 5–9pm, Sun noon–9pm.

At the **Holyoke Super 8,** Rte. 5, Holyoke, MA 01040 (tel. 413/536-1980), there are comfortable, fully equipped motel-style rooms.

Rates: $60 double.

NORTHAMPTON

Area Attractions

From Holyoke it's a short drive up I-91 to Northampton. En route you may want to stop off at South Hadley to visit **Mount Holyoke College,** the nation's oldest women's college, founded in 1837. The campus, designed by Frederick Law Olmsted (of Central Park fame), is as might be expected most picturesque, landscaped with brooks and Dutch-style and Victorian buildings. The college's museum is strong in Oriental art. For a campus tour call 413/538-2023.

Northampton is an attractive town with some fine architectural stock. At one end of the main street stands **Smith College,** the largest women's college in the country, founded in 1871 and built in a largely Gothic Revival and romanesque style.

The college's **art museum** (tel. 413/585-2770) is internationally recognized for its outstanding holdings in 19th- and early 20th-century art. The basis of the permanent collection is 19th-century French paintings, including Courbet's *Preparation of Dead Girl,* wrongly identified previously (and somewhat ironically) as *Preparation of the Bride;* Degas' *The Daughter of Jephthah;* three lyrical canvases by Monet; and paintings by Renoir, Cézanne, Gauguin, Vuillard, Sisley, and Boudin. America is represented by Hudson River School landscapes, folk art, and paintings by such major artists as Bierstadt, Inness, Homer, Sargent, and Whistler. Thomas Eakin's late masterpiece *Portrait of Edith Mahon* and the *Mourning Picture* by regional artist Edwin Romanzo Elmer are signature works from the period. Visitors exploring this area for the first time will also want to see *View of the Connecticut River from Mount Holyoke* (1840). The 20th-century American holdings range from Charles Sheeler's *Rolling Power* to Frank Stella's 40-foot canvas *Damascus Gate (Variation III)* and recent work by Smith alumna Sandy Skoglund. Scultures by Barye Rodin, Arp, Giacometti, Calder, and others complement the painting collection. The sculpture court is particularly serene.

Hours: July–Aug, Tues–Sun noon–4pm; Sept–June, Tues and Fri–Sat 9:30am–4pm, Wed and Sun noon–4pm, Thurs noon–8pm. **Closed:** Major holidays.

The college's **Botanic Garden** includes a campus-wide arboretum and the greenhouses of the Lyman Plant House. These 12 greenhouses display major botanical collections arranged according to climatic zones—Palm House, Temperate House, Succulent House, and so on. The Spring Bulb Show opens the first weekend in March and the Chrysanthemum Show the first weekend in November. Other gardens around the campus include the Capen Garden with its rose arches, the wildflower garden, a Japanese garden, and the Rock Garden.

Hours: Daily 8am–4:15pm.

Northampton Lodging

The **Hotel Northampton,** 36 King St., Northampton, MA 01060 (tel. 413/584-3100), is a 1927 Georgian Revival building. In the entranceway, display cases are filled with old wooden dolls and other antique collectibles, while the lobby, with its square chestnut columns, is large. Each of the 85 rooms (with bath, color TV, phone, and air-conditioning) is adequately furnished with wall-to-wall beige carpeting,

Wedgwood-blue walls, a bed, a reproduction Chippendale desk, and a couple of armchairs. Suites feature Jacuzzis. Because of the hotel's age, the closets have good wood doors. Besides Wiggins Tavern (see "Northampton Dining," below), there's a bar with an outdoor brick patio for summer cocktails.

Rates: $80–$155 double; from $220 suite.

The **Autumn Inn,** 259 Elm St., Northampton, MA 01060 (tel. 413/584-7660), has comfortable motel units set around a pool.

Rates: $96 double.

Northampton Dining

Seafood lovers will want to try the **North Star,** at the corner of Green and West streets (tel. 413/586-9409). In the modern high-ceilinged bar dining area or in the main dining room attractively filled with tables spread with royal-blue cloths, cane-seated Breuers, and tall ficus, you can obtain an assortment of fresh fish. For example, there's swordfish au poivre (with shallots, black pepper, brandy, red wine, and cream) and baked salmon with sweet-and-sour roasted-pepper glaze. Good meat dishes are also available, like the duck with raspberry/green-peppercorn sauce or loin of lamb with roasted garlic and mint-apple chutney. Prices range from $11 to $18. The courtyard in back is an ideal summer dining spot.

Hours: Tues–Sun 5–10pm.

At **Panda's Garden,** 34 Pleasant St. (tel. 413/584-3858), the decor is plain but the Szechuan, Mandarin, Cantonese, and Hunan cuisine is well recommended by the locals. Try the orange beef or the shrimp with walnuts. Prices run $6 to $12.

Hours: Mon–Thurs 11:30am–9:30pm, Fri–Sat 11:30am–11pm, Sun 2–9:30pm.

The **Wiggins Tavern,** 36 King St. (tel. 413/584-3100), in the Hotel Northampton, is wonderfully atmospheric. It's not a tavern—it's two post-and-beam dining rooms, with fireplaces. At night it glows golden, lit by oil-style lamps. The trestle-style wood tables are set with pewter platters and napkin rings while the room is decorated (but not overly so) with farm implements, candles hanging from the beams, and ceramics in corner cupboards. The menu offers traditional favorites like the Yankee pot roast and chicken pot pie, several steaks, and some more interesting seafood selection like grilled swordfish with kiwi-apple butter and pan-seared salmon with pecan/honey/mustard sauce. Prices run $13 to $25.

Hours: Wed-Sat 5:30–10pm, Sun 9:30am–1:30pm (brunch) and 4:30–9pm.

The **East Side Grill,** 19 Strong Ave. (tel. 413/586-3347), receives strong local recommendations. From the bar, which also serves as a raw bar, steps lead into the modern oak-and-brass dining room where food with a Cajun inspiration is served. For example, there's chicken Créole, barbecued shrimp, pasta jambalaya (shrimp, scallops, and broccoli in Créole sauce over pasta made with spinach, tomato, and egg), blackened prime rib and fish, plus steaks and a Cajun burger. The appetizers reflect the same style—gumbos, barbecued shrimp or shrimp rémoulade, and Louisiana fried oysters. Key lime pie, mud pie, and pecan pie are among the desserts. At lunch it's soup, salad, sandwiches, and several items mentioned above.

Hours: Mon–Thurs 11:30am–3pm and 5–10pm, Fri–Sat 11:30am–3pm and 5–11pm, Sun 5–10pm.

For a budget lunch or dinner, **Pinocchio's,** 122 Main St. (tel. 413/586-8275), offers pizzas, lasagne, eggplant parmigiana, soups, subs, and meat-and-spinach calzone. The atmosphere is pleasant—exposed brick, bentwood chairs, and old Italian prints. The serving counter is in back.

Hours: Mon–Thurs 11am–midnight, Fri–Sat 11am–2am, Sun 3–10:30pm.

South Hadley Dining

Across from the Mount Holyoke campus in the village of South Hadley, **Woodbridge's,** 3 Hadley St. (tel. 413/536-7341), is a good place to stop for lunch or dinner for such items as chicken or steak teriyaki, baked stuffed shrimp, and London broil, as well as burgers and sandwiches. Prices run $5 to $13. The cathedral-ceilinged room is decorated with a few country items like decoys and the wood tables are set with green gingham napkins. In summer, sit out on the pretty brick terrace under yellow-and-white umbrellas at tables set under the maple tree.

Hours: Mon–Thurs 11am–5pm and 5–10pm, Fri–Sat 11am–5pm and 5–11pm, Sun 11am–3pm (brunch) and 5–10pm.

AMHERST

Amherst Attractions

Among the attractions here are all those associated with old college towns and fine campuses, plus the **Emily Dickinson Homestead** at 280 Main St. (tel. 413/542-8161), where she lived for all but 15 years of her life and where she wrote close to 2,000 poems—only 7 of which were published while she was alive. Her grandfather Samuel was a founder and benefactor of Amherst College, but his generosity led him into financial difficulties and so his son Edward and his wife moved into the western half of the house with their son, Austin. Here on December 10, 1830, Emily was born. Although it's primarily an Amherst College faculty residence, the rooms and halls open to the public do contain many Dickinson possessions, including several portraits. Her grave can be visited in the West Cemetery on Triangle Street.

Hours: May–Sept, Wed–Sat with tours (mandatory) at 1:30, 2:15, 3, and 3:45pm; reservations necessary. The rest of the year, by appointment. **Admission:** $3.

Amherst College (1821) occupies the area beside the town Green (which is home to a farmer's market on Saturday mornings through summer). The college is worth exploring for its architecture and the American paintings and decorative arts in the **Mead Art Museum** (tel. 413/542-2335), an impressive small museum.

Hours: During academic year, Mon–Fri 10am–4:30pm, Sat–Sun 1–5pm; summer, Tues–Fri 1–4pm. Campus tours led by student guides are given usually on weekdays when school is in session. For information, call the public affairs office at 413/542-2321.

Compared to Amherst's intimate groves of academe, the **University of Massachusetts** is vast and largely a collection of high-rises. From the top of one, the Campus Center, you'll be rewarded with a view of the valley. The Fine Arts Building has a strange, haunting, futuristic effect: great slabs of concrete and huge triangular supports dwarf the individual, creating an awesome landscape. (It reminds me of the ancient observatory in Jaipur, India.) Go over to the art gallery just to view the huge timberlike object caught in time and space by a sculptor as it seems to glide down the concrete steps. The university's art gallery also has a good collection of 20th-century American drawings, photographs, and prints. For information on tours, which are usually given daily at 11am and 1:15pm (weekdays only in summer), head for the information desk in the Campus Center, at the east end of the second-floor concourse (tel. 413/545-4237).

Amherst Lodging & Dining

Amherst's prime dining and lodging place is the **Lord Jeffery Inn,** 30 Boltwood Ave., Amherst, MA 01002 (tel. 413/253-2576), named after the town's hero of the French and Indian Wars, Lord Jeffery Amherst; it's located in a handsome Georgian brick building facing the Common. Chestnuts, pine, and other shade trees give it a bucolic appearance, and so do the lawn and the begonias, petunias, and other flowers that bloom on the grounds. The 50 guest rooms are individually furnished with locally crafted furniture and feature a phone, air conditioning, and a TV. Some have working fireplaces; others have balconies looking down onto the garden courtyard. The sitting room has a walk-in fireplace and comfortable seating arrangements. The dining room offers formal dining in a colonial atmosphere created by the Windsor-style chairs and brass chandeliers. Dinner entrees ($14 to $20) might range from vegetarian pasta to veal au poivre, from grilled swordfish with orange, lime, and lemon butter to duck breast served with blackberry coulis and pâté on a croûton. Boltwood's Tavern features traditional sandwiches and flatbreads spread with such combinations as clam, garlic, bacon, diced pepper, and goat cheese.

Rates: $83–$118 double; from $125 suite. **Dining Hours:** Mon–Sat 11:30am–1:30pm and 5–9pm, Sun 11:30am–2pm and 5–9pm. Tavern stays open later Fri–Sat.

Other Amherst accommodations include the **University Motor Lodge,** 345 N. Pleasant St., Amherst, MA 01002 (tel. 413/256-8111), a motel designed in neo-Colonial style.

Rates: $95 double weekends, $55 double weekdays.

Or you might like the **Campus Center Hotel,** at the University of Massachusetts (tel. 413/549-6000), where you can secure modern air-conditioned accommodations with grand panoramic views. Extra amenities include four parlors with kitchen facilities, five dining choices in the complex, and health club on the campus.

Rates: $85 double.

A cafelike atmosphere prevails at **Judie's,** 51 N. Pleasant St. (tel. 413/253-3491). Dine on everything from lobster salad and seafood bisque to paella and southwest sirloin (with bacon, provolone, and cilantro pesto sauce), from stuffed popovers and sandwiches to pasta dishes. Prices range from $7 to $15. The greenhouse-style dining room is enhanced by hand-painted impressionist tables and copies of famous paintings by Matisse, Degas, and Manet. The desserts are renowned.

Hours: Sun–Thurs 11:30am–10pm, Fri–Sat until 11pm.

After Dark in the Area

Evening entertainment is centered on the campuses, where varied performances—ballet, jazz, classical music—are given. Call the universities for information. Also check the *Valley Advocate*, a free paper, for event listings.

For a coffeehouse charged with youthful debate and aspiration, head for the **Iron Horse,** 20 Center St. in Northampton (tel. 413/584-0610), which offers 52 beers and a full schedule of evening entertainment, from the best local talent to nationally known folk, jazz, and blues artists. Purchase tickets for the concert at the Northampton Box Office.

TO NORTHFIELD

While you're in the Pioneer Valley, you may want to take a rustic drive up Rte. 63 from North Amherst, making a few stops along the way. For example, you can turn off to **Lake Wyola Park,** in Shutesbury (tel. 413/367-2627), and go for a swim or a picnic.

Hours: Mid-Apr to Labor Day. **Admission:** $5 adults, $2.50 children.

In Northfield, on the broad street lined with gracious homes that cuts through town you'll find **The Country Store** and **Northfielder Antiques and Gifts,** both browsing stops.

The **Northfield Mountain Recreation and Environmental Center,** 99 Millers Falls Rd. (tel. 413/659-3714), offers a whole range of environmental and recreational programs and weekend workshops—bird and animal watching, nature photography, night experience, organized hikes, orienteering, and so on—lasting a few hours or a whole day. This is also prime cross-country skiing territory. For a recorded snow report call 413/659-3713. Other available activities are picnicking, camping, canoeing, and nature walking at Barton Cove (for reservations, call 413/659-3714 in preseason, 413/863-9300 during camping season). An interpretive river cruise is given aboard the *Quinnetukut II* lasting 1½ hours (for reservations, call the Recreation and Environmental Center at the above number). Summer only.

Northfield Lodging & Area Dining

Northfield Country House, School Street (R.R. 1, Box 79A), Northfield, MA 01360 (tel. 413/498-2692), is a lovely quiet retreat on 16 acres. Innkeeper Andrea Dale, a longtime director of credit for Saks, had stayed here and so fell in love with the place that she was moved to say to the owners, "If you ever want to sell, keep me in mind." They did, and now Andrea is the proud owner of this handsome 1901 home built by a wealthy Boston shipbuilder as a weekend residence for use when he attended the revivalist meetings led by the Reverend Moody in Northfield. The rooms are large and luxuriously comfortable. The living room's focal point is a large stone fireplace with a mantel supporting two bronze stag candlesticks. Beams and an Oriental rug make it cozy; two couches and plush wing chairs provide ample and restful seating; musically inclined guests may play the grand piano that stands in the bay window. A full breakfast of eggs, juice, fruit, and homemade muffins is served in the intricately carved cherry-paneled dining room.

The seven guest rooms (sharing four baths) are individually decorated, three with working fireplaces. My favorites are Rooms 5 and 6. The latter is large, has a fireplace, and comes lavishly furnished with an Oriental carpet, an iron-and-brass bed sporting frilly linens, a chest of drawers supporting an ormolu mirror, a blanket chest, and a cozy loveseat; chintz wallpaper and a dried-flower wreath complete the country look. Room 5 contains several wicker pieces set against a dark-blue floral wallpaper and has the added charm of a small Palladian-style window. There are two large decks, with sturdy stone pillars, on which you can relax in cane-seated rockers. An outdoor pool completes the facilities. In winter, excellent cross-country skiing is right there at the Northfield Recreation Area; in spring, magnolia and cherry trees blossom in the backyard.

Rates: $60–$100 double (highest price for room with fireplace).

One reason for going to the **Andiamo Restaurant,** Huckle Hill, off Rte. 10 in Bernardston (tel. 413/648-9107), is the view from the top of the mountain out over the Pioneer Valley and the Connecticut River to the Berkshires. The large terrace is designed to take advantage of this vista. The menu offers a full range of Italian cuisine, with pastas like linguine with clams, eggplant parmigiana, veal marsala or piccata, and chicken saltimbocca—all the traditional fun favorites. Prices range from $14 to $18.

Hours: Daily 5pm–closing.

ALONG THE MOHAWK TRAIL

From Bernardston it's a short run down I-91 to Greenfield, where you can pick up Rte. 2, also known as the Mohawk Trail. On this route you'll be following an old footpath, known to the Native Americans, which was opened as the New Mohawk Trail in 1914, making the area of mountains, forest, and streams more accessible.

The first stop of any interest is at **Shelburne Falls,** where you can marvel at the glacial potholes in the riverbed, some as wide as 39 feet, and view the old trolley-track bridge that's now abloom with all kinds of flowers. Incidentally, Linus Yale of lock fame was born here. Browse the country stores while you're here.

Then your drive will take you through awesome scenery, with mountains and forests rising on either side, past the 900-pound bronze *Hail to the Sunrise* memorial to the Mohawk Indians, taking you from summit to summit around hairpin curves first to Charlemont, then to Florida, and then to **Whitcomb Summit,** the trail's highest point, where there's a place for you to stop and dine. From here, it's a short run into **North Adams,** and from there only a short trip past brooding **Mount Greylock** (at 3,491 feet, the highest point in Massachusetts) into Williamstown. For further details on the last two towns, see the earlier Berkshires section.

STURBRIDGE

Sturbridge Attractions

From Springfield it's only a short drive to Old Sturbridge Village (people even stay in Sturbridge and attend Tanglewood from there).

At **Old Sturbridge Village,** Sturbridge (tel. 508/347-3362), authentically dressed "interpreters" perform the tasks of life in this re-creation of an early 19th-century American village consisting of 40 buildings located on 200 acres. Farmers haul logs with a team of oxen and fashion split-rail fencing, women cook open-hearth style, and many of the old crafts—from blacksmithing and tinsmithing to spinning, weaving, printing, and shoemaking—are practiced and explained.

Hours: Apr–Nov, daily 9am–5pm; Dec–Mar, Tues–Sun 10am–4pm. **Closed:** New Year's Day and Christmas. **Admission:** $15 adults, $13.50 seniors, $7.50 children 6–15.

En route to Sturbridge from the Springfield area on Rte. 20, you'll pass through **Brimfield,** famous for its bustling flea markets held in early May, mid-July, and mid-September. If you're visiting then, make sure you have reservations in Sturbridge or elsewhere. For information, call 413/245-7479.

Sturbridge Lodging & Dining

The Sturbridge favorite, the **Publick House on the Common,** Rte. 131 (P.O. Box 187), Sturbridge, MA 01566 (tel. 508/347-3313), is a large, tremendously popular complex of four lodgings and three restaurants that manages to retain a degree of country atmosphere (60 acres helps) despite the crowds, the huge jam-packed parking lot, and the general "busyness."

On weekends the dining room overflows with people. Be prepared to wait—you'll be lucky if you can find a seat on one of the loveseats, Windsor chairs, or wing chairs in the downstairs bar, decked out with pewter plates and brass candlesticks. A musical duo (flautist and pianist the night I visited) will entertain. The upstairs dining rooms are large and faux colonial, but the typical traditional food—prime rib, stuffed chicken breast, swordfish in lime butter, lamb chops, and roast turkey (Sunday only)—is quite good and there's plenty of it. A bread basket filled with cinnamon buns and other rolls will begin the meal. Entrees are priced from $16 to $23.

The accommodations vary. On top of the hill behind the original inn, the Country Motor Lodge is a two-story motel-style block in which the management has tried to add character to what are essentially modern motel rooms (with TV, phone, and overhead fan) by adding beams, chintz wallpaper, wing chairs, and reproductions of Early American "primitive" portraits. Rooms also have balconies overlooking an orchard of apple trees, which provides a sense of being in the country. The inn rooms are decorated in country chintz and furnished with antique reproductions, some with canopied four-posters. Similarly furnished suites are found in the Chamberlain House. The prime accommodations are at the Colonel Ebenezer Craft Inn, about which I'll say more more later. At the main inn you'll also find a tennis court, an outdoor pool, bicycles for rent, and a children's play area to keep everyone entertained.

In winter the Yankee Winter Weekend package provides, among other items, a glass of syllabub (a blended mixture of chablis and cream), roasted chestnuts, hot mulled cider, a Yankee buffet along with tavern entertainments, sing-alongs, and sleigh rides. Breakfast brings cornmeal mush, sausages, and (oddly enough) deep-dish apple pie. Dinner consists of wild boar with Cumberland sauce, roast venison, and other game.

Rates: In Publick House or adjacent Chamberlain House, $60–$125 double; $125–$170 suite.

The choice accommodations in Sturbridge are found at the **Colonel Ebenezer Craft Inn** (affiliated with the Publick House but about 1⅓ miles from it), a 200-year-old residence on Fiske Hill. Here you'll find eight rooms—six in the main house and two in the cottage adjacent—all with bath and/or shower and air conditioning. Apples and cookies are placed in the rooms, and a basket of amenities in the bath. All are taste-fully decorated in country style. Rooms 2 and 6 have canopied beds; Room 5 is a twin, decorated in sage green and containing, among other furnishings, a desk and wrought-iron floor lamp. The small suite, Room 4, is ideal for a family and brightly decorated in sunshine yellow and chintz. The cottage suite has a separate bedroom and sitting room.

For guests' pleasure there's a sun room off the comfortable antique-filled sitting room. Music lovers and performers can enjoy the grand piano. In the back the fenced-in pool is prettily landscaped. A continental breakfast of homemade muffins is served from 8 to 10am.

Rates (including breakfast): $75–$160 double. For reservations, call the Publick House (above).

Sturbridge Area Lodging

The **Wildwood Inn,** 121 Church St., Ware, MA 01082 (tel. 413/967-7798), is full of wonderful surprises. Though it's on a residential street, it has 2 acres of grounds that extend back into the woods through which guests can walk to reach Grenville Park, with tennis courts and a swim-ming hole, or the Ware River, on which they can paddle the Wildwood's canoe. Inside the 1880 house the rooms are imaginatively furnished. All kinds of interesting pieces fill the parlor—an old carpenter's chest now used to store board and other games, several cradles (including one filled with books), a spinning wheel, and a shoemaker's bench that serves as a coffee table. Comfy chairs, rugs, and a fireplace make it homelike, and so do the many books about the region and about antiques that sit in the bookcases.

There are nine attractively furnished guest rooms, seven with bath. Electric blankets or down comforters and country quilts are found on all the beds. In the cranberry afghan room an old wringer/washing machine serves as a luggage rack and a saddle vise as a night table. The flower-garden quilt room's bed sports a quilt and pretty eyelet linen. Here an old school desk affords postcard-writing space. The patchwork quilt room room has an old wicker cradle with a fish-net hood among its furnishings. Baskets of herbs and dried flowers and rural pictures add to the Early American country look of all the rooms.

Fraidell Fenster supplies a breakfast of homemade breads (popovers, muffins) served with homemade fruit butters, juice, tea, and coffee, plus one country entree, like maple-cheese squares, bread pudding, or chipmunk pie (a type of apple pie using a particular blend of spices). In summer, if you really want to relax, climb into the hammock or swing on the porch. Behind the house are two garden areas: The first, secluded by fir trees, makes an excellent cookout spot, while the second, a large open spread of grass, is great for star-gazing.

Rates: Nov–Apr, $55–$75 double. May–Sept, $60–$80 double. Holiday weekends, College Parents' Day, and foliage season (late Sept to late Oct), $65–$85 double.

IN CONNECTICUT'S NORTHEASTERN CORNER

Area Attractions

Here just southeast of Sturbridge there's real country—fields and trees and winding backroads where you'll pass farms and barns and quiet somnolent villages. It's an unspoiled area—one of the few last retreats. This is the prime reason to visit the area, although architecture buffs and those with a historical bent will enjoy visiting **Roseland Cottage** (or the Bowen House) in Woodstock, Conn. (tel. 860/928-4074). The classic Gothic Revival cottage has a bright-pink exterior. It was designed by English-born architect Joseph Collins Wells for Henry C. Bowen, a Woodstock boy who had gone to New York City and amassed some wealth. The cottage is the central building in a complex of structures, including a barn (with one of the earliest surviving interior bowling alleys), an icehouse, and an aviary. The ornamental woodwork shaped variously into pointed arches, trefoil, quatrefoil, and other motifs is accented by brilliant stained-glass windows. The interiors were refurbished in the 1880s when the earlier gothic decoration on the first floor was updated with what was then a newly introduced product, Lincrusta Walton, a composition wallcovering heavily embossed to resemble richly tooled leather. The furnishings date from 1840 to 1880 and belonged to the Bowen family.

Henry Bowen enjoyed quite a full life. After securing a fortune in the dry-goods business he lost it in the late 1850s and went bankrupt in 1861. Thereafter, he directed his energies to *The Independent,* a Congregationalist weekly that supported abolition and the Republican party. Here at Roseland, Bowen entertained prominent literary and political figures, including President Ulysses S. Grant in 1870, on which occasion Henry Ward Beecher was the principal orator. The cottage exists today as an important document of mid-19th-century life.

Hours: Memorial Day to mid-Sept, Wed–Sun noon–5pm; mid-Sept to mid-Oct, Fri–Sun noon–5pm. **Admission:** $4 adults, $3.50 seniors, $2 children 5–12.

Nearby **Putnam** is an antique lover's haven.

Area Lodging

The **Inn at Woodstock Hill,** 94 Plaine Hill Rd. (P.O. Box 98), South Woodstock, CT 06267-0098 (tel. 860/928-0528), stands on 14 acres surrounded by tree-edged meadows and wooded hills. The large white house with a pitched roof and dormer windows shelters 22 rooms and suites, each decorated differently using chintz fabrics and country furnishings. Some rooms have four-poster canopied beds; others have typical modern beds. All are extra-spacious, and have a bath, a TV, a phone, and air-conditioning; some have fireplaces. There's a dining room also.

Rates (including breakfast): May–Oct, $85–$160 double; Nov–Apr, $75–$150 double.

The **Samuel Watson House,** 374 Thompson Rd., Thompson, CT 06277 (tel. 860/923-2491), built in 1767, has retained much of its original character. Joann and Bob Godfrey have opened their wonderful home to guests, providing four rooms (one with bath) with a mix of furnishings— a queen with a fireplace, a twin with a TV, a double, and a single. A full breakfast is served in the dining room or more cozily in the country kitchen complete with fireplace.

Rates (including breakfast): $60–$75 double.

Area Dining

In this quiet corner of Connecticut there's a truly beautiful place that shouldn't be missed: the **Golden Lamb Buttery,** Hillandale Farm, Bush Hill Road, off Rte. 169 in Brooklyn (tel. 860/774-4423), created by Robert Booth and his wife, Virginia (Jimmie)—peaceful, serene, rejuvenating, blissful. From the refurbished red barn you have a view of a pond across meadows bordered by stone walls and hedgerows and dotted with sheep and horses.

The whole experience begins with cocktails, either on the porch or aboard a hay wagon that winds through the fields, usually to the sweet accompaniment of a folk singer. After this romantic beginning you return to the cozy country-style dining rooms, where the beams are hung with baskets and herbs and fresh flowers grace the candlelit trestle tables. There's no menu: The waitresses simply announce the four or so entrees, all beautifully and artistically presented thanks to the talents of Jimmie, who discovered this lovely corner of the world while she was scouring the country as a buyer for Lord & Taylor. Obviously the choices vary, but you might start with a broccoli bisque, follow with chateaubriand with béarnaise sauce or duckling with orange sauce, and finish with strawberry rhubarb pie, cheesecake, or chocolate crêpes. In summer, the soup might be peach-strawberry or cold cucumber. The vegetables accompanying these dishes are remarkable and will often be as many as eight, brought to the table in heaping bowls—herbed marinated mushrooms, peas tossed with mint, carrot slivers in a white-grape sauce, and quite often one or two raw specimens. In December a special Elizabethan dinner featuring roast pork is served to the accompaniment of madrigal singers. Dinners cost $60 per person.

Hours: Fri–Sat at 7pm. **Open:** Mid-May or thereabouts to New Year's Eve. Reservations are essential, preferably at least six weeks in advance.

The Pioneer Valley & the Mohawk Trail
Special & Recreational Activities

Bicycling: For rentals, repairs, and touring information, contact Peloton Sports in Northampton (tel. 413/584-1016), which charges $17 per day for a bike.

Boating: Canoes can be rented at the Northfield Mountain Recreation Area, Rte. 63 (R.R. 1, Box 377), Northfield, MA 01360 (tel. 413/659-3713). Also contact them for information about one-hour cruises on the Connecticut River.

Camping: The areas along the Mohawk Trail provide dramatic wilderness camping. The Mohawk Trail State Forest Camping Area, in Charlemont (tel. 413/339-5504), has 56 sites, plus swimming, fishing, hunting, hiking, cross-country skiing, boating, snowshoeing, and snowmobiling. Mount Greylock State Reservations, in Adams (tel. 413/449-4263), has 35 sites, and the Savoy Mountain State Forest, in Florida (tel. 413/663-8469), has 35 summer-only sites off Rte. 2, east of North Adams, plus log cabins available year round. There's good camping in the Stoney Ledge section of Mount Greylock, and tent camping at Barton Cove, in Gill (tel. 413/863-9300 in season, 413/659-3714 off-season). Closed after Labor Day.

Also on Mount Greylock, from May to October lodging and meals are available at the summit at Bascom Lodge (tel. 413/743-1591). The visitor center (tel. 413/449-4262) is 2 miles from Rte. 7 on Rockwell Road.

Fishing: There's good fishing in the Connecticut and Deerfield rivers and at several lakes in the area. For information, call the Franklin County Chamber of Commerce at 508/528-2800. Or contact the Division of Fisheries and Wildlife, 100 Cambridge St., Boston, MA 02022 (tel. 617/727-3151).

Fruit Picking: Write the Department of Food & Agriculture, 100 Cambridge St., Boston, MA 02202.

Golf: Crumpin' Fox Club, Parmenter Road, Bernardston (tel. 413/648-9101); Mohawk Meadows, Greenfield (tel. 413/773-9047); and Oak Ridge, West Gill Road, in Gill (tel. 413/863-9693).

Hiking: Great hiking is found in the Mohawk Trail State Forest in Charlemont, at Mount Greylock, and at Erving State Forest, east of Greenfield. There's also a trail along the Connecticut River in the Northfield Recreation Area (tel. 413/659-3713). The Savoy

Mountain State Forest, east of North Adams (tel. 413/663-8469), also has trails.

Horseback Riding: The only stable that offers trail rides in the area is Agawam Stables in Agawam (tel. 413/786-1690).

Shopping: For information about crafts studios and galleries, of which there are many throughout the valley, contact the Arts Extension Service, Division of Continuing Education, University of Massachusetts, Amherst, MA 01003 (tel. 413/545-2360).

Skiing: In a lovely setting on the Mohawk Trail, Berkshire East, River Road (P.O. Box S), Charlemont, MA 01339 (tel. 413/339-6617), has 34 trails served by one triple and three double chairs and a J-bar. A basic weekend costs $32.

The Mount Tom Ski Area, Rte. 5 (P.O. Box 1158), Holyoke, MA 01040 (tel. 413/536-0416), has downhill skiing on 17 slopes served by eight lifts. The lifts are also open in peak summer months from 10am to 10pm. In summer the alpine slide and water slide provide the thrills.

There's also cross-country skiing at the Northfield Mountain Recreation Area, Rte. 63 (R.R. 1, Box 377), Northfield, MA 01360 (tel. 413/659-3713).

State Parks & State Forests: *Florida:* The Savoy Mountain State Forest, Rte. 2 and Rte. 116, in Savoy (tel. 413/663-8469), has bicycling, boating, fishing, camping, hiking, horseback riding, picnicking, cross-country skiing, snowmobiling, and swimming. *South Deerfield:* Mount Sugarloaf Reservation, off Rte. 116 (tel. 413/545-5993), has picnicking, hiking, and cross-country skiing.

For general information on State Parks, contact the Department of Environmental Management, Division of Forests and Parks, 100 Cambridge St., Boston, MA 02202 (tel. 617/727-3180).

Swimming: Savoy Mountain State Forest and Mohawk Trail State Forest.

Tennis: Courts can be found at area high schools. Call the Franklin County Chamber of Commerce at 508/528-2800 for details.

NEW JERSEY

Cape May

Distance in Miles: 150

Estimated Driving Time: 3 hours

⊸⟨o⟩⊶⟨o⟩⊶⟨o⟩⊶⟨o⟩⊶⟨o⟩⊶

Driving: Take the New Jersey Turnpike to the Garden State Parkway all the way to the end, which will bring you right into Cape May on Lafayette Street. Turn left on Madison and you'll be at the beaches.

Bus: New Jersey Transit (tel. 201/762-5100) operates daily express buses from the Port Authority Bus Terminal to Cape May. The trip takes four hours.

Further Information: For more about New Jersey in general, contact the **New Jersey Division of Travel & Tourism,** 20 W. State St. (C.N. 826), Trenton, NJ 08625-0826 (tel. 609/292-2470). For specific information about the Cape May area, contact the **Chamber of Commerce of Greater Cape May,** P.O. Box 556, Cape May, NJ 08204 (tel. 609/884-5508).

⊸⟨o⟩⊶⟨o⟩⊶⟨o⟩⊶⟨o⟩⊶⟨o⟩⊶

When you arrive in Cape May you'll find yourself in a different world and a different era. Drive or walk through the streets to see lovely old Victorian homes painted white, sage green, pale blue, gray, or pink, with swing seats and rockers on wraparound verandas, intricate towers, turrets, and cupolas rising from fish-scale mansard roofs and deep projecting bays; row after row, they line the streets running down to the promenade and the sea. What's even more exciting is that you can stay in them, for many have been restored by young professional couples who've chosen Cape May as their refuge from the treadmill of corporate and urban life and now run these marvelous homes as guesthouses. Here you can sleep on lace-trimmed pillows and sheets under antique quilts spread on brass or Renaissance Revival beds; wander through rooms filled with Mission-style furniture, Eastlake sofas, Empire-style couches, brilliant chandeliers, and ornate clocks and mirrors; or spend time rocking gently on the veranda enjoying the cool sea breezes that waft in from the shore. During the day, cycle around town or out to Cape May Point to survey the lighthouse, the marshlands, and—best of all—the rolling dunes that back the sand beach. Or you can go fishing, swimming, birdwatching, or boating; watch the catch arrive at the main dock; play some tennis or golf; and enjoy a whole slew of summer events—clambakes, bandstand concerts, and even some special winter holiday events.

You'll enjoy pleasures similar to those that brought as many as 3,000 people a day aboard steamboats to the resort in the 1850s, making Cape May a national spa of international acclaim. Its life as a resort had begun much earlier, in 1816, when the first of several Congress Hall hotels was built. From then on, Cape May received a steady stream of notable visitors: Henry Clay and Abraham Lincoln came in the 1840s, then much later such artists as Lillie Langtry and John Philip Sousa. Between 1850 and 1890 five presidents chose it as their temporary escape from the round of government—Franklin Pierce, James Buchanan, Ulysses S. Grant, Chester A. Arthur, and Benjamin Harrison.

Even during its heyday, from 1850 to 1913, Cape May experienced a series of natural disasters. Fire struck in 1869 and 1878, destroying whole sections of the town, including the 3,500-room Mount Vernon, which had been the biggest hotel in the world. Each time, the town was rebuilt in the same bracketed Italianate style that had existed before the fire, which is why so many of these lovely houses have survived. At the confluence of the Delaware River and the Atlantic, the town is extremely vulnerable to storms. The major storm of 1962, which buried Cape May under sand and water, prompted many to think seriously about preservation. This set the course that ensured the survival of the town's great Victorian legacy and rescued it from the doldrum days when it survived only as a military base and a commercial fishing port visited by a handful of loyal tourists who stayed at rather run-down roominghouses. Today Cape May is again playing the role of the grand resort and it's a lovely place to reexperience the charm and grace of an intimate seaside resort that's escaped the ugly overlay of honky-tonk entertainment and gross modern development.

Getting Around
Cape May is easy to walk around and great for bicycling. Rental bikes are available in town at **Village Bike Rentals** in the Acme parking lot.

The **Mid-Atlantic Center for the Arts,** 1048 Washington St. (tel. 609/884-5404), offers a variety of tours—trolley, walking, historic homes, and more. The trolley tours last 30 minutes ($5 adults, $2.50 children 3–12) and leave daily in July, August, and September, weekends only in October and at other times, from the information booth on the Washington Street Mall. (Locations do change, so call for the schedule.) Half-day

Events & Festivals to Plan Your Trip Around

April: The Tulip Festival, displaying hundreds of tulips around town, Dutch food, crafts, dancing, and music (usually late April).

June: Seafood Festival, dedicated to the fishermen lost at sea, also celebrates Cape May's position as a Coast Guard training center and as the largest commercial fishing port in New Jersey. Events include exhibits, dramatic Coast Guard rescue demonstration on Friday night, and seafood tasting (usually second weekend).

October: Victorian Week—a 10-day celebration featuring fashion shows, historic house tours, antiques and craft shows, and other appropriate entertainments (around Columbus Day weekend). Contact the Mid-Atlantic Center for the Arts at 609/884-5404.

December: Christmas in Cape May is filled with events, including a Christmas Candlelight house tour that visits 10 historic homes and inns, evening wassail tours, crafts fairs, and more. Many guesthouses offer special packages then, and the stores along the Mall offer special shopping discounts along with the festive wine and cheese.

walking tours usually leave on Saturday mornings from the information booth on Washington Mall ($5 adults, $2.50 children 3–12). Gaslight tours of the Physick House, the Abbey, and the Humphrey Hughes House are given on Wednesday during summer ($10 adults, $5 children). June to September, trolleys serve the whole area from 10am to 10pm daily.

Cape May Attractions

Start at the **Welcome Center,** across from the bandstand at 405 Lafayette St. (tel. 609/884-9562). Here you'll find a hotline phone center for conducting your own accommodations search if you've come without reservations. The staff is exceedingly friendly and helpful; coffee is available, as is plenty of written information about all kinds of events—concerts at the bandstand, foot races, quilt and decoy shows, barbecues, fish fries, clambakes, vintage movies, contests (kite flying, bike racing, and so on), and other summer frolics. During summer, information is also dispensed from the booth on the Washington Mall.

Hours: May–Oct, daily 9am–4pm.

Most people will want to spend much of their time at the **beach,** swimming, fishing, sailing, windsurfing, birdwatching, sunbathing, and enjoying other shore pastimes, but for those with an interest in history and architecture, Cape May offers a lot. First on the list, of course, are the 150 or so Victorian homes that still stand in the heart of town.

I recommend that one of the first things you do is take the one-hour **walking tour,** for you'll learn an incredible amount about architecture and the history of Cape May. The tours depart from the information booth on Washington Mall (see "Getting Around," above). If you prefer to ride, take the trolley tours.

Strolling Around Town

Even if you don't take the walking tour, spend some time exploring the area between Congress and Franklin streets and from Beach Drive to Lafayette, where the greatest number of Victorian gems are concentrated.

Start at Beach Drive and Congress Street, where you'll find **Congress Hall,** an L-shaped three-story mansion screened by a multistory colonnade; this served as the summer White House for President Benjamin Harrison. Turn right on Congress Place past nos. 203, 207, and 209 onto Perry Street to see the much-photographed **Pink House** (1880) at no. 33, absolutely encrusted with gingerbread ornamentation. Cross Perry to Jackson Street, turn right, and stroll toward the sea past some beauties—the **Queen Victoria,** the **Carroll Villa** (now The Mad Batter), the **George Hildreth cottage** at no. 17, and the seven identical cottages commissioned in 1891 (they were considered unusual in their time, less so today in our standardized age). Turn left on Beach Drive, pass the **Colonial Hotel** at Ocean Street (where Wallis Warfield, long before Edward VIII abdicated the throne of England for her and she became the duchess of Windsor, had a coming-out ball), and turn left at Gurney Street. Here you'll find a whole row of highly ornamental homes—the **Baldt House** at no. 26, the **1869 house,** the **Gingerbread House**—all culminating at the corner of Columbia Avenue in **The Abbey,** built by Stephen D. Button for John B. McCreary from 1869 to 1870. Turn right along Columbia Avenue and at no. 635 you'll find the **Mainstay Inn,** originally designed to serve as a gambling house. Take a detour down Howard Street to view **Chalfonte** at no. 301, built in 1875 for Henry Sawyer, Cape May's Civil War hero, and then double back, turning right on Columbia Avenue and then left on Franklin Street, going up to Hughes Street, which is the oldest street in Cape May and still has the original gaslamps, stepping stones, and hitching posts that were used in the truly horse-powered era. There are some marvelous houses on this street, including the mauve-and-gray **White Dove cottage,** the 1868 **Joseph Hall House** with a lot of acroteria decoration, and many others with shark's-tooth and fish-scale tiles, witch's cap towers, intricate verge board carving, and more. Note, too, the **Albert Hughes House** (1838), which stands out because it's the only structure in a typical Federal style.

At Ocean Street, turn right and go over to Washington Avenue and take another right to the **George Allen House** at no. 720, an opulent bracketed mansion worthy of Newport. Continue down Washington to the Physick House (below) if you have the time and the energy.

The Physick House

In contrast to the fussily ornamental gingerbread style that flourished in Cape May stands the simplicity of Frank Furness's masterpiece, the Physick House at 1048 Washington St. (tel. 609/884-5404), which is so much more rewarding to visit than most because you can actually go into the rooms and experience what it was like to live among the period furnishings, instead of having to peer in from behind a set of ropes. A mentor of Louis Sullivan (who was in turn a mentor of Frank Lloyd Wright), Furness turned away from the extravagant Italianate style and developed his own elaborate stick style, of which the Physick House is such a good example. Commissioned in 1878 to build a summer home for Frances Ralston, Furness finished this 18-room mansion in 1881. He designed both the exterior (note his trademarks—the inverted chimneys, jerkin-head dormers, and oversize porch brackets) and the interior and even some of the furniture, including a bedroom set that's classic in its simple geometric decoration. Other highlights include several fireplaces easily identifiable by their geometric detailing and classic lines; unusual lincruster (a kind of papier-mâché) wainscoting and ceilings in the hallway and some rooms; a golden oak staircase with linear grooving; a parlor with an Eastlake couch and a magnificent ceramic tureen that defies description; a William Morris print fabric in the dining room; and (a favorite with children) a kitchen filled with all kinds of early gadgetry. The eccentric owner, Dr. Physick himself, had a curious life story. Admission includes the Carriage House, now the home of the Cape May County Art League, and an outbuilding containing a collection of antique tools.

Tours: Daily, call for times (weekends only in Jan). **Admission:** $6 adults, $3 children 3–12.

The Wilbraham Mansion

A less classic but nevertheless entertaining tour is given by the resident owners of this Victorian home (tel. 609/884-2046) whose modest facade belies the endless number of rooms and the wealth of its treasures. Built in 1840, it was not until a millionaire steam-engine producer purchased it in 1900 that it acquired its grand dimensions. The present owners have tried to recover the furniture that was sold in an estate sale, but what they already have here is a plentiful feast for the eye. The wallpapers throughout the house will probably shock you—exotic in the extreme—and 12- to 15-foot-high Empire mirrors dominate the main parlor, along with a weird and whimsically painted chandelier. The house is stuffed with treasures of all sorts that would take several days to really examine. Highlights include museum-quality Dresden lamps that have been matched with rather odd shades, several lovely 18th-century porcelain communion pieces now used as liqueur sets, majolica urns, a Sears bed purchased for the grand sum of $22 and a dresser for $19 (both still showing the price), and an early simple fire extinguisher that looks like a light bulb. It's really worth the visit.

Cape May

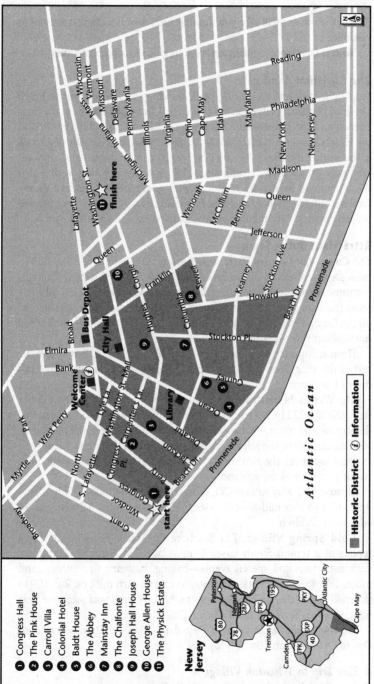

Congress Hall
The Pink House
Carroll Villa
Colonial Hotel
Baldt House
The Abbey
Mainstay Inn
The Chalfonte
Joseph Hall House
George Allen House
The Physick Estate

Historic District *i* Information

New Jersey

Paterson
Newark
Trenton
Camden
Atlantic City
Cape May

Atlantic Ocean

start here
finish here

Welcome Center
City Hall
Bus Depot
Library

199

One of the owners will take you through and answer as many questions as possible.

Tours: Given occasionally on weekends. Call for information.

The Christian Admiral

Stop in at this austere-looking brick building on the seafront at Beach Drive and Pittsburgh Avenue just to see the Tiffany-glass dome in the front portico and the stained-glass windows on the staircase. Built in 1905 as the Hotel Cape May, it had already changed its name to the Admiral when it was acquired in the 1950s by Carl McIntire, a fundamentalist minister who now uses it as his headquarters. When it was first built it provided the ultimate in luxury—350 rooms, with grand lobbies and vast dining rooms costing $1 million, twice the estimated costs. The lobby is wainscoted in Siena marble, and the iron columns are painted to simulate marble.

Attractions Out of Town

The **Cape May County Historical Society,** Rte. 9. (tel. 609/465-3535), possesses a collection of local memorabilia that includes period rooms, maritime objects like the original flag from the *Merrimac,* and a children's room featuring toys, dolls, and needlework. Take Stone Harbor Boulevard off the Garden State Parkway to Shore Road (Rte. 9). Turn right and travel north about three-quarters of a mile.

Hours: Summer, Mon–Sat 10am–3pm; Dec–Feb, Sat 10am–3pm; the rest of the year, Tues–Sat 10am–3pm. **Admission:** $2 adults, 50¢ children 11 and under.

The **Wetlands Institute,** on Stone Harbor Boulevard in Stone Harbor (tel. 609/368-1211), is a research facility whose aquarium and educational displays would interest naturalists and others who share similar interests. Visitors can follow the salt marsh trail, walk out on the marsh boardwalk and the pier over the tidal creek, or climb the observation tower for a panoramic view of the wetlands.

Hours: Mid-May to mid-Oct, Mon–Sat 9:30am–4:30pm, Sun 10am–4pm; mid-Oct to mid-May, Tues–Sat 9:30am–4:30pm. **Admission:** $4 adults, $2 children.

Cold Spring Village, 731 Seashore Rd. (tel. 609/898-2300), is a replica of a typical South Jersey farm village that features all kinds of demonstrations and special events—baking, basketry, tinsmithing, and more. Take the Garden State Parkway to Exit O, turn right on Rte. 109 to the traffic light, then follow the signs to the ferry until you reach the next light, which is Seashore Road. Turn right.

Hours: Memorial Day–Labor Day, daily 10am–4:30pm; after Labor Day to Oct, Sat–Sun 10am–4:30pm.

A Side Trip to Wheaton Village

Only a 30-minute drive away in Millville, you may enjoy a visit to Wheaton Village, 1501 Glasstown Rd., between 10th and G streets (tel. 609/825-6800), a 60-acre museum/cultural center dedicated to American glass and regional crafts. In addition to the museum, where you can view all types of glass from early bottles through art nouveau to modern, visitors can see demonstrations in the glass factory and pottery and wood-carving studios. It's worth the trip.

Hours: Daily 10am–5pm. **Closed:** Mon–Tues Jan–Mar. **Admission:** $6 adults, $5.50 seniors, $3.50 children 5–18.

Cape May Lodging

Note: On weekends, most of the following accommodations require a two- or three-night minimum. Also, most of them (some exceptions) don't encourage children under 12 or so, not because they don't like kids but simply because children are boisterous and find a weekend when they're asked to keep quiet a big bore. If you plan to visit during summer, make your reservations far in advance. Owners will usually provide complimentary beach tags.

Most of the accommodations lack air-conditioning, but don't let that deter you. Many rooms have ceiling fans or louvered doors, and the sea breezes arising from the confluence of the Delaware and the Atlantic are perfectly adequate on even the hottest day.

A Note on Parking: In summer, parking is particularly difficult and you'd do best to leave your car at home and walk or cycle around. Some accommodations do provide free parking; others will charge for the privilege of parking on the property. Always check first.

"Inns at Christmas" Package: A number of the Cape May inns and guesthouses—like the Queen Victoria, Captain Mey's, the Victorian Rose, the Brass Bed, the Manor House, the Windward House, Alexander's Inn, and the Summer Cottage Inn—have gotten together to offer a special "Inns at Christmas" package. At each establishment the theme is different: the history of Victorian decorations at the Queen Victoria, children's Christmas at the Brass Bed, Dutch celebrations at Captain Mey's, winter floral celebrations at the Victorian Rose, the lights of Christmas at the Manor House, the music of Christmas at the Summer Cottage Inn, vintage fashions for the holiday season at the Windward House, and an elegant setting at Alexander's.

The Guesthouses

The Cape May showpiece that's been featured so many times in magazines is the **Mainstay,** 635 Columbia Ave., Cape May, NJ 08204 (tel. 609/884-8690), a beauty designed by Stephen D. Button to serve as a gambling house. It's certainly impressive, with a pilastered cupola, green shutters flanking 13-foot-high Italianate windows, and a wraparound porch supported by exquisitely fluted and turned columns encrusted with gingerbread. You may find it too overwhelming and too perfect, depending on your taste. Making this a particularly idyllic spot are the well-tended gardens spilling over in early spring and summer with roses, hydrangea, iris, pinks, pansies, and tiger lilies, all set around a small fountain.

Devoted preservationists Tom and Sue Carroll have spent their time and energy restoring this place to its former magnificence. The public rooms with 14-foot-high ceilings, ornate plaster moldings, and elaborate chandeliers have been furnished with extravagant Victoriana—like 12-foot-high carved mirrors in the hall and a wrought-iron stove in the small front parlor. The drawing room boasts gilt-framed oils and colorful paintings on glass, richly patterned Oriental rugs, and a grand piano standing against a long-case clock and a graceful wrought-iron floor lamp. Here you'll always find fresh-cut flowers on the marble-topped table. In the dining room the formal table seats 12 and the tall windows are draped with lace, capped by a scarlet tasselled valance.

The six large guest rooms (all with bath) are furnished with thick pile carpets and beds with walnut Renaissance Revival headboards; one of the baths features a copper tub. Sue and Tom also have accommodations in "the cottage next door," another pleasant Victorian where there are an additional six rooms, all similarly furnished. Across the road, the Officer's Quarters contains four luxurious suites, each with a large whirlpool tub, a kitchenette with minirefrigerator, and a color TV with a VCR.

Guests are invited to enjoy a full breakfast on the porch in summer (strawberry crêpes, anyone?) or in the formal dining room at other times. Afternoon tea is served on the porch.

Rates (including breakfast and afternoon tea): Memorial Day to mid-Oct and all weekends and holidays, $140–$200 double in the inn and the cottage; $215 suite. Oct to mid-May, weekdays, $105-$170 double in the inn and the cottage; $145 suite. Three-night minimum stay required in summer.

The other lodging that's museumlike in the quality of its decor is **The Abbey,** Columbia Avenue and Gurney Street, Cape May, NJ 08204 (tel. 609/884-4506). You can't miss its steep mansard roof and soaring 60-foot tower. Owners Jay and Marianne Schatze enjoy entertaining at breakfast and in the early evening, when guests gather in the drawing room to get to know one another over a glass of wine. Jay, in particular, is a real ham. In the morning he'll be setting the breakfast table wearing a hat of one sort or another (a leather pilot's cap, a boater, a Derby, or a sea-captain's cap) from his collection. At breakfast he'll regale you with one tale or joke after another. Marianne is a creative designer and needlewoman who fashioned the lambrequins that cover the gothic windows of the double parlor, elaborately furnished with High Victorian sofas, side chairs, and a huge Empire mirror over the mantel, on which stands an ornate French clock from the same period.

It's hard to imagine that when the Schatzes took over the house in late 1979 pigeons were inhabiting the upper floors. Now, upstairs you'll find a series of rooms, many with large armoires, floor-to-ceiling mirrors, Victorian sofas, walnut beds, and ornate gas fixtures. Even the smallest room is charming. In the morning sunlight streams through the gothic-style ruby stained-glass windows, lighting up the white eyelet lace bedspread and scallop-edged pillows. All rooms have a bath, a small refrigerator, and air-conditioning or a fan.

You can look forward to a luxurious breakfast served at a large formal table in the dining room, whose most exquisite piece is a sideboard carved with Indian heads, eagles, and wolflike creatures. Your gourmet breakfast will consist of juice, a choice of teas or coffee, an egg dish of some sort—perhaps quiche with wide noodles or a delicious concoction of poached eggs with onions and bacon in a cream sauce and served over grits—plus muffins, jams, honey, and always a fresh fruit cup, sometimes laced with brandy. After breakfast Jay will take you up to the tower for a splendid view of the whole Cape May area.

Rates (including breakfast): Apr–Dec, $100–$225 double. Free parking.

Several blocks farther from the beach, away from the central cluster of Victorian hostelries, stands the **Barnard-Good House,** 238 Perry St., Cape May, NJ 08204 (tel. 609/884-5381). This stunning purple clapboard house topped with a mansard roof is run by the effervescent Nancy Hawkins and her husband, Tom. Enter through the small picket gate, pass the white picket fence, and step up onto the porch with its intricate fretwork, further enlivened by one or two hanging ferns and a windowbox with colorful pansies.

Although Nancy doesn't pretend to have furnished the house authentically, it does have a period charm and warmth. The dining room features what she calls a Turkish corner, with a tasselled brocade Victorian-style sofa beneath a tented effect; a foot-pedal organ, an old gas fire, heavy mirrors, and a Victorian glass dome filled with a silk flower arrangement add character to the front parlor.

Upstairs are three air-conditioned rooms and two suites (all with bath). The rooms are uniquely and eclectically furnished: One has a four-poster with lace curtains, another a brass bed with a candlewick spread, and another a delicate Empire-style dressing table created by Nancy herself. One of the most popular rooms has been dubbed the purple passion room, because the iron-and-brass bedstead is extra-large, with a purple quilt, leaving room for only one white wicker chair, an oak chest, and a porcelain wash bowl; its bath is worth noting for its original zinc-coated copper tub, marble sink, and old-fashioned pull-chain toilet. Another favorite is the top-floor compact suite, decorated in white and pink with a small sitting room, complete with a fainting couch, and a full bath.

Nancy is an extremely skilled cook who relishes even the challenge of catering to a special diet (if she's informed ahead). Her gourmet breakfast might consist of a cream of almond soup; tangerine-lime juice (never standard grapefruit or orange); Swiss enchilada crêpes filled with celery, onions, chiles, and tomato sauce, topped with cheese and served with assorted homemade breads; and desserts. Beach chairs, beach towels, and an outdoor shower are available.

Rates: Apr–Nov, $93–$130 double. Free parking. *Note:* Allergy sufferers—no cats reside here.

For the last 16 years Joan Wells and her husband, Dane, have been creating a warm, homelike atmosphere at the **Queen Victoria,** 102 Ocean St., Cape May, NJ 08204 (tel. 609/884-8702), a trio of restored landmark buildings. The lovely sage-green Italianate building with striking corner bays, a curvaceous fish-scale mansard roof, and ornamental porch was built in 1881. The Prince Albert Hall is a Stick Style 1882 home in mustard yellow with signature green trim. And the Queen's Cottage, across the street, is a Queen Anne painted in a historic shade of brown, complete with a porch and garden. On the ground floors of the first two are handsome dining rooms with the inn's signature wallpaper, designed by William Morris for Queen Victoria's Balmoral Castle. The parlors feature Mission and Arts and Crafts furniture and here guests can sit and browse through one of the many art and architecture books that Joan collected when she was executive director of the Victorian Society. You'll really be welcomed as friends of the family, which includes Elizabeth, whom you might find practicing her piano lesson at the Mission upright player piano. The parlor of the Prince Albert has a TV.

The 23 air-conditioned rooms and suites (all with bath) are named either after legendary Victorians—Disraeli and Lillie Langtry are the smallest, for example—or after romantic Victorian places—like Kew Garden and Hampton Court, which are suites with whirlpool tubs and TVs. The smallest rooms are on the third floor of the first house and have space only for a lowboy, a chair, and a brass iron bed. Most rooms have ceiling fans and all have colorful Mennonite quilts and a vase of fresh flowers. Additional accommodations are in the Carriage House and the Queen's Cottage.

In the morning, Joan will fortify you with a variety of egg casseroles or soufflés served buffet style in each of the main dining rooms, along with homemade muffins, nut and fruit breads, the Queen's Oats, granola, and fresh fruit. Later in the day, a casual tea is served. The side porch is a sheltered spot for rocking (50 rockers available). Bicycles are available free, and Joan and Dane also provide a useful package of information on activities and entertainment available in the area. If you stay here, you'll also receive a regular newsletter, which keeps you in touch and makes you really feel like part of the family.

Rates (including breakfast): Mid-June to mid-Sept, $165–$220 double; $220–$250 suite. Less in other months to lows of $110–$145 double and $155–$165 suite in Jan–Feb. Extra person $20. Two-night minimum stay Nov–Mar; three- and four-night minimum in summer and during holidays.

The **Queen's Hotel,** 601 Columbia Ave., Cape May, NJ 08204 (tel. 609/884-8702), is also owned by Dane and Joan Wells (above). It was built in 1876 as a commercial structure with a pharmacy on the first floor and a gambling casino above. The second-floor rooms have very high ceilings and elegant plaster cornices and medallions reflecting their past use as casino rooms. The third-floor rooms are cozier, with sloping ceilings that follow the lines of the steep mansard roof. The nine rooms are well furnished with antiques, comfortable chairs, good reading lights, and handsome appointments. All have a bath, a TV, a phone, air-conditioning, and a coffee maker. This is a "green hotel," practicing conservation by providing soap dispensers, recycling, and energy-conserving towel laundering services. No meals are included and the accommodations appeal more to those who value their privacy and appreciate modern conveniences.

Rates: Summer weekends, $150–$240 double; the rest of the time, $105–$200 double.

The **Virginia Hotel and Ebbitt Room,** 25 Jackson St., Cape May, NJ 08204 (tel. 609/884-5700), was opened as a hotel in 1879. Today this Victorian with its lacy wood porches has been restored and turned into a small hotel with modern amenities and services. Each of the 24 rooms has a bath, a phone, a TV and VCR, and air-conditioning. The furnishings are not overwhelmingly Victorian. The polished wood beds are covered with down comforters and the furnishings are minimal—a white-painted chair and desk, a tall planter, and similar accents. What makes the hotel unusual by Cape May standards is that it offers room service, valet parking, and complimentary morning newspaper with your continental breakfast.

It also boasts the Ebbitt Room for fine dining and an innovative cuisine. Among the 10 or so entrees you might find pan-seared yellowfin tuna in sesame-seed crust with crisp rice paper, hoisin, and wasabi; sea scallops with mango-jicama reserve and Thai curry sauce; filet mignon with caramelized shallot sauce; or chicken breast with prosciutto, roasted red peppers, and fresh mozzarella over pesto risotto with porcini mushroom jus. Among the appetizers, the chilled grilled shrimp with mixed Asian greens, citrus fruits, ginger confit, and soy, lime, and scallion vinaigrette hit the spot. Prices range from $19 to $28. Guests can relax in front of the hearth in the sitting room or on the front porches.

Rates (including breakfast): Spring, $170–$235 double weekends, $110–$165 double weekdays. Summer (until mid-Oct), $200–$270 double weekends, $140–$230 double weekdays. Fall, $170–$235 double weekends, $90–$130 double weekdays. Holiday season, $190–$260 double weekends, $100–$140 double weekdays. Winter, $150–$195 double weekends, $90–$130 double weekdays. **Dining Hours:** Daily 5:30pm–closing.

The **John F. Craig House,** 609 Columbia Ave., Cape May, NJ 08204 (tel. 609/884-0100), dates back to 1866, though parts of the house were built before 1850. It has had several rather flamboyant owners but is named after John Fullerton Craig, a wealthy sugar broker and Philadelphian who summered here for many years at the turn of the century. It's a Carpenter Gothic house with 10-foot ceilings and floor-to-ceiling windows that open to expansive porches. The nine guest rooms (seven with bath) and one suite are furnished with Eastlake and Renaissance Revival antiques and decorated with reproduction period wallpapers. Guests enjoy the pillared living room with a fireplace, the book-lined library, and the formal dining room where an elaborate breakfast is served.

Rates (including breakfast): $75–$125 double without bath, $95–$155 double with bath; $115–$175 suite.

The pretty lavender-and-cream **Captain Mey's Inn,** 202 Ocean St., Cape May, NJ 08204 (tel. 609/884-7793 or 884-9637), is named after the Dutch explorer and discoverer of Cape May, Capt. Cornelius Mey. The Dutch motif is seen in the dining room's Delft-tile fireplace and the parlor's Delft collection. A lovely oak staircase leads to the nine guest rooms (two with bath, seven sharing five baths). Great care has been taken to provide each with a unique atmosphere, using a variety of styles and textures— Victorian bedroom suites, handmade quilts, and lace curtains among them. Throughout the house are several mannequins wearing Victorian dresses and lingerie from owner Kathleen Blinn's collection. A full breakfast of fresh fruit, breakfast meats, and homemade breads is served by candle-light—a charming, romantic way to start the day. It can also be enjoyed on the front porch, furnished with wicker and hanging ferns. In late afternoons, guests gather for tea.

Rates (including breakfast): $115–$175 double. Free parking.

Some 100 rosebushes were planted around the property on which stands the **Victorian Rose,** 715 Columbia Ave., Cape May, NJ 08204 (tel. 609/ 884-2497), a blue-gray building made colorful by the cream-and-rust gingerbread fretwork. The rose theme is followed throughout on sheets, towels, wallpaper, and dining room place settings.

Lively owners Linda and Bob Mullock offer eight rooms, most featuring oak pieces. Number 3 in the front is their largest and comes with an oak sideboard, a king-size bed, a couch, wall-to-wall carpeting, and louvered doors that open into the bath with its clawfoot tub. The other rooms vary, but most feature high-back oak beds, oak dressers, candlewick spreads, and cane-seat chairs. Ceiling fans and sea breezes substitute for air-conditioning.

Linda and Bob are not interested in maintaining a perfectly authentic Victorian atmosphere; rather, they have a romance with the 1930s and 1940s, which explains the Glenn Miller–style sounds that waft through the house. Former nursery-school teacher Linda serves a light breakfast of fresh fruit, quiches, peach soufflé pancakes, or homemade sweet rolls and breads in the dining room, which contains a large sideboard purchased from the Boardman estate (Mr. Boardman supposedly built the boardwalk in Atlantic City).

At the back of the house is a pleasant cottage with a full kitchen and room enough to sleep five; it's available for weekly rental, but you'll need to call well ahead.

Rates (including breakfast): $90–$150 double.

In 1979 John and Donna Dunwoody and two of their three children took over a classic 1872 home that had belonged to the Dannenbaums of Philadelphia until 1930, when it was turned into a tourist home. They camped out through the winter of 1979–80 while they, their family, and their friends worked day and night restoring it and converting it into a friendly bed-and-breakfast open year round, the **Brass Bed,** 719 Columbia Ave., Cape May, NJ 08204 (tel. 609/884-8075). Period perfection was not their aim, though the house is comfortably furnished with antique pieces: 19th-century brass beds, elegant wallpapers, and billowy lace curtains. During the restoration it was discovered that many pieces were original to the first owners and still had shipping tags attached to the backs—dated 1872! Collectibles like statuary and early photographs are on view, including a portrait that looks like a Victorian version of John himself. The parlor boasts an 1890s upright piano, a five-piece Renaissance Revival set of chairs and a settee, and a turn-of-the-century phonograph.

The Dunwoodys offer a relaxing, convivial atmosphere to guests, who have the choice of eight rooms (six with bath). Furnishings vary: In the room named in honor of the famous Congress Hall Hotel there's a brass bed, needlepointed chairs, a walnut armoire, and an oak dresser, much of the furniture original to the house. The Stockton Room has a cozy air, achieved by the area rug, floral wallpaper, Eastlake settee, antique brass bed, and large walnut armoire. Third-floor rooms are tucked under the eaves, and one of them, the Mount Vernon, enjoys a private bath with a clawfoot tub. A full breakfast and afternoon refreshment are served year round. Half the front veranda has been enclosed to make a comfortable sun room with wicker that offers a variety of games, books, and puzzles.

Rates: $60–$100 double without bath, $80–$185 double with bath. "Inns at Christmas" package offered (see above).

The **Windward House** (1905), 24 Jackson St., Cape May, NJ 08204 (tel. 609/884-3368), boasts some really outstanding architectural details, especially stained glass (check out the stained-glass double doors leading to one of the guest rooms). It also has some very personal features in Sandy Miller's vintage clothing and accessories displayed on mannequins around the house and Owen's collection of German bisque bathing beauties and figurines. The parlor is accented with many eye-catching objects, including a blue glass collection on the window pelmets.

All eight rooms (with bath) are well furnished, with a refrigerator, a ceiling fan, and air-conditioning; three have a TV. My favorite is the Summer Suite: It's tucked away behind the dining room on the first floor and has its own entrance; its bedroom has a carved Victorian bed that's complemented by marble-topped pieces, and its tiny sitting room features a cozy loveseat, an armoire, and a small refrigerator. Room 5 is decked out in Rococo Revival splendor, with lemon peony wallpaper. Third-floor rooms like no. 7, the Wicker Room, are tucked under the eaves. In this room the iron-and-brass bed is draped with white lace; wicker chairs and a couch add a dash of comfort, and there's an adjoining single room that makes it ideal for a trio. Up here there's also a large deck at the back of the house from which there's a great ocean view. More seating is available on the ground-floor front porch set with wicker.

A full breakfast is served at the lace-clothed table in the dining room, in which there's still another collection—egg cups this time. This is one of Cape May's quirkily and appealingly personal accommodations.

Rates (including breakfast): In season (summer), $110–$150 single; $120–$160 double. Off-season, $80–$120 single; $90–$130 double. Extra person $25.

The **Humphrey Hughes House,** 29 Ocean St., Cape May, NJ 08204 (tel. 609/884-4428), was built in 1903, a little later than many in Cape May, and as a consequence the rooms are larger. The porch is really wide and expansive and has a fine ocean view. The seven rooms and four suites, all with a bath and air-conditioning, are well furnished with an eye for detail. One of my favorites is the Ocean View Room, featuring a Renaissance Revival carved bed made up with eyelet bed linen, a large armoire, sidetables set with gas-style lamps, and a polished floor covered with Oriental-style rugs. Other rooms are decorated in iron and brass and wicker. A full breakfast is served at 9am. Tea, served at 4pm, consists of iced tea, cakes, pies, cheese, and crudités. A large well-furnished parlor is available for guests.

Rates (including breakfast): $135–$225 double.

The owners of the **Sea Holly Inn,** 815 Stockton Ave., Cape May, NJ 08204 (tel. 609/884-6294), recently won an award for the quality of the restoration that they accomplished with alacrity, turning a neglected building into a Victorian beauty. The six rooms, all with air-conditioning, electric blankets, and a bath, have been painstakingly decorated with Schumacher papers and fine fabrics and furnishings. Room 9, at the back of the house, has a bed covered with French blue satin and lace-trimmed pillows, with a brilliant ruby-red upholstered Eastlake chair among the furnishings. Room 8 has a highly ornate iron bed covered with lace and satin, rose carpeting, and pretty chintz wallpaper. Room 2 houses a crested Victorian bed and mostly wicker furnishings set against gold chintz wallpaper.

No breakfast is served in summer; continental breakfast is served in spring and fall. Guests gather in the parlor on the camelback and wicker sofas or on the concrete porch's wicker rockers. A refrigerator is available for guests.

Rates: Mid-Feb to New Year's Eve, $110–$190 double.

The **Sand Castles,** 829 Stockton Ave., Cape May, NJ 08204 (tel. 609/884-5451), a Carpenter Gothic cottage, has to be one of Cape May's best buys. It's operated by Bill Bianco and Jill McAfee, both corporate escapees, she from advertising and he from the auto industry. On the porch stand inviting rockers, and inside warm green, peach, and red tones in the parlors provide a very hearty welcome, especially with their fireplaces in winter. There are eight guest rooms (four with bath) and two suites. Each of the rooms is charming and many are under the eaves, which gives them interesting cozy shapes. Room 3 contains an old brass bed, a couch, an oak dresser, and an appealing "steeple"-pointed gothic window. This same style of window is also found in Room 4, along with a highback oak bed covered with a Marseille-style bedspread, an oak dresser, and a sidetable. A full breakfast is served in the breakfast room complete with ornate sideboard and gilded chairs. Afternoon tea is also served.

Rates (including breakfast and afternoon tea): $90–$135 double.

One of the famed Stephen D. Button houses (known as "The Seven Sisters"), the **Seventh Sister Guesthouse,** 10 Jackson St., Cape May, NJ 08204 (tel. 609/884-2280), is very different from the establishments discussed so far. Artist Joanne Echevarria, who shares the house with her husband, Bob Myers, has chosen to decorate the house with white-painted furniture and wicker so that the whole place positively blazes with light. It's also filled with examples of her art—abstract pastels, collages, and conceptual art. Not surprisingly, many of her guests are artists, photographers, or other like-minded visitors who need privacy and quiet to pursue their inspirational muse. Of the six rooms sharing two baths, four have ocean views. The back porch is great for idling, while the lawn at the side of the house makes a pleasant change from the beach, which is only 100 feet away.

Rates: June–Aug, $95 double. May and Sept, $90 double. Apr and Oct, $85 double. Nov–Mar, $80 double. Children over 7 are welcome.

Across town, Joanne's brother, Fred Echevarria, and his wife, Joan, run the year-round **Gingerbread House,** 28 Gurney St., Cape May, NJ 08204 (tel. 609/884-0211), one of the Stockton Row cottages that surrounded the old Stockton Hotel, built in 1869 by railroad money and designed by Stephen D. Button. Here Fred exhibits his talent for photography (note the striking pictures of Nova Scotia and Maine throughout the house) and for furniture making; you'll see in front of the fireplace in the parlor the coffee table he built to display their seashell collection. Apart from this table, though, the house is furnished with Victorian-style sofas, lowboys with marble tops, and many other period furnishings. Among the six guest rooms (three with bath), the highest priced is large enough to accommodate two double beds and comes with a spacious private porch. A breakfast of fruits, cereal, and homemade breads and afternoon tea is served.

Rates (including breakfast): $110–$200 double (discounts available off-season).

Geraniums were spilling out of the hanging baskets on the ocean-view porch when I last visited **Holly House,** 20 Jackson St., Cape May, NJ 08204 (tel. 609/884-7365), a sage-green boxlike house decorated with Chinese-red trim; this is also one of the seven cottages built by Stephen D. Button deliberately facing away from Jackson Street. Up the visually striking staircase, you'll find six guest rooms, all informally furnished, primarily with oak pieces—a desk, a cane-seated chair, a dresser, a double towel rack, and an iron bedstead, for example—and kept very simple, because Bruce and Corinne Minnix want to keep it as a home away from home. The parlor has a platform rocker, a Victorian sofa, the original coal-burning fireplace, a Baldwin piano, and a comfortable spot to sit quietly and read as though you were settled in at your own cozy place.

Rates: Memorial Day–Columbus Day, $65–$80 double. Off-season, $45–$55 double.

The **Albert G. Stevens Inn,** 127 Myrtle Ave., Cape May, NJ 08204 (tel. 609/884-4717), is an impressive home built in 1898 as a wedding present for the first owner's bride. It still has the original floating staircase. Prime Victorian pieces can be found throughout—like the parlor's late Empire couch and side chairs in front of the oak mantel. The seven rooms and two suites, with a bath and air-conditioning, have a beautifully color-coordinated decor featuring exquisite individualized French wallpapers and wall-to-wall carpeting. Some rooms have Eastlake or iron-and-brass beds, while others feature Lincoln and even art deco bedroom sets. A hearty three-course Norwegian-style breakfast is served. Owners Diane and Curt have established a special Cat's Garden that provides a safe haven for Cape May's strays; here they provide food, shelter, and medical attention. Guests can enjoy afternoon tea in the gazebo on Thursday, Saturday, and Sunday (for a small charge that helps support the Cat's Garden) and relax in the hot tub.

Rates (including breakfast): $75–$165 double. Free parking.

Since it was built in 1876 the venerable 103-room **Chalfonte,** 301 Howard St., Cape May, NJ 08204 (tel. 609/884-8409), has drawn loyal families year after year to rock on its veranda, sample its southern-style cuisine, and generally enjoy its simple charms. Two short blocks from the beach, this three-story building, screened by a two-story colonnade and crowned with a cupola and some fine gingerbread ornamentation, has been reno-vated by owners Anne Le Duc and Judy Bartella. It's the only real chance you'll have to experience the kind of hotel accommodations that used to keep Cape May so crowded in its heyday. Only 11 of the rooms have a bath (most have sinks), and all are (at least at the time of my visit) furnished spartanly with iron bedsteads and marble-topped dressers. The dining room is famous for its family-style meals of southern fried chicken, crab cakes, leg of lamb, or roast beef at dinner, and biscuits, spoonbread, fish, grits, and bacon and eggs at breakfast. The dining room is open to the public and complete dinners are only $19.50. A Sunday tradition is kidney stew. On the ground floor are the King Edward Room bar, a writing room, a library, and a comfortable hall/lounge with a fireplace and TV.

The place also caters several special events, including a Victorian dinner with songs supplied by the famous Savoy company, chamber-music concerts, and a week-long children's festival. Workshops are given in such subjects as watercolor painting and massage.

Rates (including breakfast and dinner): May–Sept and weekends to late Oct, $80–$100 single; $100–$165 double (the higher prices are for rooms with bath and reflect whether room is on the second or third floor). Weekly rates and special packages available; on Work Weekends in May and Oct you can stay for free (bring your own sleeping bag or linens) and receive three meals a day for two days while you help spruce the place up.

The owners of **Alexander's Restaurant,** 653 Washington St., Cape May, NJ 08204 (tel. 609/884-2555), rent four rooms to guests in a home built in 1883. Each room is decorated in Victorian style. In the Rose Room the brass bed with its pink satin eiderdown looks very inviting. The walls of the Green Room sport a wallpaper originally designed to celebrate the opening of the Suez Canal—a truly Victorian touch. Breakfast is served on the veranda or delivered to your room. Afternoon tea too.

Rates (including breakfast): June to mid-Oct, $110–$135 double week-days, $400–$500 double two-night weekend package. Mid-Oct to June, $100–$130 double weekdays, $300–$375 double two-night weekend package.

Built around 1896, the cream-and-rust **Duke of Windsor Inn,** 817 Washington St., Cape May, NJ 08204 (tel. 609/884-1355), with its quirky 45-foot conical tower (where two rooms are located), makes a lovely stopping place in a more secluded area, midway between the town and the harbor, within walking distance of the Physick Estate and the tennis club. On the first floor the tower has a well-used games and conversation room, just large enough to accommodate a wicker couch and two wicker armchairs. A double parlor with a corner fireplace, an ornate plaster ceiling, swag drapes, solid-oak accents, and a crystal chandelier is divided in two by an archway supported by two solid-wood Colonial Revival pillars. One half is used as a reading area and contains large bookcases; the other half is used as a sitting area. It's well furnished with Victoriana, but for me, the handsomest piece is the Burmese table, intricately carved with birds, elephants, and lions. The back parlor adjoins the dining room, which possesses a lovely gilt molded ceiling, several chandeliers, a reproduction of the wallpaper from Queen Victoria's throne room, and refurbished lincrusta on the walls. Here a full breakfast is served amid mirrored sideboards at one large table.

A staircase climbs past a brilliant stained-glass window to the 10 air-conditioned guest rooms, all tastefully furnished. One room, for example, contains a Renaissance Revival bed set against gray-and-burgundy wallpaper; the carpet is rosy-red burgundy and the furnishings oak, and the bath has a hand-painted porcelain sink. The most charming rooms are the tower rooms, which have space for only one brass bed, an Eastlake chair, and a dresser. Lace curtains and fringed lampshade or gas-style lamps are only some of the period effects used. The porch, with its upholstered rattan chairs, is a favorite musing spot. The full breakfast includes a hot entree, fruit, home-baked breads, juice, and coffee. An informal tea is also served.

Rates (including breakfast): Feb–Dec, $75–$120 double without bath, $95–$195 double with bath. Free parking.

Woodleigh House, 808 Washington St., Cape May, NJ 08204 (tel. 609/8847123), in the same area as the Duke of Windsor, is run by a friendly couple (he's an elementary school principal and she's a teacher) and has a genuine homelike atmosphere. In the comfortably modern sitting room you'll find a personal collection of Danish plates, and in the dining room is another colorful collection of glass and china. Here a continental breakfast is served, unless the weather is clement, when it's served on the porch. Each of the four guest rooms has a bath. One of the nicest is off the ground-floor kitchen; it's decorated with cherubs and furnished with a high-backed oak bed, a dresser, a rocker, and a washstand, on top of which are a pair of high-button boots! In the back there's a secluded small porch and brick patio and a small garden area where guests can barbecue.

Rates (including breakfast): $105–$175 double.

Carroll Villa, 19 Jackson St., Cape May, NJ 08204 (tel. 609/884-9619), is one of Cape May's more moderately priced accommodations. Its 21 rooms, all with air-conditioning and a phone, are attractively decorated with wall-to-wall carpeting, pretty drapes and fabrics, and a mixture of antique and modern furnishings. Some feature high Victorian cottage-style bedroom furnishings. The downstairs living room with a TV is for guests only, as is the garden terrace out back. The accommodations are in the same building as the Mad Batter restaurant and (depending on the location of your room) you might be disturbed by the early-morning kitchen staff. If you're an early riser it won't matter a fig, but if you're not. . . . The breakfast is great and served on the front porch, in the dining room, or on the garden terrace.

Rates: In season, $100–$135 double. Winter, $68–$85 double.

The Manor House, 612 Hughes St., Cape May, NJ 08204 (tel. 609/884-4710), boasts some fine architectural features, like oak door frames with geometric decoration and stained glass. There are nine rooms, seven with bath. Several are on the small side, but all are prettily decorated with chintz/floral wallpapers, iron beds or similar, and such accents as floor lamps with fringed lampshades. Room 6 has a whirlpool tub and separate shower plus a sitting room. Most of the beds are made up with colorful quilts. Room 8 has a cross-stitch quilt on a brass bed, warm cranberry-colored chintz wallpaper, a chaise longue, a chest, and a Windsor chair. In Room 4 there's a lovely star quilt. Amenities include a hairdryer, an iron and ironing board, and bathrobes. In refreshing contrast to the country decor, the walls throughout are adorned with bright contemporary art. Guests may use the parlor with plenty of classic books on hand; the wraparound veranda is also a favorite spot. An added advantage is the location on one of the town's less trafficked streets. A four-course breakfast is served at 8:30 and 9:30am on lace-covered oak tables. It might include fresh fruit, a cinnamon sour-cream coffeecake, lemon-ricotta pancakes, and sausage, plus freshly squeezed juice.

Rates (including breakfast): $89–$178 double.

You can't miss the **Inn at 22 Jackson,** 22 Jackson St., Cape May, NJ 08204 (tel. 609/884-2226), an 1899 house with brilliant jade-and-mauve exterior and double porches. There are four suites available, all with a bath, a wet bar with microwave and small refrigerator, a cable TV, and air-conditioning. My favorite is the two-bedroom turret suite, on the third floor with an ocean view and a private deck. A two-bedroom cottage is also available. The furnishings may include a cottage-style Victorian bed and antiques, plus the innkeepers' eclectic collections of novelties—like the bawdy ladies, painted dishes, and toys and games found in the public areas. There's even an 1880 pump organ to play if you're so inclined. In summer the verandas are lined with rockers for afternoons when you just want to relax and breathe the salt air. Innkeepers Barbara Carmichael and Chip Masemore take pride in their buffet breakfasts. Afternoon tea is also served.

Rates (including breakfast): $105–$185 suite for two; $145–$250 turret suite and cottage.

At **Poor Richard's Inn,** 17 Jackson St., Cape May, NJ 08204 (tel. 609/884-3536), artists Richard and Harriet Samuelson attract a younger crowd to their casual home, where the furnishings are more eclectic than most, a trifle faded and less "picture-perfect" than those at many of the other guesthouses. They aim to provide unpretentious comfortable surroundings at moderate prices. Richard and Harriet are also one of the few couples who'll accept children (they have a couple of their own). The house itself is quite magnificent, built in 1882 for a man named George Hildreth, with a wonderfully steep fish-scale mansard roof, deep projecting bays, and an unusual hexagonal porch. There are nine rooms, all with air-conditioning; some have a bath, while others share two baths. The two top-floor rooms are pleasantly furnished with wicker rockers, a painted country bed, a

Mission rocker, and an oak dresser. Other rooms mix painted cottage beds with oak and pine, really old patchwork quilts, hook rugs, and other Victoriana. There are also two apartments with a kitchen available. Throughout the house hang Harriet's collages, which I wanted to purchase on the spot—they're stimulating, weirdly affecting visions.

Rates: July–Aug and weekends Memorial Day–Sept, $65–$90 double without bath, $95–$135 double with bath. Mar–June and Sept–Dec, $50–$75 double without bath, $80–$115 double with bath. Apartments rented by the week only, $500–$750. No parking.

The Mooring Guest House, 801 Stockton Ave., Cape May, NJ 08204 (tel. 609/884-5425), offers 12 rooms (5 with bath), most with air-conditioning and all furnished in Victorian style but not stiflingly so. One of the most appealing is Room 10, the largest, which boasts an intricately carved high-backed cherry bed, an acorn chest with a marble top, and French doors that lead directly to the front porch with an ocean view. Other rooms are pleasantly furnished with mixtures of wicker, white iron, and oak. The halls are extremely wide—a reminder of earlier days when steamer trunks needed accommodating. A full breakfast is served at tables for two in the spacious dining room.

Rates (including breakfast): Apr–Jan 1, $95–$180 double.

The **Twin Gables Guest House,** 731 Columbia Ave., Cape May, NJ (tel. 609/884-7332), is run by friendly Regina and Harry McCaren. The 1879 house is one of the few houses (if not the only one) to possess a screened-in porch with wicker rockers and hanging plants. Guests gather in the comfy parlor on the sofa, around the old pump organ, or on the windowseats. The four rooms (all with bath) are homey. Room 2 has pink-striped wallpaper, an Eastlake bed, a teardrop dresser, an armoire, and marble sidetables. Room 3 has a gold bed coverlet and carpet matched with yellow wallpaper. At breakfast there's always fresh fruit, home-baked breads, and an entree such as banana-stuffed french toast. Open year round.

Rates (including breakfast): $105–$120 double.

Other Accommodations

Cape May also has a goodly number of modern motels, many located on the seafront. The **Marquis de Lafayette,** 501 Beach Dr. (between Ocean and Decatur), Cape May, NJ 08204 (tel. 609/884-3431, or 800/582-5933, 800/257-0432 in New Jersey), offers package plans and the full facilities of a pool and two restaurants.

Rates: Summer weekends, $230–$265 double. Spring/fall weekends, $172–$204 double. Winter weekends, $100–$125 double. Packages available.

The **Motel Surf and Apartments,** 211 Beach Dr., Cape May, NJ 08204 (tel. 609/884-4132), is open year round; the **Montreal Inn,** at Beach Drive and Madison, Cape May, NJ 08204 (tel. 609/884-7011), is open March to November.

Cape May Dining

In season, reservations are a must; on weekends you'd do best to reserve ahead if you don't want to be disappointed. Most of the restaurants lack liquor licenses. For the largest liquor selection and the best prices, go to **Colliers** on Jackson Street, the big green place across from the bandstand. It's open on Sunday.

Breakfast, Lunch or Dinner

The best breakfasts, as you'll have gathered from the previous section, can be found at your guesthouse. If you're not staying at such an accommodation, don't despair; simply head for **The Mad Batter,** 19 Jackson St. (tel. 609/884-5970), for a choice selection of omelets, pancakes, French toast with fresh-fruit sauce, and all kinds of egg dishes with bacon and sausage and so on, priced from $5.50 to $8. You can dine either out under the yellow-striped awning at white pedestal tables or inside. At lunch there are sandwiches, burgers, pasta dishes, and salads, plus many exciting chalkboard specials, from $7 to $9. And at Harry's Juice and Java Bar you can also sample fresh-squeezed fruit and vegetable juices and cappuccinos and lattes, which can be accompanied by finger foods.

The dinner menu offers imaginative dishes, many inspired by trips undertaken by the kitchen staff to such places as Thailand or Greece. Choices might include pan-seared salmon served with an Oriental basil-and-ginger glaze and chicken breast rolled around Parma ham, vegetables, and fresh herbs with a mushroom-and-madeira sauce. Prices range from $16.50 to $23. Save some room for dessert, especially the Key lime tart or chocolate-chip cheesecake. By the way, you're dining in another of Cape May's Victorian beauties, built in 1882 complete with a cupola.

Hours: Feb 14–Dec, daily 8am–2:30pm, noon–2:30pm, and 5:30–9:30pm.

Brunch & Dinner

For top gourmet restaurants, number one has to be **Alexander's,** 653 Washington St. (tel. 609/884-2555). Lace doilies, roses on the table, and coffee served from a silver coffeepot on a swing add a dash of romance to tables set in the Victorian manner—the silverware placed face down. Dinner is served in four intimate candlelit rooms decorated with gilt-framed pictures. The food is exciting, never dull. The menu changes daily but specials always include a fish of the day, like swordfish with black-bean sauce. Other entrees might be duckling with blackberry-honey glaze, rabbit poached with onions and finished with Portuguese chocolate-burgundy sauce, and rack of lamb with béarnaise. Prices range from $22 to $27. To start, I recommend the soup du jour (like cream of crab and wild mushroom) or the well-textured sausage-nut strudel (almonds, walnuts, pecans, cream cheese, and sausage wrapped in flaky pastry). The desserts will undoubtedly include chocolate profiteroles and their very special brandy Alexander pie, flavored with brandy and crème de cacao, in a graham-cracker crust.

The tuxedoed service is impeccable, if a little too so: The bread appears in a silver basket, the cream comes in a Victorian-style silver jug with a lid carved in the shape of a lion's head, and the maître d' sports tails. The porch, bedecked with ferns and lace curtains, is a favorite spot for a brunch that's more lavish than most. Juice and a plate of seasonal fruit precede such main courses as Belgian waffles, omelets, and eggs Alexander. Dessert and coffee follow. Brunch runs $15.

Four guest rooms are available here (see "Cape May Lodging," above).

Hours: Memorial Day to late Sept, Mon and Wed–Sat from 6pm, Sun 9am–1pm (brunch) and from 6pm; mid-Apr to Memorial Day and late Sept to mid-Dec, Fri–Sat from 6pm, Sun 9am–1pm (brunch) and from 6pm.

Lunch & Dinner

A longtime favorite on the Cape May scene is the pretty **Washington Inn,** 801 Washington St. (tel. 609/884-5697), set in a large rambling house. It contains a screened-in side porch overlooking the colorful garden for summer dining, a pleasant piano bar with comfortable sofas and brocade Victorian chairs, and a front porch with wicker furniture for cocktails. The dining room is made especially attractive by an attached greenhouse filled with a brilliant show of orchids. Veal, beef (steaks), poultry, and seafood are available, including a popular henlopen's catch with shrimp, scallops, lobster, mussels, calamari, and clams in a seafood broth. Prices range from $18 to $25. Fresh homemade pies like apple-walnut and strawberry, plus such mouth-watering delights as blackberry mousse, are added attractions.

Hours: Mid-May to Oct, daily 5–9pm; mid-Mar to mid-May and Nov to Christmas, Thurs–Sun 5–9pm.

Dining at the **Lobster House,** on Fisherman's Wharf (tel. 609/884-8296), is an old Cape May tradition. The dining rooms are large and lacking in any spectacular decor, but people come for the steamed lobster or the popular schooner dinner, including a 1-pound lobster, clams, sea scallops, gulf shrimp, and king crab legs. Other selections depend on the seasonal catch—bluefish, softshell crab, clams, and other bounties of the sea. Entrees include salad, potato, and vegetable, and coffee or tea and start at $17, rising to $38 for the lobster tails.

This restaurant grosses millions in sales a year and on most nights, especially weekends, expect a two-hour wait. Names are announced over a loudspeaker and somehow the people get fed.

My favorite reason for going to the Lobster House, though, is to arrive about 5pm and go aboard the schooner *America* for a waterside seat where you can enjoy a cocktail and watch the families of ducks paddling back and forth, boatmen training their retrievers, seagulls casting moving shadows on the surface of the water, large vessels gliding into port, and the sun going down. You can order a clambake, crab sticks, steamed shrimp or crab, barbecued clams, and so on.

At the fresh seafood market, you can pick up a lobster to take home or take out some clams, scallops, or fresh fried fish with french fries onto the dock and watch the sun set while you enjoy a good meal for a fraction of the restaurant price. Get there early because the market usually closes about 6pm.

Hours: Mon–Sat noon–3pm and 5–10pm, Sun 4–10pm.

If you desperately want seafood but don't want to wait at the Lobster House (the food might even be a fraction better here), you can always go across the street to the **Anchorage Inn** (tel. 609/898-1174), at the foot of the canal bridge. The decor is nautical style, the tables are set with red gingham, and there's usually entertainment on weekends. At lunch I had a delicious crab soup filled with crab in a tomato-based stock. The clam chowder was equally well stocked with clams and potato and far less cornstarch. Dinner prices run $12 to $37 for shrimp, flounder, swordfish, sautéed crabmeat, fried or broiled scallops, baked crab Imperial, and some meat dishes. Real seafood fans will want the clambake feast for two—lobster, steamed clams, mussels, shrimp, scallops, corn, and garlic bread, accompanied by potato and vegetable, for $33. Luncheon prices are about half those at dinner.

Hours: Mid-May to mid-Sept, daily 5–10pm; mid-Sept to mid-Oct, Fri–Sat 5–10pm.

Cucina Rosa, 301 Washington Mall (tel. 609/898-9800), serves somewhat-overpriced Italian cuisine, at least for the typical veal parmigiana and piccata. Here it's best to stick to the specialties—tried-and-true favorites like manicotti, lasagne, and baked ziti. Prices range from $10 to $20.

Hours: Feb–Dec, Sun–Thurs 5–9pm, Fri–Sat 5–10pm.

Dinner Only

410 Bank Street (that's the address too) (tel. 609/884-2127), is Cape May's top-rated restaurant and certainly deserves praise for bringing the latest Cajun, Créole, and Caribbean cuisine to this waterfront town raised on seafood and prime rib. The specialties include a fine Cajun shellfish gumbo studded with lobster, sea scallops, shrimp, and mesquite-smoked sausage and a Jamaican steak that sizzles with one of the kitchen's Caribbean sauces. About six fish are offered every night and can be grilled with any one of the restaurant's famous sauces. To start, try the Bahamian yellowfin tuna beignets or crawfish bisque. Prices range from $21 to $25.

Hours: Mid-May to mid-Oct, daily 5–10pm.

Frescos, 412 Bank St. (tel. 609/884-0366), is all its name implies: lively and fun and serving some up-to-the-minute Italian cuisine. Choose among a dozen pastas—the richest is the smoked salmon and porcini mushrooms in a parmesan cream sauce over fettuccine, while the shrimp sautéed with feta, tomatoes, and fresh basil over fettuccine is on the lighter side. There's always a risotto of the day. Heartier eaters will appreciate the well-prepared saltimbocca or the swordfish in crabmeat-mushroom chardonnay-cream sauce.

Hours: Mid-Apr to Nov, daily 5–10pm.

Many people favor a tiny hole-in-the-wall called **Louisa's Café,** 104 Jackson St. (tel. 609/884-5882), which seats only 16. Even early in the season you'll be lucky if you secure a table; during summer you'll have to join the line. People flock here for the quality and freshness of the food, which includes homemade pasta and sauces flavored with herbs picked in the owner's garden. Daily specials are scrawled on a small chalkboard. When I was here it offered a choice of a delicious smooth soup of carrot with dill and cayenne, artichoke vinaigrette, and three or four main dishes—mahi mahi with Thai spice rub, tuna with tamari and ginger, and chicken breast in mustard-orange Jamaican jerk sauce. The desserts are excellent, ranging from a scrumptious chocolate-mousse pie and several fresh-fruit cobblers to vanilla bread pudding with brown-sugar/whisky sauce. Prices range from $10 to $17. You may bring your own wine, which you can pick up at Colliers, just down the street. No credit cards and no smoking.

Hours: Apr–Sept, Tues–Sat 5–9pm; Oct–Nov, Fri–Sat 5–9pm.

Maureen's, 429 Beach Dr., at Decatur (tel. 609/884-3774), is a successful Philadelphia restaurant that has been transplanted to the shore. The menu features several cuisines—French, Italian, Japanese, and southwestern. For example, among the appetizers might be Santa Fe duck, which is duck roasted with smoked apples and seasoned with chipotle barbecue sauce, wrapped in a soft warm tortilla, topped with a sassy corn relish. The main courses ($20 to $28) might range from poached salmon Natsuka served in a sauce of Mirin, sake, soy, ginger, and tangerines to a veal chop with red, yellow, and green peppers with fontina cheese and marsala sauce.

Hours: Apr–Oct, daily 5–10pm.

Peaches at Sunset, 1 Sunset Blvd. West (tel. 609/898-0100), in a remodeled Victorian home, offers fine dining in a tropical ambience. The cuisine features fresh seasonal ingredients combined into richly flavored dishes like roast Cornish game hen with Italian pancetta, rubbed with lemon and rosemary, and served in its natural juices; or medallions of venison marinated in olive oil with cranberries, sautéed and oven browned, then served on a bed of onion jam and drizzled with cranberry-orange oil. The signature appetizer is the roasted garlic Gilroy, spread on sourdough bread along with mascarpone cheese.

Hours: Apr–Oct, daily 4:30–9:15pm; Nov–Mar, Fri–Sun 4:30–9:15pm.

The **Rose Garden Restaurant** (The Bayberry Inn), on Perry Street at Congress Place (tel. 609/884-8336), has developed a good reputation for serving eclectic cuisine. The favored dining spot is out under the soaring arcade/terrace. The dining room itself is simple and derives its character largely from the huge fireplace accented by copper pots.

Hours: Thurs–Tues 5:30–10pm.

Watson's Merion Inn, 106 Decatur St. (tel. 609/884-8363), is a Cape May tradition serving an updated American menu that features plenty of seafood—grilled swordfish with lime-cilantro butter served with mango salsa, grilled tuna with sesame-ginger glaze, and crab Imperial served in a giant scallop shell. Steak and additional chicken and veal dishes round out the menu. Prices range from $13 for penne with grilled vegetables and smoked mozzarella to $32 for surf and turf. The substantial atmosphere is created by the gilt portraits and pictures on the walls and the handsome sturdy cherry-and-oak bar.

Hours: May–Oct, daily noon–2:30pm and 5–10pm; Apr, Sun–Thurs noon–2:30pm, Fri–Sat noon–2:30pm and 5–10pm.

My choice for seafood would be **A & J Blue Claw,** Ocean Drive, south of the Wildwood Crest toll bridge (tel. 609/884-5878). The decor is plain and simple, but the fish is well cooked and this is one place where you can select your lobster from the tank. Specialties include a New England clambake (lobster, clams, potatoes, onions, and an ear of corn steamed together); a deluxe seafood medley of lobster, filet, shrimp, scallops, and clams casino; seafood kebab; and clams and oysters at the raw bar. Four crab dishes are offered and several other fish items, along with steak and a chicken dish. Prices run $22 to $38.

Hours: Summer, Sun–Thurs 5–8:30pm, Fri–Sat 5–10pm; the rest of the year, Fri–Sat 5–10pm.

For simple soups, salads, burgers, and a good filet mignon with house salad, try **Oyster Bay Steak and Seafood,** on Lafayette Street right across from the Acme supermarket (tel. 609/884-2111). Prices range from $10 to $18. There's no real decor here.

Hours: Open seasonally.

After Dark

During summer, the **Mid-Atlantic Center for the Arts,** 1048 Washington St. (tel. 609/884-5404), offers musical and drama performances on their outdoor stage at the Physick Estate. Bring your own chair.

Relaxing **cocktail spots** include the schooner at the Lobster House, the Washington Inn's porch and piano bar, the Merion Inn's lounge bar, and the King Edward Room at the Chalfonte.

On the mall there are a couple of typical tavern-style places that offer musical entertainment—the **Ugly Mug,** at 426 Washington Street Mall (tel. 609/884-3459), where numerous mugs belonging to the Ugly Mug club members adorn the ceiling; and the **Old Shire Tavern,** at 315 Washington Street Mall (tel. 609/884-4700).

For loud raucous nightlife, you'll have to head for **Wildwood.**

| **Cape May** |
| Special & Recreational Activities |

Beaches: The town beaches are pleasant and sandy, with a minimum of honky-tonk. Beach passes are required and readily available at the information center. More natural, secluded beaches, backed by high undulating dunes, are located at Cape May Point; take Cape Avenue off Sunset Boulevard.

At Sunset Beach, not a particularly attractive sunning or swimming beach, you'll probably see a lot of people bent double, scouring the sands for the famous and elusive Cape May diamonds. They're milky in color and when polished glitter like diamonds. Here you can also see the concrete bulkhead of the World War I S.S. *Atlantis* rising from the ocean. After several Atlantic crossings, this impractical vessel was sunk for use as a jetty.

Bicycling: At Village Bike Rentals, Ocean and Washington streets (tel. 609/884-8500), in the Acme parking lot across from the Mall's information booth, bikes rent for $3.75 per hour, $9.55 per day. There are also a couple of surreys for two or more that rent for $12 per hour.

Birdwatching: Long before Cape May was famous as a resort, Audubon made it famous for its birdlife. A million and half migrating shore birds pass through Cape May. Prime sights are the harlequin and eider ducks in winter, warblers in spring, herons and egrets in summer, and the largest raptor migration in the nation, which takes place in fall when as many as 88,000 hawks have been recorded massing.

In Cape May State Park, P.O. Box 107, Cape May Point, NJ 08212 (tel. 609/884-2159), blinds and platforms have been built for viewing the marsh and sea birds over the tall stately reeds. Turn left off Sunset Boulevard onto Lighthouse Avenue; the park is by the lighthouse.

At the Cape May Bird Observatory and Sanctuary overlooking Lily Lake, you'll find the offices of the Audubon Society (open Mon–Fri 9am–5pm). For their special weekends led by trained naturalists, contact the Cape May Bird Observatory, East Lake Drive (P.O. Box 3), Cape May Point, NJ 08212 (tel. 609/884-2736).

For special birding and other wildlife ventures, contact Jersey Cape Nature Excursions, P.O. Box 254, Cape May, NJ 08204 (tel. 609/884-3712).

At the nearby Stone Harbor Bird Sanctuary, American egrets, Louisiana and green herons, black-crowned and yellow-crowned night herons, and ibis all nest. From 111th to 116th streets on Third Avenue in Stone Harbor. Call the Wetlands (tel. 609/368-1211).

Farther north at Avalon lies one of the last high dune areas in the state, filled with all kinds of flora and fauna (tel. 609/967-8200).

Camping: Cold Spring Campground, 541 New England Rd., Cape May, NJ 08204 (tel. 609/884-8717), has pleasant secluded sites among sycamore, beech, and hickory. It's near Higbee Beach, where you can walk between 10-foot-high reeds to a small, albeit shingly, beach. Open May to Columbus Day, it charges $15.

The closest wilderness camping can be found at Belleplain Forest, P.O. Box 450, Woodbine, NJ 08270 (tel. 609/861-2404), which has 193 sites and opportunities for bathing, boating, fishing, and hiking. Open all year.

Cruises: The 80-foot schooner *Yankee* (tel. 609/884-1919) gives three-hour cruises leaving from the marina on Ocean Drive between Cape May and Wildwood. The ship usually leaves at 10am and 2 and 6pm, charging $26.50 per person.

The Cape May–Lewes Ferry that leaves from Lower Township, North Cape May on Lincoln Boulevard, is a fun 70-minute trip to take from Cape May to Lewes in Delaware. It costs about $20 for a car and driver. For reservations call 800/717-7245; for information call 609/886-9699, or 800/643-3779.

Fishing: South Jersey Fishing Center (tel. 609/884-3800) is the dock to head for, with daily sailings from April to November for about $35 per person. Write P.O. Box 641, Cape May, NJ 08204.

Golf: Avalon Golf Club, 1510 Rte. 9 North (tel. 609/465-4389), is 18 holes, par 71. Semiprivate. Take Exit 13 off the Garden State Parkway.

Ice Skating: Often fun on Lily Lake.

Picnicking: Pick up staples in town at the supermarkets or main stores. There's a good fresh-produce stand just beyond Junction 607 on Sunset Boulevard en route to Cape May Point beaches, one of the prime picnic sites.

Sailing: Cruise aboard *The Free Spirit,* a 27-foot yacht. The charge is $20 per person for a two-hour cruise. Call 609/884-8347 between 8am and 1pm and 3 and 5pm.

Tennis: The William Moore Tennis Center, on Washington Street just before the entrance to the Physick Estate (tel. 609/884-8986), has four all-weather and four clay courts. It charges $5 per person per hour.

Whale-Watching: From April to December boats leave port in search of whales, dolphins, and sea birds. Contact either the Cape May Whale Watch & Research Center, 1286 Wilson Dr., Cape May NJ 08204 (tel. 609/898-0055), or Cape May Whale Watcher, Second Avenue and Wilson Drive, Cape May, NJ 08204 (tel. 609/884-5445).

NEW YORK

The Hudson River Valley

Distance in Miles: Newburgh, 66; Poughkeepsie, 77; Kingston, 97
Estimated Driving Time: 1 to 2 hours

◄O►◄O►◄O►◄O►◄O►

Driving: For west-bank destinations, take the Palisades Parkway to West Point and the New York Thruway to points farther north—like New Paltz and Kingston. For east-bank destinations, you can do the same; cross the river at either Poughkeepsie or Kingston. Or you can take the Taconic Parkway, a far more scenic route.

Bus: Adirondack/Pine Hill Trailways (tel. 800/225-6815) goes to New Paltz and Kingston.

Train: Amtrak (tel. 800/872-7245) travels up the east bank of the Hudson, stopping at Rhinecliff (just west of Rhinebeck). Metro North's Harlem-Hudson line (tel. 800/638-7646) stops at Garrison, Cold Spring, and Poughkeepsie.

Further Information: For more about the east-bank areas, contact the **Columbia County Chamber of Commerce,** 507 Warren St., Hudson, NY 12534 (tel. 518/828-4417); **Dutchess County Tourism,** 3 Neptune Rd., Poughkeepsie, NY 12601 (tel. 914/463-4000, or 800/445-3131); and **Putnam County Tourist Information,** ℅ Cold Spring Area Chamber of Commerce, P.O. Box 71, Cold Spring-on-Hudson, NY 10516 (tel. 914/265-9060).

For more about the west-bank areas, contact **Greene County Tourism,** P.O. Box 527, Catskill, NY 12414 (tel. 518/943-3223); **Orange County Tourism,** 30 Matthews St., Goshen, NY 10924 (tel. 914/294-5151); and the **Ulster County Public Information Office,** P.O. Box 1800, Kingston, NY 12401 (tel. 914/331-9300).

For general New York State information, contact the **New York State Department of Economic Development,** Division of Tourism, One Commerce Plaza, Albany, NY 12245 (tel. 518/474-4116).

Although many New Yorkers may simply regard the Hudson River as a dirty brown line separating Manhattan from New Jersey, they need only travel to the Cloisters and Fort Tryon Park to get a very different perspective. Here they'll marvel at the beauty and majesty of this broad swath of river that travels 315 miles from the Adirondacks, where it rises as a trout stream, cuts between the Catskills and the Berkshires, and flows past the unique bluffs of the Palisades, down to New York Bay, and out into the ocean. It's a river that has spawned many legends and mysteries, inspiring such authors as Washington Irving and William Cullen Bryant and such painters as Thomas Cole and Frederic Church, whose work gave rise to one of the first schools of American painting.

In 1609, representing the Dutch East India Company, Henry Hudson sailed up the river aboard the *Half Moon* as far as present-day Albany, but failing to find passage beyond there he withdrew and dropped anchor at Athens, where he encountered the Native Americans and remarked upon their corn and pumpkins. In 1624 the Dutch founded the first colony of New Netherland at Fort Orange (now Albany), and great estates and patroonships were later established along the fertile river valley, which is still famous for its apples, produce, dairy goods, horse farming, and horticultural wonders (Rhinebeck, for example, was once the world's violet capital). The English took over the area in 1664.

Two-thirds of all the Revolutionary War battles were fought in New York State, many along the banks of the Hudson, making the area rich in historical associations. Remnants of General Burgoyne's army straggled back from the Battle of Saratoga and encamped just outside Catskill. The spy Maj. John André, en route through the patriots' lines from a meeting with Benedict Arnold, was captured in Tarrytown and executed at Tappan Hill. Washington spent 17 months at Newburgh while discussing the nature of the peace. At West Point, an early garrison against the British, remnants of the chain barrier erected across the river to stop the British advance can still be seen. During the turmoil, the governing body of the state was forced to flit about, settling briefly in Hurley and later in Kingston, where their meeting place survived the city's burning by the British and can be visited today. Many of these historical events and dramas can be captured by visiting West Point, Newburgh, Kingston, and New Paltz and Hurley, where stone houses from the original Dutch settlements remain.

In the 19th century, the river became the very lifeline of New York City. All kinds of supplies were shipped downriver—ice blocks and bricks from Athens; cement and bluestone for the base of the Statue of Liberty and the caissons of the Brooklyn Bridge; fruit and livestock; and, most important, anthracite coal from Pennsylvania mines, which traveled via the Delaware-Hudson Canal to Kingston and from there was shipped down the Hudson. The river was lined with bustling ports: Kingston was the largest and busiest; Newburgh, Poughkeepsie, and Hudson were important whaling towns; and ice houses flourished at Athens. Many of these communities have

Events & Festivals to Plan Your Trip Around

East Bank Events

May: Great Hudson Valley Balloon Race, at the Dutchess County Airport, Wappingers Falls. More than 30 balloons, sky diving, aerobatic shows, and more.

Hudson River Valley Antique Auto Show, at the Dutchess County Fairgrounds, Rhinebeck.

Rhinebeck Antiques Show, at the Dutchess County Fairgrounds, Rhinebeck. Call 914/876-4001.

Rhinebeck Crafts Fair, at the Dutchess County Fairgrounds, Rhinebeck. More than 350 craftspeople display their work. Call 914/876-4001.

August: Bard Music Festival Rediscoveries, Bard College, Rte. 9G, Annandale. Series of lectures and performances concentrating on particular composers' works. Call 914/758-2869.

Dutchess County Fair, Rhinebeck (mid-August). Second largest fair in the state. Call 914/876-4001.

October: Pumpkin Festival, Clearwater. The sloop *Clearwater* sails the Hudson, celebrating at various riverside locations along the way. Call 914/454-7673.

Rhinebeck Crafts Fair, at the Dutchess County Fairgrounds, Rhinebeck. Call 914/876-4001.

Rhinebeck Antiques Show, at the Dutchess County Fairgrounds, Rhinebeck. Call 914/876-4001.

West Bank Events

July–September: New York Renaissance Festival, at Sterling Forest, Tuxedo (every weekend from the end of July to the second weekend after Labor Day). A celebration of pageantry, jousting, wandering minstrels, and other fitting entertainments. Call 914/351-5171.

October: Chrysanthemum Festival, in Seamon Park, Saugerties.

Oktoberfest, Kingston.

long slumbered—almost as if waiting for another call from the river to return to life, since railroads, automobiles, and airplanes stole their livelihoods. Now many are being revived, and in summer they're lively with celebrations and festivals, fairs, and all kinds of fun. A maritime museum and a trolley museum are bringing the Kingston Rondout back to life; in Hudson, many lovely old town houses are being restored; Cold Spring Harbor's Victorian hotel has been refurbished and reopened, and the town has established a reputation as a major destination for antiques lovers. Life has returned to the Hudson, and even the striped bass and the shad are running and spawning again. Naturalist John Burroughs would no doubt applaud the efforts to rescue the river from the destruction of pollution, and for the visitor there's no better way to get acquainted with the Hudson than to ride the sloop *Clearwater,* which leaves daily from Beacon and has brought so much publicity to the campaign to save this national treasure. Other cruise boats leave from Kingston, Catskill, Poughkeepsie, and Albany.

When Washington Irving first sailed up the river in 1800, the trip to Catskill took anywhere from 4 to 10 days, depending on the weather, but Robert Fulton's first steamboat, the *Clermont* (1807), changed all that, reducing the trip to a mere 24 hours. The river became a steamboat lane and tall smokestacks could be seen gliding upriver, sidewheels churning and decks crowded with tourists headed for the Catskill Mountain resorts via Kingston and Catskill Point. Sometimes their captains raced each other and accidents resulted, like the one that killed architect Andrew Jackson Downing and Nathaniel Hawthorne's sister.

Tourists still come to the valley to explore the river towns. They browse for antiques; attend festivals, fairs, and other special events; visit the mansions and homes of early settlers, artists, or such political figures as Franklin Roosevelt and Martin Van Buren; attend parades and football games at West Point; drive through the sculpture field at Storm King; cruise on the river; hike, fish, and camp in the state parks; stay at old country inns; and enjoy the landscape. All seasons bring beauty to the river valley: In spring the river is high and fast-flowing and the orchards along its banks are in full blossom along with the dogwoods. In summer the river is filled with sailboats that tack from side to side, while other pleasure craft tow waterskiers or just cruise along past towns that are celebrating summer with river festivals, antiques and craft fairs, and other events. In fall the trees are radiant and the natives congregate at country fairs or in the orchards or fields, where the busy fruit and vegetable picking testifies to the abundance of the harvest. In winter the scene resembles a Dutch painting: iceboat parties take to the river and people go skating and walking on the ice, their breath trailing momentarily in the air.

No wonder so many prominent families—the Van Cortlandts and Verplancks and later the Livingstons, Jays, Harrimans, Astors, and Roosevelts—chose to build mansions here. Today their homes are marvelous places to visit, providing some of the best vantage points from which to view the river—Boscobel in Garrison, Roosevelt's home at Hyde Park, the Vanderbilt and Ogden Mills mansions, Livingston's Clermont estate, and Olana, which commands a view of the famous bend in the river that Church so loved to gaze upon and paint.

So why not follow in their footsteps and head for the Hudson, returning laden with stories and produce, memories and more?

Sightseeing Suggestions

If you anchor in Rhinebeck, you can visit the FDR Museum Library and home in Hyde Park and the Vanderbilt mansion during one day, lunching at the Culinary Institute of America and doing some antiquing in between. You can spend the next day exploring Rhinebeck and nearby attractions like Clermont, Olana, and Lindenwald.

On the west bank you can spend a day visiting wineries or the historic spots along the river from West Point to Newburgh. You can spend the second day at lovely Lake Minnewaska, discovering the Dutch settlements at New Paltz or Hurley, or seeing what's going on at the Kingston Rondout.

THE EAST BANK

In this section I haven't included the Sleepy Hollow Restorations—Philipsburg Manor, Sunnyside, and Sleepy Hollow—as I consider them day trips from Manhattan. Instead, I begin south of Poughkeepsie and travel all the way up the river to Hudson. On this side of the river there's not an abundance of accommodations, so your choice is restricted to the Beekman Arms in Rhinebeck and several bed-and-breakfasts in Rhinebeck and environs. If none of these appeals to you, then your best bet is to anchor on the other side around New Paltz, where the Mohonk Mountain House offers delightful accommodations and there are several outstanding B&Bs. From there, you can cross the river at either Poughkeepsie or Kingston to view the sights on the opposite bank.

POUGHKEEPSIE

Poughkeepsie Attractions

At **Samuel F. B. Morse's Locust Grove,** on Rte. 9 just south of Poughkeepsie (tel. 914/454-4500), you'll discover that Morse was far more than just the inventor of the Morse Code. He was also the inventor of the telegraph, which he made out of the canvas stretchers (among other things) he used in his primary career as a painter of portraits and landscapes. Indeed he regarded his inventions as ways of supporting his painting career—an attitude supported in this century by the sale of his *Gallery of* *the Louvre* for $3.25 million. When Morse purchased the estate from the Livingstons it included an early 19th-century Georgian home. Morse hired Andrew Jackson Downing to remodel it to look like a Tuscan villa, and the Morse family lived in it from 1847 to 1901. A good interpretive tour is given of the site. One room is filled with Morse memorabilia, including a model of the first telegraph. Other rooms contain the 18th- and 19th-century furnishings of later owners, including several Duncan Phyfe pieces. Afterward, you can explore the flower and herb gardens and 4¹/₂ miles of riverfront trails.

Hours: Memorial Day–Sept, Wed–Sun 10am–4pm; Oct, Sat–Sun 10am–4pm; all Mon holidays 10am–4pm. **Admission:** $4 adults, $3.50 seniors, $1 children.

The **Frances Lehman Loeb Art Center,** at Vassar College 914/437-5632 or 437-5235), is housed in Cesar Pelli's dramatic series of buildings, which opened in 1993. The galleries are devoted to antiquities, European Renaissance and baroque paintings, 19th- and 20th-century European and American art, Asian art, and prints and drawings. The two sculpture courts are very appealing. The collection comprises 12,500 objects, but only 400 are exhibited in the Main Gallery. Among the highlights of the historic collections are the red granite head of Viceroy Merymose (1391–53 B.C.); a rhyton in the shape of a dog's head; an Eastern Han Dynasty tower (A.D. 25–220); paintings by Pieter Brueghel the Younger, Cézanne, Delacroix, and Doré; and works by John Singleton Copley, William Hamilton, and George Innes. The 20th-century galleries include notable sculptures by Calder and Anthony Caro as well as paintings by Francis Bacon, Marsden Hartley, Georgia O'Keeffe, Jackson Pollock, Balthus, and Mark Rothko.

Hours: Tues–Sat 10am–5pm, Sun 1–5pm. **Admission:** Free.

While you're here, you can also view the home Andrew Jackson Downing built for Matthew Vassar: **Springside,** 185 Academy St. (tel. 914/452-6538).

Tours: By appointment.

From Poughkeepsie, detour along Rte. 44. Take the Taconic Parkway north to the Salt Point Turnpike and turn right at the end of the exit. This will bring you to Clinton Corners, site of one of New York's small picturesque wineries, **Clinton Vineyards** (tel. 914/266-5372). Proprietor/winemaker Ben Feder produces high-quality Seyval blanc table wine and Johanissberg riesling dessert wine as well as *méthode champenoise* Seyval natural. Tours and tastings are offered on weekends year round. During summer the winery is open on Friday too. The tasting room also offers wine accessories and picnics that can be enjoyed on the grounds. To reach the vineyard, go through Clinton Corners until you come to a 10-m.p.h. sign, where the road curves to the right. Make a sharp left onto Schultzville Road and look for the vineyard sign on the left.

Poughkeepsie Lodging & Dining

The **Inn at the Falls,** 50 Red Oaks Mill Rd., Poughkeepsie, NY 12603 (tel. 914/462-5770), belies its name since it's absolutely new and modern, from the exterior of red brick and shingles to the blond-wood reception desk, but it does look out onto Wappinger Creek and falls. The 36 air-conditioned guest units include 20 doubles, 2 minisuites, 8 suites, and 2 rooms for the disabled. A standard double contains a brass bed, a wing chair, a blond pine desk, and a wardrobe. Jade and dusky rose are the chosen colors. A TV, a pushbutton phone in both the room and the bath, and toothpaste, shampoo, mouthwash, tissues, and a terry-cloth robe are among the nice amenities. The toilet is separate from the bathroom.

The suites are spectacular: The Contemporary Suite has a dramatic black-tile bath with a Jacuzzi and a platform bed with a polished black headboard and dusky-rose comforter. The English Suite has a king-size four-poster with a crocheted canopy, a polished roll-top desk, brass lamps, a gaming table, and Queen Anne–style chairs among its antique reproductions. The country minisuite sports a Pennsylvania Dutch–style chest, a Windsor chair, and a leather wing chair among its furnishings. A high-ceilinged sitting room is available for guests. The continental breakfast is served in your room.

Rates (including breakfast): $120–$130 double; $135–$160 suite.

After Dark

Poughkeepsie's **Bardavon Theater,** 35 Market St. (tel. 914/473-2072), is a historic theater where the ornate stucco and decorative work has been restored to its 1869 splendor. It now hosts a variety of performers along with popular Broadway and Off Broadway shows.

HYDE PARK

Hyde Park Area Attractions

You can spend a day or more at Hyde Park exploring this moving memorial to Franklin Delano and Eleanor Roosevelt, for there are several parts to the whole. First, the **FDR Museum and Library,** Albany Post Road (tel. 914/229-8114), documents the life, political campaigns, triumphs, and tribulations of Roosevelt through a superb collection of memorabilia, letters, speeches, and documents. The most important exhibits are the photographs that dramatize the great and tragic moments of history—the 1945 capture of thousands of German soldiers in the Ruhr; the liberation of Paris on August 25, 1944; perfectly disciplined Allied soldiers under attack waiting to be rescued at Dunkirk; the famous picture of the abandoned baby crying in the ruins of Shanghai during Japan's invasion of China.

The Hudson River Valley

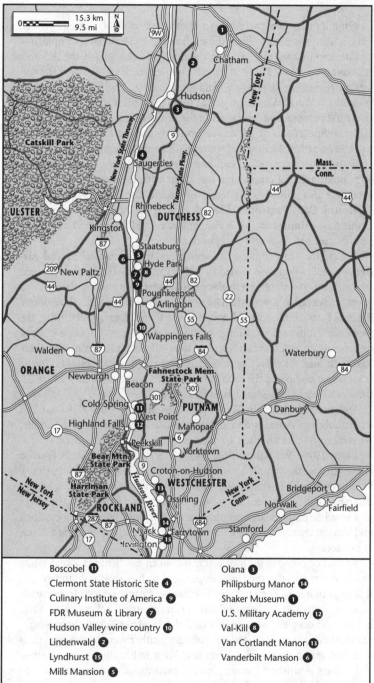

Boscobel 11
Clermont State Historic Site 4
Culinary Institute of America 9
FDR Museum & Library 7
Hudson Valley wine country 10
Lindenwald 2
Lyndhurst 15
Mills Mansion 5

Olana 3
Philipsburg Manor 14
Shaker Museum 1
U.S. Military Academy 12
Val-Kill 8
Van Cortlandt Manor 13
Vanderbilt Mansion 6

On a lighter note, there's also a photograph of FDR's famous Scottie, Fala, which was used to libel Roosevelt in the 1944 election campaign—certain Republicans charged that the dog had been left on the Aleutian Islands and recovered at great expense to the American taxpayer. The collection makes for riveting viewing and reading. There's also a stirring multimedia World War II exhibit that features a replica of the "Map Room," the secret communications center in the White House basement. An interactive computer exhibit allows visitors to assume the role of commander-in-chief and make tactical and strategic decisions. The more personal side of Roosevelt is captured in exhibits about his younger years, his battle with polio, and, of course, his love affair with Eleanor, whose life and career are also portrayed through exhibits and displays.

Hours: Daily 9am–6pm. **Closed:** New Year's Day, Thanksgiving, and Christmas. **Admission** (for home, museum, and library): $5 adults, $4 seniors, free for children 16 and under.

Behind the museum, you can walk down to the **rose arbor and garden** where Franklin was buried in 1945 (Eleanor in 1962), then proceed to the 32nd president's **birthplace and home** overlooking the Hudson River, preserved as it was when he died. Tour the house while listening to Eleanor Roosevelt's recorded comments and anecdotes, which bring the various features and furnishings of the house to life and provide insights into the historic events that took place here—the office, for example, where Roosevelt and Winston Churchill signed the agreement resulting in the first atomic bomb and the room where he was born on January 30, 1882, the son of James and Sara Delano Roosevelt.

Hours: Apr–Oct, daily 9am–5pm. **Closed:** Mon–Tues Nov–Mar and major holidays. **Admission** (for home, museum, and library): $5 adults, $4 seniors, free for children 16 and under.

From 1926, **Val-Kill,** on Rte. 9G (tel. 914/229-9115), was Eleanor Roosevelt's weekend and vacation place. After leaving the White House following Franklin's death, she made it her home from 1945 until her death in 1962. The name means "Valley Stream" and here, along the banks of a small stream, Eleanor would often picnic with friends Nancy Cook and Marion Dickerman, but FDR was the first to suggest building a house at this location.

At the beginning of the tour you're shown an excellent black-and-white film that captures the amazing compassion, enthusiasm, and humanity of this great first lady. Born in 1884 to Elliott and Anna Roosevelt, she was a disappointment to her beautiful mother and aunts, all belles of New York, but her n'er-do-well father nevertheless doted on her. When she was eight her mother died and she and her younger brother went to live with their maternal grandmother; two years later their father died. Perhaps these early losses nourished Eleanor's humanitarianism. Soon she was sent to the Allenswood School in England, where she was encouraged in her studies by the headmistress, Mlle Souvestre. At 18 she renewed her acquaintance with her distant cousin Franklin, with whom she'd been friends, and, over the objections of his mother, married him in 1905. The film then charts the birth of their five children and FDR's political career up until he contracted polio in 1921, when Eleanor began actively to promote her husband's aspirations. Later, it follows them as they bring attention to the unjust conditions that prevailed among women, minorities, youth, and the unemployed.

During FDR's presidency, Val-Kill became a center of Eleanor's social life, with swimming and picnicking parties, and also a tranquil retreat about which she wrote in her newspaper column "My Day." After FDR's 1945 death she withdrew to Val-Kill but continued to involve herself in the U.N., human rights, and politics, campaigning for Adlai Stevenson in 1956 and for Jack Kennedy in 1960. On November 7, 1962, she died at age 78 and the *New York Times* obituary eulogizing her stated that "she was a humanitarian who won over many of her critics by the greatness of her heart." Take some time to look at the photos in the theater, including an intimate moment of her picking roses.

From here, the tour of the house proceeds into the office/sitting room, where cocktails were apportioned five minutes' time. The desk and some of the other furnishings were hers, including the filing cabinet crafted to look like a chest by workmen in the Val-Kill Industries furniture factory—an enterprise she helped establish to provide for farm youth and to preserve old skills.

The overwhelming response to this residence is "how simple, how home-like and unpretentious, how ordinary." The rooms are filled with mementoes, bric-a-brac, and photographs. Eleanor loved to sleep on the porch overlooking the garden rather than in her bedroom. Note the bathroom mirror placement—she was 6 feet tall.

Hours: May–Oct, Wed–Sun 9am–5pm; Mar–Apr and Nov–Dec, Sat–Sun 9am–5pm. The tour takes 80 minutes. **Admission:** Free.

Antiques lovers may want to travel up the road a little to the **Hyde Park Antiques Center,** 544 Albany Post Rd. (tel. 914/229-8200), where 50 dealers are located under one roof.

Hours: Daily 10am–5pm.

Hyde Park Dining

Make arrangements at least three months in advance for one of the four dining rooms at the **Culinary Institute of America,** Rte. 9 (tel. 914/471-6608), the nation's leading culinary school. For reservations, call 914/471-6608 Monday to Friday from 8:30am to 5pm. If you'd like to take a tour of the school, call 914/451-1544.

The French-style Escoffier Room, with chandeliers, is the most formal space. It features modern interpretations of classic French cuisine—like sole normande, canard aux pêches, and côte de veau bonne femme. Lunch entrees run $12 to $16; dinner entrees, $17 to $25. Book at least six months ahead for weekends.

Hours: Tues–Sat noon–1pm and 6:30–8:30pm.

The **American Bounty**—my favorite dining room—celebrates the country's diverse cultural heritage with seasonal menus emphasizing regional ingredients and preparations: ham stuffed with crabmeat and corn from Maryland and chili/jack-cheese pie from Texas, for example. Each day, the Julia Child Rotisserie prepares a special roast. There are always several soups offered, served smörgåsbord style if you wish, along with a variety of breads and salads. You can see the chefs cooking in the glassed-in kitchen hung with copper pots. A sumptuous array of produce is displayed in front, and the walls are adorned with mouth-watering color pictures of food and ingredients. Among the regional specialties may be crawfish pie New Orleans style, barbecued salmon filet, or southern-style fried chicken with gravy and corn custard. Prices run $15 to $24 at dinner, a little less at lunch.

Hours: Tues–Sat 11:30am–1pm and 6–8pm.

In the **St. Andrews Cafe,** the contemporary menu includes wood-fired pizza, vegetarian dishes, and other grilled items. Outdoor dining is available in season.

Hours: Mon–Fri 11:30am–1pm and 6–8pm.

The **Caterina de Medici Dining Room** offers fixed-price menus of regional Italian specialties and seasonal selections. The prix-fixe lunch is $21; dinner is $27.95.

Hours: Mon–Fri 11:30am–12:30pm and 6:30–7:30pm.

For a convenient nearby lunch after visiting Hyde Park or Val-Kill, stop at the **Easy Street Cafe,** on Rte. 9 (tel. 914/229-7969), which has deli sandwiches and burgers priced under $6.

Hours: Daily 11:30am–10pm.

Attractions North of Hyde Park

Vanderbilt Mansion

Just north of Hyde Park, also on Rte. 9, is the "smallest" Vanderbilt residence (tel. 914/229-9115), designed by McKim, Mead and White for Frederick Vanderbilt. He was the third grandson of Commodore Cornelius Vanderbilt, who began by ferrying fruit and vegetables from Staten Island to New York City and had amassed a $1-million fortune by 1830. Although the house cost $660,000 and contains 59 rooms, 14 baths, and 22 fireplaces, it's considered modest (especially when you compare it to other remaining family homes—like the Breakers and Marble House in Newport, R.I., and Biltmore in Asheville, N.C.). Frederick, in fact, received the smallest inheritance from the family because they disapproved of his marriage to Louise Anthony, a divorcée 12 years his senior, whom he'd wed in secret. Still, the house is pretty opulent, as the 45-minute tour reveals, progressing from the den through the oval main hall and walnut-paneled drawing room where many a gala ball was held. Upstairs, Mrs. Vanderbilt's bedroom was modeled after a French queen's boudoir. Mr. Vanderbilt's bedroom features solid carved-walnut columns, a gigantic marble fireplace, and a vast bath. Astute, Frederick managed to increase his inheritance seven times to a total of $80 million, and he never missed a detail, as many of the house's features indicate. For example, though the house was used in spring and fall only, it had a central heating system, its own power plant, light dimmers, and sleeping quarters for 60 servants. After touring the house, explore the grounds north of the mansion for an unsurpassed view of the Hudson.

Hours: Wed–Sun 9am–5pm. **Closed:** New Year's Day, Thanksgiving, and Christmas. **Admission:** $2 adults, free for children 16 and under.

Mills Mansion

A few miles farther north on Rte. 9, in Staatsburg, is the lesser-known Mills mansion (tel. 914/889-4100), reflecting the grand living style of the well-to-do in early 20th-century America. Through the trees you'll glimpse the mansion's classical proportions, embellished with pilasters, a balustrade, and statuary, located on a small bluff. The grounds sweep down to the Hudson River, making it an ideal picnicking spot. The 65-room home was built by Morgan Lewis, a Revolutionary War general and governor of New York. It later became a home for one branch of the Livingston family when Lewis's great-granddaughter, Ruth Livingston, married financier Ogden Mills. They enlarged and remodeled the 1832 Greek Revival house with the aid of McKim, Mead and White. Marble fireplaces, gilded plasterwork, and oak paneling provide an opulent backdrop for ornate furnishings, tapestries, and objets d'art. Consider, though, that this was only one of the Millses' retreats—they also owned homes in Paris, Newport, New York City, and California.

Hours: Memorial Day–Labor Day, Wed–Sat 10am–5pm, Sun noon–5pm; Labor Day–Oct, Wed–Sun noon–5pm. Free guided tours of the first floor.

RHINEBECK & RED HOOK

Rhinebeck Area Attractions

Just 5 miles up Rte. 9 is the delightful village of Rhinebeck, where you can enjoy a cocktail in the tap room at the Beekman Arms, browse through the stores and boutiques, see what's on at the old movie theater that runs classic and foreign films (often attended by their directors), and attend any number of special events that are scheduled during summer and fall at the Dutchess County Fairgrounds (like the county fair or big spring antiques fair). Sadly, the renowned American Craft Enterprises Rhinebeck Crafts Fair has moved on, but there's another good crafts show now in its place.

Rhinebeck boasts another exciting attraction, the **Rhinebeck Aerodrome,** northeast of the town on Stone Church Road, off Rte. 9 (tel. 914/758-8610). During summer, daredevil pilots perform spectacular flying stunts, restaging mock battles in World War I triplanes and biplanes, recreating an era when propellers still whirled and flying was a true pioneer's pastime associated with smoke, grease, and risk. Besides viewing the thrilling air show when the Black Baron threatens the skies, you can take a ride in a 1929 vintage flyer and admire the many antique aircraft housed here.

Three buildings contain exhibits from the various flying eras. My favorite is the Pioneer Building, which displays Bleriot's machines, the Wright brothers' glider, the 1912 Passett ornithopter (it was built with the intention of the pilot to fly by flapping its wings and was specially constructed for use in *Those Magnificent Men and Their Flying Machines*), and a peculiar (looking like an insect) 1912 Thomas Pusher, which Cole Palen (the museum's founder) actually flew to Flushing Airport. The two other hangars exhibit planes from the Lindbergh and World War I eras, including a Waco Model 10 that cruised at 84 m.p.h. and had a 385-mile range. Among the World War I exhibits are the Sopwith 7F1, a 121-m.p.h. British fighter; the Fokker D VII, a German fighter that downed 275 Allied craft; the Fokker DR-1, a triplane with a two-hour range that Baron Manfred von Richthofen favored; and the Spad in which Capt. Eddie Rickenbacker achieved fame piloting as a member of the renowned "Hat in the Rug" squadron. Some are original; some were built by Palen. Sunday air shows feature World War I craft; Saturday shows use planes from the pioneer and Lindbergh eras. Before and after, you can fly in a 1929 open-cockpit biplane.

Hours: May 15–Oct, daily 10am–5pm. **Shows:** Mid-June to mid-Oct, Sat–Sun at 2:30pm. **Admission:** $4 adults, $2 children 6–10; $10 and $5, respectively, for weekend air shows.

An aside on the history of the town: After Henry Hudson arrived, the area was settled by the Dutch and later the Palatine-Rhine refugees who founded Rhinebeck in 1686. One of the early inhabitants was a Judge Beekman, whose daughter married the grandson of the lord of Livingston Manor, and their son, Robert R. Livingston, was the gentleman who attended the first Continental Congress, signed the Declaration of Independence, and helped his son-in-law, Robert Fulton, invent the first steamboat. This vessel was named the *Clermont* after Livingston's estate north of Rhinebeck, where today you can picnic blissfully overlooking the Hudson.

Just south and west of Rhinebeck stands **Wilderstein,** Morton Road (tel. 914/876-4818). The house was built in 1852 for Thomas Suckley in an Italianate style, but his son updated the design in 1888 to a Queen Anne, complete with five-story round tower with curved windows. It's a very appealing residence. The main floor, which can be toured, was decorated by J. B. Tiffany and features many stained-glass windows. The landscaping was completed by Calvert Vaux and the original trails and layout are still being researched and restored. There are lovely views downriver and in summer tea is served on the veranda after 3pm.

Hours: May–Oct, Thurs–Sun noon–4pm. **Admission:** House, $4 adults; grounds, free.

Red Hook Attractions

The town of Red Hook, about 6 miles north of Rhinebeck on Rte. 9, actually possesses little of note, except a wonderful old library and an attractive lodging and dining place called the Red Hook Inn. Both **Bard College** and Montgomery Place are nearby in Annandale, about 4 miles north. On the bucolic campus of the college, the **Center for Curatorial Studies** (tel. 914/758-2424) often features art exhibits worth stopping for.

Hours: Wed–Sun noon–5pm.

The Bard Music Festival is also a renowned summer event.

Montgomery Place, River Road, Rte. 103, Annandale on Hudson (tel. 914/758-5461), is the 23-room mansion at the center of the 434-acre Livingston family estate. Tours are given of the house's main floor and kitchens, and along the way you'll learn some family history. You might want to bring a picnic lunch because after the tour you can walk the trails, stopping to eat and enjoy the river and mountain views.

Hours: Apr–Oct, Wed–Mon 10am–5pm; Nov–Dec, Sat–Sun 11am–6pm. **Closed:** Major holidays. **Admission:** $6 adults, $5 seniors, $3 students.

North of Red Hook is a favorite place for locals: **Greig Farm** on Pitcher Lane off Rte. 9 (tel. 914/758-1234), which always has something that's in season to pick or some event going on, like the Maple Festival in March and the Easter Egg Hunt or the Asparagus Run in May. Then it's strawberry time and soon enough apple and pumpkin time. The farm has a nice store where you can purchase locally produced food items.

Rhinebeck Lodging

The **Beekman Arms,** Rte. 9, Rhinebeck, NY 12572 (tel. 914/876-7077), has been serving travelers since it was established in 1766 at the junction of the road to Hudson and the road to Albany. It still possesses an authentic colonial tap room with dark-wood paneling, oak tables, and a brick hearth, and people love to come here to drink and dine.

A typical guest room here may contain a canopied oak bed, an oak desk, a brass candlestick lamp, chintz or striped wallpaper, a table, and comfortable side chairs. Additional touches include a decanter of sherry, a coffee maker, and a small selection of books. Amenities include a phone, a TV, and an English trouser press. The most fetching accommodations are in the gothic Delameter House (1844), a few doors away. High gables with ornamented carved verge boards, a rustic porch, and bay and mullioned windows characterize this striking building fashioned by Alexander Jackson Davis, who also designed robber baron Jay Gould's Lyndhurst in

Tarrytown. The eight rooms are furnished with wicker, colorful quilts, and large armoires, all in keeping with the American gothic architecture. You'll also find a parlor furnished with wicker that offers a TV and comfortable seating. Swagged drapes, diamond-pane windows, a marble fireplace, and equestrian prints complete the Victorian ambience.

Behind the Delameter, several houses are clustered around a grassy area. The Germond (1820) has four guest rooms. Room 69 features a pencil four-poster standing on wide-plank floors, a country towel rack, a Wedgwood-blue rocker strategically positioned in front of the fireplace, and an adjacent parlor furnished with wing chairs, a desk, and Windsor chairs—a lovely accommodation for $100. The Carriage House rooms have cathedral-style ceilings with crossbeams and furnishings that include a brass bed, armchairs, Windsor chairs, a pine table, and a selection of books. All rooms have air conditioning and a TV; many have fireplaces. In the morning coffee cake and danish are served on the patio. With all these separate buildings, the Beekman Arms offers 59 rooms.

The cuisine features local Hudson Valley ingredients in finely prepared dishes. At dinner you might find such entrees as salmon nestled in a soft roasted-corn pudding with a sauce of leeks and chanterelle mushrooms, grilled New York sirloin with a merlot sauce, and venison stew with root vegetables and herbs. There are also daily specials. An appetizer I can recommend is the warm Brittany hollow-potato and goat-cheese terrine, wrapped in applewood-smoked bacon and drizzled with rosemary oil.

Rates (including breakfast): $95–$150 double (the lower price for rooms in the main building, the higher for the Germond and Delameter Courtyard rooms). **Dining Hours:** Mon–Fri noon–3pm and 5–10pm, Sat noon–3pm and 5–11pm, Sun 10am–2pm (brunch).

If you can't secure a room at the Beekman Arms, try **Veranda House,** 82 Montgomery St., Rhinebeck, NY 12572 (tel. 914/876-4133). Linda and Ward Stanley offer four guest rooms in their attractrive Federal-style home. Two rooms have Shaker four-posters, while another features a brass bed. Guests enjoy the library containing many art and achitecture titles and the living room with a fireplace; the signature feature of the house is the veranda, furnished with wicker chairs. Complimentary wine and appetizers are offered on Saturday evening.

Rates (including full breakfast): $85–$110 double.

The **Belvedere Mansion,** P.O. Box 785, Rhinebeck, NY 12572 (tel. 914/889-8000), is a few miles south of Rhinebeck on Rte. 9. It stands on 10 acres atop a hill looking out over the Hudson River to the Catskill Mountains—an impressive Greek Revival mansion with a classical pediment supported by four columns at its entrance. The original was commissioned by Maj. John Pawling, who fought in the Revolution in 1760, but it was rebuilt in 1900 after a fire burned it to the ground. There are seven lavishly decorated guest rooms in the mansion itself. The most extravagant boasts a hand-painted French armoire, a large ormolu mirror, a Persian rug, and a four-poster dressed with a richly patterned antique silk coverlet and a Battenburg lace canopy. Several possess beautiful views. Other accommodations are in cottages on the grounds. These are small rooms for the most part (with bath). Early American and other antiques and folk art are used in the rooms. The beds are covered with quilts and the pillows sport lace-fringed linens. A full breakfast is served by the fireside in the dining room or in the gazebo overlooking the fountain and pond. Facilities include an outdoor pool. The owners are planning a restaurant and spa.

Rates (including breakfast): $185–$260 double in the mansion; $95–$135 cottage.

Rhinebeck does have some **bed-and-breakfasts,** but they seem to come and go, so your best bet, if you're looking for this type of accommodation, would be to contact the Rhinebeck Chamber of Commerce, 19 Mill St., Rhinebeck, NY 12572 (tel. 914/876-4778).

Rhinebeck Dining

Besides the **Beekman Arms** (see above), for an atmospheric place for lunch, dinner, or Sunday brunch, there are several choices.

Just around the corner is **Le Petit Bistro,** 8 E. Market St. (tel. 914/876-7400), a charming and thoroughly French restaurant even down to the lace curtains in the windows. The cuisine is classic French—duck with black currants, steak with peppercorn sauce, filet mignon with madeira sauce, dover sole meunière, and coquilles St-Jacques. Prices range from $15 to $20. Start with the smoked trout or pâté and finish with the crème brûlée or marquise au chocolat.

Hours: Mon–Sat 5–10pm, Sun 4–9pm.

More French dining can be found at **Chez Marcel,** Rte. 9 (tel. 914/876-8189), a few miles north of Rhinebeck. In a cozy paneled room with a few small pictures of Paris, you can dine on owner/chef Marcel Disch's cuisine. Although the menu changes frequently, you'll probably find a selection of about eight fish dishes, like scampi Créole or provençal, sole bonne femme or amandine, and a dozen or so meat dishes (including roast duckling, chateaubriand, rack of lamb, and calves' liver Bercy). There'll always be three or four specials—when I visited they were a creamy blanquette of veal, skate with beurre noir and capers, and rabbit in red-wine sauce. Prices range from $11 to $18.

Hours: Tues–Sun 5–10pm.

South of Rhinebeck on Rte. 9, there's also the **Fox Hollow Inn** (tel. 914/876-4696), a warm, unpretentious place that serves some Italian fare. Prices range from $8 to $18 for linguine with red or white clam sauce, spaghetti with meatballs, manicotti, veal or eggplant parmigiana, and daily specials.

Hours: Apr–Dec, Wed–Sun 5–8:30pm (sometimes until 9 or 10pm weekends).

For breakfast or lunch, head for **Schemmy's,** 19 E. Market St. (tel. 914/876-6215), a genuine old-fashioned drugstore now operating as a restaurant, coffee shop, and soda fountain. It's a fun atmosphere.

Hours: Mon–Thurs 7:30am–5pm, Fri–Sun 7:30am–7pm.

Red Hook Lodging & Dining
The **Red Hook Inn,** 31 S. Broadway, Red Hook, NY 12571 (tel. 914/758-8445), has been pleasantly restored with a colonial flavor. There are five rooms, all with bath and furnished with antique country pieces; some have fireplaces. In the dining room (with a blazing hearth in winter) the menu features contemporary American cuisine with some Thai and Italian accents. Prices range from $13 to $19.

Rates (including breakfast on weekends): $105–$135 double. **Dining Hours:** Tues–Sat noon–2:30pm and 5:30–10pm, Sun 5–9pm.

In nearby Tivoli, **Santa Fe** (tel. 914/757-4100) is one of the most happening places in the valley and the best place to secure spicy southwestern cuisine. What makes the food extra-special are the local ingredients, used in such dishes as the quesadilla with sun-dried tomatoes and Pine Plains Coash Farm goat cheese. Another great appetizer is the quesadilla with Baja shrimp and spinach. Among the entrees are mole poblano or, for a change of pace, sushi rolls with smoked salmon, avocado, and wasabi. Otherwise, there are plenty of enchiladas, tacos, and burritos to enjoy. My favorite taco is one made with crabmeat sautéed with jalapeños and Jamaican curry on blue-corn tortillas. Prices range from $10 to $15. The wall and furniture colors are brilliant and the atmosphere is lively. Entertainment is provided late on Saturday.

Hours: Tues–Sun 5–10pm.

Rhinebeck After Dark
Upstate Films, 26 Montgomery St. (tel. 914/876-2515), shows American independent films as well as foreign-language movies and old classics. It features a great guest speaker/director series too.

FROM RHINEBECK TO HUDSON

Area Attractions

Clermont
About 13 miles north of Rhinebeck (just south of Germantown) up Rte. 9G, you'll come to the **Clermont State Historic Site** (tel. 518/537-4240), the Livingston family seat and former home of Chancellor Robert R. Livingston, a member of the committee that drafted the Declaration of Independence. Here the Livingston-Fulton steamboat,

known as the *Clermont,* stopped on its maiden voyage up the Hudson in 1807. The estate remained in the family from 1728 until 1962, when it was acquired by the state. The house has been restored to its 1730 appearance. The gardens are lovely, especially when the magnolias are in bloom, and the grounds provide a glorious riverside site for picnicking; for your picnic supplies, stop in Red Hook or nearby Tivoli. You can find good cross-country skiing here as well.

Hours: House, Apr 15–Labor Day, Wed–Sat 10am–5pm, Sun noon–5pm; Labor Day–Oct, Wed–Sun noon–5pm. Grounds, year round, daily 8:30am–sunset.

Olana

Just south of Hudson is Olana (tel. 518/828-0135), artist Frederic Church's magnificently whimsical home, which has been meticulously restored to even the minutest detail in an effort to recapture his vision and intention. The restoration is a fitting tribute to a man who had so great a passion for design that he drew 200 sketches of the staircase alone, and who extended that passion to the landscape itself—every tree on the property was chosen by him, and he created the lake at the bottom of the hill specifically to mirror and balance the Hudson.

Church (1826–1900) came from a very wealthy New England family. His father, a silversmith, paper-mill owner, and banker who was on the board of Aetna Insurance, was appalled at his son's desire to become a landscape artist and agreed to let him become apprenticed to Thomas Cole only because Cole was so deeply religious. Because the decor of the house has been maintained as an authentic period creation, the many artworks are not displayed to maximum advantage, but on the walls hang many of Church's masterpieces or sketches for them—*Twilight in the Wilderness, Niagara,* the *Memorial* paintings, *Sunrise and Moonrise,* and *Pilgrim in the Valley of the Shadow of Death.*

The 37-room house was built between 1870 and 1874, soon after a visit Church made to Persia and the Near East. Inspired by Near Eastern culture, he incorporated many Persian elements into the decor—like gold- and silver-stenciled doors and richly colored and decorated patterned tiles for the fireplaces. The doorway bears the inscription "Mahaba," meaning "welcome." Throughout the house Church exhibited his painterly instincts by his use of color—in the vestibule, a vivid purple on the walls and pumpkin on the ceiling, and in the Court Hall, a pink ceiling that's echoed by the Erastus Dow Palmer roundels on the walls.

Much of the furniture was shipped from Persia and other faraway places: for example, painted chairs from Kashmir and 10-sided tables of mother-of-pearl from Syria. The Court Hall, where the lower landing was used as a stage by the family, reflects Church's careful attention to detail. Light from the golden staircase window, which Church created by using yellow paper, gives the effect of sunshine falling on the brass banister; the ombra arch window is placed to capture the "spectacular moment in Nature"— the famous bend in the Hudson River. Toward the end of the century Church paid several visits to Mexico, and in his studio is piled a wonderful collection of sombreros and pre-Columbian Mexican pottery. His wife used to play the piano here to stimulate his creative inspiration.

Outside, you can walk down to the informal scatter garden that blooms in harmonious confusion below the walls encircling the mound on which the house is built. Linger a while and perhaps spread out a picnic. Better yet, join one of Olana's special period picnics attended by magicians and other entertainers. Christmas is also a good time to visit, when the house is authentically decorated according to late-Victorian custom and with appropriate musical accompaniment.

Hours: House tours (mandatory), May–Aug, Wed–Sun first tour at noon and last at 4pm; Sept–Oct, hours vary so call ahead. Reservations recommended. **Admission:** $3 adults, $1.50 children 5–14, free for children 4 and under.

HUDSON

Hudson Attractions

From Olana, you can continue up Rte. 9G into the former whaling town of Hudson, where the many **19th-century town houses** have been restored and the stores are now occupied by antiques shops. At the west end of Warren Street, take a moment to stroll up on **"Parade Hill,"** a promenade lined with benches from which you can look down to and across the river. The major attraction besides the antiques stores is the **American Museum of Firefighting,** on Harry Howard Avenue (tel. 518/828-7695 for information). Although it may not seem that enthralling a prospect initially, the museum is marvelous, boasting fascinating collections and equally fascinating guides—retired firemen like Bill Rhodes who've "lived" through much of what they explain.

This museum houses one of the largest collections of its kind in the country. The old fire engines have the biggest impact on visitors. Among them are the first mobile fire wagon, standing on wooden wheels with steel bands, which was used for 154 years (1725–1879); the most expensive, an 1846 double-decker engine of hand-carved and painted wood with copper hubcaps that required 45 men to operate for 15 to 20 minutes; and a splendiferous 1883 parade carriage, sporting gold-plated hubcaps and silver-capped hub bands, a silver-plated metal-engraved reel jacket, and the 1845 Piano Engine, the first to have a volume control ensuring a steady stream of water instead of short spurts. Later models are steam powered, many of them made by La France Company in Elmira,

N.Y., and used locally. Favorites include an 1882 horse-drawn steamer called Hercules, last used in 1940, that was built to travel on trolley tracks, and the 1870 Clapp & Jones Steamer, built in Hudson, which vibrated (or "walked") so much it had to be staked down or tied to a tree.

Around the walls display cases hold uniforms, helmets, medals, badges, banners, photographs, Currier & Ives prints, and other memorabilia. But the pièce de résistance appears at the end of the tour—a beautiful 1890 parade carriage with 68-inch wheels. Its reel is finished in etched mirrors and supported on each side by two silver-plated lions couchant. Over the reel stands a fireman holding a child and trumpet. The lamps and other artistic details are also elaborate.

Hours: Daily 9am–4:30pm. **Admission:** Free.

The Daughters of the American Revolution operate a museum at the 1811 **Robert Jenkins House,** 113 Warren St. (tel. 518/828-9764). Works by Hudson River artists—Henry Ary, Bert Phillips, Arthur and Ernest Parton—are on display along with other local memorabilia, including items documenting the town's whaling heritage.

Hours: July–Aug, Sun–Mon 1–3pm. **Admission:** $2.50 adults, $2 seniors, free for children 11 and under.

Hudson Dining

Try **Charleston,** 517 Warren St. (tel. 518/828-4990), which offers eclectic American cuisine. The menu changes frequently but among the popular appetizers is smoked trout with mustard-dill sauce and grilled portabello mushrooms on orzo salad. Among the entrees you'll find several pasta dishes—with mussels, garlic, white wine, and herbs, for example—as well as roasted Cornish game hen with Thai garlic, ginger, and coconut sauce; grilled pork loin with mustard-bourbon sauce and deep-fried yams; and tuna with mango-cilantro salsa. Prices range from $14 to $17.

Hours: Thurs 11:30am–3pm and 5:30–9:30pm, Fri–Sat 11:30am–3pm and 5:30–10pm, Sun 11:30am–3pm and 5:30–8pm.

For other dining choices convenient to the attractions of Olana, Hudson, Lindenwald, and even Clermont, cross the river to Catskill (see the upcoming chapter on the Catskills).

FROM HUDSON TO OLD CHATHAM

Area Attractions

Lindenwald

Farther north, on Rte. 9H, 2 miles south of Kinderhook, is Lindenwald (tel. 518/758-9689), Martin Van Buren's retirement home, which has been restored to its 1850–62 appearance. Van Buren was born in Kinderhook in 1782 and left in 1801 to study law in New York City, where he met Aaron Burr and DeWitt Clinton, among others. Later, he returned to practice law and continue the political career that carried him into the White House (1837–41). Although Lindenwald was built in 1797, Van Buren acquired it in 1839 during his presidency. Ten years later architect Richard Upjohn designed substantial alterations to the mansion, giving it its present eclectic appearance. The former president lived here from 1841 to his death in July 1862 and was buried in the Reform Church cemetery. The house features original French wallpaper and a reproduction of the extra-large banquet table that could seat 30. Besides personal furnishings and objets d'art, the house contains memorabilia from Van Buren's long political career—attorney-general, senator, and governor of New York; secretary of state; vice-president; and president (he was the first president born an American citizen).

Hours: Mid-Apr to Oct, daily 9am–5pm; Nov–Dec 5, Wed–Sun 9am–4:30pm. **Closed:** Thanksgiving and Dec 6 to mid-Apr. The grounds are open year round.

Van Alen House

Just off Rte. 9H in Kinderhook, the Van Alen House (tel. 518/758-9265) is worth visiting to view the fine Dutch architecture and collection of Hudson Valley paintings. The house is especially lovely in spring, when a special flower festival is celebrated.

Hours: Memorial Day–Labor Day, Thurs–Sat 11am–5pm, Sun 1–5pm; the rest of the year, by appointment. **Admission:** $3 adults, $2 seniors and children 12–18.

Old Chatham

From Kinderhook it's a short trip to Old Chatham and the **Shaker Museum,** Shaker Museum Road (tel. 518/794-9100). For information about the Shakers' history and background, see the Pittsfield section of the chapter on the Berkshires of Massachusetts. You can tour about eight buildings—a small chair factory, a cabinet maker's shop, a blacksmithy, textile and weaving shops, a herbal house—the whole representing a premier study collection of Shaker material and culture with over 32,500 items. There are also a library, bookstore, and gift store.

Hours: May–Oct, daily 10am–5pm; Nov–Dec 17, Sat–Sun 10am–5pm. **Admission:** $6 adults, $5 seniors, $3 children 8–17.

After Dark

The **MacHaydn Theater** (tel. 518/392-9292) in Chatham (*not* Old Chatham) is one of the finest summer stock theaters around that features musicals.

East Bank
Special & Recreational Activities

Antiquing: The greatest concentrations of stores are in Millbrook, in Hyde Park at the Hyde Park Antiques Center, in Rhinebeck at the Beekman Arms barn, and along the main street of Hudson.

Ballooning: Blue Sky Balloons, 246 Mountain Rd., Pleasant Valley (tel. 914/635-2461), charges $150 per person for a hot-air-balloon ride. Open April to October daily.

Boating: Boat rentals are available in Lake Taghkanic State Park, Rte. 82, in Ancram (tel. 518/851-3631); and Taconic State Park, Rudd Pond Area, off Rte. 22 in Millerton (tel. 518/789-3059).

Camping: The best camping is in the state parks, open from mid-May to October: Lake Taghkanic State Park, Rte. 82, Ancram, NY 12502 (tel. 518/851-3631), offers 51 sites, swimming, fishing, and boat rentals; Taconic State Park, Copake Falls area, Rte. 344, Copake Falls, NY 12517 (tel. 518/329-3993), has 112 sites that stay open until mid-December, plus swimming and fishing; the Rudd Pond area also in Taconic State Park, on Rte. 22, Millerton, NY 12546 (tel. 518/789-3059), has 41 sites and the most facilities, including a camp store and recreation building; Margaret Lewis Norrie State Park, Rte. 9, Hyde Park, NY 12538 (tel. 914/889-4646), offers fishing and a children's area. The basic fee for all is $10.

Fishing: At Lake Taghkanic (tel. 518/851-3631); at Taconic State Park, both the Rudd Pond and the Copake Falls areas; and at Norrie State Park (tel. 914/889-4646).

Fruit Picking: Philip Orchards, Rte. 9H, Claverack (tel. 518/851-6351), for pears and apples; Greig Farm, on Pitcher Lane, north of Red Hook off Rte. 9 (tel. 914/758-5762), for asparagus, peas, raspberries, strawberries, blueberries, apples, and cut-your-own flowers.

Golf: Dinsmore Golf Club, right off Rte. 9 in Staatsburg (tel. 914/889-4071 or 889-4751), with a panoramic view of the Hudson; James Baird State Park Golf Course, Freedom Road, Pleasant Valley (tel. 914/452-1489), offers an 18-hole course and a driving range.

Hiking: James Baird State Park, LaGrange; Norrie Point State Park, Hyde Park; Lake Taghkanic State Park, Rte. 82, Ancram. For more information on the state parks, contact the Taconic Region, Staatsburg, NY 12570 (tel. 914/889-4100), or the main office at New York State Office of Parks, Recreation and Historic Preservation, 1 Empire State Plaza, Albany, NY 12238 (tel. 518/474-0456).

Picnicking: Along the banks of the Hudson are several magnificent picnicking spots, all granting views over this river. Starting at the farthest south, there's the Mills mansion in Staatsburg, 5 miles south of Rhinebeck, where you can pick up your supplies in one of the many delis or supermarkets. Just north of Rhinebeck in Germantown, at Clermont, the home of Robert R. Livingston, the rolling parklands and gardens are open from 8:30am to sunset daily year round. Pick up supplies in nearby Red Hook (there's a deli on the corner at the main crossroads). And, finally, at Frederic Church's Olana, you can picnic high on a hill overlooking the bend in the river that he made famous. Olana even organizes occasional period picnics at which people arrive dressed in costume and are entertained in a 19th-century manner with magicians, jugglers, and so on.

Skiing: Catamount Ski Area in Hillsdale (see the chapter on the Berkshires in Massachusetts). Cross-country skiing: Lake Taghkanic State Park and Mills-Norrie State Park.

Swimming: Lake Taghkanic, Taconic State Park—Rudd Pond and Copake Falls areas.

Tennis: Call the individual chambers of commerce for information. Most public schools open their courts to the public in the evening and on weekends. Public parks sometimes have courts too. In Hudson you can play at Hudson's Columbia-Greene Community College by the Rip Van Winkle Bridge.

THE WEST BANK

This side of the river offers several towns that are gateways to the Catskills. Here you'll find an assortment of accommodations (far more than on the east bank), ranging from bed-and-breakfasts and motels to the impressive Mohonk Mountain House. But first, let's examine what there is to do.

NEW PALTZ, HIGH FALLS & LAKE MINNEWASKA

Area Attractions

New Paltz boasts the "oldest street in America with its original houses"—six stone houses all built before 1720. The most notable is the **Abraham Hasbrouck House,** an outstanding example of Flemish stone architecture, built in 1712 by Hasbrouck, reputed to have served in the British

The Wine Country

Along the river just south of New Paltz stretches the Hudson Valley wine country, around Marlboro and Milton. The best time to visit is during harvest in early fall.

Benmarl, Highland Avenue, Marlboro (tel. 914/236-4265), began working in 1957 to revive the Hudson Valley wine industry. Tours and wine tastings are offered daily from noon to 5pm. The café is open summer weekends from noon to 4pm.

In Milton, the **Royal Wine Corp. (Kedem),** Dock Road (tel. 914/795-2240), features a video show and tasting. You can also picnic by the river in relative peace. The winery is open May to October, Sunday to Friday from 10:30am to 3:30pm (closed Jewish holidays).

Perhaps the best known is the **Brotherhood Winery** in Washingtonville (tel. 914/496-3661), near West Point. The vineyard claims the largest underground cellars in the nation. In summer there are tours ($4) Monday to Friday at 12:15 and 2:30pm, and Saturday and Sunday from noon to 4pm; in winter, only on Saturday and Sunday from noon to 4pm; closed January. On weekends there's also an art gallery and shops to browse through.

army and to have been a friend of Governor Andros. (The kitchen was the scene of many a cockfight.) For over 250 years these houses have stood, passing from one generation to another of the original Duzine (or 12 men) who founded this community in 1677; they named it after die Pfalz, the temporary retreat they'd found in the Palatinate during years of exile from their native France.

This gem is usually included on the tours given by the **Huguenot Historical Society,** 18 Broadhead Ave. (tel. 914/255-1889), which maintains the houses. There are several tours to choose from: The full tour takes 2½ hours, visits five houses and the French church, and costs $7 for adults, $6 for seniors, $3.50 for children 7 to 12; the second takes 1½ hours, visits two houses and the church, and costs $4, $3, and $2, respectively; the third takes half an hour, visits one house, and costs $2.75, $2, and $1.25, respectively. Tours start from Deyo Hall. The society also maintains the Howard Hasbrouck Grimm Gallery and a museum, both open to the public free of charge, their hours coinciding with the tour hours.

Hours: Memorial Day–Oct 1, Wed–Sun 9:30am–4pm; Oct 2–31, Sat–Sun 9:30am–4pm; the rest of the year, by appointment.

At the **D&H Canal Museum,** on Mohonk Road in neighboring High Falls (tel. 914/687-9311), you can view the brief history—from 1828 to

1898—of the 108-mile-long Delaware-Hudson Canal, built in 1825 to ship coal from Pennsylvania to the Hudson River and thence to New York City. By the 1870s its role was usurped by the railroads. Maps, photographs, dioramas, working models of locks, and a replica of the suspension aqueduct by John Roebling (of Brooklyn Bridge fame) tell the story.

Hours: Memorial Day–Labor Day, Mon and Thurs–Sat 11am–5pm, Sun 1–5pm; May and Sept–Oct, Sat–Sun 1–5pm; Nov–Apr, Sat 9am–5pm.

A little farther up the road, the **grist mill** at the base of the falls is another fun place to visit.

From New Paltz, it's a short distance along Rte. 299 to brilliant-turquoise **Lake Minnewaska** (tel. 914/255-0752), rimmed by a forest of high hemlocks, set atop the Shawangunk Mountains. A resort very similar to Mohonk once functioned here. Today it's a state park open for day-use only, providing opportunities for hiking, swimming, canoeing, picnicking, and cross-country skiing. Entry to the area is $3 on weekends. In winter you can ski past frozen waterfalls and streams, between snow-covered hemlocks to points with views over the Hudson Highlands, Berkshires, and Catskills—40 miles of trails in all. Rentals are available.

Following Rte. 209 will bring you to another geological and natural wonder, **Ice Caves Mountain** at Ellenville (tel. 914/647-7909), an impressive array of ice formations, canyons, and rugged rock formations. One of the highest points in the area, it also delivers five-state views and is great for picnicking.

Hours: Apr–Nov, daily 10am–3:15pm. **Admission:** $6.75 adults, $4.50 children 6–12.

An Extra-Special New Paltz Lodging

The historic **Mohonk Mountain House,** New Paltz, NY 12561 (tel. 914/255-1000, or 800/772-6646), is an attraction in itself. A 2-mile drive through curving wooded lanes brings you to a large, rambling, primarily stone structure capped by towers that broods on the mountaintop looking out over the Rondout Valley. From the rockers or Mission settees on the veranda that wraps around the back, you can gaze across the crystalline turquoise mountain lake, surrounded by craggy rocks and dotted with gazebos, and contemplate the stillness of the lake at eventide. This is the last of many fine resorts that once dotted the area and attracted wealthy vacationers. It has retained its Victorian flavor with shuttered windows, oak pieces and mantels in the rooms, and old-fashioned bathroom fittings, including tubs that actually come with footstools. The grounds are a delight any time of year, but especially in summer, at spring blossom time, and in early June when the surrounding 2,200 wooded acres are aglow with pink and white mountain laurel. A magical spot where visitors are asked to drive slowly and quietly up the approach road "to harmonize with nature," the whole place exudes a sense of tranquillity, contemplation, love of nature, and reverence for life.

In short, it still bears some resemblance to the original idea of its Quaker founders and teachers, Albert and Alfred Smiley, who established the house in 1869 as a place where "like-minded people can gather to savor the earth and the sky." Their educational mission continues today in the 35-plus programs that are operated during the year. There have been weekends dedicated to mystery novels, antique and folk art, the wonderful world of words, Scottish country dancing, the reflective life, and even a hot 'n' spicy food lovers weekend. Mohonk also offers a tremendous range of activities—tennis; horseback riding (April to October); nine-hole golf; rowboating, paddleboating, and canoeing; lawn bowling; putting; croquet; ice skating; and 35 miles of cross-country skiing trails. Among the famous visitors have been John Burroughs, Andrew Carnegie, and Presidents Teddy Roosevelt, Taft, Hayes, and Arthur.

This was also the site of the famous conference on Indian Affairs and International Arbitration between 1883 and the outbreak of World War I. Photographs of these gatherings and prominent visitors line the corridors leading from the quiet library and parlors to the incredible oak-columned and -ceilinged dining room that seats 500. While the food is not haute cuisine, as they say, there's plenty of it. Though there's no bar, liquor is available at dinner.

Rates (including full board, excluding tax and gratuities): $230 double with sink, $275–$475 double with bath; two rooms with connecting bath, $245 for two, $446 for three, $608 for four. For children 2–15, add $60. There are special charges for some activities. You can be met at the Adirondack Trailways at New Paltz or at the railroad station in Poughkeepsie. On most weekends two- or three-day minimums are required.

New Paltz Area Bed-and-Breakfasts

The area offers several outstanding B&Bs. The two finest are probably Baker's and Captain Schoonmaker's House.

The old stone house known as **Baker's,** Old King's Highway (R.D. 2, Box 80), Stone Ridge, NY 12484 (tel. 914/687-9795), off Rte. 209 just south of town, was built in 1780 and commands a magnificent view that has remained unspoiled since the days when the highway was the east-west route (before the canal was constructed). The house then served as a stopping place for travelers—and Doug Baker and Linda Delgado continue that tradition. This is the seventh house that Doug has restored with great care and artistry; he even installed the Rumford-style fireplace, which has a high inner hearth and fire box and a tiny five-by-five-inch-hole flue opening. The house is furnished with Early American hutches, 18th-century Dutch-German wing chairs in the parlor, and other Early American and Federal pieces.

There are six guest rooms, two sharing a bath, and one suite with a sitting room and wood-burning stove. They have beamed ceilings, wide-board floors, stencil decoration, and cannonball beds with real down comforters. Linda, who teaches and functions as a counselor at the local college, turns out fine breakfasts consisting of juice, fresh fruit, and a variety of dishes like venison medallions, ham poached in homemade maple syrup, smoked trout, and the more usual egg dishes.

Attached to the side of the house is a solarium/greenhouse where they've installed a hot tub—a pleasant pastime for one and all. The pond provides skating or swimming and also some nice black bass. Chickens, ducks, and geese roam the property, while cows graze peacefully on the adjacent 20 acres.

Rates (including breakfast): $80 double without bath, $94 double with bath; $102 suite.

Captain Shoonmaker's House, Rte. 213 (R.D. 2, Box 37), High Falls, NY 12440 (tel. 914/687-7946), between High Falls and Rosendale, is the sixth house Sam and Julia Krieg have restored. They've completed this 1760 stone house immaculately, furnishing it with antiques and placing quilts on all the brass and canopied beds. Several rooms have fireplaces. Downstairs, the Kriegs have created a solarium around an old well whose stone now serves as a coffee table. Here a seven-course breakfast—apricot, cherry, or almond strudel, homemade breads, fresh fruit, soufflés, bacon, and so on—is served, with tea provided in the afternoon and sherry at night. The books there are for guests' use. Look at the album depicting the various stages of the restoration process; it should only add to your respect for this interesting, dynamic couple. Sam has also restored the 1840 barn on the property, turning it into four rooms, each looking out over the Coxing Kill stream and waterfall. And there are four rooms sharing two baths in a Greek Revival–style house down on the D&H Canal.

Rates (including breakfast): $90 double without bath, $100 double with bath and fireplace.

Just outside New Paltz, **Ujjala's,** 2 Forest Glen Rd., New Paltz, NY 12561 (tel. 914/255-6360), offers accommodations with a distinctly personal flavor, for Ujjala herself specializes in holistic health and teaches stress management—but only if you feel you need it, of course. Boy, is she kidding! A stay at her sunny Victorian home nestled among apple, pear, and quince trees on 4½ acres should amply restore your spirit. All the rooms (two with bath, three with shared bath) are prettily decorated and contain a bowl of fruit and nuts upon your arrival. The large skylit room has a fireplace and a sitting room. The large country kitchen with an outside deck for summer breakfasts—in fact, the whole house—is filled with plants and life. Ujjala also tends a fruitful vegetable garden. Breakfast will usually bring forth fresh fruits, granola, homemade bread, omelets, and crêpes. Although she's a former fashion model, don't be misled—Ujjala is not your stereotypical model. To get here, take Rte. 208 south off Rte. 299 for 3½ miles, passing Dressel farms on the right. Take the second right onto Forest Glen Road. The house is the second on the left.

Rates (including breakfast): $83–$100 double.

Across from Ujjala's is **Jingle Bell Farm,** 1 Forest Glen Rd., New Paltz, NY 12561 (tel. 914/255-6588), a lovely stone house with dormer windows. It looks positively charming, but no one was home when I stopped by, so I couldn't examine the inside. Do check it out.

Rates: $115–$130 double.

Stone Ridge & High Falls Lodging & Dining

The **Inn at Stone Ridge,** P.O. Box 76, Stone Ridge, NY 12484 (tel. 914/687-0736), occupies a beautifully mellow Dutch colonial stone mansion known as the Hasbrouck House, set on 40 acres of lawns, gardens, and woods. The guest rooms are furnished with antiques. The public areas include a large guest parlor featuring a full-size billiard table, a sitting room with a library, and a TV room. Milliways Restaurant offers modern American cuisine served either in the formal dining room or in the tavern and Jefferson Room.

Rates: $70–$105 double; $155 suite. **Dining Hours:** Mon–Fri 7:30–10am, noon–3pm, and 5–10pm; Sat noon–3pm and 5–10pm; Sun 10:30am–2pm and 5–10pm.

At the **De Puy Canal House,** Rte. 213, High Falls (tel. 914/687-7700 or 687-7777), dining is treated as an art. This landmark 1797 stone house with polished wide-plank floors, multiple fireplaces, pewter, and old china was built by Simeon De Puy, who catered to the needs of the bargemen and is recalled by memorabilia throughout the tavern rooms. The prix-fixe dinner choices always include a vegetarian entree and a selection of meat and fish dishes like poached salmon in clam bouillabaise (with cavetelli pasta in broth made with yellow tomatoes, saffron, leeks, and fennel) or duck breast and polenta with dandelion timbale on a brown sauce of red wine, shallots, and roasted garlic. The $25 three-course menu includes salad, certain menu items, and custard with biscotti. The four-course menu (from $33) includes complimentary hors d'oeuvres, soup or pasta, sorbet, an entree, and mesclun salad and a fruit bowl. The $45 seven-course menu adds both soup and an appetizer, plus dessert and coffee. Linger as long as you wish. The most luscious dessert is the chocolate-brandy soufflé with chocolate-custard sauce.

Hours: Feb 14–Dec, Thurs–Sat 5:30–9:30pm, Sun 11:30am–2pm (brunch) and 4–9pm.

For a weekend lunch or a casual dinner, try the **Egg's Nest,** Rte. 213, High Falls (tel. 914/687-7255). Giant sandwiches are the specialty at this 19th-century canal house, which has uneven floors. You'll see hanging from the low ceiling everything from a watering can and an old pair of beaten-up shoes to a miniature of the Red Baron's plane. You can't get your hands around the deli sandwiches, so filled are they with turkey, ham, corned beef, or whatever else. Other specialties include fish and chips, zesty chili, pizza with a variety of toppings, and dishes like enchiladas with black-bean sauce and pasta with chiles, tomatoes, and chicken. Prices range from $7 to $9.

Hours: Sun–Thurs 11:30am–11pm, Fri–Sat 11:30am–midnight.

The **Northern Spy Cafe,** Rte. 213, High Falls (tel. 914/687-7298), offers what can only be described as around-the-world cuisine. Among the entrees might be roasted duck with hoisin sauce and ginger, pan-seared salmon with Jamaican voodoo salsa, a clasic pad Thai, and shell steak with dark-beer butter and garlic mashed potatoes. The menu is rounded out by a selection of pasta dishes, pizzas, burgers, and salads. Prices range from $7 to $17.

Hours: Mon and Wed–Thurs 4:30–10pm, Fri–Sat 4:30–11pm, Sun 9:30am–3pm (brunch).

New Paltz Dining

The **Locust Tree Inn and Golf Course,** 215 Huguenot St. (tel. 914/255-7888), occupies a pretty setting at the head of a fir-lined drive that winds past a duck pond. The restaurant occupies an stone house dating to 1759 and an addition built in 1847. Of the restaurant's three rooms, the most appealing is the low-beamed tavern, where Delftware is displayed on both sides of the mantel. The menu changes weekly but among the specialties might be scallops dillonais (sautéed with spinach, tomatoes, and mushrooms in a garlic-cream sauce), veal fines herbes, and pheasant and venison in season. Prices range from $14 to $20. This place is lovely for summer dining overlooking the golf course.

Hours: Tues-Fri 11:30am–2:30pm and 5:30–10pm, Sat 5:30–10pm, Sun 11am–2pm (brunch) and 3–8pm.

Other choices include the **Wildflower Cafe,** 18 Church St. (tel. 914/255-0020; open Wed–Mon noon–3pm and 5–9pm), for health and vegetarian fare; **Barnaby's,** North Chestnut Street (tel. 914/255-5542 or 255-9831; open Tues–Thurs and Sun 11:30am–9:30pm, Fri–Sat 11:30am–10:30pm), for burgers, salads, and sandwiches, all under $6, and dinners from $8 to $17; and **Bacchus,** 59 Main St. (tel. 914/255-8636; open Sun–Thurs 11:30am–9pm, Fri–Sat 11:30am–10pm), for Mexican fare as well as seafood and continental dishes, served in a pine-and-plants atmosphere.

HURLEY & KINGSTON

Area Attractions

From Stone Ridge you can travel Rte. 209 via Hurley to Kingston. **Hurley** was the state capital for a month in 1777, when the Council of Safety, then the state's governing body, retreated here from the advancing British. After the Revolution it became a major stop on the Underground Railroad and is noted for being the birthplace of Sojourner Truth. The prime reason for a visit is to view the **10 privately owned Dutch stone houses,** which open their doors to the public on the second Saturday in July, revealing such secrets as the iron "witch catcher" hanging in the chimney of the Polly Crispell House and the gun holes puncturing the shutters on the stone porch of the Ten Eyck House.

Kingston was the first capital of New York State, where the first state constitution was adopted and the first governor, DeWitt Clinton, was sworn in. The original settlement had been established soon after Hudson's visit to the area but had been destroyed by the Esopus Indians in 1653. To ward off similar attacks, Peter Stuyvesant ordered a stockade built, and today in this **Stockade District** are found some of the city's finest homes—17th-century stone houses as well as Federal, Victorian, Italianate, romanesque, and art deco examples. These constitute a veritable walking tour through American architectural history. It's sad that the town has so obviously seen better days, but it still has a flavor and strong sense of history. The best way to explore Kingston is taking the self-guided **walking tour** you can obtain from the chamber of commerce (tel. 914/338-5100) in the Governor Clinton Hotel. A couple of stores you won't want to miss are **Anyone Can Whistle,** 323 Wall St. (tel. 914/331-7728), and **Joyous Kitchen** (see "Kingston Dining," below). The first offers terrific musical gifts in all price ranges and displays a full range of musical instruments—stringed, reed, and percussion—from around the world. The place is fun, educational, and magical. It also sells the famous Woodstock chimes.

Abraham Van Gaasbeek's home, where the Senate met during the Revolution and the first Constitutional Convention was held, is now the **Senate House,** 312 Fair St. (tel. 914/338-2786); it was one of the few houses that miraculously survived the sack of the town by the British. It exhibits many Dutch features, like Delft tiles and a beehive oven, and the adjacent museum relates the birth of New York State government and displays John Vanderlyn's and Ammi Phillips's paintings.

Hours: Wed–Sat 10am–5pm, Sun 1–5pm. **Admission:** Free.

In the 19th century Kingston became a thriving commercial port. The Cornell Steamship Company made its headquarters here and shipped coal, bricks, cement, ice, fruit, and other supplies downriver to New York City, while a steady tourist flow made the city one of the gateways to the Catskills. Activity once again returned to the Rondout Landing with the opening of the **Hudson River Maritime Center,** 39 Broadway (tel. 914/338-0071; open daily 11am–5pm; admission $2), and the **Trolley Museum of New York,** 89 E. Strand (tel. 914/331-3399), which also sponsors rides along the waterfront; and with the establishment of various stores in buildings that've been rehabilitated. At the Maritime Center, photographs, models, and artifacts reveal the history of Rondout Creek, from the days when its population was greater than Kingston's is today to the Great Depression, which finished off the shipyards. In its golden years the port bustled with steamers, sloops, tugs, and freighters, especially from 1828 to 1898, when the D&H Canal was operating and coal was shipped from Pennsylvania into the Rondout and then elsewhere. Steamboats like the *Mary Powell* (1861–1917), the most famous and fastest on the river, made daily round-trips to Manhattan. After the canal closed in 1898, shipyards continued to operate, building ships for World Wars I and II, but thereafter the decline was permanent.

From here boats are now plying the river, leaving the pier at the foot of Broadway for afternoon, sunset, and dinner cruises on weekends. A fun cruise aboard the *Lindy* is operated in conjunction with the Maritime Center. It crosses the river to Rhinecliff, stops at the Rondout lighthouse for a guided tour, and then returns to the Rondout. The $6 charge includes admission to the museum and the lighthouse. For information on other cruises, call or write **Hudson River Cruises, Inc.,** P.O. Box 333, Rifton, NY 12471-0333 (tel. 914/255-6515 or 473-3860). The cost is about $12.50 for adults and $5.50 for children.

Kingston Lodging
The best accommodations choice is across the river in Rhinebeck at the Beekman Arms or on the same bank of the river at the Mohonk Mountain House or one of the B&Bs around New Paltz (see above). In Kingston there's the **Skytop Motel,** Rte. 28 (R.D. 2, Box 220), Kingston, NY 12401 (tel. 914/331-2900), charging $80 to $100 double; a **Holiday Inn,** 503 Washington Ave., Kingston, NY 12401 (tel. 914/338-0400), charging $105 double on weekends; and a **Ramada Inn,** Thruway Circle, Rte. 28 (R.D. 2, Box 212), Kingston, NY 12401 (tel. 914/339-3900), charging $90 double on weekends.

Kingston Dining
The bar at **Jake and Peppers Steakhouse,** 614 Broadway (tel. 914/338-2600), is a popular hangout for locals after work. The dining room in back is dark and casual with forest-green walls and tablecloths. The fare is traditional steak and barbecue, plus some pasta dishes—all priced from $10 to $14.

Hours: Thurs–Mon 4:30–10:30pm.

The Thymes, 11 Main St. (tel. 914/338-0434), may be Kingston's most formal restaurant, but its decor is rather plain, consisting of tables set with forest-green cloths combined with Windsor chairs and modern lithographs on the walls. Brass wall sconces provide the lighting, and there's a bar at the center of the room. The food is updated American, ranging from pasta dishes like penne with Gorgonzola and sun-dried tomatoes to filet mignon with peppercorn-whisky butter, pecan-crusted chicken with honey-mustard sauce, and pork with apples, brandy, and cream. Prices range from $13 to $19.

Hours: Tues–Sat 11:30am–closing.

Schneller's, 61 John St. (tel. 914/331-9800), is a fun place to go for German sausages and schnitzels washed down with over 25 varieties of fine beer. The dining room, upstairs from the retail fish-and-meat store, is decked out with beer steins and other German decorative elements. You can enjoy outdoor dining in summer. Prices range from $9 to $12.

Hours: Mon–Thurs 11:30am–4pm and 5–9pm, Fri–Sat 11:30am–4pm and 5–10pm, Sun 1–7pm.

Around the corner is **The Joyous Kitchen,** 307 Wall St. (tel. 914/339-2111), serving excellent, imaginative lunch fare in the café at back. The soups are hearty and flavorsome, the sandwiches nicely presented along with salads, egg dishes, and daily specials priced from $4 to $7. The specials might be anything from poached salmon with caper-dill sauce to grilled chicken, scallion, and pepperjack quesadilla. The store is operated by a Culinary Institute of America graduate who knows how to turn out quality food. Upfront, the store sells fine kitchenware, utensils, china, and glass.

Hours: Mon–Sat 10am–3:30pm.

Down at the Rondout on the river are several choices. The **Armadillo Bar & Grill,** 97 Abeel St. (tel. 914/339-1550), offers somewhat mildly spiced southwestern cuisine in a colorful atmosphere. The tables and chairs are brilliant blue, pink, and turquoise and the usual southwestern accents— cacti and desert-bleached skulls—set the scene. All the traditional favorites are on hand—chimichangas, quesadillas, enchiladas, chiles rellenos, and fajitas, priced from $10 to $14.

Hours: Tues–Sun 11:30am–3pm and 4:30–10pm.

The Golden Duck, 11 Broadway (tel. 914/331-3221), serves good Chinese cuisine in a light and modern atmosphere. A carved gilt arch leads into the dining room, where the tables are covered with brown cloths and white overlays. For $12.50 you can choose wonton or hot-and-sour soup, an eggroll or chicken wings, and an entree. There are other combinations available, or you can choose à la carte. The great specialty is Peking duck ($28), carved tableside and served with pancakes, or any of the duck dishes—crispy duck, duckling Hunan style, or Mongolian duck. Crispy chicken, shrimp Imperial, Maine lobster Cantonese, chicken with cashews, orange beef, and beef Szechuan are dishes featuring other major ingredients. Prices run $8 to $26 (for lobster).

Hours: Mon–Thurs 11am–2:30pm and 3–9:30pm, Fri 11am–2:30pm and 3–10:30pm, Sat 3–10:30pm, Sun 3–9:30pm.

In addition, the **Sturgeon Wine Bar,** 23 Broadway (tel. 914/338-5186), has an extensive selection of wines by the glass. There's also an outdoor café on the waterfront, an ice cream and cookie store, and other shops for browsing.

Hours: Sun–Thurs noon–2am, Fri–Sat noon–4am.

On the outskirts of Kingston, the **Hillside Manor,** Rte. 32 (tel. 914/331-4386), offers about 17 pastas, everything from linguini al gusto with lobster to paglie e fieno. Among the entrees are rack of lamb, filet mignon, veal, and chicken, though the specialty of the house is really seafood—trout meunière; red snapper with mussels, shrimp, clams, and white wine; lobster; fried calamari; and more. To start, perhaps choose carpaccio, escargots, or stuffed clams Florentine, and to finish, select from the enticing items on the dessert cart. Prices run $13 to $19.

Hours: Mon–Thurs 5–9pm, Fri 11am–2pm and 5–10pm, Sat 5–10pm.

Other dining choices can be found nearby along or off Rte. 28 in Woodstock, Bearsville, and Mount Tremper or north along Rte. 9W to Saugerties, all only 20 to 30 minutes away from Kingston. For details, see the upcoming chapter on the Catskills.

After Dark
Kingston's **Ulster Performing Arts Center,** 601 Broadway (tel. 914/339-6088), offers a broad range of entertainment—from rock to classical, drama to comedy.

West Bank
Special & Recreational Activities

Boating: There are a number of marinas along the Hudson, but boat rentals are scarce. Your best bet is the Great Hudson Sailing Center in Kingston (see "Sailing," below). *Catskill:* Riverview Marine Services, 101 Main St. (tel. 518/943-5311), has powerboat rentals.

Camping: Open from mid-April to mid-October, Beaver Pond, Harriman State Park, RFD, Stony Point, NY 10980 (tel. 914/947-2792), has swimming, fishing, and boating facilities (no rentals) and 52 campsites. For more information, contact the Palisades Interstate Park Commission, Bear Mountain, NY 10911 (tel. 914/786-2701).

Fruit Picking: *High Falls:* Mr. Apples, Rte. 213 (tel. 914/687-9498), for apples and pears. *Milton:* Westervelt-Clarke Farm, off Rte. 9W, 13 miles north of Newburgh Clarke's Lane (tel. 914/795-2270), for apples, pears, peaches, plums, and pumpkins. *New Paltz:* Dressel Farms, Rte. 208 (tel. 914/255-0693), for apples and strawberries; Wallkill View Farm, Rte. 299, a mile west of New Paltz (tel. 914/255-8050), for pumpkins only. *Stone Ridge:* Davenport Farms, Rte. 209 (tel. 914/687-0051), for strawberries only.

Golf: *Accord:* Rondout Country Club, Whitfield Road (tel. 914/626-2513). *High Falls:* Stone Dock Golf Course, Berme Road (tel. 914/687-9944). *New Paltz:* New Paltz Golf Course (tel. 914/255-8282), nine holes; Mohonk Mountain Golf Course, Rte. 299 (tel. 914/255-1000).

Hiking: Bear Mountain State Park and Harriman State Park offer a network of trails. Contact the Palisades Interstate Park Commission, Bear Mountain, NY 10911 (tel. 914/786-2701). For the Appalachian Trail, contact the Appalachian Trail Conference, P.O. Box 807, Harpers Ferry, WV 25425 (tel. 304/535-6331), the national organization for the entire trail from Maine to Georgia. Or for information on those sections of the trail in New York and New Jersey, contact the New York–New Jersey Trail Conference, 232 Madison Ave., New York, NY 10016 (tel. 212/685-9699). Black Rock Forest on Rte. 9W, just northwest of West Point, has marked and unmarked trails. Crow's Nest is in the Storm King section of the Palisades Park on Rte. 9W south of Storm King Mountain.

Horseback Riding: *New Paltz:* Mountainview Stables (tel. 914/255-5369) offers guided trail rides for $20 per hour.

Sailing: Myles Gordon operates a nationally accredited sailing school at the Kingston Rondout in summer. You can attend "Learn to Sail" weekends and other lessons series for intermediates. Gordon also operates two-hour sunset sails on weekends, featuring wine, cheese, and music. He relates the history of the river's life. Sailboat and motorboat rentals. For a schedule of programs, contact the Great Hudson Sailing Center, P.O. Box 3542, Kingston, NY 12401 (tel. 914/338-7313).

Skiing: Cross-country in Bear Mountain and Harriman state parks. Also, great trails at Mohonk Mountain House (tel. 914/255-1000).

Tennis: Contact the individual towns' chambers of commerce for information about using school, college, and park courts in the region. The Woodstock Tennis Club, Zena and Sawkill roads (tel. 914/679-5900), is also open to the public.

A wonderful weekend can be constructed around a stay at one of the several inns located in Garrison, Cold Spring, or nearby, and from there you can explore both sides of the river.

GARRISON & COLD SPRING

Garrison itself was used as a setting for the Barbra Streisand film *Hello, Dolly!* and possesses a lovely park along the river, complete with a gazebo affording views of the majestic cliffs and river in either direction. Stop in at the **Garrison Arts Center,** Depot Square (tel. 914/424-3960), the artisan's workshops near the railroad tracks, and the station that now houses a theater, The Depot.

Hours: Daily noon–5pm.

From Garrison it's a short way north to more crowded Cold Spring, where you can browse in the antiques stores lining both sides of the main street, then explore one of the loveliest mansions on the Hudson, **Boscobel,** Rte. 9G (tel. 914/265-3638), built in the early 19th century by States Morris Dyckman. It contains fine collections of porcelain, silver, furniture, crystal, and rare books and commands spectacular views of the Hudson. The flower, herb, and vegetable gardens and orangerie are particularly enchanting, especially when the roses are in full bloom.

Hours: Mar–Dec, Wed–Mon 10am–4:15pm. **Admission:** Mansion and grounds, $6 adults, $5 seniors, $3 children 6–14; grounds only, $3 adults and seniors, $2 children 6–14.

WEST POINT, STORM KING & NEWBURGH

Area Attractions

Across the river, the **U.S. Military Academy** was founded at West Point in 1802 and has been turning out eminent leaders, both military and civilian, ever since—Robert E. Lee, Ulysses S. Grant, George S. Patton, and Dwight D. Eisenhower, to name only a few. The time to visit is spring or fall, when you can view the cadets on parade or attend one of the football games or other sports events. The museum displays military regalia, medals, and other objects relating to military history. From West Point's location on a high bluff above the river, you can look down to Constitution Island and at Trophy's Point see the remnants of the iron chain that was stretched across the river to stop the British advance. For information on parade times, contact the visitor center at 914/938-4011. For tickets to athletic events, call 914/446-4996 or write the Director of Intercollegiate Athletics, West Point, NY 10996.

From West Point, take the Storm King Highway to Cornwall, visiting the **Storm King Art Center,** Old Pleasant Hill Road, off Rte. 32, Mountainville (tel. 914/534-3115), a 400-acre park where more than 120 modern sculptures, many of them monumental, stand starkly against the horizon. Among the artists represented are Alexander Calder, Alice Aycock, Mark di Suvero, Henry Moore, Louise Nevelson, Isamu Noguchi, Richard Serra, and David Smith. Special exhibitions are on view indoors. Tours are given in summer daily at 2pm; call for a calendar of other events.

Hours: Apr–Nov 15, daily 11am–5:30pm (indoor galleries, from mid-May). June–Aug, the park is open until 8pm on Sat with free admission from 5pm. **Admission:** $7 adults, $5 seniors, $3 children 5–12.

From here you can go into Newburgh to visit **Washington's Head-quarters,** 84 Liberty St. (tel. 914/562-1195). Washington commanded his troops from here during 1782–83, the crucial period when peace was being concluded. Your visit begins in the Museum Building, which offers an audiovisual program and several exhibits recalling the events of 1782–83, when, even though Cornwallis had surrendered at Yorktown, Washington and his troops stood ready for battle in the Hudson Highlands, while the British continued to control New York City. The Hasbrouck House, which was Washington's headquarters for 16½ months, has been furnished to reflect the period and the events; you'll find a mix of utilitarian folding furniture and elegant appointments—from quill pens and camp beds to the decorative sewing of Martha.

On April 19, 1783, Washington gave the order for a "cessation of hostilities" and a monument commemorates this event. In the critical months afterward Washington dealt with serious problems of supply, pay, and morale among his troops and had to handle a contentious Congress. Washington also faced down the Newburgh Conspiracy, which called for an army mutiny and a takeover of the government to settle claims for back pay and pensions. Washington quelled the movement in a dramatic speech he made to the troops at the **New Windsor Cantonment,** Temple Hill Road (tel. 914/561-1765), about 4 miles from Newburgh. Today some of the buildings that were here have been reconstructed (there were 700, housing 8,000 troops) and are used for ceremonies, demonstrations, and other reenactments of historic events. The biggest celebration is on Washington's birthday in February. The other historic site that can be visited is Knox's Headquarters in Vails Gate.

Hours: Mid-Apr to Oct, Wed–Sat 10am–5pm, Sun 1–5pm.

Garrison Lodging & Dining

The Bird & Bottle, Rte. 9, Garrison, NY 10524 (tel. 914/424-3000), a tiny double-porched Colonial home set in the woods, has only four rooms for rent. The floors creak and slope, the iron door latches are original, and in your room a fire will be laid in the hearth and someone will come up to light it. The whole place is highly evocative. The small tavern room is delightful. A four-course prix-fixe dinner ($35 to $50, depending on the entree) is served in a romantically low-lit paneled dining room. It might offer roast duck with balsamic vinegar and orange sauce, salmon in a potato crust with tomato-and-basil beurre blanc, or roast pheasant with pâté and truffle sauce. Brunch is a similar four-course affair with choices ranging from egg dishes to much more hearty items.

Rates (including dinner and breakfast): $220–$250 double. **Dining Hours:** Wed 6–9pm, Thurs–Sat noon–2pm and 6–9pm, Sun noon–2pm and 4:30–7pm.

Xavier's, at the Highlands Country Club on Rte. 9D (tel. 914/424-4228), is the area's consistently recommended dining spot. Waterford crystal and fresh flowers grace the tables. On the $72 prix-fixe menu you can select from two menus. For example, the five-course menu might start with champagne-and-oyster soup, followed by either molasses-cured salmon or smoked chicken with gemelli and oyster mushrooms. After a refreshing

Campari-and-grapefruit sorbet, you might enjoy a roast rack of lamb with goat cheese and vegetable timbale, then a dessert of Tahitian vanilla-bean soufflé and chocolate sorbet. Coffee and petit-fours complete the meal, which is accompanied by a choice selection of wine for each course, starting with a Bellini Cipriani made from champagne and peach nectar. Reservations are required and no credit cards are taken.

Hours: Fri–Sat 6–9pm, Sun noon–2:30pm (brunch).

Cold Spring Lodging & Dining

At the foot of Main Street, **Hudson House,** 2 Main St., Cold Spring, NY 10516 (tel. 914/265-9355), looks across to the Storm King bluffs. It was built in 1832 to accommodate passengers disembarking from steamboats at the first stop between Albany and New York City. The once-forlorn place has been delightfully transformed into a comfy countrified lodging where lacquered wine decanters serve as bedside lamps and cookie cutters as wall decoration. The 11 guest rooms are comfortably old-fashioned, none with a phone, a TV, or air conditioning. The second-floor rooms open onto a broad balcony; the third-floor rooms are tucked under the mansard roof. The doors have iron latches; the sconces are Shaker style.

The favored summer dining place is the riverside porch. An additional summer dining area is under a colorful canopy with fresh-flower trimmings. The dining room has plank floors, tables set with gingham cloths, and chairs upholstered in blue. The menu is seasonal. Entrees might include duck served with a sauce of sour cherries and fresh thyme; roast loin of pork served with minted country apple sauce; salmon with a fresh dill, lemon, and caper butter; or filet mignon with a sauce of roasted shallots and burgundy. Prices run $17 to $24. The most famous dessert is a special chocolate "moose," a caramelized chocolate mousse shaped like a moose with antlers (Mary Pat Sawyer shopped everywhere to find an artisan who'd forge the molds for her). The goldbrick pudding, a flan with a crystalline crust, is another favorite. The Half Moon Bar is prettily furnished with wing chairs in front of the fireplace, pale-blue Windsor chairs, and blue chintz.

Rates (including continental breakfast): Summer, $135–$160 double; $160–$210 suite. Lower in winter. **Dining Hours:** Mon–Thurs noon–2:30pm and 6–9pm, Fri–Sat noon–2:30pm and 6–10pm, Sun noon–2:30pm and 5–9pm. **Closed:** Jan.

The owners of the **Olde Post Inn,** 43 Main St., Cold Spring, NY 10516 (tel. 914/265-2510), have the original map that labels the inn as the post office and assessor's office built in 1820. From the front porch the door opens into a raftered room with wide-plank floors that serves as a comfortable parlor with chintz sofas, a heavy country rocker, and other seating arrangements around a wood-burning Franklin stove. Dried herbs hang from the rafters, a pineapple-shaped tin chandelier provides light, and a Hoosier cabinet filled with china and pine-cone wreaths add country flair. A breakfast of homemade breads, croissants, coffee, and juice is brought to your room. Follow the scrolled staircase to three guest rooms, with bath and air-conditioning. Two appealing rooms on the attic floor have skylights. Most are furnished with oak dressers and chests, desks, country quilts, and cannonball beds.

In the old cellar, complete with a beehive oven, the innkeepers operate a jazz club on summer weekends ($5 cover), and featured artists have included Junior Mance and Ray Bryant. The tavern is open Wednesday to Sunday. A brick patio and garden are available for guests' pleasure.

Rates (including breakfast): $115 double.

At **Plumbush,** Rte. 9D, Cold Spring, NY 10516 (tel. 914/265-3904), the food reaches a high standard. Among the appetizers are a tasty venison sausage and mushrooms vinaigrette, a delicious smoked rainbow trout with horseradish sauce, escargots, terrines, and a satisfying onion soup gratinée with the unusual touch of Calvados. At a recent meal, the duck with a brandied-peach sauce, served with rösti potatoes, was perfectly crisp, not fatty; the turban of sole stuffed with crabmeat was delicately moist. Other entree choices ranged from medallions of pork with apples and chestnuts to steak bordelaise. Among the desserts, the Swiss apple fritters, Sachertorte, cherry napoleons, and orange Grand Marnier soufflé are all recommended. The atmosphere in each of the series of dining rooms is elegant, effected by chintz, lace curtains with floral-patterned pelmets, gilt-framed oils, fresh flowers, and glass hurricane lamps on the tables. The prix-fixe meal is $32; à la carte prices run $24 to $29.

Plumbush also has three rooms (including a suite) with bath available. Each is tastefully decorated in Victorian style: iron-and-brass beds, Empire chests, potted ferns, wicker pieces, marble-topped tables, and so on—remarkably fine rooms for an establishment that's first and foremost a restaurant.

Rates: $105 double; $135 suite. **Dining Hours:** Wed–Sun noon–2:30pm and 5:30–9:30pm.

A Hopewell Junction Bed-and-Breakfast

From Cold Spring, take Rte. 301 to Rte. 9 north to Rte. 82, which will bring you to Hopewell Junction, a trip of 25 to 30 minutes.

At **Le Chambord,** 2075 Rte. 52, Hopewell Junction, NY 12533 (tel. 914/221-1941), gracious accommodations and a well-respected dining room are combined. Antiques abound throughout the high-ceilinged 1863 Victorian residence built originally for a doctor on 9 acres. The hallway has a magnificent Victorian sideboard that once belonged to the Astor estate on Long Island, plus one of the largest old-fashioned wine coolers in existence, which was originally used as the refrigerator for the family with a block of ice in the center. The nine large high-ceilinged guest rooms (all with bath) are eclectically furnished with antiques from various periods. Room 2 mixes American and French; Room 8 affects an Empire style.

Some have reproduction Queen Anne furniture too. The third-floor rooms, tucked under the eaves, are particularly cozy. The 16 rooms in the addition (Tara) are minisuites furnished with fine fabrics. All rooms have a TV, a pushbutton phone, and air-conditioning.

A continental breakfast is served either in the dining room or on the flower-adorned terrace. The dining room has an excellent reputation, where pink napkins, white tablecloths, Villeroy & Boch china, lace-ruffled curtains, small crystal chandeliers, a fireplace, and gilt-framed pictures make for an elegant setting. At dinner you might begin with marinated salmon roulade, duck pâté, or almond- and pecan-encrusted Brie. Bouillabaisse, duckling with raspberry sauce, and braised veal chop filled with lobster are a few possible entrees. Extravagant soufflés, double-chocolate pâté, and crêpes Suzette are the prime dessert choices. Downstairs, the Marine Bar is especially inviting in winter, when a fire blazes in the copper-sheathed hearth. The tapestry-covered sofas are comfortable. Portholes and an authentic ship's wheel are the marine touches.

Rates (including breakfast): $120 double. **Dining Hours:** Mon–Fri 11:30am–2:30pm and 6–10pm, Sat 6–11pm, Sun 3–9pm.

Lower Hudson
Special & Recreational Activities

Boating: Fahnestock State Park, Rte. 301 (R.D. 2), Carmel, NY 10512 (tel. 914/225-7207), has a boat-rental facility.

Camping: Fahnestock State Park, Rte. 301 (R.D. 2), Carmel, NY 10512 (tel. 914/225-7207), is open all year, offering swimming, fishing, boat rentals, and 81 campsites.

Golf: Garrison Golf Club (tel. 914/424-3604).

Hiking: Hudson Highland State Park, just north of Cold Spring, has great hiking. The Manitoga Nature Preserve, just south of Garrison, has 4 miles of hiking trails. The Appalachian Trail cuts right through Fahnestock State Park, Rte. 301, (R.D. 2), Carmel, NY 10512.

The Catskills

Distance in Miles: Port Jervis, 68; Catskill, 115; Shandaken, 120

Estimated Driving Time: $1^{1}/_{2}$ to $2^{1}/_{4}$ hours

Driving: For the southern Catskills, take the George Washington Bridge to the Palisades Parkway north and follow this to the New York State Thruway north; take Exit 16 (Harriman) to Rte. 17 west. For the northern Catskills, continue up the Thruway to Kingston and Catskill.

◄o►◄o►◄o►◄o►◄o►

Bus: Adirondack Trailways (tel. 800/225-6815) travels to Hunter Mountain, Woodstock, Shandaken, and Margaretville. Shortline (tel. 201/529-3666, 212/736-4700, or 800/631 8405) travels to Sullivan County only.

For skiers there's special transportation to Hunter Mountain from Manhattan, Westchester, New Jersey, and Long Island. Call 800/552-6262.

Train: Metro North stops at Tuxedo, Harriman, and Port Jervis. For information, call 212/532-4900, or 800/638-7646.

Further Information: For more about New York State in general, write to the **Division of Tourism,** New York State Department of Commerce, One Commerce Plaza, Albany, NY 12245 (tel. 518/474-4116).

For specific information about the Catskills, contact the **Greene County Promotion Department,** P.O. Box 527, Catskill, NY 12414 (tel. 518/943-3223); the **Hunter Mountain Lodging Bureau,** P.O. Box 335, Rte. 23A, Hunter, NY 12442 (tel. 518/263-4208); the **Sullivan County Office of Public Information,** County Government Center, Monticello, NY 12701 (tel. 914/794-3000); the **Ulster County Public Information Office,** P.O. Box 1800, Kingston, NY 12401 (tel. 914/331-9300); the **Ulster County Chamber of Commerce,** 7 Albany Ave., Suite G3, Kingston, NY 12401 (tel. 914/338-5100); the **Delaware County Chamber of Commerce,** 97 Main St., Delhi, NY 13753 (tel. 607/746-2281); or the **Woodstock Chamber of Commerce,** P.O. Box 36, Woodstock, NY 12498 (tel. 914/679-6234).

Events & Festivals to Plan Your Trip Around

February–April: Maple Sugar Festivals, especially the Greene County Maple Sugar Festival, Windham.

June: Strawberry festivals, early June.

June–September: Hunter Mountain summer festivals.

"When the weather is fair and settled, they are clothed in blue and purple and print their bold outline on the clear evening sky; but sometimes, when the rest of the landscape is cloudless, they will gather a hood of gray vapours about their summits, which, in the last rays of the setting sun, will glow and light up like a crown of glory." Thus wrote Washington Irving of his beloved Catskills. Irving was certainly not their only herald, for one of the artists that painted them, Thomas Cole, wrote home from Europe that "neither the Alps, Apennines, nor Etna himself have [sic] dimmed in my eyes the beauty of our own Catskills." Thoreau put it even more dramatically when he said of the landscape, "it was fit to entertain a traveling god."

To this day there are parts of the Catskills that look like the Austrian or French Alps, where the mountains are majestic and the fast-running rivers, streams, brooks, cascading waterfalls, and deep quiet leave a visitor dumbfounded by the natural beauty. This is the Catskill area (around Shandaken, Margaretville, Roxbury, Stamford, the towns nestled along the Esopus Creek and the eastern branch of the Delaware—Mount Tremper, Phoenicia, Glenford—and the northern fringes of Greene County) that attracts skiers, mountaineers, hunters, hikers, canoers, and others who relish nature and the outdoor life. In the southern Catskills, around Monticello, Fallsburg, and Liberty, are those renowned resorts, known collectively as the Borscht Belt, that nurtured and developed so many American comedians and actors and delivered them to the TV and entertainment industry. Today they still offer a total vacation with a fantastic array of facilities for a very fair price, catering as they always did to the latest immigrants to arrive in New York. There really are two Catskills: the northern wonders of the Catskills forest preserve and the southern resort belt.

From the mid-1800s until the advent of the motorcar, the Catskills were the playground of the wealthy and eminent. The first resort hotel had been built in 1824, and from then on the Hudson Day Line brought thousands of tourists to the mountains, depositing them at Catskill Point, which became a bustling port and passenger terminal. Horse-drawn carriages and hacks, eagerly awaiting the arrival of the ferry steamers from

New York, transported tourists all over the county, though the most dramatic trip was aboard the Catskill Mountain Railroad to Palenville, where the Otis Elevating Railway (installed in 1894) scooped visitors up the face of the mountain to the Catskill Mountain House. (The gash in the mountainside can still be made out from Rte. 23A.) From the Mountain House the whole sweep of the Hudson River, from north of Albany and south of Kingston, could be seen against the backdrop of the New England mountains. Other tourists continued on to the Hotel Kaaterskill

Two Driving Routes Through the Northern Catskills

From Catskill, Rte. 23A brings you through some of the area's most dramatic scenery, as it snakes around between the mountains and forests cut by cascading waterfalls and gulleys past Kaaterskill Falls through Palenville, all the way to Hunter Mountain. Then take Rte. 296 to Windham, where you can choose either to loop back along Rte. 23, going over the dramatic Point Lookout with a five-state view into Catskill, or continue west along Rte. 23 to Grand Gorge, turning down Rte. 30 past the Burroughs Memorial all the way to Margaretville for a final loop back along Rte. 28 (detouring to Woodstock) into Kingston.

From Kingston, take Rte. 28 to Rte. 375, the turnoff into Woodstock. Return to Rte. 28 and take it to Winchells Corner. Turn left for a quick look at the Ashokan Reservoir. Cross the reservoir and turn right and then right again, looping along Rte. 28A, which will return you onto Rte. 28 near Mount Tremper. Turn left on Rte. 28 and continue through the towns of Mount Tremper and Phoenicia (both of which have some decent dining choices), all the way to Shandaken and Margaretville to the upper reaches of the Delaware. The scenery is beautiful all the way, and from here you can take Rte. 30 along the Pepacton Reservoir down to Hancock, whence you can canoe the Delaware, or to Roscoe, trout capital of the Catskills.

There are, of course, many possible routes through the mountains. Unless you know the mountains intimately, don't attempt shortcuts along dirt roads, especially at night, and always travel with plenty of gas, because if you do get off the beaten track, you can go for miles seeing nothing but trees and streams and could well be stranded for a long time.

The sections that follow have been organized according to the first route above.

or more remote resorts. The Kaaterskill, built in 1881, was absolutely palatial and could house 1,200 guests in a three-story building shielded by soaring columns, with a French Renaissance tower at each end. It fell victim to fire in 1924, a more dignified end than that experienced by the Mountain House, which was demolished in 1963.

For today's weekend visitor the Catskills offer a supreme outdoor experience. You can come to contemplate the mountains; ski at Hunter, Windham, or Belleayre; hike through the wilderness of the forest preserve; climb or ride to the summits of mountains granting vistas over five states; fish the Wallkill, Beaverkill, and Esopus; canoe the Delaware; swim in the lakes; or soar above the mountains from Ellenville and Wurtsboro. The landscape is the prime attraction, though you'll also find numerous festivals and events to attend, like those at Hunter in summer or the chamber concerts at Woodstock, but the greatest thrills and rewards await the activist willing to traverse, explore, and challenge these brooding mysterious mountains from dawn to dusk. A typical weekend could be centered on Woodstock, Saugerties, or Windham.

CATSKILL & CAIRO

Area Attractions

Since I discussed Kingston in the Hudson Valley chapter, I'm beginning with Catskill, which has three or four mostly family-oriented attractions.

The 140-acre **Catskill Game Farm,** off Rte. 32 (tel. 518/678-9595), specializes in keeping and raising hoofed creatures, so you can see rare wild horses (Przewalski) in their natural surroundings. Kids love to pet the llamas, donkeys, sheep, and lambs; see the antics of the chimpanzees; and ride the elephants. Peacocks wander freely about the grounds, stopping by the many food stands on the off-chance of receiving a treat. Bringing the makings of a picnic is a great idea. The full tour takes about two hours.

Hours: Apr 15–Oct, daily 9am–6pm. **Admission:** $12 adults, $8 children 4–11.

Although it's not open to the public, in this depressed town stands the **home of Thomas Cole,** one of the great artists of the Hudson River School. He lived from 1836 to 1848 in a house just south of the junction of Rtes. 23 and 385, where the property originally extended down to the Hudson River. Among his most famous paintings are *Sunny Morning on the Hudson, View from Tivoli, View from Kaaterskill Falls,* and his allegorical series, *The Course of Empire.* Cole was married in this house in 1836.

Also in Catskill, you can play out a western fantasy by going to **Carson City,** Rte. 32 just 2 miles north of the game farm (tel. 518/678-5518), the scene of gunfights, saloon shows, magic entertainment, and pony rides for kids. Summer rodeos are popular on Tuesday, Thursday, and Saturday.

Hours: Late June to Labor Day, daily 9:30am–6pm; May 28 to late June and Labor Day to Columbus Day, Sat–Sun 9:30am–6pm. **Admission:** $12 adults, $8 children 2–11.

For more active pursuits, head for the **Funtastic Family Fun Park,** on Rte. 32 in Cairo (tel. 518/622-3330), half a mile south of Rte. 23. There are three go-kart tracks, miniature golf, an arcade, and a picnic area.

Hours: Summer, daily 10am–10pm; spring and after Labor Day, Sat–Sun 10am–10pm.

In South Cairo anyone interested in Eastern religion may want to drop by the **Mahayana Buddhist Temple** (tel. 518/622-3619), a Buddhist retreat with a Chinese temple.

Catskill Dining

You may have difficulty finding **La Rive** (tel. 518/943-4888), but the food and the Gallic welcome at this country French restaurant will be worth it. (From Catskill travel 7 miles west on Rte. 23A to County Road 47; then follow the signs that'll take you down a dirt road to the restaurant.) In this old farmhouse you can dine either on the enclosed porch or more cozily in the house itself. Begin your meal with a selection of hors d'oeuvres from the trolley—like lamb pâté, cod mousse, cucumber with sour cream, celery rémoulade, eggs à la Russe—or opt for the shrimp rémoulade or escargots à la bourguignonne. The classics have been somewhat updated here, so you'll find duck with raspberry, thyme, and ginger sauce; filet mignon with a sauce of sage and brandied-mushroom duxelle; or grilled lamb chops with lamb demiglaze and flageolet beans topped with rosemary mayonnaise. In addition to fruit and cheese, desserts include crème brûlée, cheesecakes, and walnut-rum cake. Entree prices range from $14 to $24.

Hours: Mid-May to Thanksgiving, Thurs–Tues 6–10pm, Sun 2–9pm.

HUNTER MOUNTAIN

Area Attractions

At 4,025 feet, **Hunter Mountain,** Rte. 23A, Hunter (tel. 518/263-4223), is the second-highest mountain in the Catskills and the best ski area within a short distance of the city. Although it attracts thousands of skiers on weekends, Hunter handles them expertly and efficiently. The vertical rise is 1,600 feet. Hunter has 49 trails and 14 lifts and tows able to accommodate 15,500 skiers per hour. It boasts the best snowmaking capacity in the area (100%) and offers three mountains featuring terrain for all ability levels. You'll find base and summit lodges, eight dining facilities, and good nursery facilities. And the price is reasonable—weekdays $35 per day, weekends $42 per day. Rentals are available. Snowboarding is permitted, and there's also 5km of cross-country trails. For snow information, call 800/FOR-SNOW. For quick access, take the Hunter Express Bus from Manhattan, Westchester, New Jersey, or Long Island—call 800/552-6262.

In summer, Hunter Mountain hosts a series of colorful events and festivals, beginning in early July with an **American Patriot Festival,** followed quickly by the **German Alps Festival** (mid- to late July) with beer, Hummel figurines, brass bands, Punch and Judy, and other entertainment. Another weekend brings the **Country Music Festival,** featuring square dancing and entertainers. In early August there's **Rockstalgia,** which is just what it sounds like, and in mid-August a five-day **Celtic celebration** mixes Irish, Welsh, and Scottish music, entertainment, dancing, food, and drink. **The National Polka Festival** follows in late August, before the **Mount Eagle Indian Festival** on Labor Day weekend. The season is rounded out by the **Oktoberfest** in late September to mid-October. For festival information, call 518/263-3800.

Hunter is also the site of World Cup and Norba **mountain-bike racing.** The lift-serviced trail network provides exciting challenges for mountain-bike enthusiasts of all levels. Rentals are available. Even if you're not a mountain biker, while you're here ride the chair lift to the summit for a magnificent vista.

Between Hunter and Windham, just north of Tannersville in Jewett, architecture buffs may want to see the incredible **Ukrainian Church and Grazhda** (tel. 518/263-3862) on Rte. 23A. It's built in the traditional manner, without nails; the interior is hand-carved—a magnificent piece of craftsmanship indeed.

For cross-country skiing, **Mountain Trails,** Rte. 23A (P.O. Box 198), Tannersville, NY 12485 (tel. 518/589-5361), offers 35km of groomed, track-set, marked trails that are patrolled. Facilities include a warming hut, a snack bar, a sales and rental shop, and ski instruction.

Admission: $10 per day.

Hunter Mountain Area Lodging & Dining

Although plenty of ski lodges cater to the needs of skiers, I'll list only a couple of particular favorites. If these are full, try the **Hunter Mountain Lodging Bureau,** Rte. 23A, Hunter, NY 12442 (tel. 518/263-4208).

For easy ski-on/ski-off access to the slopes you can't beat the **Liftside Condominiums** (tel. 518/263-3707), right on the mountain, with slopeside views from each unit's deck. Each has a full kitchen, a washer/dryer, a fireplace, a TV/VCR, a phone, and a whirlpool bath. One-bedroom units sleep up to four, two-bedrooms up to six.

Rates: $250 one-bedroom condo; $340 two-bedroom condo.

The **Scribner Hollow Motor Lodge,** Rte. 23A, Hunter, NY 12442 (tel. 518/263-4211), is a fun place primarily because of its themed rooms. You might stay in one of the futuristic duplexes, with mirrored ceilings and walls, ultramodern white and beige furnishings, and a bathtub area

The Catskills

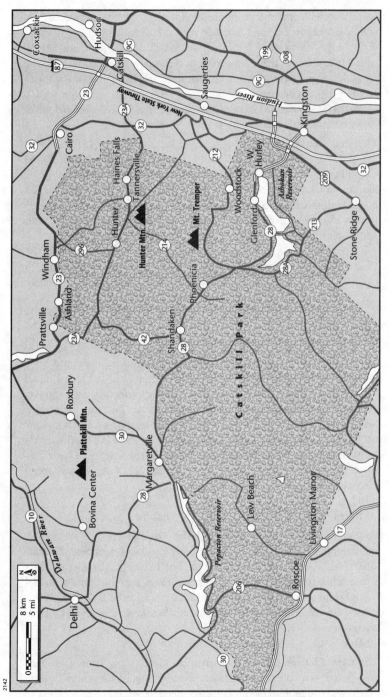

with a waterfall; or perhaps a hunting lodge might be more to your taste— with a large bearskin rug (complete with the animal's head), cozy cabin walls, beams, and a stone fireplace. Others include penthouse and South- west adobe themes. Even the pool area is specially designed to look like an underground cave/grotto, with waterfalls. The regular rooms are less fun, but they're cheaper.

Rates (MAP): $85–$120 per person double; $145–$185 special double. Two-night minimum on weekends.

The Red Coat's Return, Dale Lane, Elka Park, NY 12427 (tel. 518/ 589-6379 or 589-9858), is 10 miles from Hunter and adjacent to the Catskill Game Preserve. The menu offers about eight traditional favorites like sirloin with green-peppercorn sauce, duck with apples, and chicken breast with artichokes and mushrooms, priced from $13 to $21. There's usually a roaring fire in the lounge's stone fireplace, antiques dotted about, and a cozy library room; these contribute to the warm, comfortable atmo- sphere of this Edwardian home overlooking fields, forests, and Schoharie Creek. The 14 guest rooms (most with bath) have been decorated with oak pieces and fluffy down comforters, conveying a pleasant homey touch. The surrounding 18 acres have trails and trout streams.

Rates (including breakfast): $85–$100 double. **Dining Hours:** Fri– Mon 6–9:30pm.

The **Eggery Inn,** County Road 16, Tannersville, NY 12485 (tel. 518/ 589-5363), has 15 guest rooms (all with bath) furnished in country style with wall-to-wall carpeting, chintz wallpaper, and old-fashioned furni- ture. On arrival, guests enter a cozy living room warmed by a woodstove. There's a TV, books, a player-piano, and old comfy furniture, some of it Mission style. The inn operates a restaurant/bar offering a panoramic view of Hunter and the mountains. Here guests are served a full breakfast that includes omelets or French toast and similar. The dining room has a fire- place, and numerous plants enliven the decor. Dishes are typical Ameri- can favorites like prime rib, chicken Cordon Bleu, veal marsala, and poached salmon.

Rates (including breakfast): $95–$115 double.

Four miles from Hunter, the **Swiss Chalet,** Rte. 23A (tel. 518/589-5445), has an alpine look—plenty of hutches, cuckoo clocks, and pine. The cui- sine is also Austrian-Swiss inspired. For example, the menu offers wienerschnitzel, wiener rossbraten, sauerbraten, and Zurischer schnitzel (with cream and mushrooms). Dishes are priced from $15 to $24. For dessert, classics like apfelstrudel, peach Melba, and pear Hélène are offered.

Hours: Daily 5–9:30pm.

The **Last Chance Cheese & Antiques Cafe,** Main Street (tel. 518/ 589-6424), is a country store selling gourmet items, like cheese, pasta, coffee, tea, and more. The café can accommodate 90 and offers a variety of oversize sandwiches, several soups, cheese platters, and fondue, priced from $3 to $10.

Hours: Mon–Thurs 10am–7pm, Fri–Sat 10am–9pm, Sun 10am–8pm.

WINDHAM

This ski area lies about 7 miles north of Hunter. It was once a private club, catering to well-to-do skiers, where many political and business leaders skied, and it still exhibits the classiest atmosphere of the local resorts. There's good skiing from the 3,050-foot summit down a 1,550-foot vertical on 33 trails, 97% of them covered with snowmaking. The five chairs (including high-speed quad) and one J-bar have a lift capacity of more than 8,000 skiers per hour. Lessons, rentals, a ski shop, and a café are all available. The mid-mountain Wheelhouse lodge is an attractive place to picnic or enjoy the views. The White Birches Ski Touring Center offers 15 miles of groomed trails through lovely terrain. There's also a large snowboard park and a Children's Learning Center. Lift rates on weekends are $40 for adults and $35 for juniors (13 and over); midweek rates are $33 and $28, respectively. For information, contact **Ski Windham,** C. D. Lane Road, Windham, NY 12496 (tel. 518/734-4300, or 800/729-SKIW).

Windham & East Windham Lodging

The town is well kept and contains many appealing Victorian homes, some of which have been converted into accommodations.

The **Windham Arms Hotel,** Main Street, Windham, NY 12496 (tel. 518/ 734-3000), is owned by Ski Windham. The lobby glows in winter with a blazing fire. The modern rooms (with bath, color TV, and phone) are in a two-story building with balconies. Facilities include two dining rooms, an outdoor pool, a family recreation center, a putting green, a movie theater, a tennis court, and croquet.

Rates: Dec 22–Mar 9, $90–$110 double. Packages available.

The **Windham House,** Rte. 23 (R.R. 1, Box 36), Windham, NY 12496 (tel. 518/734-4230), is a small handsome resort. A stately 1805 house forms the nucleus of four Colonial-style buildings. Old timbers, plank walls and floors, Hitchcock chairs, and a sheaves-of-wheat railing along the upper veranda give the main house immense character. In Room 18 you'll find items like a wooden butter bowl and ladle, along with a marble-topped stand; in Room 2C there's a spool bed and washstand. Some rooms are in the carriage houses; some have only sinks; most have a bath. The loft of the old barn on this former farm now serves as a place for evening entertainment. The fields have been turned into a nine-hole golf course. There are also swimming and tennis facilities and a 2-mile hiking trail.

Rates: $260–$360 per person per week AP, $80–$90 per person daily; winter, $100–$115 room plus continental breakfast. **Closed:** Columbus Day–Dec.

At the **Albergo Allegria Bed & Breakfast,** Rte. 296, Windham, NY 12496 (tel. 518/734-5560, or 800/6-ALBERGO), two old houses have been joined by a new section that has been carefully designed to imitate the gingerbread, brackets, and stained glass of the original Victorians. Some of the 20 rooms are on the ground floor; others are located up the staircase, each step of which bears a stenciled angel. They're nicely furnished with dusky-pink carpeting and a brass bed covered with lacy pink eider, a pillow, and a bed ruffle; each has a pushbutton phone, TV, and tiled bath. In most there's plenty of room—enough for tables and chairs and a chest of drawers. Dried-flower arrangements add a country air. There are two sitting rooms with fireplaces, a few books, and polished wood floors covered with a braided rug. The one downstairs has couches, while the upstairs area has a more Victorian feel, thanks to the wicker, rattan, and Eastlake furnishings. Oak chairs and tables fill the dining room, where a full breakfast is served. In summer the small patio under a colorful awning is the breakfast spot. This B&B is right across from the Windham Country Club's 18-hole golf course, ranked no. 3 in the state by the PGA.

Rates (including breakfast): Winter, $115–$125 double weekend, $65–$95 double weekday. Summer, $75–$95 double. Fall, $115–$125 double weekend, $65–$85 double weekday. Off-season, $65–$85 double weekend, $55–$75 double weekday. Suites and a Jacuzzi suite are more expensive.

The **Pointe Lookout Mountain Inn,** Rte. 23 (P.O. Box 33), East Windham, NY 12439 (tel. 518/734-3381), takes full advantage of a magnificent view over New York, Connecticut, New Hampshire, Vermont, and Massachusetts. Most of the rooms have decks, and all have a TV and bath. The three dining rooms and deck share the spectacular view. They offer a variety of Italian dishes, from scampi to ravioli and chicken parmigiana; vegetarian specialties and steaks are also available. Prices range from $11 to $17. More than 20 beers and a dozen wines by the glass are on hand, plus a selection of Californian and Italian wines. For breakfast you can select from a long list of fillings for omelets or frittatas, as well as pancakes.

Rates (including breakfast): Christmas to early Mar, $125–$135 double. The rest of the year, $65–$105 double. **Dining Hours:** Mon–Sat 11am–9:30pm, Sun 10am–9pm. **Closed:** Early spring.

Windham Area Dining

Vesuvio, Goshen Road, Hensonville (tel. 518/734-3663), offers an elegant setting (a fireplace and gilt-framed pictures) for some good continental cuisine, including steaks; rack of lamb; chicken Vesuvio (sautéed with peas, mushrooms, and prosciutto in a wine sauce); veal with fresh mushrooms, lemon, and white wine; and assorted seafood like snapper, lobster, mussels, and squid. Prices run $13 to $22.

Hours: Daily 4–10pm.

At **Chalet Fondue,** Rte. 296, Windham (tel. 518/734-4650), you can cozy up to the Swiss alpine stove while waiting for a table in one of three dining areas—two stucco style, the other a solarium. Here you can feast on jaegerschnitzel, sauerbraten, wienerschnitzel, and more, finishing with a fine Sachertorte or apfelstrudel. Prices run $10 to $22.

Hours: Winter, Thurs–Sat 5–10pm, Sun 4–9pm; the rest of the year, Mon and Wed–Sat 5–9:30pm, Sun 4–9pm.

Theo's, Rte. 23, Windham (tel. 518/734-4455), offers continental cuisine with a hint of Greek flavor. On the menu are Greek-style lamb chops and also some Italian dishes, along with seafood. Prices ($10 to $30) include soup, salad, a main course, a dessert, and coffee. The atmosphere is simple and homey.

Hours: Jan–Mar and July–Aug, daily noon–11pm; Apr–June and Sept–Dec, Thurs–Tues noon–11pm.

A B&B Hideaway

The **Greenville Arms,** South Street, Greenville, NY 12083 (tel. 518/966-5219), is indisputably an isolated hideaway and has been used as such by many a celebrity in search of rest and anonymity. Cupolas and dormers crown the roof of this lovely Victorian house, built in 1889 for William Vanderbilt and now operated by Eliot and Tish Dalton as a country inn. There are 14 rooms, all with bath (4 rooms and one suite in the main house and 9 in the carriage house). The most pleasant is probably Old Will's Room, which contains a canopied bed and wing chairs set against rose wallpaper; it has the added attraction of a balcony. Miss Penny's Room contains a four-poster, an oak dresser, and a cozy reading nook.

A full breakfast is served in the dining rooms, both with floor-to-ceiling brick fireplaces. At dinner on weekends an American Bounty Buffet offers appetizers, roasts from the carving board, fresh fish and vegetable dishes, and homemade desserts and breads. Midweek dinner is prepared for guests only and dishes like roast chicken with orange-cranberry relish might be offered. There's a comfortable sitting room on the ground floor and a TV/VCR room on the second floor. Fine paintings can be found throughout. Out back is a lovely secluded outdoor pool you'd never expect to find, a lawn for croquet and other games, and 7 acres with a bubbling stream and wooded trails. The proprietors also offer Hudson River Valley Art Workshops, an annual series of classes in painting and drawing. Bicycles are available.

Rates (including breakfast): $120–$160 double.

FROM WINDHAM TO MARGARETVILLE

If you're following the second itinerary route outlined in the "Two Driving Routes Through the Northern Catskills" box above, from Windham take Rte. 23 west to Grand Gorge. Here you can either take Rte. 30 south to Margaretville or continue on Rte. 23 to the attractive town of Stamford. From Stamford, Rte. 10 south travels through Hobart to Delhi. En route, a scenic side trip through horse-and-farm country along Rtes. 5 and 6 to Bovina Center and New Kingston will eventually return you to Rte. 28 just west of Margaretville. You'll have completed a small loop touching on Schoharie and Delaware counties.

If you travel down Rte. 30 toward Margaretville, you'll pass naturalist **John Burroughs's Memorial,** just outside Roxbury, down Burroughs Memorial Road. You can sit here and quietly reflect on nature in the Catskill Mountain pasture as he did when he was a boy. Later, when he was a renowned naturalist/philosopher whose books had changed the way many Americans looked at their world, he still returned here for inspiration. Today he stands out as a brilliant naturalist/environmentalist who wrote this as early as 1913: "We can use our scientific knowledge to poison the air, corrupt the waters, blacken the face of the country, and harass our souls with discordant noises, or we can mitigate and abolish all these things."

Lodging & Dining En Route

A warm and friendly welcome will greet you and some unexpected facilities will surprise you at **Breezy Acres Farm,** Rte. 10 (R.D. 1, Box 191), Hobart, NY 13788 (tel. 607/538-9338), just less than 2 miles south of Stamford on Rte. 10. Joyce and David Barber love having guests at their 300-acre crop farm. Joyce serves a hearty breakfast—enough to carry you through the whole day—of fresh fruit, muffins, and eggs. For example, you might enjoy baked apples, pumpkin muffins, and French toast with homemade bread, accompanied by their own farm syrup and bacon. Guests are free to gather in the sitting room, a typically homey room with a sofa and chairs. And there's a pleasant TV room with a leather sofa and chairs, display cases filled with Winchester commemoratives, and a couple of deer trophies, including a mule deer taken in Wyoming.

There are three guest rooms, all with bath. One has solid-oak furniture crafted by Joyce's great-great-grandfather, including a fine headboard that required each tiny spindle to be lathed individually. Another has wall-to-wall carpeting, a peach- and jade-colored quilt on the carved-oak bed, and louvered closets. The other rooms have polished wood floors. Joyce usually places nuts or some other small treat in the rooms. Guest may use the Jacuzzi, and there's a Ping-Pong table in the garage.

Rates (including breakfast): $65–$80 double weekends, $60–$70 double weekdays.

A Scenic Drive

From South Kortwright, drive over the mountains to Bovina. The climb up affords beautiful views and the drive across the top takes you past black-and-white Holsteins and grazing horses against green fields, silos, and rust or gray barns topped with weather vanes.

Bovina Center is a tiny community with a firehouse, a community hall, and a one-room museum filled with local memorabilia—clothes, pictures, agricultural implements, photographs.

The **Hidden Inn,** Main Street, South Kortwright (tel. 607/538-9259), is a fine old white clapboard house with a prominent pediment supported by Corinthian pillars. Family run, it offers a small lounge with a fireplace and three plain country dining rooms: the Colonial Room, with a wood-burning fireplace; the Sunset Room, where the tables are set with burgundy napkins; and the Kortwright Room, used locally for meetings and weddings. On Friday and Saturday there's either a chuckwagon or a seafood buffet. The regular menu is short and simple, listing such favorites as veal parmigiana, duck à l'orange, chicken piccata, surf and turf, and steaks. Prices run $10 to $17.

Hours: Mon–Sat 5–9pm, Sun noon–7pm (may be closed Mon–Tues in winter).

Margaretville Dining
In the center of Margaretville, the **Binnekill Square Restaurant** (tel. 914/586-4884) is built over the narrow creek. The dining rooms have a combination of butcher block, stained glass, and comb-back Windsor chairs. The menu features a variety of beef, veal, seafood, and chicken dishes, priced from $12 to $20.

Hours: Tues from 5pm, Wed–Sat noon–3pm and from 5pm, Sun from 5pm.

Beaverkill Valley Lodging & Dining
The **Beaverkill Valley Inn,** Beaverkill Road, Lewbeach, NY 12753 (tel. 914/439-4844), located in a wonderfully restful wilderness spot, makes a marvelous, unpretentious retreat. Built in 1895 especially for sport fishermen, it stands on the banks of the Beaverkill—you can fall asleep to the sound of flowing water. The emphasis in restoration has been on solid comforts—really comfortable armchairs and sofas in the sitting room, real logs burning in the fireplace, plenty of books about the Catskills for readers to peruse, and ceramic lamps on the tables.

This is the kind of place you look forward to coming home to from a good day's fishing—where you can relish a good meal in the oak-furnished dining room, relax in front of the fire, play cards in the games room in front of a blazing fire, or enjoy a game of billiards downstairs in the plushly furnished billiard room. Also on the property are a tennis court and an indoor pool housed in a converted barn, fully equipped (can you believe it!) with an ice-cream parlor. The grounds are well kept, the lawn has a finely trimmed smooth croquet court, and there are 6 miles of Beaverkill waters for private fishing in spring and fall. The pond is perfect for skating. The stained-glass panels found throughout the ground floor are quite beautiful, especially the one in the sitting room. They were created by Cynthia Richardson, an artist from Massachusetts. On Friday a buffet-style dinner is served from 7:30 to 10pm; Saturday lunch is also a buffet. You can make special dietary requests. Hors d'oeuvres are placed in the bar at cocktail hour.

The inn offers 20 guest rooms. In the inn itself they're not large, because space was used to add baths during the renovation. Most have iron-and-brass beds, colorful quilts, oak dressers, chairs, sidetables, and solid-wood closets. Additional, somewhat simpler accommodations are available at Ardsley House and at the Quill Gordon Lodge, which some people prefer because it's almost austere, has a huge fireplace, and has always been a fishing lodge. Finally, the house has a wraparound porch furnished with wicker and a swing seat for positive relaxation.

Rates (AP): $270 double without bath, $340 double with bath.

FROM SHANDAKEN TO MOUNT TREMPER

Shandaken & Pine Hill Lodging & Dining

Albert Pollack, who owns a chain of movie theaters, and interior designer Gisele took over the **Shandaken Inn,** Shandaken, NY 12480 (tel. 914/688-5100), in 1972. At the time it was meant to be a quiet retreat from city life, but as more and more friends came to visit, they decided to continue the practice of having only their friends and friends' guests and referrals stay with them for weekends in very proper houseguest fashion. Consequently, the inn requires no advertising.

Originally a dairy barn, the house has experienced several incarnations, from a golf clubhouse to a ski lodge to a country inn. It has been tastefully decorated by Gisele, who installed a glowing copper bar, decorated the stone fireplace with copper pans and utensils, and scattered about all manner of antiques—decoys, samplers, basketry—that impart a delightful country air to the comfortable sitting areas. Each of the 12 guest rooms has been decorated individually but rather simply, some with wicker.

A typical weekend might begin with your arrival on Friday in time for dinner, prepared by Gisele for 8:30pm. The ingredients would be fresh local produce—striped bass, filet mignon, and rack of lamb, accompanied by appetizers, salads, and desserts (such as her classic raspberry tarts—the kind that only the French seem to know the secret of baking). For the rest of the weekend you can relax, go skiing, or pretty much do whatever you like, returning in the evening for cocktails, dinner, and an informal soirée with other houseguests. There's also a tennis court and a pool. No children are accepted.

Rates (including breakfast and dinner): Weekends only, $225–$245 per day per couple.

The impressive 1896 **Birch Creek,** Rte. 28 (P.O. Box 323), Pine Hill, NY 12465 (tel. 914/254-5222), is set on 23 wooded acres and approached via a tree-lined road. You'll enter a long center hall/sitting area warmed by a wood-burning stove and furnished with Empire-style furniture, wicker, and other large pieces of Victoriana. The hall leads to a large wraparound porch furnished with Adirondack chairs that overlook the creek. There are seven guest rooms, all with bath. Most are simply huge, like the champagne room, which boasts a brass bed, a large armoire and couch, and an equally large bath with a tub for two and a shower. Other rooms might feature spindle or wicker or antique Victorian beds and suitable furnishings. A full breakfast is served in the dining room. Upstairs, guests may use the book-filled library with fireplace and glass bookcases. The vintage billiard room contains a tournament-size pool table, a piano, and plenty of board games for entertainment. A TV is available on request.

Rates (including breakfast): $85–$120 double.

The **Auberge des 4 Saisons,** Rte. 42, Shandaken, NY 12480 (tel. 914/688-2223), has been well known for its cuisine ever since Edouard (Dadou) LaBeille, a waiter at Le Pavillon, Henri Soulé's legendary Manhattan restaurant (now closed), established this hunting lodge in 1954. The classically French menu changes frequently. Among the appetizers may be rabbit pâté, hors d'oeuvres variés, and stuffed mushrooms. The entrees might include duck with honey-cider apple sauce, pork loin with grapes, rabbit in white wine, breast of chicken in Calvados, trout meunière, and filet mignon béarnaise. Soufflé glacé au Grand Marnier is the dessert to choose. Prices range from $15 to $21.

The inn has 18 rooms, each just large enough for a bed and a sink, and in a chalet (separated from the inn by a tennis court) are another 18 offering more modern amenities, including baths. There's also an outdoor pool. Belleayre is only 6 miles away.

Rates (MAP): $178–$198 double. **Dining Hours:** June–Sept, daily 5:30–9:30pm; the rest of the year, Fri–Sun 5:30–9:30pm.

Dining En Route

The **Jake Moon Restaurant and Cafe,** 8373 Rte. 28, Big Indian (tel. 914/254-5953), is popular for its creative new American cuisine. You can enjoy duck breast with a fig-and-honey glaze, peppered salmon broiled with a raspberry-vinegar butter, or filet mignon with wild mushrooms and a rich beaujolais sauce. The appetizers are similarly appealing, like blue-corn-and-garlic pancakes with smoked salmon and horseradish sour cream, pheasant pâté with cranberry-orange relish, and crab cakes with tomato chutney. The desserts are more traditional—cheesecake, chocolate mousse, and a delicious banana flan with dark-rum sabayon. Prices run $13 to $18. You can dine in the plant-filled solarium or in a cozy dining area warmed by a woodstove.

Hours: Mon and Thurs–Fri 4:30–9:30pm, Sat–Sun noon–3pm and 4:30–9:30pm. Also open Tues in summer.

Sweet Sue's, Main Street, Phoenicia (tel. 914/688-7852), is a great breakfast place for raspberry, blueberry, and peach pancakes or four-grain pancakes like whole wheat and fruited oatmeal. The soups are soul-satisfying and the sandwiches are prepared on home-baked whole-grain bread. It's down-home and simple, with tables sporting floral cloths. Prices range from $2.75 to $6.

Hours: Daily 7am–3pm.

Mount Tremper Lodging

The **Mount Tremper Inn,** at the corner of Rte. 212 and South Wittenberg Road (P.O. Box 51), Mount Tremper, NY 12457 (tel. 914/688-5329), is a very inviting 1850 Victorian with white clapboard siding, green shutters, and a porch gaily hung with flower baskets and set with Adirondack chairs. All the rooms have sinks; some have baths. The rooms are on the small side but decently furnished. The parlor is strikingly furnished with Victorian antiques, with comfortable seating in front of the bluestone fireplace. Games, puzzles, and books are provided for relaxation, with badminton, volleyball, and shuffleboard for the more active. Classical music adds to the serenity at breakfast.

Rates (including breakfast): $70–$75 double without bath; $85 double with bath; $100 suite.

The **Zen Mountain Monastery,** P.O. Box 197, Mount Tremper, NY 12457 (tel. 914/688-2228), offers bunk accommodations in dorms to those who are seriously interested in Zen. The daily schedule runs from 4:45am wakeup and dawn meditation to evening meditation.

Rates: $185–$260 double for a weekend retreat.

Mount Tremper Dining

At **La Duchesse Ann,** 4 Miller Rd., Mount Tremper (tel. 914/688-5260), lace tablecloths, oak columns, and a wonderfully ornate woodstove make for romantic dining in a creekside setting. Try the terrines, soups, or escargots to start, then follow with a warming lapin provençal, entrecôte au poivre, or a simple sole meunière. Prices range from $14 to $22. The adjacent crêperie is open on weekends for delicious savory and dessert crêpes—from ham and bacon to chocolate, banana, and apples. To get here, turn off Rte. 28 onto Rte. 212 north, then turn left onto old Rte. 28. The restaurant is on the right, set back from the road.

Hours: Mon–Thurs 5:30–9pm, Fri 5:30–11pm, Sat 10am–2pm and 5:30–11pm, Sun 10am–4pm and 5:30–9pm. **Closed:** Wed in winter (and possibly Tues or Thurs as well).

WOODSTOCK

Area Attractions

Woodstock lies at the foot of the Ohayo and Overlook mountains, and its scenic location attracted artists at the turn of the century. In 1902 Ralph Whitehead established the Byrdcliffe Art and Crafts Colony. Shortly thereafter the Art Students League established its summer school in Woodstock, and in 1910 the Woodstock Artists' Association was founded. In 1916 one of the oldest chamber-music concert series was begun here, the Maverick Concerts founded by Hervey White. Sadly, the landmark Woodstock Playhouse that opened in 1937 burned down in the 1980s; funds are being raised to build another modern facility. So for a long time people— creative ones in particular—have been been attracted to Woodstock, the town that gave its name to a whole generation when 400,000 people came in 1969 to celebrate the Woodstock Music Festival. Though the festival actually took place about 60 miles west in a farmer's field in Bethel, Woodstock became its moniker, and a second Woodstock was held in 1994, this time in neighboring Saugerties, about 20 minutes north of Woodstock. It degenerated into a mud bath during the weekend rainstorm but again drew attention to the region.

Today, all the early organizations remain, except the Art Students League, which has been replaced by the Woodstock School of Art (tel. 914/679-8746 or 679-7558) and the Woodstock Playhouse. The town is crowded on summer weekends and still has a 1960s hippie air. Freaks still hang out on the green, and there's usually an aspiring singer entertaining with a guitar. The main street is lined with an eclectic mix of clothing boutiques, New Age outlets, candle stores, souvenir shops, and more utilitarian shops selling books, hardware, wine, and health foods/remedies.

Among the shopping highlights are **The Golden Notebook,** 29 Tinker St. (tel. 914/679-8000), an excellent bookstore that seems to cram more stock onto its shelves than any other store in the nation and is run by an extremely helpful and knowledgeable proprietor and staff. Similar expertise is dispensed about wine by **Woodstock Wines & Liquors,** next door. Survey the beautiful kilims stocked at **Anatolia Tribal Rugs and Weavings** (tel. 914/679-5311), tucked away behind Tinker Street; also back here is **Dharmaware,** selling Eastern religious books and statues of gods and goddesses as well as meditation cushions and clothes from Asia. Other stores to look for are **Blue Mountain Villager,** Rtes. 375 and 212 (tel. 914/679-4118), selling country furniture plus draperies, blinds, wallpaper, and other interior design accessories; **The Gilded Carriage,** 95 Tinker St. (tel. 914/679-2607), for everything for the art of setting a table, including French Quimper and Italian majolica; **Mirabai Books,** 23 Mill Hill Rd. (tel. 914/679-7819), which specializes in spiritual and metaphysical books; the **Woodstock General Store** (tel. 914/679-8140), appreciated by those suffering from acute nostalgia; and **Reader's Quarry** (tel. 914/679-9572), for a broad selection of secondhand books and first editions at decent prices.

A shopping stop crafts lovers won't want to miss is **Crafts People** (tel. 914/331-3859), owned and operated by craftspeople and housed in several buildings. They sell some beautifully crafted glass and ceramics as well as jewelry and other craft items. Call for directions. From Kingston, take Rte. 28 west to the West Hurley traffic light and turn left on Basin Road. Follow the signs from there.

Hours: Summer, daily 10am–6pm; winter, Fri–Mon 10am–6pm.

There's still a handful of galleries in town and nearby. Stop in at the **Woodstock Artists' Association,** 28 Tinker St. (tel. 914/679-2940), for their changing exhibits and lectures.

Hours: Mon and Thurs–Fri noon–5pm, Sat–Sun noon–6pm.

Also contact the **Woodstock Guild,** 34 Tinker St. (tel. 914/679-2079), which, besides holding classes/workshops, operates the Kleinert Arts Center, which offers year-round contemporary exhibits and musical and other performances.

Hours: Wed–Mon 11am–6pm.

The guild also operates the **Crafts Shop,** 34 Tinker St. (tel. 914/ 679-2688), which sells fine regional crafts.

Hours: Thurs–Mon 11am–5:30pm.

Other galleries of note are **Lily Ente** (tel. 914/679-6064); **James Cox,** 26 Elwyn Lane (tel. 914/679-7608); and in nearby Shady, **Elena Zang,** 3671 Rte. 212 (tel. 914/679-5432), which sells some eye-catching and beautifully crafted ceramics and fine arts and sculpture.

From May to October, the famous **Byrdcliffe Arts and Crafts Colony** offers residences and studios to artists, craftspeople, musicians, and writers. The Byrdcliffe Barn is the site of extensive programming during summer, including classes and performances. You can obtain a pamphlet outlining a walking tour of the arts and crafts colony from the Woodstock Guild.

In the heart of the mountains, Woodstock is also home to Buddhist monasteries and other inspirational retreats. For example, at the top of Meads Mountain Road you'll find the **Tibetan Buddhist monastery** (tel. 914/679-4271), easily identified by the prayer flags blowing in the wind out front. Tours are given of the temple and you can also visit the bookstore selling statuary and other religious objects too.

Just outside Woodstock, in High Woods, Saugerties, **Opus 40** is the site of summer musical and other events. This monumental environmental sculpture, carved out of an abandoned bluestone quarry, covers more than 6 acres and is made of thousands of tons of finely fitted blue-stone; it was contructed over a period of 37 years by sculptor Harvey Fite. At the center of it stands a 9-ton monolith. Fite had meant the entire sculpture to be a backdrop for his large stone carvings, but the backdrop took over and he removed the carvings to the surrounding lawns, woods, and pools, where they can still be seen.

Hours: Memorial Day–Oct, Fri–Sun noon–5pm. Call ahead because Sat is often reserved for special events. **Admission:** $5 adults, $4 seniors and students, free for children 11 and under.

Woodstock Lodging

Twin Gables, 73 Tinker St., Woodstock, NY 12498 (tel. 914/679-9479), is homey and attractive and retains the ambience of the time when many artists chose to lodge here in the 1940s; however, it possesses the expected modern comforts. There are nine rooms, three with bath and air conditioning; the rest share 2¹/₂ baths. The many paintings by Woodstock artists gracing the rooms add an authentic accent.

Rates: $65 double without bath, $82 double with bath.

Woodstock & Nearby Dining

On Woodstock's main street, **Joshua's Cafe,** 51 Tinker St. (tel. 914/679-5533), can be trusted to serve large portions of healthy Middle Eastern fare—hummus, baba ganoush, and shaslik, along with a dozen or so salads and a very extensive menu. Main courses include shish kebab, kilic sis (skewered swordfish with tomatoes, celery, mushrooms, and peppers), batata charp (potato pies filled with vegetables or meat), and paella couscous (clams, mussels, chicken, sausage, shrimp, peas, tomatoes, and onions). Dishes are priced from $5 to $18. At brunch 10 or so omelets are offered, from fried bananas and melted cheese to sautéed onions, potatoes, tomatoes, and parsley, along with a dozen egg dishes, whole-grain pancakes, and challah French toast. A small place—1960s style, with polished wood tables and chairs—Joshua's is always crowded with an interesting-looking artsy crowd.

Hours: Sun–Thurs 11am–9pm, Fri–Sat 11am–11pm.

Also in town, a more atmospheric choice is the **Blue Mountain Bistro,** Rtes. 212 and 375 (tel. 914/679-8519), in a gristmill at the Woodstock Golf Course. You'll find two dining rooms—one overlooking the Sawmill Creek and the golf course, the other with a large, rough-stone fireplace. The inspiration for the cuisine is Mediterranean; for the most part, the food is good, although I'd recommend, over some of the other dishes, the poulet rôti grandmère (a tasty free-range chicken roasted with thyme and mushrooms) and the salmon en papillote (topped with julienne vegetables, cooked with fresh herbs and a white-wine sauce with shallots, and baked to retain the flavors). Steak and frites, a vegetarian dish like couscous, and a pasta dish round out the menu. Prices range from $11.50 to $17. For dessert try the unusual crème brûlée Catalan, flavored with vanilla beans, lemon, and fennel.

Hours: Tues–Thurs and Sun 11:30am–2:30pm and 5–9pm, Fri–Sat 11:30am–2:30pm and 5–10pm.

Another town veteran is **Christy's,** 85 Mill Hill Rd. (tel. 914/679-5300), which has been serving locals for years. It has a cozy atmosphere, with a beamed ceiling and fireplace and a small bar in the back. The food is good for the price and consists of traditional dishes like roast pork and stuffed filet of sole. Prices range from $10 to $16.

Hours: Tues–Sat 5–10pm, Sun 4–10pm.

Mountain Gate, 4 Deming St. (tel. 914/679-5100), offers decent Indian cuisine. The atmosphere is more comfortable than that at most traditional Indian restaurants—cane-seated Breuer chairs and dark-green tablecloths combined with golden napkins. The service can be slow and erratic though. The menu offers all the usual favorites, priced from $10 to $18. Spice lovers will want to try the lamb, beef, or chicken vindaloo; the tandoori fish and the lobster malabar are other specialties. A full range of vegetarian dishes is also available.

Hours: Sun–Thurs noon–3pm and 5–10pm, Fri–Sat noon–3pm and 5–11pm.

The famous bakery **Bread Alone** has a store at 22 Mill Hill Rd. (tel. 914/679-2108), selling its great breads (try the seven-grain health loaf) plus sandwiches, pizza, salads, and pastries and cakes. The breads are first-class but the pastries are rather disappointing.

Hours: Mon–Fri 7:30am–5pm, Sat–Sun 7:30am–7pm.

Just out of town, the **New World Cafe,** at the corner of Zena and Sawkill roads (tel. 679-2600), serves the best cuisine in the area. The emphasis is on spicy Caribbean-style dishes. Jerk chicken and jerk pork come smothered with a spicy sauce; the Purple Haze shrimp is cooked in a sauce made of thyme, onions, rum, pineapple, habañeros, and more—it certainly sparks the taste buds; barbecue dishes are similarly piquant, and if you want more heat, several hot sauces are on the table. The menu also offers five or so vegetarian dishes, like the red-bean vindaloo, plus salmon puttanesca or mango-basil shrimp. Ten wines are available by the glass; bottle prices are reasonable and the selections appropriate to the food. The restaurant occupies a 1760 stone building where the ceilings are low and beamed but the decor isn't dreary colonial style. Instead, the white walls and modern art and the colorfully covered tables make for a light country ambience.

Hours: Mon–Thurs 11:30am–2:30pm and 5–10pm, Fri 11:30am–2:30pm and 5–11pm, Sat 5–11pm, Sun 5–10pm.

Decent Chinese cuisine is found at **The Little Bear** (tel. 914/679-8899), in nearby Bearsville, where you can dine on Hunan, Peking, Cantonese, and Szechuan fare on a patio overlooking the creek (illuminated at night) or inside in a woodsy atmosphere. It's especially haunting in fall, when a series of lit pumpkins is placed along the banks of the creek. Prices begin at $8.

Hours: Sun–Thurs noon–10:30pm, Fri–Sat noon–11pm.

Another recommended Bearsville restaurant, right next door and on the creek, is the **Bear Cafe,** Rte. 212 (tel. 914/679-5555). The food is excellent, but some people may find the place too noisy. If you want to relax and have a quiet conversation, this isn't the place because you really do have to shout if you want your dining partner to hear. It has a barnlike air, with cathedral ceilings and plenty of wood beams. The nice thing about the place is that it offers two menus—a lighter, lower-priced café menu featuring sandwiches, quesadillas, pasta, or similar items as well as a more fulsome menu. Among the entrees may be grilled salmon with grapefruit salsa, filet mignon with port-garlic sauce and Stilton cheese, and grilled seasonal vegetables with polenta. Prices range from $9 to $20.

Hours: Wed–Mon 6pm–closing.

Saugerties Dining

About 20 minutes north of Woodstock, some of the region's best dining is found at **Cafe Tamayo,** 89 Partition St. (tel. 914/246-9371). It occupies a handsome Victorian building, and diners can choose to dine either upfront in the bar area, complete with a beautifully carved and mirrored mahogany bar, or in the rooms behind. The atmosphere is casually elegant. The menu changes seasonally, but whatever appears will use the freshest ingredients and will have been carefully prepared to bring out the natural flavors. You might find chicken piccata enlivened by a sauce with white wine and lemon juice and that extra touch of capers, calves liver enriched by a madeira sauce, or grilled lamb that's been marinated in onion, garlic, lemon juice, and oil to produce a delicious au jus. Prices range from $15 to $17. The menu suggests wines to accompany each dish and offers them all by the glass. Among the appetizers, the seared tuna au poivre is coated with peppercorns and served with pickled ginger and soy vinaigrette, and locally grown portobello mushrooms are marinated and grilled and served with wilted arugula and balsamic vinegar. The desserts are not innovative, but the lemon tart with sesame crust is my choice for the end of a wonderful meal.

Hours: Wed–Sat 5pm–closing, Sun 11:30am–3pm and 5pm–closing.

The Catskills
Special & Recreational Activities

Boating: In Catskill, Riverview Marine Services, 103 Main St. (tel. 518/943-5311), offers 16- to 20-foot powerboats for rent to use on the Hudson River.

Camping: Backpackers can camp anywhere on state-owned land in the Catskill Forest Preserves and State Reforestation Areas as long as the site is designated or at least 150 feet from the trail, road, or body of water and below 3,500 feet altitude. They can also use the lean-tos provided along the trails. Contact the Bureau of Preserve Protection and Management, New York State Department of Environmental Conservation, 50 Wolf Rd., Room 412, Albany, NY 12233-4255.

From May 23 to September 1, campsites in the Catskill State Forest Preserves can be reserved at least 8 days in advance through Ticketron for stays of 3 to 14 nights.

North Lake, on Rte. 23A, 3 miles northeast of Haines Falls, NY 12436 (tel. 518/589-5058), open from May 1 to late October, offers 219 sites plus spectacular scenery, swimming, fishing, and boat rentals on two lakes.

There's also camping at Devil's Tombstone, Rte. 214, Hunter (tel. 914/688-7160), from May to October. There are only 24 sites, making for a quieter scene.

Other New York Environmental Conservation camping areas, charging around $10 for camping and all open from May 1 to at least September 30, are at Beaverkill, RR.3 (P.O. 243), Roscoe (tel. 914/439-4281), offering swimming and fishing; Kenneth L. Wilson, Wittenberg Road, Mount Tremper (tel. 914/679-7020), with swimming and fishing, has camping until Columbus Day; Mongaup Pond, De Bruce Road, north of De Bruce (tel. 914/439-4233), with swimming, fishing, and rowboat and canoe rentals, offers camping until mid-December; and Woodland Valley, 1319 Woodland Valley Rd., near Phoenicia (tel. 914/688-7647), which stays open for camping until Columbus Day. The central Conservation Authority number is 914/256-3099.

Canoeing: Canoeing-camping can be enjoyed along 75 miles of the Delaware from Hancock to Port Jervis. For information, contact Lander's River Trips, Rte. 97 (P.O. Box 376), Narrowsburg, NY 12764 (tel. 914/252-3925), which rents canoes, kayaks, and rafts for $26 to $30 per day and runs canoe-camping or canoe-lodging packages. Two-day/two-night lodging packages start at $90 per person; similar camping packages start at $60 per person. Children 12 and under are half price. Free transportation is included.

Silver Canoe Rentals, 37 S. Maple Ave., Port Jervis, NY 12771 (tel. 914/856-7055), rents canoes and rafts for $22 per day.

Esopus Creek also offers canoeing, kayaking, and tubing opportunities. Bring your kayak, canoe, or tube and board the Catskill Mountain Railroad open train, P.O. Box 46, Shokan, NY 12481 (tel. 914/688-7400), which will bring you from Mount Pleasant to Phoenicia, where you can ride the river back to your car. It's usually a bit of a bumpy ride because the water's not that deep. Trains operate daily from early July to Labor Day. Tubes can be rented.

Fishing: Roscoe, at the junction of the Beaverkill and the Willowemoc rivers, is known locally as Trout Town, where the Antrim Lodge Hotel (tel. 607/498-4191) is a favorite fisherman's haunt. Esopus Creek is one of the Northeast's most famous angling rivers, known for its rainbow, brown, and brook trout. Other fine waters include the Beaverkill, Plattekill, Rondout, Sawkill and Woodland Valley creeks. You can also fish in the Ashokan and Rondout Reservoir but special permits, in addition to the regular fishing license, are required (call 914/657-2213). Shad and bass are also found in the Hudson River. At least two fly-fishing shools operate in the region. The most famous is the Wolff Fishing School (tel. 914/439-4060); it offers weekend courses (May and June only) on the serene mysteries of fly-fishing. Book as soon as possible just to get on the waiting list.

Fruit Picking: For information, contact any one of the county public information offices or local chambers of commerce.

Golf: Catskill Golf Club, 27 Brooks Lane, Catskill (tel. 914/943-0302), has nine holes. Windham Country Club, South Street (tel. 518/734-9910), has 18 holes, par 71. Pleasant Valley, Rte. 23, Windham (tel. 914/734-4230), has nine holes. Colonial Country Club, Main Street, Tannersville (tel. 914/589-9807), is another nine-holer.

Hiking: Trails abound in the Catskills. Hiking-trail maps of the region can be purchased at the Golden Notebook or Catskill Art Supply in Woodstock. Closest to Woodstock is the trail that leads to the summit of Overlook Mountain. To access it, take Rock City Road from the center of Woodstock and Meads Mountain Road to a parking area opposite the Tibetan Buddhist monastery. An accessible trail up Mount Tremper starts on the old state highway about a mile east of Phoenicia. The Wittenberg-Cornell Slide Trail gives access to Slide Mountain, the highest peak in the Catskills. It offers wonderful rewards at any time of year. Access is either from the Woodland Valley Campground just outside Phoenicia or from Rte. 47 near Winnisook Lake. The trail is under 10 miles but is strenuous and crosses three mountains.

Horseback Riding: *Catskill:* Bailiwick ranch, Castle Road (tel. 914/678-5665), offers trail rides, all-day trips, and instruction. Ponderosa Ranch, Rte. 32, Catskill (tel. 914/678-9206), offers half- and one-hour trail rides plus pony rides and even hunting trips. *Delhi:* Hilltop Stables, New Road, Bovina Center (tel. 607/832-4342), charges $10 per hour and also offers overnight trail rides (groups only). *Haines Falls:* Silver Springs Dude Ranch, Rte. 25 off Rte. 23A, Haines Falls (tel. 914/589-2624), offers overnight horse trips. *Tannersville:* Silver Springs Ranch, Rte. 16 (tel. 518/589-5559), offers one- and two-hour trail rides start- ing at $24 per person. Reservations are needed for one-day and overnight trips. *Olive:* Ashokan Riding Club, 363 Beaverkill Rd. (tel. 914/657-8021), offers trail riding.

Skiing: The best is undoubtedly at Hunter Mountain (see earlier in this chapter), but there are other choices, notably the already- mentioned Windham and Belleayre, P.O. Box 313, Highmount, NY 12441 (tel. 914/254-5600, or 800/942-6904), which is good for beginners and experts. The vertical rise is 1,265 feet. There are 33 trails, five chairs, two T-bars, and one J-bar and 91% snow- making capacity.

For cross-country there's Belleayre Mountain, Highmount (tel. 914/2545601), and Frost Valley YMCA Camp, Oliverea (tel. 914/985-2291); Hunter Mountain's area is at Mountain Trails at Hyer Meadows, Rte. 23A Tannersville (tel. 518/589-5361), which has 35km of trails. In Haines Falls Vilaggio Resort has 14km of marked trails and offers rentals. In Windham, White Birches Ski Touring Center off Rte. 23 (tel. 914/734-3266) has 35km of trails and all facilities.

Soaring & Hang Gliding: Centers for this are on the southern edge of the Catskills at Wurtsboro and Ellenville. For hang gliding, contact the Mountain Wings Hang Gliding Center, 150 Canal St., Ellenville (tel. 914/647-3377), which provides introductory programs ($120) and two- and six-day training programs. It also offers the newest, most exciting form of foot-launched flying—paragliding—which uses parachutes that are launched like a hang-glider. The introductory program costs $135. Wurtsboro Flight Service, Inc., Wurtsboro Airport, Rte. 209, Wurtsboro, NY 12790 (tel. 914/888-2791), offers complete courses for beginners in soaring as well as sailplane rentals for the rated pilot. You can take a 15- to 20-minute demonstration ride.

Tubing: Enjoy a bumpy ride along the Esopus. Tube rentals are available from the Town Tinker, Bridge Street, Phoenicia (tel. 914/688-5553). The cost is $10 per day for a tube with a seat. A deposit is required.

Saratoga Springs

Distance in Miles: 186
Estimated Driving Time: 3 hours

◄◊►◄◊►◄◊►◄◊►◄◊►

Driving: Take the New York State Thruway to Albany, then I-87 to Exit 13 north. Take Rte. 9 north.

Bus: Greyhound (tel. 800/231-2222) goes to both Albany and Saratoga Springs.

Train: Amtrak's *Adirondack* stops in Saratoga Springs. For information, call 800/872-7245.

Further Information: For more about the area's festivals and events and about Saratoga Springs, contact the **Greater Saratoga Chamber of Commerce,** 494 Broadway, Suite 212, Saratoga Springs, NY 12866 (tel. 518/584-3255).

For Albany information, contact the **Albany County Convention & Visitors Bureau,** 52 S. Pearl St., Albany, NY 12207 (tel. 518/434-1217).

◄◊►◄◊►◄◊►◄◊►◄◊►

Normally the population of Saratoga Springs is a modest 25,000, but in summer it swells to 75,000 for the party centering on the old Victorian Clubhouse at the Saratoga Race Course. The races are on, the steeds are running, and Saratoga is the place to see the silks flashing by and the horses' flanks sweating in the sun, to feel the air of increasing excitement as the horses fly out, their hoofs pounding on the green turf. People also come for the now-famous arts festival that begins in June—a unique affair blessed with two national companies as regular visitors: the New York City Ballet and the Philadelphia Orchestra. During both of these events the hotels and motels are full, with people staying as far away as Albany and even farther south. The large Victorian residences on North Broadway are filled with house parties and house guests as "the season" swings into high gear.

Though having experienced some ups and some severe downs, Saratoga has nearly always had a special summer sheen. You can easily see why this spa became such a great social mecca in the 1800s and early 1900s. The park and the springs were always, and still are, prime attractions; casino gambling, and the excitement and glamour it engendered, was another; horse racing was still another. Grand hotels sprang up. Large Victorian summer cottages were constructed, and people flocked here at the turn of the century, for it had become de rigueur for the American barons to migrate to Saratoga for at least a part of the summer.

Gideon Putnam built the first hotel in 1803, and soon crowds were coming to take the waters, as many as 12,000 by 1825. They came to drink, inhale the steam, or bathe in the waters (which you can still do), and if they had no physical complaints, they simply drank the waters in fashionable Drink Halls with elegant Greek Revival columns and long colonnades, where they strolled to the strains of lilting bands and orchestras. By 1840 the era of the grand hotels had fully arrived, the most famous Saratoga examples being the Grand Union and the United States, both vast and palatial. Sadly, neither has survived. The United States was torn down in 1946, the Grand Union following in 1952.

In 1861 John Morrissey, a sometime U.S. heavyweight boxing champion and a congressman from New York City, boldly opened the first casino so he could indulge his wealthy passion. Two years later he built the racetrack, thus making Saratoga a veritable playground for the rich and famous. Among the most colorful were Diamond Jim Brady and his lavish companion, actress Lillian Russell. Brady, a railroad equipment salesman and steelcar magnate of prodigious girth and appetite, was known to drink gallons of fruit juice along with a daily diet of three dozen oysters in the morning and eight dozen at night, plus eggs, steaks, chops, joints of beef, several lobsters and crabs, and whole fowls accompanied by vegetables, salads, and desserts. His eminently suitable companion carried her 200 well-corseted pounds with such prodigious charm that she was able to capture five husbands. Less flashy were the Whitneys, Vanderbilts, Morgans, and other old families who came to romp here until 1907, when reformers closed the casino and Saratoga embarked on a roller-coaster phase.

From 1910 to 1913 the casino and the racetrack were closed, but by the 1920s the resort was thriving again. Many more lavish cottages were built; the social scene was populated by dashing figures once again. However, this was only a brief renaissance, for in the 1930s the class of Saratoga habitués deteriorated. Gamblers, bookies, pimps, and prostitutes took over, and decay settled in until the casinos were finally closed in 1951 after a national crime investigation. Only racing kept alive the spirit of Saratoga's golden era, and that's what the recent revival has been built around—the 24-day meet when traditions return and the magic and splendor of those languorous, extravagant summers return.

Events & Festivals to Plan Your Trip Around

January–February: Winter Carnival Weekends.
April–November: Harness racing. Call 518/584-2110.
June–September: The Performing Arts Festival. Contact SPAC, Spa State Park, Saratoga Springs, NY 12866 (tel. 518/587-3330 in season, 584-9330 off-season). Tickets go on sale in early May.
Late July to Late August: The Saratoga Race Meeting. Call 518/584-6200 for dates.

Saratoga Springs Attractions

Congress Park

This lovely 33-acre park, just off Broadway, was surrounded by great hotels when Saratoga was the most renowned American spa in the late 19th century. The two most famous—the Grand Union and the United States—were torn down in the late 1940s and early 1950s. At the center of the park stands Daniel Chester French's *Spirit of Life* statue and fountain, a memorial to Trask, who led the movement to revitalize the mineral springs. Today you're more likely to find craft and art shows than ladies in veiled hats strolling with parasols, though the bandstand concerts given today do recapture the era of Saratoga's heyday. At the Canfield casino (tel. 518/584-6920), built from 1870 to 1871, also in the park, Willie Vanderbilt lost $130,000 while waiting for his lady friends to dress for dinner. Today the two top floors are set up with museum exhibits, although the ballroom has been retained and is still used by socialite Marylou Whitney for her annual ball.

North Broadway's Architectural Treats

From Congress Park, go back out onto North Broadway to view the Victorian homes or cottages built for brief stays during the season. Fantasize what it must have been like to attend a house party here. You can look at the house rented by Diamond Jim Brady and Lillian Russell, the home of the Cluetts of Arrow shirt fame, the Gaines family home, the Ogden Phipps house, and those belonging to other racing folk. The styles vary from Jacobean to bracketed Italianate, from Federal to Victorian gothic and French Renaissance. As you pass you'll catch glimpses of stained glass, turrets, vine-covered porches, and gazebos; if you drive down the road behind the houses, you'll find ornate carriage houses, many of which have been converted into living quarters.

From here you can drop down into the Lower Village, past the Olde Bryan Inn, where High Rock, the first mineral spring, was discovered when the Mohawk Indians carried Sir William Johnson, then superintendent of Indian affairs, on a litter from Johnstown to the springs in August 1771. He was cured and the springs' reputation established. You can take the waters today. There are several springs in and around town—Big Red at the racetrack, one in Congress Park, and a number in the spa park, distinguished by their carbonation and saline or alkaline characteristics.

Yaddo

Famous now as a writer's retreat, this lovely Georgian mansion was once the home of New York City financier Spencer Trask and his wife, Katrina, who decided to turn it into a retreat in 1926 after all four of their children died of illnesses. Among the artists, writers, and songwriters who've found inspiration here are Carson McCullers, Philip Roth, Saul Bellow, Ned Rorem, Leonard Bernstein, Virgil Thomson, Malcolm Cowley, Katharine Anne Porter (who supposedly wrote *Ship of Fools* here), and Truman Capote (who wrote *Other Voices, Other Rooms* here). Although you can't go inside the gray stone mansion, do visit the fountains and rose garden, complete with a pergola covered with rambling roses, and the peaceful Japanese rock garden. Every year in September a tour of the mansion is given. Call 518/584-4132 for information.

The Racetrack

If you visit during the 24-day meet, you'll want to breakfast at the clubhouse, resplendent with ivied window boxes, while you watch the horses exercise. Even if the races aren't on, a visit to the racetrack is a must. It's the oldest thoroughbred track in the country, the first race having been run in 1863, when John Morrissey formed the first racing association. He didn't think it would be that popular because it was during the Civil War and most of the horses were down South, but it was a great success and has been ever since. Known as "the graveyard of favorites," it's famed for several stunning racing upsets. In 1919 Man o' War, which had been bested only once before, was defeated at Saratoga by a horse aptly named Upset. In 1930 the Travers Triple Crown winner, Gallant Fox, fell victim to Jim Dandy, the 100-to-1 shot. Secretariat was also upset here in 1973. Post time is usually 1:30pm.

The most famous race, the Travers Stakes, is the occasion for a whole week of spectacular events—parades, craft shows in Congress Park, golf and tennis tournaments, and concerts. The Whitney Handicap and the Saratoga Cup are also run in the season.

Note: When planning your trip to Saratoga, try to make it at the beginning or end of the second week of August, when you can share the eager anticipation in the Humphrey S. Finney Pavilion, as tuxedoed auctioneers preside over the yearling sales. Some people swear that this is *the* most

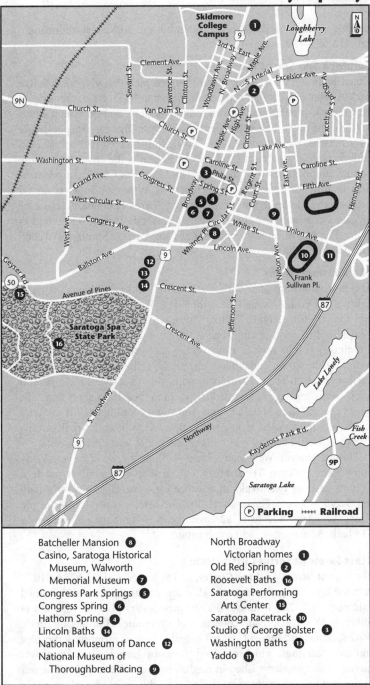

Saratoga Springs

Parking (P)   **Railroad** ++++

Batcheller Mansion **8**
Casino, Saratoga Historical
  Museum, Walworth
  Memorial Museum **7**
Congress Park Springs **5**
Congress Spring **6**
Hathorn Spring **4**
Lincoln Baths **14**
National Museum of Dance **12**
National Museum of
  Thoroughbred Racing **9**

North Broadway
  Victorian homes **1**
Old Red Spring **2**
Roosevelt Baths **16**
Saratoga Performing
  Arts Center **15**
Saratoga Racetrack **10**
Studio of George Bolster **3**
Washington Baths **13**
Yaddo **11**

exciting event in Saratoga. See for yourself. For additional information, call 516/584-4700.

Saratoga Spa State Park

Noted hydrotherapist Simon Baruch helped plan the whole 2,000-acre park as a spa, and his son, Bernard, finished it in 1935. Inside the park are 26 springs—primarily laden with sodium, lithium, and potassium—plus a 9-hole and an 18-hole golf course, the Peerless Olympic-size pool, eight tennis courts, the Gideon Putnam Hotel, and the Victoria Pool, favored bathing place of dancers and artists who appear at the arts center, whose natural amphitheater is in the park. The New York City Ballet performs here in July, the Philadelphia Orchestra in August. A buffet is served before performances in the Hall of Springs. There's a nominal entrance fee for cars. For information about the park, contact the Park Superintendent's Office, P.O. Box W, Saratoga Springs State Park, Saratoga Springs, NY 12866 (tel. 518/584-2000).

The Roosevelt Baths

Also in Saratoga Spa State Park, the Roosevelt Baths are among the highlights of any visit. Although the bathhouse looks like a utilitarian hospital and a far cry from a typically luxurious modern spa, the treatment given here is euphoric and certainly one of the best buys in Saratoga. For about 20 minutes you lie back in a tub, up to your neck in hot brown mineral water; it's like sitting in bubbling seltzer with a pillow at your head and a stool at your feet. The masseur then wraps you in hot sheets and gives you a top-to-toe massage before tucking you into bed for a short nap. The whole process takes about an hour. You emerge feeling relaxed, content, and totally rejuvenated as you walk out into the beautiful park setting. Everyone should be entitled to this experience at least once a week.

Hours: Summer, Wed–Mon 8:30am–4:40pm; the rest of the year, Wed–Sun 8:30am–4:40pm. The last bath is given at 3pm. In summer you need to book at least two weeks in advance for a massage, not for a bath (tel. 518/584-2011). The Lincoln baths, also here, are open July–Aug only. **Cost:** Weekdays, $12 bath, $23 massage, $34 combination; weekends, $15 bath, $26 massage, $40 combination.

Other Saratoga Springs Attractions

The **Regent Street Antique Center,** 153 Regent St. (tel. 518/584-0107), is in the first college building of Skidmore, constructed in 1903 (named Skidmore in 1922); it houses 30 antiques dealers plus the Museum of Antiques & Art, a private collection of stoneware, Hummel figurines, bottles, canes, and (when I visited) a local collector's exquisite scrimshaw and ivory carvings, which included pieces by French prisoners of war carved while they languished in English prisons around 1800. The rest of the building is occupied by dealers who display clocks, glass, music boxes, jewelry, weathervanes, architectural elements, silverware, Victorian furniture, oak and other antiques, and collectibles. You can spend hours browsing here. Best of all, it's open year round.

Hours: Daily 10am–5pm. **Closed:** New Year's Day, Thanksgiving, and Christmas. **Admission:** Free.

Even for those who aren't particularly interested in architecture, the **Batcheller Mansion** on Circular Street, at Whitney Place, appeals to the fantasy in all of us with its scalloped gables and Chambord-style towers capped with minarets, all built in 1873. It has been magnificently restored and now operates as an inn (see "Saratoga Lodging," below).

For a real sense of what Saratoga was like in its heyday, stop in to what was once the **studio of photographer George Bolster** at 1 Phila St. (tel. 518/587-6650). The collection of his photographs of Old Saratoga is now housed here, organized by subject for use by researchers. You can view whatever is up in the studio or request a particular subject that interests you. The space is also occupied by photographer Michael L. Noonan, who was Bolster's assistant for many years. Although he's a very busy man, he's a fount of information about the Saratoga of yesterday if you can get him talking.

Hours: Collection, Mon, Wed, and Fri 10am–3pm; store, Mon–Fri 10am–6pm. **Admission:** Free.

The **National Museum of Thoroughbred Racing,** Union Avenue (tel. 518/584-0400), displays racing silks, equine art, trophies, and memorabilia of legendary names in turf history.

Hours: Summer, Mon–Sat 10am–4:30pm, Sun noon–4:30pm; Aug, daily 9am–5pm.

The **Historical Society Museum of Saratoga Springs** and the **Walworth Memorial Museum** (tel. 518/584-6920) are located atop the casino building and contain exhibits relating to the history of Saratoga and a series of period rooms.

Hours: Summer, Mon–Sat 10am–4pm, Sun 1–4pm (July–Aug, daily 9:30am–4:30pm); winter, Wed–Sun 1–4pm. **Admission:** $2 adults, $1 seniors.

The **polo games** are also exciting, usually scheduled throughout August. Contact the Saratoga Polo Association, P.O. Box 821, Saratoga Springs, NY 12866 (tel. 518/584-3255).

Dance lovers will want to view the **National Museum of Dance** (tel. 518/584-2225), in the Washington Bath building, on South Broadway (Rte. 9) in Saratoga Spa State Park. Modern, jazz, ballet, and other dance forms are explored through a variety of exhibits.

Hours: Memorial Day–Labor Day, Tues–Sat 10am–5pm (longer hours Thurs from mid-July to Aug 21).

A Nearby Attraction

Some 20 miles or so north in Glens Falls, the **Hyde Collection,** 161 Warren St. (tel. 518/792-1761), is well worth seeing. Housed in an

Italian Renaissance–style villa, the collection includes works by Rembrandt, Rubens, and the impressionists, plus Italian Renaissance and 18th-century French antiques, all collected by Charlotte Pruyn Hyde in the early part of this century.

Hours: Tues–Sun 10am–5pm.

Albany—A Stop En Route to or from Saratoga

For the average New Yorker, Albany may not spring to mind as the first place to visit, but the state capital does have some very interesting sights and pleasures to offer and it's certainly worth stopping in en route to or from another destination—Saratoga Springs, for example.

For me the prime attraction is the New York State Museum, followed by the Capitol Building, Empire State Plaza, the Museum of History and Art, Cherry Hill, and the Schuyler Mansion.

The **Capitol Building,** State Street (tel. 518/474-2418), cost $24 million to build—double the cost of the nation's capitol in the late 19th century—and took 30 years to complete. The facade of the building exhibits a hodgepodge of styles: It stands on an Italian Renaissance base, topped by a romanesque middle, which is capped by a pitched French Renaissance–style roof. This peculiar melange arose from a typical human conflict. The original architect, Thomas Fuller, was pulled off the project, and a team including H. H. Richardson, Leopold Eidlitz, and Frederick Law Olmsted was engaged to complete it. Fuller built the base; the team built the rest. It's not surprising that it took 30 years to complete, for the actual construction was a feat in itself. Huge granite blocks were brought to Albany by water and hauled up to the site by the Albany Horse Railway. Each block was then worked on by the 200 to 250 stonecutters employed to cut and fit the stones.

The opulence exhibited in the Million Dollar Staircase and in Richardson's masterpiece, the Senate Chamber—a radiant blend of Siena marble, Mexican onyx, and Scottish red granite combined with carved mahogany and tooled red leather—reflected the wealth of 19th-century Albany, whose manufacturers and traders had amassed great fortunes from their control of and proximity to the Erie Canal, then the main east-west trade route.

Tours: Free tours daily on the hour 9am–4pm (in summer every 30 minutes). **Closed:** New Year'ms Day, Thanksgiving, Christmas.

Across from the Capitol stretches the vast wasteland of **Empire State Plaza,** dominated by 11 marble-and-glass towers and the peculiar flying-saucer–shaped Convention Center, known as the Egg (that's its polite name). In 1962 when the development was planned, costs were estimated at $350 million. When it was finished in 1978 costs had escalated to over $2 billion. The whole complex houses the offices of the state legislators and of another 11,000 who help run the government. On summer weekends the mall is enlivened by international festivals, special events, and people roller skating or just sunning themselves.

During the week, bureaucrats, politicians, workers, and visitors stride the quarter-mile-long underground concourse, scuttling along these Wellesian burrows past the great collection of modern art (Motherwell, Rothko, Nevelson) decorating the walls. (Special art tours are given of the whole plaza.) Three good cafeterias are open weekdays in the complex.

Tours: Free tours of the plaza, leaving from Room 106 on the concourse, daily at 11am and 1 and 4pm (more frequently in summer).

The **New York State Museum,** at the south end of the plaza (tel. 518/ 474-5877), really makes Albany a worthwhile stop—and moreover, admission is free. What's so amazing is the absence of the usual glass barriers and dull display cases. Instead, the museum presents spectacular, open-to-view, life-size dioramas, like a prehistoric wilderness with Ice Age mastodons or the Adirondack forest with birds singing, stags leaping, and a waterfall cascading across the rocks; one follows another in a kind of phantasma. Kids love it, and adults find it a refreshing change from the humdrum run-of-the-mill museum.

Half the space is devoted to exploring the geology, flora, fauna, and history of upstate New York and the Adirondacks, from prehistoric times through industrialization (logging, iron working, mining), all presented in an interesting, creative way. The other half of the space (believe it or not, New Yorkers) is entirely devoted to the history of New York City and presented in a dramatic fashion by tableaux further explicated by lively commentary and audiovisual effects. You'll find everything from a diorama demonstrating skyscraper construction to a complete stage set of the Lower East Side at the turn of the century, from the interior of Delmonico's, the restaurant that originated the à la carte menu, to a series of tableaux showing ships docking at the South Street Seaport, immigrants passing through Ellis Island, and the sweatshops they so often worked in once they settled in the city. Also on display are assorted memorabilia—storefronts rescued from Chinatown, a 1930s West Side barbershop, a 1950s subway car with straw raffia seats, the original "Sesame Street" set—all revealing the vibrant history of this fantastic city. You could easily spend the whole day here. It's a definite hit with adults and kids alike.

Hours: Daily 10am–5pm. **Admission:** Free.

From the museum you can ride up 42 floors above the city to the **Observation Deck of the Tower Building** and peer down onto the Governor's Mansion, complete with a pool and tennis courts. (The mansion is open one day each week—usually Thursday—from 1 to 4pm. Reservations are required: call 518/473-7521.)

Hours: Observation Deck, daily 9am–4pm.

For the art lover, the focus at the **Museum of History and Art,** 125 Washington Ave. (tel. 518/463-4478), will surely be on the Hudson River School collection and the early American portraits. The collection also contains 18th- and 19th-century furniture, silver, pewter, and archival material.

Hours: Wed–Sun noon–5pm. **Admission:** $3 adults, $2 seniors and students, free for children 11 and under, free for everyone on Wed.

The remarkable fact about **Historic Cherry Hill,** 523 S. Pearl St. (tel. 518/434-4791), which marked its 200th anniversary in 1987, is the continuity of its ownership—it remained in the Van Rensselaer family from 1787 to 1963—and the unique opportunity it allows you to view the changes from 18th-century to 20th-century lifestyles and decor.

Hours: Feb–Dec, Tues–Sat 10am–3pm, Sun 1–3pm. **Admission:** $3.50 adults, $3 seniors, $2 students, $1 children 6–17.

At the **Schuyler Mansion,** 32 Catherine St. (tel. 518/434-0834), in the springtime you can enjoy the fragrance and color of magnolia and crabapple in bloom. This lovely 18th-century brick mansion was once the isolated estate of Gen. Philip Schuyler (1733–1804). Two interesting episodes that are part of the house's story: Alexander Hamilton was married to Schuyler's daughter, Elizabeth, here in the parlor; and General Burgoyne was held prisoner-cum-guest here after the 1777 victory at Saratoga.

Hours: Apr–Oct, Wed–Sat 10am–5pm, Sun 1–5pm; Nov–Apr, Tues–Fri by appointment. **Closed:** New Year's Day, Thankgiving, Christmas. **Admission:** Free. **Bus:** 6 or 8.

Easy Side Trips from Albany

When you've finished exploring downtown Albany, there are still some wonderful places to see and things to do only a short distance away. For example, in **Glens Falls** you can experience the excitement of rising at dawn, having brunch accompanied by music to order, and then stepping into a hot-air balloon and lifting off into the air for a spectacular ride above it all. Contact **Adirondack Balloon Flights** (tel. 518/793-6342). Even if you don't want to take off yourself, you can attend the hot-air-balloon festival, usually held on the third weekend of September, a colorful exciting event. It even features a strange leaf-picking contest, in which contestants stay or hover by a tree, picking as many leaves as possible! For information, call Adirondack Regional Chambers of Commerce at 518/798-1761.

In fall, the surrounding counties of Rensselaer and Washington are magnificent for **foliage viewing.**

Only 15 miles southwest of the city, on Rte. 157, **John Boyd Thacher State Park** (tel. 518/872-1237), set on the Helderberg escarpment, commands incredible views of the Hudson and Mohawk valleys and the peaks of the Adirondacks and Green Mountains. Miles of hiking trails, an Olympic-size pool, and playing fields make it a fine summer spot, while the cross-country skiing, tobogganing, and snowmobiling are excellent in winter.

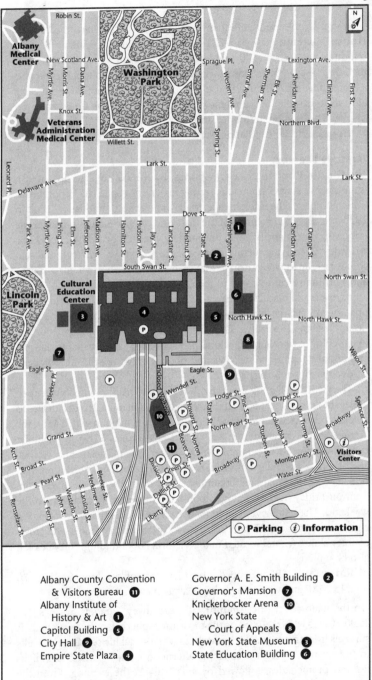

Robin St.

Albany Medical Center

New Scotland Ave.

Washington Park

Sprague Pl.

Lexington Ave.

Myrtle Ave.
Morris St.
Dana Ave.

Knox St.

Veterans Administration Medical Center

Willett St.

Spring St.

Western Ave.
Central Ave.
Sherman St.
Elk St.
Sheridan Ave.
Clinton Ave.
First St.

Northern Blvd.

Leonard Pl.

Delaware Ave.

Lark St.

Lark St.

Dove St.

Park Ave.
Myrtle Ave.
Irving St.
Elm St.
Jefferson St.
Madison Ave.
Hamilton St.
Hudson Ave.
Jay St.
Lancaster St.
Chestnut St.
State St.

Washington Ave.

Sheridan Ave.
Orange St.

1

2

South Swan St.

North Swan St.

Lincoln Park

Cultural Education Center

3

4

P

5

North Hawk St.

6

8

North Hawk St.

Wilson St.

7

Eagle St.

Bleeker Pl.

Eagle St.

9

Enclosed Walkway

Wendell St.

Lodge St.
Pine St.
Chapel St.
Van Tromp St.
Spencer St.
Broadway

10

Howard St.
Norton St.
Beaver St.
State St.
North Pearl St.
Steuben St.
Columbia St.

Grand St.

Montgomery St.

P

(i) Visitors Center

Arch St.
Broad St.

11

P P P

Green St.

Division St.

Broadway

P

Water St.

S. Pearl St.
Bleeker St.
Herkimer St.
Westerlo St.
S. Lansing St.
John St.

Dallius St.

Rensselaer St.
S. Ferry St.

Liberty St.

(P) **Parking** (i) **Information**

2144

About 25 miles south of Albany on Rte. 9W in Coxsackie is the **Bronck House Museum** (tel. 518/731-6490), a fascinating cluster of nine buildings that reflect 300 years of Upper Hudson Valley history. They include an early 1663 stone house with an Indian lookout in the loft and a more affluent 1738 brick house. The barns and adjacent slave cemetery are fun to explore. Some memorabilia of artist Thomas Cole is also on display. This is good for a brief stop en route to or from Albany.

Hours: Late June to Labor Day, Tues–Sat 10am–5pm, Sun 2–6pm.

Saratoga Lodging

The **Gideon Putnam**, Saratoga Springs, NY 12866 (tel. 518/584-3000), is *the* place to stay. Certainly the setting in Saratoga Spa State Park is beautiful, but I prefer the Adelphi or a similar smaller accommodation. Built in 1935 and named in memory of the man who came to Saratoga to enter the lumber business and wound up building the first boarding house, this red-brick Georgian structure offers spectacular views, whatever the season. A tree-lined circular drive that seems more appropriate for a coach-and-four than a car leads up to the Corinthian-columned portico, giving entry to a grand marbled, mirrored, chandeliered lobby. The parlor suites opening onto large bamboo-furnished screened porches are the most desirable of the 143 rooms. The other rooms are quite ordinary, decorated in dark blue or rust with large floral-print curtains, candlewick bedspreads, and antique reproductions. TVs and phones are standard. All rooms are gradually being refurbished.

The Georgian Dining Room, with handsome hand-painted wallpaper, is elegant for dinner. It offers a rather traditional menu with such dishes as chicken primavera, seafood Fra Diavolo, and filet mignon with a red-wine demiglaze. Prices range from $17 to $22. The typical $16 Sunday buffet brunch—a spread of scrambled eggs, lasagne, ham, beans and carrots, and so on—is popular but desperately overrated. You'll need a reservation. The drinks, piano entertainment, and hors d'oeuvres (served from 5pm on Friday in the Saratoga Room bar) make for a good start to the weekend. The hotel gives you immediate access to all the park's facilities: eight tennis courts, a 27-hole golf course, three outdoor pools, and cross-country skiing (center located in the Victoria Pool building). Bicycles can also be rented.

Rates: Aug, $255–$450 double. The rest of the year, $135–$170 double. MAP and weekend packages available.

On the main street, the **Adelphi**, 365 Broadway, Saratoga Springs, NY 12866 (tel. 518/587-4688), is the most atmospheric fantasy place here. It survives from that legendary opulent era when social life consisted of walks to the springs, courtyard concerts, afternoon garden parties, and high-fashion promenades, followed by gala balls in the evening. From the piazza of this elegant hotel rise slender columns capped by delicate gingerbread fretwork, while the interior is furnished with luxurious, well-stuffed, and richly colored Victoriana.

Gregg Siefker and Sheila Parkert bought the Adelphi a decade ago after it had stood empty for 10 years. They've gradually restored it, filling it with authentic period furnishings. The only pieces original to the hotel—it had been stripped—are the front desk and the valanced, draped, and tasseled floor-to-ceiling mirror. The lobby, with lofty 14-foot ceilings and square fluted wood pillars, invites lounging with an assortment of Victorian sofas and chairs, each beautifully upholstered in the finest brocades and fabrics. My favorites are the French polished Empire couch secured from the Schuyler mansion and the camelback sofas in the center. Large flower arrangements, fringed lampshades, and one or two potted palms complete the Victorian ambience.

Sheila has decorated all 28 rooms in her unique, inspired style. All have a bath, a phone, air-conditioning, and Crabtree & Evelyn soap and hand cream; a TV is available on request. One or two front rooms have balconies overlooking the sweep of Broadway. Here are just a few favorites: Room 19, a small suite with candy-striped wallpaper in pink and jade, contains a Victorian acorn bed adorned with a spectacular Oriental tent. Complementary furnishings include gilt-framed pictures, a dresser, and a sink with a pink marble surround. The sitting room has a dusky-rose carpet, a settee, and overstuffed comfy chairs. Suite 16 has a mix of Mission and Adirondack furnishings set against geometric-patterned wallpaper in dark green and tan, plus a fabulous paneled bath with an old-fashioned tub and separate shower. Suite 3 is large, boasting a private balcony furnished with wicker and a Victorian-style fireplace with a grate. The curtains are valanced, the wallpaper is brocade, and chairs are slipcovered (so is the bathtub); white damask covers the sofa. The parlor is filled with Stickley and assorted Victorian furnishings and artifacts. Room 1 is typical—the bed has an inlaid headboard, the pillows are damask with lace trim, brocade molded wall panels adorn the walls, the curtains are valanced, the sofa is brocade, and the desk is elegant French style. The pièce de résistance is the Riviera Room, complete with murals of the region. Throughout the hallways, statuary, quilts, Victorian pictures, prints, and engravings abound. A favorite quiet corner is the third-floor "Turkish cozy," a tented sofa created by Sheila, with Mughal-style paintings and luxuriously covered cushions.

During the season, breakfast is served out in the piazza, where Adirondack chairs are set under a colored awning surrounded by roses, pansy-filled urns, and other flowers. At the Cafe Adelphi, among camelback sofas, draped chintz banquettes, and gilt mirrors you can enjoy cocktails, exotic coffees, and wines. In July and August a limited menu is served here, including items like grilled tuna with warm lime-cilantro vinaigrette; Delmonico steak with a chutney made from roasted red peppers, onions, tomatoes, and currants; and a delicious pork loin marinated in olive oil, lime juice, and coriander and served with Indonesian hot peanut sauce and black-bean sauce. Prices run $15 to $18. Sandwiches and other light fare are also available. The ballroom, opulently arrayed with scarlet drapes and valances, is reserved for special celebrations and weddings. The classically landscaped pool set in a garden is a wonderful place to relax.

Rates (including breakfast): July weekends, $125–$195 double. Racing meet weekends, $190–$305 double. The rest of the year, $100–$180 double.

The **Batcheller Mansion Inn,** 20 Circular St., Saratoga Springs, NY 12866 (tel. 518/584-7012), is an extraordinary architectural treasure. This 1873 house with minarets, towers, and turrets was built for Judge George S. Batcheller, a brigadier general in the Union Army and a diplomat who employed the finest craftsmen to create this fantasy home. The restoration has taken close to 20 years to complete, and the house's integrity has been maintained while modern amenities like air-conditioning and efficient heating and plumbing have been added. It has been carefully decorated to reflect accurately the late 1800s.

All nine rooms come with a TV, phone, refrigerator, and bath (some with a Jacuzzi). Among the most dramatic is the Diamond Jim Brady, large enough to contain a regulation-size pool table, a king-size canopied bed, a large desk/study area, and a sitting area; the bath has a double Jacuzzi and shower. Another eye-opener is the Katrina Trusk, with its own circular porch, a king-size canopied bed, and a bath containing an old-fashioned tub plus a tiled shower. The wallpaper design in the Rip Van Dam depicts 4,000 horses all racing around this tower room tucked under the mansard roof. The common areas are equally lavish. The library offers plush velvet sofas on Oriental rugs, books arrayed in glass-fronted bookcases, and a 48-inch TV. Breakfast is served in the very Victorian dining room on tables set with lace and fine crystal and china. The living room's focal point is the marble fireplace surmounted with a gilded mirror, plus a floor-to-ceiling gilded mirror. Potted ferns, a grand piano, and a variety of comfortable seating completes the effect. The kitchen is flooded with so much light from its 20-foot-tall windows that some guests prefer to take their breakfast here. Two porches, one affording views of Whitney Street, the other well located to catch the last rays of the evening sun, make ideal relaxing spaces.

Rates (including breakfast): Summer weekends, $120–$240 double. Racing season, $240–$350 double. Other times, slightly less.

Saratoga now has a fine modern hotel downtown, the **Sheraton Saratoga Springs,** 534 Broadway, Saratoga Springs, NY 12866 (tel. 518/584-4000). All 189 guest rooms are attractively furnished in soft pastels—peach carpets, for instance, matched with peach- and blue-floral bedspreads. The furniture consists of antique Queen Anne and other reproductions.

Conveniences include an alarm clock, a vanity mirror, a hairdryer, and a phone in the bath. Green Carrara marble floors, ormolu mirrors, potted ferns, Queen Anne–style chairs, brass chandeliers, and horse portraits set the elegant tone in the Sandalwood Restaurant, which is light and airy because of its atrium. Continental American cuisine is served. The indoor pool has a pleasant patio for sunning; there's also an exercise room containing Universal equipment. The lounge swings on Thursday, Friday, and Saturday with live entertainment.

Rates: Sept–July, $140 double; from $185 minisuite. Aug, from $275 double.

The **Inn at Saratoga,** 231 Broadway, Saratoga Springs, NY 12866 (tel. 518/583-1890), has 38 large rooms, each with a TV, a phone, air conditioning, and a spacious bath. Color schemes vary from dark blue and beige to dusky rose and jade. The tasteful furnishings include chintz or striped wallpapers, a free-standing full-length mirror, pelmeted drapes, comfy chairs, and a circular table with floor-length cloth; a desk and chest of drawers are tucked into a foyer.

The dining room and adjacent bar are elegant, with chintz wallpaper, potted ferns, French-style chairs, and white tablecloths providing a formal Victorian ambience. Among the appetizers might be artichoke-and-spinach hummus with grilled pita or bloody Mary–marinated shrimp cocktail (garnished with red and green peppers). The cuisine is contemporary American and the entrees might include chicken breast with bourbon barbecue sauce, grilled strip steak with port-wine / porcini butter. There'll always be a pasta of the day and a vegetarian dish. Prices run $16 to $22. On weekends a pianist entertains in the bar with its bamboo club chairs, marble bar, and glass-topped cloth-draped tables. A serene garden dining area is also available.

Rates (including breakfast, except July–Aug): $117–$157 double. Racing season, $255–350 double. Weekend package available.

The **Union Gables Bed & Breakfast,** 55 Union Ave., Saratoga Springs, NY 12866 (tel. 518/584-1558), is a handsome 1901 Queen Anne Victorian complete with a witch's cap turret and a wide covered veranda. Each of the 10 spacious rooms has a bath, air-conditioning, a TV, a phone, and a refrigerator. The rooms are nicely furnished but not in an overly fussy or pretentious way. The furnishings are homey, as they are in the parlor. Additional facilities include an outdoor hot tub, exercise equipment, and bicycles. It's located one block from the racetrack on a street lined with similar handsome Victorians.

Rates (including continental breakfast): $90–$210 double, depending on season.

Painted in seven colors, the **Westchester House,** 102 Lincoln Ave., Saratoga Springs, NY 12866 (tel. 518/587-7613), certainly stands out, and its cupola, gables, and fretwork are striking. It was built in 1885 and features the original handcrafted chestnut moldings and wainscoting and the elaborately carved fireplace that's the focal point of the parlor. The rooms are attractively furnished with Oriental rugs on the hardwood floors and lace curtains on the windows. All are air-conditioned, though they also have ceiling fans. Fresh flowers and chocolates add that extra little touch. Stephanie Melvin, one of the innkeepers, is an opera singer, so it's hardly surprising to find a baby grand in the parlor. Breakfast includes freshly squeezed juice, home-baked breads, and fresh fruit.

Rates (including breakfast): Summer, $105–$135 double. Racing season, $190–$235 double. Special packages available at other times.

Saratoga Bed & Breakfast, 434 Church St., Saratoga Springs, NY 12866 (tel. 518/584-0920), consists of two buildings: the 1860 wood-frame Farmhouse and the 1850 House, a brick Federal that stands on lawns sloping down to a creek. Noel and Kathleen Smith have patterned their B&B on those they've stayed at in Ireland, and they provide warm hospitality. In the Farmhouse, the rooms have been furnished with maple and oak, the beds covered with locally made quilts; one room has a fireplace. The 1850 House contains four much more lavish suites, individually decorated with walnut and mahogany antiques and equipped with a gas fireplace, TV, and phone. They've been lovingly decorated with family heirlooms like the cradle Kathleen's mother brought from Ireland. Noel, an ex-restaurateur, goes out of his way to cook up marvelous country breakfasts, while Kathy is the socializer of the team.

Rates (including breakfast): Farmhouse: May–Oct, $75–$105 double in the Farmhouse, $120–$145 double in the 1850 House. Racing season, $105–$145 double in the Farmhouse, $195–$220 double in the 1850 House. Nov–Apr, $75–$95 double in the Farmhouse, $110–$135 double in the 1850 House.

Although the **Saratoga Downtowner,** 413 Broadway, Saratoga Springs, NY 12866-2245 (tel. 518/584-6160), looks like a conventional motel, it's exquisitely kept and you'll probably get a surprise when you walk in. After you register at the desk, taking a few steps will lead you to rooms set around a long, narrow indoor pool—a welcome blessing in the summer heat. The color-coordinated rooms are large and well furnished. Hosts Lois and Gene Collins are extremely attentive. Breakfast of homemade muffins and coffee or tea is always available—help yourself.

Rates (including breakfast): Sept–June, $50–$60 double. July, $65–$75 double. Racing season, $110–$150 double. Winter weekend package (including two nights' accommodation, dinner, tickets to harness racing, and lift tickets for nearby skiing), $140 double.

Other reliables include the **Holiday Inn,** Broadway at Circular Street, Saratoga Springs, NY 12866 (tel. 518/584-4550), with 150 standard rooms, a couple of restaurants, and a pool.

Rates: Aug, $205 double. The rest of the year, $90 double.

The **Carriage House Motel,** 178 Broadway, Saratoga Springs, NY 12866 (tel. 518/584-0352), has large units with kitchenettes, furnished in typical motel style. The top-floor rooms have brass beds and cathedral-type ceilings.

Rates: Summer, $75–$95 double. Aug, $160–$185 double. Winter, $34 double.

There's also Best Western's **Playmore Farms Motel,** on Rte. 9 (South Broadway), Saratoga Springs, NY 12866 (tel. 518/584-2350).

Rates: Summer, $80 double. Aug, from $150 double. Winter, $54 double.

Nearby Lodging

Seven miles west of Saratoga Springs, **The Mansion,** 801 Rte. 29 (P.O. Box 77), Rock City Falls, NY 12863 (tel. 518/885-1607), has been lovingly restored and decorated by innkeepers Tom Clark and Alan Churchill. An Italianate villa complete with a central cupola, it was built in 1866 as the summer home of industrialist George West, owner of the Empire and Excelsior Mills as well as several other paper mills, two woolen factories, and three cotton factories. His greatest fame, though, derives from his invention of the paper bag. The five rooms are furnished with handsome Victorian pieces and floral fabrics and wallpapers, but they're not decorated in pretentious "museum" style. The first-floor suite has its own sitting room. The public areas where guests can relax and gather make it an appealing accommodation: There are two parlors (one furnished in Eastlake, the other in Empire), a library, and a second-floor sitting room. One parlor is particularly striking, with a dramatic mirrored mantel, a Victorian sofa and side chairs, and a plush Oriental rug. Guests may use the porches. Breakfast also sets this establishment apart: A five-course breakfast is served to guests at individual tables between 7 and 9am. A well-landscaped pool is on the 4 acres of grounds.

Rates (including breakfast): Racing season, $175 double weekdays, $195 double weekends. The rest of the year, $105 double.

The **Inn on Bacon Hill,** P.O. Box 1462, Saratoga Springs, NY 12866 (tel. 518/695-3693), provides a peaceful haven 15 minutes or so from Saratoga. It has a welcoming air. A red-brick pathway leads past planted borders to the lovely 1862 white home (built for state legislator Alexander B. Baucus), with a porch, bay windows, and a portico entrance. Innkeeper Andrea Collins-Breslin, who left General Electric to run the inn, now uses her psychology skills to make all her guests feel comfortable and at ease. The four guest rooms (two with bath) overlook farmland. The most fetching rooms are the Tulip Room, with a four-poster, and the Queen Anne's Lace Room, with a spindle bed. The Victorian Parlor Suite contains a cannonball bed and a parlor complete with a baby grand. Guests can relax in front of the parlor's marble fireplace or on the porch's wicker furnishings. The gazebo is the favored spot for afternoon beverages.

Rates (including breakfast): Racing season, $120–$140 double or suite for two. The rest of the year, $70–$95 double or suite for two.

About 25 minutes west of Saratoga, **Salt Hill Farm,** 5209 Lake Rd., Galway, NY 12074 (tel. 518/882-9466), has a venerable history. This farm on 3 acres was built in the 1700s as a stagecoach stop and tavern. In the 1960s it became the Salt Hill Club, a retreat for wealthy Saratoga visitors named after its famous namesake in Galway, Ireland. Today it welcomes visitors to three rooms (with bath) as well as a two-bedroom/two-bath cottage. All rooms have four-poster beds. There are several places for guests to gather—in front of the large fireplace in the family room, around the pool table in the recreation room, or around the piano in the more formal living room. In summer guests gather in the pool house to enjoy drinks from the refrigerator.

Rates (including breakfast): Summer, $95 double. Racing season, $115 double. Winter, $75 double.

If you're looking for a real farm experience, **Agape Farm Bed & Breakfast,** 4894 Rte. 9N, Corinth, NY 12822 (tel. 518/654-7777), is for you. It's about 13 miles from Saratoga (16 miles from Lake George) and offers accommodations in a farmhouse surrounded by 33 acres of woods and fields, complete with trout stream. The five rooms (all with bath) are simply and comfortably decorated in different colors. Available for weekly rental is a cottage that sleeps four and numbers a fully equipped kitchen and a TV among its amenities. Guests can gather around the piano for a sing-along if they're in the mood, stroll the fields gathering cackleberries or raspberries in season, feed the horses and chickens, relax on the wraparound porch, go birdwatching, or indulge in whatever country pursuits interest them.

Rates (including breakfast): $65–$135 double or cottage for two (higher July–Labor Day).

Saratoga & Area Dining

Breakfast

When in Saratoga, obviously the place to enjoy breakfast is the **racetrack,** even though it can be expensive, with items priced up to $12. Other good breakfast spots are the **43 Phila St. Bistro** and **Bruegger's Bagel Bakery** (both recommended below).

Lunch & Dinner

The place to be seen lunching is the **Turf Terrace,** but unless you've booked months in advance, forget it.

The **43 Phila St. Bistro** (tel. 518/584-2720), provides a sleek dining ambience for some exciting contemporary cuisine. French posters and art decorate the walls, the tables are set with white linen, and the warm peach/terra-cotta color scheme is lit by track lights. The menu changes daily but dinner items will likely include lamb chops with cider-shallot sauce, smoked bacon-Gorgonzola flan and wilted Swiss chard, filet of tenderloin with mushroom dark-beer sauce, organic chicken breast simmered in a portobello-and-marsala sauce, and trout with cranberry-apple sauce. Each dish shines. Prices run $16 to $26. To start, try the sesame-crusted salmon cake with Asian plum sauce and wasabi yogurt. This is the place to come for Sunday brunch, for waffles and omelets and egg dishes, plus the restaurant's extra-special salmon hash, flavored with cilantro, Cajun spices, and Old Bay. Hot jazz, blues, or classical music plays in the background. The wine list is international, including selections from Argentina, Spain, and Australia, with an emphasis on California varietals.

Hours: Mon 5:30–11pm, Tues 11:30am–2:30pm, Wed–Sat 11:30am–2:30pm and 5:30–11pm, Sun 8am–1:30pm and 5:30–11pm.

For a quick bagel fix, **Bruegger's Bagel Bakery,** 453 Broadway (tel. 518/5844372), serves an assortment of bagels and bagel sandwiches for under $3, plus bags of bagels to take out. Eat inside or outside on the deck on Broadway.

Hours: Aug, Mon–Sat 6am–9pm, Sun 6am–7pm; the rest of the year, daily 6am–7pm.

The **Olde Bryan Inn,** 123 Maple Ave., at Rock Street (tel. 518/587-2990), supposedly Saratoga's oldest building, is named after Alexander Bryan, a Revolutionary War hero who spied on Burgoyne, thus directly contributing to the victory at the Battle of Saratoga in 1777. He purchased the inn in the late 1780s, and the place certainly possesses a well-seasoned air. In cold weather the red glow from the two fireplaces (one at each end of the polished-wood dining room) make you feel warm and welcome. In the adjacent bar another fire roars beneath a picture of Leda and the Swan, and you can sit cozily ensconced beneath the old beamed ceiling. In summer, you can enjoy alfresco dining in the courtyards. Making up the menu are salads, sandwiches, omelets, and burgers (most under $8), plus a selection of entrees, like prime rib, Cajun blackened steak, fettuccine gamberi, and fish du jour ($11 to $17).

Hours: Daily 11am–11pm. No reservations are taken.

Locals rely on **Sperry's,** 30½ Caroline St. (tel. 518/584-9618), to deliver good honest food in down-home surroundings. The dinner menu offers such standard favorites as Maryland crab cakes, chicken Dijon, steak au poivre, and a popular jambalaya chock full of ham, chicken, hot sausage, onion, and green peppers. Prices range from $14 to $19. For an appetizer try the wasabi shrimp wrapped in bacon.

Hours: Mon–Sat 11:30am–3pm and 5:30–10pm, Sun 5–9pm.

If you like pasta, you'll like **Wheatfields,** 440 Broadway (tel. 518/587-0534), which delivers pasta in every conceivable manner. There's paglia e fieno, spaghetti puttanesca, two kinds of lasagne, and fettuccine primavera—more than 30 choices in all. Even the regular soup on the menu (besides the soup of the day) is pasta fagioli. Prices range from $10 to $17.

Hours: Mon–Wed 5–9pm, Thurs and Sun 11:30am–5pm and 5–9pm, Fri–Sat 11:30am–5pm and 5–10pm.

Hattie's, 45 Phila St. (tel. 518/584-4790), is no longer presided over by Hattie Mosley, though she still drops by occasionally to check on the place. It's changed little since she turned it over to younger shoulders, for this is still the place where dancers, musicians, and other visiting stars love to gather. Their photographs, notes, and tokens of appreciation that cover the walls give thanks for a home away from home serving good fresh food and lots of it. Hattie started her cooking career when she worked for Chicago starch millionaires, the Staleys. Over 50 years ago she settled in Saratoga Springs and began serving the spiciest barbecue and southern fried chicken and ribs to happy customers. Hattie's still does. Collard greens and other special daily vegetables appear on the menu, along with "dirty rice." Dinner dishes—southern fried chicken, spareribs, lamb and pork chops, for example—are priced from $7 to $13.50, and include soup, salad, biscuits, mashed potatoes, another vegetable, a slice of apple cobbler, and coffee.

Hours: In season, daily 11am–10pm; July–Aug, daily 8am–11pm; winter, Tues–Fri 5–9:30pm, Sat noon–9:30pm, Sun 12:30–8pm. Reservations needed in season.

Scallions, 404 Broadway (tel. 518/584-0192), is a busy little place serving great salads, sandwiches, and hearty entrees in a sleek ambience of black-and-white tile, green bentwood chairs, and painted lemon tables. In the back the display case is filled with salads—chicken and sun-dried tomato, crabmeat and shrimp, and more—and desserts to go. Among the desserts, my favorites are the chocolate-chip-and-walnut pie or any of the cheesecakes, locally made by New Skete monks. Among the entrees are several chicken dishes—garlic, walnut pesto, and wild mushroom, for example. Soups and sandwiches complete the fare. Prices run $7 to $14. This is a good place to pick up the makings for a picnic.

Hours: Mon–Sat 11am–9pm, Sun 11am–8pm.

Not a particularly pretty place, **Gaffney's,** 16 Caroline St. (tel.518/587-7359), nevertheless offers an eclectic mixture of Mexican, Italian, and continental dishes in a bistro atmosphere. Lunch specialties include chicken or beef tostadas, enchiladas, sandwiches, and pastas. Dinner fare is less casual: You'll find veal marsala; linguine al pesto; chicken sautéed with mushrooms, white wine, and lemon; and more. Prices range from $10 to $17. It's pleasant to dine in the patio/garden, where music is featured in July and August.

Hours: Mon–Sat 11:30am–3pm and 5:30–10:30pm, Sun 10:30am–3pm.

For lakeside viewing, seek out the **Waterfront,** 626 Crescent Ave. (tel. 518/583-2628), which has two decks hanging literally out over the water. The place is plain and tavernlike, with large windows and a fireplace for cooler months. Sandwiches, nachos, salads, and pasta, plus dishes from the barbecue—steaks, burgers, and seafood—are the choices here ($5 to $15). To find it, take Union Avenue to Crescent Avenue and turn left at the sign.

Hours: Daily 11:30am–10pm.

The Weathervane, on Rte. 9 south of Saratoga Springs (tel. 518/584-8157), is famous—and rightly so—for a 1-pound lobster dinner for only $9, served with a baked potato.

Hours: Daily 11am–9:30pm.

Dinner Only

In recent years one of the places to dine in Saratoga has always been **Chez Sophie** (tel. 518/583-3538). You can still dine here, but you'll have to repair to 2853 Rte. 9 in Malta Ridge, just south of Saratoga, a quarter mile south of Exit 13. Here in a classic 1940s diner you can sample fine cuisine made with the freshest local ingredients and garden herbs. Sophie learned to cook when she was growing up on the Belgian-French border. One or two of husband Joseph C. Parker's fluid metal-and-wire sculptures fit into the ambience. The menu changes daily but always features a fish of the day and six or so entrees (priced at $20), such as duck breast with apricots and green peppercorns; pork tenderloin braised in balsamic vinegar; steak with mustard sauce; and the house special, a superb rack of lamb with natural juices ($25). Start with the onion soup gratinée, escargots bourguignons, or pâté de la maison.

Hours: Feb–Dec, Tues–Sat 6pm–closing, Sun 11:30am–3pm (brunch). Reservations are essential.

At the **Springwater Inn,** 139 Union Ave. (tel. 518/584-6440), the tables are set with pretty Libby's glass lanterns and burgundy napery, with burgundy Victorian chairs alongside. The restaurant has two areas—a more formal room with tables set in front of a Federal-style fireplace and a more casual skylit room overlooking Union Avenue. The food is continental. You might start your meal with the shiitake-mushroom ravioli with roasted-pepper coulis and follow with venison with a merlot-wine sauce or duckling with a raspberry demiglaze. Pasta and pizzette are also available. Prices range from $7 to $18. Lighter fare is offered in the atmospheric wood-paneled taproom, which combines old English and Adirondack styles.

Hours: July–Aug, daily 5–11pm; mid–Feb to June and Sept–Dec, Tues–Sun 5–10pm. **Closed:** Jan to mid-Feb.

The **Caunterbury,** Union Avenue (tel. 518/587-9653), is on Rte. 9P, 3 miles south of the track. The focus of this delightful restaurant, created out of two barns, is a room with cascading waterfalls and a large indoor pool around which are several rooms, each individually designed and decorated. The whole effect is quite spectacular, especially at night when the moonlight falls on the water. Ficus plants, mirrors, and sun streaming into the upstairs bar make it an exceedingly pleasant spot for early-evening meals or late-afternoon cocktails. At dinner the cuisine is a mix of regional American and French plus some pasta dishes. You might find grilled tuna with smoked-shrimp salsa or fettuccine with feta, roasted tomatoes, and arugula. Prices range from $11 to $20.

Hours: Mon–Sat 5:30–10pm, Sun noon–9:30pm.

Ye Olde Wishing Well, 4 miles north on Rte. 9 (tel. 518/584-7640), a real racing hangout, has all kinds of racing memorabilia and track/turf paintings donated over the years by owners and trainers. The stone fireplaces and low ceilings epitomize Saratoga's country charm. Softshell crabs, prime rib, filet mignon, roast turkey, veal Oscar, and lobster are the favorites here, priced from $14 to $25.

Hours: Racing season, daily 5–11pm; Feb–Dec, Tues–Fri 5–10pm, Sat 5–11pm, Sun noon–9pm.

Chez Pierre, on Rte. 9, 8 miles north in Wilton (tel. 518/793-3350), is well known in the area for its fine classic cuisine—tournedos (chasseur, Henri IV, or Rossini), frogs' legs with garlic-butter sauce, coquilles St-Jacques, veal Oscar, sole marguery (with chablis and brandy-cream sauce)—all served in the comfortable but elegant surroundings of a converted home. Red napkins and white tablecloths, French sayings, and Paris-style kiosks and murals completed by a Glens Falls artist all give it a very Gallic feel. Entrees range from $15 to $25.

Hours: Summer, daily 5–10pm; winter, Mon–Sat 5–10pm.

At **Panzas Starlight Restaurant,** Rte. 9P at the south end of Saratoga Lake (tel. 518/584-6882), the Panza family has built a fine culinary reputation over the years by giving customers a genuine welcome and exquisite Italian/continental cuisine served in a simple, unpretentious, but very comfortable setting. Pastas, veal dishes (piccata, marsala, and parmigiana), chicken, and seafood make up the menu, all entrees served with a relish tray, a salad, spaghetti or potato, and a vegetable. The desserts are equally famous. Prices range from $15 to $19.

Hours: July–Aug, daily 5–10pm; the rest of the year, Wed–Sat 5–10pm, Sun 2–9pm. It may close Dec–Feb, so check.

After Dark

Skidmore College provides a number of cultural entertainments—films, musical concerts, lectures. For information, call 518/584-5000.

For some rollicking country entertainment, there's the Friday-night **rodeo** over in Ballston Spa at the Double M Arena on Rte. 67. A western barbecue precedes the show. Tickets to the rodeo are only $10 or so.

There are plenty of cocktail spots: the **Olde Bryan Inn,** 123 Maple Ave. (tel. 518/587-9741); **Professor Moriarty's Dining and Drinking Salon,** 430 Broadway (tel. 518/587-5981); **Gaffney's,** 16 Caroline St. (tel. 518/587-9791); and **Parting Glass,** 40–42 Lake Ave. (tel. 518/

583-1916), for a bit of the Irish. For a piano bar (during racing season only), try **Siro's,** 168 Lincoln Ave. (tel. 518/584-4030).

If none of this appeals to you, then **harness racing** (tel. 518/584-2110) can be enjoyed between May and mid-November and on weekends from January to March. For information, contact Saratoga Harness Racing, Nelson Avenue, Saratoga Springs, NY 12866. Or you might attend a **polo game,** usually played on Friday and Sunday at 6pm during August. For information, contact the Saratoga Polo Association, P.O. Box 5071, Saratoga Springs, NY 12866 (tel. 518/584-5108).

Besides the New York City Ballet, which performs in July, and the Philadelphia Orchestra, which performs in August, the **Saratoga Performing Arts Center** hosts the New York City Opera, the Newport Jazz Festival, theater, and a number of special guests, who have included Judy Collins, Elton John, and John Denver. For information, call 518/587-3330.

In addition, the **Baroque Music Festival** is held in nearby Greenfield during summer. For information, call the Foundation of Baroque Music Studio (tel. 518/893-7527).

A Side Trip to New Skete

A trip to the **New Skete Monastery** in Cambridge (tel. 518/677-3928) will take you through Washington County, the countryside Grandma Moses portrayed so vividly in her now-famous landscapes. You'll travel past russet-red barns, yards filled with scurrying chickens and pigs, and rolling hillsides where horses are quietly grazing, until you reach the monastery high on a hill overlooking the quiet valley. Here Greek Orthodox monks paint eggs and icons; make sausages and cheeses; smoke poultry, bacon, and hams; and bake delectable cheesecakes—Kahlúa, chocolate, and a simple deluxe, priced from $15—for which people travel miles. The monks are also noted dog trainers and operate good kennels. You can purchase their goods and their poetry and contemplative writings in the store here before going up the hillside to the small onion-domed chapel, built by the monks themselves (the dome is made of Styrofoam, fiberglass, and polyurethane). This is a retreat for all faiths, and there's room for three or four guests in shared rooms with bunk beds and spartan furnishings. No radios, no tape recorders, and no alcohol are allowed.

While you're in Cambridge, visit **Hubbard Hall** (tel. 518/677-2765), a terrific old Victorian turreted building that now houses the Valley Artisans Market, filled with ceramics, woodcarvings, art, and basketry. Stuffed animals, candles, and other country items are found next door in the Village Store and Coop.

Hours: Mon–Sat 10am–5pm.

From Cambridge, Rte. 40 north takes you to another typical country site: the **Log Village Grist Mill Museum,** Rte. 30, 2 miles off Rte. 40, in East Hartford (tel. 518/632-5237). I must admit that this mill was not a major destination on my visit, but I spent several hours, so fascinated and charmed was I by Floyd Harwood's enthusiasm and natural gift for teaching. A retired "shop" teacher, Floyd rescued and spent five years restoring the mill as a retirement project, remaking the parts from old patterns. The mill now works—you can go down and watch the 17-foot-diameter, 10-ton wheel with its 54 buckets (each holding 450 pounds of water) driving the original 1810 French burr stones that have natural pockmarks for good grinding. Corn and wheat are ground. The original stove, plus the desk with records, kept from 1874, are in the mill.

In the nearby mill barn Floyd displays a collection of old farm machinery and household items, gas and steam engines, sewing machines, typewriters, a dog-powered churn, and all kinds of woodworking tools, including a 150-year-old treadle wood lathe, an old band saw originally advertised in the 1922 Sears Roebuck catalog, and a scroll saw advertised in an 1888 catalog. Harwood has a collection of 400 planes alone. In the room above are pump organs, sewing machines, washing machines, calendars, prams, carpet cleaners, antique clothes, and much more reflecting the daily life of earlier eras. Anyone interested in early newspapers and antique books will want to look at his collection of old newspapers, agricultural books, and calendars.

Hours: Memorial Day–Oct, Sat 10am–6pm, Sun noon–6pm; weekdays by appointment. **Admission:** $2.50 adults, 50¢ children.

North to the Lakes

Lake Luzerne

Lake Luzerne is a small and serene lake about 20 minutes from Saratoga, southwest of Lake George. From here you can take trips to Lake Sacandaga, go antiquing, attend the Friday-night rodeo in Lake Luzerne, go horseback riding and lake swimming in summer, or enjoy cross-country skiing in winter.

The **Lamplight Inn,** 2129 Lake Ave., Rte. 9N (P.O. Box 70), Lake Luzerne, NY 12846 (tel. 518/696-5294), occupies an 1899 home that proud owners Gene and Linda Merlino restored. Each of the 10 rooms (with bath and air-conditioning) is individually decorated with chintz wallpapers, quilts, and lace curtains. Some have gas-burning fireplaces. Room 2 has a mahogany canopied bed. Room 10 is decked out in forest green, peach, and white, with a draped white-iron canopied bed as the focal point. Guests can relax in the extra-large comfortable sitting room, with two wood-burning fireplaces, a TV, high beamed ceilings, chestnut wainscoting, and a keyhole staircase. Guests can admire the personal doll and turtle collections and amuse themselves with the marble chess game and Scrabble. The porch with a swing is great for unwinding in summer. A full breakfast of eggs, cereal, and fruit is served at tables set with damask cloths and pink napkins and fine china. The grounds are pretty and the whole place is surrounded by majestic white pine. In summer there are wooded nature trails to explore; in winter they're great for cross-country skiing. No children under 12 are allowed.

Rates (including breakfast): $90–$160 double, depending on season.

Lake George's Ultimate Resort

The Sagamore, P.O. Box 450, Bolton Landing, Lake George, NY 12814 (tel. 518/644-9400), lies resplendent on Lake George ensconced on 70-acre Sagamore Island, surrounded by crystalline blue waters and tree-covered mountains. The Colonial Revival white clapboard building with green shutters has been restored to its earlier magnificence. When it opened in 1883 it served as a focal point for social and recreational activities for the exclusive folks who'd built summer mansions on the island. Damaged by fire in 1893 and 1914, it was completely reconstructed in 1930 and old age didn't catch up with the grande dame until 1981, when it closed its doors. Now it combines 19th-century charm and luxury with 20th-century technology, making it a world-class resort.

Although the landward approach presents a hodgepodge of standardized condominium clusters, the hotel really should be viewed from the water. From the stylish Oriental-accented lobby, step out onto the semicircular veranda, supported by 20-foot-high classical pillars, that overlooks the mountains and lake. Here you can enjoy tea at 3:30pm or cocktails to piano accompaniment among the potted palms, wicker, and marble ambience. Pathways and stairs lead across terraced lawns to the lake, where you can sunbathe on a series of wooden decks or at the beach. The indoor pool and pool terrace are also down here. The *Morgan*, a special wooden lake cruiser, operates from here, sailing at 11am, 2:30pm, and 7pm for dinner. In winter its hull is protected from ice by a circle of warm-air bubbles.

The hotel's premier dining room, Trillium, offers an elegant setting of plush pink chairs, tables draped with magnolia damask, and fine china for both Sunday brunch and dinner (entrees run $16 to $22). Appetizers may include grilled butterflied shrimp with champagne-Dijon vinaigrette or a vegetarian napoleon made with grilled portobello mushrooms, turnip gaufrette, and smoked-tomato coulis. The dozen or so entrees are hard to choose from—breast of duckling with honey-Dijon balsamic demiglaze, seared pepper tuna with sesame vinaigrette, and medallions of veal with artichokes, lobster mousse, smoked mozzarella, and brandy-sage demiglaze are three examples. For a delirious dessert experience, select the trio of chocolate (consisting of chocolate mousse, chocolate terrine, and chocolate-and-vanilla swirl) or the banana rumba (coconut ice cream with a pecan tuille and carmelized banana-brandy sauce).

There are 100 guest rooms in the main building and 250 in "cottages" or condo units. The rooms in the main building are furnished with pencil four-posters and half-posters, peach wallpaper and carpeting, botanical prints, wing chairs, and candlestands (plus a TV, a phone, and air-conditioning); baths are tiled and feature mahogany towel bars and shower curtain rods. Most of the cottage suites have small balconies with wicker rockers; fireplaces, modular couches, TVs, and Adirondack-style chairs set the tone inside. An open kitchen with an electric stove and refrigerator and a bath and bedroom complete the layout.

Myriad facilities are available: a games room, a beauty salon, a gift shop, an art gallery, a spa (massage, facials, loufa scrub room and Universal-equipped exercise room, sauna and steam, whirlpool), an indoor/outdoor pool, two indoor and five outdoor tennis courts, racquetball, movies, an 18-hole par-70 golf course, cross-country skiing, ice skating, and a toboggan run. Use of canoes and rowboats is free. Besides the dining and entertainment facilities already mentioned, there's an attractive plush coffee shop, Mister Brown's; Van Winkle's for jazz and dancing; and the Club Grill, perhaps the most appealing of all, located on the mainland up on Federal Hill at the golf club. Free round-trip transportation is provided to the golf course and to Gore Mountain and West Mountain for downhill skiers.

Rates: July–Aug, $180–$320 double. The rest of the year, $160–$210 double; $240–$400 suite, depending on season. MAP available.

Friends Lake

Only 20 minutes north of Lake George and a mere 15 minutes from Gore Mountain, this unspoiled lake has a couple of fine inns on its shores. Sharon and Greg Taylor took over **Friends Lake Inn,** Friends Lake Road, Chestertown, NY 12817 (tel. 518/494-4251), in 1982 and restored the 1860s building to its former glory (in the 1920s there used to be six inns on this small lake). From the dining porch and the front rooms there's a restorative lake view. The four traditional guest rooms are simply and nicely decorated, with chintz wallpapers, lace curtains, oak chests and dressers, cannonball or iron-and-brass beds, and floral spreads or quilts. The larger junior suites have sitting areas and feature Waverly fabrics, four-posters, and Jacuzzi tubs. There are 14 rooms total, all with bath. Cottage accommodations are also available in adjacent buildings. Each of these has a deck, a wood-burning stove, a fully equipped kitchen, and simple homey furnishings.

In the dining room, solid-cherry square columns support the stamped-tin ceiling; the wainscoting and a fire in the brick hearth make it cozy in winter. In summer the screened-in porch is the best dining place. Dinner might begin with wood-grilled portobello mushrooms with blue-cheese polenta or Jamaica jerk shrimp with mango coulis and pineapple salsa. Among the entrees ($14 to $23) are likely to be wood-grilled salmon with tossed cherries and chanterelles, duck marinated in ginger-soy and served with peach slices, and rack of lamb with a reduction of blackberries and plums. A couple of vegetarian dishes are always available too. Among the desserts, the chocolate-walnut pie and the mud pie are rich but delicious. The wine list is good.

For after-dinner relaxing, the sitting room affords several couches, a TV with VCR, and some board games plus the opportunity to loll in front of the fire. There's also a bar with a view of the lake and umbrella-shaded tables outside. The grounds have 30km of groomed trails for hiking, biking, and cross-country and there are a few sailboats and rowboats for guest use.

Rates: $130–$200 double; $165–$250 double MAP. Wide selection of special packages available. **Dining Hours:** Wed–Fri 5–9pm, Sat 5–10pm, Sun 4–8pm.

A soaring tower and peaked gables identify the **Balsam House,** Friends Lake, Chestertown, NY 12817 (tel. 518/494-2828, 494-4431, or 494-2510). Built in 1845 as a farmhouse, the property recently suffered damage and although the owners plan to reopen, the date is unknown at press time. The rooms were charmingly decorated, the dining room served fine food, and the property also offered (and presumably still will) a private beach, rowboats, sailboats, canoes, an antique paddleboat, and bicycles. It's only 15 minutes from Gore Mountain.

Saratoga Springs
Special & Recreational Activities

Antiquing: Plenty of antiques shops can be found in town and the surrounding area. For example, try driving Rte. 29 west or east. Or pop south to Ballston Spa.

Bicycling: Rentals are available from Paradox on Church Street (tel. 518/583-7706) for $25 per day and $40 per weekend.

Boating: Rowboat and canoe rentals are available at Ballston Lake beside the Good Times Restaurant (tel. 518/399-9976). Saratoga Lake is also a good boating spot.

Camping: Located out toward the lake, Interlaken Camp, Union Avenue (R.D. 1), Saratoga Springs, NY 12866 (tel. 518/583-3447), is an ideal spot with 200 camp and tent/trailer sites. Facilities include showers, pools, a full grocery, a restaurant, and a lounge. Open summer only.

Golf: There are two golf courses in Saratoga Spa State Park (tel. 518/584-2000)—an 18-hole championship course and a par-27 9-hole course.

Picnicking: At the track, your best bet is at the Top O' the Stretch picnic area. Otherwise, Saratoga Spa State Park is ideal.

Skating: There's an illuminated rink in Saratoga Spa State Park for speed and ice skating.

Skiing: Cross-country skiing can be enjoyed in the Saratoga Spa State Park. Headquarters is at the spa park office (tel. 518/584-2535). Downhill is available at West Mountain (tel. 518/793-6606), where there are 22 trails and three chair lifts. A day pass on weekends is around $30. Take I-87 north to Exit 18W.

Swimming: Two pools are available in the park—one Olympic-size; the other, the Victoria Pool, a favorite with the dancers and other performers at the Arts Center. A beach and a pool also exist at Kaydeross Amusement Park on the edge of the lake.

Tennis: Saratoga Racquet Club (tel. 518/587-3000) and in Saratoga Spa State Park. Also city courts on Division Street.

The Hamptons

Distance in Miles: Westhampton, 81; Hampton Bays, 90; Southampton, 96; East Hampton, 106

Estimated Driving Time: 2 to 4 hours, depending on Long Island Expressway traffic.

◄○►◄○►◄○►◄○►◄○►

Driving: Take I-495 (Long Island Expressway) to Exit 70 (Rte. 111 south), then take Rte. 27 east.

Bus: The Hampton Jitney offers express service—and they mean it. Despite the odds of beating the traffic back on Sunday night, their drivers are given instructions on all the side roads and back routes and often arrive in the city to standing ovations from passengers. Reservations are required. Call 516/283-4600, or 800/936-0440 from Tri-State area codes. The jitney leaves from 86th Street between Lexington and Third, from 69th Street and Lexington, from 59th Street and Lexington, and from 41st Street between Lexington and Third.

Train: The Long Island Rail Road from Penn Station stops at each of the Hamptons. Call 718/217-5477 for timetable information.

Further Information: For more about New York in general, contact the **Division of Tourism,** New York State Department of Economic Development, One Commerce Plaza, Albany, NY 12245 (tel. 518/474-4116).

For general information about Long Island, contact the **Long Island Convention and Visitor's Bureau,** 350 Vanderbilt Pkwy., Suite 103, Hauppauge, NY 11788 (tel. 516/951-3440).

For specific information, contact the **Hampton Bays Chamber of Commerce,** Montauk Highway (P.O. Box 64), Hampton Bays, NY 11946 (tel. 516/728-2211); the **Westhampton Chamber of Commerce,** 173 Montauk Hwy. (P.O. Box 1228), Westhampton (tel. 516/288-3337); the **Southampton Chamber of Commerce,** 76 Main St., Southampton, NY 11968 (tel. 516/283-0402); the **East Hampton Chamber of Commerce,** 37A Main St., East Hampton, NY 11937 (tel. 516/324-0362).

In Paris they're promoted as New York's Riviera; in a *New York* magazine article in the mid-1980s, journalist Marie Brenner described them acidly as "suburbia by the sea." Of course, I'm talking about the legendary Hamptons, seven or so villages clustered along Long Island's South Fork, with access to miles and miles of white-sand Atlantic beaches backed by undulating dunes—a miracle coastline for any uptight urban dweller. The beaches here are certainly as good as any in the world, which is one reason to come to the Hamptons. The other is to participate in the social season, a fashion scene that *Women's Wear Daily* regards as trend-setting and sees fit to comment upon.

The Hamptons didn't always engender such opposing opinions and tart commentary. Since their founding in the mid-17th century by colonists from New England, most of these villages on the east end of Long Island remained quiet farming towns—at least until the late 19th century, when they began to attract urban emigrants. As early as 1890 a journalist observed that on the South Fork people wore fancy blazers, dressed up a good deal, played tennis, and attended hops. The scene really hasn't changed that much. The game is still tennis (along with a few others), people still dress up a good deal and wear fancy blazers, but their hops tend to be a little more camp and far more frenetic. The resort image didn't really jell, though, until the 1920s when the auto emerged as a popular mode of transportation and the Maidstone Club opened its bathing facilities. Today's celebrity-studded scene, however, can be traced more directly to the mid-1940s, when Jackson Pollock and Lee Krasner arrived and were soon followed by the de Koonings, Frank O'Hara, Larry Rivers, Nick Carone, and Barney Rosset, who in turn were followed by waves of celebrities who still lend a distinct cachet to the area—Betty Friedan, Edward Albee, Woody Allen, Craig Claiborne, Charles Addams, E. L. Doctorow, and many more. In addition to the writers and artists, actors and directors have followed and the area (East Hampton in particular) is now commonly referred to as Hollywood East. Steven Spielberg, Sidney Lumet, Alan Pakula, Kim Basinger and Alec Baldwin, Kathleen Turner, and Chevy Chase were among the first film actors and directors to summer here. They were soon joined by Robert DeNiro, Alan Alda, and moguls like David Geffen, Barry Diller, and the late Steve Ross, plus Billy Joel and Barbra Streisand.

Their homes appear in *Architectural Digest* and other glossy magazines, their social lives get into the gossip columns, and inevitably there's a certain Peeping Tom quality to any visit to the Hamptons. Being seen and trying to see are an important part of the scene for some.

When Pollock arrived the potato fields were intact and land sold for a high-priced $1,000 an acre. Today that same land sells for anywhere from $60,000 an acre and up, and the potato fields are blighted with jagged glass-and-wooden houses standing starkly on the flatlands behind the sand

Events & Festivals to Plan Your Trip Around

June: Old Whaler's Festival, Sag Harbor (early June).

July: Fireworks at East Hampton Main Beach (after 9pm on July 4 or on closest weekend).

East Hampton Ladies Village Improvement Society Fair (usually the last Saturday). Call 516/324-1220.

August: Westhampton Beach Art Show (early August).

Clothesline Art Sale, Guild Hall, East Hampton. Call 516/324-0806.

Artists and Writers Baseball Game, East Hampton (mid-August)

Hampton Classic Horse Show, Bridgehampton (late August to early September).

September: Shinnecock Indian Reservation Powwow (Labor Day weekend). Contact the Shinnecock Nation Cultural Center Museum Complex (tel. 516/287-4923).

October: Hamptons International Film Festival (late October). Call 516/324-4600.

December: Annual tour of Historic Inns and House, East Hampton Chamber of Commerce. Call 516/324-0362.

dunes. Designer-labeled hordes descend every summer, clogging the streets with their Mercedes, Jaguars, and de rigueur BMWs and Acuras. And with those 173,000 summer visitors have come the required gourmet food markets, boutiques, restaurants, and discos that shatter the night's quietude. For those who wish to ignore the scene, the beaches remain; for those who relish participating in the scene, then you can't find a better one outside New York City. The only real problem is the Long Island Expressway. My advice is to hole up here permanently for the entire summer—never mind weekending!

Friday Night Hassles

If you have time only to weekend, take heart. There are those who pride themselves on not having to punish themselves by driving anywhere on Friday night—they're the lucky ones. Those who have to leave on Friday night have their ways of beating the traffic—leaving early, leaving late, taking this route instead of that. My best advice is to check the *Times,* which publishes a map of potential bottlenecks where roadwork is being done. Stay tuned to your radio and hope for the best.

Friday Night Suppers

If you're headed all the way to the East End, you'll probably suffer hunger pangs en route. You can either stop at the diner at the Hampton Road turnoff into Southampton; wait until you reach Water Mill and drop into Meghan's Saloon, a pubby bar/restaurant serving some great burger combinations; or wait until you reach East Hampton's O'Mally's. Of course, there are plenty of other possibilities along the way.

East End Bed-and-Breakfasts

For bed-and-breakfast accommodations throughout the East End, contact **A Reasonable Alternative, Inc.,** 117 Spring St., Port Jefferson, NY 11777 (tel. 516/928-4034).

WESTHAMPTON BEACH, QUOGUE & HAMPTON BAYS

There are those who say the Shinnecock Canal divides the more socially conscious Hamptons—Southampton and East Hampton—from the less socially conscious Hamptons.

Westhampton Beach, closest to the city, attracts a fast-paced crowd, as well as a sizable number of blue bloods. Down along Dune Road, rows and rows of modern multifaceted glass-and-wood structures stretch along the beachfront. Here, on weekends you can drive past, catching the echoes of many a party and passing the crowds and cars that jostle around the party and disco spots. Neighboring Quogue has a far quieter, low-key approach to life (even though the name means "ground that shakes like thunder"), while around the corner across Tiana Bay, Hampton Bays has the most down-to-earth reputation of all and attracts families and avid fishermen.

Westhampton Beach Lodging

Staying at either the **Dune Deck Hotel,** 379 Dune Rd. (tel. 516/288-3876), or the **Westhampton Beach, Bath and Tennis Club,** 231 Dune Rd., Westhampton, NY 11978 (tel. 516/288-2500), gives you access to a full range of facilities—10 tennis courts, two pools, a dance club, and, most important, the beach. Plus you have the opportunity to dine at one of the most romantic and most highly rated restaurants in the Hamptons—Starr Boggs.

Rates: Memorial Day–Labor Day, $170–$370 double.

Quogue Lodging

The **Inn at Quogue,** 47–52 Quogue St., Quogue, NY 11959 (tel. 516/653-6560, or 212/371-3300), is one of the few accommodations that contributes to the town's reputation as a quiet stylish enclave. A mile from the beach, this 210-year-old home has 18 rooms (including two cottages), all tastefully furnished with a country combination of pine, quilts, chintz wallpapers, and an occasional wicker piece. Across the street are nine more rooms in the East Building, dating back 175 years. The rooms here are more modern-looking than those in the main house. All have phones, and some have air-conditioning and color TV. The restaurant (tel. 516/653-0666) has a fine reputation and a daily-changing menu. Herbs come from a garden out back. Dinner specialties may include swordfish scented with lemongrass or steak with bordelaise sauce. Prices are $19 to $32. Also available are beach passes, bikes, and discounted membership at a nearby health club with indoor tennis courts.

Rates (including continental breakfast in summer): In season, $180–$280 double. Off-season, $122–$192 double. **Inn Closed:** Jan to mid-Apr. **Dining Hours:** Summer, Mon–Thurs 5:30–9pm, Fri–Sat 6–10pm, Sun noon–3pm and 5:30–9pm; spring and fall, Fri–Sat 6–10pm, Sun noon–3pm and 5:30–9pm. **Restaurant Closed:** Jan to mid-Apr.

Westhampton Dining

Starr Boggs at the Dune Deck Hotel, 379 Dune Rd. (tel. 516/288-5250), and **Starr at Hampton Square,** Beach Lane (tel. 516/288-1877), are the dining hits in Westhampton Beach, at least for the summer crowd. At both the menu is limited, listing about eight or so entrees (the menu changes seasonally at the Hampton Square branch, which stays open during winter). The dishes are simple in their preparation but use the finest ingredients. There might be grilled free-range chicken with lemon and applesauce, grilled free-range pheasant with lingonberries and herbed Savoy cabbage, almond-crusted flounder with lemon-herb butter, and seared tuna with fresh tomato and basil with bok choy. A couple of steaks are also usually offered. Prices range from $22 to $32. Special prix-fixe dinners are available in fall and winter.

Hours: Dune Deck: Summer, daily 11:30am–2:30pm and 5pm–closing; spring, Thurs–Sun 11:30am–2:30pm and 5pm–closing; closed in winter. Hampton Square: Summer, daily 5pm–closing; fall–spring, Sun noon–3pm, Wed–Sun 5pm–closing.

The **American Grill,** 141 Montauk Hwy. (tel. 516/288-2255), offers an eclectic variety of American and Italian dishes from barbecue and blackened items to penne a la vodka, grilled salmon piccata, and surf and turf. Prices range from $17 to $24. The ambience is appealing, with plush banquettes and a warm hearth.

Hours: Mon–Thurs 5–9pm, Fri–Sat 5–10pm, Sun 3–9pm. In summer lunch and brunch are usually served.

Hampton Bays Dining

Villa Paul, 162 Montauk Hwy. (tel. 516/728-3261), has survived the fashions and trends and remains an institution frequented by local business folks and others who appreciate the reliable, good Italian cuisine. The traditional favorites are available—veal parmigiana, veal

Long Island

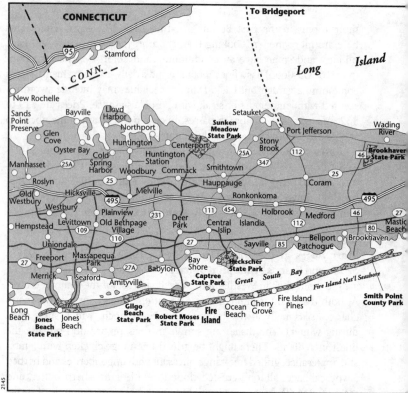

marsala, saltimbocca, and scampi with white wine, garlic, and butter, plus steaks and local duckling with apple-raisin stuffing and a sauce of the day. Prices range from $14 to $17.

Hours: Daily 4:30pm–closing.

Tully's, 78 Foster Ave. (tel. 516/728-9111), which also operates a fish store next door, assures that the fish served here is some of the freshest around. It's not fancy and the fish is simply prepared, but that's all that's required when it's so fresh. Come for the steamers, mussels, oysters, shrimp, swordfish, and other selections priced from $11 to $20.

Hours: Apr–Columbus Day, daily 5pm–closing.

Indian Cove, Canoe Place Road (tel. 516/728-8833), is near the Shinnecock Canal and set down beside a boatyard. The menu features locally produced meats and fish prepared in innovative ways. On the seasonally changing menu you might find crusty baked fluke with caramelized banana, mango, and melon salsa or salmon in a lemongrass broth. Among the meats might be chicken with Hunan garlic sauce, duckling with Catalina plum sauce, or loin of veal with merlot glaze. Prices range from $22 to $30.

Hours: In season, daily 4pm–1am. **Closed:** Winter.

Hampton Bays & Westhampton Beach
Special & Recreational Activities

Bicycling: The Hamptons are ideal for biking because the area is so flat, with only some minor hills in Sag Harbor. Shelter Island in particular is a favorite touring ground. In Westhampton Beach, bikes can be rented at Bike 'n' Kite, 112 Potunk Lane (tel. 516/288-1210).

Boating: Boats can be rented in Hampton Bays at the Colonial Shores Resort & Marina, Inc., West Tiana Road (tel. 516/728-0011); Shinnecock Fishing Station, 22 Shinnecock Rd. (tel. 516/728-6116); and Hampton Watercraft & Marine, 99B Old Riverhead Rd., Westhampton Beach (tel. 516/288-2900), which rents boats, jet skis, and surf equipment.

Fishing: Two open boats—*Capt. Clark III* (tel. 516/728-9084) and *Jenny Rose* (tel. 516/325-1309)—dock at the Indian Cove Marina.

Golf: Hampton Hills Country Club, Moriches Road (tel. 516/727-6862).

Horseback Riding: Hidden Echo Ranch, Rte. 24, Hampton Bays (tel. 516/668-5453)—take Exit 65 off Sunrise Highway north 1½ miles—offers one- and two-hour trail rides. Special sunset rides are also arranged. Choose either Western or English saddle. Sears Bellows Stables, Rte. 24, Exit 65N off Sunrise Highway (tel. 516/723-3554), offers trail rides, including a special 30-minute ride for families and children.

Soaring: Sky Sailors, Inc., at the Suffolk County Airport, Building 313, Rust Avenue, Westhampton Beach, NY 11978 (tel. 516/288-5858), offers several flight packages, including a trip for two. Prices depend on how high you go and range from $70 to $120.

Tennis: Try the Bath & Tennis Club of Westhampton Beach, Dune Road (tel. 516/288-2500); high school courts are also available in Hampton Bays and Westhampton.

SOUTHAMPTON

Southampton Attractions

Founded in 1640 by colonists from Lynn, Mass., Southampton was the first English colony established in New York State, but it became one of the most famous resorts about a century ago, when a summer colony was established here by 200 wealthy and socially prominent New York families. Their impressive estates can still be seen along Halsey, Captain's and Coopers Neck lanes, and the oceanfront Meadow Lane, South Main Street, and Gin Lane. It was they who built the Meadow Club, on Meadow Lane, with its grass tennis courts and shingle-style clubhouse. You can best explore the town by securing a **walking-tour map** from the Southampton Chamber of Commerce at 76 Main St. (tel. 516/283-0402). To some, Southampton means money and high society, and certainly a glance at the prestigious shop names on Job's Lane will only confirm that impression.

The **Parrish Art Museum**, 25 Job's Lane (tel. 516/283-2118), is the town's cultural center and boasts significant collections of William Merritt Chase and Fairfield Porter artworks. Besides art exhibitions and lectures, the museum offers concerts in the garden on several Saturday nights during summer. Bring a blanket. The gardens are a lovely, restful haven, enhanced by several della Robbias.

Hours: In season, Mon–Tues, Thurs, and Sat 11am–5pm; Sun 1–5pm. Off-season, Mon and Thurs-Sat 11am–5pm, Sun 1–5pm. **Admission:** Donation suggested.

The **Halsey Homestead** (1648), South Main Street (tel. 516/283-3527), is the oldest English saltbox in the state and furnished appropriately.

Hours: Mid-June to mid-Sept, Tues–Sun 11am–4:30pm.

The **Southampton Historical Museum,** 17 Meeting House Lane (tel. 516/283-2494), provides an overview of local history from Indian and colonial times onward.

Hours: Mid-June to mid-Sept, Tues–Sun 11am–5pm.

Southampton is also the site of the **Shinnecock Indian Reservation,** where the famous Powwow is held on Labor Day weekend.

Southampton Lodging

Obviously, your first choice would be to stay with friends who have a house, preferably south of the highway. If this cannot be arranged, then there's at least one very attractive alternative.

Marta Byer and Martin White have created some of the most original, inspired accommodations in the Hamptons at the **Village Latch Inn,** 101 Hill St., Southampton, NY 11968 (tel. 516/283-2160), only minutes from Job's Lane and a block from the beach. Set behind a privet hedge, the handsome clapboard building was once the annex of the Irving Hotel, then the area's premier accommodation. Throughout the house today you'll come upon all kinds of fascinating collectibles Marta has gathered on travels around the world, especially dolls and puppets arranged in strikingly original ways—a doll's head cupped in a bird's nest, another doll seated on a small chair, an open parasol on the stair landing—and in the parlors you'll find an intriguing assemblage of Marta's artworks.

Each of the main house's 24 rooms is furnished individually. Room 68 has a pair of comfy wing chairs and a fireplace; Room 58's centerpiece is a sleigh bed, while one of the spacious suites offers a bedroom with a handsome bed covered with a hand-woven quilt, an oak chest and rocker, and a sitting room with wicker chairs in front of the fireplace.

Marta has spent the last few years carefully restoring and decorating several historic houses that now stand on the 3 acres behind the main house. Each one is more appealing than the next. For example, the 100-year-old Homestead now has nine rooms and eight baths; the spacious shared living room is filled with leather and Victorian couches and a large Regency dining table set close to the kitchen, which has a fireplace, a brilliant Mexican tile floor, and a vast Garland range. From the Homestead guests can step out into the "spa," located in a Victorian-style greenhouse furnished comfortably with wicker. On the other side of the "spa," another house has been beautifully transformed with plush furnishings and objects from around the world—masks, puppets, and other objets d'art from Africa's Ivory Coast, South America, and India.

The Hamptons, Shelter Island & the North Fork

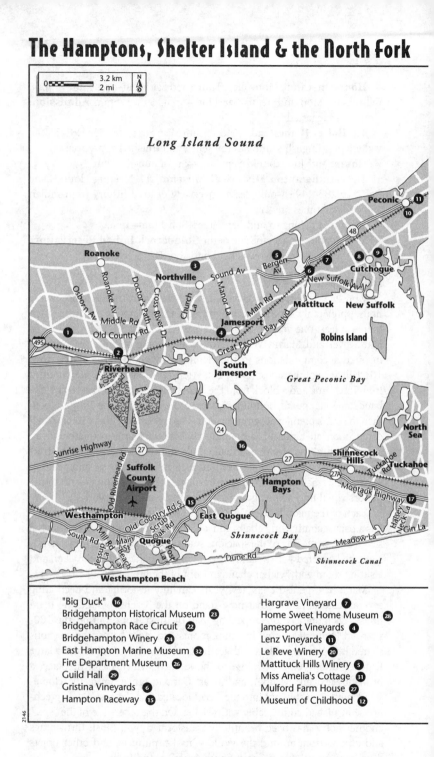

Long Island Sound

Roanoke

Roanoke Av

Osborn Av

Doctor's Path

Cross River Dr

Northville

Church La

Sound Av

Manor La

Bergen Av

Peconic

Cutchogue

New Suffolk Av

Mattituck

New Suffolk

Middle Rd

Old Country Rd

Jamesport

Main Rd

Great Peconic Bay Blvd

Riverhead

South Jamesport

Robins Island

Great Peconic Bay

North Sea

Sunrise Highway

Suffolk County Airport

Shinnecock Hills

Tuckahoe Rd

Tuckahoe

Hampton Bays

Montauk Highway

Westhampton

Old Country Rd S.

Scrub Oak Rd

East Quogue

Shinnecock Bay

Meadow La

Hatsey Neck La

Gin La

South Rd

Mill Rd

Main St

Jessup La

Beach La

Quogue

Post La

Dune Rd

Shinnecock Canal

Westhampton Beach

"Big Duck" 16
Bridgehampton Historical Museum 23
Bridgehampton Race Circuit 22
Bridgehampton Winery 24
East Hampton Marine Museum 32
Fire Department Museum 26
Guild Hall 29
Gristina Vineyards 6
Hampton Raceway 15

Hargrave Vineyard 7
Home Sweet Home Museum 28
Jamesport Vineyards 4
Lenz Vineyards 11
Le Reve Winery 20
Mattituck Hills Winery 5
Miss Amelia's Cottage 31
Mulford Farm House 27
Museum of Childhood 12

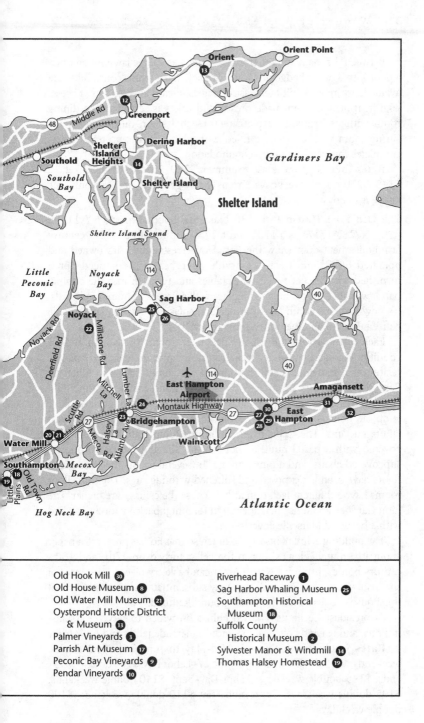

Old Hook Mill ㉚
Old House Museum ❽
Old Water Mill Museum ㉑
Oysterpond Historic District
    & Museum ⓭
Palmer Vineyards ❸
Parrish Art Museum ⓱
Peconic Bay Vineyards ❾
Pendar Vineyards ❿

Riverhead Raceway ❶
Sag Harbor Whaling Museum ㉕
Southampton Historical
    Museum ⓲
Suffolk County
    Historical Museum ❷
Sylvester Manor & Windmill ⓮
Thomas Halsey Homestead ⓳

Between the main and other houses stretches a large lawn for croquet, a pool with a privet hedge providing privacy, and a tennis court. Bikes are available for rent. A full breakfast of bagels, cream cheese, ham, cheese, yogurt, fruit, and homemade breads and cakes is served in the dining room with its brilliant-purple director's chairs. An ultra-comfortable sitting room with a fireplace filled with plants and appealing objects completes this very inviting accommodation.

Rates (including breakfast): Summer, $180–$350 double weekends, $145–$250 double weekdays. From Thanksgiving to late Apr only one house is open.

The **Old Post House Inn,** 136 Main St., Southampton, NY 11968 (tel. 516/283-1717), is a 1705 and a 1730 addition to the 17th-century farmhouse next door (now the Post House restaurant). It's owned and operated by Ed and Cecile Courville. Step across the latticed porch furnished with wicker rockers and tables and turn left into the original parlor with its 1705 beams and fireplace with adjacent warming cupboards. It's now furnished with comfy armchairs, sofas, and an Eastlake marble coffee table. An antique quilt adorns the walls.

Each of the seven individually decorated rooms (with bath and air conditioning) is named after a local historical figure and contains a plaque relating that individual's contributions to the community. The Albert G. Post Room contains an attractive walnut bed and matching armoire, a chair, a dresser, a sidetable, two comfy chairs, and a wrought-iron floor lamp; its floor is covered with dusky-rose carpeting, its windows with chintz curtains. The Captain John Halburt Room features an iron bed covered with a pastel quilt, a chest with a shaving mirror, turquoise-slipcovered chairs, and a pine armoire. In several rooms the wide-plank floors have been left exposed and softened with rag rugs. The third-floor rooms have a different feel, primarily because the ceilings are higher. The Lion Gardner Room has height enough for a highback Victorian oak bed with a beautiful Marseille coverlet.

The building is full of history, so much so that Ed has prepared a paper about it. An archeological dig in the cellar turned up 17th- and 18th-century bottles, primitive Native American basketry pieces, and traces of shellfish, vegetables, and fruit that may substantiate the local stories that this house was a stop on the Underground Railroad.

At breakfast Cecile uses varied chinas on which to serve croissants, muffins, and tea and coffee, along with homemade jellies and fresh fruit.

Rates (including breakfast): Mid-May to June 26, $150 double weekends, $115 double weekdays. June 27–Labor Day, $195 double weekends, $145 double weekdays. Labor Day–Sept, $140 double weekends, $105 double weekdays. Oct to mid-May, $110 double weekends, $100 double weekdays.

Other Southampton accommodations fall into the motel category. The **Southampton Resorts,** 1655 North Hwy. (Rte. 27; P.O. Box 1275),

After Dark in the Hamptons

The volatile, electric night scene changes from season to season. Your best bet is to check the listings in the *East Hampton Star* or pick up one of the many local papers, like *Dan's Paper* (free in supermarkets) and see what's happening. Here's a rundown on 1995's spots—it's anyone's guess whether they'll survive to see another "season."

In Hampton Bays, the **Canoe Place Inn,** Montauk Highway (tel. 516/728-4121), had live bands and a DJ, plus pool and video pinball; **Dublin Over,** 17 Canal Rd. (tel. 516/728-0707), featured a DJ. In Westhampton Beach, **Casey's,** on Montauk Highway, featured Top-40 sounds and attracted a youngish crowd; **Club Marrakesh,** 133 Main St. (tel. 516/288-2023), was another crowd-pleaser. On Dune Road in East Quogue, **Summer's** (tel. 516/653-5777) was the most happening singles' scene.

In Southampton, despite the high cover, people clamored to get into the **Club at Conscience Point,** 1976 N. Sea Rd. (tel. 516/283-5550); on Saturday nights **M80,** 1976 North Sea Rd. (tel. 516/283-5550), was *the* place; and Wainscott's **The Swamp,** Montauk Highway at East Gate Road (tel. 516/537-3332), catered to the gay crowd as it has done for decades.

In East Hampton, **Danceteria,** 44 Three Mile Harbor Rd. (tel. 516/324-2221), offered a variety of scenes and music.

In Montauk, **The Dancing Crab,** West Lake Drive (tel. 516/668-2722), and the **Mimosa Beach Cafe,** 148 S. Edison (tel. 516/668-3676), were the main contenders with **Kenny's Tipperary Inn,** West Lake Drive (tel. 516/668-3754), offering live Irish music.

In Sag Harbor, people showed up at the **Amazon Deck** (tel. 516/725-9000), overlooking the harbor.

Perhaps the longest-running live music venue is in Amagansett—**Stephen Talkhouse,** 161 Main St. (tel. 516/267-3117).

Other entertainment? The **East Hampton Cinema** (tel. 516/324-0596 or 324-0448) offers an eight-screen complex where matinees are shown daily during summer. This is a good refuge from the rain.

Southampton, NY 11968 (tel. 516/283-7600), has 60 pleasant modern accommodations, each with a TV, air-conditioning, and a phone. You can choose from among standard motel-style rooms, efficiencies, or one- or two-bedroom units complete with a kitchen/living room, a full view of the beach, and barbecue facilities on a patio. There's also a pool and two tennis courts.

Rates: In season, $290–$590 double weekends. Off-season, $99–$170 double weekends.

The **Southampton Inn,** 91 Hill St., Southampton, NY 11968 (tel. 516/283-6500), offers fully appointed modern rooms, plus an outdoor pool, two tennis courts, and dining facilities.

Rates: Summer, $460 double weekends. Off-season, $130 double weekends.

Southampton Dining

Breakfast

The best place for breakfast is **Doobie's Italian Diner,** 20 North Hwy. (tel. 516/287-3705). This diner also offers great lunches with Tuscan flair and has gleaned some fine reviews for its good contemporary American cuisine offered at night.

Hours: In season, daily 8am–closing.

Lunch & Dinner

Basilico, 10 Windmill Lane (tel. 516/283-7987), is a study in cream and sage. It affects a distinctly Tuscan air with its rough-cast walls and terra-cotta tiles, rush-seated chairs, and tall green plants. The menu offers a limited number of pasta, seafood, and meat dishes plus pizzas. There might be rigatoni alla buttera (with tomatoes, cream, sausages, cheese, and peas), which you can have as a main course or as an appetizer followed by bouillabaisse or free-range chicken served with wild mushrooms and madeira sauce. Three or so vegetarian dishes are offered.

Hours: Mon–Thurs 5:30pm–closing, Fri 6pm–closing, Sat noon–3pm (brunch) and 6pm–closing, Sun noon–3pm (brunch) and 5:30pm–closing.

Savanna's, 268 Elm St. (tel. 516/283-0202), was at the top of the dining scene in 1995. The space is unpretentious and tucked away in a historic building in a remote neighborhood at the edge of town. The frequently changing menu offers southern coastal cuisine using local ingredients and some real down-home American accompaniments. You might find pan-fried local flounder served on stone-ground creamy grits and collard greens. The chicken comes from North Sea farms and might be served with sage dumplings in a natural jus; Long Island duck breast and confit is paired with wild rice, winter squash, and cider-vinegar sauce. Prices range from $16 to $22. The appetizers are simple— local mussels and oysters or salads like the beet and Roquefort married with a luscious walnut vinaigrette. The pièce de résistance among the desserts is the pecan pie with vanilla crème Chantilly and bourbon-cara-mel sauce; the gâteau of Valhrona extra-bitter dark chocolate on toasted vanilla sauce is not far behind. A special $18 prix-fixe menu is offered from 5 to 7pm Wednesday. On Sunday you can enjoy a country breakfast featuring dishes made with organic eggs, nitrate-free bacon, and home-made sausages and country ham. Prices range from $6 to $12.

Hours: Wed–Sun 5–9:45pm, Sun 10am–2pm.

The favored seating at the **Post House,** 136 Main St. (tel. 516/283-9696), is the cozy low-beamed barroom with a fireplace or the adjacent room, also with a fireplace. The fare is contemporary American. Prices run from $16 for orecchiette with broccoli rabe, chorizo sausage, and Bermuda onion to $24 for grilled loin of venison with pearl onions, melted Brie, and morel demiglaze. Other dishes might be oven-roasted halibut with saffron beurre blanc or Long Island duckling with caramelized apples and champagne sauce. Among the appetizers are sautéed assorted wild mushrooms with Parma-prosciutto and truffle oil and Maine crab cakes. The desserts include crème brûlée of the day, ice creams, cheesecakes, and a chocolate-mango delight consisting of a tower of thin chocolate wafers combined with a light mango mousse.

Hours: Summer, Sun–Thurs noon–4pm and 5–10pm, Fri–Sat noon–4pm and 5–11pm; winter, Fri–Sat 5–10pm, Sun noon–4pm and 5–10pm.

People continue to flock to **John Duck, Jr.,** at Prospect and North Main streets (tel. 516/283-0311), for the reliable duckling with apple-raisin dressing. The decor is unpretentious. Other menu items—sauerbraten, wienerschnitzel, scampi, softshell crabs, prime rib, and steaks—are served with soup and coleslaw and priced from $14 to $23. In addition, many daily specials are offered.

Hours: In season, daily 11:30am–10:30pm; off-season, Tues–Sun 11:30am–10:30pm.

Old Guard Southamptonites still dine at **Balzarini's,** 210 Hampton Rd. (tel. 516/283-0704), a simple home-style restaurant whose windows are thrown open during summer. Northern Italian specialties predominate—lasagne, veal piccata, and scampi—supplemented by steak and other meat dishes, priced from $15 to $20.

Hours: July–Aug, Sun–Thurs to 10pm, Fri–Sat to 11pm; mid-Mar to June and Sept to mid-Jan, Thurs–Sun 5:30pm–closing.

Barristers, 36 Main St. (tel. 516/283-6206), has been here for years, which testifies to the quality-to-price ratio of its food, the appeal of its menu, and the comfort of its casual ambience. At night, the lunch menu of salads, sandwiches, and burgers (all under $8) is supplemented by specials like seared pepper-crusted tuna with Dijon-and-brandy cream sauce or braised chicken breast with artichoke hearts, sun-dried tomatoes, vermouth, and basil; all are priced from $14 to $20, with most averaging $14. The pleasant shaded courtyard is a favorite for summer dining.

Hours: Sun–Thurs 11:30am–10:30pm, Fri–Sat 11:30am–11pm.

The other famous in-town lunching spot is **The Driver's Seat,** 62 Job's Lane (tel. 516/283-6606), offering sandwiches, burgers, salads, and omelets that can be enjoyed inside or out. At dinner such entrees as New York strip steak and shrimp teriyaki or chicken piccata are priced from $13 to $18.

Hours: Mon–Thurs 11:30am–11pm, Fri–Sun 11:30am–midnight.

Le Chef, at the corner of Main and Nugent streets (tel. 516/283-8581), is a pleasant restaurant where the tables sport crisp white cloths and bentwood chairs. This place is good for lunch, when salads, sandwiches, and quiches are available. The three-course $18 prix-fixe dinner offers excellent value. You might start with duck pâté or snails with garlic butter, then follow with grilled tuna with sun-dried tomatoes and black-olive coulis, breast of duck with orange and ginger, or veal marsala. Finish with cheesecake or crème caramel.

Hours: Daily noon–3pm and 5:30–10pm.

Southampton
Special & Recreational Activities

Beaches: For beach information, contact the Parks and Recreation Department, Hampton Road, Southampton, NY 11968 (tel. 516/283-6000, ext. 233). Stickers are required at most beaches, except for South Main Street and Wyandanch Beach.

Bicycling: Rentals are available at the Cycle Peddler, 360 Magee St. (tel. 516/283-0330).

Golf: There are fine courses on the East End, but in Southampton you'll have to settle for the Golf Range on North Highway (tel. 516/283-2158).

Picnicking: Picnic hampers can be filled at the Village Cheese Shop, 11 Main St. (tel. 516/283-6949); Loaves and Fishes (tel. 516/537-0555), which offers special lunchbox menus; or more modestly at Ted's Market, 264 Hampton Rd. (tel. 516/283-0929), which specializes in creating well-stuffed heroes, and Southampton Deli, Hampton Road and North Highway (tel. 516/283-1774).

Tennis: Sandy Hollow Tennis Club, Sandy Hollow Road, County Road 52 (Exit 8 off Rte. 27) (tel. 516/283-3422), offers a seasonal membership for $850; it has 14 Hartru courts. Try also contacting the Southhampton Beach and Tennis Club, Gin Lane (tel. 516/283-1188) and Shinnecock Tennis, 240 Montauk Hwy. (tel. 516/283-7919). Southampton High, on Narrow Lane (tel. 516/283-6800), has courts open to the public. For additional public courts, call the chamber of commerce at 516/283-0402.

Windsurfing/Sailing: Windsurfing Hamptons, 1686 North Hwy. (County Road 39) (tel. 516/283-WIND), has windsurfers and sailboats for rent. Instruction is given. Windsurfers cost $30 for two hours; a Sunfish costs $85 per day.

WATER MILL, BRIDGEHAMPTON & WAINSCOTT

Area Attractions

A few miles east of Southampton, the village of Water Mill is on the edge of Mecox Bay. The **Water Mill Museum,** Old Mill Road (tel. 516/726-4625) displays early American tools and features craft demonstrations, an operating waterwheel, and a working grist mill, plus historic photographs and temporary exhibitions. The watermill windmill was moved here in 1814 from North Haven, hauled by 12 yoke of oxen, and was used until 1887.

Hours: Mid-May to mid-Oct, daily 11am–5pm, Sun 1–5pm. **Admission:** $2 adults, $1.50 seniors, free for children.

Quite a lot of literary figures hang out in Bridgehampton, and their literary gossip flies around the bar at Bobby Van's (see below). There are several antiques stores on Main Street and a landmark windmill built in 1820.

Besides the bars, Bridgehampton has a **historical museum** at the Bridgehampton Historical Society (tel. 516/537-1088), on Main Street, which has a blacksmith's shop on the grounds and another building housing antique engines and farm machinery.

Hours: June–Labor Day, Thurs–Mon 10am–4pm.

The constant roaring of engines that can be heard from May to early November on most weekends emanates from the **Bridgehampton Race Circuit,** Millstone Road (tel. 516/725-0888). And Bridgehampton has one of the few public golf courses–the **Poxabogue Golf Course,** Montauk Highway (tel. 516/537-9862).

The **Bridgehampton Winery,** Sag Harbor Turnpike (tel. 516/537-3155), offers tours and tastings.

Hours: May–Oct, daily 11am–6pm.

Water Mill Dining

The **Station Bistro,** Station Road (tel. 516/726-3016), is a very inviting place with banks of colorful window boxes. Located in the station, the restaurant seats only 40, and the menu is appropriately limited and carefully prepared using the freshest of ingredients. It always features such items as fish and stew du jour in addition to rack of lamb with shallots, wine, and mint sauce; chicken tarragon; and calves' liver with sweet onions and balsamic vinaigrette. To start there's sausage, tarte du jour, and house pâté served with brandied prunes. The desserts change, but if the chocolate cup filled with white-chocolate mousse and a touch of raspberry sauce is offered, order it. Ditto for the lemon mousse with raspberry sauce. Prices run $18 to $26. The room positively glows and the service is always winning.

Hours: Summer, Wed–Mon 6–10pm; the rest of the year, Thurs–Sat 6 –10pm, Sun noon–3pm (brunch).

Tucked away in Water Mill Square, **Mirko's** (tel. 516/726-4444) makes a statement for the chef/owner from the former Yugoslavia. In these two simply decorated rooms separated by a patio, continental cuisine is offered along with an occasional specialty from the Balkans—for example, among the appetizers might be Croatian stuffed cabbage. You might find warm vegetable-and-goat-cheese terrine with red-pepper oil and herbs de Provence or chili corn cakes served with caviar. To follow, there'll be about eight entrees. Seasonal examples may include sesame-coated tuna with soy-ginger vinaigrette; filet of beef with bleu cheese and port-wine sauce; or duck with a sauce of honey, lime, and vinegar. For dessert, the caramelized oranges with Grand Marnier over vanilla ice cream hits the spot, but chocoholics may prefer the chocolate sorbet or the white- and dark-chocolate-mousse terrine. Prices run $19 to $26.

Hours: Summer, Sun–Mon and Wed–Thurs 6–10pm, Fri–Sat 6–11pm; winter, Thurs–Sun 6–10pm. **Closed:** Jan.

Meghan's Saloon, Montauk Highway (tel. 516/726-9657), is a convenient place to stop on Friday nights en route to the East End.

Bridgehampton Lodging
The **Bridgehampton Motel,** Montauk Highway (P.O. Box 623), Bridgehampton, NY 11932 (tel. 516/537-0197), is the brainchild of Martha Stewart's daughter and certainly has shock value when you compare it to the genteel country inns and homes of the area. You can't miss the low-slung building with brilliant jade shutters. At the back of the parking lot is a nicely landscaped pool with a lawn alongside holding decorous iron lawn chairs for guest use. Inside, it's modern with a vengeance. All 10 rooms have a cable TV/VCR, a CD/cassette player, air-conditioning, a phone, and a minibar (without alcohol). The furnishings are starkly modern, but the amenities emphasize comfort—Frette sheets, down comforters and pillows, and terry-cloth bathrobes. It's a matter of taste whether you warm to the retro-1950s decor.

Rates: Summer, $175 double weekdays, $255 double weekends. Spring and fall, $135 double weekdays, $175 double weekends. **Closed:** Winter.

Bridgehampton Dining
Karen Lee's, 2402 Montauk Hwy. (tel. 516/537-7878), draws raves from locals and visitors alike. The room is simple and there's an outdoor porch

for dining. The cuisine is well spiced and the ingredients are fresh. Though the menu changes daily, some dishes regularly appear. Start with the hot peppered shrimp or homemade three-cheese tortellini with prosciutto and browned sage butter. Among the main courses the fish dishes shine—like the Montauk striped bass on sweet-corn fricassee with tomatoes, basil, and haricots verts or the crab cakes with a spicy scallion tartar. The chef isn't afraid to serve strong zesty vegetables like the broccoli rape that accompanies the rosemary- and sage-crusted ribeye steak. Prices range from $17.50 to $30, the most expensive item being the grilled veal chop with roasted lobster, mushrooms, spinach, and mashed potates. There's a nice selection of wines by the glass.

Hours: Summer, Mon and Wed–Thurs 6–10pm, Fri–Sat 6–11pm, Sun 5:30–9:30pm; fall and winter, Thurs 6–10pm, Fri–Sat 6–11pm, Sun 5:30–9:30pm.

Made famous by Truman Capote, **Bobby Van's,** Main Street (tel. 516/537-0590), provides a good bar, pleasant enough food, and plenty of gossip (you can meet everybody here). The restaurant has recently been remade and is now very comfortable. Its cuisine has been refashioned along Mediterranean lines so you'll find dishes like swordfish with purée of capers and lemon or tuna with fresh tomatoes, Gaeta olives, and pignoli nuts. Less Mediterranean is veal valdostana for those who relish the richness of fontina and prosciutto. Several pasta dishes and grilled steaks and fish round out the menu. Prices range from $14 to $26.

Hours: Sun–Thurs 11:30am–4:30pm and 5:30–10:30pm, Fri–Sat 11:30am–4:30pm and 5:30–11:30pm.

95 School Street (tel. 537-5555)—small, plain, and tasteful—serves some powerfully good food. The chef uses local ingredients whenever possible, like the Iacono farm chicken that's simply pan-roasted and served with garlic mashed potatoes and sugar snap peas, or the Crescent Farm duck breast with fresh mango and mixed-berry chutney. The fish dishes are extraordinary and fresh—the halibut baked in parchment with spinach, tomato, fennel, and onions, seasoned with fresh herbs and Pernod, is just what this fish deserves. The sautéed softshell crabs are made even more vivid with leeks, tomatoes, and capers. Vegetarians will appreciate the platter of grilled portobello mushrooms, spinach-potato pancake, corn pudding, garlic mashed potatoes, vegetable burrito with fresh tomato salsa, and rice. Prices range from $17 to $23. Even the appetizers are thrilling—crispy calamari with spicy tomato purée, crab cakes with cilantro and lime sauce, and warm organic bean salad with fennel, onion, arugula, and white Cheddar in a herb vinaigrette. This is a celebrity hangout.

Hours: Summer, Mon–Sat 6pm–closing, Sun 5pm–closing; winter, Mon–Tues and Thurs–Sat, 6pm–closing, Sun 5pm–closing.

The **Candy Kitchen,** at the corner of Main and School streets (tel. 516/537-9885), is everyone's breakfast and newspaper pickup spot.

Hours: Daily 7am–6:30pm (to 10pm in summer).

Wainscott Dining

Roger's, Montauk Highway at Townline Road, Sagaponack (tel. 516/537-7100), has been offering Hamptons visitors a fine piano bar and comfortable country dining for years. Chintz napkins, stucco, and gabled walls create a country ambience for duck with ginger-rhubarb or kumquat/green-peppercorn sauce, flounder meunière, or veal curry, all from $16 to $22.

Hours: Wed–Sat 5:30pm–closing, Sun noon–3pm (brunch) and 5:30pm–closing.

Bridgehampton & Area
Special & Recreational Activities

Beaches: The beach at the end of Job's Lane requires no sticker.

Golf: Poxabogue, Montauk Highway, Bridgehampton (tel. 516/537-0025), has nine holes.

Kayaking/Windsurfing: Main Beach Surf & Sport, Wainscott (tel. 516/537-2716), arranges kayaking tours and rents windsurfers.

Tennis: The Bridgehampton High School courts, on Montauk Highway, are open to the public (tel. 516/537-0271).

EAST HAMPTON

East Hampton Attractions

East Hampton was once voted the most beautiful village in the United States by the readers of the *Saturday Evening Post,* and you can easily see why. At one end of the town, stately elms arch over the street and the Village Green, their branches reflecting in the still water of the old pond, while at the other end of town the old cedar-shingled Hook Mill stands on a grassy knoll as it has since it began grinding in 1806. And in between along the Main Street stand lovely 18th- and 19th-century buildings that represent the town's venerable architectural heritage from 1649.

Note that East Hampton Town is a political entity that runs from the eastern border of Southampton Town to Montauk Point—thus including East Hampton village, Amagansett, and Montauk. The best way to explore the village is to pick up a **walking tour** at the chamber of commerce, 37A Main St. (tel. 516/324-0362; open Mon–Sat 10am–4pm), in a passageway that runs from Main Street to the parking lot behind.

On the other side of the town pond, south cemetery, and the Village Green stands the **Home Sweet Home Museum,** 14 James Lane (tel. 516/324-0713), so called because it was the boyhood home of John Howard Payne (1791–1852), actor, dramatist, and author of "Home Sweet Home," a song he wrote in Paris in the 1820s when he was homesick for this very house.

Hours: July–Aug, daily 10am–4pm; Sept–June, only five days a week; call ahead for hours. **Admission:** $4 adults, $2 children (infants free).

Next door, the **Mulford Farm,** 10 James Lane (tel. 516/324-1850), built in the 1650s, is the most intact 17th-century property in the village. Costumed interpreters demonstrate 18th-century chores in the house and barn; the period garden contains plants used in cooking and medicine.

Hours: Call for schedule.

The **Guild Hall,** 158 Main St. (tel. 516/324-0806), is East Hampton's cultural center, site of exhibitions featuring well-known and emerging contemporary artists. The galleries are open evenings before theater events. The Guild Hall also presents year-round programming—plays, a writer's series, a music series, and related educational classes and activities.

Hours: Summer, daily 11am–5pm; winter, Wed–Sat 11am–5pm, Sun noon–5pm.

Across the street, the **East Hampton Library,** 149 Main St., is worth a visit just to see the reading room's luxurious comforts. At the same address stands the **Town House** (tel. 516/324-6850), the first town meeting hall and one-room schoolhouse. It provides visitors with an interactive history class about 1860 led by a costumed interpreter. Next door, the **Clinton Academy,** 151 Main St. (tel. 516/324-1850), built in 1784, was the first chartered secondary school in New York State but now features an ever-changing collection of artifacts and furnishings culled from homes on eastern Long Island.

Hours: Town House and Clinton Academy, July–Aug, daily 1–3pm; Labor Day–Oct and Memorial Day–June, Sat–Sun 10am–5pm.

Art lovers will want to make an appointment to see the **Pollock-Krasner house and studio,** 830 Fireplace Rd. (tel. 516/324-4929), where Jackson Pollock (1912–56) worked. He and fellow artist Lee Krasner purchased the 1¼-acre farm overlooking Accabonac Creek in 1945, and here he created his innovative works that stunned the art world and made him the leader of the abstract expressionist movement. In the converted barn that served as his studio, visitors can see a photo essay chronicling the evolution of his art as well as the artists' milieu, including the paint-laden floor. The house can also be visited. It remains much as Krasner left it and contains prints by both artists, plus their furniture and personal library.

Hours: May–Oct, Thurs–Sat 11am–4pm by appointment only.

Beyond the junction of Main Street and Newtown Lane, on a brilliant-green lawn stands the lovely and fully functioning **Hook Mill** (tel. 516/324-0713), which began grinding in 1806 and continued until 1922 (it's still in working order). The burying ground behind the mill contains some stones dating to 1650, which are ideal for rubbing. Bring large paper and charcoal or chalk.

Hours: June–Labor Day, daily 10am–4pm.

Just north of the village is the area known as The Springs. The **Boat Shop** on Gann Road, off Three Mile Harbor Road, maintained by the Historical Society, is interesting, as is the **East Hampton Town Marine Museum** on Bluff Road, Amagansett (tel. 516/267-6544), which houses a collection of fishing, whaling, and other nautical artifacts, along with educational dioramas.

Today East Hampton is the center of Hollywood East thanks to such part-time residents as Steven Spielberg, David Geffen, Sidney Lumet, Kim Basinger and Alec Baldwin, and Kathleen Turner.

East Hampton Lodging & Dining

For authentic and exquisite lodgings coupled with friendly, unassuming hospitality, the only choice is the **1770 House,** 143 Main St., East Hampton, NY 11937 (tel. 516/324-1770). Eighteen years ago, Mr. and Mrs. Sidney Perle took it over and restored this beautiful old beamed home, filling it with their carefully selected personal collections: tall Morbier clocks, mantel clocks, and wall clocks of all sorts (Sidney's passion), plus eclectic objects that enliven and fill a room with character—like the Dobbs Fifth Avenue hatbox on top of a scallop-shell highboy in Room 3. Today their daughter Wendy brings her own talents to both the kitchen and the house.

All seven guest rooms are furnished with a distinct aesthetic sense— from the No. 11 attic room with twin beds, to the No. 10 suite with a private entrance, which is furnished with a hand-carved oak bed, a fainting couch, an oak fireplace, and a breakfront displaying some of the Perles' china collection. In the garden room (No. 12), richly decorated in blue, a leaded-glass window looks out on spring daffodils, while a sled sits at the foot of the canopied bed.

The same attention to detail is evident in the dining room, where fine oak tables are set with flowers in china shaving mugs and brass candlesticks crowned with hand-blown globes. Oriental rugs add a sense of luxury, and the room must contain about 10 antique clocks. The menu changes daily, featuring seasonally fresh ingredients. It might feature such summer appetizers as poached salmon or arugula with goat-cheese salad, followed by swordfish en papillote, stuffed filet mignon, or classic rack of lamb. Prices range from $20 to $24. The wonderful desserts range from strawberry-and-rhubarb crisp to a luscious fudgy house chocolate cake.

Rates (including breakfast): $125–$205 double. **Dining Hours:** July–Aug, Thurs–Sun three seatings beginning at 6:30pm; Sept–June, Sat 6–9pm.

The **Maidstone Arms,** 207 Main St., East Hampton, NY 11937 (tel. 516/ 324-5006), is a longstanding local favorite, across from the town pond and Village Green. This white clapboard building with green trim has the casual but semiformal ambience of a venerable beach house—wicker chairs and tables are on the front porch, and rhododendrons blossom in the garden out back.

There are 17 rooms in the main building and two cottages. All have a bath and are eclectically and individually furnished with brass-and-iron beds or Shaker four-posters with country quilts. The furnishings might include a butler's table and wing chair or a candlestand and club chair with bull's-eye mirror over the mantel if the room has a fireplace. Some rooms have painted furniture. Suite 61 is particularly attractive, tucked under the eaves and flooded with sun from the skylight.

Downstairs, the Victorian parlor has a book collection for guests' reading pleasure, and so does the oak bar. This bar leads immediately into the dining room, whose fine reputation rests on consistently well-prepared dishes like lacquered duck with Chinese five-spice sauce, tenderloin of beef with onion-thyme marmalade, and wild striped bass with beet purée, herb butter, and an inspired Stilton polenta. Prices range from $20 to $28. The favorite appetizer? Try either the cornmeal-and-cilantro fried Peconic oysters with black-bean mayonnaise and tomato salsa or the seared New York foie gras with a sauté of star fruit, curry, and Chinese black vinegar.

Rates (including breakfast): Summer, $185–$260 double; from $285 suite. The rest of the year, $175–$245 double; $285 suite. **Dining Hours:** Sun–Thurs noon–2:30pm and 6–9:30pm, Fri–Sat noon–2:30pm and 6–10:30pm. **Closed:** Usually two weeks in Mar.

You can't miss the rambling green-shuttered, white clapboard **Huntting Inn,** 94 Main St., East Hampton, NY 11937 (tel. 516/324-0410), sheltered by some very old elms and maples in the heart of the village. The 20 guest rooms are furnished individually, with unpretentious pieces. You might find a white-painted queen-size bed with a duvet set against chintz wallpaper, a Victorian-style chair and armchair, and a small secretary with a Queen Anne chair. Some rooms have brass beds with oak desks and chairs; others have wicker pieces. Room 201 possesses a delicate peach-colored fainting couch, while Room 211 overlooks the English-style herbaceous garden, where a brick path winds among the bright colors of the foxgloves, lavender, lupines, poppies, daisies, and roses. A wood-paneled cocktail lounge with a spectacular long carved oak bar and the Palm restaurant are on the ground floor.

Rates (including breakfast): In season, $160–$285 double. Off-season, $135–$185 double. **Closed:** Apr.

The **Hedges Inn,** 74 James Lane, East Hampton, NY 11937 (tel. 516/324-7100), occupies a classic old clapboard house with chocolate-colored shutters just down from the town pond. This property was granted to William Hedges in 1652 and remained in the family until 1923. It has an inviting air: Geranium-filled window boxes redden each of the five front windows, a brick path lined with flowers leads to the front door, a crazy paved patio fringed with flower boxes beckons with white wooden chairs and umbrella tables, and a small parlor with a TV and fireplace is available for guest use.

The rooms feature country furnishings. You might find a carved wooden bed combined with a sidetable draped with fabric and set against chintz wallpaper. The 11 rooms are large, with a bath, air-conditioning, and solid-wood closet doors. Several have fireplaces. Room 2 contains a king-size brass bed, two draped sidetables, a chest, and comfortable chairs. Room 1's bed sports a pretty eyelet lace eider; there's also a Windsor chair and a chintz couch that opens into a bed. Crabtree & Evelyn soaps, bath cubes, shampoo, and other amenities are placed in each bath, and a nighttime chocolate is set on the pillow.

A breakfast of croissants, danish, and muffins is served in a small bright dining room, where the wide-plank floors and oak chairs give a country feel. So do the flower displays—when I visited, a half dozen great sunflowers worthy of van Gogh's brush. The restaurant, the **James Lane Cafe,** specializes in traditional American/Italian cuisine. Prices run from $15 for linguine aglio e olio (with garlic and oil) to $25 for veal chop Chiara. The rest of the menu consists of dishes like swordfish, red snapper, veal marsala, filet mignon, and prime rib. The best place to dine is on the elegant flagstone terrace furnished with tables with market umbrellas. The interior dining room is sunny and bright and made even more so with its bleached wood decor.

Rates (including breakfast): Memorial Day–Sept, $160 double. The rest of the year, $135 double. **Dining Hours:** Mid-May to early Oct, Mon–Thurs 5–10pm, Fri–Sat 5–11pm, Sun 4–10pm. **Closed:** Early Oct to mid-May.

Outside of town at Three Mile Harbor you can stay at Jerry Della Femina's resort complex, **East Hampton Point Cottages,** 295 Three Mile Harbor Rd. (P.O. Box 847), East Hampton, NY 11937 (tel. 516/324-9191). The one- and two-bedroom cottages are individually decorated in country style and feature a living/dining room, a kitchen, and a skylit bath with a Jacuzzi. All have a TV and a phone and are air-conditioned. Facilities include a tennis court and a pool and the **East Hampton Point Restaurant** (tel. 516/329-2800), which offers dining outside overlooking the marina or inside in the mirrored dining room. The cuisine is fresh and the menu limited. Depending on the season, there'll likely be about seven dishes available, ranging from potato-wrapped Alaskan halibut with braised fennel, to pan-seared local striped bass with sautéed escarole and shiitakes, to steak with wild-mushroom hash. Prices range from $20 to $22. Appetizers concentrate on shellfish and fish selections. In season, transportation is provided to East Hampton.

Rates: May–Sept, $210–$335 one-bedroom cottage; from $360 two-bedroom cottage. Mar–Apr and Oct–Nov, $135–$260 one-bedroom cottage; $285 two-bedroom cottage. Dec–Feb, $100–$235 one-bedroom cottage; from $260 two-bedroom cottage. **Dining Hours:** Summer, Sun–Thurs noon–10pm, Fri–Sat noon–11pm; spring and fall, Fri–Sat 5:30–10pm, Sun noon–4pm. **Restaurant Closed:** Dec to late Apr.

More East Hampton Lodging

The Pink House, 26 James Lane, East Hampton, NY 11937 (tel. 516/324-3400), is a very hospitable and comfortable place. The house was built in the mid-1800s for a whaler captain and it's located by the town pond and Village Green, a short walk from the village center. Owner Ron Steinhilber is an architect with a fine eye for interior decoration and has made this an aesthetically pleasing lodging. Throughout the house are marvelous watercolors painted by his grandfather and other interesting objects. The rooms are well furnished with fine antiques, but always with a concern for comfort. Each is unique, but all have a bath, a phone, and air-conditioning. The Garden Room holds a pencil four-poster; the Country Room offers windowseats and wicker furnishings; the Attic Room is the standout, with deer trophies, a saddle, and blankets. As for the public spaces, the sitting room is inviting with a fireplace, books, a TV, and a good music collection; the wicker seating on the front porch with its hanging baskets is great for whiling away an afternoon, and the secluded pool in back has plenty of grass around it to lounge on. Start the day with a full breakfast, served inside or on the back porch, that might include house specialties like sourdough French toast and banana-walnut pancakes.

Rates (including breakfast): Summer, $255–$295 double. Spring and fall, $175–$210 double. Winter, $145–$165 double.

What makes **Centennial House,** 13 Woods Lane, East Hampton, NY 11937 (tel. 516/324-9414), extra-special is the quality of its decor and its 1¼ acres of secluded gardens complete with a pool. Near the Village Pond, this gracious home was built in 1876. The downstairs parlors are very comfortably yet beautifully furnished. The chairs and sofas are upholstered with glazed chintzes and silk damasks; the windows are similarly draped with valances; the walls support prints and art or ormolu mirrors like the one above the marble hearth. There's even a grand piano for those who wish to entertain. In the five rooms upstairs, guests will find lavish extras like down-filled comforters, fresh flowers, sweets, cordials, silver bowls of potpourri, and terry bathrobes along with standard amenities like phones, baths, and air-conditioning. The Rose Room contains an unusual corkscrew four-poster with a canopy, and all are beautifully furnished with antiques, including clawfoot tubs in several baths. My favorite room is on the third floor tucked under the eaves. If you're seeking complete privacy there's a three-bedroom guesthouse in the gardens. An elaborate candlelit full breakfast is served in the dining room, richly decorated with Schumacher and Scalamandre silk. The gardens are lovely—shaded by venerable trees, roses and perennials bloom. The pool is well landscaped and is an inviting alternative to the beach crowds in summer.

Rates: Summer, $210–$360 double weekends. Winter, $160–$310 double weekends.

At his early to mid-18th-century Ezekiel Jones house the **Bassett House,** 128 Montauk Hwy., East Hampton, NY 11937 (tel. 516/324-6127), friendly Michael Bassett caters to guests at a long refectory table in the kitchen, where he'll prepare whatever you like for breakfast (within reason). Good music fills the sunken parlor, where guests gather to read one of the many volumes in the bookcase or cozy up to the Franklin stove in winter. There are 12 rooms (8 with bath, 1 with whirlpool), for which Michael has painstakingly collected the furnishings at auctions and where he's spent many hours stripping paint from the original woodwork. His handiwork shows most exquisitely in the ground-floor room with wide-plank floors and worm-chestnut paneling on the walls and ceiling; a couch in front of the fireplace and a small rolltop desk set the tone. Other rooms vary in size and ambience, from a small single with enough room for a sink, a table, and a closet to a large double with an adjacent dressing room furnished with a hand-painted Victorian bed, ladder-back chairs, and a wrought-iron standing lamp. Two have fireplaces.

Rates: $80–$215 double, depending on season and whether the room has a bath.

132 North Main, East Hampton, NY 11937 (tel. 516/324-2246), offers an eclectic assortment of 13 accommodations. The seven rooms in the main house (two with bath) are typically homey and often small and basic. The nicest is a double immediately off the wide deck that's covered with flowers and plants: It contains a double bed covered with a colorful quilt, two sidetables, an oak chest, and a wicker folding chair. The cabanas by the spectacular private (thanks to the trees) pool are the choice accommodations because of their location: sliding doors open poolside, and the furnishings are simple in these cedar cabins—a double bed / couch, a refrigerator, and a bath. Midway between the main house and the pool, a small cottage shelters a studio with a fully equipped kitchen and a living room/bedroom heated by a wood-burning stove. Muffins and coffee are available at breakfast—help yourself. The grounds between the buildings are prettily landscaped and make you feel in the country.

Rates (including breakfast): May–Sept 15, weekends, $130–$170 double without bath, $160–$245 double with bath; weekdays, $85–$170 double.

The **Mill House Inn,** 33 N. Main St., East Hampton, NY 11937 (tel. 516/324-9766), is operated by friendly Katherine and Dan Hartnett. The Dutch colonial, with a front porch overlooking the windmill green across the street, was built in 1790. All eight guest rooms have a bath (three with a Jacuzzi), air-conditioning, and a phone; TVs are available on request. Each room is decorated in a different color scheme: The Rose Room for example, features rose-patterned wallpaper, wall-to-wall rose carpeting, plenty of lace, a fireplace, and a Jacuzzi. Furnishings range from wicker and pine to painted armoires. There's a parlor with a fireplace for relaxing.

Rates (including continental breakfast in summer, larger breakfast off-season): Summer, $190–$235 double. Off-season, $135–$170 double.

East Hampton House, 226 Montauk Hwy., East Hampton, NY 11937 (tel. 516/324-4300), offers motel-style accommodations in three modern buildings on 5 acres. The 52 units have air-conditioning, a TV, a phone, and a sundeck or patio. Facilities include a landscaped pool, two all-weather tennis courts, and a fitness room.

Rates: Late July to Labor Day, $170–$205 double weekends, $135–$175 double weekdays. Early June to late July, $160–$195 double weekends, $125–$165 double weekdays. Early May to early June and Labor Day to late Oct, $109–$115 double weekends, $95–$105 double weekdays. Late Oct to early May, $72–$85 double.

The **Dutch Motel,** 488 Montauk Hwy., East Hampton, NY 11937 (tel. 516/324-4550), is an appealing property. Although it's on busy Montauk Highway, the buildings are set perpendicular to the road so the noise is minimized. At the rear, the pool is pleasantly secluded by a high fence and landscaped with shrubs, a lawn, and a deck. The standard rooms are furnished with rattan—desk, chairs, and bed. The most dramatic accommodations are the Jacuzzi suites, flashily decorated in gray or dusky pink or beige and tan, each containing a mirrored circular bar, a bold floral bedspread, and a couch with upholstery to match. The large geranium-filled tubs and other shrubbery in front of the units add charm. Each air-conditioned room has a cable color TV, a phone, and various amenities in the bath.

Rates: Oct to about May 22, $60–$70 double. May 23–June and Labor Day–Sept, $65–$80 double. July–Labor Day, $99–$120 double. Rooms with Jacuzzi cost slightly more in each season.

East Hampton Dining

Breakfast & Snacks

For breakfast, sandwiches, and snacks at any time of day, head for the **Windmill Deli,** Main Street and Newtown Lane (tel. 516/324-9856), which sports a couple of tables outside; it's also a good spot to pick up the city newspapers. The best hamburgers are found at **O'Mally's** saloon, 11 E. Main St. (tel. 516/324-9010)—a good Friday-night revival spot.

Hours: Daily 11:30am–midnight.

Lunch & Dinner

For serious dining I've mentioned the **1770 House** and the **Maidstone Arms** above. There are also the following:

Nick & Toni's, 136 N. Main St. (tel. 516/324-3550), is the star of the current dining scene—a stylish place that wins for its food, ambience, and service. The scene is electric, made so by the rush of celebrities—writers, Hollywood stars, and others who like and can afford to drop in every weekend to see and be seen. Certainly the restaurant has an immediate appeal with its terra-cotta tile floors, French café chairs, and upfront bar displaying a broad selection of grappa. The dining room is artfully designed, with sculptural objects used as fetching accents. The new American cuisine, using local ingredients wherever possible, positively shines. It's fresh, bursting with flavor, and healthful. Among the appetizers you'll find several salads, like wild mushroom with toasted pine nuts, Smithfield ham, and sherry vinegar or wood-roasted Coach Farms goat cheese with grilled eggplant and spicy basil charmoula. Among the six or so main courses might be wild striped bass with Manila clams and saffron broth; grilled tuna with local corn, tomato, grilled red onion, and parsley-garlic oil; and grilled quail with chanterelle mushrooms. For an intensely flavored treat, try one of the wood-burning oven specials, like the free-range chicken with roasted potatoes, pancetta, garlic, and rosemary or the local lobster with corn, balsamic vinegar, rosemary, and thyme. Prices range from $15 for pasta dishes to $34.

Hours: Summer, Mon–Thurs 6–11pm, Fri–Sat 6–11:30pm, Sun 11:30am–2:30pm (brunch) and 6–11pm; winter, Wed–Thurs 6–10pm, Fri 6–10:30pm, Sat 6–11pm, Sun 11:30am–2:30pm (brunch) and 6–10pm.

Della Femina, almost diagonally across from Nick & Toni's at 99 N. Main St. (tel. 516/329-6666), is the other port of call for stars and the portraits here prove it, with those of owner Jerry Della Femina and his wife, Judy Licht, at the center. The discretion displayed by the small brass plaque that marks the restaurant is matched by the serenely neutral decor. The bilevel space is handsomely appointed in a Tuscan manner with tile floors, light maple chairs set at tables covered with white cloths, and little decoration except for such natural accents as wheatsheaf bouquets.

The menu is limited and the cuisine highly rated. To start, you might opt for the lobster-and-sweet-corn chowder with herb oil and tarragon or the grilled Sonoma foie gras with Sag Harbor honey and hazelnuts. You can follow with one of the pasta dishes ($19), like the simple spaghetti with toasted garlic, broccoli rabe, and baby clams. As for the entrees, you might find wild striped bass with red chard and pearl-onion sauce; roasted chicken with wild mushrooms, sweet corn, and roasted shallot potatoes; or ribeye with red-wine essence. Prices range from $23 to $28. It's notable that there are more desserts than main courses and they're certainly memorable—like the chocolate-and-banana tart with dark-chocolate ice cream or the terrine with crunchy dark chocolate and peanut butter.

Hours: Summer, daily 6pm–closing; spring and fall, Wed–Sun 6pm–closing. **Closed:** Mid-Oct to mid-Apr.

New York's famous **Palm** (tel. 516/324-0411) is located at the Huntting Inn, 94 Main St. Oak banquettes and brass accents in the dining room and an enclosed porch provide a conservative setting for their renowned 4-pound lobsters, huge steaks, and portion of prime rib priced from $28; less awesome fare include some veal, chicken, and seafood dishes, like veal marsala and française, sautéed shrimp, or filet of sole, priced from $17 to $23. The experience conjures up another time and place, but it's good when you're in that kind of mood.

Hours: Summer, Sun–Thurs 5–10pm, Fri–Sat 5–11pm; winter, Sun–Thurs 5–9pm, Fri–Sat 5–10pm. **Closed:** Mon–Tues or Tues–Wed.

Santa Fe Junction, 8 Fresno Place, off Railroad Avenue (tel. 516/324-8700), brings the Southwest to the Hamptons and does a pretty good job of it. The cuisine offers more than just typical chile- and cheese-daubed dishes. Here you'll find appetizers like quesadillas made with barbecued duck and wild mushrooms, tamales topped with wild mushrooms and chorizo in a madeira sauce, or delicious cornmeal-coated oysters with a rémoulade sauce. The main courses are similarly refreshing and surprising: free-range chicken grilled over mesquite with a jalapeño, sweet pepper, and cactus-pear glaze or the grilled jumbo shrimp marinated in citrus and grilled with ancho chiles and a fresh herb mix, served with tomatillo and roasted tomato salsa. Then there are the tried-and-true fajitas. Prices range from $14 to $18. The walls are decorated with those desert sun-bleached skulls, photos of the Southwest, and Native American patterns; the tables are set with burgundy cloths and cacti and the jade banquettes are evocative of the Southwest.

Hours: Daily 5:30pm–closing.

Michael's at Maidstone Park, 28 Maidstone Park Rd., The Springs (tel. 516/324-0725), offers typical American favorites: barbecued ribs, chicken piccata or marsala, steak with green-peppercorn sauce, and a variety of fish that can be prepared blackened, grilled, broiled, or baked in horseradish sauce. Prices range from $15 to $23. On Saturday night the $16 prix-fixe (with soup or salad and dessert) is a good value.

Hours: Summer, Sun–Thurs 5–10pm, Fri–Sat 5–11pm; winter, Mon–Tues and Thurs–Sat 5–10pm, Sun noon–3pm and 5–9pm.

The Laundry, 31 Race Lane (tel. 516/324-3199), has been a traditional favorite for years and is still a favorite of locals who appreciate a good meal in a comfortable casual atmosphere after all the weekenders have departed. The menu offers eveything from tapas, salads, and such appetizers as grilled portobello mushrooms with sage-roasted garlic and parmesan to pasta and a variety of entrees. You might find grilled swordfish with tomato coulis or local striped bass on a bed of black trumpets, cèpes, and chanterelles among the seafood dishes. Diners relish the mashed potatoes that accompany the meatloaf, the pan-roasted chicken with garlic and rosemary, and the fries that arrive with the steak and burgers. Prices run $12.50 to $21. In summer, ogle the crowd and the always-decorous flower arrangements; in winter, nod off in front of the fire.

Hours: Daily 5:30pm–closing.

AMAGANSETT

Amagansett Attractions

Only 4 miles east, Amagansett seems far less concerned with social events than does East Hampton. There are only a dozen or so stores along Main Street as well as a farmer's market. A block away, **Atlantic Avenue Beach,** a favorite singles' gathering spot, is known as Asparagus Beach because everybody stands, showing themselves off to maximum advantage.

More seriously, the **East Hampton Town Marine Museum,** on Bluff Road (tel. 516/267-6544), houses displays about the East End's fishing, whaling, and nautical heritage. Two discovery rooms for infants and toddlers house rotating exhibitions. At the back of the museum, kids can ring ships' bells and clamber over a fishing trawler jungle gym that's moored in the sand.

Hours: July 4–Labor Day, daily 10am–5pm; mid-May to July 3 and Labor Day–Dec, Sat–Sun 10am–5pm. **Admission:** $2 adults, $1.50 seniors, $1 children 2–12.

Amagansett Lodging

Bluff Cottage, 266 Bluff Rd., Amagansett, NY 11930 (tel. 516/267-6172), is 100 yards from Atlantic Beach, and from the front porch you can feel the sea breezes and look out at the ocean stretching beyond the neatly trimmed privet hedge. The handsome house was built in 1892 for a doctor and editor at Funk & Wagnalls. Each of the four rooms is well furnished with antiques—one features a carved rice four-poster, another a mahogany four-poster. Each is decorated a different color and everything is selected to blend with the particular color. One room is dark green, another peach, another rich cameo blue, and the last Windsor beige. The public areas are super-elegantly furnished with great personal style but with the warmth that comes from the sense that the objects have been carefully selected and acquired with love. In the living room is an old confessional in the corner, a beautifully carved partners' desk, and a French chasseur rug. The kitchen possesses a collection of antique English ironstone as well as faïence and Quimper. The grounds are well tended and contain stately horse chestnuts and well-coiffed shrubs, including attractive topiary.

Rates (including breakfast): $195–$220 double.

The Mill Garth, Windmill Lane (P.O. Box 700), Amagansett, NY 11930 (tel. 516/267-3757), a 100-year-old lemon-yellow clapboard house, has its own windmill and offers an astounding assortment of well-kept rooms with charmingly idiosyncratic furnishings. These are located in the old original farmhouse or in cottages around the property. The suites in the main house have a living room, a bedroom, a kitchenette, and a bath. Among the cottages my favorites are the English Cottage, with a private little garden area out back, an eat-in kitchen, two bedrooms (one with a four-poster), and a remarkable octagonal paneled living room; and the Carriage House, which contains a huge living room with exposed beams and fireplace, two bedrooms, two baths, and a private patio. Also attractive is the Dairy House with its skylit living room, screened breezeway, and private patio. None has a TV or a phone. Bikes are available; babysitting can usually be arranged. The beach is about a mile away, and the grounds are quite lovely.

Rates (including continental breakfast): $145–$195 studio for two; $155–$270 suite for two; $210–$270 cottage for two.

Gansett Green Manor, Main Street (P.O. Box 799), Amagansett, NY 11930 (tel. 516/267-3133), offers secluded cottage/apartments, each with a private picnic area furnished with an umbrella-shaded table and a grill. All are nicely furnished and contain a bedroom, a living room, a kitchen, a bath, and a TV; most have electric fireplaces. The pebbled pathways are prettily landscaped and everything is meticulously maintained.

Rates: In season, $140–$170 double. The rest of the year, $95–$140 double.

Amagansett Dining

Restaurants may come and go, but **Gordon's,** on Main Street (tel. 516/267-3010), continues to offer carefully prepared *and* served food in unpretentious surroundings. The only concessions to decor are a few hanging plants in the window and a central crystal chandelier, yet at night the low-lit room looks especially inviting. Specialties include scampi, sea trout, filet of sole meunière, veal piccata or marsala, mignonette of beef bordelaise, and excellent salads, including arugula that's grown in the backyard. Prices run $20 to $27. During the week there's also a four-course wine menu for $25 including two glasses of wine and choices from a limited menu that'll always have two fish dishes, a chicken breast dish, and a veal dish that can be preceded by a pasta dish or baked clams or mussels.

Hours: In season, Tues–Sun 6pm–closing; off-season, Tues–Sat noon–2pm and 6pm–closing. **Closed:** Feb.

Mount Fuji, Montauk Highway (tel. 516/267-7600), offers truly fine sushi in a typical Japanese ambience decorated with lanterns, sake drums, and a kimono. In addition to the sushi, a full Japanese menu is served—teriyaki, tempura, noodles, and other dishes. Prices range from $10 to $20 (the sushi-sashimi combination).

Hours: Mon–Thurs 11:30am–3pm and 5–11pm, Fri–Sat 11:30am–3pm and 5pm–midnight, Sun noon–11pm.

Estia, 177 Main St. (tel. 516/267-6320), is a comfortable place to repair for breakfast, lunch, or dinner. By day it's a luncheonette complete with a counter and red vinyl stools, and at night the lights are dimmed and the place is transformed into a bistro serving consistently good food. It's famous for its pasta, made on the premises and served with a variety of sauces. The pasta and the salads are served in huge bowls with portions large enough for three. Start with the turtle rolls—quesadillas that are filled with avocadoes, beans, tomatoes, onions, cheese, and sour cream—and follow with a pasta of your choice and a sauce selection (there are about a dozen; my favorite is spinach and sun-dried tomato with garlic and goat cheese). Or there are such special dishes as pan-roasted venison and oven-roasted striped bass stuffed with spinach, onions, carrots, and celery. For breakfast you can choose from an array of omelets and egg dishes, plus some eye-opening tortilla dishes. The wine list offers more than 20 selections.

Hours: Summer, Sun–Thurs 7am–2:30pm and 5:30–9pm, Fri–Sat 7am–2:30pm and 5:30–10pm; winter, daily 7am–2:30pm.

East Hampton & Amagansett
Special & Recreational Activities

Beaches: Access to beaches is rather complex. Parking permits are issued by both the village and the town (which stretches all the way to Montauk), but village permits may not be used at town beaches and vice versa. For information about town beaches, contact the Town Clerk's office at the Town Hall, Pantigo Road, East Hampton (tel. 516/324-4142 or 324-4143). For information about village beaches, contact the beach office at Main Beach (at the end of Ocean Avenue) or the Village Hall, 1 Cedar St., East Hampton (tel. 516/324-4150). Don't park without paying a fee or obtaining a permit—you'll certainly be fined and your car could be towed. You can park at Main Beach and in Amagansett at Atlantic Avenue Beach without a sticker, but you must pay a fee. Check with your accommodations about securing temporary stickers.

Bicycling: For rentals, try Bermuda Bikes, 36 Gingerbread Lane, East Hampton (tel. 516/324-6688).

Boating: Uhleins is the only place that rents boats. See the Montauk chapter that follows.

Picnicking: Lavish picnic ingredients can be found at the Barefoot Contessa, 46 Newtown Lane, East Hampton (tel.516/324-0240), where even potato salad can set you back several dollars. But it's worth the visit for the luscious displays and for the people-watching. Less exotic picnic fare can be found at the Windmill Deli on Main Street in East Hampton.

Tennis: Three town courts are located at the Springs Recreation Area, off Old Stone Highway; four courts are available at Abraham's Path Park, Abrahams Path, Amagansett. Behind the East Hampton high school on Long Lane, about a dozen courts are open to the public for a nominal fee. Some courts are open to the public at the following: Buckskill Tennis Club, Buckskill Road (tel. 516/324-2243); East Hampton Racquet Club, Buckskill Road (tel. 516/324-5155); and Green Hollow Tennis Club, Green Hollow Road (tel. 516/324-0297).

Windsurfing: For surfing equipment, try Main Beach Surf & Sport, Montauk Highway, Wainscott (tel. 516/537-2716).

Montauk

Distance in Miles: 124

Estimated Driving Time: 2 to 4 hours, depending on Long Island Expressway traffic.

◄o►◄o►◄o►◄o►◄o►

Driving: Take the Long Island Expressway to Exit 70, taking Rte. 111 south to Rte. 27 east.

Bus: The best bet is the Hampton Jitney. Call 212/895-1941 or 516/936-0440 for reservations.

Train: Take the Long Island Rail Road from Penn Station (tel. 718/454-5477).

Further Information: For more about New York in general, contact the **Division of Tourism,** New York State Department of Economic Development, One Commerce Plaza, Albany, NY 12245 (tel. 518/474-4116).

For specific information about Montauk, contact the **Montauk Chamber of Commerce,** Montauk Highway (P.O. Box 5029), Montauk, NY 11954 (tel. 516/668-2428).

For general information about Long Island, contact the **Long Island Convention and Visitor's Bureau,** 350 Vanderbilt Pkwy., Suite 103, Hauppauge, NY 11788 (tel. 516/951-3440).

◄o►◄o►◄o►◄o►◄o►

Montauk is different from the rest of the Hamptons. Once you get out of East Hampton and onto Old Montauk Highway, the two-lane road rolls along beside the dunes and the ocean as if cutting through a Marsden Hartley painting, until suddenly there below you huddles Montauk like some isolated western frontier town. Compared to the frenetic chic of East Hampton and Southampton, Montauk remains the Cinderella left behind for family-style vacationing. It has a far less contrived air—there are no boutiques here, only the sea, the gulls, the gorse and beachplum, the sand and the sky, all sometimes blotted out by the mysterious mist that rises off the ocean and rolls in as if it were peeled from a great cylindrical drum.

Events & Festivals to Plan Your Trip Around

June: Blessing of the Fleet, Town Dock (early June).
July: Shark Tag Tournament, Montauk Marine Basin (mid-July).
August: Concert at Deep Hollow Ranch.
October: Full Moon Bass Tournament at the Marine Basin.

Besides the landscape, Montauk has some of the most romantic history in the area. Montauk is almost an island—surrounded by water on three sides and on the fourth by Hither Hills and the state park. In fact, you go "on" and "off" Montauk, a local expression used ever since the English settlers bought the land from the Montaukett Indians in 1655. Adrian Block was the first white man to set foot on Montauk. Lord Gardiner, who moved across from Saybrook, Conn., was the first to take possession of his land grant, which has remained in the Gardiner family since 1639.

The Old Montauk Highway was traced out in the 1700s by Hampton ranchers who in spring and summer grazed horses, sheep, and cattle on the 15,000 acres patterned with 2,000 acres of lakes and ponds and in late fall herded them off the peninsula. Animals were driven here from as far west as Patchogue; and the cattle drive was quite an event until well into the 1900s, when volunteer cowboys rode alongside the herd. Teddy Roosevelt and his Rough Riders fitted in very well with the 29,500 veterans of the Spanish-American War who came here to recuperate from diseases caused by bad food and water.

Three houses were built for the keepers of the herds, and they remained the only buildings—except for the lighthouse, which was built in 1796 and has stood here ever since. **First House** was built in 1774; **Second House,** now a museum run by the Historical Society (tel. 516/668-5340), with an interesting herb garden in back, was built in 1797 (the original had been erected in 1746).

Hours: Thurs–Tues 10am–4pm. **Admission:** $2 adults, $1 children.

Third House was first built in 1742, although the present structure dates from 1806. The houses also served as inns for the hardy travelers who braved the mosquitoes and the atrocious roads to come for the fine fishing (which still draws thousands) and game shooting.

In 1879 the heirs of the early proprietors sold Montauk for $151,000 to Arthur W. Benson of Bensonhurst, who brought railroad magnates and his cronies from Standard Oil out for visits, and they built a few "cottages" at the Point, calling themselves the Montauk Association. In 1895 Benson sold 5,500 acres to Austin Corbin and Charles M. Pratt, who brought the Long Island Rail Road from Sag Harbor out to Montauk and had dreams of making the town a major port of entry for the whole country. Those dreams were never realized, and the dreams of another man, Carl Graham Fisher, were also dashed (thank goodness), for he wanted to turn Montauk into a northern version of Miami Beach, which he'd developed. He laid out the town and built the golf course, the polo field, the Manor, the tall office building in town (now a condominium), indoor tennis courts, and a theater. The Surf Club and Yacht Club were established, as well as the casino on Star Island. He also opened the jetty into Lake Montauk. His dream collapsed along with the stock market in 1929.

Several legendary characters and romantic tales are attached to the area—tales of pirates and bootleggers lying off Montauk Point waiting to bring their illicit cargo ashore, legends of Native Americans and their burial grounds. One such tale reveals the relationship that developed between the sachem of the Montauketts, Wyandanch, and Lion Gardiner, proprietor of Gardiner's Island and one of East Hampton's founders. Wyandanch and Gardiner had gone through the rite of blood brotherhood, and when the Narragansett Indians came down from Rhode Island and carried off Wyandanch's daughter, Gardiner arranged for her ransom. For this, in 1659 Wyandanch gave Gardiner much of the land that's now Smithtown. Indian Stephen Pharoh, known as Stephen Talkhouse, who thought nothing of walking to Brooklyn, was exhibited by P. T. Barnum as the greatest walker of all time. Another Indian associated with the area was Samson Occom, a Mohegan who came from Connecticut to the Montauketts to preach. He wrote hymns that are still sung today and raised in England the £12,000 sterling with which Dartmouth College was founded in 1769.

Montauk Attractions

For beach and seascape lovers, Montauk offers an incredible variety of things to do (see "Montauk Special & Recreational Activities," later in this chapter) and many things to see. The first destination is usually the **Montauk Point Lighthouse** (tel. 516/668-2544). Built in 1797 by order of George Washington at a cost of $23,000, it stands 108 feet high, its flashing lantern visible for 25 miles. Originally it stood 297 feet from the cliff's edge; now, because of erosion, it's only 50 feet away. The antique lens was donated by the French in 1860 and has been operating ever since. The light marks the craggy shoreline, standing strongly isolated against the sea and sky, surrounded by masses of wild dogwood roses that ramble all over the terrain.

Hours: Mon–Fri 10:30am–4:30pm, Sat–Sun 10:30am–6pm. **Admission:** $2.50 adults, $1 children 6–11.

Montauk Harbor is a second major attraction. Always alive with commercial fishing activity, the harbor is also the site of a shopping complex that attracts many browsers. The harbor at Montauk holds more fishing records than any other single port in the world, and 1986 added to them. Excitement ran through the whole East End when two world shark

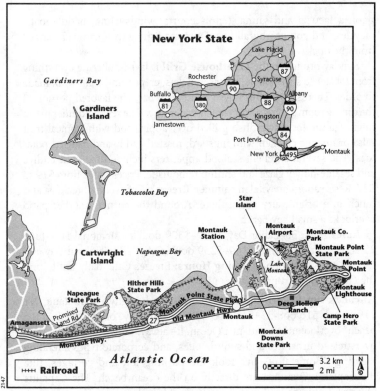

records were broken within a few days of each other. Crowds gathered to view the 17-foot-long great white shark weighing 3,540 pounds, caught by rod and reel.

The town consists of a strange, amorphous collection of motels and shops clustered around the Florentine-looking **tower-folly** built by Carl Fisher. Just east of town, the famous **Manor** stretches along the bluff and continues to survive despite the perpetual rumors that it's about to be turned into a resort-condominium.

Montauk Lodging

The **Montauk Resort and Marina,** 32 Star Island Rd., Montauk, NY 11954 (tel. 516/668-3100), has a sea resort air. The property is located on an island with its own 232-slip marina alongside, with a lighthouse towering above the accommodations. Dining facilities include a classic outdoor cabana-style bar at waterside. Luxury detailing extends to the decor of the 107 rooms, where louvered doors lead to the tiled baths (with robes and oversize fluffy towels), the closets are large, and gray-and-purple-upholstered bamboo furnishings and marble-topped tables and dressers are set against weathered-wood paneling. An extra touch is nightly turn-down. The extensive facilities include two outdoor pools and one indoor pool, a Jacuzzi and sauna, tennis courts, windsurfing, paddleboats, bicycles, and golf nearby, all free. Deep-sea fishing trips can be arranged from the dock.

Sunday brunch in the **Lighthouse Grill** is lavish, offering everything from lobster to steak Diane, pastas, omelets, crêpes, and waffles, all made to order. There's also a fresh oyster and clam bar. The favored portion of the dining room affords a spectacular water view. The regular dinner menu might feature local swordfish grilled over applewood with tropical fruit salsa or organic chicken with mustard, roasted garlic, and mashed potatoes. The several excellent seafood appetizers include tuna with endive and sesame-honey glaze and shrimp rémoulade. Prices range from $19 to $27. Reservations are vital in summer. **Breeze's Cafe** serves breakfast and lunch in a bright, airy atmosphere. Around the corner, another patio overlooks a small bay beach.

Rates: June 30–Labor Day, $209–$309 double. Memorial Day–June 29 and Labor Day–Sept, $169–$259 double. Apr 28–Memorial Day and Oct, $129–$209 double. **Dining Hours:** Breeze's Cafe, daily until 3pm; the Grill, daily 6–10pm.

Gurney's Inn Resort and Spa, Old Montauk Highway, Montauk, NY 11954 (tel. 516/668-2345 or 668-3203), is directly "on the brink o' the beach" overlooking the Atlantic Ocean. It's always crowded with the rich, overstressed urbanites and suburbanites, and corporate types attending meetings. Some units overlook the parking lot, and cottages, like the Captain's Quarters, are directly on the ocean beach. The Captain's Quarters features such luxuries as two double beds; a color TV; a phone in the living room and bedroom; two baths; a dressing room; a 30-foot terrace; a corner double divan in the living room; a butler's pantry with a sink, a refrigerator, and an electric range; and individual heat and air-conditioning controls. The Crow's Nest has all of the above plus a fireplace. In several buildings, terraced into the hillside, there are time-share units that've been completely soundproofed and furnished in a modern manner, featuring beds with light-oak mirrored headboards, oak partitions supporting a collection of brass objects, a phone in the bath, a personal doorbell, and a refrigerator tucked under the vanity. All units at the resort have a color TV with free HBO, a phone, a coffeemaker, a refrigerator, and a tiled bath with amenities.

The famous attraction, of course, is the spa, using seawater for therapies and treatments in luxurious Roman baths and a large heated indoor swimming pool with floor-to-ceiling windows opening out to the ocean. Guests may use the pool, Finnish rock saunas, Russian steamrooms, Swiss showers, and exercise and weight rooms. The spa is open to the public for a daily charge.

The Sea Grille overlooking the ocean offers classic Italian cuisine. Among the entrees are several carefully grilled items—steaks as well as seafood, like swordfish with red-pepper/basil beurre blanc. Other dishes include duck with Catalina peach glaze, lobster Diavolo, and locally raised rack of lamb with rosemary jus, priced from $18 to $30. To start, choose among carpaccio, smoked salmon, or oysters on the half shell; to finish, sample any of the luscious desserts—pecan pie, tiramisù, amaretto cheesecake, or chocolate chiffon cake. Breakfast and lunch buffets are served on weekends. Spa cuisine is available: low in calories, salt, fat, sugar, cholesterol, and refined carbohydrates.

Rates (including breakfast and $30 allowance at dinner): Memorial Day–Sept 10, $165–$210 per person; spring and fall, $150–$200 per person. Extra person $100 in season, $80 at other times. Four-night minumum July–Aug.

In town, **Montauk Manor,** Edgemere Street (R.D. 2, Box 226C), Montauk, NY 11954 (tel. 516/668-4400), occupies a Tudoresque manor house on Signal Hill surrounded by 12 acres. It was built in 1927 as a luxury resort hotel by Carl Fisher. Today it's a restored National Landmark. When you enter the vaulted lobby with its massive beams, rounded arches, and stone floor you'll feel as if you're stepping into the Middle Ages. The 140 accommodations are studios or one- or two-bedroom units with kitchens. Many are duplexes with two baths, terraces, and private patios. The furnishings are typically modern. There's a restaurant on the premises, **Laurentide** (tel. 516/668-4400), between the building's two wings; it provides alfresco dining on the terrace in summer. The limited menu offers such simple classics as grilled salmon with dill sauce, leg of lamb with rosemary, and duckling with Grand Marnier glaze. Prices range from $16 to $23. To start, choose the duck pâté with apricots or the array of smoked salmon, gravlax, and salmon tartare. Facilities include a fitness center, indoor and outdoor pools, three tennis courts, and a squash court. Complimentary jitney service is offered to the beach.

Rates: Late June to Labor Day, $155-$205 studio or one-bedroom unit. Labor Day–Columbus Day, $105–$150 studio or one-bedroom unit. The rest of the year, $95–$140 studio or one-bedroom unit. **Dining Hours:** Daily 7am–10pm.

One of Montauk's nicest accommodations is **The Panoramic View,** Old Montauk Highway, Montauk, NY 11954 (tel. 516/668-3000), set on 10 acres that've been carefully landscaped to create privacy and serenity through the abundant use of pine shrubs. The grounds are immaculately kept and always blazing with seasonal colors—begonias, scarlet pimpernels, flame flowers, and the like.

The management is extremely friendly and obliging, offering a variety of accommodations to suit most tastes in buildings that are terraced into the hillside at different elevations. Barbecues are conveniently tucked away around the property. Highpoint and Point of View are older-looking but pleasantly furnished in country colonial furnishings; Salt Sea is closest to the 1,000-foot ocean beach; Valley View is an ultramodern three-story unit with less charm and privacy. The rooms here are also furnished in colonial-country decor. The games room is located inside this building, and the kidney-shaped outdoor pool is very convenient. Three beach homes with two bedrooms, two baths, a living room with a fireplace, a porch, and a patio are also available. All rooms are air-conditioned and have individually controlled heat, a kitchenette, a color TV, and a phone. The only drawback for beach buffs is the steep steps cut into the hillside that go down to the ocean. No children under 10 are accepted.

Rates: In season, $102–$192 1½-room unit; $168–$218 2½-room suite; $418 cottage for four. Apr 7–June 23 and Sept 11–Nov 5, $76–$112 1½-room unit; $102–$120 2½-room suite; $256 cottage for four.

Sadly, more and more condominiums are going up along the dune approach to Montauk, obscuring the dunes and the ocean with boxlike monstrosities. Most are managed and rented out. They often make ideal accommodations for two couples traveling together since they usually offer suitelike accommodations. There's really very little to distinguish one from the other (unless you're planning to buy, of course). All have immediate access to the beach.

The most attractive of these to me is **Sea Crest**, Old Montauk Highway, Amagansett, NY 11930 (tel. 516/267-3159), which has a more rustic appearance than some of the others. The best accommodations are in the second-floor units whose balconies have ocean views. Other buildings are clustered closer to the pool area. Accommodations are either studios or one- or two-bedroom units, each with air-conditioning, a TV with HBO, and an equipped kitchen. The grounds are pleasantly landscaped with shrubs and conifers, and barbecues are available in one area. Facilities include a pool, two tennis courts, handball, shuffleboard, and basketball courts.

Rates (weekends): Mid-June to mid-July, $195–$215 studio; $175–$255 one-bedroom unit; $235–$375 two-bedroom unit. Mid-July to mid Sept, $220–$235 studio; $195–$275 one-bedroom unit; $265–$415 two-bedroom unit. May to mid-June and mid-Sept to early Oct, $115–$119 studio; $95–$145 one-bedroom unit; $125–$220 two-bedroom unit. Mid-Oct to Apr, $100–$105 studio; $85–$130 one-bedroom unit; $115–$160 two-bedroom unit. Weekday rates slightly less.

Windward Shores, Old Montauk Highway (P.O. Box L), Amagansett, NY 11930 (tel. 516/267-8600), is equidistant from Amagansett and Montauk. Here apartments arranged around a central grass courtyard with a pool offer a choice of oceanfront and ocean-view locations. The open-design units are spanking modern, featuring semi-equipped kitchens (with an electric stove, a refrigerator, a dishwasher, a toaster, and flatware) opening into a skylit living room with a pull-out couch, a TV, and a dining area; a spiral staircase leads to a double bedroom, all furnished in beige. From the decks you can literally jump down onto the Napeague dunes bordering the ocean. Two all-weather tennis courts and an outdoor pool complete the facilities.

Rates: Late July to Labor Day, $230–$470 double weekends, $175–$370 double weekdays. Late June to late July, $205–$415 double weekends, $140–$325 double weekdays. Early May to late June and Labor Day to early Oct, $105–$210 double weekends, $75–$155 double weekdays. Early Oct to early May, $75–$160 double weekends, $70–$135 double weekdays.

At **The Hermitage,** Old Montauk Highway (P.O. Box 1127), Amagansett, NY 11930 (tel. 516/267-6151), the units are furnished individually by their owners. All have balconies, two bedrooms, a living and dining room, and full kitchen facilities. There's a pool and also access to the beach—beach chairs, umbrellas, and towels are provided. Two tennis courts complete the scenario.

Rates: Late July to Labor Day, $390–$440 double weekends, $320–$385 double weekdays. Late June to late July, $305–$390 double weekends, $250–$320 double weekdays. Mid-May to late June and Labor Day to early Oct, $135–$210 double weekends, $100–$160 double weekdays. Mid-Mar to mid-May and early Oct to Jan, $100–$160 double weekends, $85–$110 double weekdays.

Driftwood on the Ocean, Old Montauk Highway (P.O. Box S), Montauk, NY 11954 (tel. 516/668-5744), is an ideal family place with direct access to the beach from motel-style units sheltered from the ocean by the dunes. A concrete-surrounded pool and two tennis courts are set behind the parking area, while a children's playground and games are set still farther back on the property. Accommodations range from cottages and two-room suites to studio efficiencies with dining, sleeping, and sitting areas, plus a small kitchenette. Furnishings are IKEA modern.

Rates: Mid-June to mid-Sept, $153–$173 double. Early May to mid-June, $91–$109 double. Mid-Sept to mid-Oct, $98–$115 double.

Wave Crest I Apartments, Old Montauk Highway (R.F.D. 1, Box 86), Montauk, NY 11954 (tel. 516/668-2141), offers several types of accommodations in several buildings terraced into the hillside overlooking the ocean. All units have a TV, a VCR, a phone, and air-conditioning. Beach Dune Place contains simple units where the decks are only 20 feet from the ocean—it's like having a cottage on the beach. Some 20 or 30 feet back, Water's Edge has rooms with kitchenettes. In Panorama, pleasant efficiencies have a TV, a phone, and Scandinavian Formica-topped furniture; a sink, electric burners, and a refrigerator are housed in one compact unit. There's an indoor pool.

Rates: Late June to Labor Day, $135–$165 double weekends. Early to late June and Labor Day to late Sept, $95–$109 double weekends. Late Apr to early June and late Sept to late Oct, $80–$95 double weekends. Mar to late Apr and late Oct, rates slightly lower. **Closed:** Dec–Feb.

The **Sun Haven Motel,** Montauk Highway, Amagansett, NY 11930 (tel. 516/267-3448), is another good family accommodation. The motel-style units face toward the restaurant across a tarmac roadway that leads to the tennis courts and ultimately to beach access. A line of conifers and other shrubs screens the units nicely, and in front of every other doorway a pleasant graveled niche has been created for relaxing on chaise longues or at umbrella-shaded tables. The rooms are adequate, featuring industrial carpeting, modern couches, wire chairs, rattan beds with print bedspreads, and refrigerators. A functional indoor pool and tennis courts complete the facilities.

Rates: Mid-June to Labor Day, $150–$155 double weekends. The rest of the year, $90–$95 double weekend.

At the **Surf Club,** P.O. Box 1174, Montauk, NY 11954 (tel. 516/668-3800), each of the 92 units is a duplex with a kitchen opening onto the living room, a deck overlooking the pool, and a skylit stairway leading to either one or two small bedrooms and bath. All have a color TV, air-conditioning, and a phone. There's a private beach, of course. The units are constructed around an outdoor pool. Two tennis courts and a bathhouse with steam baths are offered.

Rates (rooms for two to four): Late June to late July, $235–$325 double. Late July to Labor Day, $265–$375 double. Mid-May to late June and Labor Day to early Oct, $115–$170 double. Mid-Apr to mid-May and early Oct to mid-Nov, $80–$105 double.

Ocean Beach at Montauk, South Emerson Avenue, Montauk, NY 11954 (tel. 516/668-4000), has accommodations in two long two-story beachfront buildings. All are sleekly modern studios with efficiency kitchens and a color TV. There's also a glass atrium with an enclosed pool.

Rates: June 30–Labor Day, $120–$160 double. Late June and Labor Day–Oct 1, $95–$109 double. Memorial Day to late June, $85–$109 double. The rest of the year, $69–$95 double.

Charm exudes from **Lenhart's,** Old Montauk Highway (at Cleveland Drive), Montauk, NY 11954 (tel. 516/668-2356), a cluster of secluded cottages landscaped into the hill; conifers, shade trees, roses, and flowering shrubs create a tranquil country air. The accommodations are in studios or one- and two-bedroom cottages, each with a color TV, air conditioning, and a kitchen. Even the pool is sheltered by a hedge and softened by a grass surround.

Rates (weekends): Late July to Labor Day, $175–$185 studio; from $230 cottage. Late June to late July, $155–$165 studio; from $205 cottage. Mid-May to late June and Labor Day to early Oct, $109–$120 studio; from $140 cottage. Early Oct to mid-May, $90–$100 studio; from $120 cottage.

For clean, well-run, family-owned motel accommodations, try the **Blue Haven Motel,** West Lake Drive (P.O. Box 781), Montauk, NY 11954 (tel. 516/668-5943), which has 30 air-conditioned units, including some with fully equipped kitchenettes and two-room apartments with full kitchens. There's no phone in the rooms, but they all have a TV, a coffee-maker, and a refrigerator. There's a sparkling-clean outdoor pool. Owners Tom and Monica Brennan will arrange fishing trips and pick you up at the train or bus stop or at the airport.

Rates: Mid-June to Oct, $88 double weekdays, $105 double week-ends. Apr to mid-June, $62 double weekdays, $72 double weekends. Three-day minimum in season.

Montauk Dining

A really spectacular brunch is served at the **Montauk Resort and Marina** and at **Gurney's Inn** (see above).

In the last few years Montauk has acquired some top dining spots.

Harvest on Fort Pond, 11 Emery St. (tel. 516/668-5574), commands a view of the lake and in summer offers elegant water-view dining at tables set on a brick terrace. The dining room is a light and airy space, but what wins people's hearts is the inspired and superb food. The chef blends flavors with great success. You might find grilled salmon with cucumbers, dates, and walnuts or roast pork with a hazelnut crust and Grand Marnier sauce. Swordfish steaks are marinated in white wine and rosemary. For an appetizer try the grilled oysters with bacon. Pasta dishes, including a divine spaghetti with lobster, shrimp, scallops, clams, and calamari, plus pizzas and bruschetta, round out the menu. Portions are meant to be shared and the waiters will advise you about this at this very friendly restaurant. Prices range from $19 to $30 ($10 for pizza).

Hours: Tues–Sun 5:30pm–closing.

Dave's Grill, 468 Westlake Dr. (tel. 516/668-9190), is a small restaurant down on the marina next to where the Viking party boats dock. The room is cozy, with a low ceiling and comfortable booths and seafaring accoutre-ments; there's also a small awning-sheltered patio for water-view dining. The food is first rate, showing traces of Asian influence and concentrating on seafood, not surprisingly, for fresh ingredients are available right there at the dock. You might find Szechuan grilled striped bass or grilled salmon with rosemary sauce. For meat eaters, the coconut chicken and shrimp is certainly not a low-fat delight, but the honey-mustard sauce and curried rice mask it well. I recommend sampling the seafood, with fried calamari with chipotle tomato sauce or littleneck clams to start. Prices range from $16 to $23.

Hours: Thurs–Sun 5:30pm–closing.

The famous place that everyone knows about is **Gosman's Dock Restaurant,** West Lake Drive (tel. 516/668-5330), where a series of restaurants feed hordes of people during summer, while herring and black-backed gulls soar and whirl above or simply stand and stare. Here,

1- and 2-pound lobsters are the prime attractions among an assortment of softshell crabs, flounder, bluefish, bass, oysters, scallops, and clams, priced from $14 to $28.50 (for a 2-pound lobster). Fancier specials also appear on the chalkboard—like yellowfin tuna with ginger and soy, bluefish Cajun style, or sole with dill-Dijon. From the open but covered dining rooms you can watch the boats coming into dock—fishing trawlers, lobstermen, and pleasure craft, with seagulls whining and whirling hungrily above.

Hours: Memorial Day–Labor Day, daily noon–10pm; mid-Apr to May and Sept–Columbus Day, Wed–Mon noon–10pm.

The **Topside Deck,** perched atop one of the Gosman buildings (tel. 516/668-2447), offers a great vantage point and is fine for casual lunches. Take-out counters below turn out an endless stream of lobster rolls, steamers, and so on to customers who take their goodies to colorful umbrella-shaded tables and feast while watching all the harbor activity. The Fishmarket is open daily from 10am to 6pm during the season. The best time to catch the fleet unloading the day's haul is 5 or 6pm at Gosman's Dock.

Hours: Memorial Day–Labor Day, daily noon–10pm; mid-Apr to May and Sept-Columbus Day, Wed–Mon noon–10pm.

For a dash of Italy in Montauk, **Luigi's,** Euclid Avenue (tel. 516/668-3212), complete with checked tablecloths and a sprinkling of chianti bottles, serves a variety of veal dishes, including veneziana with artichoke hearts, as well as classic scungilli and calamari marinara or Diavolo and the ever-popular chicken parmigiana. Entrees run $10 to $23.

Hours: Summer, daily 5–10pm; spring, Fri–Sun 5–10pm. **Closed:** Mid-Oct to Mar.

The Blue Marlin, at Edgemere and Flamingo streets (tel. 516/668-9880), is known for its steaks. Wood tables and chairs set the scene in this unpretentious place. Carnivores enjoy 1½- or 1¾-inch-thick prime sirloin, double-cut lamb chops, prime rib, and seafood specials. Prices run $13 to $20.

Hours: In season, Wed–Mon noon–2pm and 5–10pm; off-season, call for hours.

It's affectionately known as "Lunch," and you'll see why when you reach **The Lobster Roll,** on Rte. 27 (tel. 516/267-3740). This shanty offers you the chance to sit and enjoy some seafood outside with the dunes stretching off into the distance or, if you prefer, inside among the nautical clutter of nets, glass floats, and ship's lanterns. Crab, lobster, or shrimp rolls; fried clams, scallops or softshell crabs; steamers; and fish and chips are just a few of the goodies that attract the crowds. Prices run $9 to $18.

Hours: Summer, daily 11:30am–10pm; after Labor Day, Sat–Sun 11:30am–10pm. **Closed:** Off-season.

After Dark

Montauk's hot spots include those listed in the "After Dark in the Hamptons" box (above), plus the **Montauk Resort and Marina** (tel. 516/668-3100) and **Gurney's Inn** (tel. 516/668-2345), where there's dancing and musical entertainment nightly in summer.

Montauk
Special & Recreational Activities

Beaches: Montauk's beaches fall under the jurisdiction of East Hampton Township. See "East Hampton Special & Recreational Activities," in the last chapter.

Birdwatching: During summer, environmentalists and naturalists lead daily nature walks spotting birds and flowers. On these walks you'll be on territory where the first cattle ranches were established in the United States. Walks leave from the Third House, East Lake Drive (Deep Hollow Ranch).

Boating: Uhlein's, Montauk Harbor (tel. 516/668-3799), rents 16- to 31-foot boats for fishing and waterskiing and plans to have kayaks in 1996.

Camping: The best and most popular camping is found at Hither Hills State Park, where sites are near the dunes. They're not for the camper in search of seclusion though—competition for reservations is so fierce that if you can get through to the camp reservation number (tel. 800/456-CAMP) you'll likely find that all the sites have been reserved. Reservations are allowed up to 90 days in advance. The average cost is $13 to $14 per day, and there's a minimum of seven days. Open from late April to November. For information, contact Mistix Corp., P.O. Box 9029, Clearwater, FL 34618 (tel. 800/456-CAMP). The campground office at the park (tel. 516/668-2554) doesn't handle reservations.

Fishing: Montauk is an angler's paradise, where 11,000 vessels and 75 charter boats hold many of the world records for sports fishing. Party and charter boats leave from Montauk Marine Basin, West Lake Drive (tel. 516/668-5700), mostly for shark or bluefish. An annual shark-fishing tournament is held (usually mid-July) when trophies as large as 1,000 pounds are brought in.

Viking Starship, Inc., P.O. Box 730, Montauk, NY 11954 (tel. 516/668-5700), sails daily for half- and full-day and/or night fishing for porgie, bass, bluefish, and tuna. A trip for blues costs

$38. Fishing tackle is available aboard. The *Marlin V* (tel. 516/ 668-2517) is another party boat. Smaller charter boats include the *Blue Fin IV*, P.O. Box 2084, Montauk, NY 11954 (tel. 516/ 668-9323), which charges $360 and up for parties of six and leaves from the Viking Dock; and the *Irish Rover* (tel. 516/ 668-1010), which docks at Captains Cove Marina on West Lake Drive.

Golf: The 18-hole, par-72 championship Montauk Downs Golf Course (tel. 516/668-5000) was designed by Robert Trent Jones and is one of the top 50 public courses in the United States. Greens fees are $20 weekdays and $25 weekends.

Horseback Riding: Ride in the footsteps of Teddy Roosevelt on a 1½-hour trail/beach ride for $37. Open year round, but by reservation only. Contact Deep Hollow Ranch, Montauk Highway (tel. 516/668-2744).

Picnicking: Pick up supplies at Gosman's Dock seafood store, which sells gourmet items and salads as well as seafood. Other sources include Herb's Market, Main Street (tel. 516/668-2335), open Sunday, and Ronnie's Deli and Grocery, Main Street (tel. 516/ 668-2757).

Sailing: Sailboat rentals can be found at Puff 'n' Putt.

State Park: Guided nature tours are given through Hither Hills State Park during summer. For information, call 516/668-2461.

Tennis: The Hither Hills Racquet Club (tel. 516/267-8525) has six courts available by the hour ($30) or the season. Facilities include a ball machine. Also at the Harborside Motel and Tennis Club, West Lake Drive (tel. 516/668-2511), where courts rent for $10 per hour. Montauk Downs State Park, South Fairview Avenue (tel. 516/668-5000), has six clay courts available for $6 per hour.

Swimming: Montauk Downs State Park, South Fairview Avenue (tel. 516/668-5000), has a pool if you don't like the beaches.

Whale Watching: This is one of Montauk's unique attractions (at least for Long Island). A scientific research crew leads a four- to seven-hour trip in search of these magnificent benevolent creatures and also dolphins, sea turtles, and sea birds. The cost is around $30 for adults. From January to mid-May seal-observation cruises also operate. Guided walks along the Montauk beaches are given. The visitor center in Riverhead, where animals are rehabilitated, is open weekends from 11am to 4pm. For information, contact Okeanos Ocean Research Foundation, 431 E. Main St., Riverhead, NY 11901 (tel. 516/369-9840).

Sag Harbor & Shelter Island

Distance in Miles: Sag Harbor, 106; Shelter Island, 110

Estimated Driving Time: 2 to 4 hours, depending on Long Island Expressway traffic.

◄O►◄O►◄O►◄O►◄O►

Driving: For Sag Harbor, take the Long Island Expressway to Exit 70, and pick up Rte. 27 east; turn left in Bridgehampton along the Sag Harbor Turnpike. For Shelter Island, take the bridge out of Sag Harbor down Rte. 114 to the blinking light and turn right for the North Haven ferry. Or you can take the Long Island Expressway to Rte. 25 to the Greenport Ferry.

Bus: The Hampton Jitney will take you to Sag Harbor (check off-season). For information, call 516/283-4600, or 800/936-0440.

Train: The Long Island Rail Road (tel. 718/217-5477) stops in Bridgehampton or East Hampton. If you come via the North Fork, it also stops in Greenport.

Further Information: For more about New York in general, contact the **Division of Tourism,** New York State Department of Commerce, One Commerce Plaza, Albany, NY 12245 (tel. 518/474-4116).

For general information about Long Island, contact the **Long Island Convention and Visitor's Bureau,** 350 Vanderbilt Pkwy., Suite 103, Hauppauge, NY 11788 (tel. 516/951-3440).

For specific information about Sag Harbor, contact the **Sag Harbor Chamber of Commerce,** 459 Main St., Sag Harbor, NY 11963 (tel. 516/725-0011).

For Shelter Island, contact the **Shelter Island Chamber of Commerce,** P.O. Box 577, Shelter Island Heights, NY 11965 (tel. 516/749-0399). During July and August, information is dispensed at the windmill on Long Wharf in Sag Harbor

◄O►◄O►◄O►◄O►◄O►

To me, Sag Harbor has always seemed the most real of the South Fork's towns, still rooted in its whaling past, unpretentious and unaffected by

361

Hampton chic and artifice. Sadly, that's changing. The boutiques and condos have arrived, and the stores displaying expensive gourmet items and the proverbial bar/restaurants done with light oak and brass are opening along Main Street. Still, nothing can really detract from the fine architecture of the town's 18th- and 19th-century homes or from the view across Gardiner's Bay from the main downtown dock.

SAG HARBOR

Sag Harbor Attractions

Like the earlier-settled Hamptons, Sag Harbor was first colonized by the English from Connecticut, who arrived and built a thriving town that, even before the Revolution, was a major port, second only to New York. In 1693 a bell for Southampton was landed here. Trade between Sag Harbor and the West Indies was initiated between 1760 and 1770. In the first session of the U.S. Congress, George Washington approved the act establishing Sag Harbor as an official Federal Port of Entry, appointing Henry Packer Dering Sag Harbor's first Customs master. The **first Custom House** (1789) in New York was located here on Garden Street (tel. 516/941-9444) and can be visited today. Here all the cargo was cleared, duties were paid, and mail was dropped. The house has been meticulously restored according to Dering's household inventory and reveals the lifestyle of a fairly affluent Long Island family between 1790 and 1820.

Hours: June–Sept, Tues–Sun 10am–5pm; Oct, Sat–Sun 10am–5pm. **Admission:** $1.50 adults, $1 children 7 and up.

During the Revolution, the town was occupied by the British, who established their headquarters at what's now the American Hotel on Main Street. Many Long Islanders fled to Connecticut. On May 22, 1777, Lieutenant-Colonel Meigs led a number of patriotic refugees across the Sound from New Haven in 13 whaleboats; raided Sag Harbor; burned 12 brigs and sloops at Long Wharf; seized 120 tons of hay, corn, and oats and 12 hogsheads of rum; and killed 6 and took another 90 prisoner. Two monuments on Union and High streets commemorate this daring raid.

After the Revolution, the town continued to thrive on trade with the West Indies and became an increasingly cosmopolitan community, with a newspaper, the *Long Island Herald,* established in 1791. When the War of 1812 was declared, Dering was put in charge of the Sag Harbor Arsenal and the populace overcame the 1813 British attack. The war, though, brought hardship and interfered with trade, and the disastrous 1817 fire made economic recovery difficult. It wasn't until the late 1820s that the port regained its importance, primarily because of increased whaling. By 1845 it had grown into the largest whaling port in the state and fourth

Events & Festivals to Plan Your Trip Around

June: The Whaler's Festival—whaleboat races, beard-growing contests, and so on.

September: The Hamptons Triathlon, a 1-mile swim combined with a 25-mile bike ride and a 10-mile run. For information, contact P.O. Box 643, Wainscott, NY 11975.

largest in the world, with a fleet of 63 vessels belonging to 12 firms. The biggest year was 1847, when 32 ships brought in 605,000 pounds of bone and 68,000 barrels of sperm and whale oil valued at $1 million. In all, during the brief period of whaling, $25 million was brought into the port.

To recapture the flavor of this era, go through the whale's jawbone into the **Whaling Museum,** at Main and Garden streets (tel. 516/725-0770), housed in a marvelous Greek Revival mansion that once belonged to Benjamin Huntting II and was designed and built by Minard LaFever. Besides the whaling equipment, the ship models, the log books describing four-year trips, and a great collection of scrimshaw, the museum features collections of guns, children's toys, and other items, all crammed into a series of rooms. You could spend several hours here looking at a portrait of Sag Harbor in 1860, a tricycle of the same date, an exquisite cameo carved on a whole shell, or the Native American artifacts excavated locally by William Wallace Tooker. You'll also come across objects that relate stories about local characters, like Fannie Tunison, an Edwardian lady who, even though she could move only her head and neck, created watercolors and all kinds of sewn and embroidered articles, some of which are on display. At the end of your visit you'll discover the differences among a bark, a brig, a ship, and a schooner (if you didn't know already).

Hours: May 15–Sept, Mon–Sat 1–5pm, Sun 2–5pm. **Admission:** $3 adults, $2 seniors, $1 children.

Across the street, the **Whaler's Presbyterian Church** (tel. 516/725-0894) also dates from this period. Designed by Minard LaFever in 1844, it was once crowned by a five-story tower that was destroyed by the hurricane of 1938. The walls slope in the manner of ancient temples on the Nile, and the parapets are decorated with rows of whaler's blubber spades that were finely crafted by ships' carpenters.

Hours: For a tour, call for an appointment at the number above.

When oil was discovered, the whaling industry declined. The population of Sag Harbor dwindled to 2,000, and the almost-deserted village languished until the Fahys opened a watchcasing factory in the 1890s. The labor used was largely Jewish, and for this reason **Temple Adas Israel,** Long Island's oldest Jewish temple and congregation, was built in

1898. It's well worth a visit to see the gothic stained glass and locally carved altarpiece. At about the same time the town was beginning to gain some fame as a resort, and this development continued, the town later attracting writers like John Steinbeck, who set out from here on his famous *Travels with Charley* trip. The tradition continues to this day. Many writers and artists have chosen Sag Harbor as their home, and you might catch them playing softball in the local park. History, tree-lined streets flanked by all kinds of old homes (from saltboxes to Greek Revival mansions to Victorian gingerbread confections), a lovely harbor where many summer visitors choose to dock and live aboard their yachts, and sunsets over bay beaches all make Sag Harbor a lovely place to go down to the bay again.

Sag Harbor Lodging

The **American Hotel,** Main Street, Sag Harbor, NY 11963 (tel. 516/725-3535), operates in a thoroughly Victorian atmosphere. Wicker chairs stand on the front porch, and the front parlor is filled with Victorian-style sofas and other pieces. The bar is dark and cozy, particularly in winter, when a fire burns; in summer, an overhead fan hanging from the stamped-metal ceiling hums quietly. Classical music in the background adds to the atmosphere. The rooms, reached by a separate entrance, are individually decorated in an antique elegant style. Room 2 has a sleigh bed set against candy-striped wallpaper, Room 6 features several Eastlake pieces, and Room 5 contains a high carved Victorian bed with a crocheted coverlet, an oak dresser, and wicker chairs. Fresh flowers grace every room.

The dining room is well known, particularly for its extensive (60 pages plus) wine list. There are several dining areas: the formal chintz room with a fireplace, where tables are set with crisp white linens; the skylit porch/conservatory, decked out with white metal chairs, rambling plants, and Mexican tile; and a third dining room in the rear. The menu changes daily but always includes extravagances like several caviar selections and foie gras to start. About a dozen main courses offer a variety of fish, poultry, and meat dishes—turbot with beurre blanc, tuna steak with béarnaise sauce, gallantine of chicken with pheasant mousse, rack of lamb with mint and garlic, and tournedos à la périgourdine. For the fitness-conscious there are items like grilled vegetables and fish. Prices run $17 to $30.

Rates: $185 double weekends, $120 double weekdays. **Dining Hours:** Daily noon–3pm and 5:30–11pm. **Closed:** Thanksgiving and Christmas.

Other lodgings are scarce in Sag Harbor. The one downtown motel, **Baron's Cove Inn,** West Water Street, Sag Harbor, NY 11963 (tel. 516/725-2100), has been converted into modern time-sharing units, although you may have some luck getting a rental. Second-floor units giving a view of the bay and the bridge are light and airy; furnished in light oak and Breuer chairs, they feature a sleeping loft. All have air conditioning, a TV, a phone, and a kitchenette. Facilities include a tennis court and an outdoor fenced-in pool.

Rates: In season, $210–$285 double weekends. Off-season, $85–$105 double weekends.

Sag Harbor Dining

Breakfast

Breakfast with the best view is enjoyed at the **Amazon Deck** on the wharf (below), but you'll have to wait until noon. Most everyone in Sag Harbor heads for **The Paradise** on Main Street (tel. 516/725-6080).

Lunch & Dinner

On the wharf, **Amazon Deck** (tel. 516/725-9000) commands a magnificent view over Sag Harbor marina out into Gardiner's Bay, one of the finest in the whole of the Hamptons. In summer the large deck is filled with happy visitors relaxing waterside. The dining room has a Mediterranean ambience, appropriate to its waterfront location. The cuisine focuses on grilled dishes like salmon, tuna, and ribeye steak. In addition you'll find a few pasta dishes, like tagliatelle with pesto and ravioli. Prices range from $12 to $24. The desserts are mainly pies and ice cream, as well as tiramisù.

Hours: Mon–Thurs noon–3pm and 6–10pm, Fri noon–3pm and 6–11pm, Sat for brunch and 6–11pm, Sun for brunch and 6–10pm. The deck is open daily noon–8pm.

At the **Bay Street Cafe,** 5 Bay St. (tel. 516/725-9613), past the small front bar area with windows looking out onto the dock lies a pretty dining room with a cathedral-style ceiling and rush-seated gatebacks set at tables spread with mauve cloths. The menu features dishes with Latin American/Caribbean accents: flounder with Cajun pecan sauce or Ecuadorian tuna steak sautéed with peppers, cilantro, shallots, and lime. There's also lobster or shrimp curry, served with peach chutney, and duckling with the sauce of the day. Prices range from $17 to $22. To start, there's a seafood appetizer of the day plus such items as clam fritters with jalapeño-tartar sauce and luscious fried Brie on a bed of spinach finished with sweet red-pepper purée. The brick patio, arrayed with tables sporting pink cloths and turquoise chairs, is a pleasant place to dine.

Hours: Summer, Mon–Thurs 6–10pm, Fri 6–11pm, Sat noon–3pm and 6–11pm, Sun noon–3pm and 6–10pm; off-season, Thurs–Fri 6–10pm, Sat noon–3pm and 6–10pm, Sun noon–3pm and 6–10pm.

Spinnaker's, 63 Main St. (tel. 516/725-9353), is a popular casual local spot for luncheon sandwiches and salads and such main dishes as crab cakes. The look is brick and brass and the food is okay for the price.

Hours: Sun–Thurs 11:30am–10pm, Fri–Sat 11:30am–11pm.

Sen, Main Street (tel. 516/725-1774), is a tiny restaurant, possessing only half a dozen or so polished wood tables. The menu offers typical Japanese dishes and good fresh sushi-sashimi.

Hours: Thurs–Mon noon–2:30pm and 6–9:30pm.

Dinner Only

Citron, 62 Main St. (tel. 516/725-7575), is a small elegant restaurant where the tables are covered with crisp white cloths and the chairs are of simple bentwood. The food is extra fine, though. The menu changes frequently but you may find such treats as rack of lamb with an olive tapenade and tuna marinated with ginger and soy and served on a nest of cappellini with Oriental vegetables. The seafood stew is filled with tuna, scallops, shrimp, and swordfish, while the duck is absolutely crisp and comes with a cranberry-pignoli sauce. Prices range from $15 to $24. To start, I heartily recommend the shrimp beignets with apricot-flavored mustard or the stuffed portobello mushroom provençal. As for dessert, try the almond brioche bread pudding with chocolate sauce or one of the seasonal cobblers.

Hours: July–Aug, daily 5:30–10:30pm; Sept–June, Wed–Fri 5:30–10:30pm, Sat–Sun noon–3pm and 5:30–10:30pm.

Locals (if you can count as locals those who come from as far away as Hampton Bays) swear by **Il Capuccino,** Madison Street (tel. 516/725-2747), a warm, comfortable place serving excellent, fairly priced food. The garden salad, tossed in a garlic dressing and served with croûtons sprinkled with cheese, is superb; the special fish of the day might come in a spicy marinara sauce; pastas include a tasty tortellini with pistachios; and standbys like veal parmigiana are available. Prices range from $10 to $17. Red gingham, red-glass candleholders, and jazz in the background give the place a lovely glow.

Hours: Summer, Mon–Thurs 5:30–10:30pm, Fri–Sat 5:30–11pm, Sun 5–10pm; winter, Sun–Thurs 5–10pm, Fri–Sat 5–10:30pm.

Tucked away, the **Inn at Mill Creek,** 590 Noyac Rd. (tel. 516/725-1116), is another favorite overlooking the busy scene, hoist, and boats at Mill Creek. The decor is simple—light oak and blue napery—and the food fresh and good value. A pianist entertains on Friday and Saturday (in season only, I believe). The menu offers a traditional selection of steak and seafood, priced from $14 for chicken marsala to $20 for twin lobster tails. Other dishes include broiled flounder, duck with orange sauce, chicken Cordon Bleu, veal parmigiana, and prime rib. During the week the price includes a trip to the salad bar. To start, try the clams on the half shell or shrimp cocktail.

Hours: Summer, Mon–Sat 6–10pm, Sun 5–10pm; off-season, Fri–Sat 6–9pm, Sun 5–9pm. **Closed:** Thanksgiving–Easter.

After Dark

The major cultural entertainment is provided by the **Bay Street Theatre,** at the Wharf, now in its fifth season. In the past it has premiered productions that went on to Broadway and other international venues—plays that starred such greats as Eli Wallach and Anne Jackson, Maria Tucci,

Mary Cleere Haran, Dianne Wiest, and Mercedes Ruehl. For tickets and information, call 516/725-9500. The season runs from mid-June to the end of August, with spring performances by cabaret artists and other singers.

There's a downtown **cinema** in Sag Harbor. Or, more interesting, there's **Canio's Bookstore** on Main Street (tel. 516/725-4926) and also down at the wharf (tel. 516/725-4462). A delightful place to poke around during the day, it hosts weekend poetry readings and other literary events in the early evening.

The Corner, Main Street (tel. 516/725-9760), is a real down-home hangout, but most nightlife action is found elsewhere, along Rte. 27 from Southampton to East Hampton.

Sag Harbor
Special & Recreational Activities

Beaches: Long Beach in Noyac is a narrow beach stretching along the bay and open to nonresidents for a fee.

Birdwatching: The Morton Wildlife Refuge, on Noyac Road (cross the bridge, along the bay beach, and turn right by the Salty Dog restaurant), is managed for migratory shore birds with emphasis on two protected shore birds—the piping plover and least tern. There are plenty of other shore and songbirds to spy, as well as pheasant, deer, and osprey. This is an ideal place for fishing and hiking on nature trails. For information, contact the Refuge Manager, Wertheim National Wildlife Refuge, P.O. Box 21, Shirley, NY 11967 (tel. 516/286-0485).

Boating: For boat rentals, see the Montauk chapter.

Fishing: In the Elizabeth Morton National Wildlife Refuge, there's good bay fishing for weakfish in summer or bluefish in fall.

Golf: Sag Harbor Golf Club, on Rte. 114 in Sag Harbor (tel. 516/725-9739).

Hiking: The Elizabeth Morton National Wildlife Refuge, where waterfowl, songbirds, mammals, and even birds of prey congregate, is lovely for nature rambles and picnicking on the small beach. For a permit, contact the Refuge Manager, National Wildlife Refuge, R.D. 359, Noyac Road, Sag Harbor, NY 11963 (tel. 516/725-2270). From Rte. 27, go 2 miles north on North Sea Road, then 4 miles east on Noyac Road. Also good for clamming, oystering, and scalloping.

Picnicking: Any of the beaches or the Elizabeth Morton Wildlife Refuge make great picnicking spots. For gourmet supplies, head to Susan's Gardens, 89 Division St. (tel. 516/725-5812), or

Provisions, at Bay and Division streets (tel. 516/725-3636); for deli and other German specialties, drop in at the Cove Deli, 283 Main St. (tel. 516/725-0216). For more mundane fare, there's always the supermarket across from the post office.

Tennis: Try the courts at Mashashimuet Park on Main Street.

SHELTER ISLAND

From Sag Harbor, it's only a short ferry ride across the bay to the rolling wooded hills and miles of white-sand beaches of Shelter Island, first settled by Quakers fleeing persecution in New England. Today it's an unspoiled haven for bicycling, hiking, horseback riding, and boating—and the residents aim to keep it that way.

From downtown Sag Harbor, cross the bridge and follow the signs to the ferry (turning right at the blinking light). Ferries leave North Haven from 6am to 11:45pm (until 1:45am during July and August and on fall weekends). For information, call 516/749-1200.

Once you're off the ferry, following Rte. 114 will take you all the way through Shelter Island Heights, where the island's few stores and restaurants are located, to the rim of Dering Harbor, where another ferry leaves for Greenport on the North Fork (see the next chapter).

Shelter Island Lodging

At the eastern tip of the island you'll find Ram Island, so called because it looks a little like a ram. It's attached by a very narrow spit of land, so the approach road appears more like a causeway. The island's most appealing lodging, the **Ram's Head Inn,** Shelter Island, NY 11965 (tel. 516/749-0811), is here on 4 acres overlooking Coecles Harbor. In this green-shuttered shingled Colonial, a group of scientists, including Einstein, gathered in 1947 for the first Shelter Island Conference on the Foundation of Quantum Mechanics. Country furniture and candlewick spreads are found in the 17 rooms (13 with bath). The grassy backyard, with shade trees and rosebushes, sweeps down to a private beach, where two sloops, two Sunfish, a paddleboat, and a two-person kayak are available for guests. A tennis court is also available. A bar/recreation room with an upright piano affords more entertainment, while the chintz dining room serves the best cuisine on the island.

The menu changes seasonally, but among the eight or so main courses might be seared striped bass with tomatoes and leeks or potato-crusted flounder, as well such local specialties as duck with fruit chutney and a tenderloin of beef with chanterelles. Prices range from $18 to $22. To start, I recommmend the warm goat cheese with grilled endive, roasted peppers, and beets or the lobster-and-corn bisque garnished with a corn fritter. The desserts are simple and seasonal.

Rates: Apr–Oct, $100–$135 double. Nov–Mar, $75–$90 double. **Dining Hours:** May–Oct, daily noon–3pm and 5–9:30pm; Nov–Apr, Thurs–Sat 5–9:30pm, Sun noon–3pm (brunch) and 5–9:30pm.

The **Chequit Inn,** 23 Grand Ave. (P.O. Box 292), Shelter Island, NY 11965 (tel. 516/749-0018), has been purchased by the proprietors of the Ram's Head and so can now be recommended as a place to stay. The guest rooms and dining room have been spruced up. The rooms in the main building are pleasantly furnished with wall-to-wall carpeting, beds covered with white spreads and decorated with lacy treatments behind the headboard, lace curtains, and floral wallpapers. The furnishings are often painted white, and there's comfortable seating and good bedside lighting for reading. The rooms across the street in the Cedar House still show signs of wear, but they're looking a lot better than they did, since they've been spruced up with repainted floors and wood paneling to provide a much lighter look.

The inn is the island's focal point and social center. People enjoy breakfast, lunch, and dinner in the dining room on the covered veranda or out on the terrace surrounded by flowering hydrangea and shaded by an enormous maple tree. Dinner prices range from $16 to $19 for such dishes as duckling with honey-citrus glaze, pork with Dijon mustard jus, salmon over lentil-and-lobster ragoût, or tortellini with pesto, prosciutto, and peas.

Rates: $90–$135 double; from $160 suite. **Dining Hours:** Summer, daily noon–3pm and 6–10pm; spring and fall, Fri–Sun 6–10pm. **Closed:** Nov to mid-Apr.

Overlooking Crescent Beach, the rambling **Pridwin,** 81 Shore Rd., Crescent Beach, Shelter Island, NY 11965 (tel. 516/749-0476), offers guest rooms plus an array of activities—swimming in the bay or the pool, windsurfing, rowing, bicycling, Sunfish sailing, pedalboating, hydrobiking, and tennis on three courts. It's certainly an ideal summer place. Wicker chairs and couches line the 40-foot-long lobby; there are 40 rooms in the main building (those with even numbers face Shelter Island Sound), all with a bath and furnished very plainly in an old-fashioned way. Six suites make ideal family accommodations. Behind the main building are eight pleasant cottages (three with fireplace)—some studios, others one-bedrooms, but all with a kitchen or kitchenette, air-conditioning, a color TV, and a private deck. Breakfast, lunch, and dinner are served on the deck in summer; there's dancing three nights a week, and the Pridwin's special Wednesday cookout is a popular island event.

Rates (weekends): June 30–Labor Day, $139–$179 double, $169–$209 double MAP; $209 cottage, $239 cottage MAP. Off-season, $82–$119 cottage only (no MAP).

Closer to the Heights, the **Dering Harbor Inn,** 13 Winthrop Rd. (P.O. Box AD), Shelter Island, NY 11965 (tel. 516/749-0900), occupies a grassy knoll overlooking the harbor. The main building has "late motel"–style rooms, some with a private patio, cable TV, and air-conditioning. Other buildings around the property offer two-bedroom/two-bath units and one-bedroom/one-bath units with a water view; these have kitchen facilities. All rooms have air conditioning and a phone. There's an outdoor pool enclosed by a hedge, tennis courts, and a full dining room with a flagstone chimney fireplace.

Rates: Summer, $170–$250 studio or one-bedroom unit; $315–$335 two-bedroom unit. Spring and fall, $150–$220 studio or one-bedroom unit; $285–$305 two-bedroom unit. **Closed:** Mid-Oct to Mar.

Also at Crescent Beach is the modern **Shelter Island Resort Motel,** 35 Shore Rd. (P.O. Box 255), Shelter Island, NY 11965 (tel. 516/749-2001), where each room has a sun deck, air conditioning, a color TV, and a phone—and you're right across from Crescent Beach. Some units have kitchenettes. Paddleboats are available.

Rates: Late June to Labor Day, $135 double weekdays, $205 double weekends. Late May to late June and Labor Day to early Oct, $89 double weekdays, $159 double weekends. Early Oct to late May, $89 double weekdays, $119 double weekends.

Despite its name, the **Olde Country Inn,** 11 Stearns Point Rd. (tel. 516/749-1633), is actually a modern building, though it has been well designed to give the appearance of age. The front door is leaded glass with a fanlight and it leads into a small lobby area where guests register at the antique desk. The eight air-conditioned guest rooms (all with bath) are furnished with a mix of antiques and antique reproductions, their oak floors covered with Oriental rugs. Breakfast is served in a light and airy room and consists of crêpes, apple waffles, French toast, and omelets that are cooked to order. In winter the owners operate a cozy restaurant with a small L-shaped bar, polished wood tables, and a brick fireplace. The limited menu might offer venison in poivrade sauce with chestnut purée and cranberries as the accompaniment or halibut in a sauce of red peppers, leeks, capers, and white wine. Prices are $18 to $20. Guests may also use the sitting room, furnished with a grand piano and comfortable seating.

Rates (including breakfast): Summer, $135–$155 double. Winter, $95–$110 double.

Annabelle's Hideaway Belle Crest Inn, 163 N. Ferry Rd., Shelter Island Heights, NY 11965 (tel. 516/749-2041), is located in a historic home surrounded by pretty gardens complete with a gazebo. It's operated by Herbert, who studied hotel management in Switzerland, and Yvonne, who used to be a psychological nurse. The parlor/dining room where guests take breakfast looks out over the gardens. It's comfortably and eclectically furnished with a grand piano topped with a calabash from Ghana, Oriental rugs, and gilt-framed paintings. The guest rooms are comfortable, decorated with a melange of patterns and colors. Some have canopied beds, some have refrigerators, and some share baths. All have a TV and air-conditioning.

Rates (including breakfast): $105 double without bath, $175 double with bath.

Shelter Island Dining

The best dining is found at the **Ram's Head Inn** (see "Shelter Island Lodging," above). Recommendable dining establishments are hard to find, and locals swear by the simple roadside fish/shellfish stands and bars like **Chips,** on Rte. 114 (tel. 516/749-8926). A step leads down from the fish market into the dining area furnished with plain wooden tables, each sporting a bottle of ketchup. The choice of fish is wide—dolphin, mako, swordfish, flounder, weakfish, and tilefish, as well as lobster, all priced from a low of $11 to a close-to-low $13.

Hours: Summer, Mon–Sat noon–3pm and 5–9:30pm, Sun noon–3pm (brunch) and 5–9:30pm; winter, Thurs–Sat 5–9:30pm, Sun noon–3pm (brunch) and 5–9:30pm.

Chamberlain's, 15 Grand Ave. (tel. 516/749-2005), in the Heights, occupies a pretty Victorian house with a narrow front porch. The dining room is decorated with the artist/proprietor's metal sculptures incorporating old car parts. Behind the dining room is a long bar. The menu emphasizes fresh seafood, with such entrees as herb-encrusted flounder, seared tuna provençal, and swordfish with roasted red-pepper butter. You'll always be able to secure a burger along with ribeye with madeira demiglaze or pork medallions with brandy-cinnamon apples. Prices range from $8 to $22.

Hours: Summer, Sun–Fri 6–10pm, Sat 6–11pm; the rest of the year, Thurs–Fri 6–10pm, Sat 6–11pm, Sun 10:30am–2pm (brunch) and 6–10pm.

Other possible lunch spots? The deck overlooking the pond at **The Dory,** Bridge Street (tel. 516/749-8871), offers sandwiches, salads, and fish and meat dishes for lunch and steaks and seafood at dinner.

Hours: Summer, daily noon–3pm and 6–10pm; spring and fall, Thurs–Tues noon–3pm and 6–10pm. **Closed:** Three or four months in winter (mid-Dec to mid-Apr).

Or try the terrace/restaurant at the **Chequit Inn** (see "Shelter Island Lodging," above), a secluded spot set behind a privet hedge and dotted with hydrangea from which you can glimpse blue waters and sailing craft through the trees.

Shelter Island
Special & Recreational Activities

Beaches: Beach permits can be obtained from the Town Hall, Ferry Road (tel. 516/749-0291).

Bicycling: For rentals, go to Piccozzi's Service Station, Bridge Street (tel. 516/749-0045), or Coecles Harbor Marina (tel. 516/749-0700).

Golf: The Shelter Island Country Club, 26 Sunnyside Ave. (tel. 516/749-8841), has a nine-hole course.

Hiking: The Mashomack Preserve, 79 S. Ferry Rd. (Rte. 114), is open Thursday to Tuesday and has 15 miles of hiking trails. Guided walks are given, but you need to reserve ahead (tel. 516/749-1001).

Kayaking: Two-hour tours are given by Shelter Island Kayak Tours, P.O. Box 360, Shelter Island, NY 11964 (tel. 516/749-1990).

Picnicking: Head for the beaches, picking up supplies at George's IGA Market or Fedi Market (open until 8pm). The Island Food Center has barbecued chickens, ducks, and sandwiches to go.

The North Fork & North Shore

Distance in Miles: Cold Spring Harbor, 37; Northport, 46; Stony Brook, 58; Greenport, 102; Orient, 107

Estimated Driving Time: 45 minutes to 2 hours

<figure>◄O►◄O►◄O►◄O►◄O►</figure>

Driving: Take the Long Island Expressway (LIE) to Rte. 25 for towns on the North Fork. Take the LIE to Walt Whitman Road for Huntington and Cold Spring Harbor; take the LIE to Deer Park Avenue for Northport and Centerport or to Nicolls Road for Stony Brook. If you drive to Sag Harbor, you can take the ferry to Shelter Island and from there to Greenport.

Bus: Sunrise Express (tel. 516/477-1200) provides rapid service to North Fork towns—the last stop is Greenport.

Train: The Long Island Rail Road (tel. 718/217-5477) stops at Cold Spring Harbor, Huntington, Green Lawn (for Centerport), Northport, Smithtown, St. James, Stony Brook, and Port Jefferson. On the North Fork it stops at Mattituck, Cutchogue, Southold, and Greenport.

Further Information: For more about New York in general, contact the **Division of Tourism**, New York State Department of Commerce, One Commerce Plaza, Albany, NY 12245 (tel. 518/474-4116).

For general information about Long Island, contact the **Long Island Convention and Visitor's Bureau**, 350 Vanderbilt Pkwy., Suite 103, Hauppauge, NY 11788 (tel. 516/951-3440).

For specific information about the North Fork, contact the **Greenport/ Southold Chamber of Commerce,** P.O. Box 66, Greenport, NY 11994 (tel. 516/477-1383); the **Southold Town Promotion Committee,** P.O. Box 499, Greenport, NY 11944 (tel. 516/298-5757); the **Port Jefferson Chamber of Commerce**, 118 W. Broadway, Port Jefferson, NY 11777 (tel. 516/473-1414); the **Three Village Chamber of Commerce** (tel. 516/689-8838) for Stony Brook information; and the **Huntington**

Township Chamber of Commerce, 151 W. Carver St., Huntington, NY 11743 (tel. 516/423-6100).

The North Fork has a far more rural feel than the well-developed South Fork. Over a third of the 121-square-mile area is still devoted to farming, compared to less than a tenth of the South Fork's much larger 212 square miles. The summer population totals only 72,000 compared to the South Fork's 173,000. The landscape consists of a lovely crazy-quilt of ponds and marshlands, hills and wooded strands, and a string of unassuming country towns. The North Fork—indeed the North Shore in general— clings tenaciously to its past rural traditions, and those traditions have been given a boost by the emergence of the North Fork as the best wine-producing area in the state (about which I'll say more later).

At the eastern tip of the North Fork, visitors can explore a string of New England–like towns: old whaling ports like Greenport, whose narrow streets boast several antiques stores; Orient, whose main street has a post office, a general store, a church, and one or two residences; Cutchogue, with its historic central Green; and many others, all enfolded into Southhold Township. All offer beaches and opportunities for sailing and other water-oriented pastimes, as well as hiking, bicycling, and the pleasures of wine tasting and dining on succulent lobster and other seafood.

Farther west are glorious farmlands, acres and acres of potatoes, sod and horse farms, orchards and fields growing all kinds of vegetables and fruits. Then there's the so-called Historic Triangle, centered on the picturesque 19th-century town of Stony Brook, site of an exquisite museum collection, and close to Old Field Point, bustling touristy Port Jefferson, and (to the west) St. James, which still possesses a wonderful old country store. This area is great for exploring, where the wealthy still live along hedgerowed roads. From St. James it's only a short distance to the charms of Northport and Cold Spring Harbor, both old whaling towns, and sandwiched in between is Centerport, site of the Vanderbilt Mansion and Observatory Planetarium.

GREENPORT & ORIENT POINT

—◄◦►—

GREENPORT

Settled in 1682, this New England–style fishing village retains the flavor of its earlier days, when it was a prominent whaling port and a major link between the cities of New York and Boston. You'll want to wander down the port's narrow streets, browsing in the stores and antiques shops. Explore the **harbor and docks** where schooners from Connecticut anchor alongside yachts and other pleasure craft.

Events & Festivals to Plan Your Trip Around

June: The Bach Aria Festival, P.O. Box 997, Stony Brook, NY 11790, a two-week festival of concerts and workshops, culminates in a waterfront picnic supper on the last evening. Call 516/689-8838. Strawberry Festival, Mattituck.
September: Labor Day Craft Show, Greenport.
October: Festival of the Sea, Greenport.

Greenport Lodging

The charming **Bartlett House,** 503 Front St., Greenport, NY 11944 (tel. 516/477-0371), was built for a state assemblyman in 1908. It's now owned by John and Linda Sabatino, who've restored its structural and decorative elements—stained-glass windows, Corinthian columns, and large porch facing Front Street. Step inside to an impressive Corinthian-columned living room with intricate molding and a classical-style fireplace. The 10 guest rooms (all with bath and air-conditioning) are up the handsome staircase. Room 2 is especially appealing, containing a working fireplace, an iron-and-brass bedstead, an oak dresser and rocker, and a marble-topped treadle table; the bath is huge. In the morning, homemade muffins, fruit cobblers, or freshly squeezed fruit juices are spread out buffet style.

Rates (including breakfast): Memorial Day–Labor Day, $89–$115 double. Labor Day–Dec, $77–$100 double. Jan–Memorial Day, $72–$94 double.

Although the white-pillared mansion bearing the name the **Townsend Manor Inn,** 714 Main St., Greenport, NY 11944 (tel. 516/477-2000), looks gracious and full of character (it was built in 1835), the varied accommodations, decorated in "late motel" style, are rather plain, many having white candlewick bedspreads and Scandinavian-style furniture; each has a TV, a phone, and air conditioning. The setting is extremely pleasant, with the secluded grounds abutting the Stirling Basin, so many yachtsmen find the place convenient for docking and staying overnight. There's a cocktail lounge/dining room serving a selection of meats and seafood, from sauerbraten and Yankee pot roast to swordfish, flounder, and fisherman's platters. Prices run $13 to $16. There's also an attractive grass-bordered outdoor pool.

Rates: June 26–Labor Day, $110–$140 double; from $150 apartment. May 30–June 25 and Labor Day–Oct 9, $85–$105 double; from $110 apartment. Apr–May 29 and Oct 10–Nov 26, $75–$95 double; from $99 apartment. Nov 27–Mar, $75–$80 double; $90 apartment.

Silver Sands, Silvermere Road (P.O. Box 285), Greenport, NY 11944 (tel. 516/477-0011), off Rte. 25, is a motel in a quiet location overlooking the bay with a prettily landscaped backyard for sitting and contemplating the vista. In fact, the motel has its own beach and nature preserve. All the air-conditioned rooms have a color TV, a phone, a refrigerator, a coffee maker, and access to the beach. A heated outdoor pool and waterskiing and sailing lessons are available.

Rates (including breakfast): Mid-June to mid-Sept, $120–$220 double. Mid-Sept to mid-June, $100–$120 double. Special packages offered off-season.

The **Sound View Inn,** Rte. 48 (P.O. Box 68), Greenport, NY 11944 (tel. 516/477-1910), right on the bay, is a down-home "customer is always right" kind of place. Accommodations are in two-story motel-style buildings where all rooms face the Sound, each with two double beds, a bath, a sundeck, air-conditioning, a TV, a phone, and a refrigerator. Some have full kitchens; others are two-room suites with a bedroom and living room; still others have two bedrooms. The furniture is typical Scandinavian-style motel or light-oak modern. Other facilities include a dining room, a lounge/piano bar, four tennis courts, an outdoor heated pool, and a private beach.

Rates: Late June to Labor Day, $90–$140 double; from $155 suite. Early May to late June and early Sept to late Oct, $90–$109 double; from $125 suite. Late Oct to early May, $75–$95 double; from $109 suite.

On the highway but set well back from the road with attractive grounds, shade trees, and flowers in front, is the **Drossos Motel,** Main Road, Greenport, NY 11944 (tel. 516/477-1339). Each room has a TV, air-conditioning, and kitchen facilities. Facilities include miniature golf and a snack bar.

Rates: June 15–Sept 15, $95–120 double. Sept 16–June 14, from $60 double.

Greenport Dining

Aldo's, 105 Front St. (tel. 516/477-1699), is famous for its breads and pastries and is perhaps the most charming and best place to dine in Greenport. The menu is very limited and you'll need to bring your own wine. You might find a fish of the day, steak au poivre, and chicken paillard, priced from $17 to $22. Antiqued walls, classical accents, and decorative majolica pieces create a warm Italian atmosphere.

Hours: Summer, daily 6pm–closing; Fri-Sun 6pm–closing.

The **Porto Bello,** Manhasset Avenue, at Stirling Harbor (tel. 516/477-1717), occupies a lovely setting overlooking Stirling Harbor toward Greenport; this makes for romantic summer dining as you gaze past the bobbing masts to the shady bank opposite, where a steepled church is etched against the sky. The decor is restful and simple—cane-seated ladderbacks, stucco arches, a stone hearth, and a pleasant bar that takes advantage of the view. The food is traditonal Italian all the way. Pasta dishes range from fettuccine to a house specialty with penne alla Mimmo (made with ground beef, prosciutto, mushrooms, mozzarella, bay leaves, marsala, and a touch of cream). Veal and seafood dishes are predictable favorites too. Prices range from $14 to $18.

To reach the Porto Bello, take Main Street out of Greenport toward Orient, then turn right. Take Manhasset Avenue to Stirling Harbor.

Hours: Summer, Sun–Tues and Thurs 5–9pm, Fri–Sat 5–10pm; winter, Sun and Thurs 5–9pm, Fri–Sat 5–10pm.

Claudio's, 111 Main St. (tel. 516/477-9800), the local favorite for fish, has been purveying food at the dock since 1870. It's a typical waterfront restaurant that serves fresh fish and steaks, priced from $11 to $25, the latter for lobster tail and New York steak. In summer, on the wharf outside, the Clam Bar offers a variety of steamers, burgers, and chowders from $5 to $15.

Hours: In season, daily 11:30am–closing; off-season, Wed–Mon 11:30am–closing. **Closed:** Jan–Mar.

At the **Cinnamon Tree Cafe** in Sterling Square, on Main Street and Bay Avenue (tel. 516/477-0012), you can dine out on a brick patio or inside in a pubby atmosphere. On the menu is usually a fish of the day that might be cooked with lemon and capers, or in a Créole style with tomatoes, peppers, and onions; as well as such meat dishes as New York shell steak with whisky-peppercorn butter or any of several other ways. Prices range from $12 to $16. On Sunday a jazz trio plays from 3 to 7pm.

Hours: In season, daily 11:30am–10pm; off-season, Wed–Sat 11:30am–10pm.

Another dining possibility is the **Rhumbline,** 34–36 Front St. (tel. 516/477-8697), a pleasantly nautical dining room serving seafood and steaks from $11 to $18.

Hours: Daily 11:30am–3pm and 5–9pm.

For a spot of afternoon tea, drop into the **Greenport Tea Company,** 119A Main St. (tel. 516/477-8744), a charming tea room that also sells teapots and other accoutrements for serving and enhancing the tea ritual. For $11 you can sample a full tea, consisting of scones and sandwiches and pastries accompanied by a pot of properly brewed tea.

ORIENT POINT

From Greenport it's only a few miles out to the very tip of the North Fork— Orient Point—where the ferries leave daily for New London, Conn. At the point, you'll find **Orient Beach State Park** (tel. 516/323-2440), providing acres and acres of shorefront for bathing, picnicking, and surf fishing. There's also a bird sanctuary at the west end.

The town of Orient was originally called Oysterponds, and this name is recalled at the **Oysterponds Historical Society,** Village Lane in Orient (tel. 516/323-2480), which consists of six museum buildings, a slave burial ground, and a consignment antiques shop, Shinbone Alley. The Village House, for example, displays an interesting parlor, dining room, and kitchen, and upstairs, portraits of local family ships' captains and toys, including an incredible locomotive built by Orrin F. Payne of Southold, who began it at age 11 in 1858 and finished it in 1881—a fine work of art.

Hours: Memorial Day–Labor Day, Wed–Thurs and Sat–Sun 2–5pm; fall and spring, Tues–Fri and Sun 2–5pm; winter, Sun 2–5pm. **Admission:** $3 adults, 50¢ children 11 and under.

You may also want to detour and see the 20 **rock carvings** commemorating the Poquatuck Indians, done by E. A. Brooks on the Sound shore via Young's Road from Rte. 25.

Greenport & Orient Point
Special & Recreational Activities

Fishing: Try either of the following open party boats. *Prime Time III* (tel. 516/323-2618) leaves from Orient by Sea Marina on Main Road. The *Peconic Star II* (tel. 516/289-6899) is based in Greenport. Both leave early in the morning.

Golf: The Island's End Club, Greenport, on Rte. 25 (tel. 516/ 477-0777), offers a scenic course along the bluffs overlooking the Sound. Greens fees are $21 weekdays and $25 weekends.

Horseback Riding: Zimmer Farm, Main Road, Orient (tel. 516/ 323-1317), offers two-hour trail rides for $40 per person.

Swimming: Orient Point State Park. Open year round.

Tennis: The Sound View Motel's courts are open to the public (tel. 516/477-1910). On Route 48, the Brick Cove Marina, Sage Boulevard (tel. 516/477-0830), has courts renting for $10 per hour.

SOUTHOLD, CUTCHOGUE & MATTITUCK

◄◦►

SOUTHOLD

Going west from Greenport will bring you to Southold, where the first settlers arrived in 1640 at Founder's Landing. Southold was once part of an independent colony that included New Haven, Guilford, and other Connecticut towns, which probably accounts for the New England/Cape Cod flavor of many North Fork towns.

In Southold you may want to view the **Old First Church** on Main Street, founded in 1640, although the present building dates from 1803. The adjacent burial ground is one of the oldest on Long Island.

The **Indian Museum,** on Bayview Road (tel. 516/765-5577), houses one of the most complete collections of Native American artifacts on Long Island—Algonquin pottery, spear and arrow heads, a variety of tools from knifes and hoe blades to gouges and drills, plus jewelry, toys, pipes, and other items.

Hours: July–Aug, Sat–Sun 1:30–4:30pm. **Admission:** Free.

The **Historical Society Museum,** on Rte. 25A (tel. 516/765-5500), features an 18th-century barn, a buttery, and collections of tools, toys, carriages, costumes, and furnishings.

Hours: July–Labor Day, Wed and Sat–Sun 2–5pm.

Southold Dining

For seafood that's excellently and imaginatively prepared, try **Ross' North Fork Restaurant,** North Road (Rte. 48) (tel. 516/765-2111). Chef/owner John Ross uses local fresh ingredients. On the menu, listing a dozen or so entrees, might be tuna with peppercorns flamed in brandy with mustard-cream sauce, swordfish with white wine and capers, or fresh sea scallops with olive oil and lime. The meat dishes are also well prepared, like the rack of lamb with braised shallots and mushrooms or Long Island duck with plum sauce. Prices run $17 to $22. To start, select any of the shellfish dishes or the hearty clam chowder. The ambience is simple but elegant.

Hours: Summer, Tues–Sat noon–2:30pm and 5–9pm, Sun noon–9pm; spring and fall, Thurs–Sat noon–2:30pm and 5–9pm, Sun 1–9pm. **Closed:** Jan to mid-Feb.

The **Seafood Barge,** Rte. 25, at Port of Egypt Marina (tel. 516/765-3010), overlooking Peconic Bay toward Shelter Island, offers ultra-fresh well-prepared seafood that's a far cry from the old fried-fish days of yore. Today you're likely to find grilled tuna with sun-dried tomato sauce, oven-roasted striped bass with fennel salad, or grilled mahi mahi in a citrus marinade. There are a couple of meat dishes, like barbecued duck, as well as pasta plates usually incorporating fish and shellfish. The decor is plain with a couple of fish trophies and ship's-wheel chandeliers the only nod to the waterfront scene. Prices range $13 to $18.

Hours: Summer, daily noon–3pm and 5–10pm; spring and fall, Mon noon–3pm, Thurs–Fri 5–9pm, Sat 1–10pm, and Sun 1–9pm. **Closed:** Dec to mid-Apr.

For classic continental cuisine in a very pretty atmosphere there's **La Gazelle,** a white clapboard house surrounded by flowering shrubs on Main Road (tel. 516/765-2656). You can enjoy such entrees as coq au vin, flounder grenoblois, or spicy steak au poivre priced from $16 to $22.

Hours: Mon–Thurs 5–10pm, Fri–Sat 5–11pm, Sun noon–9pm.

CUTCHOGUE

Cutchogue Attractions

Next is the historic town of Cutchogue, which clusters around the Village Green, where you can visit the **Old House** (tel. 516/734-7122, or 516/734-7113 for the historical society), a fine 1649 shingled frame house with leaded casement windows, a great chimney, and stairs that arch over closets below.

Hours: July–Aug, Sat–Mon 1–4pm; Memorial Day–June and Sept, Sat–Sun 1–4pm. **Admission:** $1.50.

Also on the Village Green there's the **Old School House Museum,** Cutchogue's first district school, built in 1840. The early 18th-century **Wickham Farmhouse** is also located here.

Hours: July–Aug, Sat–Mon 1–4pm; Memorial Day–June and Sept, Sat–Sun 1–4pm.

Since the pioneers of **Hargrave,** County Road 48 (tel. 516/734-5111), started their winery in 1973 in Cutchogue, more and more vineyards have opened and the area has become the premier wine-producing region of New York. In fact, there are now close to 20 wineries on the North Fork. Hargrave offers wine tastings daily from 10am to 5pm in the front barn.

Among the area wineries offering self-guided tours and tastings (most are open from 10am or 11am to 5pm daily in season, weekends only in winter) are **Bedell Cellars,** Rte. 25, Main Road, Cutchogue (tel. 516/734-7537); **Palmer Vineyards,** Sound Avenue, Aquebogue (tel. 516/722-WINE); **Jamesport Vineyards,** Rte. 25, Jamesport (tel. 516/722-5256); **Lenz Winery,** Rte. 25, Peconic (tel. 516/734-6010); **Peconic Bay Vineyards,** Rte. 25, Cutchogue (tel. 516/734-7361); and **Pindar**

Vineyards, Rte. 25, Peconic (tel. 516/734-6200). Visit **Pellegrini Vineyards,** 23005 Main Rd., Cutchogue (tel. 516/734-4159), for their elixir—Finale, an extraordinary dessert wine. There are about another 10 vineyards producing a variety of wines, which gives you some idea how rapidly the East End has developed as a wine-producing region.

To go with the wines, oyster fanciers will want to stop in at the **George Braun Oyster Co.,** Main Road (tel. 516/734-6700), to purchase some oysters, clams, scallops, or lobster.

Wickham Fruit Farm, Rte. 25 (tel. 516/734-6441), is a great place to stop for really choice fruits and vegetables. In season, you can pick your own.

Hours: Mon–Sat 9am–6pm.

Cutchogue Lodging

For an immaculate motel that offers 60 spotless, very large rooms (yes, I mean it), all with a refrigerator and color TV, some with a supermodern kitchenette with full-size stove and refrigerator, turn off Rte. 25 onto Depot Lane and head north for **Aliano's Beachcomber,** 3800 Duck Pond Rd.(at the foot of Depot Lane; P.O. Box 947), Cutchogue, NY 11935 (tel. 516/734-6370). Added bonuses are the 800-foot private beach on the Sound, outdoor pool, and bocce court.

Rates: Memorial Day–Oct 15, $125–$145 double. Apr–Memorial Day and Oct 16–31, slightly less.

Cutchogue Dining

The **Fisherman's Rest,** Rte. 25 (tel. 516/734-5155), is a down-home spot for steamers, lobster, and other seafood mixed with some Italian specialties, all at modest prices (under $12). For lobster lovers, there's the best treat of all—a 1-pounder for $11 and a 1¼-pounder for $13.

Hours: Summer, Tues–Thurs 3:30–9pm, Fri 3:30–10pm, Sat 11:30am–9pm; the rest of the year, Tues–Thurs 3:30–8pm, Fri 3:30–9pm, Sat 11:30am–8pm.

MATTITUCK

Mattituck extends from the Sound to the bay and possesses the only harbor on Long Island Sound east of Port Jefferson. Among its points of interest are the old **Presbyterian church** (1715); the **general store** on Main Street, located in the Octagon House (1856); and the **North Fork Theater,** occupying a former church on Sound Avenue.

From Mattituck you can travel west along Sound Avenue through fertile countryside, where **berry farms** stretch for miles, abutting green-velvet sod farms, fields of white-flowering banked potato plants, or horse farms where horses graze behind white rail fences. It's a lovely way to spend an afternoon rambling, especially if it's the fruit season, when you can stop at one of the many farms—Levin's, Friar's Head, Young's, and Briermere are the names to look for—along Sound and North avenues around Centerville. Farther south, you'll also want to visit **Calverton,** famous for its strawberries.

NEW SUFFOLK DINING

Legends, 835 First St. (tel. 734-5123), is a popular sports bar and the ambience of the dining room continues the theme with a crew boat suspended from the ceiling and the occasional saddle or baseball bat as a decorative accent. People are drawn to the bar because it offers more than 125 international beers. The fare in the dining room is honest and reasonably priced—barbecued ribs, sole or salmon with lemon-butter sauce, stuffed shrimp, and grilled chicken breast marinated in soy oil and garlic. Prices range from $11 to $15.

Hours: Sun–Fri noon–9pm, Sat noon–10pm.

Southold, Cutchogue & Mattituck Area
Special & Recreational Activities

Beaches: The main beaches with lifeguards and other facilities are New Suffolk Beach on Jackson Street, Kenny's Beach in Southold at the end of Kenny's road, McCabe's Beach on North Sea Road in Southold, and the Town Beach on North Road (Rte, 48) in Southold, which is the most used. Parking at all these beaches is by permit only. For additional information, call 516/765-5182.

Boating: Strong's, Camp Mineola Road, Mattituck (tel. 516/298-4770), rents small runabout motorboats. Sunfish can be rented for $50 per day at Capt. Marty's, First Avenue at King Street, New Suffolk (tel. 516/734-6852).

Fishing: Capt. Marty's, First Avenue at King Street, New Suffolk (tel. 516/734-6852), rents boats, tackle, and bait for $75 per day.

Golf: The Cedars, Case's Lane, Cutchogue (tel. 516/734-6363), offers nine holes.

Hiking: For nature rambles there are 34 acres at Goldsmith's Inlet and another 37 acres to explore at Inlet Point, good birding terrain, where naturalists lead guided walks.

Swimming: Southold Town Beach, North Road, Rte. 48.

THE NORTH SHORE'S HISTORIC TRIANGLE

The so-called historic triangle area stretches from Stony Brook and Setauket all the way west via Smithtown–St. James, Northport, to Huntington and Cold Spring Harbor, an area worth exploring on any weekend. There's even a historic old inn to stay at right in Stony Brook.

STONY BROOK

Stony Brook Attractions

Stony Brook is a beautifully restored 19th-century shipping and fishing village, complete with a mill pond, a grist mill, a rock garden, a brook, and a harbor.

The **Museums at Stony Brook,** Rte. 25A (tel. 516/751-0066), comprise a superb museum complex of four major collections devoted to history, art, period buildings, and carriages, the last of international renown. The carriage collection's 250 vehicles include cabriolets, grand Victorias (by manufacturers like Abbot-Downing, Studebaker, Brewster, and Million Guiet), royal coaches, and a brilliantly painted ornate Gypsy wagon said to have belonged to Queen Phoebe, a Gypsy who lived on Long Island in the early 1900s. The art collection contains most of the works by William Sidney Mount (1807–68), a major figure in 19th-century American art noted for his painting of everyday life and his sympathetic depiction of African Americans. Other highlights include 15 exquisite miniature period rooms, a fine costume collection, and carved decoys. Period buildings on the site also include a one-room schoolhouse, blacksmith shop, and barn.

Hours: July–Aug and Dec, Mon–Sat 10am–5pm, Sun noon–5pm; the rest of the year, Wed–Sat 10am–5pm, Sun noon–5pm. **Admission:** $4 adults, $3 seniors, $2 children 6–18.

The **Stony Brook Mill,** Grist Mill Road (tel. 516/751-2244), is one of the few fully operational 18th-century mills whose millstones are original. Kids love to feed the ducks on the pond afterward.

Hours: June–Sept, Wed–Fri 11am–4:30pm, Sat–Sun noon–4:30pm; spring and fall, Sat–Sun noon–4:30pm. **Closed:** Jan–Mar. **Admission:** $1 adults, 50¢ children 11 and under.

Stony Brook Lodging & Dining

At the center of this classic 19th-century village stands the delightful **Three Village Inn,** 150 Main St., Stony Brook, NY 11790 (tel. 516/751-0555). Sloping creaky floors, rooms tucked under the eaves, iron door latches, and costumed bonneted waitresses add color and character to this hostelry once (1751) the home of shipbuilder Jonas Smith and later the site of the religious conference, the Stony Brook Assembly. Rooms in the main building (with a TV and air conditioning) are furnished with comfy country-style antiques set against floral wallpapers and exposed beams. A series of cottages house pleasant, modern, superior-grade motel rooms, some opening onto lawns facing the harbor. The parlor is more classically furnished, with wing chairs, Martha Washington chairs, clubfoot tables, and a handsome writing desk, all placed to take full advantage of the large fireplace.

The dining room specializes in American cuisine—prime rib, Long Island duckling, flounder, and lobster—that's plain and good. Prices begin at $19.95. On Friday, Saturday, and Sunday people gather around the piano for a jovial song session. In summer the patio is a lovely place to sit out under the shade trees surrounded by flowers.

Rates (weekends): $105–$139 single or double. **Dining Hours:** Sun–Thurs 7am–11am, noon–4pm, 5–9pm; Fri–Sat until 10pm. **Closed:** Christmas.

A more colorful summer setting would be hard to find than the one at the **Country House Restaurant,** at Main Street and Rte. 25A (tel. 516/751-3332). Fresh flowers adorn the three bright dining rooms, each painted variously green, blue, and lilac and pink. Lemons and oranges garlanded with ivy form the centerpiece on the Good Luck Penny bar, flanked in summer by dishes of strawberries or peanuts and cheese puffs. On weekends a pianist entertains. The menu varies according to the season and might feature filet of sole almondine with a lemon, butter, and wine sauce; salmon and scallops with a pepper-brandy/cream sauce; steak with a mushroom-wine sauce; or duck breast with house pâté and a touch of bleu cheese. Prices range from $16 to $23. Brunch is prix fixe at $16 and offers a variety of fare, from steak and poached salmon to chicken pot pie and egg dishes.

Hours: Sun–Thurs noon–3pm and 5–9pm, Fri noon–3pm and 5–10pm, Sat 5–10pm.

SETAUKET & PORT JEFFERSON

Area Attractions

From Stony Brook, take Rte. 25A into Setauket, turning off for a detour to the **Old Field Lighthouse,** from which you get an inspiring view all the way along the Sound. Here there are a couple of old houses for history or architecture buffs to visit.

The **Thompson House,** on North Country Road (tel. 516/941-9444), dating to the early 1700s, displays a collection of early Long Island furniture, including the distinctive double-paneled blanket chest, the Dutch-influenced kas, several rural chair types, and a 1797 clock made by

Nathaniel Dominy IV of East Hampton. There's also a colonial herb garden to view.

Hours: May to mid-Oct, Fri–Sun 1–5pm. **Admission:** $1.50 adults, $1 seniors and children 7–14.

The 18th-century **Sherwood-Jayne House,** Old Post Road, Setauket (tel. 516/941-9444), located in a bucolic setting, is also filled with a varied collection of furniture and objects. The hand-painted frescoes in the east parlor and bedroom are fine examples of Early American wall decoration.

Hours: Memorial Day to mid-Oct, by appointment only. **Admission:** $1.50 adults, $1 seniors and children 7–14.

From here it's a short run into Port Jefferson, docking point for the Bridgeport, Conn., **ferry,** which during the summer deposits hundreds of day trippers who swarm into the dockside restaurants, boutiques, and antiques stores.

You may want to visit the **Mather House Museum,** 115 Prospect St. (tel. 516/473-2665), a complex of buildings and exhibits featuring costumes, shell craft, Indian art, ship models, and much more.

Hours: July–Aug, Tues and Sat–Sun 1–4pm; May–June and Sept–Oct, Sat–Sun 1–4pm.

Port Jefferson Lodging & Dining

Danford's Inn, at Bayles Dock, 25 E. Broadway, Port Jefferson, NY 11777 (tel. 516/928-5200), occupies a prime waterfront spot with views of the prettier side of the harbor. The lobby is accented with mallard and pheasant trophies, powder horns, guns, rifles, and other hunting paraphernalia. Tucked into an area created by a bay window is a TV and couch for guests' convenience.

Accommodations are in several two- or three-story buildings connected by a brick walkway bordered by stores reminiscent of St. Thomas, Nassau, and other pleasant shopping areas. There are 80 rooms, many overlooking the water and all quite large and furnished with good-quality antique reproductions; the baths contain the full list of amenities. Two buildings in particular have extremely large rooms with beds decorated in a special draped effect, a desk with a Queen Anne chair, an armoire, a pink-burgundy carpet, and a sitting area furnished with a couch and armchairs. The design layout of rooms in another building make them suitable for families or two couples traveling together; though they contain two double beds, there's a bath in between.

The **Restaurant** serves continental cuisine—duckling with raspberry sauce, grilled salmon with basil beurre blanc, or pasta of the day, which might be lobster-stuffed ravioli in Alfredo sauce. Buffet brunch and buffet dinner are available on Sunday. On weekends there's dancing in the sail loft.

Rates: $130–$210 (the higher price for suites). **Dining Hours:** Sun–Thurs 7am–midnight, Fri–Sat 7am–1am, Sun 8:30am–noon.

Port Jefferson & Setauket Dining

Fusion Grille, 316 Main St., East Setauket (tel. 516/751-2200), has won top ranking on the North Fork's dining scene. The cuisine reflects the name insofar as the prepared dishes fuse the flavors and ingredients from several world cuisines—Asian, European, Caribbean, and Latin American. For example, among the appetizers you might find tuna sushi tempura alongside grilled portobello mushrooms with herbed viniagrette; among the pastas are black linguine with pan-seared calamari, plum tomatoes, golden raisins, black olives, pine nuts, and hot red peppers as well as ravioli with portobellos, asparagus, and ricotta in a spicy chipotle-cream sauce. Main courses range from a terrific macadamia-crusted shrimp with tamarind-ginger glaze and guava-habañero syrup to filet mignon with pinot-noir sauce and basil mashed potatoes. Exciting indeed. Prices range from $17.50 to $26. A special five-course dinner is offered weekdays accompanied by wine with each course for $65—an excellent value. The wine bar stocks some great wines and even offers Opus 1 by the glass for $19! The artworks on the walls complement the art on the plate. On Friday and Sunday there's piano/jazz entertainment.

Hours: Mon–Thurs 11:30am–3:30pm and 4–10pm, Fri–Sat 11:30am–3:30pm and 4–11pm, Sun 1–9pm.

Costa de España, 9 Traders Cove (tel. 516/331-5363), has a small bar, tables with red cloths, a pleasant warm atmosphere, and fine Spanish food. The emphasis is on seafood—paella valenciana con langosta (with sausage, chicken, and lobster) or seafood combination dishes in a variety of sauces from green and garlic to hot and egg. There's also such meat dishes as veal in almond sauce, chicken in garlic sauce, and a special chicken with onions, mushrooms, wine, and tomato sauce. Prices run $12 to $22.

Hours: Mon–Thurs noon–3pm and 5–10pm, Fri–Sat noon–3pm and 5–11pm, Sun 1–10pm.

Printers Devil, Wynne Lane (tel. 516/928-7171), is a pubby local favorite decked out in typical oak, stained glass, and plants. Chicken Cordon Bleu, surf and turf, filet mignon, veal français, and burgers typify the fare, priced from $8 to $22.

Hours: Mon–Thurs 11:30am–4pm and 4–11pm, Fri–Sat 11:30am–4pm and 4pm–1am, Sun 11am–3pm and 4–11pm.

SMITHTOWN & ST. JAMES

Area Attractions

If you head west on Rte. 25A from Stony Brook you'll pass **Wicks Farm Stand,** famous not only for fresh produce but also for their imaginative Halloween display that the kids all love. Turn left at Moriches Road and head for the **St. James General Store** (tel. 516/862-8333), established in 1857. The porch is lined with baskets of all sorts, a big old teddy bear, and a cigarstore Indian. The interior offers all kinds of old-fashioned favorites, sugarcanes and candies, jams, preserves, cookie jars, quilts, spices, and craft items, all displayed on the original counters, on shelves, or in old cases. In winter the place is warmed by an old pot-belly stove.

From here, Moriches Road north takes you through Nissequogue, a land mass that separates Stony Brook Harbor from the Nissequogue River. Follow Moriches Road until it loops around into Nissequogue Road, which leads into River Road. All through here you'll be driving along winding, tree-shaded lanes bursting with rhododendron and mountain laurel that in early summer shield the grand houses from the prying eyes of the passing motorist.

Getting back on Rte. 25A brings you into Smithtown, one of the nation's fastest-growing townships, which, paradoxically, has several historic landmarks: The **Caleb Smith House,** on Rte. 25A (tel. 516/265-6768; open Mon–Fri 8am–4pm, Sat noon–4pm; admission by donation), is the home of the Historical Society. The **Epenetus Smith Tavern,** Middle Country Road (tel. 516/724-3091; open only on Heritage Day, usually the second Sun in Sept), is where memories of mirth and mead are preserved in the one-room bar, as is the lifestyle of an earlier era in pictures, sea chests, tea caddies, and rockers. Also look for the first **Presbyterian church** (1675) and the **Old Smith House** (1664) on Long Beach Road (open only by appointment; call 516/265-6768).

Smithtown Area Lodging

Unfortunately, there are no attractive country inns (the closest is Stonybrook's Three Village Inn), but there are plenty of fine dining establishments. First, a place to stay.

The **Sheraton Smithtown,** 110 Vanderbilt Motor Pkwy., Smithtown, NY 11788 (tel. 516/231-1100), has 209 rooms, two dining rooms, two lounges, and an indoor pool and exercise room.

Rates: $136–$146 double. Ask about special weekend packages.

Smithtown Area Dining

Smithtown Haus, 65 E. Main St., Smithtown (tel. 516/979-9113), offers good German fare in a warm wooden room with a large bar: sauerbraten, bratwurst and sauerkraut, jaegerschnitzel with mushrooms in cream sauce, sole almondine, and filet mignon, from $13 to $20.

Hours: Tues–Fri noon–3pm and 5–9pm, Sat 5–11pm, Sun noon–9pm.

Fine-quality Italian cuisine draws crowds to **Casa Rustica,** 175 W. Main St., Smithtown (tel. 516/265-9265). From the cozy fire-warmed bar a ramp leads into the stucco-and-timbered country dining room. Start with carpaccio with radicchio and parmesan dressed with a pink sauce or a delicious seafood salad of calamari, scungilli, octopus, mussels, and shrimp.

More unusual, try the polenta salsiccia—cornmeal porridge flavored with savory sausage and pinot grigio wine. There are several pastas, like meat-filled agnolotti, risotto with porcini mushrooms or with champagne and caviar, along with more common dishes like veal piccata, veal valdostana, and steak fiorentina. Prices run $15 to $20.

Hours: Mon–Thurs noon–3pm and 5–10pm, Fri noon–3pm and 5–11pm, Sat 5–11pm, Sun 2–9pm.

Due Torri, 330 Vanderbilt Motor Pkwy., Hauppauge (tel. 516/435-8664), is on the top (fourth) floor of an office building and offers a more limited menu than nearby Mario's (below), slightly lower prices, and a more modern Italian ambience with a sleek tiled service area and plush semicircular burgundy banquettes. Penne alla vodka, tortellini Duchessa (with chicken, prosciutto, mushrooms, and peas), and other pastas are good starters or main courses. Veal scaloppine with mushrooms, veal piccata, striped bass alla Livornese (with garlic, onion, olives, and capers in a light tomato sauce), rack of lamb, and chateaubriand are a few of the many choices. There's dancing on weekends.

Hours: Mon–Thurs noon–3pm and 5–10pm, Fri noon–3pm and 5–11pm, Sat 5–11pm, Sun 2–10pm.

Mario's, 644 Vanderbilt Motor Pkwy., Hauppauge (tel. 516/273-9407), features an extensive menu offering chicken breast marsala, veal with artichokes and mushrooms, saltimbocca, red snapper with spinach, and such pastas as cannelloni, manicotti, and linguine alla vongole. The decor is rich: gilt pictures, chandeliers, banquettes, and chairs covered in floral fabric. Prices run $9 to $18.

Hours: Mon–Thurs noon–2:30pm and 5–9:30pm, Fri noon–2:30pm and 5:30–10:30pm, Sat 5:30–10:30pm, Sun 3–9:30pm.

Mirabelle, 404 North Country Rd., St. James (tel. 516/584-5999), serves the best food in the area and has a rather spare modern decor that relies on color—pink with gray trim, red banquettes—for effect. The menu changes but may feature steamed salmon with beet vinaigrette and anchovies, roast loin of venison with a sauce of red wine and port, and grilled duck breast followed by confit leg. Prices run $21 to $30. Begin with the quail stuffed with foie gras and grapes served with celeriac and walnut salad and prunes with Armagnac or with the splendid tray of oysters, mussels, lobster, clams, and shrimp. The natural finish for the meal is a soufflé.

Hours: Tues–Thurs noon–2pm and 6–10pm, Fri noon–2pm and 6–11pm, Sat 6–11pm, Sun 5–9pm.

At **Garden Grill,** 64 North Country Rd., Smithtown (tel. 516/265-8771), the cuisine is classically traditional—like steak marchand de vin and chateaubriand. Prices run $14 to $22. The decor is country French.

Hours: Mon–Fri noon–3pm and 5:30–10:30pm, Sat 5:30–10:30pm.

NORTHPORT

Northport Attractions

From Smithtown, Rte. 25A brings you all the way to the outskirts of Northport. Turn right down into the harbor area that looks out across lovely Northport Bay to the wooded bluffs opposite.

At Eaton's Neck Point, which cuts between Northport and Huntington bays, you can visit the 175-year-old **lighthouse** erected at the request of the citizens after the terrible wreck of the brig *Salley*. Today light from the 73-foot-high beacon flashes a warning to ships as far as 17 miles out at sea. The lighthouse is open to the public only for group tours, which must be requested by writing to the commanding officer at USCG Station Eatons Neck, Lighthouse Road, Northport, NY 11760.

At 215 Main Street, the **Northport Historical Society Museum** (tel. 516/757-9859) tells the story of the village's shipbuilding past. **Hours:** Tues–Sun 1–4:30pm. **Admission:** By donation.

Northport Dining

Some 1½ miles east of Northport, at the **Australian Country Inn,** 1036 Fort Salonga Rd. (tel. 516/754-4400), the waitresses wear khaki shorts and bush shirts while they heft tropical chooks (chicken breast encrusted with crushed nuts and a hint of coconut served with a lime-zest beurre blanc) and beef tucker bags (sirloin stuffed with broccoli and Swiss cheese) amid the kangaroos and other Australian fauna. Dinner prices range from $9 to $27. There's a very pleasant shrub-sheltered terrace for evening cocktails. Fosters is available, of course.
Hours: Mon–Thurs 11:30am–3pm and 4:30–10pm, Fri 11:30am–3pm and 4:30pm–1am, Sat 4:30pm–1am, Sun 11:30am–3pm (brunch) and 4:30–10pm.

Pumpernickel's, 640 Main St., Rte. 25A (tel. 516/757-7959), offers excellent German cuisine, seafood, and a full selection of beers for accompaniment. There's delicious sauerbrauten, flavorsome goulash, wiener and other schnitzels, and sausages, as well as simply prepared seafood dishes. Prices range from $13 to $25 (the latter for surf and turf).
Hours: Mon–Sat 11:30am–3pm and 5–10pm, Sun noon–10pm.

CENTERPORT

Centerport Attractions

Leave Northport and get back on Rte. 25A and you'll soon be in Centerport, at the entrance to the land spit known as Little Neck Point. Here there's an outstanding attraction: the Vanderbilt Museum and Planetarium.

The **Vanderbilt Museum,** 180 Little Neck Rd., Centerport (tel. 516/854-5555), a 24-room mansion of Spanish-Moroccan design, was built in 1910 for William K. Vanderbilt (1878–1944) and added onto in the 1920s. It commands a magnificent view of Northport Harbor from the interior and from the pool area and balustered terrace. You'll begin in a room filled with models of the villa itself and a museum filled with animal trophies from Africa and India, all set against colorful dioramas. Many of the living areas are furnished in Spanish/Portuguese style, with impressive tile fireplaces and floors. In fact, there's only one American piece in the house—a Philadelphia lowboy in the organ room. The bedrooms are filled predominantly with French Empire and ormolu.

Though the house is splendid and filled with museum-quality antiques, the most interesting part of any visit has to be the collection of 17,000 varieties of marine and wildlife that Vanderbilt amassed. On display in the **Marine Museum** are all kinds of species—starfish, limpets, Samoa sea lily, and painted sea worms. Rapacious fiddler crabs, praying rock crabs, and sharp-horned spider crabs are only three of this genus. The shells are beautiful, and some are very rare. There are green turbans, conch abalone, chambered nautilus, Triton's trumpet shell, and an engraved tiger cowrie among them. In the same room are collected artifacts from the Philippines, Fiji, and Samoa, all catalogued in detail, plus birds from all over the world—quetzal, scarlet ibis, penguins, and incredible birds of paradise. In a separate room is a butterfly and insect collection. Certainly you could spend many hours poring over these natural treasures.

The final attraction is the **planetarium** (tel. 516/854-5544) and a small glass-enclosed observatory with a professional-grade reflecting telescope. Besides the planetarium sky shows, there's a Young Peoples Show on Saturday morning for kids under 6.

Hours: House, Tues–Sat 10am–4pm, Sun and holidays noon–5pm. Planetarium, Labor Day–June, Fri–Sun 10am–4pm; summer, the schedule is expanded. **Admission:** $5 adults, $1 children 4–12.

Centerport Lodging & Dining

The **Chalet Motor Inn,** Rte. 25A, Centerport, NY 11721 (tel. 516/757-4600), is a perfectly good motel, set well back from the main road.

Rates: Summer, $80 double; winter, $74 double.

The **Mill Pond Inn,** Rte. 25A (tel. 516/261-5353), overlooking Northport Bay, offers moderately priced steaks and seafood; complete dinners run $10.50 to $16. There's usually a fresh catch of the day special.

Hours: Mon–Thurs 11:30am–10pm, Fri 11:30am–midnight, Sat 4pm–midnight, Sun 11:30am–10pm.

COLD SPRING HARBOR

From Centerport, Rte. 25A brings you to Cold Spring Harbor, an old whaling town where the industry boomed from 1836 to 1862. Although the port only ever had nine ships, it was Long Island's second-largest whaling port. The **Whaling Museum** on Main Street (tel. 516/367-3418) recaptures this era. The highlights of the collections include a fully equipped whaleboat from the brig *Daisy,* whaling implements, marine paintings, ship models, and scrimshaw. The "Wonder of Whales" exhibit entertains children well, for they can touch whale bones, listen to the song of the humpback whale, and marvel at the size of a sperm whale's jawbone. A permanent exhibit, "Mark Well the Whale!" documents Long Island's whaling industry.

Hours: Memorial Day–Labor Day, daily 11am–5pm; the rest of the year, Tues–Sun 11am–5pm. **Admission:** $2 adults, $1.50 seniors, $1.50 children 6–12.

Anyone interested in nature/ecology might like to stop at the **Cold Spring Harbor Fish Hatchery & Aquarium,** Rte. 25A (tel. 516/692-6768). Here the 20 aquariums contain over 60 species, including freshwater turtles, fish, and amphibians. Trout are still hatched here by the thousands. Great for kids who love to feed all the trout.

Hours: Daily 10am–5pm. **Admission:** $2.50 adults, $1.25 seniors and children 5–12.

HUNTINGTON

En route to Cold Spring Harbor you'll pass through Huntington, a historically conscious town where landmarks include **The Arsenal,** 425 Park Ave., used during the Revolution to store arms and ammunition; the **Conklin House,** 2 High St. (tel. 516/427-7045), a local history and decorative-arts museum located in a 1750 house (open Tues–Fri and Sun 1–4pm, but call ahead for appointment); **Fort Franklin,** Lloyd Harbor Road, Lloyd Harbor, a British fort and Loyalist hangout; the **Jarvis Fleet House,** 424 Park Ave., the oldest house in Huntington; the **Village Green,** where the Liberty Flag was first flown on July 23, 1776; **Mother Chick's Inn,** 124 Bay Rd., where reportedly spy Nathan Hale was betrayed to the British by his cousin; the **Old Burial Ground,** at Main Street and Nassau Road, where 35 Revolutionary soldiers are buried; the **Old Presbyterian Church,** 125 Main St., built in 1665, whose bell was cast in 1715 and still sounds today; and perhaps most interesting of all, the **Kissam House** at 434 Park Ave. (tel. 516/427-7045; open Tues–Fri and Sun 1–4pm, but call ahead for an appointment), where antiques buffs gather for the occasional auctions and sales sponsored by the Huntington Historical Society.

Huntington also possesses a couple of lovely areas for walking and picnicking (see below), including the **Target Rock Refuge,** West Neck Road, the 80-acre former estate of Ferdinand Eberstadt, which has a quarter-mile beachfront and a 10-acre formal garden.

Whitman fans will want to take New York Avenue south from Huntington into Walt Whitman Road, which runs past **the old farmhouse,** 246 Walt Whitman Rd. (tel. 516/427-5240), where **Walt Whitman** spent his boyhood. It's worth visiting to pay homage to America's first major poet.

Hours: Wed–Sun 10am–4pm.

The North Shore
Special & Recreational Activities

Beaches: *Huntington:* Crescent Beach, Crescent Beach Road; Fleets Cove, Fleets Cove Road; Gold Star Battalion, West Shore Road; Hobart, Eaton's Neck; and West Neck, West Neck Road. *Northport:* Swimming beaches include Asharoken Beach on Asharoken Road, and Crab Meadow Beach, reached via Waterfront Street West, complete with boardwalk, concessions, and parking for 600 cars; Geissler's Beach, on Makamah Road, is a beach for sunning and walking, not bathing.

Birdwatching: Makamah Nature Preserve, Huntington.

Boating: *Port Jefferson:* Craftis Fishing, Barnum Avenue (tel. 516/473-2288), rents small fishing boats.

Golf: Crab Meadow, Waterside Avenue, in Northport.

Hiking: *Huntington:* West Hills County Park, Sweet Hollow Road (tel. 516/854-4949), has 854 acres crisscrossed by nature trails, and Target Rock Refuge, West Neck Road; the Makamah Nature Preserve has great hiking in 160 acres of woodland, streams, and marsh.

Picnicking: West Hills County Park, Target Rock Refuge, and Makamah Nature Preserve, all in Huntington.

Swimming/Picnicking: *Port Jefferson:* West Meadow Beach, West Meadow. *Smithtown–St. James:* For fishing, ice skating, rowboats, camping, and hiking, Blydenburgh Park (tel. 516/853-4966) has 588 acres that are all yours. The Nissequogue River State Park is great for hiking. A permit is required.

Tennis: At SUNY at Stony Brook.

PENNSYLVANIA &
DELAWARE

New Hope & Bucks County

Distance in Miles: Erwinna, 60; Upper Black Eddy, 65; New Hope, 78

Estimated Driving Time: 1½ hours

◄○►◄○►◄○►◄○►◄○►

Driving: For Upper Black Eddy, Erwinna, and Point Pleasant, take the New Jersey Turnpike to Exit 10, Rte. 287 north to Exit 10, and then Rte. 22 west to the Flemington-Princeton exit, onto Rte. 202 south. At the Flemington circle, bear right onto Rte. 12 to Frenchtown and cross the river to Rte. 32. For New Hope, continue down Rte. 202 south to Rte. 179, which brings you to Lambertville and then across the river into New Hope.

Bus: Trans Bridge Lines (tel. 800/962-9135) goes to New Hope, Doylestown, Buckingham, Lahaska, Lambertville, and Upper Black Eddy.

Further Information: Contact the **Bucks County Tourist Commission,** 152 Swamp Rd., Doylestown, PA 18901 (tel. 215/345-4552), or the **New Hope Information Center,** P.O. Box 141, New Hope, PA 18938 (tel. 215/862-5880).

◄○►◄○►◄○►◄○►◄○►

In the county of Buckinghamshire, England (known as beechy Bucks), is a tiny village called Penn, whence William Penn set forth to settle in America. He must've had this area in mind when he named the valley that borders the Delaware—like England's Bucks, Pennsylvania's Bucks County is a bucolic landscape of woods and glades, gentle hills, and pleasant pastures. Although today you may be disturbed by the commerce and crowds that have overtaken the Main Street of New Hope, you have only to set out along the lanes and hedgerows or along the river or the towpath and your sense of tranquillity will be restored.

In 1681 Penn granted the 1,000 acres that now constitutes the borough of New Hope to Thomas Woolrich, who never even saw the land because he remained in England. Not until John Wells was licensed to operate a ferry in 1722 and to keep a tavern in 1727 did the town's life really begin. The tavern was known as the Ferry Tavern, and when you visit the core of the Logan Inn you'll be standing in that early establishment. Whenever the ferry operator changed, the name of the town changed, and it was as Coryell's Ferry that the community played an important part in the Revolution, when the people aided the retreating Continental Army and helped take them downriver to McConkey's Ferry, where they began the march on Trenton.

After the Revolution, the town prospered because of the river and because of its location on the main Philadelphia–New York road. Real prosperity began when Benjamin Parry established a flaxseed-oil mill and a lumber factory here in the 1780s. They were destroyed by fire and Parry rebuilt only the lumber and grist mills, calling them the New Hope mills. When the Delaware Canal opened in 1832, it brought even greater prosperity, as barges—as many as 3,000 in 1860—traveled the canal carrying Bushmill's whisky and coal to Bristol and returning to Easton with manufactured and imported goods. The prosperity was brief, for in 1891 the railroad arrived on the other side of the river and New Hope slipped back into being a quiet backwater; however, we should be grateful for this, since it ensured the survival of the old inns and buildings that make such delightful lodging places today.

At the turn of the century, the beauty of the area was discovered by a group of landscape and impressionist artists like Edward Redfield, Daniel Garber, and Charles Demuth, who made their homes in the area, turning New Hope into an art colony of worldwide repute between 1905 and 1935. Their artistic ranks were swelled when the old grist mill was turned into the Bucks County Playhouse and opened in 1939, drawing the New York theater crowd, like Moss Hart and his friends from the Algonquin Round Table, Dorothy Parker, S. J. Perelman, and George Kaufman. They were in many ways the vanguard of the tourists who flocked here later, turning New Hope into a very commercial, crowded weekend destination by the mid-1960s.

The town is still crowded on weekends, but only a few miles outside you can experience the tranquillity of the banks along the Delaware River, of the towpath along the canal, or of the surrounding countryside. In nearby Doylestown you can ponder the eccentric brilliance of Henry Chapman Mercer, archeologist, historian, anthropologist, and collector, and the legacy he left behind—a museum containing 40,000 preindustrial American tools, a tile-making factory, and a 39-room home, all built out of reinforced concrete. To the south lies Washington Crossing State Park, the site of Washington's dramatic crossing of the Delaware; Pennsbury, William Penn's 17th-century plantation; and, in contrast, Sesame Place, an ultra-20th-century playground for kids and parents alike.

Events & Festivals to Plan Your Trip Around

April–May: Lambertville Shad Festival.

Spring at Lenteboden to view hundreds of crocus, daffodils, and tulips blooming at bulb specialist Charles Mueller's, at Phillips Mill Road and Rte. 32 (tel. 215/862-2033).

May: Great Bike Adventure to Six Flags. Call 215/230-8411.

June: Bucks County Balloon Festival, Quakertown Airport (tel. 215/538-3055)—hot-air-ballooon race, aerobatics, airplane, helicopter rides, and more.

August: New Hope Auto Show, Doylestown. Call 215/862-5665.

September–October: Phillips Mill Art Exhibition runs through October at the Phillips Mill Art Gallery. Call 215/862-0582.

October: State Craft Festival in Tyler State Park, Richboro (tel. 215/579-5997), with more than 200 craftspeople.

Great Teddy Bear Halloween Festival, Doylestown—complete with a teddy bear masquerade and Old Teddy contest. Call 215/230-8411.

Bucks County Wine and Food Festival, a week of wines and food from the area's restaurants and wineries. Call 215/230-7533.

Historic Fallsington Day (second Saturday). Call 215/295-6567.

November: New Hope Antiques Show. Call 215/345-6410.

December: Reenactment of Washington's crossing of the Delaware. Call 215/493-4076.

Throughout the area are comfortable historic inns to stop at, antique stores and art studios galore to browse through, haunted houses to visit, barge rides to enjoy, and all kinds of activities on the river and the canal. And wherever you look are trees and fields, the bucolic surroundings that first moved William Penn to remark on the valley's great beauty.

Bucks County Area Attractions

New Hope

Besides the pleasures afforded by the Delaware River and the grassy towpath of the historic Delaware Canal, which is great for hiking, picnicking, canoeing, and even cross-country skiing, New Hope has several other attractions.

Start at the **New Hope Information Center,** at the corner of South Main and Mechanic streets (P.O. Box 141), New Hope, PA 18938 (tel. 215/862-5880), and obtain as much free information as possible.

Hours: June–Sept, daily 10am–6pm; Oct–May, Sat–Sun 10am–6pm.

The best way to spend a lazy summer afternoon is gliding along the canal in a **mule-drawn barge** under leafy glades, past old inns and homes, for an 11-mile journey from New Hope to Centre Bridge and back. For information, contact the New Hope Barge, P.O. Box 164, New Hope, PA 18938 (tel. 215/862-2842).

Hours: May–Oct, daily departures at 11:30am and 1, 2, 3, 4:30, and 6pm; Apr and Nov 1–15, Wed and Sat–Sun departures at 1, 2, 3, and 4:30pm. **Admission:** $6.95 adults, $6.50 seniors, $5.50 students, $4.25 children 11 and under.

You can go from the canal age into the steam age by boarding the **New Hope & Ivyland Railroad** steam train, which leaves from New Hope's 1892 station, with its unusual witch's peak, for a 9-mile round-trip journey to Lahaska. For information, contact the New Hope & Ivyland Railroad, P.O. Box 634, New Hope PA 18938 (tel. 215/862-2332).

Hours: Apr–Nov, daily 11am–4pm; Jan–Mar, Fri–Sun 10am–4pm, with special Santa rides in season. **Admission:** $7.95 adults, $6.95 seniors, $3.95 children 2–11, $1 children under 2.

For a different kind of trip from June to November you can sign up for a **Ghost Tour** of New Hope's many haunted sights. Contact Ghost Tours, P.O. Box 3354, Warminster, NY 18974 (tel. 215/957-9988).

In town, between the historic Logan Inn and the Bucks County Playhouse stands the **Parry Mansion Museum** (tel. 215/862-5652), erected by mill owner Benjamin Parry in 1784. Each room is decorated to reflect the changes in interior design and lifestyle from colonial times to the early 1900s.

Hours: May–Dec 10, Fri–Sun 1–5pm. **Admission:** $4 adults.

From New Hope, you may want to take the shuttlebus (Saturday only) that runs to the landscaped and heavily touristed **Peddler's Village** in Lahaska, which contains stores featuring everything from porcelain and crystal to crafts and apparel.

Wine enthusiasts can visit the **Buckingham Valley Vineyard and Winery,** Rte. 413, Buckingham (tel. 215/794-7188).

Hours: Tues–Fri noon–6pm, Sat 10am–6pm, Sun noon–4pm.

Bucks County is also one of the few areas to have saved its **covered bridges.** There are 13 in the county and the information center will gladly furnish you with a tour pamphlet.

And bear in mind that **Princeton** and **Trenton,** N.J., are only about 15 miles away—you can visit the tranquil groves of academe and the Princeton University Art Museum or the Capitol, planetarium, and art and natural history museum in Trenton.

River Road—Rte. 32 North of New Hope

Whatever you do, don't miss driving this undulating road that parallels the river and canal, stopping to browse in antiques stores or at farm stands, to stay or dine in quaint country inns or do whatever tickles your particular fancy. You'll pass through the tiny hamlet of **Phillips Mill,** where landscape painter William Lathrop made his home in 1900. In 1929 a group of area residents, many of them artists, formed an association and bought the mill to preserve it as a landmark and community center. Yearly art exhibitions, concerts, and theatrical productions were held, and Phillips Mill is still a cultural center.

Next door to the inn, **Bucks County Carriages,** West End Farm (tel. 215/862-3582), runs escorted trail and carriage rides. Farther up the road is **Centre Bridge,** home of Edward W. Redfield at the turn of the century. At **Lumberville,** you'll want to stop at the old-fashioned country store that's been here since 1770 and walk across the footbridge over the river to **Bull's Island,** a New Jersey state park that's well known to birdwatchers for being the nesting ground of the cerulean and yellow-throated warbler. While you're here, stop in at the Black Bass.

The next community is **Point Pleasant,** the most popular base for canoeing the Delaware and site of Ralph Stover State Park, great for swimming, fishing, camping, and hiking. A little farther north is **Erwinna,** where the EverMay on the Delaware was a popular resort in the late 19th century, frequented by the Barrymore family. Pick up some Gentlemen Farmer jams at River Road Farms before heading for Upper Black Eddy, passing through **Uhlerstown,** where you'll find the only covered bridge over the canal at Lock 18. The final stop after Upper Black Eddy is **Riegelsville,** a small town with an inn, some antiques stores, and a few other shops nestled in beautiful countryside.

By the way, while traveling this route you may want to detour from Erwinna west to Perkasie to visit **Green Hills Farm,** on Dublin Road (tel. 215/249-0100), home of author **Pearl S. Buck.** Buck was the first American woman to win the Nobel Prize and Pulitzer Prize for literature (for *The Good Earth*). She was born to missionary parents in China but returned to the United States to this 60-acre farm where she continued to write and raise her eight children. Today the Pearl S. Buck Foundation operates an adoption agency and assists displaced and Amerasian children.

Tours: Mar–Dec, Tues–Sat at 10:30am, 1:30pm, and 2:30pm, Sun at 1:30 and 2:30pm. **Admission:** $6 adults, $5 seniors, $2.50 children 6 and up.

Rte. 32 South to Washington Crossing & Pennsbury Manor

Having retreated from the British across the Delaware safely to Pennsylvania and ordered all boats to be taken from the New Jersey side of the river, Washington regrouped only a few miles south of New Hope. He and 2,400 men made their famous crossing of the Delaware in a blinding snowstorm to his victory at Trenton on December 26, 1776. The 500-acre area is now **Washington Crossing State Park.**

The northern section, 2 miles south of New Hope, contains **Bowman's Tower,** a 110-foot observation tower marking the spot where the sentries watched the movements of the enemy. There's also a **wildflower**

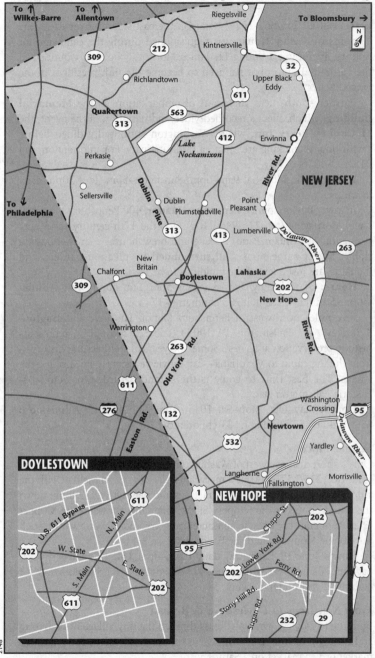

New Hope & Bucks County

To ↑
Wilkes-Barre

To ↑
Allentown

Riegelsville

To Bloomsbury →

N
0

309

212

Kintnersville

32

Richlandtown

Upper Black
Eddy

611

Quakertown

563

313

412

Erwinna

Lake
Nockamixon

Perkasie

NEW JERSEY

River Rd.

Sellersville

Dublin Pike

Dublin

Point
Pleasant

To ↓
Philadelphia

313

Plumsteadville

413

Lumberville

Delaware River

263

Chalfont

New
Britain

Doylestown

Lahaska

202

309

New Hope

River Rd.

Warrington

263 Rd.

Old York Rd.

611

Washington
Crossing

95

276

132

Easton Rd.

Newtown

Delaware River

532

Yardley

Langhorne

Fallsington

Morrisville

1

DOYLESTOWN

U.S. 611 Bypass

611

N. Main

202

W. State

E. State

S. Main

202

611

NEW HOPE

Chapel St.

202

95

Lower York Rd.

202

Ferry Rd.

202

Stony Hill Rd.

Sugan Rd.

232

29

1

2148

399

preserve (tel. 215/862-2924) here. On the east side of River Road, the **Thompson-Neeley House** was requisitioned during the campaign for officers, including a young Lt. James Monroe, who was wounded at the Battle of Trenton but survived to become the fifth president of the United States.

Farther south, near the point of embarkation, is the **Memorial Building,** which offers a recorded video and narration of the event; the **McConkey Ferry Inn,** where Washington supposedly dined before embarking; picnicking areas; and a bird sanctuary. For information, call 215/493-4076.

Hours: Park, Mon–Sat 9am–5pm, Sun noon–5pm (to 4:30pm daily in winter).

In lower Bucks County, **Pennsbury Manor,** 400 Pennsbury Memorial Lane, Morrisville (tel. 215/946-0400), was the 17th-century residence/plantation of William Penn. A bake-and-brew house, a smokehouse, a stable, and a barge house, all surrounded by pleasant gardens and orchards, are just a few of the buildings to be seen.

Hours: By tour only, Tues–Sat 9am–5pm, Sun noon–5pm. **Admission:** $5 adults, $4 seniors, $3 children 6–17.

Five miles northwest of Pennsbury Manor, **Historic Fallsington,** 4 Yardley Ave., Fallsington, PA 19054 (tel. 215/295-6567), represents historic preservation at its best. Some 300 years of architectural history—from the log cabin to Victoriana—can be viewed simply by strolling the streets. The best time to come is the second Saturday in October—Historic Fallsington Day.

Hours: May–Oct, Mon–Sat 10am–4pm, Sun 1–4pm. **Admission:** $3.50 adults, $2.50 seniors, $1 children 6–17.

Sesame Place

Only a short distance west of Washington Crossing in Langhorne, Sesame Place (tel. 215/752-4900) is a marvelous place to spend the day with the whole family exploring the 50 attractions and play activities. Romp down the Zoom Flume or the Slippery Slope, enjoy live shows in the Muppet Theater, operate the latest in computer gadgetry, and eat your way through the Cookie Mountain and the Food Factory.

Hours: June 18–Labor Day, daily 10am–8pm; Labor Day to early Oct, Sat–Sun 10am–5pm. **Admission:** $21.95 adults, $18.65 seniors, free for children 2 and under. Parking: $4.

From New Hope to Doylestown & Beyond

En route to Doylestown, you'll pass through the tiny village of **Holicong** and the town of **Buckingham,** where you might happen upon a farmer's market or flea market on a Saturday.

In **Doylestown** I suggest that you view the extraordinary landmarks created by archeologist/anthropologist/dandy/bachelor Henry Chapman Mercer, who was considered somewhat of an eccentric in his early years but was awarded many academic honors in later life. Mercer was one of the first individuals to realize the unique properties of concrete—plasticity, fireproofness, and durability. All three of the structures you can visit are of poured reinforced concrete built between 1908 and 1916, well before the medium became popular.

Fonthill, Mercer's 39-room home on East Court Street, was begun in 1908 when he was already 52, and he designed it and supervised the construction. Today it illustrates Mercer's many accomplishments as an architect, an archeologist, a tilemaker, a historian, and a creator of museums. It's an amazing concrete warren, where even the bookcases, windows, steps, and pillars are constructed of concrete. The walls, columns, and vaulted ceilings in every room are covered with an incredible array of brilliantly colored tiles, either collected from the world over (Delft tiles around the windows, Chinese roof tiles on a hallway ceiling, Persian tiles elsewhere) or manufactured at his Moravian Pottery and Tile Works (see below).

Many of the tiles relate stories or themes. For instance, in the Columbus Room all the tiles encrusted on the ceiling relate to the New World and its exploration. The rooms also contain treasures from Mercer's world travels and more than 900 prints. The house is amazing in its conception: It contains 44 rooms, 18 fireplaces, 32 staircases, and 200 windows of different shapes and sizes. Oddly enough, though, there's no formal dining room, for Mercer apparently preferred to dine wherever his whim decided at the moment. For information and reservations, call 215/348-9461.

Tours (mandatory; advance reservations necessary): Mon–Sat 10am–5pm, Sun noon–5pm. **Admission:** $5 adults, $4.50 seniors, $1.50 children 6–17. **Closed:** New Year's Day, Easter, July 4, Thanksgiving, and Christmas.

The **Moravian Pottery and Tile Works,** at Rte. 313 and East Court Street, is adjacent to Fonthill. Mercer had been moved to make tiles when he discovered that this old Pennsylvanian German art was dying. After several attempts, he succeeded in making a satisfactory tile and by the turn of the century his tiles were in great demand. For example, they were installed in John D. Rockefeller's estate at Pocantico Hills, N.Y.; in the Traymore Hotel in Atlantic City; and in the Isabella Stewart Gardner Museum in Boston. Most of the designs were adapted or copied from the old German stove plates. Like Fonthill, this building is of concrete and looks like a Spanish mission. A short film precedes a self-guided tour on which you'll see the machinery, kilns, molds, tiles, and tools. The tiles are still manufactured according to Mercer's original formulas and methods, and you can purchase them in the store. For information, call 215/345-6722.

Hours: Daily 10am–4:45pm. **Admission:** $3 adults, $2.50 seniors, $1 children 6–17.

Mercer built the concrete **Mercer Museum,** on Pine Street (tel. 215/ 345-0210), to house his collection of over 50,000 preindustrial artifacts, tools, and folk art that he'd amassed ever since he realized that what most people considered junk was in fact the essence of history. The work performed by these tools had cleared the forests of North America, opened a continent, and built a nation. In his museum he intended to illustrate America's history from a new point of view. It's an amazing place, and the exhibits are extraordinarily displayed. Walk into the central court and you'll see a Conestoga wagon, an old stagecoach, whaleboats, and antique fire engines suspended from the ceilings. The many alcoves house a complete watch and clock maker's shop, a room filled with candy molds, another with redware pottery, and many more displaying the tools of over 60 early American crafts and trades. Among the folk art on display are cigarstore figures, weather vanes, and decorated chests.

Hours: Mon–Sat 10am–5pm, Sun noon–5pm. **Admission:** $5 adults, $4.50 seniors, $1.50 children 6–17.

Another famous artist/author who was born in Doylestown is James Michener, which is why the **James A. Michener Art Museum** is at 138 S. Pine St. (tel. 215/340-9800). It's located in the imposing old Bucks County prison and features 20th-century art and sculpture in changing exhibitions. Naturally, the collection includes a number of works by artists who made the area home: William Lathrop and Edward Redfield, who arrived in 1898, and the later New Hope group who lived at Cuttalossa in Lumberville around 1916—Daniel Garber, Charles Rosen, Robert Spencer, and Charles Sheeler among them.

Hours: Tues–Fri 10am–4:30pm, Sat–Sun 10am–5pm. **Admission:** $5 adults, $4.50 seniors, $1.50 students, free for children 11 and under.

New Hope Area Lodging & Dining

New Hope & Lambertville, N.J., Lodging & Dining

At the center of town stands the impressive 260-year-old **Logan Inn,** 10 W. Ferry St., New Hope, PA 18938 (tel. 215/862-2300), built by the first ferryman and originally known as the Ferry Inn. Friends of Moss Hart and members of the Algonquin Round Table—Dorothy Parker and George S. Kaufman, among others—and the theater crowd gathered here in the 1930s. The inn has hosted stars from Tallulah Bankhead to Robert Redford over the years. It's still a favorite gathering place. The old tavern is a must. Or you can have a cocktail on the front terrace and dine either in the conservatory, brimming with plants, or in the more formal Gallery Room. The menu lists a variety of American/continental dishes—from filet mignon and broiled chicken to sauerbraten with Bavarian cabbage.

The inn offers 16 air-conditioned guest rooms (all with bath, color TV, and phone) furnished in colonial style with four-poster canopied beds and other period pieces. Original art adorns the walls and lace curtains and country flower baskets are set in the deep casement windows.

Rates: Weekends and in season, $105–$160 double; weekdays off-season, $85–$110 double. **Dining Hours:** Daily 11:30am–5pm and 6–10pm. **Closed:** Jan to mid-Feb and Mon until Memorial Day.

The **Wedgwood Inn,** 111 W. Bridge St., New Hope, PA 18938 (tel. 215/862-2570), occupies a gracious gabled 1870 Victorian with a large veranda decorated with scrolled-wood brackets and turned posts, as well as a historic Classic Revival stone manor house (ca. 1833). Pennsylvania Dutch–style surreys transport guests to and from New Hope. Carl Glassman and Nadine Silnutzer offer 12 rooms, all with bath and air-conditioning and brass ceiling fans. One room has a spool bed with lilac lace ruffles, a treadle sewing machine, a towel rack, and an oak dresser; another well-lit room has a large bathroom and an iron bedstead with a candlewick spread; and still another has a brass bed with a colorful quilt. On the ground floor, the grandest room boasts a four-poster with a lace canopy and more formal Federal-style highboy furnishings. There are also six suites, four with a fireplace—ask for rates. And in another Victorian, the Aaron Burr House just up the street, are another seven accommodations. At night you'll find your bed turned down and a complimentary carafe of amaretto awaiting you.

A breakfast of fresh-squeezed juice, muffins, zucchini bread or croissants, and fruit salad is served out in the gazebo, on the back porch, or in your room. In summer, guests have swimming and tennis privileges at a nearby private club. In the evenings guests can settle into the Victorian chairs in front of the parlor fire and enjoy a quiet read or conversation. Carl and Nadine also operate an innkeeping school offering consultations, seminars, and even apprenticeship programs to anyone interested. And they're quick to offer any information about Bucks County.

Rates (including breakfast): $100–$170 double weekends, 20% discount weekdays.

Chimney Hill Farm, 207 Goat Hill Rd., Lambertville, NJ 08530 (tel.609/397-1516), is a lovely 1820 stone-and-woodframe home atop a ridge with glorious views of the countryside. The 8 acres of grounds are well tended and in summer the perennial gardens bloom in colorful abundance; there's even a boxwood maze. There are eight guest rooms with bath; several have fireplaces. The Hunt Room contains an exotic canopied bed; the Terrace Room is decorated with lovely tapestry fabrics and offers a balcony. The public rooms are extremely comfortable: The living room, for example, is furnished with Persian rugs and period reproductions, plus an antique baby grand. A full breakfast is served in the dining room—candlelit tables for two surround the fireplace and classical music plays in the background. In summer it can be enjoyed on the garden patio. Little extras that guests appreciate are the complimentary snacks and refreshments offered in the Butler Pantry. The library and sun room are other places to relax while looking out over the beautiful gardens.

Rates (including breakfast): Apr 15–Dec, $120–$155 double weekends, $85–$115 double weekdays. Jan–Apr 14, $95–$115 double weekends, $85–$105 double weekdays.

The **Inn at Lambertville Station,** 11 Bridge St., Lambertville, NJ 08530 (tel. 609/397-4400), is a brand-new accommodation right down by the Delaware River. The rooms (all with bath, phone, and color TV) are variously furnished to re-create the Victorian era and have been decorated to suggest particular places during that period—Hong Kong, New Orleans, Paris, and London. Some rooms have fireplaces; some have whirlpool tubs.

Rates (including continental breakfast and complimentary newspaper): $95–$135 double Sun–Thurs, $140–$190 double Fri, $160–$235 double Sat (discounted if you stay two nights).

Lodging & Dining Along the River Road (Rte. 32) North of New Hope

The first accommodation you'll come to is the **Hotel du Village,** Phillips Mill Road and North River Road, New Hope, PA 18938 (tel. 215/862-9911). This estate, which most recently served as a girls' school, is quite lovely, set on spacious grounds studded with trees, shrubs, and flowers (some popped into tubs). The 19 air-conditioned guest rooms (all with bath) are in a large rambling building. While they're not spectacular, they are good-sized and fairly priced. The furnishings are all different, but expect to find simplicity—like a king-size bed, a mahogany chest, an armchair, and a coat-and-hat stand. On the grounds there's also a nicely landscaped secluded pool and two tennis courts. The dining room is extremely fetching and has a good reputation in the area. Oriental rugs cover the flagstone floors; rich chestnut paneling and fireplaces at each end of the room add warmth. There's also an outdoor flagstone dining area prettily arrayed with begonias and other plants and sheltered by a vine. It looks out onto a sylvan backdrop.

The menu might feature sole in curried butter, scallops with garlic butter and tomatoes, filet mignon with béarnaise sauce, chicken with tarragon-cream sauce, and similar classic French dishes. To start, perhaps try escargots with garlic sauce, pâté maison, soup, or a salad. The desserts are always special, and so are the fresh vegetables and the bread that accompanies the meal. Prices range from $15 to $20. Breakfast brings coffee or tea, flaky croissants, and coffee cake or similar to your room. Dried-flower bouquets, hand-painted trays, and embroidered clothes on the night tables are extra little touches.

Rates (including breakfast): $90–$110 double. **Dining Hours:** Wed–Thurs 5:30–9:30pm, Fri–Sat 5:30–10:30pm, Sun 3–9:30pm.

The **Inn at Phillips Mill,** 2590 N. River Rd., New Hope, PA 18938 (tel. 215/862-2984 for the inn, 862-9919 for the restaurant), is a small stone building (formerly a barn built around 1750) bedecked with ivy and other vines. The five charming guest rooms all have air-conditioning and are exquisitely furnished. One room, for example, has a four-poster, weathered barnboard paneling, a beamed ceiling, and colorful throw rugs on the wide-board floors; another has a unique chest and a bath with a clawfoot tub (no shower). Godiva chocolates are placed in each room. Downstairs is a large parlor, with huge roughhewn beams and a massive stone fireplace, where you can lounge on a leather couch. The original hand-cranked elevator is an affecting anachronism. The dining room has an excellent reputation for French continental cuisine. For vegetarians there's a spring garden plate. Prices range from $13 to $23. In winter the fireplace makes the tiled dining room cozy, while in summer French doors open to an outdoor dining area. Bring your own wine.

Rates (including breakfast): $90–$100 double. **Dining Hours:** Sun–Thurs 5:30–9:30pm, Fri–Sat 5:30–10pm. **Closed:** Jan–Feb 6 or thereabouts.

Although the whitewashed **Centre Bridge Inn,** 2998 N. River Rd., New Hope, PA 18938 (tel. 215/862-9139 or 862-2048), with maroon shutters and dormers, doesn't look that inviting (largely because it was built in the 1950s, after the 1706 structure had burned down), it's beautifully decorated inside with a mix of authentic antiques and reproductions; the rooms and terraces overlook the canal and the river. In summer, barges drift right by as you dine on the brick terrace graced with a fountain, hibiscus, and clematis. For guest use there's a parlor with a fieldstone fireplace, an Oriental rug placed atop royal-blue carpeting, and Williamsburg blue-and-salmon sofas and wing chairs.

The grandest of the nine rooms is No. 9, on the ground floor, which has a large private terrace alongside the canal, a four-poster canopied bed with a colorful quilt, and a rocker. The spacious bath has double louvered closets and cedar (yes) paneling. This is also one of five rooms that has a TV. While the other ground-floor room lacks the view, it has a separate sitting room, a fine marble Eastlake-style dresser, and a brass bed. In all rooms great attention is paid to quality products—the soap is Crabtree & Evelyn, the wallpapers from Schumacher. Upstairs, each of the more standard but still large rooms has sitting chairs, a chest, sidetables, and a pretty decor.

The dining room is typically country, with a low beamed ceiling and a fieldstone hearth; it serves well-prepared grilled lamb chops glazed with rosemary, mint, and pecan pesto; salmon with fresh dill and chardonnay beurre blanc; duck with plum-and-thyme chutney; and a daily fish and pasta special, among 10 or so items on the menu. The temptingly displayed desserts may include amaretto Bavarian cream pie, baked Alaska, and mocha-walnut pie. Prices for entrees run $19 to $29.

Rates: $110–$155 double weekends, $80–$125 double weekdays. **Dining Hours:** Mon–Thurs 5:30–9:30pm, Fri–Sat 5:30–10:30pm, Sun 11:30am–2:30pm and 3:30–8:30pm.

Stockton, N.J., Lodging

Set on 10 acres, the **Woolverton Inn,** 6 Woolverton Rd. (R.D. Stockton), Stockton, NJ 08559 (tel. 609/397-0802), provides a pastoral retreat. It occupies a historic 1793 home built by industrialist John Prall as a wedding gift for his new bride, Amelia Coryell. The second owner, Maurice Woolverton, turned it into a Victorian by adding the mansard roofs and most of the architectural details—the elaborate scrollwork on the porch, the fanlight transom, and the wrought-iron cresting over the roof ridge. Whitney North Seymour, a leader of the American Bar Association for 50 years, added still more gingerbread and planted the formal gardens. St. John Terrell, who purchased it in 1957, hosted many of the celebrities who performed at his famous Lambertville "Music Circus" with lavish parties on the estate.

The house was converted into an inn in 1980 and innkeepers Elizabeth and Michael Palmer today continue the tradition of hospitality. From the sitting room formally furnished with a grand piano, sofas, wing chairs, and French side chairs, all set around an Adam-style fireplace, you can step onto the porches and take in the view across the fields. A full breakfast is served either in the formal dining room, out on the flagstone patio, or in your room. There are 11 rooms (10 sharing five baths) and a suite in the carriage house, each with a canopied bed, a chest, stenciled rockers, stoneware lamps, and soft rugs on the wide-board floors; there are no TVs or phones. Second-floor rooms lack air-conditioning, but third-floor rooms, under the eaves with dormer windows, do have air-conditioning. Croquet and horseshoes are available for guests. No children under 14 and no pets are accepted.

Rates (including breakfast and afternoon tea): $105–$170 double weekends, $85–$125 double weekdays.

Established in 1710, the **Stockton Inn,** 1 Main St. (Rte. 29, Box C), Stockton, NJ 08559 (tel. 609/397-1250), tucked away in the center of Stockton, inspired Richard Rodgers to write the song "There's a Small Hotel with a Wishing Well." The wishing well is still here, but the place has been completely renovated while retaining an elegant old-world ambience. Two suites (each with a fireplace, a bath, a sitting room, a balcony, and a bedroom) and a cozy studio with a fireplace and bath are available in the inn. A suite and one large room with canopied beds and a shared veranda are in the carriage house. The Wagon House has two suites with canopied beds. An additional four rooms are across the street in the Federal House. Each room has a bath and many have working fireplaces.

The restaurant serves contemporary American/continental cuisine in the Glass Room's formal ambience, created by murals depicting 18th-century life in Hunterdon County; it overlooks the garden. Or you can dine in the garden itself, complete with a trout pond and waterfalls. Among the entrees might be roasted salmon with pineapple salsa, roast tenderloin of pork with red-onion marmalade and thyme jus, duck with

Cointreau-orange glaze, and filet mignon with Gorgonzola and bordelaise sauce. Prices range from $14 to $28.

Rates (including continental breakfast): $95–$175 double weekends, $70–$135 double weekdays. **Dining Hours:** Mon–Sat 11:30am–2:30pm and 4:30–9:30pm, Sun 11:30am–2:30pm and 3–9:30pm.

From Lumberville to Riegelsville—Lodging & Dining

The **Black Bass Hotel,** 3774 River Rd. (Rte. 32), Lumberville, PA 18933 (tel. 215/297-5815), could be taken and deposited in the English countryside and the locals would hardly notice. In this pre-Revolutionary hostelry, the parlor fireplace is suitably blackened, Tudor-style settles keep the heat in, and portraits of Queen Victoria and of Prince Charles stare down from the walls. The seven rooms with shared bath and three suites with bath all have air-conditioning. The room known as the Place Vendôme has a massive carved oak Victorian bed, marble-topped dressers, and sidetables. The Grover Cleveland features a half-canopied bed, an Eastlake-style dresser, and a fireplace, while a suite overlooking the river has a sleigh bed, a Victorian bed, and a separate sitting room. In the dining room (tel. 215/297-5770) and also in the tavern, which has a solid pewter bar rumored to be from Maxim's in Paris, the owner displays his varied and large collection of Royal commemorative porcelain and china. The food is continental/American, offering everything from rack of lamb with orange-Guinness sauce and minted crumb topping to poached salmon with little-neck clams and scallops in tomato-fennel broth; prices run $17 to $26. The desserts are traditional—ice creams, sorbets, pies, and cheesecakes.

Rates (including continental breakfast): $90 double weekends, $65 double weekdays; $160–$185 suite weekends, $160 suite weekdays. **Dining Hours:** Mon–Sat noon–3pm and 5:30–9pm, Sun 11am–2:30pm and 4:30–8:30pm.

Tattersall, Cafferty Road (P.O. Box 569), Point Pleasant, PA 18950 (tel. 215/297-8233), is the name given to this early 1800s double-porched house among conifers and shade trees. Innkeepers Gerry and Herb Moss offer six air-conditioned rooms, each with a bath. The Highland Room (No. 1) has Black Watch plaid draperies and chair upholstery and an Irish chain quilt on the mantle-style bed; Room 4 contrasts strongly, with its walls covered in lavender silk, a four-poster with crocheted lace canopy, and wicker furnishings. Many of the rooms have the original wainscoting. Breakfast is served in the dining room, on the veranda, or in your room. Apple cider, coffee or tea, and cheeses are placed in front of the fireplace in the tavern in the midafternoon. Gerry's needlework and paintings can be seen throughout the house, and Herb enjoys demonstrating and talking about his old phonographs displayed in the dining room. There's a small reading room and parlor with a beamed ceiling and a large fireplace.

Rates (including breakfast): $95–$119 double weekends, $15 less weekdays.

For elegant romance, head for the **EverMay on the Delaware,** River Road, Erwinna, PA 18920 (tel. 610/294-9100), an imposing Victorian mansion set well back from the road and approached via a semicircular drive. Built in the 1700s, it functioned as an elegant small hotel between the Civil War and the Great Depression, hosting such vacationers as the Barrymores. Fifteen years ago it was purchased by Ronald Strouse and Frederick Cresson, who have restored it to its earlier glory. There are 16 rooms (all with bath), ranging from the large Colonel Erwin room (with a towering Eastlake bed, needlepoint side chairs, Victorian velvet sofa, marble-topped dresser, and fireplace) to the smallest room, the Edward Hicks (with a bed, a small chest, and a dresser). Fresh flowers, potpourri, and bowls of fruit and nougat are placed in each room, along with miniature bottles of liqueurs. Tea and sherry are served in the formal Victorian parlor with a grand piano, two fireplaces, and rare walnut paneling. The dining room serves a $48 prix-fixe meal that begins with a champagne apéritif and hors d'oeuvres, followed by six courses. The menu changes daily, but the entrees might include grilled yellowfin tuna with lime-caper hollandaise or roast loin of veal with lentils and wild mushroom sauce; the desserts are freshly made and might be chocolate-chestnut torte or coffee-Kahlúa honey-almond ice cream.

Rates (including breakfast, tea, and sherry): $110–$200 double. **Dining Hours:** Fri–Sun and holidays at 7:30pm.

The **Golden Pheasant Inn,** River Road, Erwinna, PA 18920 (tel. 610/294-9595), is a lovely historic inn nestled between the canal and the river (but lacking a view); it was built in 1857 to serve as an overnight stop for the bargemen traveling the canal. Now owned by Michel and Barbara Fauré, it offers fine hospitality in its 14 guest rooms and superb cuisine prepared by Michel, who trained at both La Tour d'Argent and Le Ritz in Paris and refined his expertise at Le Bec Fin and the Hotel duPont on this side of the Atlantic. All rooms are furnished with great flair. You might find a brass or cherry bed or a four-poster canopied bed, combined with appropriate antiques.

Each of the dining rooms is wonderfully atmospheric too. The solarium, lit by candles only and with lights twinkling in the trees outside, is positively magical at night, while the French country dining room glows with copper pots, Oriental rugs, and Barbara's Quimper collection. It's made even more intimate when the fire is blazing in winter. The cuisine is wonderful—roast duck with apricot-and-ginger sauce, roast pork loin with currant-and-cassis sauce, filet mignon with bordelaise sauce, and bay scallops with garlic, shallots, and tomatoes. Game is offered in season. Prices range from $17 to $23. Start with the pheasant pâté served with peach chutney or the wonderful croustade of wild mushrooms with bordelaise sauce. For me, the only dessert is the Beglian white-chocolate mousse with raspberry coulis.

Rates (including continental breakfast): $120–$155 double weekends, $105–$135 double weekdays. **Dining Hours:** Tues–Sat 5:30–10pm, Sun 11am–3pm and 4–9pm.

Set back from the road, the **Isaac Stover House,** 845 River Rd., Erwinna, PA 18920 (tel. 610/294-8044), is a Victorian Federal-style mansion with a steep mansard roof and a bracketed porch along the front. It's owned by talk-show host Sally Jessy Raphaël. There are seven rooms, four with bath. Each is stylishly decorated in a different carefully coordinated decor. Your room might feature Oriental blue wallpaper or English ivy or blue-and-cream stripe. The bed might be canopied or iron or carved oak. A full breakfast of breads and muffins and omelets or similar is served. You'll find Swiss chocolates by your bedside and a full cookie jar for midnight snacking. There's no minimum weekend stay, which is a real plus.

Rates (including breakfast): $160–$185 double.

Beatrice and Charles Briggs rescued the 1836 **Bridgeton House,** Rte. 32, Upper Black Eddy, PA 18972 (tel. 610/982-5856), from decay and have faithfully restored it, revealing the original fireplace and floor boards. They've furnished the living room with old pine chests and other Early Americana. At the back, French doors lead to a porch overlooking the river. The Briggs offer 11 rooms, many with screened-in porches and river views, all with bath. Throughout, Charles and Bea have decorated in their inimicable way, creating a variety of effects with murals; the plank floors are covered with hook rugs, rag rugs, or Chinese rugs. The furnishings are eclectically mixed.

Room 1 has a four-poster; Room 2 has an Eastlake look; Room 3 sports a four-poster with eyelet-lace pillows and sheets and a sidetable draped with floor-length cloth. There are also several suites, the most spectacular being the third-floor penthouse, boasting a marble-and-mahogany bath with an oversize soaking tub, a fireplace, a TV, a separate dressing room, a bar, and a panoramic river view. Each room has fresh flowers, baskets of fruit, and chocolates. In the baths are English toiletries: soap, moisturizer, shampoo, and so on. A country breakfast of fresh fruit, omelets, and breads is served, and afternoon tea and sherry are available in the sitting room. This is one of the few B&Bs right on the riverbank, where you can swim, fish, and even tube.

Rates (including breakfast, tea, and sherry): Weekends, $89–$149 double; $149–$209 suite or penthouse. Weekdays, $79–$169 double or suite.

The Delaware flows in front of and the canal drifts behind the **Riegelsville Hotel,** 10–12 Delaware Rd., Riegelsville, PA 18077 (tel. 215/749-2469), a simple double-porched house. The main dining room is pleasantly old-fashioned, with polished wood tables, Victorian loveseats, a tin ceiling, and Oriental-style upholstery. The food is continental—steak au poivre, rack of lamb, chicken Rockefeller (with wine, spinach, tomatoes, cheese, mushrooms, and spices)—and prices run $20 to $28. At brunch you can opt either for the country table buffet with baked ham, sausage, breads, fruits, and so on or choose something à la carte. Twelve simply furnished guest rooms are available, some with bath.

Rates (including continental breakfast): $80 double without bath, $95–$100 double with bath. **Dining Hours:** Tues–Sat 4pm–closing, Sun 11:30am–2:30pm.

Gardenville Lodging

Maplewood Farm, 5090 Durham Rd., Gardenville, PA 18926 (tel. 215/766-0477), is run by energetic and enthusiastic Cindy and Dennis Marquis. The stone farmhouse was built in 1792; the second story was added in 1826. Today it's surrounded by 5½ acres on which a flock of sheep graze and chickens roam—you can even pick your own eggs. Seven air-conditioned rooms (five with bath) are offered. The largest is the suite, featuring a sleeping loft (with a queen-size bed) that's reached by a fine tongue-and-groove oak staircase. Another room features an acorn four-poster combined with an oak dresser, a dry sink, a rocker, and a blanket chest to create a cozy country ambience. Quilts and stenciled walls are found in all rooms. The full breakfast—of French toast, fluffy omelets, and the like—is served in the breakfast room with its inspiring "Tree of Life" mural painted by a local artist. The summer kitchen with its double walk-in fireplaces makes a great reading room, and the sun porch (with a drink-stocked refrigerator) is an ideal relaxing and chatting spot.

Rates (including breakfast): $90–$150 double weekends, 10% less weekdays.

Frenchtown, N.J., Lodging & Dining

Across the river in Frenchtown, the **Frenchtown Inn,** 7 Bridge St. (tel. 908/996-3300), offers some of the finest cuisine in the area. The old red-brick building contains a handsome bar on one side and an attractive dining room on the other. The high beamed ceilings and natural elegance of the candlelit space enhance the dining experience. On Saturday a $48 prix-fixe dinner is offered. A recent menu offered such hors d'oeuvres as house-smoked salmon layered on a potato napoleon with crème fraîche, diced red onions with a country rémoulade, and an autumn-squash soup. Among the five or so main courses were roast red snapper with grilled chanterelles and a balsamic-vinegar reduction, filet of beef and a caramelized onion-and-Roquefort pithivier with roasted apples on a confit-garlic essence, and venison with cured foie gras and a wild-mushroom jus. The à la carte menu features similar dishes priced from $20 to $27.

Hours: Tues–Fri noon–2pm and 6–9pm, Sat noon–2pm and 5:30–9:30pm, Sun noon–3pm and 5:30–8:30pm.

Hunterdon House, 12 Bridge St., Frenchtown, NJ (tel. 908/996-3632), was built in 1865 by a local banker. The handsome Italianate house has seven guest rooms, all with bath (tub or shower). The Henri Prevost Room is painted in a terra-cotta color and furnished with a high-back Victorian bed and some comfortable seating. In the Ruth Aspgar Room are found an Eastlake dresser combined with a marble-topped sidetable and a camelback sofa. The Daniel Bray Room contains an ornately carved walnut bed, while the Charles Lindbergh/Ann Morrow Room, tucked under the eaves, has an iron-and-brass bed and a charming circular window among its attractions. Guests can enjoy reading in the parlor with its slate coal fireplace. A full breakfast of omelets or Belgian waffles is served.

Rates (including breakfast): $120–$155 double weekends, $95–$110 double weekdays.

Newtown Lodging & Dining

Jean Pierre's, 101 S. State St. (tel. 215/968-6201), has a very French atmosphere and some fine French cuisine. Up front is a small bar and sitting area with French music playing in the background. Behind are two small dining rooms, including an upstairs room. The changing menu is supplemented by specials, which included fresh foie gras, quail Chinese style, and jumbo shrimp with balsamic vinegar when I visited. Among the 10 or so entrees might be sautéed breast of chicken with truffle sauce, filet of red snapper with Cajun sauce, and steak bordelaise. Prices range from $23 to $29. For an appetizer, try the crab cakes with a champagne sauce or snails in garlic butter.

Hours: Tues–Fri 11:30am–2pm and 5:30–9pm, Sat 5:30–9pm, Sun 4–8pm.

The **Temperance House,** 5–11 S. State St., Newtown, PA 18940 (tel. 215/860-0474), in the heart of town, combines a Colonial stone building with two dormers and a Victorian. The 13 rooms have all the modern conveniences—bath, air-conditioning, TV, and phone. They vary in color and decor. The Violetta is decorated in violet and contains white-painted furniture. The Benetz suite boasts a twig bed with a canopy, a Mission desk, an acorn chest, and even a comfortable chaise longue. The Granny McMinns features a Shaker four-poster with a crocheted canopy. The Edward Hicks suite is more formal, with mahogany furnishings and walls hung with reproductions of the famous artist's work. A continental breakfast is served in the Checkers dining room. There are three other dining rooms, plus the tavern, offering a Dixieland brunch on Sunday afternoons. The **Edward Hicks Dining Room** has two open hearths and murals painted in Hicks's style. The food is served on cherry tavern tables set on plank floors. It offers an eclectic menu featuring traditional American, Italian, continental, and even some Thai dishes. You might find veal chop with portobello-mushroom/cabernet-sauvignon reduction, salmon with sweet citrus butter, fresh brook trout Cajun style, or venison with roasted shallots, Kentucky bourbon, and cracked black pepper; six or so pastas can be ordered as appetizers or main courses. Prices range from $15 to $25.

Rates (including breakfast): $105–$145 double. **Dining Hours:** Mon–Fri 11:30am–2pm and 4–10pm, Sat 11:30am–2pm and 6–10pm, Sun 10am–2pm and 4–9pm.

Holicong & Buckingham Lodging

A narrow tree-lined lane, yellow with daffodils in spring, leads to **Barley Sheaf Farm,** Rte. 202 (P.O. Box 10), Holicong, PA 18928 (tel. 215/ 794-5104), one of my favorite lodgings anywhere. This 30-acre farm with sheep, chickens, and beehives was formerly playwright George S. Kaufmann's residence. The barn, secluded landscaped pool, pond, and majestic old trees round out the beautiful setting overlooking fields, dappled with cattle and horses. The original part of the house dates from 1740, and the parlors and rooms contain comfortable antiques. There are five rooms and two suites in the main house, all with bath and all furnished differently and attractively. Many have four-posters. The cottage, which used to be the ice house, contains three rooms with bath and a cozy living room with a fireplace and hooked rugs. One of the accommodations is known as the Strawberry Patch because of the wallpaper and comes with a handsome bed, plank floors covered with hooked rugs, a pie cupboard, and a Mexican-tiled bath. The bedroom has a French door, which you can throw open and gaze out over the pastures beyond or step through onto a small flagstone terrace set with a table and chairs. Breakfasts are abundant—fresh juice, seasonal fruit, granola, followed by farm-fresh eggs scrambled with salmon or a frittata with sweet peppers and onions, plus a variety of baked Swiss breads, jams, and honey from the hives.

Rates (including breakfast): Summer weekends, $150–$205 double. Winter weekends and summer weekdays, $140–$185 double. Nov–June weekdays, $115–$165 double.

Mike and Suella Wass run the **Whitehall Inn,** 1370 Pineville Rd. (R.D. 2), Buckingham, PA 18912 (tel. 215/598-7945), located 5 miles south of town. This 1794 home is set on 12 acres with an adjacent barn and stables. There are six air-conditioned guest rooms: four with fireplace, four with bath. All are attractively furnished. Extra touches include fine linens, Crabtree & Evelyn amenities, bathrobes, and chocolate truffles embossed with a W at turndown. The most sumptuous part of the experience is the four-course breakfast served by candlelight. Fresh fruit and freshly squeezed juice and freshly made bread precede an entree like spinach-and-pine-nut tart or similar. Afternoon tea is also served. The parlor provides a welcome retreat for guests who can relax in front of the fire and on the contemporary seating. There's a pool, tennis, and horses for guests' pleasure.

Rates (including breakfast and tea): $140–$190 double.

Mill Creek Farm, P.O. Box 816, Buckingham, PA 18912 (tel. 215/ 794-0776), is a truly secluded retreat situated on 15 acres and surrounded by 100 more. Thoroughbred horses are raised on the property, giving it a real country feeling. Five well-appointed guest rooms are offered in the 18th-century stone house. Each is decorated in a different color (peach, green, or pink) and furnished with antiques that might include cottage-style Victorian beds, marble-topped dressers, wicker chairs, floor lamps, trunks, and similar pieces with character. A full breakfast is served in the sun room overlooking the pond that's stocked with bass and serves as an ice-skating rink in winter.

Rates (including breakfast): $100–$145 double.

Doylestown Area Lodging & Dining

The **Sign of the Sorrel Horse,** 4424 Old Easton Rd., Doylestown, PA 18901 (tel. 215/230-9999), dates to 1710 and was originally a grist mill. The dining room is rated highly for its cuisine, always artistically presented. Diners may choose from either the traditional menu featuring favorites of an American table or from the seven-course tasting menu, which offers an array of European creations. The former might offer a luscious boneless rack of lamb with peach-and-mint sauce, chicken stuffed with mango and prosciutto, duck breast with maple syrup and toasted hazelnut-Frangelico sauce, grilled filet of mahi mahi and salmon steak with mango sauce, or a splendid wild-game combination of wild boar chop, elk loin, and pheasant breast with lingonberry-and-cassis sauce. The desserts are French classics. If you really want to spoil yourself, order the Deadly Sin—crème brûlée, chocolate-hazelnut terrine, and passionfruit sorbet. Prices range from $16 to $35. A light menu is offered in the Waterwheel Lounge and the Sunday brunch ($14.95) brings soup, fresh-baked goods, fresh fruit, and salads, plus many hot favorites like eggs Baltimore (made with sherried crabmeat) and beef Stroganoff.

There are also five guest rooms available (three with bath). They're furnished with country pieces; a couple have canopied beds. The fireplace suite is a favorite; there's also a suite with a Jacuzzi.

Rates: $105–$135 double; $160–$185 suite. **Dining Hours:** Wed–Sat 5:30–9:30pm, Sun 11:30am–2pm (brunch).

Highland Farms, 70 East Rd., Doylestown, PA 18901 (tel. 215/340-1354), was once the estate of lyricist Oscar Hammerstein II. The stone house stands on 10 acres surrounded by sheep-filled meadows. Each of the rooms, decorated with great flair, is named after a musical. The King & I Room has bold floral wallpaper and an elaborate crown treatment over the bed. Among the furnishings is a loveseat with a nearby floor lamp, making it an ideal reading place. The pink-and-sage Carousel Room has a carousel horse painted on the wall, the windows are draped with striking valances, and the bed is piled high with pillows. This room also features a fireplace and a comfortable loveseat. Lovely bed treatments are found in the Show Boat Room, decorated with coral floral wallpaper. The Oklahoma Room is a little more masculine, with a high-back oak bed, a wingback chair, and an acorn oak dresser.

The common rooms are welcoming too. The original music room has been converted into the dining room, where a four-course breakfast of fruit, breads, cereal, and a hot entree like eggs Oscar is served. The living room contains a grand piano, two comfortable sofas, and numerous books. The sun room, with flagstone floors and wicker furnishings, is a favorite spot for relaxing; so is the second-floor wraparound porch. Other facilities include a sylvan landscaped pool and a tennis court.

Rates (including breakfast): $135–$185 double.

Past the gatehouse, a long driveway leads to the ivy-draped **Inn at Fordhook Farm,** 105 New Britain Rd., Doylestown, PA 18901 (tel. 215/345-1766), an entrancing building with diamond-paned leaded windows and several dormers along the roof line. It was built for W. Attlee Burpee of seed fame in 1880 and back then the estate was 100 acres; today it's only 60 acres. In the mid-19th century it served as a boys' school but now it's as a comfortable country inn where guests are welcomed by Jonathan and Carole Burpee. Some of the original Burpee furnishings—an Empire-style sofa, ormolu mirrors, a secretary, and ancestral Burpee portraits—adorn the large living room/parlor. Breakfast is served on Mrs. Burpee's china in front of the Mercer tile fireplace. It might start with poached pears and oatmeal or a similar cereal, baked items, fresh fruit, and French toast stuffed with cream cheese. Afternoon tea is served from 4 to 6pm in the living room or on the terrace shaded by 200-year-old linden trees. The study, added in 1903, is a wonderful place to withdraw and savor the surroundings—book-filled bookcases, leather chairs, a beamed ceiling, a large fireplace, and an immense world globe. Here W. Attlee Burpee wrote the first Burpee Seed catalogs.

There are five guest rooms (three with bath) and two rooms in the carriage house. Each is well decorated with authentic antiques. The 18- by 22-foot Burpee Room contains a rice four-poster, a peer mirror, an Empire dresser, wing chairs, and fine paintings over the Mercer tile fireplace; it also has a private balcony. The Attlee Room boasts a brass bed, a working fireplace, and a private balcony. The third-floor Curtiss Room has sloping ceilings, a cannonball bed, a desk, a blanket chest, and stack bookcases, plus a tiny bath. The Carriage House is a large self-contained suite with two bedrooms and the most striking room of all, the Great Room. This was Mr. Burpee's private library and is richly paneled in chestnut with chestnut beams, rafters, and bookcases and lit by Palladian windows.

Rates (including breakfast): $110–$210 double.

The original core of the **Simon Butler Mill House,** 116 E. Butler Ave., Chalfont, PA 18914 (tel. 215/822-3582), was built in 1720 and added to in 1846. It stands on 10½ acres. Innkeepers Bob and Maryanne Showalter cherish the past and love to frequent fleamarkets, and they're the source of much of the fanciful decor. The library is enlivened by bottles and other objects that were turned up in an archeological dig on the property and also by a pile of quilts and an old typewriter and phonograph used as decorations. Comfortable seating and a TV can be found in the living room. The dining room has a deep walk-in fireplace, and here a breakfast of stuffed French toast or similar is served. All seven guest rooms (with bath) are air-conditioned. Most of the beds are covered with colorful quilts, including a signed-and-dated one in the Amish Room. The Simon Butler Room has a Shaker four-poster and nine small windows overlooking a creek. An Eastlake suite can be found in another room, which is accented with a parasol and a trunk flung open to reveal a beautiful state bird quilt.

Rates (including breakfast): $135–$155 double weekends, $85 double weekdays.

Pine Tree Farm, 2155 Lower State Rd., Doylestown, PA 18901 (tel. 215/348-0632), is set down an oak-shaded lane on 16 acres. The 1730 fieldstone farmhouse is now a rambling place that has been added to over the years, operated by Ron and Joy Feigles. Joy was trained in hotel administration and always dreamed of opening an inn. She has filled the house with beautiful antique furnishings and her personal collections of redware and antique china. There are four guest rooms with bath, each furnished differently but with an eye to guest comfort and convenience (a phone is available on request). For example, each has a writing desk and comfortable armchairs upholstered with fine fabrics. In one room you'll find a twig four-poster, in another a wrought-iron bed. Extra touches include nightly turndown and free morning paper with breakfast, which is served in the dining room or at poolside. The breakfast may include such dishes as Grand Marnier French toast and omelets, plus fruit, muffins, and more. There are plenty of super-comfortable common rooms—from the keeping room with its blazing hearth to an upstairs sitting room, a library with a Mercer tile fireplace, and a bright solarium. In addition to the pool there's a tennis court.

Rates (including breakfast): $145–$175 double.

The **Curley Mill Manor,** 776 N. Limekiln Pike, Chalfont, PA 18914 (tel. 215/997-9015), was built in 1831 and has been faithfully restored by the Rauschers. It's set on 4¼ acres and has an inviting rose-garden terrace and a small pool surrounded by grass. Guests can enjoy croquet, badminton, and volleyball in the warmer months. Four air-conditioned guest rooms are offered. The largest is the Manor Room, which boasts a carved rice four-poster, swagged window treatments, an antique armoire, a sofa, and a cane-back rocker. Extra touches include a decanter of amaretto and chocolate-covered nuts in each room. Guests may use the small but comfortable living room and the sun room with a pump organ and TV. A full breakfast is served inside or on the patio.

Rates (including breakfast): $85–$105 double.

New Hope Area Dining

I've already discussed a couple of places that rank among the very best in the area, notably the **Inn at Phillips Mill** and the **Hotel du Village**. Other first-rate choices previously covered include the **Centre Bridge Inn**, the **Black Bass**, the **Golden Pheasant**, and the **Stockton Inn**.

Some of the best dining in the area lies across the river from New Hope in such New Jersey towns as Lambertville and Frenchtown.

Lambertville Dining

The **Ferry House,** 21 Ferry St. (tel. 609/397-9222), is certainly a gem. Sleek and modern, a study in black and white, the room is a perfect foil for the cuisine, presented on striking faux-marble plates. The limited menu offers exciting well-flavored food. Among the entrees might be grilled peanut-crusted swordfish with curried banana and green-chile sauce, pan-seared beef tenderloin topped with bourbon-mushroom sauce, or grilled pork loin with black-bean salsa and melted Monterey Jack cheese. Prices range from $17 to $26. To begin, opt for the roast portobello mushroom with baby greens and balsamic vinaigrette. Finish with a perfect crème brûlée.

Hours: Mon–Sat 5pm–closing, Sun noon–3pm and 5pm–closing.

By the river in a little cul-de-sac known as the Porkyard, **Hamilton's Grill Room,** 8 Coryell St. (tel. 609/397-4343), is a pretty local favorite. Up front is a raw bar and a fresh fish display in front of the open grill. The inner dining room is more formal, with a mirrored ceiling and trompe-l'oeil sky. The woodstove is garlanded with plants and flowers in summer. Among the eight or so entrees might be grilled salmon with Dijon mustard and lime, pork loin with caramelized fennel and apricot, or grilled duck breast with honey, mustard, and green peppercorns. Start with the grilled sea scallops with prosciutto, lemon, and sage or baked chèvre with roasted vegetables. Prices range from $15 to $22.

Hours: Summer, Mon–Fri 6–10pm, Sat 5–10pm, Sun 5–9pm; the rest of the year, Mon–Sat 6–10pm, Sun 5–9pm.

Anton's at the Swan, 43 S. Main St. (tel. 609/397-1960), changes its menu monthly. The modern American cuisine uses the freshest local ingredients. The limited menu features only six or so entrees—grilled salmon with ginger-pumpkin sauce, roast monkfish on cilantro and scallions, grilled beef tenderloin with ancho chile sauce, or grilled venison with quince-and-apple relish, depending on the season. To start, you might find softshell crab; risotto of shrimp, tomatoes, and basil; or a tart with potatoes, olives, and sun-dried tomatoes. The ambience is warm, with wood paneling, brass sconces, and mirrors; a short menu is served in the bar.

Hours: Wed–Sat 6–10pm, Sun 4:30–8pm.

Manon, 19 N. Union St. (tel. 609/397-2596), is a small pretty dining room decorated with old photographs and posters of Provence and fresh potted plants. The menu features hearty bistro and regional cuisine. The chicken breast is enhanced by a full-flavored garlic sauce; a green-peppercorn sauce accompanies the sirloin, while provencal herbs bring out the flavor of the tender lamb chops. Seafood lovers will enjoy the bouillabaisse. The salted-codfish mousse in puff pastry with tomato coulis is a good start, or try the more subtly flavored grilled portobello mushroom with red-pepper oil on a bed of mesclun. On Wednesday and Thursday a prix-fixe menu is usually offered for around $20; otherwise, prices range from $17 to $22. The desserts are classics—smoooth rich chocolate terrine with raspberry coulis or golden apple or pear tartin. BYOB.

Hours: Wed–Thurs 5:30–9:30pm, Fri–Sat 5:30–10pm, Sun 11:30am–2:30pm and 5:30–9:30pm.

Back on Bridge Street at no. 23, **The Full Moon** (tel. 215/397-1096), is a casual spot with a light-oak and modern-graphics look. Here you can have a full breakfast (omelets, egg dishes) or savor a chocolate croissant or two. Salads, omelets, burgers, and sandwiches are the prime lunch items, while dinner features such dishes as walnut-breaded chicken with Dijon sauce, duck stuffed with apples and walnuts and served with either apple or cassis sauce, grilled tuna with capers and parsley, or filet mignon au poivre. Prices run $14 to $17. Bring your own wine.

Hours: Mon and Wed–Thurs 8am–3pm, Fri–Sat 8am–10pm, Sun 9am–3pm.

At the restored 1867 stone **Lambertville Station,** 11 Bridge St. (tel. 609/397-8300), there are a series of restaurants, a bar, and a lounge. Etched glass, oak, mirrors, period light fixtures, and Victorian furnishings create the atmosphere. About a dozen entrees are featured on the menu—trout almondine, swordfish with lemon butter, sesame chicken with raspberry sauce, veal chanterelle, and roast duck with sauce du jour. Prices range from $10.25 to $21.

Hours: Mon–Thurs 11:30am–3pm and 4–9pm, Fri–Sat 11:30am–3pm and 4–10pm, Sun 10:30am–3pm and 4–9pm.

New Hope Dining
Set in a condominium development known as Village 2, on a hill above New Hope, **La Bonne Auberge** (tel. 215/862-2462), a charming old stone inn, is a lovely surprise. The dining here is quite fine. Specialties include rack of lamb with provencal herbs, veal with morels, and grilled salmon with lobster sauce. Prices range from $27 to $34. Among the luxurious appetizers are Beluga caviar and foie gras, along with plainer items like avocado vinaigrette.

Hours: Wed–Sat 6–10pm, Sun 5:30–9pm.

Odette's, South River Road (tel. 215/862-3000), occupies a pretty stone house and offers several dining rooms overlooking the river. The atmosphere is warm and inviting, made even more so by the fireplace in the bar and the soft piano sounds (except Tuesday). In summer there's outdoor dining on the terrace and on Friday, Saturday, and Sunday year round there's cabaret and dancing in the Theater Room. The fare is continental and American—veal saltimbocca, chicken francais, filet mignon finished with port-wine/tarragon demiglaze, and grilled tuna steak topped with toasted pine nuts and shallot-herb butter. Prices range from $17 to $25.

Hours: Mon–Thurs 11:30am–3pm and 5–10pm, Fri–Sat 11:30am–3pm and 5–11pm, Sun 11:30am–3pm and 4–9pm.

The Forager House, 1600 River Rd. (tel. 215/862-9477), is a refreshing change from many area dining rooms because the decor is sleek and modern. The cuisine offers a range of dishes from several ethnic traditions. For example, among the appetizers on the seasonal summer menu might be everything from grilled Cajun shrimp with a barbecue cream to smoked chicken and Thai noodles with a peanut dressing, plus mussels steamed with white wine, garlic, and herbs. In addition to such main courses as wood-grilled salmon with gazpacho sauce and duck with honey-soy glaze, several pizzas, calzones, and pastas are available. Prices range from $8 to $21.

Hours: Mon and Wed–Thurs 5:30–9pm, Fri 5:30–10pm, Sat 11:30am–2:30pm and 5:30–10pm, Sun 11:30am–2:30pm and 4:30–9pm.

The Landing, 22 N. Main St. (tel. 215/862-5711), offers, as its name implies, river-view dining in the dining room and on the patio in summer. The seasonal menu will likely offer a mixture of traditional continental dishes, plus some regional American and Asian-accented items. There could be veal chop with green-peppercorn/mustard sauce; salmon glazed with tea, sesame, and soy and served with a tomato-and-ginger concassée; catfish served with a New Orleans rémoulade sauce and salsa; and smoked barbecued pork chop with apricot-and-chile barbecue sauce. Prices range from $18 to $25. To start there'll be a pâté and two soups of the day, plus some terrific smoked trout and smoked scallops and even Beluga caviar. Good lunch dishes include the traditional Muffaletta; sloppy toms made with ground turkey, tomatoes, green peppers, and spices; and other sandwiches and entrees.

Hours: Sun–Thurs 11am–4pm and 5–10pm, Fri–Sat 11am–4pm and 5–11pm.

The Raven, 385 W. Bridge St. (tel. 215/862-2081), is about a mile out of New Hope on Rte. 179. Here you can enjoy such entrees as duck with honey-ginger sauce; salmon with herb pesto of sage, rosemary, capers, sun-dried tomatoes, and garlic; chicken cacciatore; or rack of lamb with rosemary-Dijon demiglaze. Prices range from $14 to $20. The handsome wood-paneled dining room looks out over a pretty garden. Lunch is also a good bet.

Hours: Mon–Thurs noon–3pm and 6–10pm, Fri–Sat noon–3pm and 6–10:30pm, Sun noon–3pm and 5–10pm.

For casual dining and great breakfasts and lunches in a warm rustic atmosphere, head for **Mother's,** 34 N. Main St. (tel. 215/862-9354). The breakfast choices are eye-opening. My favorite is the Santa Fe scramble, made with peppers, onions, and jack cheese and wrapped in a tortilla with salsa. At lunch all kinds of burgers (meat, salmon, vegetable), sandwiches, pizza, pasta, and salads are available, plus such specialties as Mother's Hot Pot filled with chicken, duck, pork, and beef braised with barbecue sauce and sweet potatoes and served over cornbread. Prices range from $7 to $12. Dinner brings more substantial dishes like duck with orange sauce, prime rib, steaks, and seafood—priced from $14 to $18. Desserts baked on the premises are also prime attractions.

Hours: Mon–Thurs 9am–9pm, Fri 9am–10:30pm, Sat 8am–10:30pm, Sun 8am–9pm.

Lake Nockamixon Dining

The **Harrowe Inn,** Rtes. 611 and 412, Ottsville (tel. 610/847-2464), is a great favorite for atmospheric dining. Although it was built around 1720 for fur trappers and Indian traders, it became an inn in 1744. Chef Tell is a celebrity chef known for fine cuisine, German in particular. You'll therefore likely find such dishes as a German sausage platter with sauerkraut, wienerschnitzel, grilled pork loin with sweet chutney, and strip steak with shallots, French mustard, and peppercorns accompanied by delicious rösti potatoes. Prices range from $10 to $20. The appetizers tilt more to the Caribbean than to Germany, featuring such items as coconut shrimp with apricot-mustard sauce and conch fritters Cayman style, along with a German onion tart.

Hours: Tues–Sat 5pm–closing, Sun 4–8pm.

New Hope Area After Dark

For theater entertainment, the **Bucks County Playhouse,** South Main Street (P.O. Box 313), New Hope (tel. 215/862-2041), stages musicals, including some Gilbert and Sullivan, in a converted gristmill. The season runs Easter through Christmas. Over in Princeton, N.J., the **McCarter Theater,** 91 University Pl. (tel. 609/683-8000), presents a full season of professional drama, dance, music, and special events.

For jazz lovers there's music Thursday to Sunday at the **Havana Bar and Restaurant,** 105 S. Main St., New Hope (tel. 215/862-9897).

In Doylestown, the **Doylestown Inn,** 18 W. State St. (tel. 215/345-6610), has a DJ Thursday to Saturday.

In Lambertville, the **Swan Hotel,** 43 S. Main St. (tel. 609/397-3552), draws crowds regularly from as far away as Princeton to its typical

English-style pub. It's open daily from 4pm to 2am. Other pleasant bars are found at the old inns stretching along Rte. 32 north, the **Golden Pheasant** and the **Black Bass.** Then, of course, there's the **Logan Inn** itself, whose tavern brings back so many memories from the 1930s. **Lambertville Station,** 11 Bridge St. (tel. 609/397-8300), has a DJ on Friday and Saturday in the downstairs bar. There are other dancing spots around, some straight, some gay. Ask the locals for details.

The New Hope Area
Special & Recreational Activities

Antiquing: The whole area is dotted with stores specializing in all sorts of items. Frenchtown has many good stores, and the road (Rte. 202) from New Hope to Lahaska is well stocked with stores. For information, write the Bucks County Antique Dealers Association, 5 Byron Lane, Yardley, PA 19067.

Ballooning: Harrison Aire, Wertsville Road (P.O. Box 73), Hopewell, NJ 08551 (tel. 609/466-3389), offers daily champagne balloon flights for $160. They've been in business for 20 years. The whole experience lasts about three hours, though flight time is only one hour.

Canoeing & Rafting: Point Pleasant Canoe, P.O. Box 6, Point Pleasant, PA 18950 (tel. 215/297-8823 or 297-8181), offers canoeing, tubing, and rafting trips on the river. There are several options available—6-mile/two-hour and 13-mile/four-hour canoe trips costing $20 and $25, respectively; 6-mile/four-hour rafting trips at $15 per person; and tubing trips that are $15 for adults and $12 for children 10 and under on weekends. Reservations are needed.

Golf: Five Ponds, 1225 W. Street Rd., Warminster (tel. 215/956-9727).

Hiking: There's a quiet, grassy towpath along the canal and some other trails in local state parks—for example, at Washington's Crossing, Bull's Run across the footbridge at Lumberville. See "State Parks," below.

Picnicking: Head for the Bowman's Hill State Wildflower Preserve or any state park, including the one along the towpath.

Shopping: Flemington, N.J., is famous for its outlets (tel. 908/806-8165)—close to 200 of them, ranging from Dansk and Reebok to Ann Klein, Calvin Klein, and Joan & David. For landscaped shopping, some people enjoy Peddlers Village at Rtes. 202 and 263 in Lahaska (tel. 215/794-7055). For confirmed tourists only.

State Parks: The Delaware Canal State Park, R.R. 1, Box 615A, Upper Black Eddy, PA 18972 (tel. 215/982-5560), stretches along the canal that's the only intact remnant from the great canal-building era. It's ideal for biking, hiking, horseback riding, cross-country skiing, and picnicking. Nockamixon State Park, 1542 Mountain View Dr., Quakertown, PA 18951 (tel. 215/538-2151), offers picnicking, swimming, fishing, hiking, boat and bike rentals, sledding, ice boating, ice fishing, and skating, in a 5,250-acre area. The 45-acre Ralph Stover Park, 6011 State Park Rd., Pipersville, PA 18947 (tel. 610/982-5560), has picnicking, fishing, hiking, sledding, and cross-country skiing. Tyler State Park, south of Washington Crossing at 101 Swamp Rd., Newtown, PA 18940 (tel. 215/968-2021), has close to 2,000 acres for picnicking, fishing, boating (rentals available), hiking, bicycling (rentals available), ice skating and fishing, sledding, and cross-country skiing. Bull's Island, N.J., across the river at Lumberville, has camping, picnicking, and birding.

Swimming: See "State Parks," above, and the Hotel du Village, Barley Sheaf, and Whitehall Farms.

Tennis: The Hotel du Village and Whitehall Farm have courts. For other locations, call the chambers of commerce.

White-Water Rafting: See "Canoeing & Rafting," above. Call 215/297-8823 for information.

Greater Wilmington, the Brandywine Valley & Valley Forge

Distance in Miles: Valley Forge, 115; Wilmington, 121
Estimated Driving Time: 2½ hours

◄o►◄o►◄o►◄o►◄o►

Driving: For Wilmington, take the New Jersey Turnpike to I-95 to the Delaware Avenue exit (Exit 7). For Valley Forge, take the New Jersey Turnpike to the Pennsylvania Turnpike (I-76) to the Valley Forge exit.

Bus: Greyhound (tel. 800/231-2222) goes to Wilmington and King of Prussia.

Train: Amtrak (tel. 800/872-7245) runs to Wilmington. It also goes from Philadelphia to Harrisburg, stopping en route at the small towns of Downingtown and Malvern (both southwest of Valley Forge).

Further Information: For more on the area, contact the following: the **Greater Wilmington Convention and Visitor's Bureau,** 1300 Market St., Wilmington, DE 19801 (tel. 302/652-4088, or 800/422-1181); **Delaware Tourism** (tel. 800/441-8846); or the **Valley Forge Country Convention and Visitors Bureau,** 600 W. Germantown Pike, Suite 130, Plymouth Meeting, PA 19462 (tel. 610/834-1550, or 800/441-3549).

◄o►◄o►◄o►◄o►◄o►

Most New Yorkers associate Brandywine with the battle of that name, but few have ever visited this lovely part of the country where the landscape is very much like the English countryside. The gently rounded hills, the big old barns, the grazing horses, the roadside wildflowers, and the driftwood and willows along the Brandywine River's banks are all on a human scale. Besides its pleasant green landscape, the area is exceedingly rich in prime attractions—the finest collection of American furniture and decorative arts anywhere at Winterthur, an outstanding American garden at Longwood, a couple of truly fine art museums displaying the works of the school of painters inspired by the Brandywine River, a château to match any in France at Nemours, and a fascinating museum capturing part of America's early industrial history at Hagley. The Brandywine may be a narrow and short river, but it possesses a great and inspiring tradition.

There are a couple of ways to explore the area over a weekend. You can go to Wilmington and stay at the venerable Hotel duPont, which Craig Claiborne ranks with London's Connaught and New York's Plaza, or you can anchor at Valley Forge, only about 45 minutes away from most of the attractions.

WILMINGTON

Wilmington Attractions

Only a few blocks from the Hotel duPont, the **Market Street Mall** has been constructed around a series of splendid old buildings, including a fine 18th-century civic building, the **Old Town Hall,** 500 block of Market Street Mall (tel. 302/655-7161), where you may want to begin to get a fix on Delaware history. Normally it would feature displays of regional decorative arts, children's toys, and other changing exhibits highlighting aspects of local history, but it's currently closed for renovation—however, it may reopen by the time this book appears. Among its treasures is one of the original chairs given by George Washington to each of the signers of the Declaration of Independence. The collection also includes an Early American primitive sculpture of Washington, carved to replace the one of George III the patriots tore down at Bowling Green in New York City, and which Sen. T. Coleman duPont found languishing outside a barbershop.

Hours: Call for further information.

Farther down Market Street, at no. 818, stands the Grand Opera House (1871), Delaware's **Center for the Performing Arts,** a magnificent Second Empire–style building with a cast-iron facade resembling chiseled marble. Restored to its original Victorian splendor, it echoes to the applause of audiences enjoying a variety of programs—from Robin Williams and Marcel Marceau to the London Philharmonic and the Academy of St. Martin-in-the-Fields—as they did when such figures as Edwin Booth (brother of John Wilkes Booth), Buffalo Bill, Ethel Barrymore, and James O'Neill (father of Eugene O'Neill) performed here. Tours of the building, which enable you to see the magnificent frescoed ceiling and lavish decor, can be arranged but you must call ahead. The season runs from September to July. For tickets and information, call 302/658-7897.

In summer you can take a stroll down the pedestrian Market Street Mall, browsing the store windows or stopping for some refreshment at one of the sidewalk cafés.

Events & Festivals to Plan Your Trip Around

February: Washington's Birthday Weekend reenactment of the winter of 1777–78 in Valley Forge Historic Park. Drilling, shooting, cooking demonstrations, and more (usually the third weekend).

April: Winterthur in the Spring, Winterthur Museum.

April to Mid-May: Blossom time in Valley Forge Park.

May: Winterthur Point-to-Point (first Sunday).

Wilmington Garden Day (first Saturday).

Devon Horse Show and Country Fair. Contact Devon Horse Show and Country Fair, Rte. 30, Devon, PA 19333 (tel. 215/964-0550), usually the last weekend.

A day in Old New Castle, 6 or so miles south of Wilmington (usually the third Saturday).

June: Festival of the Arts, Longwood Gardens. Call 215/388-6741 (third week).

July: Old-Fashioned Fourth at Rockwood Museum, Wilmington.

August: Goschenhoppen Folk Festival, authentic noncommercial Pennsylvania Dutch Festival on Rte. 29, Green Lane (usually the second weekend).

September: Reenactment of the Battle of the Brandywine. Contact Brandywine Battlefield State Park, P.O. Box 202, Chadds Ford, PA 19317 (tel. 610/459-3342).

October: Chester County Day in West Chester—historic house tours, hunt and hounds (first Saturday).

Laerenswert ("worth doing"). Craftspeople demonstrate and invite audience participation at the Peter Wentz farmstead (usually the second Saturday).

December: Candlelight tours at Hagley, Winterthur, and Rockwood Museums. Also of Historic Old New Castle.

Valley Forge Music Fair: Though it operates year round, full billings really begin in March and run to December. Contact P.O. Box 917, Devon, PA 19333 (tel. 215/644-5000).

Just outside Wilmington are several more attractions. The closest is the **Delaware Art Museum,** 2301 Kentmere Pkwy. (tel. 302/571-9590 for information, 571-9594 for tour reservations), internationally known for its collection of pre-Raphaelite paintings hanging in a gallery decorated with period wallpaper specially designed for the museum by William Morris. The museum also displays illustrations of pirates, soldiers, and fictional characters depicted by Howard Pyle, father of the Brandywine School of Art, and examples of other fine American artists, like John

Sloan and Edward Hopper. To get here, take I-95 to Wilmington Exit 7 (Rte. 52 north).

Hours: Tues–Sat 10am–5pm, Sun noon–5pm. **Closed:** New Year's Day, Thanksgiving, Christmas. **Admission:** $5 adults, $3 seniors, $2.50 students.

Rockwood, 610 Shipley Rd. (tel. 302/761-4340), is one of the few American examples of rural gothic architecture and the Gardenesque school of landscape design. In the rooms you'll find decorative arts from the 17th to the mid-19th century, reflecting the lifestyles of the Bringhurst family who lived here. It's also famous for its conservatory, collections of overlay glass, and archives of photographs, documents, and wallpaper designs.

Hours: Guided tours of house, Tues–Sat 11am–4pm, Sun noon–4pm (the gardens can be toured during the same hours). **Admission:** $5 adults, $4 seniors, $1 children 5–16.

Named after the French ancestral home of the duPonts, **Nemours** (tel. 302/651-6912) is as close as you'll get to a French château in this country. On this 300-acre country estate, Alfred I. duPont had Carrère and Hastings of New York build a 102-room mansion where he entertained lavishly. On arrival, you'll receive a glass of fresh juice, then will be ushered through the house to feast your eyes on the exquisite European art and furnishings. The ornate wrought-iron gates were commissioned by Henry VIII as a gift for his sixth wife, Catherine Parr; another set of gates came from Catherine the Great's palace in St. Petersburg; one of the many clocks was made for Marie Antoinette; and there are many tapestries, rugs, and paintings, some dating to the 15th century. The rooms give a wonderful insight into the family's opulent lifestyle—vintage automobiles, a billiard room, a nine-pins alley, a bottling plant, and an ice plant. Throughout you'll notice personal items (a fishing trophy taken by Mrs. duPont, for example) and will learn about the character of the owner, who had the statuary washed every day and who personally inspected the boiler and heating system. The formal gardens are splendid, some of the finest examples of the French style to be found anywhere in America. The obligatory guided tours take about two hours. The mansion is on Rockland Road between Rtes. 141 and 202, just north of Wilmington across the Brandywine River.

Tours: May–Nov, Tues–Sun at 9am, 11am, 1pm, and 3pm. **Admission:** $8. Reservations are required and visitors must be 16 or over. Contact the Nemours Mansion and Gardens, Reservations Office, P.O. Box 109, Wilmington, DE 19899 (tel. 302/651-6912).

Wilmington Lodging

The **Hotel duPont,** 11th and Market streets (P.O. Box 991, Rodney Square), Wilmington, DE 19899 (tel. 302/656-8121), is a venerable establishment where you immediately feel welcome. It's not in the least ostentatious— the luxury comes from service and attention to details: 24-hour room service; towels that are changed twice daily; a croissant, coffee, and a newspaper delivered to your room in the morning; turndown service; and a chocolate mint on your pillow and similar little touches. Each of the 206 large rooms features a service bar, a TV/VCR, a large leather-inlaid desk, an in-room safe, and two phone lines with voice mail in three languages. Many famous personalities have bedded down here since it opened in 1913—Duke Ellington, Amelia Earhart, Eugene O'Neill, Tallulah Bankhead, Dorothy Gish, and even Paderewski, who angered other guests by playing his piano well into the night.

Even if you don't stay here, you might think of attending the justly famous $27.50 brunch (reservations necessary), where you can treat yourself to a lavish spread of appetizers—smoked salmon, shrimp-and-tomato salad, veal terrine with duck sausage and morels, and many more. Then you have a choice among several entrees, like a chanterelle-and-crab omelet, grilled filet mignon with celeriac and red-wine sauce, and brioche French toast with fruit compote. It's served in the formal Green Room, an imposing oak-paneled space with majestic 18-foot Palladian windows draped and valanced in gold fabric, a coffered ceiling that's carved and gilded ornately, and gilt chandeliers and sconces; there's also a musician's loft. The tables are set with Rosenthal china.

At dinner the menu features such items as pheasant breast with roasted garlic flan and black trumpet mushrooms, filet mignon with potato crust finished with a cabernet sauce and portobello mushrooms, grilled lamb loin with a sesame sauce, or grilled red snapper with an olive crust served with slow-roasted plum-tomato confit and basil oil—all priced from $20 to $29. My favorite desserts are the stuffed white-chocolate timbale with fresh fruit and orange sauce and the lemon crème brûlée with a cherry coulis. The Brandywine Room is richly paneled and enhanced with originals by Howard Pyle and three generations of Wyeths; it's noted for its fine cuisine too—duck with a cider-ginger sauce, striped bass with lemongrass broth, and veal Chesapeake with jumbo lump crabmeat and sauce béarnaise. The lower-level grill serves cafeteria-style breakfast and lunch. Facilities include fitness club and shopping arcade.

Rates: $119–$169 double weekends, $179–$239 double weekdays.

The **Hilton,** I-95 and Naamans Road, Claymont, DE 19703 (tel. 302/792-2700), is on the outskirts of Wilmington (about 8 miles, or 10 minutes, from downtown) and offers modern rooms with full amenities. The Evergreens restaurant offers New American cuisine. There are 187 bedroom/sitting rooms and 7 suites. The seventh-floor executive rooms are spacious, with enough room for a desk and couch and a coffee table. On the same floor is a convenient lounge area and plenty of business and other magazines to read. Whispers lounge is crowded, especially on weekends, when a DJ spins for dancing. The hotel has an outdoor kidney-shaped pool.

Rates: From $109 double. Special weekend packages available.

The **Holiday Inn Downtown,** 700 King St., Customs House Plaza, Wilmington, DE 19801 (tel. 302/655-0400), is in a modern nine-story building. The 217 rooms are tastefully furnished and you can opt for a

Wilmington & the Brandywine Valley

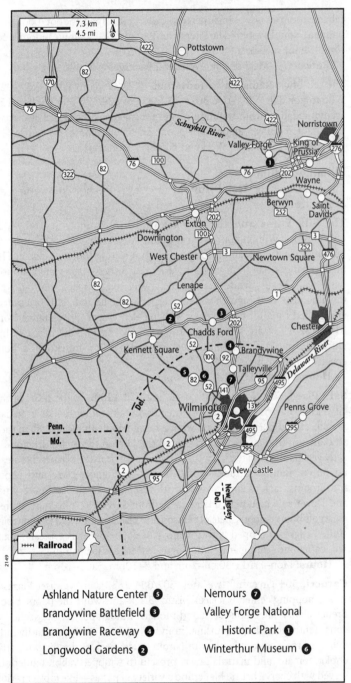

Ashland Nature Center ❺

Brandywine Battlefield ❸

Brandywine Raceway ❹

Longwood Gardens ❷

Nemours ❼

Valley Forge National
Historic Park ❶

Winterthur Museum ❻

427

cabana room overlooking the tropically landscaped indoor pool or a standard double room. The American Bar and Grill and an indoor pool complete the facilities.

Rates: $79–$103 double. Weekend packages available.

The red-brick **Radisson Brandywine,** 4727 Concord Pike (Rte. 202), Wilmington, DE 19803 (tel. 302/478-6000, or 800/325-3535), offers 154 accommodations with standard modern furnishings. The hotel also has a restaurant, a lounge, an outdoor pool, and six outdoor tennis courts.

Rates: $129 double. Weekend packages available.

Wilmington Dining

The brunch at the **Hotel duPont** (above) is the best known and an elegant treat.

The Silk Purse and the Sow's Ear, 1307 N. Scott St. (tel. 302/654-7666), is Wilmington's premier dining spot. In an obscure white brick building, it provides an understated elegant setting for fine cuisine. The menu changes daily but offers a variety of dishes—pan-seared salmon with black beans, white-bean purée, sweet red peppers, and smoked tomato sauce; venison with soft mascarpone polenta and chili corn sauce; and grilled tuna on fried greens with pickled ginger. Prices range from $16 to $25. To start, select the corn-coated oysters on salsa fresca with a chipotle cream or the crabmeat quesadilla with yellow-tomato salsa, both specialties of the house.

Hours: Tues–Sat 5:30–9 or 9:30pm.

Sal's Place, 603 N. Lincoln St. (tel. 302/652-1200), in the heart of the city's Little Italy, is one of the top three restaurants. It looks like an Italian neighborhood place, and that's what a lot of people think it is when they stray in—until they see the prices and the fare on the menu. It's not exactly veal parmigiana territory. Instead, the menu features classics like steak au poivre flambée; duck with cabernet-sauvignon glaze and cèpes mushrooms; rack of lamb roasted with rosemary, thyme, and port wine; and Dover sole meunière. Prices range from $18 to $27. To start, there's escargots bourguignons, pâté of venison and black truffles, and Gorgonzola-stuffed eggplant topped with tomato sauce. The decor is typical—plain red leatherette seating and undistinguished landscape paintings.

Hours: Mon–Fri 11:30am–2pm and 5–10pm, Sat 5–10pm.

Carucci, 504 Greenhill Ave. (tel. 302/654-2333), in Wawaset Plaza, a small shopping center, is a sleek bistro. Black-and-white tile floors, black Breuer chairs, large bouquets, and modern lithographs set the scene for consistently good Italian cuisine, from $14 to $22. Dishes might include delicious roast rack of lamb with barolo sauce; beef tenderloin with artichoke, tomato, and marsala sauce; prosciutto-wrapped rabbit tenderloin served with chervil beurre blanc; and a variety of pastas—like lobster ravioli and penne with spicy tomato-basil sauce.

Hours: Mon–Fri 11:30am–2:30pm and 5:30–10:30pm, Sat 5:30–10:30pm.

Dinardo's Seafood, Fourth and Lincoln streets (tel. 302/656-3685), is a traditional regional favorite for crabs, although ironically they actually come from Louisiana. Still, crabs here are steamed, sautéed, deviled, or Imperial. Noncrab fanciers can sample clams and mussels as well as stuffed flounder and barbecued shrimp, from $7 to $15 (with king crab legs going for $38). The room is plain—wood tables and Hitchcock chairs—but it's a real Wilmington treat.

Hours: Mon–Sat 11am–11pm, Sun 3–10pm.

AN EXCURSION TO NEW CASTLE

New Castle Attractions

Only a 15-minute drive south of Wilmington lies historic New Castle, one of Delaware's oldest settlements and a lovely town to visit for a full day or just an afternoon. In 1631 the Dutch established the fishing settlement of Zwannendael (Valley of Swans) on the site of present-day Lewes. This settlement was destroyed by Native Americans, and so it was left to Sweden to plant the first settlement at the mouth of the Christina River in 1638. The Dutch conquered this little colony in 1655 and renamed it New Amstel, a name the English changed to New Castle when they took over.

There's bound to be something happening on the **Green**—like an art or craft show. Around it are beautiful historic buildings, all still used and many still fine residences. For example, on the east side of the quadrangle is the **Academy** (1799). Adjacent to it, the oldest part of the handsome **Imanuel Episcopal Church** dates to 1703, although the congregation was established in 1689. Its graveyard contains many stones from the 1700s.

On the north side of the square are rows of old residences, including the **Old Dutch House** at 32 E. Third St. (open Jan–Feb, Sat 11am–4pm, Sun 1–4pm; Mar–Dec, Tues–Sat 11am–4pm, Sun 1–4pm). Also on this side is the **Old Library Town Museum,** 40 E. Third St., an interesting hexagonal structure built in 1892 in which you can research local history (open Sat 11am–4pm, Sun 1–4pm). On the west side is the **Old Court House.** In May many homes are open to the public (see the "Events & Festivals" box at the beginning of this chapter). For details, call the New Castle Historical Society at 302/322-2794.

As you walk along the brick sidewalks, note the rise and fall of the pathway around the roots of the old trees that line the streets.

At a point not far from the Delaware River, a marker indicates the spot where William Penn landed on October 27, 1682. For additional information on New Castle, call 302/323-4453.

New Castle Lodging & Dining

The **David Finney Inn,** 216 Delaware St., New Castle, DE 19720 (tel. 302/322-6367), well known for its tavern/dining room and historic atmosphere, was recently severely damaged by fire. It's currently being restored and will open sometime in 1996. It should retain its style and quality, so I suggest you call and check it out.

Serenely facing the tree-lined cobblestone street in Old New Castle, with its back to the Green, is the **Arsenal on the Green,** 30 Market St. (tel. 302/328-1290). The two dining rooms—one decorated in cranberry, the other in Wedgwood blue, both with sparkling white tablecloths and pink napkins and several pieces of sculpture and other artwork—are lovely spots for sampling traditional American cuisine. The regional specialties are the Delaware crab cakes. There's also veal Arsenal with lemon sauce; pork medallions Créole with a Créole mustard sauce; and chicken Chesapeake—chicken breast topped with crab Imperial and hollandaise. Prices range from $13 to $20. For an appetizer, try the shrimp rémoulade or stuffed mushrooms. Some folks will want to try the traditional drinks like grog (rum, water, and sugar, served hot or cold) or the 18th-century favorite, Sangaree (madeira with lemon and orange juices and a dash of soda).

Hours: Mon–Sat 11am–2pm and 5–9pm, Sun 11am–2pm and 3–8pm.

THE BRANDYWINE RIVER VALLEY

Area Attractions

Three miles northwest of Wilmington, more of the duPont legacy can be viewed at the 230-acre **Hagley Museum** (tel. 302/658-2400), bordering the Brandywine River. This is where Eleuthère Irénée duPont established his first powder mills in 1802, after hearing, according to family legend, a retired artillery colonel complain about the inferiority of American gunpowder compared to European. These mills were simple stamping and rolling operations, where workers blended sulfur, saltpeter, and charcoal into black powder. Water was diverted from the river and channeled through a series of wooden waterwheels, and later turbines provided power to turn the massive granite stones that ground the ingredients.

Today you can see this process as the powderman opens the millrace gates and lets the water do its work. In the 1850s steam engines were used, and the museum has one of these operating. In the main museum building, exhibits trace the change from water to giant steam-powered industries. At one time, 33 mills stretched along the river (part of 21 of them can now be seen). To minimize the devastation that an unexpected explosion could cause, the mills were designed with an opening over the river to direct a blast away from the duPont home and the workers' cottages on the bluff above.

From the powder yards a bus takes you to **Eleutherian Mills,** a handsome Georgian residence built for E. I. duPont in 1803; it has been furnished to reflect the changing tastes of the five generations of duPonts who lived here until 1958—with the exception of the years 1890 to 1923, when a blast drove them out. The modest office building can be seen, along with the workshop of Lammot duPont, whose discovery of how to make explosives with Peruvian nitrate gave the Union forces superior firepower in the Civil War. The mills became obsolete after World War I and were closed in 1921. Allow three or four hours for a leisurely visit.

Hours: Mid-Mar to Dec, daily 9:30am–4:30pm; Jan to mid-Mar, Sat–Sun 9:30am–4:30pm, one tour daily at 1:30pm. **Closed:** Major winter holidays. **Admission:** $9.75 adults, $7.50 seniors and students, $3.50 children 6–14.

Kids always enjoy the **Delaware Museum of Natural History,** Rte. 52, Greenville (tel. 302/658-9111), which has, among other displays, a renowned shell collection of over a million items and possesses the egg of an elephant bird, which weighs 27 pounds! Exhibit highlights include a visit to an African waterhole, a walk over the Great Barrier Reef, and an introduction to Delaware fauna.

Hours: Mon–Sat 9:30am–4:30pm, Sun noon–5pm. **Closed:** New Year's Day, July 4, Thanksgiving, and Christmas. **Admission:** $4 adults, $3 seniors and children 3–17.

Winterthur

Antiques lovers, craftspeople, historians, and interior designers may want to spend a whole day at Winterthur (tel. 302/888-4600), 6 miles north of Wilmington, for this collection of furniture and decorative arts is extraordinary. It was amassed by Henry Francis duPont, who began collecting in the 1920s and had acquired before his death in 1969 a matchless collection of antiques made or used in America between 1640 and 1860. The collection includes furniture, textiles, paintings, prints, pewter, silver, ceramics, and glass. Highlights are a set of six silver tankards made by Paul Revere; John Trumbull's portrait of George Washington at Verplanck's Point; and Chinese export porcelain including a 66-piece dinner set made for Washington. DuPont also purchased interior architecture to use in several rooms, including the Port Royal Parlor from Frankford, Penn.; a drawing room from Richmond County, Va.; a Commons room from a Delaware inn; the Montmorency staircase from a house in North Carolina; and a 17th-century room from Ipswich, Mass.

The collection is displayed in two buildings. The 175 Period Rooms are seen only on guided tours. As you go from room to room, you'll see beautifully crafted highboys and lowboys made by Townsend and Goddard, Shaker furniture, a stair hall filled with miniatures, exquisite pie-crust tables, lusterware, glass, and textiles. On a first visit you'll see only a fraction of the rooms.

The galleries offer a more traditional museum experience. On the first floor, "Perspectives on the Decorative Arts in Early America" in the Walter J. Laird Gallery introduces you to 200 years of American decorative arts. On the second floor, the Henry S. McNeil Gallery has three display areas focusing on furniture and traditions of craftsmanship. These galleries feature some interactive exhibits.

The whole collection is at the home duPont occupied until 1951. During his lifetime Winterthur was a self-contained, nearly self-sustaining community with turkey and sheep farms, vegetable gardens, greenhouses, a golf course, a sawmill, a rail station, a post office, and a prize-winning herd of Holstein Friesian cattle. Today the estate covers nearly 1,000 acres. DuPont's first love was horticulture, and he designed the garden with an eye to color, shapes, and vista, planning it so that it'd have to have color almost year round. Spring presents the most glorious color show—lilacs, daffodils, azaleas, and dogwoods—while fall offers the changing hues of the foliage.

If you decide to spend the day or arrive around lunch for the afternoon, the Garden Restaurant and Cafeteria offer lunch, afternoon tea, and Sunday brunch. After your meal, stop at the museum stores in the Pavilion and on Clenny Run across from the museum for a selection of licensed reproductions, gifts, books, jewelry, home accessories, and plants. Special events include the Winterthur Point-to-Point races, the first Sunday in May, and County Pride Pops, an outdoor concert with the Delaware Symphony Orchestra in July.

Hours: Mon–Sat 9am–5pm, Sun noon–5pm. **Closed:** New Year's Day, Thanksgiving, Christmas. **Admission** (including a self-guided garden walk and the galleries): $8 adults, $6 seniors and students, $4 children 5–11. **Special Tours:** Guided tour of selected period rooms, add $5 (reservations recommended); one-hour decorative arts tour, add $9; two-hour tour, add $13 (reservations required). Mid-Nov to Jan, over 20 rooms highlight the holiday celebrations of the 18th and 19th centuries during the annual Yuletide tour.

Longwood Gardens & Environs

Longwood Gardens is on Rte. 1, over the state border in Kennett Square, Penn. (tel. 610/388-1000 for information, 388-6771 for the restaurant). I envy the curator of Longwood, for he can enjoy the beauty of the gardens in all seasons and weathers.

The conservatory is breathtaking year round, but the outdoor gardens are in their prime during spring and summer, when they burst forth with magnolias, flowering crab apples, cherries, dogwoods, rhododendrons, wisteria, and thousands of annuals and perennials. The show continues through summer, when the formal Rose Garden blossoms and 5 acres of fountain gardens in front of the conservatory play, cooling the air with magnificent jets of water (along with the Italian Water Garden fountains), and the other specialty gardens of topiary, vegetables, and wildflowers can be seen to full advantage.

The 4-acre **conservatory** is radiantly filled with the colors, scents, and textures of seasonal displays. Spring begins here in January, when cyclamen and narcissus bloom, followed by tulips, crab apples, and acacias in February, then magnolias, wisterias, azaleas, freesias, stocks, daffodils, hyacinths, primrose, Easter lilies, and velvet-sheened deep-red pocketbook flowers in March (a display that'll gladden any winter-wearied heart). November is the time for a fantastic display of 20,000 chrysanthemums, while at Christmas the garden conifers sparkle with 400,000 lights and the conservatory is filled with red, pink, and white poinsettias and red-berried hollies.

Besides the special displays in the main conservatory, you can view orchids (6,000 plants are cultivated here, 1,200 or so hybrids or species, with only the best culled for display), centuries-old bonsai, all kinds of exotic tropical plants and cacti, and, at the center of it all, the **lily pond**—a true highlight—where lily pads as large as 7 feet in diameter float along with lilies that vary from tiny, perfect flowers to large orbs of deep purple, magenta, magnolia-pink, and yellow, many of which open even on the dullest of days. There's also a **children's garden** with a fun maze.

Longwood has other delights, like the 2,100-seat **theater,** inspired by the Villa Gori near Siena, Italy, which is set amid a copse of trees and hosts music, drama, and dance performances in summer. In place of the traditional curtain a brilliant screen is created by a row of illuminated fountains. After a performance additional fountains in the stage floor rise as high as 50 feet into the trees. Tinted lights shine on the water to create a liquid kaleidoscope.

Another show is given in summer: For three nights a week the 5 acres of **fountains** in front of the conservatory are illuminated in all colors of the rainbow as they shoot 130 feet into the air, bringing to mind a marvelous inverted Niagara Falls. After the show, visitors are free to wander through the conservatories and admire the exotic night-blooming water lilies, which are artfully lighted.

For those who enjoy music, a mammoth **pipe organ,** whose pipes are housed in nine rooms, is played regularly from October to April. Located in the conservatory ballroom with its wonderful pink-glass ceiling, the instrument boasts 10,010 pipes, some as long as 32 feet, and a full array of percussive devices, like drums, castanets, cymbals, a grand piano, and a Chinese gong.

Finally, there's the old **Peirce-duPont house,** open for self-guided tours. The Longwood property was granted to the Peirces by William Penn in 1700, and it was two Peirce brothers who laid out an arboretum of ornamental trees. The impending destruction of this arboretum prompted

Pierre duPont, great-grandson of founder Eleuthère, to purchase Peirce's Park (as it was called in 1906) and develop it into a horticultural showplace. The house is filled with photos and memorabilia tracing Longwood's history from 1700 to the present, with special emphasis on duPont's accomplishments. Here in the den duPont designed much of what you'll see at Longwood—1,050 acres tended by a full- and part-time staff of 444, including 55 full-time gardeners.

Longwood is frequently open evenings for fountain shows and holiday displays. For a current schedule of events, send a self-addressed stamped envelope to Schedule, Longwood Gardens, P.O. Box 501, Kennett Square, PA 19348. Longwood also has a very fine restaurant and self-service café.

Hours: Apr–Oct, conservatories, daily 10am–6pm; outdoor gardens, daily 9am–6pm. Nov–Mar, conservatories, daily 10am–5pm; outdoor gardens, daily 9am–5pm. **Admission:** $10 adults ($6 on Tues), $6 youths 16–20, $2 children 6–15.

Mushroom Capital

While you're in the area you really should savor, or at least take home, some of the local delicacy—mushrooms. Kennett Square is known as the mushroom capital of the world and only half a mile south on Rte. 1 from Longwood Gardens, you can stop at **Phillips Mushroom Place**, 909 E. Baltimore Pike (tel. 610/388-6082), and pick up a basket or baskets of mushrooms—portobello, crimini, oyster, and shiitake. According to the wisdom of the place, you can partially cook and then freeze the mushrooms. You may want to buy them before you go into the museum and discover the growing process to which they've been submitted. The store is also filled with all kinds of mushroomabilia.

Hours: Daily 10am–6pm.

Chadds Ford

A few miles east along Rte. 1 you'll come to Chadds Ford, heart of the Brandywine Valley and home of the famous **Brandywine River Museum** (tel. 610/388-2700), an old grist mill that has been artfully converted into a museum displaying American art, including the works of the region's most famous artists—the Wyeths. Around the mill the architect has wrapped several brick terraces and added dramatic towers of glass that give views over the creek and surrounding pastoral scenery. The galleries with plaster walls and hand-hewn beams seem appropriate to the art, which is firmly rooted in a sense of place. On the second floor the works of the Wyeths are displayed—N. C. (illustrator of *Kidnapped* and *Treasure Island*), Jamie, Carolyn, and Henriette. On the first floor is a gallery devoted to the Brandywine River and its artists, including Howard Pyle, father of them all, Horace Pippin, W. T. Smedley, Frank Schoonover, and Maxfield Parrish. The third floor features a gallery devoted to the works of Andrew Wyeth and another used for changing exhibitions. Special events are held throughout the year in the Belgian block–paved courtyard.

Hours: Daily 9:30am–4:30pm. **Admission:** $5 adults, $2.50 seniors and children 6 and up.

Just east of Chadds Ford, **Brandywine Battlefield Park,** Rte. 1 (tel. 610/459-3342), makes a lovely setting for a picnic. Great rounded hills, with sturdy old trees, overlook a brook that runs down toward a fieldstone Georgian-style church, whose weathered gravestones stand silently brooding. Although the Battle of Brandywine was fought around the church, it remained neutral, and no soldier from either side is buried here. Dioramas in the visitor center tell the story of the battle on September 11, 1777, while Washington's headquarters and the Marquis de Lafayette's quarters show life during the Revolutionary War.

Hours: Tues–Sat 9am–5pm, Sun noon–5pm.

At the junction of Rtes. 1 and 100, behind the Chadds Ford Inn, the **Christian Sanderson Museum** (tel. 610/696-3234) grants an intimate look at a community. There are paintings and sketches from every member of the Wyeth family, including a very early Andrew Wyeth painting done for Chris Sanderson's mother. A close friend of the Wyeth family, Sanderson also happened to collect everything that passed into his hands. He even kept the notes people wrote on the pad he provided at his door. Here you'll see it all—valentines, autographs, rocks, and more.

Hours: Sat–Sun 1–4:30pm. **Admission:** By donation.

Brandywine Area Lodging & Dining

The **Fairville Inn,** Rte. 52 (Kennett Pike; P.O. Box 219), Mendenhall, PA 19357 (tel. 610/388-5900), has been completely restored by Ole Retlev, an experienced Scandinavian-born Vermont innkeeper, and his wife, Patricia. They offer 13 rooms and 2 suites, each with a bath, a TV, a phone, and individually controlled heat and air; 7 have a fireplace. Though they have an obvious newness and are furnished with antique reproductions, the accommodations are attractive. All the cut-out lampshades were made by Patricia; the sidetables are classic drop-leaf. Some rooms have canopied beds; the washbasins are separate from the bath. Carriage House rooms are set well back from the road and have small decks overlooking a bucolic scene. A light continental breakfast is served in the main dining room between 7 and 10am or can be brought to your room. There's also the sitting room with a couple of sofas placed in front of a white brick fireplace with a large copper coffee table in between.

Rates (including breakfast and afternoon tea): $135–$200 double.

Meadow Spring Farm, 201 E Street Rd. (Rte. 926), Kennett Square, PA 19348 (tel. 610/444-3903), has been a family farm for over 50 years. Anne Hicks and her daughter Debbie run the B&B, providing six accommodations. Each is nicely decorated and has a TV and air-conditioning. One room has a canopied bed; the quilt is stacked high with cushions, the plank floors are softened with rag rugs, and the furnishings include an Empire dresser and chest. The Fireplace Room boasts a fireplace, of course, and a high-back Victorian bed combined with a chaise longue. Character is bestowed throughout by the collections Anne displays, like her 100-plus dolls, some of which are over 75 years old. Orchids, too, can be found throughout the house. The kitchen is made cozy by its beams, hung with baskets and the cow figures that seem to be everywhere.

Breakfast is served in a fairly formal dining room with an Empire-style sideboard and Chippendale chairs set around an oval table. Anne's signature dish is a mushroom omelet, but you might also enjoy apple pancakes or French toast. In summer, breakfast is served on the porch. For relaxing, the sitting room with a fireplace is ideal, or even better are the pool in summer and the hot tub in winter. There's also a games room with a pool table and a Ping-Pong table, a pond for fishing, and plenty of fields for leisurely strolls. Kids love the cows, rooster, chickens, and rabbits.

Rates (including breakfast): $85–$95 double.

Scarlett House, 503 W. State St., Kennett Square, PA 19348 (tel. 610/444-9592), occupies a solid, almost Richardsonesque stone house with a wraparound porch that was built in 1910 for Robert Scarlett, a prominent local. The interior features beautifully crafted chestnut elements—solid pocket doors in the parlor and a fireplace flanked by solid bookcases. There are four air-conditioned guest rooms, two with a bath. The Senator's Suite features an antique Jenny Lind walnut bed. The Victorian Rose Room, so named because of the rose-motif wallpaper, contains a high-back walnut Victorian bed. The Bayard Taylor Room has a mahogany canopied bed and Queen Anne–style furnishings. The Chanterell Room is ornamented with stenciling and offers a small sitting area. There are two Victorian parlors with fireplaces; each is furnished comfortably—one in a warm red with velvet-covered Victorian sofas and sidechairs. One also offers a cable TV. There's a small sitting area on the landing. The continental breakfast buffet includes chocolate-chip scones, bread pudding, and more.

Rates (including breakfast): $85–$110 double; $120 suite.

Just down Rte. 52 not far from Winterthur, the **Mendenhall Hotel and Conference Center,** P.O. Box 208, Mendenhall, PA 19357 (tel. 610/388-1181), offers 70 hotel rooms furnished with North Carolina country pine furnishings. The front lobby is traditionally furnished with antique reproductions and the place has a cozy ambience. The elegantly appointed dining room is candlelit at night. It serves classic country French and American cuisine—prime rib, lobster tail, and crab cakes, as well as pheasant and quail. Prices range from $20 to $30. Facilities include a fitness center.

Rates: $105 double. **Dining Hours:** Mon–Sat 11:30am–2pm and 5–10pm, Sun 10am–2pm and 4–8pm.

Sweetwater Farm, Sweetwater Road, Glen Mills, PA 19342 (tel. 610/459-4711), has to be one of the most idyllic inns I've ever visited. The large stone farmhouse on 50 acres was built in 1734 and added to in 1815. It contains six exquisite guest rooms on the second floor, three with a bath and four with a fireplace. The Lafayette Room, complete with a working fireplace, features a four-poster bed and a variety of antique furnishings—a comb-back Windsor chair, a cherry sidetable, and a blanket chest on which magazines are displayed. The Garden Room, my favorite, is in the oldest part of the house where the ceilings are lower. It's furnished with a four-poster and colonial-style pieces. On the ground floor are two parlors, a library, and (best of all) an eat-in kitchen, all with fireplaces. An elegant country breakfast is served either in the formal Queen Anne dining room or in the country kitchen at a harvest table. The beams are hung with baskets, and in winter a fire blazes in the brick hearth. From the back porch, with wicker chairs, you can look out across the lawn to a well-landscaped pool and hay fields and meadows beyond. A truly special place.

Rates (including breakfast): $155–$175 double.

An elegant drive sweeps up to the forecourt of **Faunbrook,** 699 W. Rosedale Ave., West Chester, PA 19382 (tel. 610/436-5788). This marveous bracketed Italianate Victorian features lovely wrought-iron work and carved woodwork. The seven rooms (one with bath) are nicely decorated with brass beds and other country pieces, plus a lot of paintings. One has a working fireplace. On cold days breakfast is served fireside in an inviting dining room. Guests have the run of the house, from the parlor (with a grand piano) to the library and the sun room. Guests love to sit on the wraparound porches overlooking the beautifully landscaped grounds with their statuary.

Rates (including breakfast): $80–$120 double.

Crier in the Country, Rte. 1 (Baltimore Pike), Glen Mills, PA 19342 (tel. 610/358-2411), is primarily known for its dining rooms. The building was constructed in 1740 and added to between 1820 and 1830. The high-ceilinged rooms are ornate. The Powel Room, set with Queen Anne chairs, has a molded gilt ceiling and chandelier. Above the fireplace in the Chamberlain Room hangs an ormolu mirror, while around the room portraits and landscapes hang from picture rails. The polished wood tables are set with lace placemats and burgundy napkins. The menu lists classic continental favorites: crab Imperial, lobster Fra Diavolo, cioppino, veal francais or fontina, and duck à l'orange, along with steaks and chops. Prices run $18 to $23. Tucked away in the back is a small tavern room with a cozy brick fireplace; the deck out back is for summer lounging.

In a long, low adjacent building are another eight rooms. Although from the exterior you might expect an upgraded motel accommodation, the rooms are surprisingly attractive, each furnished with a four-poster with eyelet lace canopy, Eastlake-style chairs, and snug rose drapes. One very large room has a fireplace and kitchenette. Another room has a Windsor chair and drop-leaf desk among its furnishings. All are air-conditioned and have a TV and phone.

Rates (including continental breakfast): $75 double; $110 suite. **Dining Hours:** Daily 5pm–closing.

Pace One, Thornton Road (off Rte. 1), Thornton, PA 19373 (tel. 610/459-3702), is a cozy restaurant in a 250-year-old converted barn with hand-hewn beams, Shaker-style tin lanterns, and Brandywine scenes adorning the walls. A meal might begin with some samples from the soup cart (which might include a homemade snapper soup), barbecued ribs, or stuffed shrimp with horseradish wrapped in bacon. Follow with a selection from such specialties as duck in cider, vinegar, white wine, and orange sauce; veal tenderloin with crabmeat filling and hollandaise; and salmon marinated in soy, citrus, and parsley and then roasted. To finish there's chocolate fondue, kiwi crêpes with raspberry sauce, and a variety of pies and cakes (including a delicious bourbon pecan). Prices run $15 to $27. Brunch offers soup and dishes like broccoli, tomato, and ham rarebit; fresh fish marinated in soy, citrus, and parsley; broiled veal tenderloin stuffed with crabmeat; and egg dishes—for $5 to $13.50. Bring your own wine.

Six guest rooms are offered, all with a bath, oak floors, rag rugs, chests, stoneware lamps, country wreaths, tattersall coverlets, and wrought-iron floor lamps.

Rates: $90 double. **Dining Hours:** Mon–Fri 11:30am–2pm and 5:30–10pm, Sat 4–10pm, Sun 10:30am–2:30pm and 5-9pm.

Brandywine Area Dining

The most comfortable place I know of in the area is the **Chadds Ford Inn,** at Rtes. 1 and 100 (tel. 215/388-7361), where you may come across one of the members of the Wyeth family in the back tavern. You'll certainly encounter their work in each of the cozy low-ceilinged dining rooms, either placed between the deep-set windows or above the wainscoting of this old 1703 building, which has served as a tavern since 1736. Butterfly Windsor chairs and pink-and-brown napery complete the comfortable ambience. The food is fine; there are usually several specials and the menu features such dishes as salmon with tomato vinaigrette over fresh basil and spinach, rack of lamb with roasted garlic jus, and duck with plum chutney. Prices range from $14 to $24. A light tavern menu is offered from 2pm to closing and brunch is served on Sunday. By the way, the colonial tavernkeeper here entertained the Americans before the Battle of Brandywine and was "plundered" when the British forces swarmed into the village.

Hours: Mon–Thurs 11:30am–2pm and 5:30–10pm, Fri–Sat 11:30am–2pm and 5–10:30pm, Sun 11am-2pm (brunch) and 4–9pm.

Buckley's Tavern, 5812 Kennett Pike (Rte. 52), Centreville (tel. 302/656-9776), is grander than it sounds. Oriental carpets cover the wide-plank floors, and molded panels and Queen Anne chairs give the dining room an elegant atmosphere. The cuisine is a mix of American traditional (like Maryland crab cakes and peach barbecued pork with cornbread) and Italian/Asian/continental dishes (like linguine with wild mushrooms and Thai curry shrimp made with coconut milk, fresh ginger, and sour Thai curry). Sandwiches and burgers are also offered at dinner. Prices range from $6 to $19. Appetizers are equally eclectic—hummus, goat cheese bruschetta, and shrimp LeJon (a tangy dish of shrimp stuffed with horseradish, wrapped in bacon, and served with a mustard-horseradish sauce). Brunch offers a varied menu: eggs Benedict to cheeseburgers to seafood salad, priced from $6 to $11.

Hours: Mon–Wed 11:30am–2:30pm and 5:30–9pm, Thurs–Fri 11:30am–2:30pm and 5:30–10pm, Sat 11:30am–3pm and 5:30–10pm, Sun 11am–3pm and 5–9pm.

Appearances at the **Lenape Inn,** Rtes. 52 and 100, south of West Chester and convenient to Longwood Gardens (tel. 610/793-2005), are deceptive. Yes, the place is large. Yes, the people crowd in. Yes, you'd expect the food to be average—but it's not, because owner Michael Person keeps a close watch on the quality of the meats he serves, what the cattle are fed, and so on. The filet mignon my dinner partner sampled literally melted in the mouth. The rack of lamb was of equally high quality. On Sunday a raw bar displays oysters, clams, and shrimp. Among the other entrees you might find duckling with cherries, filet of sole topped with lump crabmeat and served with a caper sauce, or veal medallions with prosciutto and shiitake mushrooms. Prices run $16 to $27. For dessert I highly recommend the Linzertorte with Chambord sauce, served hot. But there are plenty of other divine choices too. The din-ing rooms have cathedral ceilings and overlook the grassy banks of the Brandywine. A resident gaggle of ducks parades by regularly, under what has to be one of the most perfectly shaped fir trees you could ever wish to see.

Hours: Mon–Sat 11:30am–3pm and 4:30–10:30pm, Sun 11:30am–3pm and noon–9pm.

For fancy dining there's the **Dilworthtown Inn,** Old Wilmington Pike, Dilworthtown (tel. 610/399-1390). You'll find it down a little country road off Rte. 202, near West Chester. The stone-and-brick inn, which functioned as a tavern in 1758, has been carefully restored to its original decor, even down to the wall stenciling. The rooms and the tavern with a large fireplace have been simply furnished with Early American art and furniture, appropriate for the traditional continental cuisine. Start with shrimp bisque flavored with Armagnac and follow with filet mignon béarnaise, chateaubriand, or lobster tail. More exciting dishes are duck with a black-raspberry/balsamic glaze, swordfish with a macadamia-and-parmesan crust in a lemon-caper sauce, and chicken with apricot-and-ginger glaze. Prices range from $15 to $24.

Hours: Mon–Thurs 5:30–8:30pm, Fri 5:30–9:30pm, Sat 5–9:30pm, Sun 3–9pm.

The **Marshalton Inn,** 1300 W. Strasburg Rd. (Rte. 162), West Chester (tel. 215/692-4367), is an Early Federal landmark from 1793 and has been serving travelers since 1814, when it became a major overnight stop on the Philadelphia–Pittsburgh road. Today it offers only victuals, American/continental in style. Among the eight or so entrees you might find grilled marinated swordfish with fennel and roasted-red-pepper relish and game dishes like roast pheasant with duck-and-rabbit sausage and huckleberry-port glaze and medallions of venison with asparagus and shiitake mushrooms. Prices range from $16 to $24. Among the desserts may be chocolate-chip cheesecake, Black Forest cake, or raspberry torte, depending on the chef's whim and the season.

Hours: Tues–Fri 11:30am–2pm and 5:30–10pm, Sat 5:30–10pm, Sun 11am–3pm and 4–9pm.

Lodging & Dining En Route to Valley Forge

The **Duling Kurtz House and Country Inn,** 146 S. Whitford Rd., Exton, PA 19341 (tel. 610/524-1830), is a romantic place to dine. The lodgings are lovely, but I'll begin with the restaurant and its seven dining rooms. Here's a rundown of the various ambiences: an enclosed porch overlooking the formal gardens; a beamed tavern with a huge fireplace, rush-seated gatebacks, and a few wicker and rush objects hanging from the beams; fey Aunt Lena's Parlor, named after a legendary local woman with enough dramatic flair to play the musical saw in St. Peter's and decorated with her hats and dashing dresses; the formal Chippendale-furnished Hunt Room; and several upstairs rooms, including a veranda that offers a beautiful view of sunsets over pastureland. For $25 a night you can even rent the Duling Kurtz Room, affording you the privacy of a table with a closed curtain set in a bay window overlooking the gardens. The cuisine is classic French/continental. Among the dozen or so entrees you might find brook trout meunière, poached salmon with champagne beurre blanc, pheasant in a port demiglaze, confit of duck with marsala, and escalope of veal with porcinis and chanterelles. Prices range from $15 to $25.

Adjacent to the restaurant, the inn contains 15 rooms, all prettily turned out and furnished with antique reproductions. The Lincoln Suite, for example, has twin canopied beds with eyelet lace linens, attractive fabric shutters, an Oriental carpet, a small sitting room, and a courtyard for breakfast or cocktails.

Rates (including continental breakfast): $90–$130 double. **Dining Hours:** Mon–Fri 11:30am–2:30pm and 5–10pm, Sat 5–10pm, Sun 3–9pm.

Tucked away on Gordon Drive, just off Rte. 100 in Lionville, the **Vickers Tavern** (tel. 610/363-6336 or 363-7998) offers fine food in five modest-size dining rooms. Each room is warmly country, lit by carriage lamps and Shaker-style tin chandeliers. In one, a high-beamed ceiling combined with brick and barnboard, comb-back Windsor chairs, a few landscapes, and farm implements evoke the atmosphere. Elsewhere, bold chintz and matching valances set the mood. Appetizers may include snails with white wine and herbs or shrimp with wild mushrooms sautéed in garlic butter and white wine. The specialties are continental/American: beef Wellington, steak Diane, roast duck with seasonal fruits, medallions of veal with morel-cream sauce, or Dover sole sautéed with lime, orange, and grape-fruit sauce. Finish with one of the fine flambéed desserts—crêpes Suzette, bananas Foster, or cherries jubilee. Entrees are $18 to $26.

Hours: Mon–Fri 11:30am–2:30pm and 5:30–10:30pm, Sat 5:30–10:30pm.

The **General Warren Inne,** Old Lancaster Highway, Malvern (tel. 610/296-3637), offers a typical continental menu with such dishes as beef Wellington and shrimp and scallop Fra Diavolo and more modern dishes like venison with honey-mustard/macadamia dressing and duck breast with orange-peppercorn sauce. To start, try the home-smoked tuna or goat-cheese-and-pear tart. The ambience is colonial. Prices range from $18 to $27.

The inn has a rich history: It was built in 1745 and served as a major carriage stop. During the Revolution it was owned by John Penn, grandson of William, and became a center of Loyalist activity. Later it returned to its role as a major stage stop. Today it offers old-world charm and modern conveniences in eight elegant suites. Some have canopied or four-poster cherry beds; others feature cannonball beds. Two have fireplaces. The Franklin Suite contains two baths, one with a Jacuzzi. All rooms have air-conditioning, a cable TV, and a phone.

Rates (including continental breakfast): $95–$145 double. **Dining Hours:** Mon–Fri 11:30am–2:30pm and 5–10pm, Sat 5–10pm.

Wilmington & the Brandywine Valley
Special & Recreational Activities

Canoeing: Northbrook Canoe Company, 1810 Beagle Rd., West Chester (tel. 215/793-2279), offers one-hour trips to full-day trips on the Brandywine River. Prices range from $18 to $48.

State Parks: The 271-acre Bellevue State Park, overlooking the Delaware River in North Wilmington, was last owned by William B. duPont, Jr., and his wife, Margaret Osborne. She was crazy about tennis (a former Wimbledon contender) and he was nuts about horses, and as a consequence the park is now blessed with eight outdoor clay and two indoor tennis courts and an equestrian center. Call the tennis center at 302/798-6686 for details. At the equestrian center, unfortunately, your chances of landing a lesson on weekends are slim, and since most of the horses are privately owned and boarded here, no trail rides are given. A 1⅛-mile fitness track circles a fishing pond stocked with bass and catfish; there are also bike paths and hiking trails. Good for picnicking too. Contact Bellevue State Park, 800 Carr Rd., Wilmington, DE 19809 (tel. 302/577-3390). You can also picnic, hike, and fish here.

Brandywine Creek State Park offers 850 acres of rolling meadows and woodlands with Brandywine Creek flowing through the center. The Nature Center (tel. 302/655-5740) offers year-round interpretive programs and special events. You can also picnic and fish. Write to P.O. Box 3782, Wilmington, DE 19807 (tel. 302/571-3534).

VALLEY FORGE

The historic park at Valley Forge is now surrounded by a medley of highways, shopping centers, and other suburban elements, a far cry from the time when you could look down across the hills and along the river to Philadelphia, as did the Continental troops while they waited through the winter of 1777–78. They were watching for the British, who were cavorting in Philadelphia 18 miles downriver. Though the suburban development is dense, there are still some places to visit from Valley Forge besides the Brandywine Valley (above). But first, the park.

Valley Forge Historic Park

"I lay there two nights and one day and had not a morsel of anything to eat all the time save half of a small pumpkin cooked by. . . making a fire on it." So wrote Pvt. Joseph Martin in the winter of 1777. He was just one of the 11,000 who retreated here on December 19, after their defeat at Brandywine and a draw at Germantown—a raggle-taggle army Gen. Anthony Wayne described as "sick and crawling with vermin" in March 1778. The winter was certainly cruel. Deep snow caused food shortages and starvation. Over 3,000 died, and according to British reports, another 1,150 deserted. Hundreds of horses starved to death. Yet by June that same pathetic army was well drilled and ready to fight, and they marched out of Valley Forge on June 19, 1778, having won a victory of will and survival.

These are some of the facts that can be gleaned from a visit to the visitor center of this 2,800-acre park, which houses various displays, including Washington's original battlefield tent. The facts will help you imagine the scene as you drive past the log cabin replicas, where 12 men were housed in a 10-by-12-foot space during that long frigid winter. From mid-April to October you can take a regular bus tour through the park or a self-guided tour past the monument to the soldiers who died in the

Revolution, down to the three-bedroom house that probably quartered 25 to 30 people, including Martha Washington, who provided food and shelter aided by two or three servants. As you look at the rooms, imagine the inhabitants dining, playing cards, smoking, planning strategies, and whiling away the time before setting up their bunks in the rooms upstairs. Stop by the Washington Memorial Chapel, parish of David and Julie Nixon Eisenhower, and hear the 58-bell carillon that rings regular recitals.

Besides the historic associations of the park, it's a wonderful place to visit any time of year, but especially from late April to mid-May, when 50,000 dogwoods bloom. In summer it's filled with people picnicking, flying kites, biking, throwing Frisbees, and sunbathing on the rolling hills or down along the creek. Fall is magnificent, while winter can bring the most enthralling sight when snow carpets the ground and the ghosts of those soldiers tread softly, always looking downriver toward Philadelphia. The big event here is Washington's Birthday. The park is located at the junction of North Gulph Road and Rte. 23 (tel. 610/783-1000). Admission charged to enter Washington's headquarters is $2 for anyone over 16. The park's hours are daily from 9am to 5pm.

Nearby Attractions

Closest to Valley Forge is **John James Audubon's Mill Grove,** Pawlings Road, in neighboring Audubon (tel. 610/666-5593), where you'll find the first home Audubon occupied after he left France in 1803 at age 18. It may seem rather large and lavish for a boy, and in fact it belonged to his father; Audubon came to board with his father's tenants. Here in several rooms you can admire the details of specimens that nature makes so beautifully—the lines on the sunset clam that radiate as if from the setting sun; the polished iridescent interior of a simple mussel shell; or any number of shells, butterflies, and birds. There's a whole case of stuffed owls, worthy characters all, from the charming long-eared specimen to the tiny saw whet and the awesome snowy owl. Besides the prints and watercolors from *The Birds of America,* examine the birds' nests and note the exquisite delicacy and dexterity that the swift exhibits in selecting, gathering, and glueing together with saliva the twigs for its nest. Early pictures and portraits of Audubon capture the young man who spent his days here happily "roaming the frontier seeking new birds and animals." Audubon began the first banding of birds, and he hit upon a method of wiring animals or birds into lifelike positions and then painting them. You'll also discover (if you didn't already know) that Audubon had been born illegitimately in Haiti but had been taken home to France and raised in the Loire Valley. From the house you can explore the nature trails on the 175 acres. It's especially beautiful at apple blossom time and at fall foliage time.

Hours: Tues–Sat 10am–4pm, Sun 1–4pm. **Closed:** Major holidays. **Admission:** By donation.

From the park, it's only a short ride up Rte. 363 to the **Peter Wentz Farmstead,** Worcester (tel. 610/584-5104), fascinating not only for Washington's visit before and after the Battle of Germantown but also for the ways restorers accomplished their detective work in uncovering the secrets of the house's construction and history. Built in 1758 in a Georgian style, the house has certain Germanic details—the blessing carved into the external wall in a German dialect, the beehive bake oven, and the dining room's fireplate stove. The house has been furnished with period pieces and restored to the way it looked in 1777. The staircase was reconstructed and the nails were placed in the same holes, which were still visible. The Washington Room, where the general planned the Battle of Germantown, still retains some of the original red milk paint, while in many places the original sponge painting can be seen. What will probably surprise visitors most are the vibrant colors—blue, yellow, and salmon—which are as they would've appeared in the 18th century. The summer kitchen is used for cooking demonstrations, and the surrounding gardens of seasonal herbs and vegetables, including flax, give some insight into the colonists' lives. On summer Saturday afternoons the public is invited to participate in the craft program—weaving, woodcarving, fireplace cooking, fraktur painting, and the like. Take Rte. 363 north to Rte. 73, the Skippack Pike, and turn right.

Hours: Tues–Sat 10am–4pm, Sun 1–4pm. **Admission:** By donation.

If you turn left on Rte. 73, you'll come to the country town of Skippack. En route you'll pass the **Ironmaster's Shop,** Art Smithy, Worcester (tel. 215/584-4441), where people love to stop and hear what Harry Haupt has to say about the world in general and about blacksmithing and iron forging more specifically. Harry's one of those rare human beings who has the capacity to inspire, teach, amuse, and stimulate some thought. Crammed into his garage is an amazing collection of iron objects—toys, mechanical banks, trains, stoves, cars, fireplates, a 1915 Wurlitzer automatic piano, wagons, a hand organ—and to each is attached a story, which Harry will sometimes relate. From here he'll lead you into his workshop, where he forges and casts articles after old designs. Then he'll take you into a room containing all kinds of blacksmithing equipment—numerous lathes, planes, hammers, anvils, bellows, and a unique spade with a pick-ax blade fashioned by a creative individual who had tired of stopping to pick up his ax every time he needed to break rocks on his soil and so combined the two into one. He left it to Harry on his death. Harry will pepper his conversation with anecdotes, philosophical commentary, and exhortations for more individuality and less conformity. He'll discourse on why there are seven nails in a horseshoe, explain the symbolism of the four-season dishes, and probably jolt you, if you're over 30, with something like "Time is love. You mustn't kill time. Time is the most precious gift you have." After an encounter with Harry, most people leave feeling a little better about the world. Lamps, lanterns, trivets, and toys are available in the shop in his home.

Hours: Call ahead to make an appointment. Or you can see Harry at the Kutztown Folk Festival, held annually on the July 4 weekend at Summit Station.

Valley Forge Lodging

The **Sheraton–Valley Forge,** North Gulph Road and First Avenue, King of Prussia, PA 19406 (tel. 610/337-2000, or 800/325-3535), is the area's most lively hostelry. Its Underground throbs every night and is packed on weekends to its 750-person capacity. Lilly Langtry's (tel. 215/337-LILY) features a Las Vegas–style revue with singing and dancing, and you can enjoy a meal before the show. The atmosphere is wonderfully gaudy— plenty of red velvet, brass, painted skylights, and waitresses scantily clad in black corsets and lace. The hotel's restaurants include Chumley's for gourmet dining and the Sunflower coffee shop for casual dining. Sunday brunch in Lilly Langtry's (10am–2pm) provides an all-you-can-eat buffet, loaded with everything from meatballs to omelets and other egg dishes, waffles, and pancakes.

In addition to the 266 large modern rooms are 60 exciting themed suites, just made for an exotic weekend experience, and the 160-room Park Tower. Each expresses a fantasy—The Sphinx, Excalibur, Kyoto, Park Avenue, and Seclusion, a re-creation of a prehistoric cave complete with stalactites and cave art. Each suite has a loft with a small TV and phone, plus a downstairs area with a color TV, a Murphy or hydraulic bed that descends from the ceiling, a stereo system, a wet bar, and an exotic hot tub or Jacuzzi in the bath. They're really fun, and you just might be lucky enough to obtain one on a weekend. Other hotel facilities include an out-door pool and health club.

Rates: $150 double; $175–$205 suite. Special packages available from $195 a night.

A stylish and quieter atmosphere can be found at the **Park Ridge at Valley Forge,** 480 N. Gulph Rd., King of Prussia, PA 19406 (tel. 610/337-1800, or 800/337-1801). The 265 large rooms are handsomely furnished, each with a balcony overlooking the pool or the golf course. All rooms have a minibar, a desk with a computer-compatible phone, a cable TV, a full-length mirror with a high-intensity light, and skirt hangers. The fourth-floor club level offers extra amenities and services—bathrobes, a concierge, a private lounge, nightly turndown, and a continental break-fast. The Coppermill Harvest restaurant serves American and Mediterra-nean cuisine. Mad Anthony's Tavern features light snacks and pool, darts, and alley bowling. Sports facilities include a landscaped outdoor pool, two tennis courts, and a Nautilus room. A golf course is adjacent.

Rates: $95 double weekends, $145 double weekdays.

About 4 miles down Rte. 202 South, the **Doubletree Suites Hotel,** 888 Chesterbrook Blvd., Wayne, PA 19087 (tel. 610/647-6700), is located in a red-brick building possessing a double atrium. All 230 accommodations are suites, set around one of the atriums. Each has a small sitting room, with dusky-rose carpeting, a couch, a table and chairs, a phone, and a remote-control TV in a cabinet. The bedroom is separated from the living room by the bath and a small open kitchen that has a refrigerator and sink. The faux-marble bath contains all the usual amenities. Another TV and phone are in the bedroom, which also has a desk, a clock-radio, a gray comforter, and a peony-fabric headboard.

A green-and-white-checked decor predominates in the Town and Country Grille, where the menu offers modern American cuisine: grilled chicken in orange-pecan glaze, tenderloin of beef glazed with wild mushrooms, and paupiettes of sole stuffed with shrimp and salmon mousse. Prices run $13 to $20. A couple of lobby lounges, a pool with an outdoor terrace, and an exercise room with a rowing machine and Nautilus equipment complete the facilities.

Rates (including full buffet breakfast and daily 5–7pm cocktail reception): $149 suite. Weekend packages available.

Valley Forge Area Lodging

About 30 minutes from Valley Forge and 20 from New Hope, the **Joseph Ambler Inn,** 1005 Horsham Rd. (Rte. 463), Montgomeryville, North Wales, PA 19454 (tel. 215/362-7500), is a charming stone farmhouse with shutters set on 13 acres of lush woodland and pasture. Built in 1734, it was added to in 1820 and 1929. The small parlor to the left of the entrance is original, and here you'll find books and games, while the large sitting room to the right with the stone hearth is a reproduction built in 1929. Rich and Judy Allman are the owners and Terry and Steve Kratz are the managers.

The 15 rooms with bath are furnished attractively with antique reproductions. The Ambler Room has an Empire-style mahogany bed with a Marseilles coverlet, a reproduction candlestand, and a marble-topped dresser, as well as a TV, a phone, and air-conditioning; the six-on-six windows are hung with blue chintz curtains, and the plank floor is covered with Oriental area rugs. The Penn Room, in the original part of the house, has a sloping ceiling, a double-poster with a Marseilles coverlet, swagged burgundy drapes, and a camelback sofa among its furnishings. The Roberts Room has a full canopy, a couch, and a TV. The most luxurious is the Allman Room, which has a private entrance and contains a rice four-poster bed, with French doors that open onto a greenhouse patio. The third-floor rooms are smaller but appealing with their sloping ceilings. The cranberry-colored cottage rooms in adjacent buildings are smaller but decorated with four-posters with fish-net canopies, stenciled walls, wing chairs, and candlestands.

A full breakfast, selected from a menu of eggs, omelets, French toast, and pancakes, along with fresh fruit, is served on cherry tables in the Early American dining room with its wide-plank floors. The old stone barn has been converted into a restaurant, where the real specialty of the house is rack of lamb prepared in three ways—with a port-wine sauce, a mild garlic sauce, or a creamy shallot sauce. Other favorite dishes are the salmon roulade rolled with a layer of salmon mousse and served with champagne butter and filet mignon marinated in Guinness and served with a demiglaze of Guinness and balsamic vinegar. Prices range from $19 to $26. The ambience is very country. The stone walls are enhanced by country wreaths and Pennsylvania Dutch quilts, the floors covered with Oriental rugs, and the pine tables matched with Windsor chairs.

Rates (including breakfast): $105–$150 double; $95–$105 cottage room. **Dining Hours:** Mon–Fri 6–9:30pm, Sat 5–9:30pm, Sun 5–8:30pm.

Valley Forge Area Dining

The **Baron's Inn**, 499 N. Gulph Rd., King of Prussia (tel. 610/265-2550), may not look like much from the outside, but the dining rooms have a plush European air and cuisine to match. The proprietor is an Austrian, and while some of the dishes, particularly the desserts, reflect that background, the food is new American. Specialties include geschnetzeltes Zuricher (veal in a light cream sauce with fresh brandy-glazed mushrooms, served on potato pancakes), wienerschnitzel, calves' liver with raspberry-onion demiglaze topped with applewood-smoked bacon, or pheasant roasted with herbs and glazed with madeira-truffle sauce. Several fish dishes are outstanding—the cedar-roasted salmon in a light ginger broth accompanied by bok choy and rice vermicelli and the lobster tails coated in a dark-beer tempura and tossed with fresh melon and tarragon. Prices run $16 to $26.

Start your meal with a delicious soup of tomatoes and roasted peppers, with shrimp and onions flambéed with vodka or gin and topped with crème fraîche and caviar; the crab galette; or the smoked fish prepared in the seasonal style. Finish with a delicious Sachertorte, a poached pear, or chocolate decadence. All three dining rooms are atmospheric. The main Von Steuben Room has gilt pictures and an effectively lit wine rack, the warm atmosphere derived as much as anything from the ruby-burgundy color scheme. In the formal Washington Room, with a crystal chandelier, burgundy velvet curtains are pulled back with tassles and hunting prints adorn the walls. The least formal is the den.

Hours: Mon–Fri 11am–2:30pm and 5–10pm, Sat 5–10pm.

Samuel's, in Spread Eagle Village, 503 W. Lancaster Ave., Wayne (tel. 610/687-2840), is one of the area's fine dining spots, popular with Main Liners. From the tiled grand entrance hall adorned with painted-wood Austrian church panels you'll be taken into a series of large dining rooms with well-spaced polished wood tables, each set with Villeroy & Boch, a posy of flowers, and a small peppermill. The waiters are properly aproned and the music is classical. The largest room has a stucco fireplace with a beam mantel and a brick hearth adorned with a few copper pots. Narrow ceiling beams and valanced chintz curtains give a French provincial air to a smaller room. There's also an atrium dining room that sparkles with Mexican floor tiles, a large ficus, and tables set with pink cloths. You can also eat in the large bar.

The menu will likely include a dozen or so entrees, like grilled swordfish with black-olive tapenade; venison with dried cherry sauce; chicken breast with mushrooms, fennel, and spinach; and duck breast with fig-Chambord sauce. Prices run $18 to $25. To start, try the vodka- and citrus-cured gravlax or the grilled portobello mushroom with smoked chicken. The desserts are made daily and worth sampling—orange crème caramel, peach tart, or chocolate-mousse cake could be on the tray. A simple grill menu is served in the bar from 6pm to closing. The wine list is extensive and there are several wines by the glass.

Hours: Mon 5–9pm, Tues–Thurs noon–2:30pm and 5–9pm, Fri–Sat noon–2:30pm and 5–10pm.

Villa Strafford, 115 Strafford Ave., Wayne (tel. 610/964-1116), is in a stone mansion with a classic portico supported by Colonial Revival pillars. The dining rooms are equally elegant. Forest-green velvet chairs are set at tables; burgundy drapes are cinched back gracefully. A bust of Schiller stands prominently on the mantel. A less formal room, though in similar style, is adorned with French posters on chintz wallpaper. There's a comfortable bar for sipping while waiting. The frequently changing menu features fresh seasonal ingredients. The menu lists about a dozen entrees ($17 to $27)—veal with wild mushrooms and marsala, salmon with roasted-tomato-flavored béarnaise sauce, filet mignon with cabernet sauce, or calves' liver with red-onion marmalade and bacon. Appetizers might range from oysters, gravlax, and caviar to grilled shrimp with coriander-barbecue sauce and black-bean salsa.

Hours: Mon–Fri noon–2pm and 6–10pm, Sat 6–10pm.

La Fourchette, 110 N. Wayne Ave., Wayne (tel. 610/687-8333), is the other contender for fine fare in this area. Lit by a row of tall Palladian-style windows and graced by an elegant central balustered staircase, the room is distinctly decorated in French style. Different types of china are used on the tables, along with fresh flowers and candles in glass globes. Dinner offers a dozen or so entrees, some with Asian accents. There might be a rack of lamb with ginger, soy, and lime glaze; Chinese five-spice salmon with a hint of green curry in the broth; or medallions of veal with a pear-and-sherry-vinegar–scented sauce. Choice appetizers are the escargots with wild mushrooms in a savory pastry with madeira and roasted garlic and the wonderful lobster wontons in a ginger-infused oil with a lemongrass, soy, and cilantro sauce. The tempting desserts are made daily by the pastry chef—lemon tart, apple-hazelnut tart, or chocolate-praline torte, for example. Prices run $14 to $21.

Hours: Mon–Fri 11:30am–2:30pm and 6–10pm, Sat 5:30–10pm, Sun 5–9:30pm.

About 1700, William Penn and his daughter visited the Welsh Quakers at Gwynedd and stopped at the Thomas Evans home, which later became the **William Penn Inn,** Rte. 202 and Sumneytown Pike, Gwynedd (tel. 215/699-9272). Here you'll find two dining rooms: The Mayfair Room is lushly formal, with plush rose banquettes, brass sconces and chandelier, forest-green napery, and large bouquets of fresh flowers; the typical colonial tavern contains booths and comb-back Windsor chairs. The Mayfair serves continentally inspired seafood, steaks, veal, and poultry— swordfish glazed with rum, orange, and lime and served with orange-and-champagne vinaigrette; salmon with vermouth and fresh basil-butter sauce; pecan-crusted rack of lamb served with gingered port-wine sauce, or duckling with a sauce of tangerines and Grand Marnier. Prices run $18 to $29. The tavern serves the same menu, except on Thursday night when there's a special seafood buffet.

Hours: Mayfair Room, Mon–Sat 11:30am–3pm and 4:30–10pm, Sun 4:30–10pm; tavern, Thurs–Sat 4:30–10pm, Sun 10:30am–2pm.

In 1954 Edward Wallis Callahan turned his home into the **Coventry Forge Inn,** Rte. 23, Coventryville (tel. 610/469-6222), something that it had been earlier from 1717 to 1818. This really is the most charming place to dine in the area—a series of low-ceilinged rooms, one with an original Franklin stove, that are lit by Shaker lanterns. The small tavern bar has wide-plank floors and a collection of fine flasks; it's particularly inviting in winter. The porch dining area is most pleasant in summer. The owners keep live fresh trout and use local Muscovy duck for their special grilled breast of duck with red wine. Other menu items include steak au poivre, rack of lamb with port-rosemary sauce, and salmon steamed with fresh fennel. Prices begin at $17. On Saturday a $38.50 prix-fixe meal is served. These main dishes can be followed with classic desserts like a lemon sorbet, profiteroles, or white- and dark-chocolate mousse with raspberry coulis.

The accommodations in the adjacent guesthouse are spacious and attractive, with large baths. The windows look out onto a pastoral wooded scene. Guests are requested to dine in the restaurant.

Rates (including continental breakfast): $75–$85 a night, depending on room and day of the week. **Dining Hours:** Tues–Fri 5:30–9pm, Sat 5–10pm.

The **Skippack Roadhouse,** Rte. 73, Skippack (tel. 610/584-9927), is a refreshing change from the many Colonial decors that predominate in the area's restaurants. From the parking lot, a wooden footbridge and crazy paving path leads into the tavern room, which features an unusual tiled bar. What follows is a series of dining rooms, all small and intimate, decorated with prints, copper lanterns, and modern lithographs and furnished with banquettes and cane Breuers or simple chairs. The food is excellent and nicely presented. Among the chalkboard-menu specialties might be almond-crusted catfish served with Dijon-mustard/cream sauce, barbecued bluefish wrapped in bacon, grilled pork medallions with pear-and-pistachio salsa, and roast duckling with brandy-orange sauce. Prices run $16 to $28. The desserts are traditional favorites like hot-fudge sundae, chocolate mousse, and peach Melba.

Hours: Mon–Thurs 11:30am–2:30pm and 5:30–9pm, Fri–Sat 11:30am–2:30pm and 5:30–10pm, Sun noon–3pm and 4:30–8:30pm.

Back on the other side of Valley Forge is the **Jefferson House,** 2519 DeKalb Pike, Norristown (tel. 610/275-3407), a magnificent mansion (modeled after Jefferson's Monticello) overlooking a duck pond and gracious gardens. The cuisine is continental. Perhaps begin with the steamed mussels with white wine and capers or oysters on the halfshell, then follow with any of the beef, poultry, veal, and many pasta dishes—salmon with horseradish crust with cabernet-sauvignon-wine sauce, veal Oscar, or spaghetti albina with shrimp, scallops, and crab in a white-wine sauce with clams. Prices range from $11 to $25. Take DeKalb Street (Rte. 202) north from Valley Forge.

Hours: Mon–Fri 11:30am–2:30pm and 5:30–10pm, Sat 5:30–10pm, Sun 1–7:30pm.

Out east along Skippack Road (Rte. 73) you'll find the **Blue Bell Inn,** 601 Skippack Rd., Blue Bell (tel. 215/646-2010), a popular local favorite. The oldest part of the restaurant dates from 1743, but it has been extensively enlarged and now offers a series of large dining rooms. Stone crabs, shad roe, frogs' legs, steaks, and similar traditional dishes are served at prices from $13 to $22.50. There's also a pleasant piano bar containing a display of fine German steins.

Hours: Tues–Sat 11:30am–2:30pm and 4:30–9:30pm.

Valley Forge Area After Dark

The best entertainment value is found at the Sheraton's **Lilly Langtry's** (tel. 215/337-LILY). Otherwise, the entertainment's rather sketchy and consists of such seasonal entertainments (spring to December) as the **Valley Forge Music Fair,** when top-name entertainers and Broad-way stage shows appear at the 3,000-seat theater-in-the-round. Contact the Valley Forge Music Fair, Rte. 202, Devon, PA 19333 (tel. 610/644-5000).

Valley Forge
Special & Recreational Activities

Antiquing: Antiques are best found in and around Skippack Village along Rte. 73.

Bicycling: Rentals are available in Valley Forge Historical Park from May to October.

Golf: General Washington Golf Club, 2750 Egypt Rd., Audubon (tel. 610/666-7602); Valley Forge Golf Club, Rte. 363, King of Prussia (tel. 610/337-1776).

Horseback Riding: There's a 120-mile trail in Valley Forge Historical Park. Call the convention bureau at 610/834-1550 for nearby stables.

Picnicking: Valley Forge Historical Park makes a perfect spot.

Shopping: King of Prussia possesses one of the largest shopping centers in the country, to which many foreigners fly specifically to shop at Bloomingdale's, Saks, Lord & Taylor, and hundreds of other stores in ease and comfort (compared to, say, shopping in New York, where you can't park and can't move for the crowds). Dedicated shoppers will love it!

State Parks: Marsh Creek has 1,700 acres and offers picnicking, a pool, fishing, boat rentals, hiking, ice boating and fishing, skating, and sledding. Contact 675 Park Rd., Downingtown, PA 19335 (tel. 610/458-5119).

Tennis: Park Ridge has a couple of courts. At the Gulph Mills Racquet Club, 610 S. Henderson Rd., King of Prussia (tel. 610/265-6730), you can play for $28 to $38 per hour.

Lancaster & the Pennsylvania Dutch Country

Distance in Miles: Lancaster, 153
Estimated Driving Time: 3 hours

◄o►◄o►◄o►◄o►◄o►

Driving: Take the New Jersey Turnpike to the Pennsylvania Turnpike west. Get off at Exit 22, where you can pick up Rte. 23 west. If you're in a hurry, take Exit 21 and Rte. 222 south.

Bus: Capitol Trailways (tel. 717/397-4861) travels to Lancaster daily from Philadelphia.

Train: Amtrak travels to Lancaster via Philadelphia. Call 800/872-7245 for information.

Further Information: For more about the state, contact the **Pennsylvania Travel Department Bureau,** Pennsylvania Department of Commerce, Harrisburg, PA 17101 (tel. 717/255-3252). For specific information, contact the **Pennsylvania Dutch Visitors' Bureau,** 501 Greenfield Rd., Lancaster, PA 17601 (tel. 717/299-8901 or 800/723-8824).

◄o►◄o►◄o►◄o►◄o►

Although many visitors come to Lancaster County to observe the lifestyles of the Amish and Old Order Mennonite communities, there are plenty of other fascinating things to do and see in this historic area that was settled by so many groups—Scottish Presbyterians, Quakers, French Huguenots, and many German sects, as well as Moravians, Roman Catholics, and German Jews—all of whom contributed greatly to the arts and the agricultural and technological development of the area. Their contributions can be viewed at many of the area's historic and other museums—the National Clock and Watch Museum, the Landis Farm Museum, Robert Fulton's birthplace, Wright's Ferry Mansion, and many more.

Lancaster itself is a lovely old historic town, which also contains President James Buchanan's home and another historic residence belonging to Edward Hand, George Washington's adjutant-general. Southeast of

Lancaster, Strasburg offers a string of delights to railroad buffs—a trip aboard a real old iron horse, a collector's museum, a fine model-railroad museum, and even a motel that's housed in 17 cabooses. On the northern side of Lancaster is the quiet, pretty Moravian town of Lititz, which possesses one of the most pleasant inns in the area, and Ephrata, site of a cloister and religious community—a historic example of the kind of groups and communities William Penn's tolerant state attracted and sheltered. For those who love to shop for antiques, the area has many stores and a fantastic collection of antiques emporiums and markets in nearby Adamstown. If discount shopping is on your mind, then the outlets at Reading, to which many New York–based corporations are taking their employees by the busload, are en route to or from Lancaster. And then there are the delights of Pennsylvania Dutch cooking and lively Pennsylvania Dutch markets and auctions, which are prime targets on most visitors' agendas, along with those attractions that pretend to explain the local Mennonite and Amish communities.

The term *Pennsylvania Dutch* refers to the many groups who fled persecution in southern Germany and settled in Pennsylvania, in such places as Germantown, before fanning across the rest of the state to establish farms and communities. Their native language was German, or *Deutsch,* which probably became corrupted to *Dutch,* and their customs, traditions, and philosophies emphasized hard work and plain living. Among them are, of course, the Amish and the Mennonites, who are sort of cousins. Both groups, formed during the Reformation in the 1500s, were Anabaptists who sought a pure church, free from state control, open to adult believers from any religion. Because they preached the priesthood of all believers, there was no one leader among them, although Menno Simons, a Catholic priest from Holland, became well known through his writings and gave his name to the group, which was bitterly persecuted. Thousands were killed; others fled to the caves in the Swiss mountains and eventually to America.

The Amish division came in 1693, when Jacob Amman, who was concerned about the purity of the church, demanded that the church socially shun anyone who'd been excommunicated from the brethren. Such divisions have occurred ever since in the history of these sects, and so today there are many, many groups around the world and in Lancaster County. For example, in Lancaster County you'll find Old Order Amish, Old Order Mennonites (Wenger), Old Order Mennonites (Pike), Beachy Order Mennonites, New Order Amish, Brethren in Christ, and the Lancaster Mennonite Conference, all adding up to about 29,000 people, or less than 10% of the county's population. The most significant division in the groups is not between Amish and Mennonite but between Old Order and the more "Modern" groups.

Events & Festivals to Plan Your Trip Around

May: Carriage and Sleigh Auction, Lebanon Fairgrounds (usually mid-May). Call 717/768-8108.

July: Kutztown Pennsylvania Dutch Festival—a nine-day celebration of the arts and crafts of the region (basketry, embroidery, woodworking, tinsmithing, decoy carving, wood whittling, toleware painting, sgraffito), along with food, music, and dancing (usually July 4th weekend). For information, contact the Kutztown Folk Festival, 461 Vine Lane, Kutztown, PA 19530 (tel. 610/683-8707, or 800/447-9269).

    Lititz—July 4th celebration, when thousands of candles are lit and reflect into the narrow waterways dotted with waterwheels in Lititz Springs Park. Contact the Lititz Borough Office, 7 S. Broad St., Lititz, PA 17543 (tel. 717/626-2044).

June–Labor Day: Crafts day and harvest days, Landis Valley Farm Museum.

December: Wheatland opens the dining room for punch and cookies in a 19th-century-style party.

Because the Old Order groups have made specific choices against the easy way of acculturation and the temptations of technology, they've often been attacked as backward and regarded as curiosities. As a visitor you might try and come to a deeper understanding of what these people intend. There may be things we can learn from them, like commitment, community, a deep love of the earth and its bounty, living in harmony with life's daily and seasonal rhythms—in short, wholeness. If you look at these people closely, you'll see a serenity, peace, and contentment you don't find in too many places today.

They have chosen to live in communities where religion and daily life intersect. They have no use for cars because cars scatter the community— a horse can travel only about 8 miles per hour and 20 miles per day; it can only help to keep the community together. In their dress they stress simplicity and modesty. They believe in peace and will not go to war. They educate their children to live self-fulfilling productive lives within the community, stressing wisdom and understanding more than knowledge and facts. They believe in looking after their own elderly and refuse to accept Social Security benefits. Similarly, if someone is widowed or disabled or suffers some calamity, the neighbors and church come forward to help indefinitely.

On the subject of buggies, while you're driving around you're most likely to see Lancaster Amish carriages with gray tops, straight sides, and rounded roof corners. The Wenger Mennonites, who are concentrated in northern Lancaster County, drive a carriage with a black straight-sided top; the Pike Mennonites, so-called because their meetinghouse is on Rte. 322 in Lancaster County, are the oldest and most conservative of the Old Order Mennonites and drive carriages with no back or side windows. By the way, the open carriage is not properly called a courting carriage at all.

Today there are 313,000 Mennonites living in North America. Of these, about 34,000 are Old Order Amish. You may be surprised to learn that the fastest growing are the Old Order groups, both Amish and Mennonite, a fact that seems to speak to our alienated ritual-less society and is certainly worth pondering on a visit to this lovely, bountiful part of the country.

Note: Obviously, many people are drawn to the area to gawk at the Amish and Old Order Mennonites. True, these communities are fascinating and their way of life certainly has lots to be said for it, but just imagine if you were suddenly to become the object of millions of staring people as you went about your daily business and every activity from shopping and gardening to simply walking down the road was stared at, scrutinized, analyzed, scoffed at, questioned, given bad press, and worse, photographed. The last is especially disturbing to the Old Order groups because their religious principles include the strict commandment that "thou shalt not make graven images." If you *must* take pictures, then please exercise some degree of sensitivity.

AMISH & PENNSYLVANIA DUTCH COUNTRY

Area Attractions

Driving along main roads like Rte. 30, you'll be assaulted by sign after sign screaming the word *authentic* and offering buggy rides in real buggies and so on. It's clear that the Amish have been horribly exploited, and my advice is to try and sift the authentic from the chaff. One way to do this is to stay off Rte. 30 as much as possible. Get out into the countryside. Go into the farms wherever you see a sign inviting you to buy eggs, quilts, plants, vegetables, ice cream, or whatever. I've tried to include only those places that will prove most rewarding. The best time to visit, for my money, is in the busy springtime of hoeing, plowing, and planting, when the farmers work night and day to beat the weather and get the crops in. The other time to visit is in October, when the fall adds a colorful dimension to the whole rewarding scene of harvesting and thanksgiving. Summer is the most crowded. Plan to see all the Amish-Mennonite attractions on Saturday, for they're closed on Sunday. That applies to many Pennsylvania Dutch restaurants as well.

The best place to begin your visit is probably the **People's Place**, Intercourse (tel. 717/768-7171). See the 25-minute film *Who Are the Amish?*

to get a very good and sympathetic idea of what these people intend, their diversity, their practices, their traditions, and what has held them together through centuries. Afterward, walk through the upstairs exhibit, "The Amish World," which gives you an opportunity to understand the eight areas in which the Amish remain in tension with the rest of American society: (1) sense of time, (2) transportation, (3) dress, (4) education, (5) peace, (6) government aid, (7) energy, and (8) mutual aid.

Kids can enjoy the "Feeling Box," dressing up, filling out an actual worksheet exercise in the one-room schoolhouse, and following Amos and Suzie through the 12 months of a typical Amish child's year. There are also several quizzes, which adults may find very enlightening. The second half of the museum is devoted to over 30 three-dimensional carved wooden paintings by Aaron Zook, each depicting a community scene—an Amish wedding, a funeral, a barn raising, planting, a marketplace, and the evening prayer. They're quite magnificent and deeply moving. You'll also find some watercolors and furniture designed by folk artist Henry Lapp, an Old Order Amishman. The final room ties the whole museum together with a moving tribute to the Old Order Amish. Downstairs you may want to browse in the bookstore and craft store.

Hours: Memorial Day–Labor Day, Mon–Sat 9:30am–6:45pm (with *Who Are the Amish?* showing continuously and a 7:30pm showing of the film *Hazel's People*, with Geraldine Page); the rest of the year, Mon–Sat 9:30am 4:30pm. **Closed:** New Year's Day, Thanksgiving, Christmas. **Admission:** $3.50 for *Who Are the Amish?* and $3.50 for "The Amish World" exhibit.

While you're in Intercourse, you'll likely want to browse through the stores across the street from the People's Place and drop into Zimmerman's, with many a buggy hitched out front.

For a quick trip through Amish country, take Rte. 772 out of Intercourse and turn left on Cat's Tail Road. All along here you can see the water wheels and windmills generating power for each farm. The road loops back to Rte. 340, which you can take west into Intercourse again, then take Rte. 772 northwest for about a mile. Turn right on Centerville Road and keep going until you come to the **Phillips Lancaster County Swiss Cheese** at no. 433 (tel. 717/354-4424). In this store you can see a video showing how the cheese is made and pick up some samples, of course.

Hours: Apr–Christmas, Mon–Fri 8am–5pm, Sat 9am–3pm.

While you're in the region you should also stop in at **Lapp's Ice Cream,** sold at a farm just off New Holland Road. Drive into the farmyard and purchase a really good creamy cone or sundae and enjoy it as the cows come and go, the turkey struts, and the dog barks wildly from his kennel.

Get back onto Rte. 340, heading for Intercourse. From Intercourse it's a short journey west on Rte. 340 to **Bird-in-Hand,** where there's a **farmer's market.** En route, if you want some handmade and hand-carved

Lancaster & the Pennsylvania Dutch Country

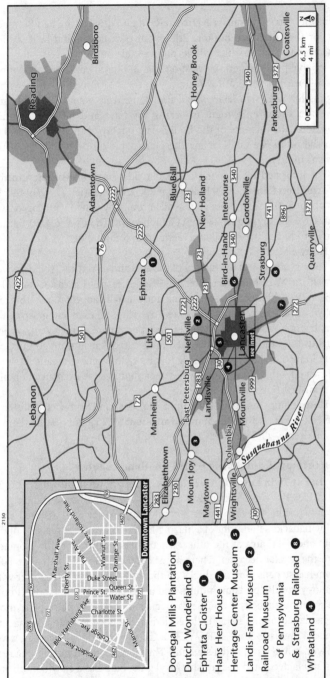

Donegal Mills Plantation ❸

Dutch Wonderland ❻

Ephrata Cloister ❶

Hans Herr House ❼

Heritage Center Museum ❺

Landis Farm Museum ❷

Railroad Museum
of Pennsylvania
& Strasburg Railroad ❽

Wheatland ❹

furniture, turn right on Weavertown Road and drive to the Red Barn and ask for **the furniture maker.** Bring your own design and he'll fashion whatever you want—like whole dining table and chair sets—for very reasonable prices. Continue west on Rte. 340 until you come to Witmer Road. Turn left and go down until you see a farm on the right with a "Quilts for Sale" sign. Here you'll find some truly wonderful quilts and have the added enjoyment of seeing the farm and meeting Hannah Stoltzfoos, the mistress of the house. The quality of the work is superb and the prices are fair. For me these are some of the highlights of the Amish country.

For informed tours along the backroads, head for the **Mennonite Information Center,** 2209 Millstream Rd., Lancaster (tel. 717/299-0954). For about $20 a Mennonite guide will accompany you in your car for two hours to explain the Pennsylvania Dutch ways. There's also a 20-minute film introducing the Amish and Mennonite communities.

Hours: Mon–Sat 8am–5pm.

For an overview of the history of the area and its settlers, you'd do well to visit the **Wax Museum,** Rte. 30, 4 miles east of Lancaster (tel. 717/393-3679). Although wax museums don't usually appeal to me, this one really is artistically created and gives any visitor an excellent grasp of the local history. Each diorama focuses on a particular period, event, or personality, from the arrival of the Mennonites and Amish through the Civil War. Some of the figures are made to speak, and some dramatic illusions are created—the whole tour capped by an impressive dramatization of a barn raising. Fun and worth seeing.

Hours: June–Aug, daily 9am–9pm; Mar–May and Sept–Oct, daily 9am-8pm; Nov–Feb, daily 9am–5pm. **Admission:** $4.75 adults, $4.25 seniors, $3 children 5–11.

Churchtown, Gordonville & Bird-in-Hand Lodging

The **Inn at Twin Linden,** 2092 Main St. (Rte. 23), Churchtown, PA 17555 (tel. 717/445-7619), occupies a 150-year-old frame house standing on 2 acres. Inside, guests discover a comfortable parlor with assorted sofas and wingbacks set in front of a blazing log fire in winter at one end of the room and a TV area at the other, where guests can also enjoy a brandy from the crystal decanter. There are six rooms, all with bath. The Polo Room has stencils of flying ducks on the walls, a Shaker four-poster with a canopy and Ralph Lauren quilt, and a sizable bath. The Linden Room has a canopied bed, a double Jacuzzi, and a gas fireplace. The most spectaular accommodation is the Palladian Suite, which has a private entrance, a fireplace/stove, a TV/VCR, a CD player, a double Jacuzzi, a wet bar with refrigerator, and a skylight. The Cottage Room has sloping ceilings and is decorated Laura Ashley style; the bath has a clawfoot tub and Mexican tile decor.

Pennsylvania Dutch Markets

The market that has the reputation for being the most authentic is held in downtown Lancaster at **Center Square** (tel. 717/291-4723), on Tuesday and Friday from 6am to 4pm and Saturday from 6am to 2pm. It's the oldest market in the area, and from 1730 to 1889 it was held at the curbside, where farmers sold produce from their wagons. If you want to view the local farmers delivering their goods, you'll have to rise about 5am or earlier. Later in the day the market is bustling, and you'll see among the vendors Mennonite ladies selling their home-baked goods, fresh flowers, fancy-looking meats, and shoofly and whoopee pies.

If you have a lot of energy when you arrive on Friday night, you might plan to attend the **Green Dragon Market in Ephrata,** a huge affair. Dust whirls over the parking lot, which is filled with cars and a few buggies. Vendors of all sorts gather outside the main buildings selling clothes, flowers, cookies, fruits and vegetables, fast foods, all manner of items. In the main market building fresh meats, cheeses, homemade baked goods, books, and much more are sold. In the barn at around 6pm an auction of animals is held and fat, frightened rabbits, turkeys, chickens, goslings, hamsters, and all kinds of other small fry are held aloft as the auctioneer sing-songs his way to the final gavel and the animal is passed out over the heads of the crowd. Kids love the action and the whole rural ritual is fascinating to observe. Other auctions of the kind of merchandise you might expect to find at Odd Job Lot are held in other market buildings. Open Friday from 10am to 10pm.

The **Meadowbrook Market,** on Rte. 23 just outside Leacock, is another good market to visit. The one in Bird-in-Hand is rather too modern and lacks any real character. On Tuesday from 2 to 9pm, **Roots Country Market and Auction,** between Manheim and East Petersburg off Rte. 72, is another fascinating market experience.

The inn is operated by Bob and Donna Leahy. Bob teaches at Temple University, while Donna is the chef, creating appetizing breakfasts and providing fine weekend dinners in the candlelit dining room or alfresco on the brick terrace. Breakfast brings tarts or cobblers, freshly squeezed juices, fresh fruit, and an entree such as raspberry croissant French toast or smoked salmon and eggs in dill crêpes. On Saturday the four-course prix-fixe menu ($36.95) will likely offer a napoleon of prosciutto, chèvre, and roasted peppers or scallops, corn, and vidalia onion soup to start, followed by a Belgian endive salad with Stilton, pears, and walnuts.

Main courses might be lobster and crab in a tarragon crêpe, rack of lamb with rosemary pesto and pecan crust, or beef tenderloin with sun-dried-tomato pesto and Gorgonzola. On Friday nights similar entrees range from $17 to $24. It's BYOB. Guests enjoy wandering the gardens and relaxing on the rear porch, which looks across the gardens to farmland. The outdoor hot tub is great fun too.

Rates (including breakfast): $110–$175 double; $220 suite.

Besides being prettily decorated, the historic **Churchtown Inn,** 2100 Main St., Narvon, PA 17555 (tel. 717/445-7794), offers some extra-special weekends thanks to the entertaining and energetic innkeepers who've dreamed up everything from An Evening of New Orleans Jazz to a full evening dress Victorian Costume Ball. They even have special fund-raising weekends for the Women's Shelter of Lancaster and other worthy causes. The inn is an 18th-century fieldstone mansion offering eight rooms (two sharing bath), and in the carriage house is the honeymoon suite. All accommodations are aesthetically pleasing. Both the James Griffin Room and the Carriage House Suite contain a four-poster with a crocheted canopy; the one in the Carriage House is dressed in a double-wedding-ring Amish quilt coordinated with swagged cherry drapes on the windows. The Edward Davis Room is decked out in purple and mauve, with a handsome crown canopy fabric treatment draping the high-back bed.

In the double parlor furnished with Eastlake pieces guests can relax in front of the fire, play the grand piano, or, better yet, be entertained by innkeeper Jim Kent, who was the music director of a choir. Another parlor offers a cozy Victorian ambience with family portraits, china, and figurines on display, along with an old phonograph. Breakfast is a five-course feast of local fruit, oatmeal and cereal, homemade coffee cake, and such items as Grand Marnier French toast—all served on Royal Doulton in a glass-enclosed garden room. The innkeepers will also arrange for you to dine at an Amish-Mennonite home. A winning place indeed.

Rates (including breakfast): $65–$105 double; $145 suite.

If you want to be in the heart of the Amish country and hear the gentle clop of their horses as they go by, then you can't beat the **Osceola Mill House,** 313 Osceola Mill Rd., Gordonville, PA 17529 (tel. 717/768-3758). It's a lovely 1766 stone house with maroon shutters set by a millstream and humpbacked bridge. A flower-lined brick path leads to the porch, and you may catch sight of one of the resident peacocks. You'll be welcomed into the beamed keeping room/parlor, atmospherically furnished with Early American antiques, or into the parlor, furnished with a comfortable sofa, chairs, and a loveseat.

Upstairs are three guest rooms, two with fireplaces. Room 1 offers a tiger maple four-poster bed dressed in an Amish quilt, set on plank floors embellished with hooked rugs. Room 2 features a high canopied four-poster requiring a step stool. Room 3 contains among its furnishings a painted German chest, and the bathroom has a clawfoot tub. Room 4's unique items include an 18th-century doll's cradle. A full breakfast is served in the dining room. It might bring German apple pancakes or baked orange French toast served with fresh fruit and fresh breads and the local sausages—smoked, sage, or apple.

Rates (including breakfast): $110–$145 double (the higher price for fireplace rooms).

The **Village Inn of Bird-in-Hand,** 2695 Old Philadephia Pike (P.O. Box 253), Bird-in-Hand, PA 17505 (tel. 717/293-8369), occupies an authentic 19th-century three-story building, with five bays fronted by a double porch with turned columns and fretwork railings. Guests stay in 11 comfortable rooms furnished with antique reproductions—wing chairs, Queen Anne chairs, Federal-style desks—combined with chintz wallpapers, lace curtains, and wall-to-wall carpeting. Four are suites, two have whirlpool baths, one has a wood-burning stove, and another has a fireplace. All have air-conditioning, a TV, and a phone. Guests have free use of nearby indoor and outdoor pools and tennis courts.

Rates (including continental breakfast): Late June to late Oct, $89–$109 double; $125–$149 suite. The rest of the year, $69–$89 double; $105–$129 suite.

The **Bird-in-Hand Family Inn,** P.O. Box 402, Bird-in-Hand, PA 17505 (tel. 717/768-8271), is a well-kept and prettily landscaped motel accommodation. The rooms are attractive and modern. The restaurant is fine for breakfast or lunch, and you'll often find a number of locals, including Amish, sitting at the counter. A few hundred yards down the road you'll find the bakery, which I can heartily recommend for their buns, cookies, shoofly pies, and more. There's also tennis courts and an indoor pool.

Rates: Summer, $85 double. Winter, special lower rates apply.

Pennsylvania Dutch Dining

Groff's Farm Restaurant, Pinkerton Road, Mount Joy (tel. 717/ 653-2048), is a wonderful choice. James Beard and Craig Claiborne have described Betty Groff's cooking as authentic Americana, and certainly Betty operates a restaurant where the ingredients are always fresh and the food is tasty and plentiful.

Ideally, you'll arrive at the old stone farmhouse as the sun is sinking and you can capture the silhouette of one of the swans gliding by on the farmyard pond against the pink-tinged sky of a Pennsylvania sunset. If you select the family-style menu, your meal will begin with a collection of relishes—corn, bean, and bread, plus chocolate cake for you to enjoy while you still have room. Then comes your choice of soup or fruit salad and the main course, served family style. You can choose any one of special combinations of classic Pennsylvania Dutch fare—roast prime rib, hickory-smoked ham, a special seasonal seafood combination, or Betty's own famous chicken Stoltzfus, consisting of succulent chunks of chicken in cream sauce placed on a bed of light pastry. Whatever combination you choose, it'll be accompanied by several vegetables, each done to a turn, and a bowl of superb whipped potatoes. Want seconds? Just ask. If you have room for dessert, select from a variety of pies and ice creams included in the price of the meal. This family-style repast will cost $15 to $25, depending on your choices. Bring your own wine.

If Betty is there the night of your visit (she nearly always is), she'll undoubtedly stop by and introduce herself, talking away in her effervescent manner, making sure everything is to your liking. At some point she may take out her trumpet to toast whoever happens to have a birthday or anniversary with a round or two of the "Anniversary Waltz" or "Happy Birthday." On the way out, you'll be invited to stop in the cellar for a glass of home-brewed wine, a nice way to wind down at the end of the evening.

Hours: Tues–Fri 11:30am–1:30pm and 5–7:30pm, Sat 11:30am–1:30pm and dinner seatings at 5 and 8pm. Lunch is by reservation only.

One of the better and larger (seats 600) places to stop for Pennsylvania Dutch fare is the **Willow Valley Inn,** 2416 Willow Street Pike (tel. 717/464-2711), located south of Lancaster in a lovely setting overlooking a golf course. The breakfast buffet is vast. Spread before you are several tables, one piled with fruit salads and dried fruits, another with doughnuts and pastries, and still another with eggs, sausage, scrapple, waffles, home-fries, and more. Help yourself, all for $15. Lunch and dinner offer equally large arrays of food, including the classic favorites associated with this part of the world: ham, beef, chow-chow, apple butter, shoofly pie.

Hours: Mon–Sat 6am–8pm, Sun 8am–8pm. No liquor.

The **Stoltzfus Farms Restaurant,** on Rte. 772, just east of Intercourse (tel. 717/7688156), is famous for its flavorsome sausages, which isn't surprising for farming and the butcher business came first. The restaurant was an afterthought and a great one. Here you can enjoy family-style meals featuring chow-chow, apple butter, pepper cabbage, candied sweet potatoes, and all the other famous area treats. No liquor.

Hours: Mon–Sat 11:30am–8pm; Apr and Nov, Sat–Sun 11:30am–8pm. **Closed:** Dec–Mar.

The **Brownstown Restaurant,** 1 South State St., Brownstown (tel. 717/656-0763), is another smaller (seating 200) dining room specializing in good home-cooking, served family style (although it also offers a regular menu with dishes like liver and onions, veal cutlet, sandwiches, and haddock at very reasonable prices). The family-style platter includes roast beef, baked ham, chicken, or turkey, and about four vegetables (corn, potatoes, and so on), dessert, beverage, and soup for only $9.50. Good for breakfast.

Hours: Mon–Sat 6am–8pm, Sun 7am–7pm.

Miller's Smorgasbord, 2811 Lincoln Hwy. East (tel. 717/687-6621), is famous for its choice of 75 items at dinner. Here you can have the privacy of your own table.

Hours: June–Oct, daily from 8am; Nov–May, daily noon–8pm.

Similar regional fare, family style, can be found at the famous 600-seat **Good n' Plenty,** Rte. 896, Smoketown (tel. 717/394-7111).

Hours: Mon–Sat 11:30am–8pm. **Closed:** Mid-Dec to Jan.

Sunday Dining

In this area Sunday dining can be a problem. Here follows a list of area establishments open on Sunday: the **Historic Strasburg Inn,** Rte. 896, Strasburg (tel. 717/687-7691), open from 7am to 9pm; **Miller's Smorgasbord,** 2811 Lincoln Hwy. East (tel. 717/687-6621), open from noon to 8pm; and the **Stockyard Inn,** Rte. 222 North, Lancaster (tel. 717/394-7975), open from noon to 7:30pm.

LANCASTER

Area Attractions

The first inland settlement and national capital for a day during the Revolutionary War—when the Continental Congress met here on September 27, 1777, during the British occupation of Philadelphia— Lancaster is a lovely old town whose streets are lined with restored 18th- and 19th-century brick town houses. The old market downtown and the jail are impressive pieces of architecture. For a full exploration of the city you can't beat the downtown **two-hour walking tours,** which begin at 10am and 1:30pm from April to October. Meet at 100 S. Queen St. (tel. 717/392-1776) for a short introductory film. The price is $5 for adults, $4 for seniors, and $2 for children 6 to 17. By the way, don't miss the ornate interior of the old Fulton Opera House.

The **Heritage Center Museum,** Penn Square at King and Queen streets (tel. 717/299-6440), displays objects relating to Lancaster's history— furniture, quilts, clocks, silver, pewter, copperware, Pennsylvania rifles, fraktur, and many other kinds of folk art.

Hours: May–Dec, Tues–Sat 10am–4pm. **Admission:** Free.

Just outside Lancaster stands the home of the only bachelor to gain possession of the White House—James Buchanan's **Wheatland,** 1120 Marietta Ave. (tel. 717/392-8721). He bought this house in 1848 for $6,750, primarily because it suited his aspirations, which were attained in 1857 when he entered the White House accompanied by his niece, Harriet Lee, who was then only 27. Her portrait can be seen, along with other memorabilia, like an unusual portrait of a young pretty Queen Victoria and a portrait of Buchanan's fiancée, Ann Coleman, who broke their engagement because he didn't pay enough attention to her. The 45-minute tour, given by costumed guides, provides insight into Buchanan's life and sensibility and that of the 19th century.

Hours: Apr to mid-Dec, daily 10am–4pm. **Admission:** $5.50 adults, $4.50 seniors, $3.50 students, $1.75 children 12–17.

West of Lancaster in Columbia, on the east bank of the Susquehanna River, **Wright's Ferry Mansion,** at Second and Cherry streets (tel. 717/684-4325), is a stone house built in 1738 for the remarkable English Quaker Susanna Wright. The house, with its wonderful collection of early 18th-century furniture, glass, and ceramics, reflects the sophisticated tastes and interests of this woman whose pursuits ranged from literature to the raising of silkworms. Well worth the visit.

Hours: May–Oct, Tues–Wed and Fri–Sat 10am–3pm. **Admission:** $5 adults, $2.50 children 6–18.

The **Watch and Clock Museum,** 514 Poplar St., just off Rte. 30 (tel. 717/684-8261), houses one of the nation's largest collections of precision watches, clocks, tools, and other related items.

Hours: May–Sept, Tues–Sat 9am–4pm, Sun noon–4pm; Oct–Apr, Tues–Sat 9am–4pm. **Closed:** Major holidays. **Admission:** $3 adults, $2.50 seniors, $1 children 5–17.

And farther south on Rte. 222 in Quarryville, New Yorkers may be surprised to discover **Robert Fulton's birthplace** (tel. 717/548-2679). The little stone house is a tribute to his diverse genius and inventive spirit, a room being devoted to exhibits showing some of Fulton's artistic and mechanical accomplishments. Among them are examples of Fulton's miniature portraits, some of the finest produced in this country.

Hours: Memorial Day–Labor Day, Sat 11am–4pm, Sun 1–5pm.

Especially for Kids

Kids probably won't let you escape without a visit to **Dutch Wonderland,** 2249 Lincoln Hwy. East, Lancaster (tel. 717/291-1888), where the Monorail whisks them into a park with many rides—a sternwheel riverboat, miniature auto rides, a wooden roller coaster, a merry-go-round, and a log flume.

Hours: Memorial Day–Labor Day, daily 10am–8pm; Easter weekend–Memorial Day and Labor Day–Columbus Day, Sat 10am–6pm, Sun 11am–6pm. **Admission:** $12 (including five rides), $17 (unlimited rides, not including Monorail); free for children 2 and under.

Historic Rock Ford & Kauffman Museum

Just south of Lancaster, **Historic Rock Ford,** 881 Rockford Rd. (tel. 717/392-7223), is well worth visiting, and you may want to take along a picnic and enjoy it along the banks of the Conestoga River in Lancaster County Central Park.

This two-story brick mansion was the home of Gen. Edward Hand and his family in the late 18th century and is one of the best-preserved late

Georgian homes in North America. Begin your visit at the barn housing the Kauffman Collection, comprised of more than 400 examples of fraktur, pewter, copper, tin, lehnware, shimmel figures, glassware, firearms, and furniture made by local artisans and craftsmen from 1750 to 1850. The collection includes some lovely bride's boxes and toleware. Then walk down to the house for a guided tour.

Edward Hand graduated from Trinity College, Dublin, in medicine and came to the colonies in 1767 with an Irish regiment when he was 23. He soon quit the British army, became a doctor in Lancaster County, and later joined the Continental Army, becoming Washington's adjutant-general. The house was built in 1792, and you'll probably be shocked by the brilliance of the colors in the rooms. They're in fact the blues and golds that would've been used at that time. On the tour you'll glean a lot of history about the house, the furnishings, and the personal quirks of Mr. Hand, who defied fashion by refusing to wear a wig (he considered such a practice dirty). Among the original pieces on display are the general's personal field desk with "secret" compartments and a special chair made to accommodate his 6-foot, 4-inch frame. Take Duke Street south and follow the signs.

Hours: Apr–Nov, Tues–Sat 10am–4pm, Sun noon–4pm. **Closed:** Thanksgiving. **Admission:** $4.50 adults, $3.50 seniors, $2 children 6–12.

Hans Herr House

The Hans Herr House, 1849 Hans Herr Dr., Willow Street (tel. 717/464-4438), is Lancaster County's oldest house, constructed in 1719. Those interested in the finer points of construction will find this an interesting place. There are few furnishings in the house—some of the more interesting are an ingenious ratchet lamp, a Swiss/German–style heating oven, and a kas (German–style wardrobe) that can be taken to pieces and doesn't contain a single nail. From Lancaster, take Rte. 222 south 3 miles. Turn right onto Hans Herr Drive and the house is on the left.

Hours: Apr to the first weekend in Dec, Mon–Sat 9am–4pm. **Closed:** Major holidays. **Admission:** $3.50 adults, $1 children 7–12.

From here, get back onto Rte. 222, taking it east to Lampeter and onto Rte. 741, which takes you all the way down to Strasburg, a railroader's paradise in the heart of Amish country farmland.

Lancaster Lodging

Gardens of Eden, 1894 Eden Rd., Lancaster, PA 17601 (tel. 717/393-5179), has an accurate name. In a beautiful red-brick Victorian house built about 1867 by an ironmaster, it's set on 3½ acres overlooking the Conestoga with terraced grounds inhabited by scores of songbirds and carpeted with wildflowers (Dutchmen's breeches, coltsfoot, trout lilly), perennials, and woodsy trails. These gardens are the source of the many flowers and floral decorations that fill the house created by innkeeper

Marilyn Ebel, who is a professional floral designer. There are four guest rooms with bath, all delightfully furnished. One has a sleigh bed and other Victorian pieces, including a rocker; another features a mahogany canopied bed. In each you'll find fetching floral weaths and decorative framed needlework. In the Quilt Room a sampler quilt and several other quilts hang on the walls. The Beecher Cottage offers a bedroom upstairs and a living/dining area with a working fireplace and an efficiency kitchen downstairs. The sitting room in the main house is extraordinarily comfortable and cozy with its fireplace and plush seating, built-in book-cases, fine art on the walls, coffee table with small piles of magazines, and grand piano displaying a collection of family portraits. Breakfast is taken on the porch or flagstone patio in summer to the sound of the nearby waterfall or in the country dining room at other times. Bill and Marilyn will also arrange a Saturday dinner at an Amish home and personal Dutch country tour.

Rates (including breakfast): $85–$105 double; $120 cottage.

A mile and half east, **Witmer's Tavern,** 2014 Old Philadelphia Pike, Lancaster, PA 17602 (tel. 717/299-5305), is the sole survivor of the 62 inns that once lined the old Philadelphia–Lancaster road, the route that led to the western frontier beyond the Susquehanna River. Here people stayed while waiting for their Conestoga wagons and Pennsylvania rifles before heading out. The 1725 inn has been restored by Brant Hartung and offers seven rooms (two with bath, five with fireplace). First- and second-floor rooms share a bath; third-floor rooms have baths. The rooms are decorated in authentic colonial pumpkin and Wedgwood blue and are furnished with either high-back Victorian or brass beds, combined with painted cottage furniture, oak dressers, and similar pieces. Peg boards function as closets. In one room there's even an acorn pine rope bed and trundle covered with an antique quilt. Deep casement windows and shutters, wide-plank floors, and original hardware add historic character to each.

Downstairs, Brant's sister runs Pandora's Antiques, which occupies the earliest part of the house and the two-room brick-floored tavern. Adjacent, the sitting room, which features a cast-iron stove and decorative corner cupboard, can be used by guests for reading or playing cards and other games.

Rates (including morning coffee, tea, and pastries): $70–$100 double.

At the **Patchwork Inn,** 2319 Old Philadephia Pike, Lancaster, PA 17602 (tel. 717/293-9078), Lee and Anne offer warm hospitality. There are six rooms (four with bath), each furnished individually in a country manner, containing high-back oak beds dressed with Amish quilts, oak dressers, blanket trunks, and the like. The suite has a private entrance, a sitting room, and a kitchenette with refrigerator; the bed sports a magnificent "Tree of Life" pine tree quilt. Lee is a collector of quilts and has about 70 or more that he has amassed over the years, many of which are on display. He also collects old phones, and these can be seen on display in a telephone booth in the homey and comfortable sitting room.

Rates (including full breakfast): $70–$95 double.

The **King's Cottage,** 1049 E. King St., Lancaster, PA 17602 (tel. 717/ 397-1017), is the name Karen Owens has given this marvelous Spanish Revival home that was built in 1913 for a dentist. Karen greets guests with genuine warmth. The interior has been beautifully decorated with antique reproductions and displays a fine eye for color and comfort. The floors are covered with Oriental rugs, the windows given swag treatments. Several sofas are set against the restful sea-green walls of the parlors, both of which have fireplaces; the library has a TV. The Florida Room sports salmon-pink walls and upholstered wicker furnishings.

The wooden staircase leads to five guest rooms with bath. The King's Room in the front harbors a brass bed and a large walnut armoire, plus armchairs. Pink is the hue of the Queen's Room, which has an old-fashioned tub and a pedestal sink in the bath. The Duchess Room contains a hand-carved mahogany four-poster and is attractively decorated in peach, with such furnishings as a cherry secretary and Sheraton chair. The Carriage House contains the most lavish of all the rooms: It features a fireplace, a canopied king-size bed, a double Jacuzzi, a refrigerator, a microwave, and handsome furnishings like a mahogany armoire inlaid with mother-of-pearl and a walnut piecrust table. A full breakfast is served at a beautifully set table.

Rates (including breakfast): May–Nov, $100–$170 double. Dec-Apr, $79–$149 double.

The **Apple Bin Inn,** 2835 Willow Street Pike, Willow Street, PA 17584 (tel. 717/464-5881), is run by very warm and friendly Barry and Debbie Hershey, who offer four comfortably furnished guest rooms (two with bath). One has a Shaker pencil four-poster covered in a down comforter and several ruffle-trimmed pillows, combined with an oak dresser, a wing chair, and a sofa. In summer a wonderful breakfast of German apple pancakes or French toast with pecan sauce is served on the patio or on pine tables in the dining room. Guests have use of a sitting room with an upright piano for anyone inspired to play; it also features several apple checkerboards made by Barry.

Rates (including breakfast): $75–$85 double without bath, $85–$105 double with bath.

The **Maison Rouge,** 2236 Marietta Ave. (P.O. Box 6243), Lancaster, PA 17607 (tel. 717/399-3033), is an architectural gem, a Second Empire–style Victorian with a steep mansard roof punctuated with dormers and a bracketed wraparound porch. Unfortunately, no one was home when I stopped by, but it looks very fetching—give it a try.

Rates: $110–$130 double.

In downtown Lancaster, the **Hotel Brunswick,** at Chestnut and Queen streets (P.O. Box 749), Lancaster, PA 17604 (tel. 717/397-4801), looks like a rather unattractive slab of concrete, but it offers a good location if you're looking for easy access to fine dining, cocktail spots, and some evening entertainment. The rooms are typically modern, and facilities include a restaurant/lounge, an indoor pool, free parking, and an adjacent movie theater.

Rates: $80–$85 double.

On the outskirts, the **Best Western,** 222 Eden Rd. (Rte. 30 and the Oregon Pike), Lancaster, PA 17601 (tel. 717/569-6444), has 230 rooms set around a courtyard or the pool; they're furnished in typical modern style. Other facilities include an outdoor pool, a health club, and a games room.

Rates: In season, $120 double. Off-season, $105 double.

Lancaster Resorts

Out on Rte. 222 south, the **Willow Valley Inn,** 2416 Willow Street Pike, Lancaster, PA 17602 (tel. 717/464-2711, or 800/444-1714), is a well-landscaped family resort run by the Thomas family, who "believe deeply in the Anabaptist way of life." There's a lake for boating, fishing, or ice skating; a nine-hole golf course; outdoor lighted tennis courts; a special children's playground; rental bicycles; and outdoor and indoor pools. The 170 rooms are very pleasantly appointed.

Rates: Mid-June to Labor Day, $102–$142 double. The rest of the year, $43–$75 double. MAP rates and packages available.

Lancaster Host Resort, 2300 Lincoln Hwy. East, Lancaster, PA 17602 (tel. 717/299-5500), is a full-facility resort with 9- and 18-hole golf courses, eight indoor tennis courts, four lighted outdoor courts, jogging trails, an exercise-fitness center, a games room, four pools, a cabaret, and a dinner theater. Kids programs too. The 330 rooms are modern and fully equipped with a refrigerator, a wet bar, a coffee or tea maker, and a color TV.

Rates: July–Labor Day, $129–$179 double. Labor Day–Nov and Apr 2–June, $119–$169 double. Dec–Apr 1, $99–$139 double. Special packages available.

Lancaster Dining

At **Jethro's,** 659 First St., at Ruby Street (tel. 717/299-1700), three-piece-suited characters rub elbows with bejeaned students and rumpled professors from nearby Franklin and Marshall College, all in a comfortable relaxed atmosphere. At the front is a long narrow bar with a couple of gray-upholstered booths for dining; the room in the back, seating only about 30, is simple but takes on a special air of elegance and even romance at night.

The food is exquisite. I can honestly say I've never tasted a filet mignon as tender as the one served here with a luscious béarnaise, or a more flavorful salmon (in lemon and capers, cooked to a perfect moistness). Other entrees may include breast of duck with vanilla glaze or roast pork tenderloin with grilled yams and mango chutney, and many daily specials are priced from a modest $12 to $22. All the desserts are homemade, and the real specialty of the house is the alluring death by chocolate—a dark-chocolate Grand Marnier terrine served with orange crème anglaise. To find Jethro's, take Orange Street West (it's one way) to Ruby Street and turn left. Go down one block to First Street; the restaurant's on the corner.

Hours: Mon–Thurs 5–10pm, Fri–Sat 5–10:30pm.

Portofino, 254 E. Frederick St. (tel. 717/394-1635), has a sleek look and serves some very fine cuisine indeed. Beyond the bar lit by lights with pink-fringed shades you'll find a dining room filled with black tables set with pink cloths and gray placemats and black moderne chairs. The menu offers a broad selection of meat, seafood, and pasta. Among the pastas, the smoked chicken with fresh rosemary, wild mushrooms, garlic, and diced tomatoes in madeira demiglaze is recommendable. Veal Madagascar is a less often found dish featuring veal, green peppercorns, shiitake mushrooms, sun-dried tomatoes, and brandy demiglaze. Chicken piccata and veal parmigiana are among the more traditional favorites. Prices range from $11 to $18.

Hours: Sun–Thurs 11am–4pm and 5–10pm, Fri–Sat 11am–4pm and 5pm–midnight.

Located upstairs, **The Loft,** at the corner of North Water and West Orange streets (tel. 717/299-0661), affects a country atmosphere with an occasional farm implement or piece of wicker hanging around or above the cozy booths. The people who run this place are gracious and considerate of their customers and have installed a special mechanical chair lift for those unable or too fragile to climb the stairs. At lunch expect a wide choice: salads, hamburgers, London broil with mushroom sauce, stuffed shrimp, and delicious crab sandwiches, all under $10. At dinner, candlelight provides the setting for steaks, including a filet mignon stuffed with crabmeat, plus veal with brandied morels and cream sauce, venison with forestier sauce, roast duck with raspberry-tamarind glaze, and poached salmon with hollandaise. Prices range from $16 to $30.

Hours: Mon–Fri 11:30am–2pm and 5:30–9pm, Sat 5:30–9pm.

In downtown Lancaster overlooking the splashing fountains, trees, and brick courtyard of Steinman Park is **The Press Room,** 26–28 W. King St. (tel. 717/399-5400). The cuisine touches base with most American favorites taken from a variety of cuisines—chicken amaretto, adobo pork marinated in brown sugar and malt vinegar, crab cakes, filet mignon with maître d'hôtel butter, calzones, pizzas, and more. Prices range from $8 to $17.

Hours: Mon–Sat 11:30am–midnight, Sun 5–10pm.

Market Fare, in the Hager Arcade, 25 W. King St. (tel. 717/299-7090), directly across from the Market Building, is a fine lunch, brunch, or dinner spot. Upstairs, the atmosphere is cafélike and the menu light—salads, sandwiches, soups—while downstairs is more formal (cushioned armchairs and 19th-century paintings) and the food consists of pasta, steak, veal, chicken, and seafood entrees, from $10 to $19. Among the favorites are steak-and-seafood combinations and veal served with tomatoes, prosciutto, and garlic topped with smoked mozzarella. The brunch menu lists such items as mushroom-crab omelet, French toast with apple-almond topping, and eggs Oscar, from $10 to $13.

Hours: Mon 11am–2:30pm and 5–9pm, Tues–Sat 11am–2:30pm and 5–10pm, Sun 11am–2pm and 5–9pm.

Although it's large and lacking any real atmosphere or decor, locals still swear by the **Stockyard Inn,** 1147 Lititz Ave., on Rtes. 501 and 222 (tel. 717/394-7975), for prime rib, steaks, and seafood at moderate prices—$14 to $25.

Hours: Tues–Fri noon–9pm, Sat noon–10pm, Sun noon–8pm.

If you enjoy diners, try **Zinn's Diner,** on Rte. 272 in Denver, 5 miles north of Ephrata (tel. 717/336-2210), famous for the statue of an Amish man standing upright with a pitchfork in hand. It's a popular place for Pennsylvania Dutch meals, with daily specials like pork mit kraut and wienerschnitzel, priced from $6 to $11.

Hours: Daily 6am–11pm.

Leola Dining

A really wonderful find for the area, if somewhat difficult to locate, is **The Log Cabin,** off Rte. 272 at 11 Lehoy Forest Dr., in Leola (tel. 717/626-1181). Tucked away in the woods and reached by the Rose Hill covered bridge spanning Cocalico Creek, as befits a spot built during Prohibition, the Log Cabin offers good food—primarily steaks—in a series of comfortable, convivial rooms. The original log-cabin room now has brass chandeliers and plenty of mirrors. Cozy booths provide the seating in another room, while Windsor chairs and a selection of portraits accent another; then there's a room with barn siding, beams, and plush armchairs. A meal begins with a hot loaf of bread and a plate of crackers and cheese. The food is straightforward: steaks, double-cut lamb chops, roast duck, lobster, and stuffed flounder with crabmeat. Entrees run $18 to $28, topping out at $35 for surf and turf. The selection of appetizers includes smoked Brook trout with strawberry-horseradish sauce, clams provençal, and fried calamari. For dessert, try a standard like chocolate mousse, cheesecake, or carrot cake. Upstairs is a lounge area with a pianist/singer entertaining.

Hours: Mon–Sat 5–10pm, Sun 4–9pm.

Lodging & Dining Across the Susquehanna

The **Accomac Inn,** Wrightsville (tel. 717/252-1521), is located in a 200-year-old stone building down by the Susquehanna River, a peaceful spot with a screened-in porch set with tables covered with blue gingham. The dining rooms are formal: tables set with white cloths, pewter candlesticks and plates, fresh flowers in pewter mugs; Queen Anne–style chairs; gilt-framed landscapes and portraits; and a white fieldstone hearth create the ambience. The bar is equally formal, in Chippendale style. The menu offers classic French/American cuisine—duck with orange sauce, steak Diane, tuna with tomato coulis, chicken breast with calamata and manzanilla olives in lemon-saffron sauce, and rack of lamb with Dijon mustard. Prices range from $17 to $28. A heart-healthy menu quantifies its dishes' fat, calories, cholesterol, and sodium. The luscious desserts include bananas Foster and crêpes Suzette as well as blood-orange crème brûlée and raspberry/chocolate ganache truffle torte with chocolate mousse and a chocolate tuille. The champagne brunch features eggs Benedict, pecan waffles, and more unusual dishes like rolled Texas eggs made with jack cheese, onions, and chiles as well as potato pancakes with sautéed apples and pheasant sausages. The price includes soup, breads, fresh-fruit salad, champagne, dessert, and coffee.

Hours: Mon–Sat 5:30–9:30pm, Sun 11am–2:30pm (brunch) and 4–8:30pm.

STRASBURG

Area Attractions

Summer is the time to ride the **Strasburg Railroad,** Rte. 741, east of Strasburg (tel. 717/687-7522), and recapture the days when the great iron horses, their bells and whistles sounding, traveled round the mountain in a billowing cloud of coal-fired smoke. En route you can stop off, enjoy a picnic, and hop the train back. The trip is 9 miles round-trip (45 minutes) from Strasburg to Paradise. Every car in the train has a history, but one is especially appealing—an open coach featured in the Barbra Streisand film *Hello, Dolly!* At the Railroad Museum next door you can see a large collection of the old iron characters.

Hours: Apr–Oct, train operates daily; the rest of the year, weekends only. **Admission:** $7 adults, $4 children 3–11.

At the **Railroad Museum,** Strasburg (tel. 717/687-8628), the history and technology of the railroad industry from the earliest steam locomotives to 20th-century innovations are preserved and interpreted through exhibits and daily programs. The collection possesses 80 railroad engines and cars. Visitors may enter the cab of a steam locomotive, view the stateroom of a private car, see the interior of a Pullman sleeper, and walk under No. 1187—the 62-ton class of locomotive swept downstream for nearly a mile during the 1889 Johnstown flood.

Hours: Mon–Sat 9am–5pm, Sun noon–5pm. **Closed:** Mon Nov–Apr and certain holidays. **Admission:** $6 adults, $5 seniors, $4 children 6–17.

At the **National Toy Train Museum,** Paradise Lane, Strasburg (tel. 717/687-8976), headquarters for the Train Collectors Association, you'll find the nation's largest nonprivate collection of toy and model trains. In the historical hall are exhibits of toy trains from the last half of the 19th century to the present. Buffs will especially appreciate the classic 1928 Blue Comet set, while the average viewer will definitely note the pink girl's train pulling pink, turquoise, and lavender freight cars, which Lionel produced in the late 1950s and which totally bombed in the marketplace. Kids and dads will love the operating layouts, reminiscent of department-store displays from the first half of this century, while wives and others can commiserate with the poor female featured in the nostalgic movie that's shown every 30 minutes or so.

Hours: May–Oct, daily 10am–5pm; Apr and Nov–Dec, Sat–Sun 10am–5pm. **Admission:** $3 adults, $1.50 children 5–12.

Kids'll also love the model railroad drama at the **Choo-Choo Barn,** Rte. 741, Strasburg (tel. 717/687-7911), complete to the finer details of motor cars running on the roads, animated figures at work, and even a "fire" in a home attended to by the fire department.

Hours: June–Aug, daily 10am–5:30pm; Apr–June and Sept–Dec, daily 10am–4:30pm. **Admission:** $3 adults, $1.50 children 5–12.

Strasburg Area Lodging

Staying on a Farm

Since 1968 Ellen Neff has been welcoming visitors to **Neffdale Farm,** 604 Strasburg Rd. (on Rte. 741, east of Strasburg), Paradise, PA 17562 (tel. 717/687-7837), a 160-acre dairy farm that also keeps sheep. Her six guest rooms (three with bath) are spick-and-span and comfortable; some have TVs. You're welcome to help milk the cows at 5:30am or 5pm.

Rates: $38–$44 double.

Rayba Acres Farm, Black Horse Road (R.D. 1), Paradise, PA 17562 (tel. 717/687-6729), is off Rte. 741 east of Strasburg. Since 1971 Reba Ranck has been illustrating a "different way of life" to visitors who come down with their "electric fans" still marveling why they bothered when "you people don't have electricity" or to families whose children shriek "Mommy, Mommy, look at the sheep" when they're looking at the family dog. Still others, she says, "wonder that she doesn't have a college education when she's so knowledgeable about so many things." Reba is amused by such antics and blithely goes about her business, maintaining the four rooms in the main red-brick farmhouse (all with double beds and shared bath), the accommodations over the garage (which include a double with a bath and TV and a large family room with two double beds and a couch, which can sleep up to eight), and the four brand-new rooms with bath. Morning coffee is available free—just help yourself. The 100-acre farm is a dairy and chicken operation, with a few sheep "for atmosphere." From the windows you'll look out across the flat landscape. You can set up picnics in the backyard with views over the fields. There's a swing for the kids.

Rates: $35–$55 double.

Other Strasburg Area Lodging & Dining

The **Timberline Lodges,** 44 Summit Hill Dr., Strasburg, PA 17579 (tel. 717/687-7472), are set on a wooded hillside outside Strasburg and provide seclusion on 15 acres. The cabins are all different. Yours might contain two double beds, a pine chest, and a sidetable in the bedroom; a fully equipped kitchen; a sitting room furnished with a couch, two armchairs, a TV, and a fieldstone fireplace; a full bath; and sliding glass doors that open onto a wooden deck. There are also some new deluxe rooms (with a small deck, a color TV, and tasteful furnishings) and some motel-style units available. The owners, the Mowrers, also run a fine country restaurant decorated in earth tones that glows in winter. The food is continental—cashew-mushroom Stroganoff, steak au poivre, and congolese (flamed with brandy and served with cream sauce). Prices run $16 to $20. The adjacent bar/lounge is one of the few convivial watering holes in the woods—a rare find around here. Facilities include a pool and games room. Take Rte. 896 south, off Rte. 30, to Strasburg. Then continue into Strasburg, picking up Rte. 896 going east and following the signs.

Rates: $105–$125 cabin for two (depending on number of bedrooms); $65 double summer, $55 double off-season.

A fine time Donald Denlinger had in trying to get 19 25-ton hulks of rolling stock he'd purchased on a lark from Gordonville, Penn., to their current resting place down in Strasburg, where they now form the **Red Caboose Motel,** P.O. Box 102, Strasburg, PA 17579 (tel. 717/687-6646).

Yes, you'll be sleeping in one of these red cabooses, built in the early 1900s. Inside each you'll find a double bed with a velveteen coverlet, an engineer's lantern swinging over the bed, a TV atop a potbelly stove, and a sink and stall shower in the bath. The larger cabooses have bunk beds as well. The rooms are small and cozy, as you'd expect; hope for a warm still night or you'll be gently rocked by the wind. At the motel you'll also find a dining car (complete with brass Pullman lanterns and gold-tasselled red velvet curtains and open March to November) and a gift shop filled with all kinds of railroad memorabilia and trains, priced from a few hundred dollars to $39,000 for a large custom-built outdoor model locomotive. By the way, Donald is the guy in the uniform.

Rates: Summer, $70–$80 small caboose for two; $90–$100 double unit with four bunks. The rest of the year, $45–$60 small caboose for two; $60–$80 double unit with four bunks.

The **Historic Strasburg Inn,** Rte. 896, Strasburg, PA 17579 (tel. 717/687-7691), is a replica of the Strasburg Washington House that served travelers from 1793 to 1921. Although it exudes all the imitation "charm" that such reconstructions inevitably seem to possess, the rooms are tastefully decorated and comfortable, with chintz wallpaper, chair rails, Lapp furniture, beds, desk, and rocker. The large dining room serves breakfast, lunch, and dinner daily, plus a Sunday brunch buffet. Dinner items like medallions of pork with sweet vermouth sauce, chicken with brandied peppercorns in Dijon cream, and crab cakes range from $19 to $27. There's an outdoor pool, and bicycles are available free of charge.

Rates: Mid-June to Oct, $109–$149 double. Apr to mid-June and Nov, $99–$139 double. Dec–Mar, $79–$125 double. Many weekend packages are offered. **Dining Hours:** Mon–Thurs 7–10am, 11:30am–2pm, and 5–9pm; Fri–Sat 7–10am, 11:30am–2pm, and 4:30–9:30pm; Sun 7–10am, 11am–2pm, and 4–9pm.

LITITZ, MOUNT JOY & ENVIRONS

Area Attractions

Only 8 miles north of Lancaster is the village of Lititz, a charming, undisturbed town that was a Moravian community until 1855.

Stop at the **Sturgis Pretzel House,** 219 E. Main St. (tel. 717/626-4354), and try to twist your own pretzel. Find out where and how the first pretzel was made, watch what it symbolizes, and see them being baked at the first pretzel bakery in the United States.

Hours: Mon–Sat 9am–5pm. **Admission:** $1.50.

Walk through the village and browse in the antiques stores and around Moravian Square, which was the town's hub in the 1700s. Here you'll find the **Brethren's House,** built in 1759, which was used as a hospital during the Revolution; the **Sisters' House,** built in 1758 and now part of Linden Hall, the oldest girls' residence school in the country. Here also stands the **Moravian Church,** built in 1787 but rebuilt several times. The July 4th weekend is special here, when a pageant of the Queen of Candles is held as more than 5,000 candles burn in Lititz Springs Park. The main street is also lined with crafts and antiques stores worth browsing.

From Lititz it's only a short run over to Mount Joy and East Petersburg, where there are several fine accommodation and dining establishments, including Groff's farm, where you ought to plan for an evening meal (see "Pennsylvania Dutch Dining," above).

At **Donegal Mills Plantation,** off Rte. 141, south of Mount Joy (tel. 717/653-2168), you can tour four buildings—a mansion, a mill, a miller's house, and a bake kitchen—and enjoy the gardens, trout hatchery, and nature rambles. First settled in 1736 by a Scotch-Irish adventurer and later by the Pennsylvania Germans or Dutch, the mansion was a simple 18th-century stone farmhouse until it was transformed into a more splendid residence in the early 19th century. It was the Krayville family who built the first half of the mansion (in 1790), the bakehouse, Grandmother's house, an extension at the rear of the mansion, and the red-brick mill (in 1832). When Jakab Krayville died, leaving a five-year-old son, the trust was squandered; later the three Watson sisters from England purchased the property as a summer home and extended the porch, adding the Monticello-style pillars. On the tour, traditional crafts and daily tasks are demonstrated. In the mansion itself people can view the incredibly cluttered Victorian parlor, complete with an organ, a tinsel print made from tea wrappings, a gas chandelier, and a magic lantern; and the adjacent dining room containing a pony rocking horse made of *real* pony hair.

Hours: Easter weekend to Columbus Day, Tues–Sat 10am–4:30pm; Columbus Day to the third weekend in Nov, Sat–Sun 1–5pm.

Tours and wine tastings are offered at the **Nissley Winery** in Bainbridge, off Rte. 441, via Wickersham Road (tel. 717/426-3514), along with a variety of special events. The place is appealing—an 18th-century–style stone building and plenty of acreage for a quiet picnic lunch (washed down by a bottle of wine, of course).

Hours: Self-guided tours and tastings, Mon–Sat 10am–5pm, Sun 1–4pm. **Closed:** Major winter holidays and Easter.

Lititz Lodging

The **General Sutter Inn,** 14 E. Main St., Lititz, PA 17543 (tel. 717/626-2115), a handsome three-story brick edifice overlooking the town square, has been famous for its unique feather beds, good food, and prohibition of dancing, cursing, gossip, and bawdy songs since it was founded in 1764 by the Moravian Church as the Zum Anker (the Sign of the Anchor). Today it's known for being one of the area's quieter retreats. Enter into the downstairs parlor with a Louis XIV medallion-backed sofa, a carved marble-topped coffee table, and a parlor organ, which are just part of the ultra-Victorian atmosphere.

The upstairs corridors, with Oriental throw rugs, lead to 14 individually decorated rooms, all with bath, air-conditioning, phone, and black-and-white TV. Ornate Victorian beds with inlaid work, shaving stands, and other eclectic pieces of Victorian country-style furniture add dash to the rooms. The dining room is as richly decorated in deep cranberry, accented with old-fashioned gaslights and antique accessories. It serves typical American/continental fare—chicken Dijon, veal Cordon Bleu, crab cakes, steaks, and similar, priced from $14 to $19. There's a pleasant

enough cocktail lounge as well. On the Broad Street side guests can enjoy sitting on the brick patio by the fountain. By the way, it's named after John Augustus Sutter, who discovered gold in California but then returned to Lititz, hoping to find a cure for arthritis in the town's famed mineral springs.
Rates: $85–$110 double.

The **Alden House,** 62 E. Main St., Lititz, PA 17543 (tel. 717/627-3363), is an 1850 brick Victorian with olive-green shutters and a gambrel portico. It has three rooms and three two-room suites, all with a bath and cable TV. The Lavender and Lace Suite contains a four-poster with a lace canopy, windowseats under the bay window, and a sitting area. A full breakfast is served in the dining room or on one of the porches.
Rates (including breakfast): $85–$115 double.

Swiss Woods, 500 Blantz Rd., Lititz, PA 17543 (tel. 717/627-3358), is indeed in the woods, overlooking Speedwell Forge Lake, and is styled like a Swiss chalet. This appealing place offers seven modern rooms with private entrances. The rooms are furnished with country pine four-posters and armoires, armchairs, and such country accents as twig wreaths and lamps bearing stenciled shades. The most luxurious room is the Lake of Geneva, so named because it has a view of the lake; it also offers a Jacuzzi in the bath. The focal point of the common room is the sandstone fireplace. Open beams, natural woodwork, handcrafted furniture, and cowbells give it a distinct Swiss air. In the mornings proprietor Debrah Mosimann prepares specialties like cinnamon-raisin French toast stuffed with strawberry cream cheese and eggs Florentine along with birchermuesli, a Swiss fruit-and-yogurt dish. Werner tends the gardens that overflow with annuals and perennials and flowers that attract hummingbirds and butterflies.
Rates (including breakfast): $85–$140 double.

Mount Joy & Manheim Lodging

The **Herr Farmhouse Inn,** 2256 Huber Dr., Manheim, PA 17545 (tel. 717/653-9852), is situated on 11½ acres of rolling farmland. The inn dates to 1738, when it operated as a tobacco plantation. It's a classic stone house with a porch along the front bays and a handsome entrance topped by a large fanlight. Inside, the original moldings, cabinets, doors, plank floors, and fireplaces have been retained and restored. There are five individually decorated guest rooms, two with a fireplace and three with a bath. The North Room features a hooped canopied bed and an assortment of antique pieces, including a washstand, a rocker, a table with lamp, and a ladderback chair; it's decorated in pale-green trim and the chair rail adds a certain elegance. All the rooms have nice touches—quilts, embroidered samplers, Shaker boxes, and glass bottles. The penthouse suite is the largest accommodation, with a king-size bed and two twins. The kitchen with a large walk-in fireplace is the heart of the house and breakfast is served here, in the dining room, or on the glassed-in patio. The common areas include a comfortable sitting room with a fireplace, a library, and a games room with a player piano.

Rates (including breakfast): $85–$100 double; $135 suite.

The **Olde Square Inn,** 127 E. Main St., Mount Joy, PA 17552 (tel. 717/ 653-4525), is on the town's square in a handsome 1917 two-story home with dormer windows and an elegant side porch. There are four rooms with bath, each decorated in a different color scheme—the Charleston Room in dark-blue wallpaper with sprays of pink and white flowers, the Garden Room in soft green. The Ivy Room contains furniture painted by a local artist. The Royal Room is splendidly decorated in red-and-blue wallpaper. All rooms have a TV, a VCR, and air-conditioning. Guests use the living room with fireplace and the porch, a favorite spot for breakfast in summer.

Rates (including breakfast): $75–$95 double.

At **Rocky Acres Farm,** Pinkerton Road (R.D. 3), Mount Joy, PA 17552 (tel. 717/653-4449), Mrs. Eileen Benner will give you a really warm welcome and provide a room and breakfast. Over a humpback bridge, along a twisting road beside a brook you'll suddenly come upon the farm around a corner. There are five rooms with bath in the 200-year-old farmhouse. If you're lucky, you'll be given the large front room, with a fireplace; it's furnished with a colossal carved and painted Victorian bed. Other rooms are pleasantly but modestly furnished with cannonball beds, perhaps a marble-topped chest; pegboards serve as closets; and the bathroom is shared. There's also an efficiency on the third floor and a private apartment that sleeps seven, with two upstairs bedrooms, a bath, a living room, and a fully equipped kitchen. Kids'll love helping to milk or feed the cows or watch the calves being born; there's also a Victorian dollhouse for them to play with and a small horse for them to ride.

Here you'll be treated to a superb country breakfast. Although the fare may vary, there'll always be heaps of it. Plates piled high with scrambled eggs, ham, pancakes, and the best home-fries anywhere, all accompanied by apple sauce, sugar cake, home-baked bread or muffins, jams, fresh milk, and coffee. There's plenty of surrounding groves and fields for walking and a creek to tube down if you wish. Eileen will steer you to all the authentic attractions in the region and can even arrange for you to have dinner in a real Amish home.

To get there, take Rte. 30 west, to Rte. 283 west, to Rte. 230 west, which will bring you into Mount Joy. In Mount Joy, take Rte. 772 west a short distance only, to Pinkerton Road. Turn left and follow the road about 3 miles over the stone arch bridge.

Rates (including breakfast Mon–Sat): $65–$75 double. Extra adult $10; extra child $5.

When you stay at **Ionde Lane Farm,** 1103 Auction Rd., Manheim, PA 17545 (tel. 717/665-4231), you really are part of the family. There's no privacy or separate entrance, and you'll be sharing the house with Elaine and John Nissley and their four children. Indeed 18 to 20 of you will probably sit down at the table in the kitchen to a farm breakfast of orange juice, eggs, bacon, toast, homemade bread or doughnuts, and coffee or tea. There are four rooms available, two on the ground floor and two upstairs, all sharing one bath. All rooms are well suited to families: One has a double bed with twin bunks; the others have doubles or two singles and a crib. The quilts were all made by Elaine. A herd of 25 cows and two chicken houses are added attractions. Elaine doesn't serve breakfast on Sunday.

Rates (including breakfast Mon–Sat): $45 double. Teenagers $10; children $6.

Mount Joy Lodging & Dining

Under "Pennsylvania Dutch Dining" (above) I've described Betty Groff's restaurant. Betty and her husband also operate the **Cameron Estate Inn,** Donegal Springs Road (R.D. 1, Box 305), Mount Joy, PA 17552 (tel. 717/653-1773), an inviting red-brick Victorian mansion set on 15 acres; it once belonged to Simon Cameron, secretary of war to President Lincoln. They've restored and furnished it lavishly with antique reproductions. The 18 rooms (7 with fireplaces) are large and spread over three floors. In each you'll most likely find a canopied four-poster or brass bed, Oriental porcelain lamps, two wing chairs, a writing desk, and Oriental rugs. The two top-floor rooms tucked beneath the eaves are a trifle smaller, are more modestly furnished, and share a bath.

Downstairs, the lounge has been made luxuriously comfortable with a brocade-covered couch, Martha Washington chairs, assorted books, and a TV. The food in the dining room is very different from the Pennsylvania Dutch fare served at the Groff's farmhouse. Veal with white-wine/caper sauce, medallions of roast pork with peach chutney, and shrimp and scallops with garlic butter and herbs are more typical of the continental menu here. Prices range from $13 to $22. Red tablecloths, candlelight, and a fire in winter make the small room glow. There's an enclosed porch for summer dining. Liquor is served. Children under 12 aren't allowed and reservations are required.

Rates (including continental breakfast): Mar–Nov, $75–$120 double. Dec–Feb (except holidays), $70–$100 double. **Dining Hours:** Mon–Thurs 6–8pm, Fri–Sat 5:30–9:15pm, Sun 10:30am–1:30pm.

Bube's Brewery, 102 N. Market St. (tel. 717/653-2160), is as much fun as it sounds, located in an old brewery. There are three distinct areas: Stone walls and rafters and thousands upon thousands of empty bottles characterize the Bottling Works (tel. 717/653-2160). Downstairs, the Catacombs (tel. 717/653-2056) is precisely that—the old cellar area— now a romantic candlelit dining room; and Alois's (tel. 717/653-2057), a plush Victorian dining room with lots of stained glass, overstuffed chairs and sofas, and oak chairs.

Steaks, light dinners, sandwiches, and subs are served in the Bottling Works. Dinner prices are $4 to $17. The Catacombs, where you'll be greeted by a serf in medieval costume, offers traditional steak and seafood dishes like coquilles Catacombs (bay scallops, onions, tomatoes, garlic, and white-wine sauce), filet mignon with herb butter, and stuffed chicken breast, priced from $16 to $22. Twice a month medieval feasts are held. At Alois's prices range from $20 to $27. Cocktails and appetizers are served in the parlor before diners move into one of the dining rooms. A sample menu offers veal Dijon, roast duck with orange-marmalade glaze, steak Diane, and spiced scallops and cashews in tomato sauce. These will be preceded by an appetizer, a soup, a salad, and a sorbet, then followed by a dessert like crème Kahlúa or chocolate-chip/banana cake.

Hours: Bottling Works, Mon–Thurs 11am–2pm and 5:30–10pm, Fri 11am–2pm and 5pm–midnight, Sat 5pm–midnight, Sun 5–10pm. Catacombs, Mon–Thurs 5:30–9pm, Fri 5–9:45pm, Sat 4:45–9:45pm. Alois, Tues–Thurs 5:30–9pm, Fri 5–9:45pm, Sat 5–10pm, Sun 5–8pm.

A Special Dining Place in East Petersburg

Haydn Zugs, Center Square, 1987 State St., East Petersburg (tel. 717/569-5746), offers traditional dining. Both dining rooms are elegant, with Queen Anne–style chairs, pewter settings, pink napkins, and a Williamsburg-blue background. The menu emphasizes steaks and meats, including Lancaster County smoked pork chops with fresh horseradish and blackened breast of duckling with a Grand Marnier sauce. Fish offerings might include grilled salmon with maître d' butter or grilled shimp with lobster sauce. Among the more unique dishes is Norwegian chicken—sautéed breasts of chicken with smoked salmon, capers, onions, tomatoes, and white wine. Prices range from $11 to $21. To start, you'll find such tasty morsels as lemon-pepper shrimp and bacon-wrapped scallops. Finish with a lemon sorbet with raspberry-and-blackcurrant sauce.

Hours: Mon–Fri 11:30am–2pm and 5–9pm, Sat 5–9pm.

FROM LANCASTER TO EPHRATA & ADAMSTOWN

Area Attractions

From Lancaster, take Rte. 501 to Rte. 272/222, which will lead you all the way past the Landis Farm Museum to Ephrata, site of a fascinating religious community, and then to Adamstown, a well-known center for antiques—a journey of 19 miles, which makes a perfect Sunday.

Henry and George Landis were avid collectors of farm and related machinery and gadgetry, and they used their collection to found the **Landis Farm Museum,** 2451 Kissel Hill Rd. (tel. 717/569-0401), in 1924. The collections are housed in 22 buildings, some original and some newly constructed, which have been laid out as a village. During summer, such crafts as tinsmithing, flax and wool spinning, and weaving are demonstrated, but whatever time you visit the museum will provide insight into rural and 19th-century American life, offering much to marvel at from our 20th-century viewpoint. For example, did you know that 1 acre of land is required to keep one sheep, that one sheep is required for one person's clothing, that between 1750 and 1850 it took roughly 25 days to go 320 miles (or from Philadelphia to Pittsburgh), that a sickler could cut only three-quarters of an acre a day, compared to the grain cradle introduced in the 1780s, which could cut 2 to 2½ acres per day, or the reaper of the mid-1800s, which could cut 10 to 12 acres a day? Progress was comparatively slow in those days. To get here, take the Oregon Pike (Rte. 272 north) exits off either Rte. 22, 230-30 (the Bypass), or 72. Entrance to the parking area is off Landis Valley Road opposite the Landis Valley Resort Inn.

Hours: Tues–Sat 9am–5pm, Sun noon–5pm. **Closed:** Nov to early Apr. **Admission:** $7 adults, $6 seniors, $5 children 6–17.

German Pietist Conrad Beissel founded the **Ephrata Cloister,** 632 Main St., Ephrata (tel. 717/733-6600), a religious communal society consisting of three orders—two celibate and a married order of householders—in 1732. From 1735 to 1750 about 300 souls lived on 250 acres as a fully self-supporting community, complete with mills, craft shops, and so on. The celibates lived in the 10 restored medieval-style buildings you can see today. The doorways, which are extremely low, were meant to ensure a bowed head, an expression of a proper sense of humility. The spartan monastic cells, where the celibates slept on wooden benches with wooden blocks as pillows, and the almost-masochistic strictures of the community testify to the almost-cultlike dedication that these followers felt for their leader, Conrad Beissel.

Beissel combined ideas from pietist, Kelpian, Jewish, Roman Catholic, Anabaptist, mystic, inspirationist, and Rosicrucian faiths. His followers rose at 5am for private devotions and passed the day alternating study periods with work periods of basket making, printing, book making, carpentry, and paper making until their 6pm vegetarian meal. This was followed by singing and music school and retirement to bed at 9pm. At midnight the bell was sounded for two hours of worship followed by additional sleep from 2 to 5am. After Beissel died, the practices became less austere and the community declined, although the group continued to occupy the property until the 1940s. The order was famous for the original music and hymns Beissel composed, the singing and music schools, the art of fraktur, and the many important books that were printed here. A small museum shows archeological fragments that were recovered when the buildings were restored, along with fraktur and documents. From late June to early September, on Saturdays and occasional Sundays, *Vorspiel,* a musical drama depicting 18th-century cloister life, is presented at dusk. Take Rte. 272 north to Ephrata, then turn right onto Rte. 322.

Hours: Tours given hourly, Mon–Sat 10am–4pm, Sun 1–4pm. **Admission:** $5 adults, $4 seniors, $3 children 6–17.

If you enjoy shopping for handmade craft items, including jewelry and quilts, go to the **Artworks at Doneckers,** 100 N. State St., Ephrata (tel. 717/738-9503).

If you have time, stay over until Monday and head out to New Holland for the regular weekly **horse auction** at New Holland Sales Stables, Fulton Street (tel. 717/354-4341)—an exciting event for any visitor from 10am to 1pm. Here the local farmers and Amish and Mennonites bid for work horses and other animals. Later in the week the auctions are for pigs, sheep, and other livestock.

Ephrata Lodging

The **Inns at Doneckers,** 318–324 N. State St., 301 W. Main St., 251 N. State St., and 287 Duke St., Ephrata, PA 17522 (tel. 717/738-9502), offer some of the area's most comfortable and best-decorated rooms. The accommodations are in four buildings: the largest (with 20 rooms) is the Guesthouse; the second largest is the 1777 House (with 12 rooms), which once belonged to famous clockmaker and member of Ephrata Jacob Gorgas; the Gerhart (5 rooms) and the Homestead (4 rooms) are the smallest.

Each room is different. In the Guesthouse, the Wheatland Suite features stained glass in the bay window, inlaid wood floors, and a Jacuzzi in the bath; it has a private entrance. In the Rock Ford Suite are lovely individualized stenciling, a fireplace, a comfy sitting area, and a Jacuzzi. The Traveler's Berth is small but still appealing, with exposed brick walls, a blanket chest, and a wingback chair among the furnishings. In the 1777 House, the Jacob Gorgas Suite contains a loveseat in front of the original green marble fireplace; the Peter Miller Suite is heavily stenciled and has a handsome kas among the furnishings (its bath features the original stone masonry and a Jacuzzi); the Blacksmith's Loft bursts with color—blue green, mustard, and spicy red—and features a loft sitting room, a fireplace, and a Jacuzzi. Rooms in the Gerhart House tend to have either iron, canopied, or cannonball beds; in the Homestead, Melba's Suite contains a unique four-poster iron bed, the original limestone fireplace, and a sitting area in the bay window.

Guests are served a buffet breakfast at long harvest tables—baked apples, croissants, cheese, fruit, and cereal. The inn also has a fine restaurant where the cuisine applies French traditions to fresh local ingredients. Additional amenities include the store, which has great home furnishings and men's and women's fashions, plus the Artworks, an old warehouse that's been converted into artists' studios and galleries selling a variety of fine art, quilts, jewelry, and designer crafts—some of the best the region has to offer.

Rates (including breakfast): $79–$105 double; $159–$195 suite. **Dining Hours:** Mon–Tues and Thurs–Sat 11am–10pm, Sun 11:30am–3pm.

Smithton, 900 W. Main St., Ephrata, PA 17522 (tel. 717/733-6094), is a B&B offering charming rooms with bath and fireplace. What can be finer for romance than a candlelit room with the strains of chamber music playing in the background and a fire in the hearth? That's what you'll find here, plus some good books and a refrigerator to store the champagne. In addition, each room has a sitting area, comfortable leather chairs, reading lamps, and a writing desk. The beds are covered with bright Pennsylvania Dutch quilts. The Red Room contains a four-poster that's covered with a magnificent handmade quilt. Ballfringe curtains, rag rugs, fresh flowers, and stenciling accent the country look. Among the Blue Room's furnishings, the rope four-poster with a velvet canopy stands out. On the third floor is a small suite—four skylights, beams, a Franklin stove, and a Red Star quilt give it wonderful character. This is one of the quietest rooms, along with the Red Room.

Guests are welcome to use the attractive living room with its stucco-brick fireplace, comfy armchairs, valanced curtains, and country knick-knacks in the windows, or to relax and read in the study filled with books. Breakfast (homemade waffles, fruits, coffee and tea) is served at a harvest table in a room that has a number of quilts, stuffed animals, and folk art for sale. There's also a brick fireplace here too.

Rates (including breakfast): $75–$150 double; $150–$180 suite.

Glenn and Mildred Wissler operate **Clearview Farm,** 355 Clearview Rd., Ephrata, PA 17522 (tel. 717/733-6333), an 1814 limestone house with Turkey red shutters. It's a fully working farm of 200 acres with 400 head of Black Angus. There are five rooms (three with bath): The Garden Room is a floral celebration with black-and-rose curtains; its furnishings include an iron-and-brass bed with a crown canopy, wicker rockers, a marble dresser, and a trunk filled with quilts. The Princess Room is very Victorian, with a hooped four-poster canopied bed, a cottage-style marble-topped dresser, and upholstered Victorian sidechairs. The Royal Room is appropriately decorated in red and gilt, with a carved walnut Victorian bed. My favorite is the Washington Room tucked up in the attic: It contains a Shaker four-poster with a ballfringe canopy and a pretty dahlia quilt; the walls are of stone and the ceilings display the original pegged rafters, and additional comforts include wing chairs and a table with a lamp for reading.

The comfortable sitting room overlooks the pond and fields, and an appealing stone patio is adjacent to the well-manicured lawns and flower beds. A full breakfast is served on fine china. Glen likes to collect chocolate pots and these are on display in the cabinet he converted from an armoire.

Rates (including breakfast): $125 double weekends, $105 double weekdays.

After Dark

Lancaster County is hardly nightlife country. Farm folk rise early, work hard, eat well, and retire early to rest for an early start to the next day. The rhythm is completely different from the urban pace we're used to.

Any evening entertainment is centered in Lancaster, where there are several bars, a prime historic theater, several cinemas, and good restaurants. Drinking spots include the **Lancaster Dispensing Company,** 33–35 N. Market St. (tel. 717/299-4602), which features bands Wednesday to Saturday, a large selection of beers served in a decor of stained and etched glass, a 1960s marble bar, bentwood cane chairs, and lots of greenery; and **Jethro's** (see "Lancaster Dining," above).

Theater

Lancaster is blessed with America's oldest theater, the **Fulton Opera House,** 12 N. Prince St., Lancaster (tel. 717/397-7425), a National Historic Landmark that's home to the Fulton Theatre Company, producer of professional regional theater. Other local arts organizations also use the facility. Tours of the marvelous gilt-and-red interior are available.

At the **Mount Gretna Playhouse,** Pennsylvania Avenue, Chautauqua side (P.O. Box 578), Mount Gretna, PA 17064 (tel. 717/964-3627), the Gretna Theatre produces plays and musicals and Music at Gretna presents chamber music and jazz concerts.

Franklin and Marshall College's **Green Room Theater** on College Avenue (P.O. Box 3003), Lancaster, PA 17604, also puts on good productions. Famous alumni include Roy Scheider. Call 717/291-4015 for information.

Lancaster County
Special & Recreational Activities

Antiquing: Adamstown is a great center, boasting 1,500 dealers every Sunday of the year at several large markets. The most famous is probably Ed Stoudt's Black Angus (tel. 717/484-4385), with over 200 dealers and a convenient steakhouse. Lititz and vicinity is another, much smaller hunting ground—there are several stores downtown. New Holland has four or five stores.

Bicycling: Rental or free bicycles are available at certain accommodations—the Strasburg Inn and Host Farm, for example. Independent cyclists should contact the Lancaster Bicycle Club, P.O. Box 535, Lancaster, PA 17608, for information on their Saturday and Sunday rides.

Golf: Hawk Valley Golf, R.D. 1, Denver (tel. 717/445-5445); Overlook Golf Course, 2040 Lititz Pike, Lancaster (tel. 717/569-9551).

Picnicking: You can picnic on the Strasburg Railroad trip or in Lancaster County Central Park, Lititz Springs Park, or Burchmiller State Park on Rte. 222 south. See also "State Parks," below.

Shopping the Reading Outlets: En route to or from the Dutch country, you can stop (or spend the whole day) at the shopping outlets at Reading for shoes, shirts, sweaters, sportswear, linens, tools, jewelry, sports equipment—you name it, it's here being sold at a discount. For more information, call 610/376-0206.

Shopping for Quilts: Quilts have a history and symbolism and offer the quilters an opportunity to express their talents and love of color. Many of the patterns are derived from the patterns of the fields, the interplay of sunshine and shadow, the bounty of the earth, and the celestial bodies.

One of the best places to shop for local crafts, including quilts, is the Studio at Donecker's in Ephrata. Another of the better places is across from People's Place in Intercourse at the Old Country Store. According to the locals, the store accepts work only from the very best, rejecting as much as 40%. Better yet, shop at Hannah Stoltzfoos's farm on Witmer Road. Dotty Lewis is known for her talent in traditional weaving; find her by calling 717/872-2756.

State Parks: Susquehannock, % Gifford Pinchot State Park, 2200 Rosstown Rd., Lewisberry, PA 17339 (tel. 717/432-5011), has picnicking and hiking areas. Samuel S. Lewis State Park, % Gifford Pinchot State Park, 2200 Rosstown Rd., Lewisberry, PA 17339 (tel. 717/432-5011), has picnicking and hiking. French Creek State Park, 843 Park Rd., Elverson, PA 19520 (tel. 610/582-9680), has over 7,000 acres for picnicking, swimming (pool), fishing, boating (rentals in summer), hiking (32 miles of trails), ice fishing and skating, sledding, and nongroomed cross-country skiing. There are also 318 camping sites.

Swimming: There's a pool in Lancaster County Park on Broad Street (tel. 717/299-8215). See also "State Parks," above.

Tennis: Six tennis courts are available in Burchmiller Park on Rte. 222, south of Lancaster. Four are available in Lancaster County Park (tel. 717/299-8215). Also, at the Universal Racquet and Fitness Center (tel. 717/569-5396) you may be able to secure a court on weekends but cannot reserve one unless you're a member.

Hershey

Distance in Miles: 170

Estimated Driving Time: 3 to 4 hours

<o><o><o><o><o>

Driving: Take the New Jersey Turnpike to I-78 to I-81, to the Hershey exit, Rte. 743 south; or the New Jersey Turnpike to the Pennsylvania Turnpike to Exit 20, then Rte. 72 north to Rte. 322.

Bus: Greyhound (tel. 800/231-2222) goes to Hershey.

Train: Amtrak travels to Harrisburg. Call 800/872-7245.

Further Information: For more about Pennsylvania in general, contact the **Pennsylvania Travel Department Bureau,** Pennsylvania Department of Commerce, Harrisburg, PA 17101 (tel. 717/255-3252). For specific data about Hershey, contact the **Hershey Information Center,** Hershey, PA 17033 (tel. 717/534-3005), or the **Harrisburg-Hershey-Carlisle Convention and Tourism Bureau,** 114 Walnut St. (P.O. Box969), Harrisburg, PA 17108 (tel. 717/232-1377, or 800/995-0969).

<o><o><o><o><o>

Imagine a theme park with four thrilling roller coasters and all kinds of other rides and entertainments, a zoo, chocolates galore (enough to feast on for several lifetimes), 23 acres of beautiful gardens, and two hotel resorts that offer everything from golf to horseback riding. You've just imagined Hershey, a wonderful town for the whole family to enjoy, which is just how Mr. Hershey would've wanted it.

Milton Snavely Hershey was a remarkable man who planned and built this utopian community in the Pennsylvania valley where he was born in Derry Township. When he was eight his family left for Lancaster and he was apprenticed to a candymaker. Ambitious and determined, Hershey began his own business at 19, making a whole line of varied candies, but it collapsed when he could no longer obtain credit to purchase sugar and other ingredients. So Hershey decided to go West, following his father, who'd left in search of a silver strike. Stopping in Denver, he learned a new candy-making process—the art of making caramels—and he returned to try again, this time in Philadelphia, where he enjoyed a modest success until once again he was driven into bankruptcy.

Undaunted, he returned to Lancaster penniless and managed to persuade a skeptical family to help start yet another business. This time he decided to specialize in caramels only, and soon orders were pouring in and outstripping supply. Hershey finally built a thriving business, which he was able to sell for $1 million at only 42. By this time Hershey had already become interested in chocolate as a foundation for a whole new industry and begun manufacturing a variety of chocolate novelties. When he sold his business he retained the right to make chocolate, and soon this enterprise also began growing so fast that additional space was required to keep pace with demand. Hershey decided to locate his new factory in the countryside, where he had been born and where he knew he had access to a hardworking labor force and also to the milk he'd require to mass-produce his single product, a milk chocolate bar made with fresh milk. Despite bankers' objections, he built his factory in 1903, and by 1911 the business had grown to $5 million and Hershey was well on his way to becoming the largest chocolate manufacturer in the world.

Around his factory he set about building his dream community. First, he built homes for the workers, taking a personal interest in each building and issuing strict instructions to make each home different. He wanted to encourage the workers to own their own homes and built only a few houses for rent. Gradually homes went up along Trinidad Avenue, Chocolate and Cocoa avenues, and other streets whose names were taken from the cocoa industry. Churches, schools, a library, a bank, a store, and finally a post office followed, the last prompting a change in the name of the town, when the U.S. government demanded to know what the office should be called. A competition for a new name was run and a woman who suggested Hersheykoko won, but the final "koko" was dropped.

At this time Hershey also designed and built his mansion at High Point, much later laying out the gardens which his wife, Kitty, had planned. In 1907 he created an amusement park, golf courses, and a zoo and went on to found his great school for orphaned children, all of which remain and continue to bring joy and happiness to a great many visitors and the community itself. In the 1930s, despite the dire economic conditions, he embarked on a second building phase, which he justified by the low cost of building materials and the needs of the workers. He created the Hotel Hershey overlooking the town, a community center, an extraordinary windowless office building, a sports arena (the first concrete monolithic structure), and Hershey Stadium (finished in 1939). All of them survive, and each continues to serve the community and the town as Hershey dreamed they would.

Events & Festivals to Plan Your Trip Around

February: Great American Chocolate Festival—demonstrations of chocolate dipping, chocolate facials/scrubs, and chocolate decorations; guest chefs; and much more (mid-month at the Hotel Hershey).

May–Labor Day: Hersheypark is open only during summer.

October: National Fall Meet of the Antique Automobile Club of America.

Hershey Attractions

Any visit should begin at the **visitor center**, on Hershey Park Drive. From here it's a short drive to the parking lot for the main thrills—Chocolate World, Tudor Square and Hersheypark, the Hershey Museum of American Life, and ZooAmerica/North American Wildlife Park. A free shuttle to all the attractions operates from June 11 to Labor Day.

Chocolate World

Hershey always appreciated the value of letting people see his business operations in action. Indeed, between 1927 and mid-1973 more than 10 million people toured the world's largest chocolate and cocoa plant on Chocolate Avenue. In 1970 close to a million visitors arrived to tour the plant, so it became necessary to cater specifically to their needs by creating Chocolate World, which now welcomes a million people each year.

Chocolate World takes you on a Disney-style ride through the chocolate-making process, from African cocoa-growing plantations, where 500 cocoa pods an hour are broken open by machete, through the manufacturing processes of cleaning, blending, roasting, milling, and grinding—all of which produces the liquor from which the cocoa and chocolate is made. Hershey pioneered the making of milk chocolate, and to this liquor is added milk (50,000 cows are needed to supply the daily requirements of the plant) and sugar, creating a mixture that's then refined, conched, and deposited in molds to create Kisses, bars, Reese's Pieces, and all the other famous Hershey products. Appetite whetted at the end of your tour, you can shop for any kind of chocolate souvenir you could ever wish for.

Hours: Daily 9am–5pm. **Closed:** New Year's Day, Easter, Thanksgiving, Christmas. **Admission:** Free.

Tudor Square & Hersheypark

In his planned community, Hershey had always wanted an amusement park, for he didn't want to create just another industrial community. Over his mother's objections that the workers required no such luxuries, he had the park laid out from 1906 to 1907. The entertainment included band concerts at the bandshell, boating on Spring Creek, dancing at the old-time pavilion, vaudeville acts, carousels, a miniature railroad, and even a roller coaster. Even though the park was remodeled in 1971, the aim to provide fun for all the family was continued. You enter via Tudor Square, a re-creation of a brick-and-stone Tudor village, where the buildings have mullioned windows and a Tudor castle looms over all. Just to the right of the castle is a guest relations building that provides tickets, tours, and information.

Rides are the park's prime drawing card—more than 50 of them, including four roller coasters. First and foremost is the Superduper Looper, which travels over 50 m.p.h. and loops riders 360°, literally turning them upside-down; second is the Comet, a wooden coaster with a thrilling 96-foot first drop and a 72-foot second drop; and third is the Trail Blazer, a sidewinding high-speed centrifugal-force roller coaster. The Looper and Comet have been listed as two of the nation's top roller coasters. The Tidal Force ride includes a 55-foot drop and a dramatic "splashdown." For the less daring there's the Kissing Tower, the Monorail, and the Skyride, 30 enclosed gondolas that cruise to a high point 113 feet above the park. Perhaps the most charming and delightful ride is the Carousel, built in 1919 with 42 jumping horses and many large stationary horses, all hand-carved by Italian craftsmen. There's also a giant Ferris wheel. For kids, there's Kaptain Kid's Kove, a fantasy playground where youngsters can enjoy finger painting, a Hound Dog Jamboree, strolling clowns, puppet shows, and encounters with the famous Hersheypark Furry Tales costumed characters in between their romps in the Kid's Krawl Rope Climb, Tubular Sliding Board, and Teeter-totter Horses. In the park is also an aqua amphitheater that features dolphins and sea lions.

Several areas are devoted to the food and crafts of the Pennsylvania Dutch and their forebears who came from Germany. At der Deitschplatz (Pennsylvania Dutch Place), candlemakers, potters, silversmiths, black-smiths, and leather makers practice their skills on items that are for sale. Over at Rhine Land, a quaint reconstruction of a German village, you'll find many gift shops and stores, three cafeteria-style restaurants (Hamburger Chalet, Der Pizza Meister, and the Alpine Ristorante), and the Rhine Land Express, which chugs along Spring Creek following the original path of the miniature train. In several theaters you'll come across entertainment of all sorts, special musicals produced by Hersheypark, and showcased top-name entertainment. For tickets and information, call 717/534-3911.

Hours: Mid-May to late Sept; for exact hours, call the number above.
Admission (including ZooAmerica/North American Wildlife Park): $24.95 adults, $15.95 seniors and children 3–8. Check for special discount packages at the information center. For information, call 717/534-3090.

From Hershey Park a bridge leads across to **ZooAmerica/North American Wildlife Park,** where two indoor and three outdoor exhibit areas feature plants and animals in natural settings from five North American regions, each demonstrating how particular species adapt to a specific type of environment—desert, swamp, forest, plains, and mountains. Although ZooAmerica is part of the park, it's open year round.

Hours: Mid-June to Aug, daily 10am–8pm; Sept to mid-June, daily 10am–5pm. **Admission:** $4.75 adults, $4.25 seniors, $3.50 children 3–12.

The Hershey Museum

This museum (tel. 717/534-3439) features collections of American Indian and Eskimo artifacts along with some Pennsylvania Dutch German objects, grouped thematically to highlight the functional and decorative beauty of items used in early America. Among these treasures is the famous Apostolic clock (moving figurines depicting the Last Supper), phonographs, music boxes, early firepumps and engines, glassware, furniture, and pottery.

Hours: Memorial Day–Labor Day, daily 10am–6pm; the rest of the year, daily 10am–5pm. **Admission:** $4.25 adults, $2 children 3–15.

Other Attractions

Away from Hersheypark Arena and the surrounding attractions, you might want to visit the famous **Hershey Gardens,** located off Hersheypark on a hillside en route to the Hotel Hershey. Here you can wander through 23 acres of gardens planted in spring with daffodils, tulips, azaleas, and rhododendron, and blooming through summer with all kinds of flowers and shrubs. Then, of course, there are the famous roses—14,000 in over 800 varieties. Once a little 3-acre garden, it has now been divided into five horticulturally themed areas—English formal garden, colonial garden, rock garden, Japanese garden, and a garden of old roses.

Hours: Mid-May to Oct, daily 9am–5pm. **Admission:** $4.25 adults, $3.75 seniors, $2 children 3–15.

You can also visit **Founders Hall** (tel. 717/534-3500), which serves as the visitors center for Milton Hershey School. Hershey and his wife founded the school in 1909 to provide education for orphaned boys. It opened in the Homestead, the farmhouse where Hershey had been born, with a total of four pupils. Today the same school owns over 50 farms and educates 1,300 boys and girls, who live in 84 student homes scattered across 10,000 acres. The school still reflects many of Hershey's ideas—that every child should learn a trade and learn by doing rather than by simply reading, that each should be imbued with some kind of religious training and learn to help others, and that each should learn how to farm and enjoy rural life. A 27-minute film at Founders Hall explains the school's history and life at the school.

Hours: Daily 9am–4pm. **Admission:** Free.

Hershey Lodging

An ochre-brick building topped by a green-tile roof and Spanish-style turrets, the **Hotel Hershey,** Hershey, PA 17033 (tel. 717/533-2171), is unique and wonderfully whimsical, representing a melange of the favorite places where Hershey and Kitty had ever stayed on their Mediterranean travels. The hotel is best entered from the terrace. Open the huge French doors and you enter a Spanish-Mexican square with brilliantly colored mosaic tile floors, a splashing fountain, stucco walls, and archways capped by a cloudless sky (yes, it's painted in).

It's unfortunate that the theme is not continued in the accommodations. The 241 rooms are decorated in beige and rust and well appointed with adequate seating (two wing chairs and a loveseat), a coffee table, and a desk, plus the usual amenities.

The circular dining room looks out onto the gardens through windows with leaded panes overlaid with delicate stained-glass images of trees, flowers, birds, and squirrels. Hershey had much influence on the design of this room, and he wanted a good view from every table. "In some places if you don't tip well, they put you in a corner," he said. "I don't want any corners."

At dinner you can choose the from a menu that features such dishes as lemon/thyme-crusted chicken breast, wasabi-crusted rack of lamb, and pan-seared tuna topped with foie gras. Prices range from $22 to $28. To start, enjoy the richly smooth lobster terrine or flavorsome mushroom ragoût. To finish, don't miss the triple-chocolate/truffle torte (if available) or the famous Hershey chocolate-cream pie.

Facilities include tennis courts, indoor and outdoor pools, 72 holes of golf, lawn bowling, and horseback riding. Live entertainment is featured in the Iberian Lounge.

Rates: Summer, $225 double. Spring and fall, $205 double. Winter, $185 double. MAP rates available. **Dining Hours:** Daily noon–2pm and 6–9pm. Special weekend and other packages offered.

Hershey Lodge and Convention Center, West Chocolate Avenue and University Drive, Hershey, PA 17033 (tel. 717/533-3311), is for the traveler who likes a large modern place with complete entertainment facilities. Shutters and old-fashioned iron latches on the bathroom doors are the only faint note of rusticity in the 457 rooms with faux burled-wood headboards and furnishings. In the recently redecorated rooms, dark-rose carpeting is combined with floral bedspreads. Bath amenities include hair conditioner, shampoo, and a shoehorn. The rooms also have coffeemakers. The recreational facilities include indoor and outdoor pools, four tennis and two paddletennis courts, golf, pitch and putt, and bicycles for rent. There are three restaurants, two lounges (live entertainment six nights a week in one), and a cinema.

Rates: May–Labor Day, $152 double. Children 17 and under stay free in parents' room. Special weekend and other packages offered.

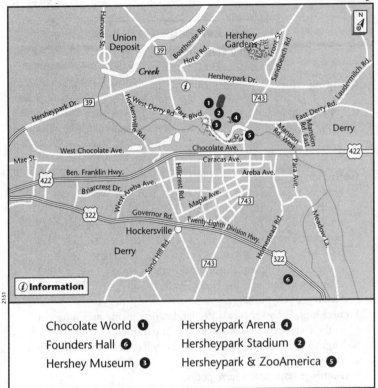

Chocolate World ❶

Founders Hall ❻

Hershey Museum ❸

Hersheypark Arena ❹

Hersheypark Stadium ❷

Hersheypark & ZooAmerica ❺

Hershey Dining

The dining room at the **Hotel Hershey** (above) is excellent and known for its fine luncheon buffets and first-rate dining. At the Hershey Lodge, the **Hearth Room** is aptly named, given the size of its fieldstone fireplace. Here you can enjoy a complete dinner of calves' liver, sauerbraten, honey-dipped fried chicken, roast beef, or similar dishes priced from $9 to $23. The pricier **Tack Room** specializes in steak and lobster dinners.

After Dark

Broadway favorites run every season at the **Hershey Theater,** Chocolate and Cocoa avenues (tel. 717/534-3405). The season runs from September to April. Hersheypark Stadium hosts football, entertainers (Aerosmith, Billy Joel, the Eagles, Phil Collins), and other events.

The **Hersheypark Arena** (tel. 717/534-3911) is home to the Hershey Bears on most winter Wednesdays and Saturdays and to such spectaculars as Disney's World on Ice, the Harlem Globetrotters, and a mixed bag of entertainers from Frank Sinatra to Reba McEntire to ZZ Top.

J. P. Mallard's lounge, in the Hershey Lodge, offers live Top-40s dance bands Tuesday to Saturday.

Hershey
Special & Recreational Activities

Camping: Hershey provides camping facilities at Highmeadow Camp, only 2 miles away on Rte. 39 (tel. 717/566-0902), on 25 acres of tree-shaded grounds. There are 297 sites, a pool, a fishing pond, playgrounds, indoor and outdoor games, movies, square dancing, and a supply store. Basic camping is $19.50. Open year round.

Golf: Hershey is often called the Golf Capital of Pennsylvania because it possesses five beautiful courses: the West Course at the Hershey Country Club (tel. 717/533-2360) is rated one of the top 100 in the United States, while the east course is also popular. The South Course, closer to Hersheypark (tel. 717/534-3450), ranks among America's top 25. There are also a couple of nine-holers, the original Hershey course, built in 1933 at Spring Creek, and the Hotel Hershey Golf course. The Hotel Hershey offers packages.

Picnicking: There's a pleasantly landscaped picnic area adjacent to the Hersheypark/Chocolate World parking lot.

Skiing: You can cross-country ski on the golf course at the Hershey Hotel.

Swimming: Both hotels have pools.

Tennis: Both hotels have tennis courts.

RHODE ISLAND

Block Island

Distance in Miles: 167

Estimated Driving Time: Allow 3¾ to 4½ hours to reach the Point Judith Ferry (you must be there 30 minutes ahead of departure).

━◁○▷━◁○▷━◁○▷━◁○▷━◁○▷━

Driving: Take I-95 to Exit 92 to Rte. 78, which will lead onto Rte. 1. Take Rte. 1 to Rte. 108, which runs down the Point to Galilee/Point Judith.

Air: Take New England Airlines (tel. 401/596-2460, or 800/243-2460) flying from Westerly, R.I., or Action Airlines (tel. 203/448-1646, or 800/243-8623), flying in summer from East Hampton, LaGuardia, and Groton airports.

Train: Amtrak (tel. 800/872-7245) service is available to New London (with easy connection to the Point Judith ferry), to Westerly (with connecting taxi service to the airport), or to Kingston (with cab connection to the Point Judith ferry).

Ferry: Interstate Navigation Co., Galilee State Pier, Point Judith, RI 02882 (tel. 401/783-4613), runs ferries year round, eight trips per day in season. The one-way cost is $6.50 for adults, $3.15 for children, and $20.25 for a car. The trip takes about 70 minutes.

Nelseco Navigation Co., P.O. Box 482, New London, CT 06320 (tel. 203/442-7891), operates one ferry daily in season (with an additional 7:15pm trip on Friday). The one-way cost is $13.50 for adults, $9 for children, and $25 for a car. The trip takes about two hours. Advance reservations are needed.

Other ferries leave from Providence and Newport, R.I., and from Montauk, N.Y.

Further Information: For more about Block Island, contact the **Block Island Chamber of Commerce,** Drawer D, Block Island, RI 02807 (tel. 401/466-2982, or 800/383-BIRI).

Even a two-day trip to Block Island will seem like a long, langorous vacation as the island's slow-paced life works its miracle of restoring peace of mind and granting serenity to even the most jaundiced frantic urbanite.

Events & Festivals to Plan Your Trip Around

June: Storm Trysail Race week (fourth weekend).
September: Annual Road Race (the weekend after Labor Day).

Going to Block Island, you'll feel as if you're making a real journey. From the minute you arrive at the Point Judith dock, you'll notice an excited, exaggerated sense of anticipation. Gulls wheel and caw overhead, fishermen unload their catch, boats chug in and out of the inlet, the houses stand swaying ever so slightly on stilts, and there's a rough-and-ready rhythm to the port that leaves Manhattan far behind. Once aboard the ferry, kids run excitedly from deck to deck, their orange and yellow oil-skins flashing here and there. And then suddenly the ship is under way and you're moving, pulling past the rock breaker, past the houses, and into the ocean, until there's only water behind and in front—gray and cold and dappled with snowlike foam or shining metallic blue, depending on the season. People settle back with their hampers or hang out by the snack bar until on the horizon the island appears, just a thin sliver, as often as not, emerging from the mist. First you can make out the undulating contours of the island, then the clay red cliffs that are indeed reminiscent of those other famous cousins. A solitary house comes into view, then another and another, and finally, if you're aboard a late-afternoon or evening ferry, the lights of the harbor sparkle ahead and the outline of the Victorian buildings appear as the gongs on the buoys sound out across the water.

You've arrived on Block Island, a largely unspoiled beautiful island only 7 miles long and 3 miles wide, which for its size offers an incredible variety of terrain. It's an island with gently rolling hillsides studded with wildflowers, windswept dunes, winding lanes bordered by stone fences, and more than 200 freshwater ponds colored with abundant water lilies. You'll find no fast-food chains here, few cars, and hardly a traffic light, although condominiums are beginning to appear, much to the dismay of the local independent islanders.

Block Island Attractions

And what, you may ask, is there to do here? Relax, loll on the beach, wander over the rose-scented cliff tops, climb down to the rock-strewn pebble beach below the cliffs, rent a bicycle and travel around the island, browse the few harbor shops, go fishing or swimming or clamming or sailing, fly a kite, or do any of those things you'd traditionally do on an island. Or you can just plain sit and read or talk to the locals who'll fill your ears with many a Block Island tale. One such tale you'll most likely hear is the saga of the *Palatine,* a vessel supposedly carrying emigrants from the German Palatinate that went down off Block Island in the 1700s. It's said that the islanders plundered the ship, ignoring the imprecations of the drowning passengers. Even today, they say, a ghostly light can be seen seeming to burn at sea, a haunting remembrance of this shameful day.

If you'd like to learn more of the island's legends and lore, pick up a copy of Livermore's *History of Block Island,* available at several stores on the island. Also stop by the **Historical Society Museum,** at the corner of Old Town Road and Ocean Avenue (tel. 401/466-2481), to view the period rooms and other local memorabilia.

Hours: In season, Wed–Mon 10am–4pm.

Block Island was originally inhabited by a tribe of Native Americans who called it Manisses, or "Isle of the Little God." In 1524, on his way to what he hoped was Asia, Italian explorer Giovanni da Verrazano spied the island and named it Claudia, after the wife of François I of France, under whose flag he sailed. Before the name took hold, along cruised Dutch navigator Adrian Block, who charted the island's location in 1614. And so it came to be called Block Island in his honor. In 1661 the island was sold to 16 settlers from the Massachusetts Bay Colony. To view the spot where they landed, take Dodge Street from the Old Harbor to Corn Neck Road, and this will lead you out past Crescent Beach northward to the area known as **The Maze,** a nature lover's delight with over 11 miles of trails that emerge on the cliff tops. From here it's only a few minutes' drive to **Settler's Rock,** where the first settlers' names are found on the monument marking their landing place. From here you can view the abandoned **North Light** at Sandy Point, which was built in 1867 and now houses a maritime museum.

At the center of the pork chop–shaped island lies the **Great Salt Pond,** on which the New Harbor is located, a fully protected basin for the docking of many pleasure boats. One or two restaurants and lodging places are also located here. If you continue out along Ocean Avenue instead of turning right at Corn Neck Road, you'll eventually come to **New Harbor.** Turn left at the harbor and the road will bring you to the island cemetery high on a hill. The decorated tombstones here stand witness to the local families and their members who contributed to the island's 300 years of history.

Nearby, **Redman's Hollow** is one of five wildlife refuges on the island, a great natural ravine, located off Cooneymus Road. Many paths wind their way down to a point below sea level where you can spend a leisurely afternoon observing the area's wildlife.

The most spectacular area, however, is the **Mohegan Bluffs,** clay cliffs extending 5 miles at the southernmost tip of the island, reached via Spring

Block Island

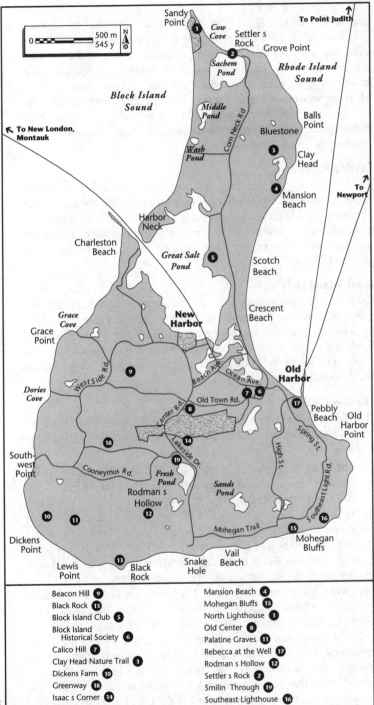

Beacon Hill 9
Black Rock 13
Block Island Club 5
Block Island
  Historical Society 6
Calico Hill 7
Clay Head Nature Trail 3
Dickens Farm 10
Greenway 18
Isaac's Corner 14

Mansion Beach 4
Mohegan Bluffs 15
North Lighthouse 1
Old Center 8
Palatine Graves 11
Rebecca at the Well 17
Rodman's Hollow 12
Settler's Rock 2
Smilin' Through 19
Southeast Lighthouse 16

Street and Southeast Light Road. Here legend has it that the Manisses routed and starved out the invading Mohegan Indians and pushed them off the bluffs into the sea. Several dirt paths lead to the sea and a view from 200 feet up out over the Atlantic and down to the rocky shoreline. Stairs lead down at one place, or you can climb down on your own. Off to the left is the **Southeast Light,** a quaint brick structure built in 1874. The lens then cost $10,000; today it would cost more like $7 million. It still warns the seafarers of the treacherous shoreline, the only perimeter to this pristinely beautiful island.

Getting Around

The island is only 7 miles long, so if you're staying in either harbor area there's no need for a car—it's less than a mile from one harbor to the other. The most suitable mode of transport is a bicycle, and many outfits rent them. Mopeds are also available. The state beach is so close to town that walking is still another option. And there are always taxis available. Cars can also be rented.

Block Island Lodging

You'll need to make reservations well in advance, especially for July, August, and all holiday weekends. Be aware, too, that if you're planning to fly in and the weather is bad enough so that your flight is grounded, most hotels will expect you to catch the ferry over. Otherwise you'll forfeit the charge for your room for that night. So make sure to check reservation and cancellation policies carefully.

The Top Choices

The island's two most sophisticated accommodations are the 1661 Inn and the Hotel Manisses, both owned by the Abrams family and both quite different.

The **1661 Inn,** Spring Street, Block Island, RI 02807 (tel. 401/466-2421 or 466-2063), has a colonial charm and looks out to the Atlantic Ocean across a pond frequented by regal swans—in short, it has a marvelous location a five-minute walk from Old Harbor. The inn is named in honor of the year Block Island was settled by courageous colonists from New England. Each of the nine guest rooms (all with bath) is named for one of the original settlers and is furnished individually, many with decks overlooking the ocean. In the Samuel Staples Room even the Jacuzzi has a view; it also has an extra-large deck. The Simon Ray Room has cathedral ceilings and a brass canopied bed. The John Ackurs Room has two brass beds, a kitchenette, and windows on two sides with great views.

In the guesthouse across the yard are 10 rooms (4 with bath). The upstairs rooms are furnished in country style with oak beds, marble-topped dressers, and lace curtains. The ground-floor rooms are more contemporary, although they also contain wicker loveseats and chairs. Each room has a deck with an ocean view. Adjacent to the 1661 Inn, the Nicholas Ball

Cottage is a replica of St. Anne's by the Sea Episcopal Church, which was destroyed in the 1938 hurricane. It contains three luxurious suites (each with a fireplace, Jacuzzi, and tiled bath), furnished with Victorian cottage pieces or similar. Two are very attractive duplexes.

There's a comfortable parlor in both the guesthouse and the main inn. A buffet breakfast—fresh fruit, cereals, waffles, hash, eggs and potatoes, bluefish, sausage, muffins, and smoked fish—is served in a pretty room with floral wallpaper at tables set with pink linen and sky-blue napkins or out on the ocean-view deck.

Rates (including breakfast): Summer, $166–$345 double weekends, $119–$345 double weekdays. Spring and fall, $110–$200 double weekends, $95–$205 double weekdays. Winter, $89–$180 double weekends, $85–$170 double weekdays. **Open:** Inn, Apr–Oct; guesthouse and Nicholas Ball Cottage, year round.

The **Hotel Manisses,** Spring Street, Block Island, RI 02807 (tel. 401/466-2421 or 466-2063), is a gracious turreted white clapboard Victorian decked out in period style. Even the staff members wear period dress. On the ground floor is a comfortable wicker-furnished parlor where you'll find board games and some fascinating old, old volumes—*Historians' History of the World,* Bulwer Lytton, and the like. There's also the small Top Shelf Bar, where guests can enjoy cocktails or flaming coffees.

The hallways leading to the 17 rooms (all with bath and phone, some with Jacuzzi and refrigerator) are lined with a variety of Victorian portraits and pre-Raphaelite pictures. A decanter of brandy and a dish of hard candy are placed in each room. The ground-floor Chelsea Room has a Jacuzzi, a high-backed oak bed, wicker chairs and table, and a marble-topped dresser. The Prince Augusta Room has similar marble-topped furnishings, along with a deep-well dresser and a Mme Récamier couch. The Pocahontas Room has its own deck. And the William Frederick Room contains an assortment of Victoriana, including a chair with a fold-out footstool, a wedding-cake table, and a Stickley-style chair.

Breakfast is served at the 1661 Inn (above); afternoon tea is served during summer. Bamboo chairs and pink-on-burgundy tablecloths contribute to the dining room's pretty ambience. For those who prefer to sit outside, the sliding glass doors lead out onto a deck set with tables sporting yellow umbrellas overlooking the fragrant garden with a fountain. Lunch fare consists of soups, salads, and sandwiches, plus a raw bar and an assortment of items like baked frittata, chicken teriyaki, fish du jour, and cheese tortellini cooked with assorted smoked fish, herbs, and cream. Many of the vegetables and herbs come fresh from the large garden behind the inn.

At dinner, start with a selection from the raw bar, a clam-filled chowder, or seafood sampler Antoinette. Follow with one of the dozen or so entrees—steaks, baked stuffed flounder (with oysters and walnuts), scallops with fines herbes, bouillabaisse, duck au poivre, or basil chicken sautéed with pine nuts, fresh basil, and tomato. Prices run $15 to $23. Dessert might be fresh strawberries, apple pie, chocolate layer cake with raspberry filling, or something similar. Guests who stay here can also enjoy the fascinating menagerie that grazes in the fields behind the house—llamas, Sicilian donkeys, Indian runner ducks, and pygmy and fainting goats.

Rates (including breakfast): See rates for the 1661 Inn above. **Dining Hours:** Mid-May to Columbus Day, daily 10pm–closing; check at other times of year. For dinner reservations, call 401/466-2836.

Other Choices

The **Atlantic Inn,** High Street, Block Island, RI 02807 (tel. 401/466-5883 or 466-2005), is an atmospheric old Victorian inn with a wraparound porch that first opened in 1879. It stands high on a bluff with the whole island and the Atlantic Ocean at its feet. Shores, hills, and ponds are spread out to view, and sunrises and sunsets too. There are 21 rooms, all with bath and wall-to-wall Wilton carpeting. The rooms are variously furnished: For example, Room 3 has a high oak bed with a floral comforter, a sidetable, a dresser, and an armoire. Third-floor rooms have knee walls (low walls under a gable or mansard roof) and shuttered windows, plus assorted oak, marble-topped, and Mission furniture.

From late May to October, a continental breakfast is served to guests. Dinner is served in the dining room at white-draped tables; candlelight, classical music, and often spectacular sunsets make it a romantic spot. If you have to wait for a table, the bar is attractively furnished with a camel-back sofa and Stickley chairs. The six-course $40 prix-fixe menu changes weekly. It might begin with a choice of three appetizers, like house-smoked salmon, and could be followed by a choice of soup and salad. The four or so entrees might include sea scallops sautéed with dried poblanos with a hint of lime and cilantro or suprême of chicken with a sauce of fresh tomatoes, rosemary, and green olives. The finale may be a bittersweet-chocolate truffle tart or a fresh blackberry flan with a light sour-cream sauce. Other facilities include a croquet court, two tennis courts, a horse-shoe pit, and 6 acres of grounds from which to view the ocean.

Rates (including continental breakfast late May to Oct): Summer and fall, $130–$230 double. Spring, $109–$175 double. **Closed:** Nov–Mar.

Tucked away behind the Atlantic Inn, the **Rose Farm Inn,** Roslyn Road (P.O. Box E), Block Island, RI 02807 (tel. 401/466-2034), is located in two buildings. The first is an 1897 farmhouse offering 10 rooms (8 with bath) that are sparkling clean and variously furnished. Some have pencil four-posters, others high-back Victorian beds, and still others iron-and-brass beds. These are combined with oak dressers and rockers and other antique country pieces. Room 9 is a favorite, with a four-poster canopied bed, nautical wallpaper, a ship's-wheel mirror, and watercolors of sea-going vessels. A couple of rooms have double whirlpool baths. There's a deck on the south side of the farmhouse furnished with chaise longues for sunning. There's also a TV lounge and such conveniences as an ice machine, a regrigerator, and a coffeemaker. The newer building contains 9 rooms, all with bath. The first-floor rooms have double whirlpool baths and the upstairs rooms have appealing sitting areas tucked under the large dormer and single whirlpool baths. They're furnished in similar Victorian style.

The breakfast room gets the morning sun and is welcoming with its tables set with blue cloths and pine Windsor chairs and its many hanging plants. Fruit, cereals, and breads are served.

Rates (including breakfast): Summer, $100–$185 double. Spring and fall, $100–$185 double weekends, $85–$160 double weekdays. Winter, $85–$135 double weekends, $75–$125 double weekdays.

Right down on Old Harbor, the **Surf Hotel,** Block Island, RI 02807 (tel. 401/466-2241 or 466-5990 in season, 401/466-2147 in winter), has a marvelous view of Crescent Beach and is typical of Block Island's hostelries before the island was discovered by the urban tourist. Each of the 40 rooms (7 with bath) has floral wallpaper, lace curtains, a bed, a dresser, and a rocker, sometimes of oak or wicker. There's often a sink in the room, plus an overhead fan. A kitchen is available to store ice and other stuff. The dining room is great fun, its tin walls hung with a pretty china collection; the tables sport blue cloths, and the room has a view of the ocean, of course. A complete breakfast can be purchased here. There's also a comfortably cluttered Victorian sitting area decked out in red with a splendid wood-burning stove from Kalamazoo, a variety of seating, a giant chess set (each piece 8 inches high), and assorted other games, plus a TV and a grand piano. Wood rockers line the porches overlooking the harbor, street, and beach.

Rates: Late June to Labor Day, $90–$100 double without bath, $120-$140 double with bath. Late May (excluding Memorial Day weekend) to late June and Labor Day–Columbus Day, $85–$95 double without bath, $115–$135 double with bath. Six-night minimum stay July–Aug.

Just down the street from the Surf Hotel, the **Blue Dory Inn,** Dodge Street, Block Island, RI 02807 (tel. 401/466-5891), is a small attractive accommodation. Past the entry porch hung with flower baskets you'll find a ground-floor parlor with a TV and Stickley furnishings. The main inn has 10 rooms with bath, some with high-backed oak beds, others with brass beds, and all with a variety of Stickley and oak furnishings and floral fabrics. The rooms are nicely decorated in a comfortable feminine style using rose-patterned and other Waverly fabrics, fringed lamps, down comforters and ruffles on the beds, plenty of pillows, fresh flowers, and potpourri. The top-floor rooms have skylights. A continental breakfast—fresh fruit, cinnamon rolls, croissants—is served at tables set with fresh flowers in a pretty room. The cottage sleeps six or seven, the Doll House has one room for romantics, and the Tea House contains an efficiency and has its own porch overlooking the sea. Out back of the main inn is a small patio with access to the beach less than 100 feet away. There are also three cottages that sleep four to eight. A charming accommodation.

Rates (including breakfast): Early June to Labor Day and weekends Memorial Day–Columbus Day, $145–$195 double. Spring and fall, $95–$160 double. Winter, $75–$105 double.

Across the street, the **Gables Inn,** Dodge Street (P.O. Box 516), Block Island, RI 02807 (tel. 401/466-2213 or 466-7721), offers a variety of accommodations. There are 13 rooms (4 with bath) in the main inn, each decorated with chintz wallpaper and featuring either an oak or an iron-and-brass bed. On the ground floor is a TV room and a sitting room with wicker armchairs. On the ground floor of Gables II are several paneled apartments, each with a fully equipped kitchen and dining area. These have immediate access to the lawn picnic tables and a barbecue.

Rates (including breakfast): Summer, $85–$120 double without bath, $105–$135 double with bath. Spring and fall, $60–$110 double without bath, $80–$120 double with bath. Apartment from $730 per week. **Closed:** Dec to mid-Apr.

The Adrian, P.O. Box 340, Block Island, RI 02807 (tel. 401/466-2693), is located in an old sea captain's house that was built in 1880 and is now on the National Register of Historic Places. It stands on a knoll with a broad porch overlooking the Old Harbor. There are 10 extremely nice rooms with bath. Each is furnished individually with rockers and armoires, occasional wicker or Mission pieces, and high-back Victorian beds. The charming guest cottage has two twins and makes for a private retreat. Guests can enjoy lounging on the 3 acres of grounds complete with a gazebo. Set on a bluff, the property offers panoramic views of the ocean and Old Harbor. It's close to town but far enough away for guests to avoid the summer hordes of day trippers.

Rates (including continental breakfast): Summer weekends, $135–$185 double. Early June and Sept 15–Columbus Day, $95–$145. **Closed:** Columbus Day–May.

The **Old Town Inn,** a little way from Old Harbor at the junction of Old Town Road and Center Road (P.O. Box 351), Block Island, RI 02807 (tel. 401/466-5958), is a B&B operated by the Gunter family, who hail from England. The inn incorporates two houses, the older dating from the mid-19th century, when it served as a merchant's residence. The East Wing was added in 1981. Six rooms are found in each, all neat and clean and nicely, if simply, furnished with maple beds and chests against chintz wallpaper. In the newer building the rooms are larger and have a full bath. Monica serves a full breakfast of eggs and bacon and a "proper" English afternoon tea around the brick hearth in the living room. The inn is surrounded by 5 acres, and in the back is a pretty garden.

Rates (including breakfast): Mid-June to Labor Day, $90 double without bath, $110–$140 double with bath. Mid-Apr to mid-June and Labor Day–Oct, $85 double without bath, $95–$115 double with bath.

Midway between Old and New Harbor on a hill overlooking the Great Salt Pond, **The Barrington,** Beach and Ocean avenues (P.O. Box 90), Block Island, RI 02807 (tel. 401/466-5510), built in 1886, is operated by friendly Joan and Howard Ballard. There are six rooms in the house (all with bath) and two housekeeping apartments in an adjacent barn. Each of the three rooms on the second floor has a private deck and fine water views; third-floor rooms also have water views. Each room is simply furnished with chintz wallpaper. In Room 5 is a brass bed and wicker rocker. On the ground floor is a large room overlooking the garden with a private porch—very cool in summer. Guests have two comfy sitting rooms with a TV/VCR and a selection of books and games. A breakfast of fresh fruit, muffins, and cereal is served in the dining room or on the deck out back with a view of the ponds. The apartments have two bedrooms, a fully equipped kitchen, and a living room. Out front are a lawn and shade trees.

Rates (including breakfast): Mid-June to Labor Day and Memorial Day weekend, $115–$159 double. May to mid-June (excluding Memorial Day) and Labor Day–Oct, $70–$115 double. Apr and early to mid-Nov, $60–$85 double.

The **Seacrest Inn,** 207 High St., Block Island, RI 02807 (tel. 401/466-2882), is an attractive well-maintained accommodation. The 17 rooms (all with bath) are sparkling clean. Each contains a maple bed, a sidetable, a dresser, and a rocker, all set against beige wallpaper; three rooms have brass beds. The grounds are prettily landscaped, with a latticework gazebo hung with flower baskets. Kids enjoy the play area. Umbrella-shaded tables are placed on the lawn. Coffee, juice, and danish are provided in the mornings. Bicycles are available for rent.

Rates (including breakfast): Mid-June to mid-Sept and holidays and weekends, $105–$140 double. Early May to mid-June and mid-Sept to mid-Oct, $65–$100 double.

The next two hotels are island classics. The **Spring House,** Spring Street, Block Island, RI 02807 (tel. 401/466-2633), is the largest and oldest on the island, built in 1852. The striking white clapboard building crowned with a cupola is on a hilltop overlooking the ocean and "The Village." The porch, set with rockers, extends along the house's front and side overlooking the swan pond. The large lobby extends into the ballroom/living room with 7-foot-tall windows and 12-foot ceilings, where the focal point is a large stone fireplace. The dining room is decked out in pink and forest green. Cocktails and afternoon tea can be enjoyed in Victoria's parlor with a long oak bar, while the sun room with its wicker seating is a wonderful place to curl up with a book. There are 49 studios, rooms, and suites (17 in a separate building), furnished with four-posters, wing chairs, and Eastlake and other reproductions. The hotel stands on 15 acres dotted with Adirondack chairs and benches. Facilities include croquet, volleyball, and horseshoes.

Rates (including continental breakfast): Mid-June to Labor Day and holiday weekends, $159–$260 double. May 30 to mid-June and Labor Day–Oct 14, $119–$210 double weekends, $109–$199 double weekdays. Apr–May 29 and Oct 15–31, $109–$179 double weekends, $69–$139 double weekdays.

The **Harborside Inn,** overlooking the ferry dock at Old Harbor (P.O. Box F), Block Island, RI 02807 (tel. 401/466-5504, 466-2693 at the Gazebo), has 52 rooms, 30 with bath. They are prettily decorated with beige/blue-striped wallpaper, color-coordinated carpets and spreads, and rattan furnishings. The quietest rooms are found at the Gazebo, about 300 yards from the inn.

Rates: July–Aug weekends, $125 double without bath, $165 double with bath. Spring and fall weekends, $85–$125 double without bath, $95–$165 double with bath.

If you're looking for a room with a TV and a phone, then the **National Hotel,** Old Harbor (P.O. Box 189), Block Island, RI 02807 (tel. 401/466-2901), is for you. It also has a series of bars, a dining room, and regular live entertainment on the porch. The hotel is located in a historic clapboard building with a cupola and gabled mansard roof.

Rates: Mid-June to Sept, $159–$209 double weekends, $99–$189 double weekdays. Mid-Apr to mid-June and Oct, $99–$149 double weekends, $89–$119 double weekdays.

Block Island Dining

Breakfast & Brunch

Certainly you ought to take one breakfast at the **Surf Hotel,** served from 7:30 to 11am (above).

Down on the Old Harbor, **Ernie's,** Water Street (tel. 401/466-2473), is another breakfast favorite, a coffee shop–style place from which you can watch ferries docking while eating eggs, omelets, or pancakes.

Hours: May to mid-Oct, daily 6:30am–noon.

Ballard's, 42 Water St. (tel. 401/466-2231), offers a self-service cafeteria-style buffet breakfast. Or you can pick up a chocolate croissant or similar at **Aldo's Bakery,** Weldon's Way (tel. 401/466-2198), just behind the Old Harbor on Main Street.

Breakfast is also served, weekends only, at the **Harborside Inn,** right on Old Harbor (above).

Lunch

The best choice is to pack yourself a picnic and take it to the bluffs or the beach. You can assemble the fixings at the Old Harbor supermarket. Or you can try the **Hotel Manisses,** Spring Street (tel. 401/466-2836) for a more formal lunch (see the lodging section above).

The **Harborside Inn,** at the ferry landing (tel. 401/466-5504), offers a variety of sandwiches and burgers, plus fish dishes like lobster roll, fried clams, baked scrod, and broiled scallops, priced from $5 to $12. Try the famous chowder. Dine inside amid the nautical rigging or outside under the umbrellas.

The **Taffy Tent Cafe,** at the Empire Theatre, offers light lunch fare plus delicious homemade ice cream. There are art galleries on the premises too.

Also on the harbor, **Finn's** (tel. 401/466-2473) has burgers, sandwiches, fried clams, scallops, lobster, and clam rolls for $3 to $9. Nearby, **Ballard's** offers a variety of sandwiches and snacks, priced from $3, plus seafood, pasta, and other Italian dishes.

Dinner

For the three top choices for dinner—the **Hotel Manisses** (tel. 401/466-2836), **Atlantic Inn** (tel. 401/466-2005), and **Spring House** (tel. 401/466-5844)—see "Block Island Lodging," above.

Another top choice is **Winfields,** Corn Neck Road (tel. 401/466-5856), a pretty beamed candlelit restaurant where the tables have fresh wild-flowers on the sparkling-white cloths. The menu offers a pasta and chicken of the day, plus a variety of seafood—like Block Island swordfish with a mustard-and-honey glaze that's succulently moist and served with aspara-gus and potatoes. Other items might include turbans of sole with shiitake mushrooms; bay scallops with a mango-champagne sauce; shrimp with garlic, wine, and Dijon-and-herb butter; tenderloin of beef with a bleu-cheese sauce. Prices run $15 to $23. Start with any one of several shellfish dishes or an oyster bisque with bourbon, and finish with the white-chocolate mousse with Chambord sauce or whatever is available that par-ticular day. (Only one dessert is made fresh daily.)

Hours: In season only, daily 6–10pm.

For a casual dinner, the **Harborside Inn,** at the ferry landing (tel. 401/466-5504), has a selection of steaks, chicken, and seafood—baked scrod, swordfish, lobster, scallops sautéed in garlic butter—priced from $12 to $18. All entrees include vegetables and salad bar.

Hours: Summer, daily 5–10pm.

After Dark

There isn't too much to do after dark except watch the sunset, curl up with a book or a loved one, and enjoy a fine dinner. But there is the **Empire Theatre and Cafe** at Old Harbor (tel. 401/466-2555), featuring first-run films and a variety of live events ranging from swing bands to standup comics and live theater. Another cinema, the **Oceanwest Theatre** (tel. 401/466-2971), is at New Harbor.

Captain Nick's, Ocean Avenue (tel. 401/466-5670), has nightly dancing—a brick fireplace is the band's backdrop. So, too, does the **Yellow Kittens Tavern,** Corn Neck Road (tel. 401/466-5855 or 466-5856), which, though open year round, in winter functions as a bar with no dancing.

There's usually some entertainment given at the **National Hotel** on Old Harbor.

Block Island
Special & Recreational Activities

Beaches: Block Island State Beach and Crescent Beach are the popular sandy beaches. For a secluded (but pebble) beach, try the base of Mohegan Bluffs or the west side of the island. There are plenty of small sandy coves you can discover on your own.

Bicycling: Bikes and mopeds can be rented at The Moped Man, 435 Water St. (tel. 401/466-5011); Island Moped & Bike, P.O. Box 280 (tel. 401/466-2700); and the Old Harbor Bike Shop, P.O. Box 338 (tel. 401/466-2029). Bikes can also be rented from the Seacrest Inn, 207 High St. (tel. 401/466-2882).

Birdwatching: In spring and fall Block Island is on the Atlantic flyway and birdwatchers congregate to watch the migrating birds. This is the third-largest migratory center in the United States and as many as 150 species have been sighted.

Boating: Sailboat rentals are available at the Block Island Club, Corn Neck Road (tel. 401/466-5939); rowboat rentals for $12.50 a day are available from Twin Maples (tel. 401/466-5547). You can attach your own motor to these fiberglass boats. Boat rentals are available from Island Tours, P.O. Box 216 (tel. 401/466-2474).

Camping: This is *illegal* on Block Island.

Canoeing/Kayaking: Oceans & Ponds, The Orvis Store, Ocean Avenue, rents canoes and kayaks as well as surf rods for fishing.

Fishing: Many boats are available for charter, like at Captain John's Charter Fishing (tel. 401/466-2526). You'll need a license to go shellfishing. If licenses are available, they're obtained at the police station.

Beach fishing is popular. For bait and tackle, try Twin Maples (tel. 401/466-5547) or Ocean & Ponds, The Orvis Store on Ocean Avenue (tel. 401/466-5131).

Horseback Riding: Rustic Rides Farm, West Side Road (tel. 401/466-5060), offers guided trail rides.

Mopeds: See "Bicycling," above.

Parasailing: Block Island Parasail, P.O. Box 727 (tel. 401/466-2474).

Tennis: Block Island Club, Corn Neck Road (tel. 401/466-5939).

Newport

Distance in Miles: 183

Estimated Driving Time: 3³/₄ hours

◄○►◄○►◄○►◄○►◄○►

Driving: Take I-95 to the Newport Bridge.

Bus: Greyhound (tel. 800/231-2222) travels to Providence, from which you can catch a local Rhode Island bus into Newport.

Train: Amtrak (tel. 800/872-7245) services Providence.

Further Information: For more about Rhode Island in general, write to the **Rhode Island Department of Economic Development,** Tourism Division, 7 Jackson Walkway, Providence, RI 02903 (tel. 401/277-2601).

For specific Newport information, contact the **Newport County Chamber of Commerce,** 45 Valley Rd., Middletown, RI 02842 (tel. 401/847-1600), or the **Newport County Convention & Visitor's Bureau,** 23 Amer-ica's Cup Ave., Newport RI 02840 (tel. 401/849-8098, or 800/326-6030).

◄○►◄○►◄○►

When Giovanni da Verrazano first landed on Aquidneck Island, he named it Rhodes, because the quality of the light here reminded him of that mysterious Greek island; indeed, when you approach the town from the west across the high-arching bridges, you'll be awestruck by the bay's beauty, especially on a sunny day when literally hundreds of white, blue, and red sails bob, adrift as if in a romantic dreamy idyll, making kaleidoscopic patterns on the deep-blue ocean.

Newport offers the perspective of an island, the excitement of a port, world-class events, wealth, and a wonderful blend of contemporary and past delights. It represents two great eras of American history—downtown reflects the boisterous 17th-century mercantile community and the mansions on Bellevue Avenue show the extravagance and outrageous fantasy and spectacle of the Gilded Age. It's a wonderful place to be.

In summer Newport swarms with life. The wharves are filled with sleek yachts and millions of dollars' worth of powerboats, clinking and rocking in the harbor, their bronzed captains and crews crowding into harborside restaurants, bars, and stores, eyeing and vetting one another as they go. Behind the harbor, the narrow streets lined with stately 18th-century clapboard houses painted muted grays and sage greens add character and grace to the scene, although their shades must wonder at the parade of the fashion-conscious and the chic that now inhabits their lusty old port. Up on the hill most of the mansions stand empty, except for busloads of visitors who come to ogle the gilt, the marble, and the lavish rooms where great balls once were held and dogs sat down to dinners of stewed liver, rice, and fricasse of bones. In these opulent surroundings daughters were pledged to dukes (like Consuelo Vanderbilt, who was coerced into becoming the duchess of Marlborough by her mother, Alva), insults were hurled, upstarts were snubbed, and the 400 members of fashionable society once cavorted so dashingly and freely.

First and foremost, Newport was a colonial town, a mecca for ambitious 17th-century merchants who risked their money, chances, and often their lives by engaging in the Triangular Trade among Africa, Europe, and the Caribbean, defying the British by taking advantage of European wars to seize a greater share of world trade and carrying slaves, molasses, rum, and sugar. The ranks of these fiercely independent souls who'd fled the narrowmindedness of Massachusetts included dissidents of every sort—Methodists, Quakers, Jews, and all manner of men who chafed under the restrictions of British rule and were the first to declare their independence, an act that brought a contingent of Redcoats into their city and led to its occupation and destruction during the Revolution. When the French arrived in July 1780, 300 buildings had been wantonly destroyed, and they found a beleaguered town that continued to languish for many years thereafter.

Its life and reputation as a resort began in the mid-1800s, when many southern planters discovered its pleasant climes and sought refuge from malaria and the oppressive southern heat. They spent their summers here in pleasant cottages like Kingscote. Soon, Julia Ward Howe's literary set and the moneyed folk from New York and Philadelphia followed. The latter built "cottages" on a palatial scale, imitating the aristocracy of Europe, vying to outdo one another in the extent of their extravagance and display. For example, William K. and Alva Vanderbilt spent $11 million on Marble House, a residence they used only two months of the year. The wealthy flocked to Newport, where society was ruled by women (the men usually came up only on weekends) and the days were spent following a rigid schedule of activities, each with a prescribed change of clothes.

Breakfast would be followed by a ride on horseback, then by a carriage ride to the Casino to watch tennis and gossip. This would be followed by

Events & Festivals to Plan Your Trip Around

May Breakfasts: Church and other civic groups hold celebrations for Rhode Island's early declaration of independence.

July: Newport Music Festival, two weeks of chamber music concerts. Contact the Newport Music Festival, P.O. Box 3300, Newport, RI 02840 (tel. 401/846-1133).

The Miller Hall of Fame Tennis Championships. For tickets and information, contact the Tennis Hall of Fame (tel. 401/849-3990).

August: The JVC Jazz Festival and Ben & Jerry Folk Festival in Fort Adams State Park.

The Wooden Boat Show.

September: The Outdoor Art Festival (usually early September).

December: Christmas in Newport with wassail parties, Bach and Handel in the churches, and climaxed by a reading of "The Night Before Christmas" and a bonfire in Washington Square.

swimming at Bailey's Beach, lunching aboard a yacht, watching a match at the Polo Fields, and participating in the afternoon carriage promenade along Bellevue Avenue. A lavish dinner and then most likely a ball lasting until dawn would cap the day. Society also brought here the two sports synonymous with Newport to this day—yachting and tennis. The America's Cup Challenge was moved from New York to Newport in 1930, and the cup remained here until 1983, when it was carried off by the Australians, only to be returned triumphantly to the United States in 1987. New Zealand won it back in 1994, and the races will be held in Auckland in 1998, when the New York Yacht Club hopes to bring it back to Newport. The U.S. National Tennis Championships were held at the Newport Casino from 1881 until they moved to Forest Hills, and if you like, you can play on those hallowed grass courts.

The mansions these families used for the season have been preserved and now stand as witnesses to this era of incredible wealth, ostentation, and spectacle. Extravagant hostesses, melodramatic scenes, colonial tales of free-booting merchants and pirates, ships and yachts, elegant pastimes—Newport has it all—chic, beauty, history, romance, the ocean, and the nerve to remain a prestigious East Coast resort, a role bestowed on it by the generations that've gone before.

Newport Attractions

The Preservation Society of Newport Mansions

Plan to see only two or three mansions in a day. Tours last one hour and you'll soon be exhausted and surfeited. On weekends you'll want to get there early, because the crowds and busloads of people can be horrendous. I'd definitely see Kingscote (1839), an example of the earlier cottages that preceded the Gilded Age, and Château-sur-Mer (1852), both of which have an added charm because they still seem lived in. The more extravagant era of the 1890s can be captured at The Breakers, Marble House, The Elms, or Rosecliff. Here are a few details about each, followed by touring and admission information.

Kingscote (1839), Bellevue Avenue, was built by Richard Upjohn for George Noble Jones of Savannah, Georgia, and later acquired by William Henry King, a China trader, after whom it's named. The house is furnished with fine Oriental export pieces. Most dramatic is the dining room, added in 1881 and designed by Stanford White: Light shimmers over the opalescent Tiffany brick tiles that surround the Siena marble fireplace at one end of the room, while an intricate spindle-work screen encloses the other. The paneling is mahogany, while the ceilings and upper walls are of cork. The tour is intimate and interesting.

Château-sur-Mer (1852), Bellevue Avenue, was built for William Shephard Wetmore, a China trader from New York; when Wetmore died, his son hired Richard Morris Hunt to transform the house into a grand château. Wetmore entertained lavishly. At one of these affairs, held for George Peabody of London in 1857 and attended by 3,000 guests from both sides of the Atlantic, Wetmore served woodcocks, plovers, and snipes among the entrees, plus confections that were molded in the shapes of Washington and Lafayette. To some the house may appear austere and somber, with its Victorian gothic granite exterior; extensive use of Eastlake ash paneling in the entrance hall, staircase, and morning room; and heavy butternut furnishings in the bedrooms. Note the dining room's extravagantly carved Italianate overmantel depicting Bacchus.

The Breakers (1895), Ochre Point Avenue, was built for Cornelius Vanderbilt II and his wife, Alice, and is the most lavish and Italianate of the cottages (the original Breakers on this site burned down, and when Vanderbilt hired Richard Morris Hunt to build this replacement he demanded that the new house be fireproof). The Breakers contains 70 rooms, 33 for the 40-strong army of servants. The most striking attributes are the beautiful multicolored (rose to gray green) marbles used throughout; the arched double loggia with mosaic ceilings, which provides dramatic ocean vistas; the music room, which was constructed in Europe and shipped here for reassembly; faucets that deliver salt and fresh water in the baths; a two-story kitchen, sealed off so that none of the odors escaped; and the billiard room of gray-green marble, yellow alabaster, and mahogany. Remember, the house was used only two months of the year. Note that Countess Szapary, a descendent of Vanderbilt, maintains a private apartment here.

Rosecliff (1902), Bellevue Avenue, was the chosen setting for scenes in the films *The Great Gatsby, The Betsy,* and *True Lies,* and certainly it does have a romantic aura with its heart-shaped staircase, well-tended rose garden, and fountains scattered around the grounds. Theresa (Tessie) Fair Oelrichs was one of the three top hostesses of Newport, the daughter of James Graham Fair, who struck the Comstock Lode, and the wife of Hermann Oelrichs. She was a stickler for perfect cleanliness and was even known to scrub the floor herself if it didn't meet her standards. Designed by Stanford White after the Grand Trianon at Versailles, it contains the largest ballroom in Newport, where Tessie staged such extravagant events as the White Ball, at which all the flowers and decorations were white, the guests were all in white, and on the ocean floated several white-sailed ships, just to complete the effect.

Marble House (1892), Bellevue Avenue, was where the socially insatiable Alva Vanderbilt held court while the wife of William K. Vanderbilt. A dashing woman, she was the first of her set to cycle in bloomers, to own a motorcar of her own, to cut her hair at the shoulders, and to divorce (she then married Oliver Belmont and lived at Belcourt Castle—see below). The $11-million cottage was modeled after the Petit Trianon at Versailles by Richard Morris Hunt and contains the most ornate gilt-encrusted ballroom you'll ever see, where daughter Consuelo became engaged to the ninth duke of Marlborough in 1895. The dining room is furnished with bronze chairs that weighed so much they required a footman's help whenever a guest wanted to sit or rise. The Chinese Teahouse was added in 1913 by Alva, who also had a tiny railroad constructed to ferry the footmen bearing tea from the main house. Later, she was one of the first to open the house to the public to raise funds for the suffragettes.

The Elms (1901), Bellevue Avenue, was built for coal magnate Edward J. Berwind by a relatively unknown Philadelphia architect, Horace Trumbauer, who based the design on the Château d'Asnières near Paris (except for the three arched entrances, which were modeled after Buckingham Palace), creating a low-key classically symmetrical mansion. The grounds, dotted with bronze statuary, gazebos, and fountains and planted with an amazing variety of trees, shrubs, and sunken gardens, are the most remarkable aspect of the house.

Hours: May–Oct (all mansions), daily 10am–5pm, sometimes later in the evening. Winter (Marble House, The Elms, and Château-sur-Mer), Sat–Sun 10am–4pm (they're decorated for the holiday season). Apr (The Breakers, Marble House, and Rosecliff), daily 10am–5pm; the other mansions, Sat–Sun 10am–5pm. For information, contact the Preservation Society of Newport County, 424 Bellevue Ave., Newport, RI 02840 (tel. 401/847-1000). **Admission:** The best bet is to purchase a strip ticket good for two ($13.50), three ($18.50), four ($23), five ($26), or six ($30) mansions. There's also a $37.50 ticket covering all six, plus Hunter House, a colonial house (1748) worth seeing for its Townsend Goddard furniture, and Green Animals, a topiary garden with 80 sculptured trees in Portsmouth.

Other Mansions

Belcourt Castle (1891), Bellevue Avenue (tel. 401/846-0669), was built for Oliver H. P. Belmont when he married Alva, the former wife of William K. Vanderbilt. It was designed by Richard Morris Hunt in the style of Louis XIII's palace at Versailles. The most dramatic displays here are the 23-karat-gold coronation coach and the stained-glass windows. Costumed guides lead the way through the house, and tea is served to visitors.

Hours: Memorial Day–Oct, daily 9am–5pm; Apr, daily 10am–5pm; Nov, daily 10am–4pm; other months, call for times. **Closed:** January, Thanksgiving, and Christmas. **Admission:** $6.50 adults, $2 children 6–12.

Beechwood (1855), Bellevue Avenue (tel. 401/846-3772), was the Italianate home of William Backhouse Astor, where the doyenne of Newport society, Mrs. Astor (*the* Mrs. Astor), born Caroline Schermerhorn, held court. With the help of southern sycophant Ward McAllister, she devised the famous "Four Hundred," a list of 213 families and individuals whose lineage could be traced back at least three generations; this was also the number of guests who could fit comfortably into the ballroom of her New York City residence. (At the time of its compilation, this list included no Vanderbilts, who were considered upstarts, but soon Alva Vanderbilt's social-climbing skills won out and Mrs. Astor was forced to recognize the Vanderbilts socially.) So resplendent were Caroline's gowns and jewels that Mr. McAllister once remarked that she resembled a spectacular chandelier. At Beechwood you'll find no roped-off rooms or historic lectures, but a re-creation of the lifestyle the Astors brought to Newport in the 1890s reenacted every day by the Beechwood Theater Company.

Hours: May–Nov, daily 10am–5pm. **Admission:** $8.50 adults, $6 children 12 and under.

Hammersmith Farm (1887), Ocean Drive (tel. 401/846-7346), was John W. Auchincloss and family's 28-room summer cottage. It was here that the daughter of Janet Lee Bouvier Auchincloss, Jacqueline Bouvier, and John F. Kennedy held their wedding feast. This is a beautiful seaside retreat, and the tour gives charming details about the summers spent here by the Kennedy family. The gardens are also worth exploring. *Note:* At press time Hammersmith Farm is up for sale, so you should call first to see if it's still open to the public.

Hours: Apr to mid-Nov, daily 10am–5pm. **Admission:** $7 adults, $3 children 6–12.

Colonial Era Attractions

Walking tours of Historic Newport are offered by the Historical Society (tel. 401/846-0813) from mid-May to October on Friday and Saturday at 10am, at a cost of $5. They leave from 82 Touro St.

Downtown, **Washington Square** is the center of colonial Newport. At the west end is the **Brick Market** (1762), now occupied by the Museum of Newport History (tel. 401/841-8770), and at the other is the **Old Colony**

Newport

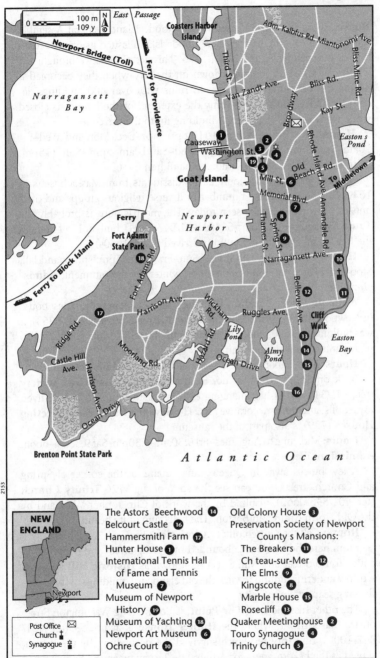

100 m
0 — 109 y
N

East Passage

Narragansett Bay

Newport Bridge (Toll)

Ferry to Providence

Coasters Harbor Island

Adm. Kalbfus Rd. Miantonomi Ave.
Bliss Mine Rd.
Third St.
Van Zandt Ave.
Bliss Rd.
Broadway
Kay St.
Rhode Island Rd.
Easton s Pond

Causeway
Washington St.

Goat Island

Old Beach Ave.
Annandale Rd.
To Middletown

Mill St.
Memorial Blvd.
Thames St.
Spring St.

Newport Harbor

Ferry

Fort Adams State Park

Ferry to Block Island

Narragansett Ave.

Fort Adams Rd.

Harrison Ave.

Wickham Rd.

Ridge Rd.

Bellevue Ave.

Cliff Walk

Ruggles Ave.

Lily Pond

Moorland Rd.

Harrison Ave.

Castle Hill Ave.

Ocean Drive

Almy Pond

Easton Bay

Brenton Point State Park

Atlantic Ocean

2153

NEW ENGLAND

Newport

Post Office ✉
Church ⛪
Synagogue ✡

The Astors Beechwood ⑭
Belcourt Castle ⑯
Hammersmith Farm ⑰
Hunter House ①
International Tennis Hall of Fame and Tennis Museum ⑦
Museum of Newport History ⑲
Museum of Yachting ⑱
Newport Art Museum ⑥
Ochre Court ⑩

Old Colony House ③
Preservation Society of Newport County s Mansions:
  The Breakers ⑪
  Ch teau-sur-Mer ⑫
  The Elms ⑨
  Kingscote ⑧
  Marble House ⑮
  Rosecliff ⑬
Quaker Meetinghouse ②
Touro Synagogue ④
Trinity Church ⑤

House dating from 1739, used by the Rhode Island General Assembly until 1900. From the balcony here Rhode Island issued its own Declaration of Independence on May 4, 1776. This act of defiance brought the wrath of the British Redcoats down on the city when they occupied it during the Revolution, leaving it in ruins with over 300 buildings destroyed. Today you can view only the exterior, for the interior is closed while work is done to bring the building up to the fire code.

Hours (Museum of Newport History): Apr–Dec, Mon and Wed–Sat 10am–5pm, Sun 1–5pm; winter, Wed–Sat 10am–5pm, Sun 1–5pm. **Admission:** $5 adults, $4 seniors, $3 children 6–16.

An independent town founded by dissidents from Massachusetts in 1639, Newport attracted a number of diverse religious groups and their houses of worship can be seen today. The most famous is probably the **Touro Synagogue,** 72 Touro St. (tel. 401/847-4794), built in 1759 (though the first member of the community arrived in the 1650s).

Hours: Late June to Labor Day, Sun–Fri 10am–5pm; spring and fall, Mon–Fri 2–3pm and Sun noon–3pm; winter, by appointment. **Admission:** Free.

A little way down Broadway from the synagogue stands the oldest house in Newport, the **Wanton-Lyman-Hazard House** (tel. 401/846-0863); it was built in the 1690s and is furnished authentically for the period. It also has an interesting colonial garden.

Hours: June–Labor Day, Thurs–Sun noon–5pm. **Admission:** $5 adults.

Back on Touro Street, at no. 82 the **Newport Historical Society** (tel. 401/846-0813) has changing exhibits of furniture, colonial silver, toys, dolls, and other decorative arts. The **Seventh Day Baptist Meeting House** (1729) is also part of the museum.

Hours: Mid-June to Aug, Tues–Fri 9:30am–4:30pm, Sat 9:30am–noon. **Admission:** Free.

A few blocks away in Queen Anne Square, at the corner of Spring and Church streets, you can see the spire of the 1726 **Trinity Church** (tel. 401/846-0660), inspired by the work of Christopher Wren and by the Old North Church in Boston. The bells ring quite beautifully.

Hours: Call the church office. **Admission:** Free.

From here the whole area bounded by Spring Street and Bellevue Avenue, Touro Street and Mill Street, is known as **Historic Hill** and well worth wandering around to view the old clapboard buildings of this once-thriving seaport community.

The other historic area, **The Point,** is down along Washington Street on the harborfront, where the **Hunter House** is at no. 54 (tel. 401/847-1000); this Tory residence survived the occupation by the British, served as the headquarters for Admiral de Ternay when the French naval forces arrived in July 1780, and is worth visiting to see the Townsend Goddard furniture and the floor-to-ceiling pine paneling.

Hours: May–Oct, daily 10am–5pm. **Admission:** $6.50 adults, $3 children 6–11.

Other Newport Attractions

Two absolute musts after (or even before) seeing the mansions: Drive or cycle **Ocean Drive,** stopping for a picnic at Brenton Point State Park; and walk along the back of the mansions the 3-mile **Cliff Walk,** which stubbornly remains a public thoroughfare, showing the rocky coastline to full advantage. Downtown, I suggest that you explore the many dining, shopping, yachting, and people attractions at such harborside complexes as **Bowen's Wharf** and **Bannister's Wharf.**

The **International Hall of Tennis Fame,** in the Newport Casino building at 194 Bellevue Ave. (tel. 401/846-4567), designed by Stanford White, exhibits trophies, art, videos, and memorabilia. The casino was commissioned by James Gordon Bennett, Jr., the publisher of the *New York Herald,* who commissioned it after a good friend had been thrown out of the Bellevue Men's Club for riding a horse through the building. The casino, with its horseshoe piazza, turretted porches, and breezy verandas, instantly became the place to see and be seen and the focal point of society, where people came to play and watch croquet, court tennis, cards, and billiards and attend many special events. The casino's courts are where the U.S. Tennis Championships were played from 1881 until they moved to Forest Hills.

Hours: Daily 10am–5pm. **Admission:** $6 adults, $3.50 seniors, $3 children 6–18.

The **Newport Art Museum,** 76 Bellevue Ave. (tel. 401/848-8200), highlights the works of artists who painted in and around Newport in the 19th century. The exhibits are staged in the Griswold House (1862), designed by Richard Morris Hunt, and in the Cushing Gallery. Throughout the year several temporary exhibitions are on view, like the recent one displaying works painted by nine members of the Vanderbilt family. There are photography shows too.

Hours: Tues–Sat 10am–4pm, Sun noon–4pm. **Admission:** $5 adult, $4 seniors, free for children 11 and under.

Sailing enthusiasts may want to visit the **Museum of Yachting** in Fort Adams State Park on Ocean Drive (tel. 401/847-1018), which offers a gallery of small craft, an exhibit about the history of yachting in Newport and the America's Cup, and a slide show of 12-meter craft.

Hours: May–Oct, daily 10am–5pm. **Admission:** $3 adults, $2.25 seniors, $1 children.

Military buffs should enjoy the **Naval War College Museum,** Coasters Harbor Island (tel. 401/841-4052), which traces the history of naval warfare and the history of the naval presence in the Narragansett Bay region; enter via Gate No. 1 of the Naval Education and Training Center.

Hours: June–Sept, Mon–Fri 10am–4pm, Sat–Sun noon–4pm; Oct–May, Mon–Fri 10am–4pm.

Newport Lodging

The **Inn at Castle Hill,** Ocean Drive, Newport, RI 02840 (tel. 401/849-3800), has to be the most picturesque accommodation here, with a commanding view of Narragansett Bay, Newport Harbor, and the ocean. It's a prime vantage point from which to watch the sailing and fishing craft bobbing around the bay or returning to port. In summer you can dine on the terrace, at the top of the grassy bluff that sweeps down to the water. There are two other dining rooms, known for their continental cuisine, where you can start with lobster mousse served hot with morel sauce; shrimp, scallops, crab, and lobster served with rémoulade; or artichoke bottoms with goat cheese, lightly grilled with basil and lime juice. Follow with any one of the fine seafood selections (like lobster Rasputin in sour cream, caviar, and sherry or monkfish in a crayfish sauce) or one of the meat selections (like saddle of lamb served with brown sauce with madeira and truffles). Prices run $23 to $30.

The inn was built in 1874 by Alexander Agassiz, son of naturalist Louis Agassiz, and it's known for the collection of Oriental furnishings he displayed here. The accommodation in the turret was inspirational for Thornton Wilder, who wrote that he could "see the beacons of six lighthouses and hear the booming and chiming of as many buoys." The 10 rooms are all different, many with exquisite paneling; some are oddly shaped, with dormer windows. Some, like Rooms 1 and 2, are undistinguished. Room 4, though, is beautifully paneled and sports a bold floral-and-bird wallpaper. Room 8, tucked under the eaves, has plenty of wicker—chairs, table, lamp, and even beds. There are also several houses for rent.

Rates (including breakfast): Summer, $125–$225 double. Spring and fall, $90–$155 double. Winter, $75–$110 double. **Closed:** Late Oct to Feb.

The **Sanford-Covell Villa Marina,** 72 Washington St., Newport, RI 02840 (tel. 401/847-0206), is a spectacular place with a marvelous view of the harbor. The house, built for Milton Sanford, a New York City industrialist, was completed in 1870 before the Newport mansions were built. It was designed in stick style by William Emerson, cousin of Ralph Waldo. Once inside, you'll be transported to a more elegant era. Among the period furnishings in the soaring foyer (with the original gaslamps) stands a peacock, a bust of Sanford, and a grandfather clock. The walls are decorated with a technique that pounds the paint into them, creating a blistered but brilliant effect.

There are only four guest rooms. My favorite is the Kate Field Room on the third floor: It has a windowseat and a deck overlooking the water, a fine selection of books in the built-in cases, a rocking chair, and a nonworking fireplace. Dolls and a chalkboard and the oak-slat paneling add more charm. It shares a bath that has a clawfoot tub, a pull-chain toilet, and two marble sinks. The Cuvalier Room faces the Newport Bridge and has plenty of character thanks to its coffered ceiling, old books, ship's model on the mantel, tiny parasol, and authentic Windsor chair. The Play Room is remarkable for its little balcony extending over the central lobby, stained-glass window, and contents (including many antique toys and the diaries of William King Covell from 1919 to 1972). The most spectacular is the Covell Room, which has a working fireplace, French-style furniture, and a large sitting room filled with antiques, Oriental carpeting, books, and a TV. Throughout there are fine decorative objects to admire, including many clocks and dolls. A continental breakfast is served in the handsome dining room with a converted oil chandelier. The parlor features two baby grands, two fireplaces, and lots of comfortable seating. Complimentary sherry is served in the evening. In summer the most glorious feature here is the broad porch furnished with wicker and below it the heated saltwater pool. Beyond stretches the entrance to Newport Harbor. A magnificent nostalgic retreat.

Rates (including breakfast): Summer, $105–$235 double. Winter, $75–$160 double.

The **Ivy Lodge,** 12 Clay St., Newport, RI 02840 (tel. 401/849-6865), is a gorgeous place. The shingled house is extraordinary with its gables and chimneys and curving veranda. Step inside the front door and an impressive entrance hall rises in front of you. The woodwork is glorious. An oak staircase zigzags to the third-floor landing, directing your eye to the stained-glass ceiling glowing above. There are eight rooms (seven with bath), each handsomely decorated in a different color and furnished with wing chairs, wicker, painted pieces, and the like. Room 1 has a spectacular highback Victorian bed. The Turret Room is among the most charming, boasting a coral-colored sitting area with boudoir-style chairs and a bath with a pull-chain toilet. In the Under the Staircase Room are a mahogany sleigh bed, a fireplace with the original Delft tiles, a large bay window, and a double Jacuzzi tub in the bath.

The public areas are lavishly decorated. A breakfast buffet is served at a table seating 14 in a paneled room with floor-to-ceiling windows, lit by a striking silk floral chandelier. Off the lobby are a small sitting area and a larger sitting room furnished with a baby grand and comfortable sofas and chairs arranged around the central fireplace. My favorite spot in summer is the swingseat on the wide porch overlooking the colorful gardens complete with a fountain.

Rates (including breakfast): Apr–Oct, $135–$175 double. Nov–Mar, $95–$135 double.

The **Cliffside Inn,** 2 Seaview Ave., Newport, RI 02840 (tel. 401/847-1811), would be my other choice Newport accommodation, even though it's out toward Middletown. The lovely Victorian residence was built in 1880 for a governor of Maryland and later occupied by the family of artist Beatrice Pastorius Turner. The 10 rooms have been personally and authentically furnished with great flair—all have air-conditioning and a

TV; some have a VCR; eight have a fireplace. In yours you may find a large four-poster spread with eyelet linens and pillowcases or a cannonball bed dressed with a floral comforter. The Governor's Suite offers lavish comforts—a king-size four-poster, a two-sided fireplace, a whirlpool, an antique Victorian birdcage shower, and a double pedestal sink. Children's prints and pictures add charm in one room; the floral brilliance of the wallpaper dramatizes another. Miss Beatrice's Room features a Lincoln bed, Eastlake chairs, marble-topped tables, a black marble fireplace, and an appealing windowseat in the bay; its bath contains a whirlpool and a double-headed shower. Several third-floor rooms have skylights. At the center of the Gazebo Room is an oval whirlpool bath set in a bay window and enclosed by a gazebo. The bilevel Country Garden Suite has two fireplaces, a double whirlpool, and a patio.

A full breakfast is served in a comfortable parlor crammed with Victorian couches, loveseats, and objets d'art. The porch is a favorite gathering place, arrayed with turquoise wicker chairs on canvas-painted flooring.

Rates (including breakfast): $155–$205 double; $235–$285 suite.

The **Elm Tree Cottage,** 336 Gibbs Ave., Newport, RI 02840 (tel. 401/849-1610), is a lovely romantic accommodation located away from the waterfront. What makes this B&B special are innkeepers Priscilla and Tom Malone, who have decorated their 1882 home with flair and welcome guests with warmth. The house in set on an acre of landscaped property two blocks from the beach. Each of the six guest rooms (all with bath) has been individually decorated in a rich tapestry of fabrics and wallpapers. The Master Suite is the largest and most elaborate, containing a carved French Louis XV bed with a partial crown canopy, a fireplace with a gilt mirror above and a ceramic French clock on the mantel, a sofa, and a French side chair; its bath is spectacular, with a skirted vanity and a sink standing on gleaming crystal legs. Room 2 is more masculine, featuring striped wallpaper with heraldic borders, a purple paisley quilt, and hunting prints; its bath is mirrored, and there's even a cushion in the deep tub.

The former owner of the house was the heiress to the Pennsylvania Railroad fortune and the bar she installed is still here, studded with hundreds of 1921 silver dollars, as well as the stained-glass porthole windows and the crest she designed symbolizing the Pekinese she regarded as the result of crossing a lion and a monkey! The other public spaces are comfortably and lavishly furnished: The sun room is filled with wicker. The living room with a grand and an upright piano offers a variety of seating (camelback sofas and wingbacks) and is accented with putti and a mirror that was rescued from a mansion. In winter there's a view of First Beach from the property. A full breakfast (pear-stuffed crêpes, orange waffles) is served in the elegant dining room. Afternoon hors d'oeuvres and iced tea or hot chocolate are also served. The pergola and statuary add panache to the gardens.

Rates (including breakfast): $125–$235 double; $235–$335 suite.

The **Francis Malbone House,** 392 Thames St., Newport, RI 02840 (tel. 401/846-0392), is on the waterfront but manages to retain a quiet air thanks to a serene landscaped garden where Adirondack chairs are set under the trees and on the flagstone patio. The house is supremely stylish, with dentil moldings, wainscoting, and glorious scallop-shell corner cupboards. It was built in 1760 for shipping merchant Francis Malbone and designed by the same architect responsible for the Touro Synagogue and Redwood Library. The nine guest rooms are decorated in colonial colors like Wedgwood blue and slate gray and elegantly furnished with colonial reproductions—rice four-posters, Oriental rugs, highboys, pier mirrors, and Martha Washingtons in front of the fireplace; seven have working fireplaces. The curtains are swagged, and in some rooms there are inviting windowseats under the casement windows. The Counting House Suite behind the main house offers a bedroom, living room, and dining room, plus a Jacuzzi in the bath.

The staff is extremely helpful and friendly. There are two parlors for guests to use, plus a library with a TV and some good books to read. The sumptuous breakfasts—including, for example, peach granola pancakes and Belgian waffles—are served in a colonial-style formal dining room at a lace-covered table lit by candles. A great place to stay.

Rates (including breakfast): May–Oct, $170–$205 double; $305 suite. Nov–Apr, $105–$160 double; $165–$205 suite.

One of the friendliest and most attractive places—and also very conveniently located—is the **Admiral Benbow Inn,** 93 Pelham St., Newport, RI 02840 (tel. 401/846-4256), built in 1855. The vibrant innkeeper has a wonderful way of tending to guests and a genuine enthusiasm for what she's doing.

The 15 guest rooms (all with bath) in this handsome Victorian are large and comfortable. For example, the room I stayed in contained brass twin beds, a dresser, a wing chair, and a couch. The curtains at the Palladian-style bay windows were cinched back; an old-fashioned gaslamp and chandelier provided light. Above the fireplace hung Oriental prints, all reminiscent of an earlier era. Other rooms are furnished variously with fish-net canopied beds, satin eiders, and a mixture of antiques and reproductions. Room 2 has a kitchenette and Room 12 has its own large deck for sunning with a view of the harbor. The room itself is small but furnished with an oak dresser, a brass bed, a sidetable, and a Mission rocker. Room 9 has a handsome hooped canopied bed. Some rooms have air-conditioning—ask.

Breakfast is served in the basement, decked out with colorful kites serving as wall hangings. Muffins, cinnamon-raisin toast, cereals, and fresh fruit are spread out for you to help yourself. Guests gather here in the evening if they want to watch TV or warm themselves in front of the woodstove. A collection of old barometers is on display and also for purchase.

Rates (including breakfast): May–Oct, $120–$235 double. Nov–Apr, $75–$130 double.

At the **Brinley Victorian,** 23 Brinley St., Newport, RI 02840 (tel. 401/849-7645), there are 17 rooms, 13 with bath. This large, rambling place occupies two houses (joined by a breezeway) a little distance from the immediate downtown area. It possesses much character, and each of the rooms is carefully and personally furnished with extra touches, like fresh flowers and magazines. On the ground floor, Room 5 has a stucco fireplace and a double-poster bed with Laura Ashley pillows and coverlet. In Room 4 a cherry bed is matched with a handsome Mme Récamier sofa against a beige chintz wallpaper. My favorite room is no. 17, featuring a high oak bed, Eastlake chairs, and a brick colonial fireplace. Room 12 sports striped floral pink-and-brown wallpaper, oak furnishings, and two brass beds. The iron bed in Room 13 is covered with a pink lace-trimmed coverlet. The second house has a comfortable parlor furnished with books and a marble fireplace. Room 6 has a large double bed set in the bay window and a single; other furnishings include a wicker sofa, a kneehole dresser, and an armoire. The third-floor rooms with knee walls are smaller and attractively furnished with oak and wicker. A refrigerator is on each floor for guests' use.

A breakfast of fresh-baked goods is served in the Victorian-style parlor filled with a loveseat and an Empire-style sofa set in front of the fireplace; the windows are covered with cream swagged drapes. In summer breakfast is served in the brick courtyard. There's also an information/library area where guests can peruse books and menus of local restaurants or enjoy an assortment of games. Both houses have porches with swings and wicker furnishings.

Rates (including breakfast): May–Oct, $100–$125 double without bath, $115–$160 double with bath. Nov–Apr, $59–$80 double without bath, $65–$90 double with bath.

The **Melville House,** 39 Clarke St., Newport, RI 02840 (tel. 401/847-0640), is a charming 1750s shingled home, located on one of the quieter downtown historic area's streets. It's run by enthusiastic innkeepers Vincent DeRico and David Horan. In the country parlor you'll find comfortable wing chairs and a sofa set in front of an old pine fireplace, home to a basket of cones and gleaming copper tea kettles. Breakfast— including buttermilk biscuits, Rhode Island johnny cakes, and stuffed French toast—is served at polished wood tables in a sunny room adjacent to the parlor. There are seven rooms (two with bath). Flowers and fruit are placed in every room, and each is nicely decorated in a colonial style. The ceilings are low and all the rooms have character. In winter a romantic fireplace suite is available and guests who stay in this room are welcomed with champagne and served breakfast in bed. Games and books are available in the corridor leading to the rooms. Afternoon tea is served (hot soup on cold days) and complimentary sherry is available when guests gather to chat in the evening. This is a hospitable, warm, and friendly place.

Rates (including breakfast): Memorial Day–Oct 15, $95–$135 double. Oct 16–Mar, $60–$95 double. Apr–Memorial Day, $70–$110 double. Year round, $175 fireplace suite.

The Inntowne, at Mary and Thames streets, Newport, RI 02840 (tel. 401/846-9200), conveniently located in the historic section, takes a contemporary approach to the interiors of its two colonial-style buildings. There are 24 air-conditioned rooms, all clean as a whistle and prettily decorated, often with matching floral prints on walls and curtains. By far the most interesting accommodations are in the Mary Street House—the Rathskeller in particular ($235 in season), named so because of the rounded pine door frames and doors, brick, and tile. It has a mirrored bedroom, a cozy sitting room with a couch and armchairs, and a full kitchen. Other rooms in this house are also attractively furnished with antique reproductions, often with coordinated wallpaper and bedspreads. Breakfast of fresh-squeezed juice, baked muffins, rolls, and a beverage is served in the pretty dining room with a polished wood table and ladderback chairs.

Rates (including breakfast): $90–$260 double.

Wayside, Bellevue Avenue, Newport, RI 02840 (tel. 401/847-0302), was built by Elisha Dyer, one of Mrs. Astor's "Four Hundred" and cotillion dancemaster for the Astors, Vanderbilts, and the other top families. It's certainly imposing and lavish. In the entrance hall a large molded stucco fireplace is carved with cherubs and a coat-of-arms that includes the fleur-de-lis. A staircase of quarter-cut oak leads to the huge rooms. In fact, some of the rooms are so large that they seem a trifle bare. All have small TVs. Room 1 has a double canopied bed along with a single bed, both covered with candlewick spreads. A wicker chaise longue, a wicker table, and a chest of drawers are among the furnishings in this room hung with blue-rose wallpaper. Broken-scroll-decorated doors lead into the ground-floor room that was once the library. Even though there's an Oriental-style bed, a couch, a loveseat, an armchair, and an Oriental chest, there are still masses of space. This room, decorated in bold blue floral wallpaper, also contains a handsome carved stucco fireplace. Coffee and pastries are put out in the morning for guests to help themselves. Facilities include an in-ground pool. For what you get, the rates are reasonable.

Rates (including breakfast): May–Oct, $145 double. Nov–Apr, $105–$115 double.

The **Admiral Farragut Inn,** 31 Clarke St., Newport, RI 02840 (tel. 401/846-4256), occupies an authentic Colonial home but has been decorated in a fresh and entertaining way; you'll see this clearly the minute you enter the hall, which boasts a large mural depicting a heron. All 10 charmingly decorated rooms contain a bath and a phone. The atmospheric low-ceilinged Admiral's Quarters contains a Shaker four-poster, a fireplace made of Dutch tiles, and walls that've been sponged to resemble pale-green marble; its bath has a lovely ceramic tile sink with a decorative floral motif. In other rooms you may find oak or pine furnishings and wing chairs and other nice pieces. The Ensigns Quarters on the third floor has a skylight, wooden beams, an enchanting sloped ceiling, and a small fireplace. In the Marquis Quarters one of the inn's most beguiling pieces can be found: a gray-and-red folk-art chair depicting two cats. A continental breakfast is served at a long harvest table in the dining room.

Rates (including breakfast): May–Oct, $95–$160 double. Nov–Apr, $55–$135 double.

The **Admiral Fitzroy Inn,** 398 Thames St., Newport, RI 02840 (tel. 401/846-4256), is in the heart of the waterfront district. A red-brick building dating to 1890, it's named after the admiral who developed the barometer and several modern versions decorate the front hallway and are for sale. All 18 guest rooms have a bath, cable TV, refrigerator, coffeemaker, and hairdryer. Each is hand-painted in a unique way, and you'll likely find a sleigh or iron-and-brass bed combined with different furnishings and color schemes. In Room 1 the walls are painted moss-gray-green and a large Eastlake dresser dating to 1853 is among the furnishings. Room 9 is particularly airy and bright and has roses and orchids hand-painted on the walls. In Room 10 the walls are adorned with a marvelous apricot tree. Each top-floor room has a skylight and a view of the harbor from its private deck. A continental breakfast is served in the basement breakfast room. Also in the basement is a functional sitting room with a TV and VCR.

Rates (including breakfast): May–Oct, $120–$235 double. Nov–Apr, $95–$175 double.

The **Victorian Ladies Inn,** 63 Memorial Blvd., Newport, RI 02840 (tel. 401/849-9960), occupies a large Victorian with a steep dormer roof. All nine rooms come with a bath, a TV, and air-conditioning; some have a phone. They're attractively furnished with a variety of antiques—carved Victorian, Shaker canopy, or iron-and-brass beds combined with loveseats and Queen Anne chairs or oak pieces. The room moods are created by dramatic use of color—forest green in one combined with silver-gray fabrics or burgundy and rose and jade in another. Guests have access to a comfortable sitting room with a fireplace; a full breakfast is served in the dining room.

Rates (including breakfast): Feb–Dec, $95–$175 double.

Hydrangea House, 16 Bellevue Ave., Newport, RI 028340 (tel. 401/846-4435), is a small attractive B&B occupying an 1876 house. It offers six rooms with bath, each attractively and tastefully furnished. The Rose Dutchess is gussied up with tasseled window treatments, candy-striped wallpaper, and rose carpeting; Joshua Reynolds prints from the 1790s adorn the walls. My favorite, even though it's the smallest, is La Petite Rouge, with lush plum-red walls and a hand-painted Edwardian chest of drawers, a fireplace, and French cartoons. In summer breakfast is served on the deck at the back of the house; otherwise it's served in the downstairs gallery where you can enjoy looking at the collection of works by local artists. The third-floor sundeck offers barbecuing facilities.

Rates: May–Oct, $99–$149 double; Nov–Apr, $65–$105 double.

The **Stella Maris Inn,** 91 Washington St., Newport, RI 02840 (tel. 401/ 849-2862), was given its name by the Sisters of Cluny who occupied it in the 1920s when it was a convent. This 1853 stone mansion stands down in the Point. Each of the eight guest rooms has a bath. Several, like the Lady Gregory Room, have a marble fireplace. The Lady Gregory also contains a carved Victorian bed, marble-topped sidetables, and a camel-back sofa; its bath has delightful porthole windows. Most rooms are large enough to have small sitting areas. The windowseat offers a fine view in the J. M Synge Room, furnished with a wicker bedroom suite and two wingbacks. The public rooms include a comfortable parlor with a TV. In the dining room is a Steinway grand piano in addition to the table and Chippendale chairs. A continental breakfast is served here or out on the wide porch that affords a peek of the harbor between the houses across the street.

Rates (including breakfast): May–Oct, $135–$160 double weekends, $120–$135 double weekdays. Nov–Apr, $120–$135 double weekends, $85–$105 double weekdays.

Cliff Walk Manor, 82 Memorial Blvd., Newport, RI 02840 (tel. 401/ 847-1300), is about a 10-minute walk out of town en route to Middletown, right on Easton's Beach. It was built in 1855 so the rooms are large and the ceilings lofty. It was originally owned by the Chandlers, relatives of the Astors. Many of the 28 air-conditioned rooms (with TV) overlook the ocean across toward Middletown, as does the terrace adjacent to the restaurant/ bar. The rooms have wall-to-wall carpeting, marble-topped dressers and sidetables, rockers, and often Renaissance Revival–style beds with Marseilles coverlets. Some have Jacuzzis.

Rates (including breakfast): May–Oct, $135–$145 double. Nov–Apr, $105–$135 double.

The **Pilgrim House Inn,** 123 Spring St., Newport, RI 02840 (tel. 401/ 846-0040), is a simple B&B occupying a gray clapboard with a steep mansard roof in Newport's historic area. There are 11 rooms, 8 with bath. They're unpretentious, with assorted furnishings—chintz wallpapers, ruffle-trimmed curtains, painted drawers, and occasional pieces of wicker. In each you'll find a plant. At breakfast, muffins, fruit, coffee, and juice is served either inside or on the top-floor deck.

Rates: In season, $65–$165 double. Off-season, $60–$90 double. **Closed:** Jan and two weeks in Feb.

If you're looking for modern accommodations in the historic area, the **Mill Street Inn,** 75 Mill St., Newport, RI 02840 (tel. 401/849-9500), may be for you. It's a converted red-brick mill in which there are 23 air-conditioned suites, including 8 two-story "town houses," featuring a downstairs sitting room and an upstairs bedroom with a sliding door leading to a deck with a view across the rooftops to the harbor. Furnishings are strictly modern IKEA. The living room has a bar area with a refrigerator, a pullout sofa, a TV, a phone, and track lighting. The one-level units have a bar with a refrigerator, a pullout sofa, and other amenities. Guests have use of the large communal roofdeck for sunning and relaxing. A continental breakfast is served at tables set with pretty pink cloths in a room with rough-hewn-stone walls. Tea is served in the afternoon.

Rates (including breakfast): Summer, $165–$265 double. Off-season, $135–$165 double.

The **Doubletree Islander Inn,** Goat Island, Newport, RI 02840 (tel. 401/849-2600), is surrounded by water and reached by a causeway. You get incredible harbor views in all directions. Parking is available (extremely important in this town) and you're a 5-minute drive or 15-minute walk from the town center. The accommodations are spacious and modern, with double sinks an added convenience. A pushbutton phone and a cable TV are standard facilities. There are two dining rooms, a lounge/entertainment room, an indoor pool and an outdoor saltwater pool, and tennis courts.

Rates: Memorial Day–Labor Day, $169–$249 double. May and Sept to mid-Nov, $149–$189 double. Mid-Nov to Apr, $89–$99 double.

The **Harborside Inn,** Christie's Landing, Newport, RI 02840 (tel. 401/846-6600), is, as the name suggests, in the center of the action. The 14 accommodations here have a nautical air. You have a choice between a room and a suite. Both have modern pine furnishings (workbench style), the only difference being that the suite has a skylit loft bed-room reached by a ship's ladder (in a water-view suite) or by a regular staircase (in a landside suite). The rooms are beamed and the beds covered with Tattersall-style comforters; each comes with a phone, a TV, air-conditioning, a refrigerator, and a full bath. Water-view rooms and suites have small decks. There's a breakfast and sitting-room area furnished with director's chairs overlooking the dock and harbor. Help yourself to continental breakfast, hors d'oeuvres, and tea in the afternoon (winter only). Parking is available.

Rates (including breakfast): July to mid-Sept, $165–$235 double weekends, $125–$185 double weekdays. Spring and fall, $125–$195 double weekends, $95–$145 double weekdays. Winter, $65–$105 double weekends, $55–$85 double weekdays.

Covell House, 43 Farewell St., Newport, RI 02840 (tel. 401/847-8872), offers five rooms with bath in a beige clapboard Colonial with a pretty front porch and an attractive breakfast room. The gardens here are quite pleasant.

Rates (including breakfast): Summer, $100–$120 double. Off-season, $85–$90 double.

The **Jenkins Guest House,** 206 S. Rhode Island Ave., Newport, RI 02840 (tel. 401/847-6801), is an authentic European-style guesthouse. Sally and Dave Jenkins raised their eight children here and today they open their home to guests, providing two comfortable rooms and serving a continental breakfast. Sally understands that some folks want their freedom and others want convivial conversation and she respects your wishes. Guests tend to gather in the kitchen or enjoy sitting on the back deck overlooking the garden and having their morning coffee. It's a relaxed, casual place. Sally and Dave have lived all their lives in Newport and will regale you with tales of the town, both past and present.

Rates (including breakfast): In season, $65 double.

Newport Dining

Breakfast & Brunch

A fine way to spend Sunday morning is looking out from the terrace at **Inn at Castle Hill,** Ocean Drive, and enjoying brunch.

Other great brunch/breakfast places include **Muriel's** (tel. 401/849-7780); the **White Horse Tavern** (tel. 401/849-3600); the **Clarke Cook House** (tel. 401/849-2900); **The Pier,** Howard Wharf (tel. 401/847-3645); **The Mooring,** on Sayer's Wharf (tel. 401/846-2260).

Lunch

You'll probably want to have lunch on the piers or at the Inn at Castle Hill and enjoy the watery vista while you dine at the places I've already described. Or you can try such casual spots as the **Brick Alley Pub and Restaurant,** 140 Thames St. (tel. 401/849-6334), which attracts a friendly young crowd to the bar and the tables for an incredible assortment of reasonably priced food. The menu spreads over several pages and the inspiration for the cuisine over several continents, offering fish, sand-wiches, salads, nachos, and all kinds of items priced from $10 to $20.

Hours: Sun–Thurs 11am–9pm, Fri–Sat 11am–11pm.

The **Music Hall Cafe,** 250 Thames St. (tel. 401/848-2330), is another fun place for lunch. Decorated in brilliant southwestern colors—sand, jade, and coral—with buffalo skulls and a kiva ladder hanging from the trompe l'oeil–painted wall it offers cuisine to match. In addition to some standard Mexican dishes you'll find swordfish with jalapeño butter or blackened salmon with guava-ginger sauce; a great appetizer is the Texas torpedoes—jalapeños stuffed with cream cheese. Prices range from $10 to $20 for dinner main courses, less for lunch items.

Hours: Sun–Thurs noon–3pm and 5–9pm, Fri–Sat noon–3pm and 5–10pm.

Salas', 341 Thames St. (tel. 401/846-8772), is a cheery, noisy, bustling place. Here you can enjoy a clambake with a 1-pound lobster, clams, corn on the cob, and clam broth for $21, washed down with beer served in pitchers and wine from jugs. Sala's is also famous for selling pasta by the pound.

Hours: Mon–Fri 5–10pm, Sat–Sun 4–10pm.

Cafe Zelda, 528 Thames St. (tel. 401/849-4002), also draws crowds for its daily luncheon specials, which often feature crab or fish of the day.

Hours: Sun–Thurs 11:30am–3pm and 5–10pm, Fri–Sat 11:30am–3pm and 5–11pm.

Breakfast, Lunch & Dinner

The Black Pearl, Bannister's Wharf (tel. 401/846-5264), is one of Newport's leading restaurants. The tavern is a cozy gathering place, the patio is great for a meal or drink and a sea breeze, and the intimate Commodore Room, decorated in forest green with brass accents and polished wood, is known for its classic French cuisine. To start, escargots are a fine choice. Prices range from $18 to $27 for such dishes as veal medallions with morels and champagne sauce, roast duck with green-peppercorn sauce, rack of lamb with roasted garlic and rosemary jus, and softshell crabs (in season) with shallots and lemon butter. Among the desserts might be cheesecake, homemade ice creams, and profiteroles. The chowders are so good I've seen people ask for several large bowls in the tavern, where prices range from $13 to $20 and the menu includes burgers, omelets, and daily specials like bluefish with lemon-caper butter.

Hours: Daily 11:30am–3pm and 6–11pm (to 10pm in winter). Jackets are required in the Commodore Room.

Away from the bustle of the wharves, another of my favorites is the **White Horse Tavern,** Marlborough and Farewell streets (tel. 401/849-3600), a 1673 tavern that has a series of dining rooms with a romantic ambience. The superb food ranges from traditional European to contemporary American. For example, you may start with either the iced shellfish or the grilled ribbons of duckling served in a flour tortilla with caramelized red onions, herbed Camembert, and a berry compote. Follow with the halibut topped with crabmeat and served in lemon-saffron beurre blanc, grilled swordfish with papaya salsa, tournedos of beef with grilled portobellos on a fresh oregano-and-balsamic-reduction sauce, or rack of lamb on a bed of bourbon-glazed wild mushrooms. Prices range from $23 to $33.

Hours: Sun–Mon and Wed–Thurs noon–2:30pm and 6–9:30pm, Tues 6–9:30pm, Fri–Sat noon–2:30pm and 6–10pm. Jackets for men are required in the evening.

The **Clarke Cook House,** Bannister's Wharf (tel. 401/849-2900), for my money, is one of Newport's finest dining places. In this old Colonial building are two dining rooms: the formal room, delightfully colonial with solid posts and beams, plank floors, and tables set with brass candlesticks and freesias or similar in silver stem vases, where black-tied waiters provide attentive service; or the Candy Store Cafe, more like a tavern/bar despite the marble tables. Here models of ships' hulls and wood-framed pictures of sailing ships are the major decoration.

At dinner, start with ravioli of lobster and wild mushrooms with morels or gravlax on a crisp potato galette with crème fraîche and osetra caviar. Follow with a selection from dishes like tuna steak with sweet-and-sour sherry-vinegar glaze, rack of lamb with minted tarragon glaze, and filet mignon with port-wine reduction and wild mushrooms. Prices run $23 to $25. Finish with crème caramel or Locke Ober's famous Indian pudding. The café menu offers lighter dishes—pastas, stir-fried chicken with snowpeas and ginger or angel-hair pasta, or shrimp gumbo on rice—from $9 to $13.

Brunch offers an interesting array of egg dishes, plus nachos with salsa, guacamole, and cheese; grilled shrimp and Cajun sausage en brochette; angel-hair pasta bolognese; codfish cakes with baked beans; delicious Mexican pizza (served on a taco shell); or Irish lamb-and-stout stew. Save room for a delicious dessert, especially the Snowball in Hell—chocolate roulade, vanilla ice cream, and hot fudge sauce with a sprinkling of coconut served in an iced wineglass coated with chocolate.

Hours: Formal dining room, Wed–Fri and Sun 6–10:30pm, Sat–Sun 11:30am–3pm (brunch) and 6–10:30pm. Cafe, Sun–Thurs 11:30am–10:30pm, Fri–Sat 11:30am–11pm.

La Petite Auberge, 19 Charles St. (tel. 401/849-6669), is among the city's top three restaurants. The service is gracious, the ambience romantic, and the food good, though not as memorable as the prices might suggest. The menu is very traditional French. Among the appetizers might be lobster bisque, goose-liver pâté, or escargots bourguignons. Main courses ($21 to $30) range from seafood—lobster tails with truffles, trout with hazelnuts—to meats, including tournedos Rossini and filet mignon au poivre, chateaubriand béarnaise, and saddle of lamb with garlic sauce. The desserts offer similar classics—crêpes Suzette, bananas flambé, peach Melba, and strawberries Romanoff. The tables are set with lovely lace cloths, lanterns, and fresh flowers. Classical music in the background, the low lighting of wall sconces, and a handsome fireplace complete the romantic atmosphere.

Hours: Mon–Sat 6–10pm, Sun 5–9pm.

Some of Newport's most exciting cuisine can be found at **Yesterday's Wine Bar & Grille,** 28 Washington Sq. (tel. 401/847-0116). It may not look like the domain of fine cuisine, but it certainly is—and will remain so if the chef stays in place. On one side is a popular wine bar; on the other is the restaurant, which has booth and traditional table seating. Among the 10 or so entrees might be maple-glazed duck with cherry sauce spiced with chipotle peppers, lamb loin in a pecan crust with balsamic-vinegar sauce, and pan-seared halibut in roasted tomato-fennel broth. Appetizers are similarly inspired—crab ravioli with chèvre and ginger served on tamari beurre blanc, scallop salad in cilantro-lime vinaigrette, and barbecued quail with sweet-onion marmalade. Prices range from $15 to $24. Those who appreciate wine will enjoy the opportunity to taste several from a so-called "flight" containing four 3-ounce glasses of different wines. This should absolutely be your first dinner stop.

Hours: Tues–Sun 5:30–10pm.

At **Elizabeth's,** Brown Street and Howard Wharf (tel. 401/846-6862), Broadway show tunes set the pace and old and new movies add to the fun—don't be surprised if hostess Elizabeth Burley, a former film producer, suddenly launches into song. The food is as theatrical as the ambience. You'll be served huge Oriental platters for two, piled high with such treats as shrimp and piselli (shrimp sautéed with garlic and oil and topped with pesto sauce), plus a pasta of the day, roasted hot herb sausage, mushrooms, peppers, and onions plus the vegetable of the day. Or there's the barbecue feast: chicken spareribs with sweet-potato pie, beans and apples, mushrooms, hot-dog sausage, cornbread and onions, and several vegetables. Prices range from $30 to $40 for the platters. The decor is charmingly eccentric with assorted chairs and tables covered in exotic fabric. There's a great deck for summer dining.

Hours: Summer, daily 5:30–10pm; winter, Wed–Sat 5:30–10pm. **Closed:** Usually Jan–Feb.

Puerini's, 24 Memorial Blvd. West (tel. 401/847-5506), is a delightful small Italian restaurant with a cozy ambience. The two dining rooms—upstairs and down—contain tables spread with black plastic cloths covered with butcher paper. The walls are decorated with evocative art photographs of Italy. The food is good and reasonably priced. Start with sweet roasted peppers in oil and garlic with provolone and follow with a pasta like the ravioli stuffed with ricotta and parmesan with pesto sauce or one of the fine chicken dishes with marsala or fiorentina (with spinach). Beer and wine are available. Prices range from $9 to $15.

Hours: Tues–Thurs 5–9pm, Fri–Sat 5–10pm.

Muriel's, Spring and Touro streets (tel. 401/849-7780), is fun for breakfast, lunch, or dinner. The walls are covered with Maxfield Parrish posters, the tables sport floral and lace-trimmed cloths under glass, and ficus trees set off the jade walls. For breakfast, choose the huevos rancheros or the French toast in spiced butter with walnuts and syrup. At lunch, salads, pasta, sandwiches, omelets, and entrees under $10 are offered. At dinner the room is transformed by candlelight. The extensive seasonal menu might offer everything from vegetable stir-fry and lasagne to chicken Bombay (with bananas, raisins, and walnuts), shrimp Louisiana, and grilled porterhouse steak with caramelized onions. Prices range from $10 to $17.

My favorite dessert is the chocolate bread pudding with vanilla ice cream, chocolate sauce, and walnuts. Beer and wine are available.

Hours: Mon–Sat 8am–5pm, Sun 9am–2:30pm and 5pm–closing.

Scales and Shells, 527 Thames St. (tel. 401/846-3474), is the quintessential waterfront fish restaurant. Up front is an open kitchen where the chefs cook the produce of the sea. The choices are many. You can start with cherrystones, littlenecks, and oysters on the half shell, calamari, or grilled shrimp. Follow with lobster Fra Diavolo or a mesquite-grilled fish— swordfish, salmon, tuna, bluefish, red snapper, or mahi mahi. Prices range from $10 to $18 (more for the lobster). There's little decor to speak of— the charged atmosphere is created by the crowds.

Hours: Summer, Sun–Thurs 5–10pm, Fri–Sat 5–11pm; winter, Sun–Thurs 5–9pm, Fri–Sat 5–10pm.

Christie's of Newport, Christie's Landing (tel. 401/847-5400), is home to the powerboat crowd and a hangout for local politicos who like to drink and dine on steaks and seafood, priced from $18 to $28. There's veal Oscar, salmon, lobster (stuffed, broiled, or served with tenderloin), swordfish, bouillabaisse, scallops, sole, a clam boil (made with lobster, steamers, corn, potatoes, and onions chourio), steaks, and lamb chops. The dining room is large and crowded, and a warm atmosphere prevails; in winter it's warmed by the large stone hearth. The long bar separated from the dining room is usually filled with locals anxiously watching the outcome of one of the Boston teams' games. Lunch brings salads, sole, seafood pie, scrod, and other dishes for $6 to $10. Many famous folks' faces line the entryway here.

Hours: Sun–Thurs 11:30am–3pm and 5–9pm, Fri–Sat 11:30am–3pm and 5–10pm.

The yachting crowd as well as the locals favors **The Mooring,** on Sayer's Wharf (tel. 401/846-2260), off America's Cup Avenue, which has a multi-level deck over the water and a large outdoor bar. The menu features steaks, lobsters, and fresh fish from $15 to $28. Favorite dishes are the seafood platter (lobster, shrimp, scallops, and mussels in a broth) and jumbo shrimp stuffed with scallops and crabmeat in a casserole. The chowders are famous; sandwiches and salads are also available.

Hours: Daily 11:30am–10pm.

The Pier, Howard Wharf (tel. 401/847-3645), is another Newport tradition, for steaks, seafood, and lobster served in half a dozen or so ways. Prices range from $13 to $33. In summer there's nightly entertainment and dancing on weekends.

Hours: Mon–Sat 11:30am–3pm and 5–10pm, Sun 5–10pm (winter, Sat–Sun 11:30am–3pm).

Canfield House, 5 Memorial Blvd. (tel. 401/847-0416), is popular among Newporters. It has been restored to its earlier splendor: The barrel-vaulted room with its ornately carved wood ceiling and solid-oak wainscoting now positively glows. If you have to wait for a table, take refuge in front of the huge fire in the bar. The food is traditional continental—baked stuffed shrimp, chateaubriand (the house specialty), filet mignon with wild-mushroom ragoût, and duck with port-raspberry sauce. Prices run $17 to $24.

Hours: Tues–Sat 5–10pm, Sun 4–10pm.

Le Bistro, Bannister's Wharf (tel. 401/849-7778), offers finer, lighter cuisine than the name suggests—bouillabaisse, sautéed lobster with three peppercorns, beef tenderloin with mustard-herb butter, duck with cranberry-merlot sauce, veal kidneys with madeira, and a full game menu (including medallions of wild boar with apples and Calvados). To start, try the feuilleté of lobster with sweet peppers, shrimp, and scallops in cabbage with caviar. Prices run $12 to $33. The dining room is comfortable country French. Lunch offers omelets, sandwiches, and salads, though the kitchen will prepare dinner items.

Hours: Daily 11:30am–9pm.

After Dark

For the most current information, ask at the convention and visitor's bureau for its nightlife paper. Sunday-afternoon jam sessions are held at the **Newport Harbor Hotel** on America's Cup Avenue (tel. 401/847-9000). **Christie's of Newport** (tel. 401/847-5400) and the **Clarke Cooke House,** Bannister's Wharf (tel. 401/849-2900), both offer bands and dancing on weekends.

For more cultural pursuits, the **Newport Playhouse,** 102 Connell Hwy. (tel. 401/848-7529), mounts a variety of productions year round. Most tend to be comedies on the order of Neil Simon.

An exciting evening can be spent at **Newport Jai Alai,** 150 Admiral Kalbfus Rd. (tel. 401/849-5000), watching the fast-paced Basque game of jai alai and wagering a few bucks. There's simulcast horseracing here also.

Newport
Special & Recreational Activities

Antiquing: There are plenty of antiques stores in Newport, though they're most concentrated along Franklin Street between Thames and Spring.

Beaches: Bailey's Beach, at Ocean Drive and Bellevue Avenue, is where the "Four Hundred" park in their monogrammed parking spaces to frolic in private. Gooseberry Beach on Ocean Drive is attractive and open for a parking fee of about $12. Otherwise, Fort Adams State Park, Ocean Drive, has a beach with a lifeguard; Newport Beach, at the eastern end of Memorial

Boulevard; Second Beach in Middletown, Sachuest Beach Road; Third Beach is around the corner at the mouth of the Sakonnet River.

Bicycling: Rentals are available April to October at Ten Speed Spokes, 18 Elm St. (tel. 401/847-5609). Daily charges average $25. Also check out Island Sports, 86 Aquidneck Ave. (tel. 401/846-4421).

Boating: Oldport Marine Services, Sayer's Wharf (tel. 401/847-9109), offers harbor cruises mid-May to mid-October. The Newport Sailing School (tel. 401/683-2738 or 246-1595) gives lessons and offers one- and two-hour tours for $12 and $20, respectively.

Viking Tours, 184 Thames St. (tel. 401/847-6921), runs cruises of the harbor (mid-May to Columbus Day only) from its Goat Island dock six times daily. The trip is a one-hour narrated cruise to Jamestown, costing $7.50 for adults and $6 for children 4 to 11.

Golf: In Portsmouth, a 10-minute drive from Newport, you can choose from three courses: Green Valley (tel. 401/847-9543), Montup (tel. 401/683-9882), and Pocasset (tel. 401/683-2266).

Hiking: The Cliff Walk is a marvelous coastal experience, from the end of Newport Beach to Bellevue and Coggeshall avenues. Brenton Point State Park is mainly a parking area off Ocean Drive with access to a fishing pier and rocky inlets. Norman Bird Sanctuary, 583 Third Beach Rd. (tel. 401/846-2577), has 7½ miles of hiking trails.

Horseback Riding: The Newport Equestrian Center, 287 Third Beach Rd. (tel. 401/848-5440), offers both beach and trail rides. The beach rides go to two beaches and cost $32.50 per hour for a minimum of two hours. The trail ride takes riders around the island and costs $65 for the two-hour ride. By reservation only. There's also a stable in Portsmouth: Glen Farm (tel. 401/846-0200) offers haunted hay rides in fall.

Picnicking: Brenton Point State Park and Fort Adams State Park are pretty spots.

Polo: Take along a picnic and watch the game, played during late August and early September at Glen Farm, off Rte. 114 in Portsmouth.

State Parks: Brenton Point State Park (tel. 401/846-8240), Ocean Drive and Fort Adams State Park, has swimming and picnicking.

Swimming: The pools at the YMCA, 792 Valley Rd. (tel. 401/847-9200), and also at Howard Johnson's, 351 W. Main Rd., Middletown (tel. 401/849-2000), are open to the public for a charge of $3 to $8. Or you can head for the beaches mentioned above.

Tennis: The biggest thrill is to play on the courts either at the Casino Indoor Racquet Club, 194 Bellevue Ave. (tel. 401/849-4777), for which the charge is $25 per hour for the court, or on the grass courts at the Tennis Hall of Fame (tel. 401/849-3990), which costs about $35 per person per 1½ hours. You can also watch or try to play the forerunner of tennis, "court tennis" (tel. 401/849-6672), at the Tennis Hall of Fame ($20 per person). Other courts are available at Aquidneck Park at Bowery and Spring Street and at Cottrell Field on Vernon Street.

Windsurfing: Island Sports, 86 Aquidneck Ave. (tel. 401/846-4421), offers rentals for $50 per day at Third Beach. It also rents kayaks and surfboards.

VERMONT &
NEW HAMPSHIRE

Dorset, Manchester & Windham County

Distance in Miles: Bennington, 180; Brattleboro, 194; Wilmington, 201; Manchester, 207; Dorset, 212; Mount Snow, 213; Newfane, 215; Saxtons River, 227; Grafton, 229

Estimated Driving Time: 4 to 4½ hours

◄◦►◄◦►◄◦►◄◦►◄◦►

Driving: You can take the New York State Thruway to Troy and then Rte. 7 into Bennington or take I-684 to I-84 to I-91. For Brattleboro, take I-95 to I-91.

Bus: Greyhound/Trailways (tel. 800/231-2222) travels to Manchester, Brattleboro, and Bennington.

Train: Amtrak (tel. 800/872-7245) travels daily from New York to Brattleboro, arriving at 4:45pm.

Further Information: For more on Vermont, contact the **Vermont Department of Travel & Tourism,** 134 State St., Montpelier, VT 05602 (tel. 802/828-3236); the **Vermont State Chamber of Commerce,** P.O. Box 37, Montpelier, VT 05602 (tel. 802/223-3443); or the **Department of Forest, Parks & Recreation,** 103 S. Main St., 10 South, Waterbury, VT 05670 (tel. 802/241-3655), for state park camping information.

For specific town information, contact the **Manchester and the Mountains Chamber of Commerce,** 2 Main St. (R.R. 2, Box 3451), Manchester Center, VT 05255 (tel. 802/362-2100); the **Dorset Chamber of Commerce,** P.O. Box 121, Dorset, VT 05251 (tel. 802/867-2450); the **Londonderry Chamber of Commerce,** P.O. Box 58, Londonderry, VT 05148 (tel. 802/824-8178); the **Bennington Chamber of Commerce,** Veterans Memorial Drive, Bennington, VT 05201 (tel. 802/447-3311); the **Mount Snow/Haystack Region Chamber of Commerce,** Main Street, Page House (P.O. Box 3), Wilmington, VT 05363 (tel. 802/464-8092); and the **Brattleboro Chamber of Commerce,** 180 Main St., Brattleboro, VT 05301 (tel. 802/254-4565).

For information on the Monadnock region, contact the **Greater Keene Chamber of Commerce,** 48 Central Square, Keene, NH 03431 (tel. 603/352-1303).

◄◦►◄◦►◄◦►◄◦►◄◦►

Southern Vermont was home to Ethan Allen and his Green Mountain Boys, where they stalked the British and fought the Battle of Bennington. Historic it may be, but today the area offers an incredible variety of activities in both summer and winter. However, Vermont is her shining best in winter, when the ski slopes at Stratton, Bromley, Magic Mountain, and Mount Snow are dotted with colored parkas streaming down the trails, the inns and lodges are warmed by blazing hearths, and people return burnished from the slopes to enjoy an evening's entertainment.

In summer there's boating and swimming on Lake Whitingham, the Marlboro Music Festival to attend, a variety of events and performances to watch at the Southern Vermont Arts Center and at Hildene Meadowlands, as well as plenty of antiquing and craft studios to visit, for this is the area (especially around Brattleboro) the 1960s generation sought out for practicing their crafts. Fall brings an even-greater glory, when the mountains are turned into great pyramids of color. And then there are the quiet villages, perfectly groomed town greens, inviting inns, and white clapboard churches that offer you the gentle relaxation of a much quieter era.

THE DORSET & MANCHESTER VALLEY

A beautiful area bordered by mountains and cut through by the famous Battenkill River, the region has much to offer. Dorset is a somnolent village that boasts the Dorset Playhouse and several fine inns. Farther south, Manchester village has always attracted visitors, often wealthy ones, especially to its grand old hotel, the Equinox. People came in the mid-19th century to take Dr. Sprague's famous water cure, a phenomenon that hotel owner Frank Orvis capitalized on when he advertised that he'd piped the precious water from the mountain and bottled it. These ads appeared briefly in subway cars and on buses in New York City, until a federal agency intervened. Today people come to the area for various reasons: to visit Hildene, the home of Robert Todd Lincoln, and to attend a variety of events held at the Hildene Meadowlands and at the Southern Vermont Arts Center; to fish, cycle, ski, canoe, or just plain relax; and also to shop the 125-plus outlets that can be found in Manchester and the area.

Events & Festivals to Plan Your Trip Around

February–March: Winter carnivals are held at Bromley Mountain and at Stratton Mountain, featuring ice skating, snow sculptures, fireworks, ski races, and more. Brattleboro holds a large carnival with more than 50 events, including an ice-fishing derby and a 70m ski jump.

March–April: Easter Weekend at Mount Snow, when a sunrise service is held at the summit along with a variety of other events, including parades and egg hunts. Call 802/464-3333.

U.S. Open Snowboarding Championships, Stratton Mountain. Call 802/297-2200.

May: Bennington County Horse show at Hildene, Manchester.

July: Old-Fashioned Fourth, a celebration complete with square dancing. Vermont Symphony concert.

Polo season opens and continues every third weekend.

Hildene and Dorset Antiques shows.

July–August: The Marlboro Music Festival.

August: Bennington Battle Day weekend, commemorating the Revolutionary War battle on August 16, 1777.

The Acura Tennis Tournament, Stratton.

Hildene Crafts Fair, exhibiting work by 250 craftspeople and an array of Vermont food specialties.

September: Stratton Arts Festival.

Area Attractions

The prime sightseeing destination in the valley is **Hildene,** off Rte. 7A, 2 miles south of Rte. 30 (tel. 802/362-1788); it was the home of Robert Todd Lincoln, eldest son of Abraham Lincoln, who first discovered Vermont when his mother brought him to the Equinox House in 1863 on a summer retreat. A visit begins in the carriage house, where a video prsents the highlights of Robert's life—his birth in August 1843; his army service (he was present at Appomattox); his years as a partner in the Chicago law firm of Isham and Lincoln, and his appointments as secretary of war under Garfield, as ambassador to Britain under Harrison, and later as chairman of the board of the Pullman Palace Car Company; and his 1902 purchase of 500 acres and building of this Georgian Revival home overlooking the Battenkill Valley.

Hildene means "hill" and "valley." During Robert Lincoln's working and retirement years, he and his family summered here. He was involved in local affairs until he died at Hildene in 1926. His widow summered here until her death in 1937, when it was briefly occupied by her daughter, Mary Lincoln Isham, then later by Mary Lincoln Beckwith, daughter of

Robert Lincoln's other daughter, Jessie. Peggy Beckwith was a fascinating outspoken woman who flew her own biplane, painted, sculpted, studied piano and guitar, and tried to operate the property as a working farm. She died in 1975, leaving her younger brother, Robert Todd Lincoln Beckwith, the last of the Lincoln line. He died in 1985.

On the house tour you can view the room where Robert Todd died and his office, containing one of Abe Lincoln's stovepipe hats and all the original furnishings. The original rolls are played for visitors on the 1908 Aeolian player pipe organ. From the top-floor rooms you can look down onto the restored formal garden, designed after a stained-glass window. It contains 25 varieties of peonies; the best time to visit is mid-June, when they're in bloom.

Being able to walk into and through the rooms is a particularly appealing aspect to a tour of Hildene. In the toy room, note the screen depicting fairy tales that Robert Todd Lincoln commissioned for his grandchildren and go down to the garden terrace for the view of the Green Mountains on one side and the Taconics on the other. Then stroll the nature trails or enjoy a picnic.

After a visit you can't help pondering how frequently the Lincoln family was beset by tragedy. Abraham and Mary Todd had four sons, three of whom died—the first at age 3, the second at 11, and the third at 18. Robert Todd Lincoln, though, lived to 82. Of Robert's children, Abraham II, the eldest, died in England of blood poisoning contracted while studying in France; his daughter Mary married Charles Isham and bore Lincoln Isham, and his daughter Jessie married Warren Wallace Beckwith and bore four children.

Hours: Mid-May to Oct, daily 9:30am–5:30pm (last tour begins 4pm). **Admission:** $7.

The **Southern Vermont Arts Center,** West Road, off Rte. 7A, Manchester (tel. 802/362-1405), is worth a visit for its setting alone. Against the woods-and-meadow backdrop, a Festival of the Arts is celebrated from early June to mid-October on the slopes of Mount Equinox. Paintings, sculpture, and photographs are displayed and music, dance, and vocal performances given in the performance barn.

Hours: Galleries and gardens, summer, Tues–Sat 10am–5pm, Sun noon–5pm; winter, Mon–Sat 10am–4pm. **Closed:** After Columbus Day to early Dec.

The **Dorset Theatre Festival** opens in June and continues through Labor Day. For information, call 802/867-5777.

Even nonanglers and those who've only read Izaak Walton on fishing might find the **American Museum of Fly Fishing,** Rte. 7A at Seminary Avenue in Manchester (tel. 802/362-3300), interesting. Tying a fly to lure a fish is a delicate art, and an exotically colorful one. The traditional feathers used in Atlantic salmon flies, for example, include peacock, kingfisher, jay, heron, and macaw. From these feathers, thread, and wool, artificial flies are created in thousands of patterns that range from literal to impressionistic and gaudy in style. Here the works of great fly tiers are displayed. The museum also displays 18th- and 19th-century fly rods, some 20 feet long, the earlier ones made from ash, hickory, lancewood, and greenheart, and the later (mid-19th century on) from bamboo. Today, of course, fiberglass, graphite, and boron are used, and these are displayed as well. Exhibits also include the fly-fishing tackle of many famous Americans: Winslow Homer, Arnold Gingrich (founder of *Esquire*), Dwight Eisenhower, Daniel Webster, and Ernest Hemingway.

Hours: Summer, daily 10am–4pm; winter, Mon–Fri 10am–4pm. **Admission:** $3, free for students.

Drop in and browse among the hunting and fishing gear at the **Orvis Company store** on Rte. 7 (tel. 802/362-3750), open daily from 9am to 6pm. Orvis operates a fly-fishing school near Manchester from April to October. A two-day course costs $340 to $395 per person and teaches you the intricacies of tying flies and casting and all the other skills of the sport. It offers a variety of packages, including one for parents and children and another for women only. Orvis also operates a shooting/hunting school.

Also along Rte. 7 you'll find several **outlet stores** selling such famous brand names as Anne Klein, Bass, and Van Heusen. There are about 125 such stores in the area, including such names as Cole Haan, Ralph Lauren, Liz Claiborne, Brooks Brothers, and Giorgio Armani. **Dexter Shoes** is at Rtes. 11 and 30 (tel. 802/362-4810) and the **Hathaway Outlet** is located in the Equinox Shops (tel. 802/864-4828). Stock up, too, on Vermont specialties—ham, cheese, and maple syrup—at **Harrington's,** at the junction of Rtes. 7, 11, and 30 (tel. 802/362-2070), open daily from 9am to 5pm.

On Rte. 7A, **Coffee, Tea and Spice** has a wide selection of gourmet items. At **Mother Myrick's Confectionary and Ice Cream Parlor,** stop by to savor ice cream or fantastic pastries and cakes you can enjoy out on the awning-shaded deck. **The Jelly Mill,** on Rte. 7A (tel. 802/362-3494), shelters a number of stores offering everything from handmade lamps to gourmet cookware, from crafts to foodstuffs; open daily from 9am to 6pm. **The Woodcarver** is special here. The town possesses two terrific bookstores: the **Johnny Appleseed Bookshop** (tel. 802/362-2458) and the **Northshire Bookstore** (tel. 802/362-2200), both on Rte. 7A.

North on Rte. 7, the **Enchanted Doll House** (tel. 802/362-1327) welcomes all ages to its 12-room toy shop featuring all kinds of dolls, stuffed animals, books, games, and creative toys; open daily from 9am to 5:30pm. The **Vermont Country Store** on Rte. 100 in Weston is also well worth a stop; open Monday to Saturday from 9am to 5pm. And, of course, take time to drive the **Skyline Drive** up to the summit of **Mount Equinox,** just to see the glorious view.

Southern Vermont & New Hampshire

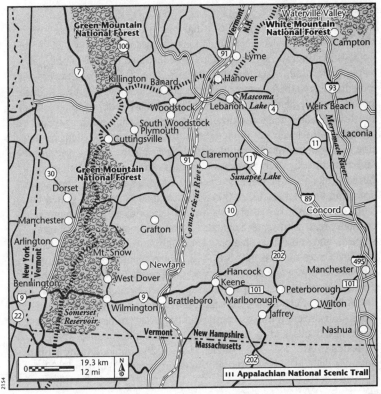

A few miles south of Manchester village in Arlington, Norman Rockwell fans will want to visit the **Norman Rockwell Exhibition & Gift Shop,** on Rte. 7A (tel. 802/375-6423), in this village that was his hometown. Over 1,000 *Saturday Evening Post* covers are on display in the gallery. A 20-minute film is shown.

Hours: Summer, daily 9am–5pm; winter, daily 10am–4pm. **Admission:** $1 adults, free for children 6 and under.

In Dorset, on Rte. 30, the **J. K. Adams Company Factory Store** (tel. 802/362-2303) stocks a whole line of gourmet woodware—spice racks, knife racks, butcher block, and other home accessories; open daily from 9am to 5:30pm.

At nearby **Bromley Mountain,** Ski Resort, Rte. 11, 6 miles east of Manchester (tel. 802/824-5522), the whole family will enjoy winter skiing or flying down the Alpine Slide in summer.

Dorset Lodging & Dining

Standing at the center of a quiet community, the **Dorset Inn,** on the Green, Dorset, VT 05251 (tel. 802/867-5500), is a genuine country inn. Ferns, lupins, and geraniums add a splash of color to the borders by the crazily paved marble paths and steps leading into the white clapboard building.

Operating as an inn since 1796, it has been extensively renovated over the years. The upstairs accommodations and decor vary: Room 24 (with bath) is invitingly arrayed with a brass bed, ruffled curtains, floral wallpaper, comfortable Martha Washingtons, and a chest of drawers. A cannonball-style bed dominates Room 26, while Room 28 offers a four-poster, a comfy Martha Washington chair, and a view of the Green. The third-floor rooms under the eaves are interestingly and cozily shaped.

Besides the lovely accommodations, the inn has an excellent reputation for its food—and it's well deserved. The same menu is served in the tavern and in the dining room and affords ample choice—from several burgers (like a simple turkey burger served with a herbed lemon-yogurt sauce) and vegetarian dishes (like baked eggplant crêpes) to grilled loin lamb chops with roasted shallots and garlic confit or grilled marinated chicken breast with sautéed shiitake, oyster, and portobello mushrooms, spinach, and sun-dried tomatoes. There's also always a pasta and fish of the day. Prices range from $8 to $18. Green paint, plank floors, plaid tablecloths, and white shutters provide the country dining atmosphere. The tap room is a cozy supper spot, especially in winter when a fire flickers. A broad selection of beers and a fine selection of wines are offered. Guests can also enjoy the two comfortable stenciled parlors with a fireplace, thick rugs, books, and such country objects as an old spinning wheel.

Rates (MAP): $90–$105 single; $160–$225 double. **Dining Hours:** Summer, daily 11:30am–2pm and 5:30–9pm; winter, Wed–Sun 11:30am–2pm and 5:30–9pm.

The **Barrows House**, Dorset, VT 05251 (tel. 802/867-4455), is a large rambling property on 11 acres that still retains a warm country feel. The 28 rooms and suites are dotted around the 6-acre property in seven buildings as well as the main house. The grounds are quite beautiful and fragrant, bursting with lupins, iris, cornflowers, tulips, honeysuckle, and lilacs shaded by hemlocks, weeping willows, and silver birches.

There are 10 rooms in the black-shuttered white clapboard inn built as a parsonage in 1804. Each is individually decorated and may contain country pine or oak furnishings, perhaps a four-poster, slipcovered chairs, a desk, and other comforts. Eight similar rooms are in the Hemlock House. The Truffle House has three double rooms and a large living room with a fireplace. The upstairs suite is really lovely, the windowseat and pencil four-poster making it especially so. These are the only air-conditioned rooms. The Schubert House holds two double rooms and a secluded private sitting room with a fireplace. The Stable suites are pleasantly rustic with plank floors, a pine hutch, and a Windsor chair among the furnishings. Each has a kitchenette and a living room with a TV. The Carriage House has ideal family accommodations. The Truffle House contains five bedrooms plus a spacious living room with a fireplace. Ping-Pong and a billiard table are located in the basement. All the accommodations are attractively furnished and very well kept.

The grounds are beautiful and the outdoor pool is idyllically situated and surrounded by grass. A sauna is located in the stables. So is the bicycle and cross-country ski shop, at which both items are available for rent. There are two tennis courts.

In the dining room, fresh flowers and atmospheric hurricane lamps grace the tables. The whole room is fresh and gardenlike, but when you're sitting in the atrium it's as if you're sitting in a garden. The Tap Room gleams with polished wood and fine books. Here people gather to chat, entertain at the piano, or play backgammon. The food is inspired continental. At dinner you might find pork chops with maple/caramelized-onion sauce, filet mignon with a rich wild-mushroom sauce, or crabmeat-stuffed sole on a sauce of red peppers and basil. For an appetizer, don't miss the crab cakes Chesapeake style or the smoked-salmon pâté with an orange/green-peppercorn vinaigrette. Prices range from $15 to $19.

Rates (MAP): $200–$260 double. Bed-and-breakfast rates available. **Dining Hours:** Dec–Mar and May–Oct, daily 6–9pm; Apr and Nov, Wed–Sun 6–9pm.

The **Inn at West View Farm,** Rte. 30, Dorset, VT 05251 (tel. 802/ 867-5715), has enjoyed a fabled reputation for its Auberge dining room's contemporary American cuisine. Among the appetizers may be a terrine of mesquite-grilled salmon with raspberry coulis and toasted walnuts, baked Brie in phyllo with poached pears and port sauce, and a daily appetizer of the day. Among the 10 or so entrees may be sesame sheared shrimp with red-pepper ravioli and ginger-and-apricot beurre blanc, loin of pork with caramelized apple and Calvados on a potato pancake, or rack of lamb with a rosemary jus. Prices range from $18 to $25. In the tavern you can enjoy such dishes as crab cakes, grilled bratwurst, or marinated rosemary chicken in a spiced tomato-herb sauce, priced from $9 to $13. Desserts include homemade sorbets and ice creams, tarts, chocolate mousse, and crème caramel. The tables are arrayed with Villeroy & Boch settings and hurricane-style lamps. The choice tables are set in the large bay window. If you have to wait, there's a small bar in which you can study the 1920s photos from the *New York Times* that cover the walls.

There are also 10 guest rooms available, all with bath. The nicest has a pineapple-style bed covered with a star quilt, a cane-seated rocker, a chest, and a sidetable. In the Carriage House, the suite has two double rooms, one with a turned four-poster sans canopy.

Rates: $95–$150 double B&B, $165–$215 double MAP. **Dining Hours:** Tues–Sun 6–9pm. **Closed:** Apr and Nov–Dec 11.

Cornucopia of Dorset, Rte. 30 (P.O. Box 307), Dorset, VT 05251 (tel. 802/867-5751), is an attractive B&B that offers extras like a champagne welcome, a wake-up tray with coffee or tea and fresh flowers, evening turndown, and a library of videocassettes. There are four air-conditioned rooms with bath, plus a cottage suite that has a skylit loft bedroom, a living room with a cathedral ceiling and fireplace, a fully equipped kitchen, and a patio. All rooms have sitting areas, and most have canopied beds covered with down comforters in winter and quilts in summer. The ground floor offers a living room and study, both with fireplaces, and a sunroom overlooking the grounds.

Rates (including full breakfast): $120–$145 double weekends, $110–$130 double weekdays; $205 cottage weekends, $185 cottage weekdays.

Manchester Lodging & Dining

Antique lovers will adore the **1811 House,** Rte. 7A, Manchester, VT 05254 (tel. 802/362-1811), a salmon-and-beige clapboard structure in the center of Manchester. It was built as a farmhouse in the 1770s. In 1811 the roof was raised and it was turned into a tavern. Later, Mary Lincoln Isham, Lincoln's granddaughter, resided here until she died in 1939. Today it's run by Marnie and Bruce Duff, who hail from Scotland.

The 14 rooms, all with bath, are exquisitely furnished. The Robert Todd Lincoln Room contains a canopied pencil four-poster with a candlewick bedspread and a Federal-style slate-blue mantel and fireplace; chintz curtains hang at the pelmeted windows. Most of rooms have desks and comfy chairs, dried-flower arrangements, clocks, and amenities like bath salt cubes. In each, you'll find a personal touch—for example, in the Grace Hoyt Singer Room, a cross-stitch rug, a small glass case filled with china cats and birds, and a handsome porcelain figure on the chest of drawers; or the framed pressed flowers in the Franklin Orvis Room. The Henry Ethel Robinson Room possesses a great bath containing a clawfoot tub with a sunflower-size old-fashioned showerhead. The Robinson Room has a private balcony with a glorious view of the mountains. The Hidden Room's 12-over-12 windows are original; so are the beams in the Burr Room.

The tavern is wonderfully authentic. Pewter mugs hang from the old beams, horse brasses adorn the fireplace and bar, brass candlesticks stand on tables smoothed by long use, and Windsor chairs and bar stools complete the scene. Bruce has a fine collection of single-malts to choose from. A breakfast of fresh fruit juice, fresh farm eggs, fried bread, and grilled tomato (typical British style) is served at the polished refectory oak table set with studded Tudor-style chairs. For relaxing, there are two comfortably furnished sitting rooms. One has a couch on an Oriental carpet before a mantel with carved plaster reliefs. Homelike touches include photos placed on a clawfoot table. The other has filled built-in bookcases, two couches, a wooden chess set, and a small TV. The basement contains a games room with a Ping-Pong table and a billiard table. The 7 acres of gardens are lovely, filled with perennial flowering plants, a sundial, and a well-manicured lawn. From here the view extends across the Equinox golf course to the Green Mountains beyond.

Rates (including breakfast): $170–$210 double.

The owners of the **Inn at Manchester,** Rte. 7A (P.O. Box 41), Manchester, VT 05254 (tel. 802/362-1793), go out of their way to welcome guests and inform them about the area. The 1880 house has 18 rooms with bath. Four are suites, including the Primrose, which has a working fireplace. No. 1 is a large front room with a bay window decorated in rose colors and furnished with an oak bed, a chest, and a rocker, among other things. No. 4 is decked out in robin's-egg blue and chintz and has an iron-and-brass bed. The third-floor rooms are charmingly decorated too. The most appealing rooms, including the Garden Suite, are perhaps those at the back, furnished with country pine and oak, pretty comforters, frilled curtains, and chintz wallpaper.

In the carriage house are four rooms offering mountain and meadow views. The Columbine Room has a handsome carved cherry bed with a Ralph Lauren blue-and-white comforter and matching drapes. The old Tiffany-style floor lamp and a beautifully carved lion's-head chair immediately catch the eye. The upstairs rooms here have cathedral-style ceilings. These rooms are particularly convenient to the pool, from which you have a lovely mountain view. They're large and will likely contain a brass bed, bold chintz wallpaper, a Victorian-style mahogany chest, a cherry sidetable, and rocking chair.

For the full country breakfasts, Stanley and Harriet whip up delicious apple-buttermilk pancakes with Vermont maple syrup, omelets, and homemade granola.

Rates (including breakfast): Foliage season and holidays, $120–$175 double. The rest of the year, $105–$140 double.

From the road you can't help noticing the celery and mauve splash of color and the hanging flower baskets adorning the front porch of the **Village Country Inn,** Rte. 7A, Manchester, VT 05254 (tel. 802/362-1792). It's run by Jay Degen and his wife, Anne, who has a natural flair for interior decoration that's amply demonstrated throughout the 1889 house. As a child she built her own dollhouses, making the furniture and picking the fabrics to go in them. Celery and mauve are the predominant colors in the large front parlor, which offers an array of seating—a corner furnished with Stickley, a high-backed Victorian loveseat, and a mauve camelback sofa—all set around a fieldstone fireplace in a room accented with a gilt mirror and a stained-glass door.

The 31 accommodations, all with bath, are highly individual. Room 111 is large and features a carved oak bed under a tent of cream lace, a wicker chaise longue, an oak dresser, a lace-draped table, bold chintz wallpaper, and inviting windowseats. Room 107 is a small country space furnished primarily with oak pieces. Other rooms might come in pale blue and wicker or Laura Ashley country or gray and lavender with a lacy swag above the bed, or more traditionally in burgundy. A couple of garden rooms by the pool, with a TV and Ethan Allen furniture, are holdovers from the inn's previous owners. Ann has brightened them by adding celery-colored quilts and mauve wallpaper. All rooms have fluffy towels and pretty eyelet linens.

The dining room's lattice trellises, floral-green wallpaper, pink and forest-green napery, glass candleholders, and celery-colored bentwood chairs create a romantic gardenlike effect. Even the fireplace is mauve. The continental menu changes seasonally. You may find medallions of veal with wild mushrooms, shallots, and madeira; fish of the day grilled with oil, oregano, garlic, and lemon; breast of chicken sautéed with shiitake mushrooms, garlic, parsley, and lemon; or loin of lamb with rosemary-and-juniper sauce. Appetizers might include chilled tomato bisque, tagliatelle in cream with wild mushrooms, or apple-smoked pheasant and oregano; desserts may be crème brûlée or pears poached in red wine. Prices run from $15.50 to $21. A pianist entertains softly at the grand piano. A comfortable tavern opens onto a summer patio furnished with wrought-iron furniture set among fountains and flowers. There's a tennis court across the street, an outdoor pool, and a boutique selling clothing, accessories, and good-quality gifts. Anne also offers different weekend packages—a champagne picnic by horse-drawn carriage, a fly-fishing workshop, golf and tennis specials—so inquire about her latest idea. No children are allowed.

Rates: Summer–fall, $120–$180 double B&B, $160–$230 double MAP (more for suites sleeping three or four). Special rates apply in Apr, May, and Nov.

You can't miss the purple-and-cream clapboard **Reluctant Panther Inn,** Rte. 7A (P.O. Box 678), Manchester, VT 05254 (tel. 802/362-2568), known for its fine restaurant as well as for its rooms. The dining room seats 60 in a highly colorful, almost tropically inspired atrium of plants, a flagstone floor, and brilliant orange, yellow, and peach napery. The stone fireplace makes it cozy in winter, while in summer the marble terrace dotted with flowers, plants, silver birches, stone ornaments, and a view of Equinox Mountain makes a lovely spot for cocktails. Or you can enjoy drinks in the unique bar. Green-leather low chairs on casters are set at Vermont marble tables; the ceiling, paneling, and shutters are a brilliant purple; and in one corner a full bear trophy, its teeth bared, stands ready to party no matter what. Elsewhere, carved gryphons are placed in niches. A fire adds warmth in winter.

The menu offers a dozen or so entrees. The seafood is imaginatively prepared—tuna with minted cilantro-walnut salsa, bacon-wrapped monkfish filet on red-wine/shallot reduction—as are such meat dishes as tenderloin of pork with black-bean/garlic sauce or pan-seared calves' liver with Calvados and apples. Prices range from $19 to $23. Among the appetizers might be a flavorsome portobello mushroom with port-wine crème fraîche or a delicious warm Brie with raspberry coulis.

There are 12 rooms in the main house, all with a bath, air-conditioning, a color TV, and a phone, six with fireplaces. Each is dramatically and differently decorated, with a half bottle of wine for guests. The wallpapers are quite extraordinary: mushrooms in Room A, purple poppies in Room C, Queen Anne's lace in Room E, for example. Room G is exceptionally attractive: Eyelet pillows grace the bed covered with a light-purple comforter and adorned by a draped lace curtain effect. Comforts include two steel-gray wing chairs, a fireplace, dusky-rose carpeting, a marble-topped table, an oak dresser, and a bath with a clawfoot tub and a pedestal sink. Room J is exceptionally large and possesses a Victorian oak bed and furniture in a matching style, while Room L contains a cherry Stickley bed, a carved oak Victorian chair, a chestnut armoire, a black-walnut chest of drawers, and two wing chairs covered in salmon-pink fabric. In the adjacent Mary Porter House are four suites with whirlpools and fireplaces and four-poster beds.

Rates (including full breakfast): Sept 15–Oct 22, Dec 22–Jan 1, and holiday weekends, $220–$305 double MAP; from $315 suite (rates $40 less if restaurant is closed). The rest of the year, $175–$225 double; from $240 suite. **Dining Hours:** Thurs–Mon 6–9pm.

The famous old resort, **The Equinox,** Rte. 7A, Manchester, VT 05254 (tel. 802/362-4700), which welcomed Mary Todd Lincoln and other dignitaries in its heyday, has been restored to its former glory. Although the Equinox is on the site of a pre-Revolutionary tavern, its life as a fashionable summer resort was really begun by the Orvis family in 1854. Behind the facade with its stately columns and veranda stretching a full block along the marble sidewalk, you'll find a large lobby with a Federal-style fireplace. The floor is covered with Oriental carpeting and comfy wingbacks and Martha Washingtons are set around coffeetables.

All 163 air-conditioned guest rooms have a TV and a phone. Most are decorated with pine furniture, chintz comforters, a couple of wing chairs or rockers, stenciled walls, and ruffle-trimmed organdy curtains. Also available are several duplex suites and accommodations with fully equipped kitchens and fireplaces in three-room town houses.

The most impressive public space is the main dining room, the Colonnade. Designed in 1913, it has a huge semicircular bay window with a splendid mountain view. The menu features about six expertly prepared entrees—filet of halibut with lemon-thyme mignonette, veal with basil-roasted tomatoes and forest mushroom strudel, and filet of beef with Guinness stout and roasted shallot demiglaze. Prices range from $20 to $25. The Marsh Tavern is authentic, dating back to 1769. Today it's furnished with Windsor chairs and polished wood tables and is open for breakfast, lunch, and dinner. The menu offers a variety of dishes, like shepherd's pie, pan-roasted chicken with cranberry jus, and rainbow trout with shiitake-and-leek ragoût—all priced from $9 to $20.

From the lobby, an elevator takes you up one story to the Lincoln Terrace, where afternoon tea is served overlooking the gardens of azaleas, tulips, and other flowers (at least when I visited). Umbrella-shaded tables are placed out there in summer. A short walk from the main building brings you to the pool area (set with yellow loungers), which is serviced by a garden lounge located in the old carriage house. Lunch and drinks are served here, and in the evening there's also dinner-dancing. Other facilities on the 1,100-acre property include two pools (indoor/outdoor), three clay tennis courts, a fitness center and spa (with massages, wraps, and scrubs), and the 1927 Walter Travis 18-hole golf course that was recently updated by Rees Jones. You can dine at the clubhouse restaurant or out under an awning and enjoy the glorious view. In winter there are 35km of cross-country ski trails, plus ice skating on the golf-course pond and snowshoeing. Rentals are available. Services include a concierge, valet, and room service. You can also stroll across and down the street to the Equinox shops—three levels that include a Hathaway outlet and other stores selling toys, flowers, and antiques. Carriage rides are also part of the fun.

Rates: $150–$300 double; from $370 suite. Special packages available. **Dining Hours:** Tavern, daily 7am–9:30pm. Colonnade, June–Oct, daily 6–9pm; Nov–May, Fri–Sat 6–9:30pm.

The **Inn at Ormsby Hill,** R.R. 2, Box 3264, Manchester Center, VT 05255 (tel. 802/362-1163), is a restored manor house standing on 2½ acres of landscaped grounds. Legend has it that Ethan Allen took refuge here from the English and the innkeepers will happily show you the secret room in which he's said to have hidden. Spectacular hand-tooled staircases and woodwork and other handsome architectural elements are found throughout. The five rooms are furnished with four-poster canopied beds and elegantly decorated with country antiques and original artwork. Four have a fireplace and whirlpool. The size of the dining room/conservatory will overwhelm you, as will the view beyond of Hildene and the Green Mountains. An excellent breakfast is served.

Rates (including breakfast): $105–$1802 double.

The Chantecleer, Rte. 7, Manchester Center (tel. 802/362-1616; fax 802/362-5756), is the premier local restaurant. The fieldstone fireplace, rafters, and barn siding give a pretty country atmosphere to the room filled with captain's chairs and tables covered in pink cloths. The inspiration is distinctly Swiss, with Oriental accents—like fondue chinoise, thin-sliced beef to dip in a special Oriental-style broth. More familiar dishes include rack of lamb with herbed garlic; sautéed pheasant; roast duck with cranberry-and-orange sauce, veal sweetbreads grandmère (with bacon, mushrooms, tomatoes, and wine-and-veal glaze); and filet mignon flamed with kirsch and served with Bing cherry sauce. The seafood terrine appetizer with tomato coulis is very special, consisting of layers of scallops, salmon, and green-pea mousse, and so is the croûte aux champignons, assorted mushrooms sautéed with garlic and fines herbes and veal glaze and served on toast. Prices run $18 to $26. It's located about 4 miles north of Manchester on Rte. 7.

Hours: Wed–Mon 5–9pm (in winter, also Sun 11:30am–2pm). **Closed:** Mid-Apr to mid-May and mid-Nov to mid-Dec.

Arlington Lodging & Dining

The **West Mountain Inn,** Rte. 313, Arlington, VT 05250 (tel. 802/ 375-6516), half a mile west of Arlington, is one of my favorite retreats for several reasons, but primarily for the spirit and the character of owners Wesley and Mary Ann Carlson. Both love animals and tend to a menagerie of Netherland dwarf lop-eared rabbits, goats, and several llamas. The 150-acre setting is lovely. Cornflowers and iris and other flowers bloom. The house looks out onto Red Mountain and the grounds are filled with hemlocks, pine, and maple. To get there, you'll have to cross the Battenkill and take a dirt road to the top of a hill.

There are 15 rooms, each named after a favorite historical figure. On the ground floor Wesley and Mary Ann have created Gwendolyn's Room, a *really* accessible room for the disabled in which all the switches are placed low, as are the bars in the closet; the bath is fully and properly equipped, even with an open-style shower to accommodate a wheelchair. The room itself is one of the nicest, with a brick fireplace, ebony sculptures on the mantel, a Stickley loveseat, and a comfy chair. In all the rooms guests will find a chocolate candy bar and a bowl of fruit. The Robert Todd Lincoln Room has a carved-oak lace-canopied bed with a hand-loomed 1830 quilt—"snowflakes on evergreen," a special Vermont pattern. Oak furnishings, including a rocker, complete the decor. In the Daniel Webster Suite are sleigh beds; Grandma Moses's small pale-blue room has a fireplace, a rocker, and, of course, her farm scenes; the Robert Frost Room has its own porch with wicker chairs overlooking the llama pasture; the Carl Ruggles Room, with a fireplace and deck, features a carved high-backed oak bed, a Stickley couch, and a rope rug. The largest room is the Rockwell Kent Suite, with a native pine cathedral ceiling and loft bed, a brick fireplace, an Indian rug as a wall hanging, and an eclectic mix of pine and Victorian furnishings. The Booker T. Washington Room has original pine paneling. In addition, there are three millhouse suites with a living room, a kitchen, and two bedrooms and bath; two have a wood-burning stove.

The dining room is basically for inn guests, who receive a six-course dinner that changes daily. The main courses may be veal marsala and a chicken and a shrimp dish. The fireplace makes it cozy in winter, and the orchids and other plants and color photos of the inn in all seasons give it a homey feel. Adjacent is a bar with Windsor-style bar stools and, oddly enough, a tank full of exotic tropical fish, plus plenty of books and magazines. Other popular gathering spots are the games room, equipped with cribbage, backgammon, and the like; and the sitting room, warmed by a Franklin stove and offering plenty of couches and armchairs and a piano at which guests entertain one another. In summer the enclosed flagstone porch set with cushioned bamboo chairs is a favorite lounging spot. At breakfast, eggs Benedict, omelets, and vanilla crêpes with butterscotch sauce are all likely choices.

Rates (including breakfast): Spring, $162–$194 double. Summer, $162–$194 double. Fall, $182–$214 double. Winter, $162–$194 double. There's a 10% discount Sun–Thurs Nov–July.

Occupying a cream-colored Greek Revival building with rust-colored shutters, the **Arlington Inn,** Rte. 7A, Arlington, VT 05250 (tel. 802/375-6532), stands behind a row of stately maples. A marble path fringed with flowers and ferns leads to the central portico. The main hallway, handsomely furnished with an Oriental carpet, carved Chippendales, and color engravings of London scenes dating back to 1848, is a refreshing change from colonial New England.

It's both an inn and a restaurant. The main dining room's tables are elegantly covered in white and set with crystal candlesticks and gold-rimmed china. The faintly Empire-style ambience is created by a couple of classical urns and an ornate clock that stands on the fireplace mantel. A meal here might start with a strudel of pheasant in a cream sauce with sun-dried cranberries or sauté of Maine crab cake with cilantro, orange, and green-peppercorn beurre blanc. Among the main courses, priced from $10 to $22, might be medallions of Vermont-raised beef tenderloin crusted with peppercorns and herbs in merlot demiglaze or rack of lamb with roasted garlic, port wine, rosemary, Vermont chèvre, and a potato croquette. Breakfast offers eggs, bagels, omelets, and pancakes. If you have to wait for your table, relax in the cozy forest-green Sylvester Deming Tavern while a pianist entertains (Friday and Saturday only). Don't miss the two huge (you'll see what I mean) Canadian rawhide rockers on the adjacent porch. The greenhouse dining room looks very summery with its green, peach, and pink color scheme and marble floor.

The accommodations are variously decorated in a 19th-century style; some have fireplaces. The Pamela Suite features flounced pillow cases, valanced windows, a Mme Récamier sofa, an Oriental throw rug, and a marble Victorian dresser in one room. The Martin Chester Room contains a broken-scroll bed, needlepointed side chairs, a camelback sofa, an armoire, a carved wood table, orange-and-green macaw and bird-of-paradise wallpaper, and a huge sideboard with a turnip foot. The tongue-and-groove ceiling makes it very cozy and unique. Some rooms are tucked under the eaves. Many of the baths have clawfoot tubs; and quilts, Victorian prints, and period pieces like a spinning wheel found are throughout. Guests have the use of the parlor furnished Stickley style, most comfortable in winter, when the fire is lit. Active folks will like the tennis court out back.

Rates (including breakfast): July–Sept 15, $90–$170 double. Sept 16–Oct, $100–$195 double. Nov–June, $80–$160 double. (The higher price is for fireplace rooms.) **Dining Hours:** Summer, Tues–Sun 5:30–9pm; winter, Thurs–Sat 5:30–9pm, Sun 11:30am–2:30pm.

Bromley & Magic Mountain Area Lodging & Dining

A trellis gate hung with fuchsias leads into the garden at the **Three Clock Inn,** Middletown Road (R.R. 1, Box 59), South Londonderry, VT 05155 (tel. 802/824-6327). This secluded establishment is best known for its restaurant, which is very good indeed. The updated American/continental cuisine features fresh local ingredients. You might find roast Statler breast of chicken served with sautéed seasonal fruits and napped with a sauce suprême, loin of pork wrapped with apple-smoked bacon and glazed with apricot and curry, or filet of salmon topped with pineapple-chile salsa. Prices range from $16 to $23. To start, there may be smoked salmon with buckwheat crêpes and horseradish cream or pâté maison. Desserts include classics like peach Melba, pear Hélène, and strawberries Romanoff. There are two small dining rooms, plus a flagstone porch enclosed with diamond-pane windows.

Upstairs are five guest rooms, including a small suite with two bedrooms. The largest has a canopied bed. Guests also can use a colonial-style furnished living room. At breakfast the gracious proprietors will serve whatever you fancy.

Rates (MAP): $85 per person. **Dining Hours:** Tues–Sun 6–9pm. **Closed:** Apr–Memorial Day and the third week of Oct to a week before Christmas.

The **Inn at Weston,** P.O. Box 56, Weston, VT 05161 (tel. 802/824-5804), which was built in 1848 as a farmhouse and was converted to a guesthouse in 1951, is set on 5 acres in the village. The atmosphere is relaxed and casual. There are 13 rooms, 7 with bath. Six additional rooms with bath and phone are in the 1830 Coleman House across the street. The inn, though, is primarily known for its continental cuisine. The menu features nine or so dishes, ranging from scampi sautéed with tomatoes, capers, and olives and ossobuco milanese to steak au poivre and breast of chicken on a cilantro-accented black-bean sauce. Prices range from $15 to $19. The ambience is country, with Windsor-style chairs set at tables draped with white linen.

Rates: Summer, $78–$122 double. Foliage season, $86–$132 double. Winter, $82–$128 double. (Higher rates are for rooms in the Coleman House.) MAP rates available.

The **Nordic Inn,** Rte. 11, Landgrove, VT 05148 (tel. 802/824-6444), offers reasonably priced accommodations, 12 miles of Nordic ski trails, and a 75-seat restaurant favored by the locals. There are five guest rooms, three with bath. The largest has a queen-size bed and two singles, and all rooms are simply furnished. The solarium dining room sports purple napkins on tables and a balcony dining area. The menu has a Nordic touch and includes gravlax (salmon cured with salt, sugar, and dill), Nordic herring, and hearts of palm and artichoke to start. The nine or so entrees might include poached salmon with dill butter, chicken glazed with maple syrup, pork with garlic and orange, veal marsala, and steak au poivre. Prices run $13 to $17. A fire blazing in the fieldstone hearth draws an after-ski crowd to the bar.

Rates: Summer, $50–$58 double (with continental breakfast). Fall, $70–$90 double (with continental breakfast). Winter, $75–$100 per person (MAP). **Dining Hours:** June–Oct, Mon and Wed–Fri 6–9pm, Sat–Sun noon–2pm and 6–9pm; May and Nov, Sat–Sun noon–2pm and 6–9pm; Dec–Mar, Wed–Mon noon–2pm and 6–9pm. **Closed:** Apr.

After Dark

The Dorset Summer Theater Festival presents a series of plays from late June to Labor Day at the **Dorset Playhouse,** Dorset Village (tel. 802/ 867-2223). The **Weston Playhouse** (tel. 802/824-5288) also produces Broadway shows.

The Manchester & Dorset Area
Special & Recreational Activities

Camping: On the Battenkill, R.D. 2, Arlington, VT 05250 (tel. 802/ 375-6663), hookups are available, with swimming, tubing, and fishing on the grounds. Open May to October.

Canoeing: Battenkill Canoe, on River Road (leading to West Arlington), off Rte. 313 (P.O. Box 65), Arlington (tel. 802/ 362-2800), rents a canoe for $44 per day and picks you up at the end of the trip. It also offers interpretive nature trips on the river and guided day trips, plus many longer trips in the Northeast and farther afield in places like Costa Rica.

Fishing: The Battenkill is one of the East's great fishing rivers. See "Area Attractions," above, for the famous Orvis Fly Fishing School (tel. 800/548-9548).

Golf: The Dorset Field Club (tel. 802/867-5553); also at the Equinox and at Stratton, which hosts the McCall's LPGA Classic Golf Tournament.

Skiing: Bromley, off Rte. 11 in Bromley, is a full-facility resort offering 39 trails serviced by nine lifts. Slopeside accommodations are available at Bromley Village. For information call 802/ 824-5522 or write P.O. Box 1130-B, Manchester Center, VT 05255.

Stratton, Stratton Mountain, VT 05155 (tel. 802/297-2200), is a full-facility resort complete with a sports center that also offers tennis, badminton, swimming, and more. There are 92 trails on 478 acres serviced by 14 lifts, including one high-speed 12-passenger gondola and four quads. Accommodations include the Stratton Mountain Inn, Stratton Village Lodge, and Stratton Mountain Village, as well as the Liftline Lodge and the Birkenhaus. Classes and seminars on a variety of subjects are given for those who don't ski. For reservations call 800/787-2886. For snow conditions call 800/297-2211. From Manchester, take Rte. 11 east and then Rte. 30 south to Bondville. The entrance to Stratton is in the village center. Follow Stratton Mountain Road 4 miles.

For cross-country skiing, the Hildene Ski Touring Center (tel. 802/362-1788) has 50km of trails. It's open daily from 9am to dusk if there's sufficient snow (usually from the third week in December to March 1). The Viking Ski Touring Centre, Little Pond Road (R.R. 1, Box 70), Londonderry, VT 05148 (tel. 802/824-3933), has 40km of trails and offers inn-to-inn and guided tours.

Swimming: There's good swimming at a lake on Rte. 30 between Dorset and Manchester.

Tennis: The Stratton Tennis School, site of the Acura Women's Tennis Tournament during summer, has 15 Har-Tru and Deco Turf II courts, four indoor courts, three racquetball courts, and other athletic facilities. Special packages, including accommodations in a variety of room types, are available. Call 802/297-2200, or 800/787-2886. From Manchester, take Rte. 7 to Rte. 11 east to Rte. 30 south to Bondville. From the center of the village follow the Stratton Mountain Road to the resort.

Courts are also available at the Equinox.

BENNINGTON

Bennington Attractions

During the Revolutionary era, Bennington was the headquarters for Ethan Allen and his Green Mountain Boys, who, with Benedict Arnold, captured Fort Ticonderoga from the British in 1775. A few years later Bennington was at the center of another famous battle that turned out to be a turning point in the war and a prelude to the victory at Saratoga. General Burgoyne was in desperate need of supplies and sent a column of Hessians north to capture the supplies stored in Bennington. The Revolutionary forces heard of the plan and intercepted the British at Walloomsac, N.Y., where they inflicted great losses on the British troops. The 306-foot-tall **Bennington Battle Monument** is a fitting memorial to this historic event. An elevator takes you to the top for a marvelous three-state view.

Much of the history and crafts of the area can be reviewed at the **Bennington Museum,** West Main Street (Rte. 9), Old Bennington (tel.

802/447-1571), filled with an assortment of glass, stoneware (including that of the famous Bennington potters), early American paintings by Erastus Salisbury Field, furniture, military items, and other household wares from the 19th century. Most appealing, though, is the gallery devoted to Grandma Moses, or Anna Mary Robertson, a New York farm girl who turned her full attention to art at age 78 and achieved her first show at age 80 at New York City's Galerie St. Etienne in 1940. She became a legendary figure who continued to paint until she died in 1961 at the age of 101, an inspiration to all aspiring artists for her late start and her untutored natural gift. Here you can view 32 of her refreshing, delightful farm and country scenes and a display of family memorabilia.

Hours: Daily 9am–5pm. **Closed:** Major holidays. **Admission:** $5 adults, $4.50 students, free for children 11 and under.

From the obelisk of the battle monument, you can stroll past gracious 18th- and 19th-century homes through Old Bennington, past the **Old First Church burial ground,** where some Hessians who fell in the battle are buried in a mass grave. Robert Frost is buried here too. You can pick up the **walking tour** of the area at the Bennington Chamber of Commerce, on Veterans Memorial Drive (Rte. 7 north).

The **Park-McCullough House** (tel. 802/442-5441) is an extremely well-kept Victorian mansion at the corner of West and Park streets in North Bennington. Besides the house itself, which is filled with period furnishings and personal effects, be sure to see the miniature "manor," used as a children's playhouse, and a cupola-topped carriage house, complete with century-old carriages.

Hours: Late May to Oct, daily 10am–4pm. **Admission:** $5 adults, $4 seniors, $3 students 12–18.

While in North Bennington, you may wish to visit the campus of the progressive **Bennington College,** whose curriculum stresses artistic creation and an acquaintance with nature.

In Bennington itself you may want to stop by **Williams Smokehouse,** 1001 E. Main St. (tel. 802/442-1000), and pick up some fine smoked hams, bacon without nitrates, or many other fresh Vermont products. Also visit **Bennington Potter's Yard** (tel. 802/447-7531), a shopping-and-gallery complex at School and Country streets.

Hours: Mon–Sat 9:30am–5:30pm, Sun noon–5pm.

Bennington Lodging

The **Molly Stark Inn,** 1067 E. Main St., Bennington, VT 05201 (tel. 802/442-9631), occupies an 1890 Queen Anne–style Victorian with a wraparound porch set on a carefully tended acre. Six rooms are available, each decorated individually in country style with quilts, oak and other pieces, and clawfoot tubs in the bath. Some share a bath. The most private accommodation is the guest cottage with a brass bed in the loft, a Jacuzzi, a wetbar, a woodstove, and many other creature comforts. Guests also may use the den and parlor, which is warmed in winter with a wood-burning stove. A hearty breakfast is served.

Rates (including breakfast): $70–$90 double; $135 cottage.

Otherwise, Bennington's accommodations are strictly motel style, including Best Western's **New Englander Motor Inn,** 220 Northside Dr., Bennington, VT 05201 (tel. 802/442-6311, or 800/528-1234).

Rates: $50–$98 double (less in winter).

Bennington Dining

The **Publyck House,** Rte. 7A, Harwood Hill (tel. 802/442-8301), is a remodeled barn that has been filled with 18th-century decor and an indoor greenhouse. Good beef and seafood are the staples here, from $11 to $16. There might be grilled halibut with herb butter, salmon with dill-hollandaise, chicken teriyaki, and several steaks and surf-and-turf combinations.

Hours: Mon–Thurs 5–9pm, Fri–Sat 5–10pm, Sun 4–9pm.

The Brasserie, in Potter's Yard (tel. 802/447-7922), is a pleasant outdoor dining spot in summer and a fine lunch or dinner spot year round. At lunch, have the Yard Special, a platter with Danish pâté, French bread and butter, and a Boston lettuce salad. Or you can choose from a variety of salads, omelets, and sandwiches under $9. Turn off Main Street at Dunkin Donuts (at 460 Main).

Hours: Summer, daily 11:30am–8pm; winter, Sun–Thurs 11:30am–3pm.

Bennington
Special & Recreational Activities

Boating: Rental boats are available in Woodford State Park, east of Bennington on Rte. 9.

Fishing: Woodford State Park has some great trout fishing.

Golf, Swimming & Tennis: The Mount Anthony Country Club, Bank Street below the Battle Monument (tel. 802/442-2617).

WILMINGTON

From Bennington, it's only about 21 miles to Wilmington, where there happen to be several charming accommodations to use as your base while exploring pretty Vermont villages and enjoying all the activities the mountains and southern Vermont have to offer—particularly, of course, Mount Snow.

Wilmington Lodging & Dining

If I could spare a weekend right now, I'd head for the warm and different hospitality of Jim McGovern and Lois Nelson at the **Hermitage Inn,** Coldbrook Road, Wilmington, VT 05363 (tel. 802/464-3511). Jim certainly has his own way of doing things: He's a renegade Connecticut gent who more than 25 years ago fled the South to the 24 acres he now occupies, where he can indulge his hobbies and enthusiasms without too much interference.

From the minute you cross the bridge over the tiny stream onto the property, you know you're somewhere special. Off to the left is a series of farm structures, which, after investigation, turn out to be houses for the game birds—geese, pheasants, ducks, wild turkeys, and partridges—that Jim raises specifically for the table and for which his dining room is famous. He also collects some 35 species of rare beauties that're worth far too much to put on any table—gold and silver pheasants, India blue peacocks, and New Zealand and Arctic snow geese, to name a few. Walk up to the house at the top of the hill and you'll discover a whole run full of wild turkeys, an area where Jim and Lois raise English setters, and a sugar house where every spring 5,000 buckets of maple sap are turned into 700 gallons of pure maple syrup; this syrup is sold in the store along with jams, jellies (including originals like Montrachet, made with Montrachet), and other McGovern favorites, notably decoys and fine wines. In the store you can also rent ski equipment to travel the 40km of cross-country trails or the downhill slopes at Mount Snow. A clay tennis court and a trout pond complete the picture.

The main inn, with a shingle roof and dormer windows, dates back 100 years. Wide pine floors and chairs cozily placed in front of the hearth in the bar engender a convivial atmosphere conducive to conversation. Several small dining areas lead off the bar (also an outdoor terrace), and here you'll enjoy some of the finest dining in the area—game, trout, wienerschnitzel, from $14 to $25—enhanced by fine wines from Jim's virtuoso wine cellar (2,000 labels with many extra-fine vintages over 30 years old). Start with mushrooms Hermitage, stuffed with caviar, and I can heartily recommend the pheasant braised in white-wine cream sauce. There's also a larger dining room in the back and a gallery where Jim has been collecting Delacroix lithographs.

The inn was once the home of Bertha Eastman Barry, the redoubtable editor of the Social Register, and it retains some original furnishings, most notably the four-poster in Room 4. In the mid-1980s Jim added a new wing, carefully constructed in the same architectural style. All 15 rooms have a bath, working fireplace, and phone; each is furnished individually, some in mahogany, some in honey oak. A typical large room contains a pineapple half-poster bed, a chest of drawers with a broken-scroll mirror, a Stickley loveseat, and a comb-back Windsor chair. From most rooms you get a glorious view looking toward Haystack Mountain. Additional rooms are a short distance down the road in Brookbound, where guests can use a pine living room with a fieldstone fireplace, a TV, and an upright piano. Rooms here vary in size. The largest, No. 42, possesses a high carved oak bed, a needlepointed Victorian rocker, a Stickley chair, a Chippendale sidetable, and a brick fireplace. Most have a bath.

This may not be the ultimate designer-stamped, glossy-magazine-quality establishment, but it offers a deeply satisfying sense of honesty, character, and individuality—and this is a place where you can relax and be yourself. In winter you can enjoy the 50km of ski trails; hunters appreciate the sporting clays and hunting preserve. The Hermitage is 2 miles north of Wilmington; from Rte. 100, turn left at Coldbrook Road and continue for about 2 miles. Turn left at the sign for the inn.

Rates: Main inn (MAP), summer, $220 double; winter, $250 double. Brookbound (including continental breakfast), $70–$135 double weekends, $60–$135 double weekdays. Add $48 per person for dinner plan. **Dining Hours:** Sun–Thurs 5–10pm, Fri–Sat 5–11pm.

You can't miss the **Nutmeg Inn,** Rte. 9, Wilmington, VT 05363 (tel. 802/464-3351), a Chinese-red clapboard house whose long front porch always supports some colorful floral display—roses in summer; potted bronze, yellow, and orange mums in fall. The place is lovingly cared for, and everything is spotless at this comfortable, homey 180-year-old farmhouse. The special warmth is most evident in the large living room in the carriage house where guests gather to read in front of the fire, watch TV, and play cards or games or to enjoy a drink at the "bring your own" bar. Out back is a lawn set up for croquet in summer, with volleyball and badminton for more active guests. Throughout the house, pine furnishings add special coziness. Each of the 11 guest rooms (all with bath and air conditioning, most with fireplace) is decorated in country fashion with pine or oak pieces, tables draped with Laura Ashley prints, brass beds or four-posters, and so on. There are also three two-room suites with a fireplace and TV/VCR. For dining you're offered two cozily furnished dining rooms—one containing a Norman Rockwell plate collection, the other warmed by a woodstove, giving a hillside view.

Rates (including breakfast): Summer weekends, $98–$145 double; $165–$185 suite. Fall weekends, $105–$165 double; $185–$205 suite. Winter weekends, $130–$185 double; $205–$225 suite. Weekday rates $10–$15 less; special higher rates on holidays.

Tall maples, manicured lawns, and a vegetable garden surround the white clapboard **Red Shutter Inn,** Rte. 9 (P.O. Box 84), Wilmington, VT 05363 (tel. 802/464-3768). This house on 5 acres was built in 1894 and inside are five guest rooms, all with bath, most furnished in chintz country fashion. Room 3 has a pineapple half-poster, a maple chest, a Queen Anne–style side chair, lace-trimmed curtains, and chintz wallpaper. In the carriage house behind the inn are three rooms, plus a fireplace suite that features a double whirlpool bath. The dining room with its stone fireplace is a welcoming retreat on a winter's night. In summer there's alfresco dining on the awning-covered porch. Guests also enjoy the woodstove's warmth in the living room/pub.

Rates (including breakfast): $115–$180 double. **Dining Hours:** Summer, Wed–Sun 6–9pm; winter, Fri–Sat 6–9pm.

Set atop a hill with a lovely view of the Deerfield Valley, **The White House,** Rte. 9, Wilmington, VT 05363 (tel. 802/464-2136), was built as a private summer home in 1914 and possesses a gracious Georgian-style portico and rows of dormers jutting from the roof line. As you might expect, the 16 rooms in the main inn are extra-large, all with bath; 9 rooms have a fireplace and 2 have a double whirlpool tub. Seven additional rooms are located in the Guest House, which has a common living room with a fireplace and cable TV. The public areas include large antique-filled sitting rooms, a dining room with rich mahogany paneling, and a bar, which was especially sunk so as not to impair the view of the sunsets across the valley. A terrace also takes advantage of the vista. The grounds are delightful. Roses climb around a trellis by a garden fountain, creating a romantic arbor, while beyond is an outdoor pool. In winter, 43km of ski trails are available. The restaurant offers a selection of continental dishes—chicken almondine, veal piccata, filet mignon with Armagnac-and-mushroom sauce, and salmon with country glaze, priced from $17 to $20. The new spa has an indoor pool, a whirlpool, and a sauna.

Rates (including full breakfast): Main inn, $138–$188 double, $150–$205 double on holidays; Guest House, $118 double, $128 double on holidays. **Dining Hours:** Mon–Sat 5:30–9pm, Sun 11:30am–2:30pm and 5:30–9pm.

About 4 miles from Mount Snow and 4 miles from Wilmington center, at the **Trails End Lodge,** 5 Trails End Lane, Wilmington, VT 05363 (tel. 802/464-2727), you'll find a real home away from home at which charming and delightful hosts Mary and Bill Kilburn will welcome you. Bill and Mary love having guests in their home and that's what makes this place extra-special. The house stands on 10 beautifully kept acres. At the back is a prettily landscaped heated pool, a clay tennis court, and plenty of sunning space.

Dinner is served to guests only, and in summer only during the Marlboro Music Festival. The menu will be on the chalkboard by the kitchen counter where you check in. It's served all-you-can-eat family style and includes soup and salad and a single entree like pork loin with madeira sauce, beef rouladen, or baked scrod, accompanied by two or three vegetables and topped off with a dessert like strawberry daiquiri. There's a guest refrigerator for storing away your choice drinks.

Breakfast consists of cereal and homemade granola, juice, muffins, and an egg dish with bacon or sausage. Guests can relax in the cathedral-ceilinged living room around the massive fieldstone fireplace on any of several cozy seating arrangements. There's also a games room equipped with board games, books, and something called bumper pool—great for the kids.

Fifteen rooms with bath are available: Four are spacious Fireplace Suites, five are queen-size rooms, three are two-bedded rooms for families, and three are suites without fireplaces. They're individually decorated in a Laura Ashley or similar country style with chintz and floral wallpapers and oak dressers and wicker loveseats or the like. One room contains a bed covered with a fluffy cream eiderdown, chintz celery-and-rose wallpaper, a small table and chair, and an oak dresser. My favorite rooms, though, are the so-called Fireplace Suites, each of which has a stone fireplace, canopied bed, cathedral ceiling, cable TV, wet bar, refrigerator, and Jacuzzi bath, plus a private entrance.

Rates (including breakfast): Summer, $100–$120 double; $150 suite. Fall, $110–$140 double; $170 suite. Winter, $120–$150 double; $180 suite. Holiday weekends add $10.

The **Misty Mountain Inn Lodge,** Stowe Hill Road (R.R., Box 114C), Wilmington, VT 05363 (tel. 802/464-3961), was once a one-room schoolhouse about 2 miles from Wilmington center overlooking the picturesque Deerfield Valley, ideally situated for the Marlboro Music Festival. There are 150 surrounding acres to walk around in summer or cross-country ski in winter. Meals are served family style in the rustic dining room and might feature roast beef with mashed potatoes and vegetables, home-baked rolls, and desserts. There's a cozy living room, warmed by a fire in winter, where guests may join in a sing-along with innkeepers Buzz and Elizabeth Cole, who play guitar or banjo. There's also TV, games, and books for the children. The eight guest rooms—four with bath and four sharing three baths—are simply furnished.

Rates: MAP, $109 double weekdays, $130 double weekends. B&B, $80 double weekdays, $100 double weekends.

Wilmington Dining

Le Petit Chef, Rte. 100 (tel. 802/464-8437), is a local favorite for superb food served in homey country surroundings. Although the dishes change frequently, you may find rack of lamb; filet of beef with green-peppercorn sauce; veal chop marinated in balsamic vinegar; poisson Méditerrané (fish, clams, mussels, and shrimp poached in tomato broth with aromatic sea herbs); venison with sun-dried-cherry sauce; and always a vegetarian dish. The desserts are tantalizing—especially the crunchy meringue pie, the chocolate torte, and any of the homemade fruit pies. Main-course prices run $15 to $25.

Hours: Sun–Mon and Wed–Thurs 6–9pm, Fri–Sat 6–10pm. **Closed:** Nov and Apr.

WEST DOVER & MOUNT SNOW

From Wilmington, **Mount Snow,** Mount Snow, VT 05356 (tel. 802/464-3333), lies only 9 miles north on Rte. 100. Mount Snow is one of the state's largest ski resorts and draws great crowds from the metropolitan areas of Boston, Hartford, and New York City (it's the Vermont resort closest to New York). The company that manages Killington took over Mount Snow in 1977, making substantial improvements, like the installation of computerized snowmaking. The trails are myriad (127 plus), serviced by 24 lifts. You'll find good skiing for beginners and intermediates, and on the North Face, for experts, with 84% snowmaking capability. Lift passes are about $45 on weekends. Facilities include a nursery, a bar, a cafeteria at the summit, rentals, a ski school, and 40 miles of cross-country trails. There's plenty to do *après ski* as well, at the Snow Barn, Deacon's Den, and Dover Bar & Grill.

Mount Snow & West Dover Lodging & Dining

Close to 100 lodges, inns, and motels are clustered near the ski area, and one or two of them are quite exquisite. I've already mentioned the **Hermitage Inn** under "Wilmington Lodging & Dining," above. The other accommodation, the **Inn at Sawmill Farm,** Rte. 100 (P.O. Box 367), West Dover, VT 05356 (tel. 802/464-8131), created by Rodney Williams and his wife, Ione, from an old farmhouse and barn, has international renown and is a Relais & Châteaux property. It's famous for the classic quality of its dining room, the designer-perfect quality of its rooms and cottages, and the understated elegance of its grounds.

The dining room positively glows. Copper pots adorn the walls, fresh flowers add color and life, fine crystal and china grace the tables in a cathedral-ceilinged room that has been carefully designed to provide intimate dining areas. Son Brill creates the cuisine. At dinner you'll find a selection for every palate—pan-seared salmon with crispy skin and saffron sauce, pheasant breast with forestière sauce, rack of lamb with eggplant provençal, or tenderloin of beef with glazed onions, mushrooms, and balsamic vinegar. Prices run $26 to $30. The appetizers are equally tempting—like lobster salad, confit of pheasant with black beans and salsa, Vermont trout with white wine, lemon, and capers. The wine list is extensive. Jackets are required for men after 6pm. The garden dining room has a sun atrium filled with huge ferns and hydrangeas; pine hutches, Windsor chairs, and burgundy floral wallpaper complete the summer atmosphere. A pianist quietly entertains in the evening.

In winter the living room is especially welcoming, as guests gather around the large fireplace and settle into the couches and wing chairs. The upstairs gallery overlooking the room contains games, chess, books, and a large TV. Tea is served at 4pm, classical music making the announcement.

The inn's 10 large guest rooms are individually decorated, boasting antiques and bright chintzes with cannonball, pencil-post, or similar beds; some have balconies and some have sitting areas. The prime accommodations, though, are in the plushly decorated cottages. Farmhouse 2 possesses a full-canopied bed and fireplace, is decorated in peach, and is furnished with handsome china lamps, a desk tucked into the bay window, a candlestand table, and floor-to-ceiling drapes. The Woodshed, Mill House, and Spring House each offer rooms with fireplaces, sitting areas, and views of the beautifully landscaped grounds and ponds. All rooms are richly appointed with fine linens and fabrics, original artwork, and fresh flowers, plus such treats as Godiva chocolates at nightly turndown.

The grounds embrace a pool, a pond with canoes, a tennis court, and two trout ponds. The Mount Snow golf course is up the road. No children under 10 are allowed.

Rates (MAP): $360–$420 double. **Dining Hours:** Daily 6–9:30pm. **Closed:** Easter to mid-May.

Across from the Inn at Sawmill Farm is the far more modest but nonetheless attractive **West Dover Inn,** Rte. 100, West Dover, VT 05356 (tel. 802/464-5207), hard against the village's white clapboard church. It occupies an informal 1846 clapboard home and offers 12 comfortably furnished rooms with plank floors, all with bath and color TV, 2 with balconies. There are also four suites with whirlpool tubs and fireplaces. Downstairs is a rustic, woody dining room serving continental/ New England cuisine, from $15 to $22.

Rates (including breakfast): Summer, $90 double; $130 suite. Fall, $100 double; $160 suite. Winter, $120 double; $195 suite. MAP rates available.

The **Deerhill Inn,** Valley View Road (P.O. Box 136), West Dover, VT 05356 (tel. 802/464-3100), a clapboard house tucked into the side of a hill, has a fine view of the valley. The new owners have spruced it up considerably. There are 15 guest rooms with bath, decorated in chintz, with oak and maple furnishings and brass or canopied beds. The prettiest room, decked out in rose and lavender, features a four-poster canopied bed with a floral dust ruffle and has French doors leading to a balcony overlooking the attractively landscaped pool. Room 6 has twin beds with an embroidered white canopy.

Guests can use the large upstairs sitting room complete with a fireplace, sofas, loveseats, and wing chairs; it offers a supply of books as well as a TV. A more formal parlor downstairs serves as a waiting area for diners. The restaurant has a good reputation. The fireplace makes it cozy in winter and it offers a view of the valley that's equally lovely in winter or summer. The menu is limited and changes seasonally but will likely feature signature dishes like the five-layered veal (three layers of veal interspersed with a layer of caramelized onions, mushrooms, and artichokes and a layer of mozzarella and tomatoes). Fish is emphasized, and another favorite is the candystripe fish (with alternating layers of white fish like bass and salmon filet). Among the appetizers, the mussels and some Cajun items are the chief draws. As for dessert, if you don't select the homemade ice cream I'd suggest the white-chocolate/pumpkin cheesecake with cara-mel sauce. Prices range from $16 to $24. The pool deck also has umbrella tables.

Rates (including full breakfast): Weekends, $120–$185 double B&B, $190–$255 double MAP; weekdays, $105–$170 double B&B, $175–$240 double MAP. **Dining Hours:** Sun–Thurs 6–9pm, Fri–Sat 6–9:30pm. **Closed:** Wed off-season, so call ahead.

For an alpine-style ski lodge, there's the nicely kept **Kitzhof,** on Rte. 100 in West Dover, VT 05356 (tel. 802/464-8310), half a mile from Mount Snow. Here no two rooms are alike except in their comfort and clean-liness. Knotty-pine boards, logs, and a fieldstone fireplace impart a moun-tain coziness; a mahogany hot tub is an added luxury. There's a BYOB bar with set-ups and a full-service restaurant. Other facilities include a heated pool.

Rates: Summer, $65 double. Fall, $89 double. Winter, $56 double weekdays, $138 double weekends. During summer many bus tours stop here.

At the **Snow Den Inn,** Rte. 100 (P.O. Box 625), West Dover, VT 05356 (tel. 802/464-9355), an 1885 farmhouse, there are eight snug rooms with bath and color TV; five have a fireplace. Most are furnished with oak beds and dressers, with braided rugs spread on pine floors. One of the fireplace rooms has a lace-canopied bed covered with a colorful fan-patterned quilt; other furnishings include a rocking chair and corner cupboard. Another fireplace room features a brass bed sporting a blue star quilt, various marble-topped pieces, and a cane-seated chair. A full breakfast is served. In win-ter, guests gather around the fire in the comfortable living room. A continental breakfast can be brought to your room.

Rates (including breakfast): Fall–winter weekends, $65–$78 per per-son per night. Spring–summer weekends, $57–$65 per person per night.

Other lodging choices include a full traditional ski lodge, the **Snow Lake Lodge,** 84 Mountain Rd., Mount Snow, VT 05356 (tel. 802/464-3333, or 800/4514211), overlooking Snow Lake and the ski slopes. The pine-paneled rooms are plain, furnished with somewhat-worn Danish-style furniture. All have a cable TV and a phone, and some even have waterbeds. Summer amenities include an outdoor pool, two lighted clay tennis courts, a cabana bar and barbecue, and boating on Snow Lake. Year-round facili-ties include two indoor hot and cool pools, entertainment in the lounge, a fitness center, and breakfast and dinner in the Lakeside Dining Room.

Rates (including breakfast): Winter, $44–$90 per person. Summer, $64 per person.

West Dover & Mount Snow Dining

Prime dining spots I've already mentioned are the **Inn at Sawmill Farm** and the **Hermitage Inn.**

Two Tannery Road (tel. 802/464-2707) has a fine reputation locally. The original old frame building, with plank floors and a piano for impromptu entertainment, offers a comfortable, romantic candlelit setting for dinner, while the high-ceilinged barnlike extension, warmed by a woodstove in winter, is most inviting in summer. Specialties include Tannery pâté with pork and veal, pine nuts, and sun-dried tomatoes, served with onion jam and crackers. For a delicious main course, try the shrimp simmered with soy sauce, ginger, honey, and sesame-seed butter or the scaloppine of veal sautéed with crumbled bacon, spinach, and madeira (the bacon and madeira give it a special kick). Desserts may be mud pie or baklava à la Nancy. Prices range from $18 to $25. The name comes from its location on the old site of two sawmills and a tannery. Take the left fork off Rte. 100 about 2 miles north of West Dover.

Hours: Dec–Mar and May–Oct, Tues–Sun 6–9:30pm; Apr and Nov, Thurs–Sun 6–9:30pm.

MARLBORO

From the West Dover and Mount Snow area, you can either cut across via East Dover, South Newfane, and West Dummerston to Rte. 30, which will take you north into Newfane, or you can double back down to Rte. 100 and continue east to Marlboro.

Marlboro is home of the famous **Marlboro Music Festival,** founded in 1951 by Rudolf Serkin and others. Each summer, dozens of the most talented musicians from America and abroad gather here for seven weeks of intensive chamber-music study and rehearsal. Weekend concerts are presented from mid-July to mid-August at Marlboro College's Persons Auditorium. If you wish to attend the concerts, you must write early for tickets to Marlboro Music, P.O. Box 10, Marlboro, VT 05344 or call 802/254-2394 (June 15 to August 15) or 215/569-4690 (before June 15).

Marlboro Lodging & Dining

Marlboro is more a state of mind than an actual place, for when you arrive at the dot on the map you'll find only a church, a post office, a few houses, and most glorious of all, an old inn right next door to the church.

At the **Whetstone Inn,** Marlboro, VT 05344 (tel. 802/254-2500), Jean and Harry Boardman welcome guests into their living room, which is lined with interesting books (from Rabelais to *Moby-Dick*) and houses a piano, a bar that first served as the post office, and a fireplace that's well used on cold Vermont days. This venerable 1786 building has always flourished as a tavern, except briefly for 15 years in the 1930s. Many of the musicians performing at the festival stay here, so you'll enjoy interesting company in addition to the fascinating conversation likely to flow from Harry, who spent a decade at San Diego's Salk Institute educating professionals about new biological developments and their effects on our society. The rooms (some with bath) vary in decor and size, but most are furnished in keeping with the inn's colonial atmosphere. All look out on the meadowed and forested grounds.

Meals are served in what was originally the big old kitchen, with a fireplace large enough to accommodate a cooking crane. Full breakfasts are $7 to $9 and complete dinners run $18 to $25. Though Jean will accommodate friends of yours at the table, dining is really for guests only. In winter, dinner is served on Saturday; in summer, on concert nights—Wednesday to Saturday. Dishes will be homemade, from the cheddar-cheese soup and roast leg of lamb or pork to the brandy-Alexander pie. In winter, the inn is ideal for cross-country skiing, sledding, and snowshoeing.

Rates: $65–$75 double without bath, $80–85 double with bath. Rates go up in July–Aug during the Music Festival, when priority is given to weekly rentals.

While in Marlboro, drive to the top of Hogback Mountain for the spectacular 100-mile view. The **Skyline Restaurant,** Rte. 9 (tel. 802/464-5535), is at the summit and makes a great spot for a Vermont breakfast of waffles and real maple syrup.

Hours: Mon–Tues 7:30am–3pm, Wed–Sun 7:30am–8 or 9pm.

BRATTLEBORO

For most shopping and services, Marlboro residents drive the 18 miles into Brattleboro, an industrial town that was the first colonial settlement in Vermont. Today it's one of the state's larger cities (pop. 13,000), a center for book and paper manufacturing and home to a major optical company. In the early 1970s the town was discovered by urban pioneers of the sixties generation, and they give the town its relaxed air. Today they are artists, potters, writers, musicians, artisans, and entrepreneurs and the results of many of their labors can be seen at **Vermont Artisan Designs,** 115 Main St. (tel. 802/257-7044). As for famous sons, Mormon leader Brigham Young was born nearby in Windham County, and Rudyard Kipling married a Brattleboro girl in 1892 and they lived here for some time.

En route to Brattleboro, book lovers will want to stop at the **Bear Book Shop,** off Rte. 9 (tel. 802/464-2260), where you'll find 30,000 categorized books housed in a big old barn. Owner John Greenberg was once a professor of philosophy in Montréal. In summer, a fun Saturday farmer's market is held west of Brattleboro along Rte. 9.

Brattleboro Lodging & Dining

The accommodations here are primarily motels. Your best bet is probably the **Motel 6,** Rte. 5N, Brattleboro, VT 05301 (tel. 802/254-6007, or 800/258-1980), where rooms rent for $45.

T. J. Buckley's, 132 Elliot St. (tel. 802/257-4922), is an unlikely local dining favorite operated by Michael Fuller; this old diner, now avant-garde looking, seats 16 maximum. Fuller is a creative cook who prepares a different menu daily, consisting of four entrees made with local and often organic ingredients. You may find swordfish with roasted lobster stock, green peppercorns, and horseradish served on a bed of fava beans and lentils in a lemongrass broth or tenderloin of beef with shiitake mushrooms and cracked peppercorns cooked in a caper-veal stock with fresh thyme. The $23 price includes salad and rolls. The desserts are prepared daily. On weekends you'll need to reserve at least a week in advance. Beer and wine only.

Hours: Tues–Sun 6pm–closing.

The other local spot is **Common Ground,** 25 Elliot St. (tel. 802/257-0855), where in summer many of the craftspeople can be seen lingering over vegetarian and natural foods on the second-floor enclosed terrace. Downstairs, the entry and stair serve as the town's alternative bulletin board. It's strictly vegetarian, with such items as cashew burgers, lentil stew, lasagne, bean-and-cheese burritos, and stir-fries with vegetables as well as tofu, tempeh, and seitan. Prices range from $4 to $10.

Hours: Mon and Wed–Thurs 11:30am–8pm, Fri–Sat 11:30am–9pm, Sun 10:30am–2:30pm and 11:30am–8pm.

NEWFANE, GRAFTON, CHESTER & SAXTONS RIVER

Area Attractions

From Brattleboro it's about 17 miles along Rte. 30 to Newfane, another 12 miles to Grafton, and another 7 miles north to Chester and east to Saxtons River.

All these villages are picture-book New England, their gracious homes and buildings set around town greens and white clapboard churches with spires. There's not an awful lot to do, but that's the whole point—this is cycling and rambling country, havens for those who just want to enjoy the bounties of the mountains and the backroads.

Newfane clusters around its Village Green with the Windham County Courthouse at the center. Two country inns and the First Congregational Church complete the scene. As you travel along the route you'll find plenty of antiques shops to stop at. East of Newfane, **Putney** is a major center for crafts lovers. Here you can stop at the **Green Mountain Spinnery** (tel. 802/387-4528), where they spin wool and other yarns. The

Brandywine Glassworks (tel. 802/387-4032) is nearby on Fort Hill Road, off Rte. 5.

Grafton was settled in 1780 and grew throughout the 19th century. Farming, milling, and soapstone quarrying were the major occupations of the villagers, and there were about 10,000 sheep grazing in the surrounding meadows in 1850. The town was on the Boston–Montréal stage route and the Phelps Hotel (now the Old Tavern) serviced overnight travelers. Around the turn of the century, however, the town declined as people were lured west or moved to the cities. By 1940 many of the community's buildings had become decrepit, and it wasn't until the Windham Foundation was founded in 1963 that serious restoration work was undertaken. Now you can stroll (or ride in a horse and carriage enjoying a narrative tour) through the beautifully restored town and visit the **Grafton Village Cheese Company,** half a mile south on Townshend Road (tel. 802/843-2221). They make their very own Covered Bridge Cheddar, and you can watch the process and take a few tangy samples home.

Hours: June–Oct, Mon–Fri 8:30am–4pm, Sat 10am–4pm.

History buffs will want to stop at the **Grafton Historical Society Museum,** on Main Street (tel. 802/843-2305), just down from the post office. Old photographs, memorabilia, historical objects, and genealogical books reflect the town's story.

Hours: July–Aug, Sat–Sun 2:30–4:40pm; June and Sept to mid-Oct, Sat 2:30–4:40pm.

Chester is another photographer's and artist's dream, with a Village Green and more than 20 pre–Civil War buildings faced in gleaming mica schist. It's a terminus for the **Green Mountain Flyer** that steams 26 miles round-trip from Bellows Falls to Chester. Trains operate in summer and during special holidays. Tickets cost $12 for adults, $10 for seniors and children 3 to 12, and $3 for those under 3.

In **Dummerston,** along the route between Brattleboro and Newfane, you'll have the chance to see one of the longest **covered bridges** in Vermont, spanning the West River.

Newfane Lodging & Dining

Before Jacques Allembert took over the classically proportioned **Four Columns Inn,** on the Common at 230 West St., Newfane, VT 05345 (tel. 802/365-7713), it was known primarily for its cuisine. Today this 150-year-old building with its Greek Revival columns and front porch houses a marvelous country inn complete with a trout pond and pool, flower and herb gardens, an old-fashioned swimming hole, and cross-country ski trails across the property. The dining room is still exceptional: Comfortable and very appealing, with large brick fireplace, old beams, Windsor chairs, and deer trophies, it's reminiscent of a European hunting lodge. The cuisine is always exciting. Among the soups may be a white bean with sausage or a fine parsley; these you can follow with an appetizer like pheasant pâté or oysters, then a choice of entrees like chicken breast in foie-gras sauce with mushrooms, duck with sour-cherry/rosemary sauce, filet mignon with cabernet sauce, and scallops and shrimp with coconut milk, lemongrass, and green-curry sauce. Prices range from $18 to $25. In the main inn, which was fashioned after the original owner's wife's southern mansion, are 12 guest rooms; several more are in the renovated barn. All have a bath and are furnished in country style with quilts on the brass or similar beds, chintz on the walls, and assorted items like armoires and wicker chairs.

Rates: Winter, spring, and summer, $120–$170 double B&B (continental breakfast). Foliage season, $220–$270 double MAP. **Dining Hours:** Wed–Mon 6–9pm. **Closed:** Apr and possibly Nov.

Eric and Gundy Weindl run the **Old Newfane Inn,** Rte. 30, Newfane, VT 05345 (tel. 802/365-4427), a typical New England inn with uneven floors, beamed ceilings, and flocked wallpaper. The dining room possesses a large warming brick fireplace and pewter lamps and offers fare that runs from filet of sole amandine and frogs' legs provençal to veal marsala, duck à l'orange, and a variety of steaks. The desserts include classics like cherries jubilee, crêpes Suzette, and baked Alaska. Main dishes go for $16 to $26. The inn's 10 guest rooms are furnished with pleasant oak pieces, rockers, and wing chairs.

Rates (including continental breakfast): $115–$155 double. **Dining Hours:** Tues–Sun 6–9pm. **Closed:** Apr to mid-May and Nov to mid-Dec.

Grafton, Chester & Saxtons River Lodging & Dining

At the center of the idyllic, meticulously kept village of Grafton, the **Old Tavern,** Grafton, VT 05146 (tel. 802/843-2231), is a town landmark dating from 1801. It occupies a main building as well as a number of historic homes in the village and has a long and proud tradition dating back to 1788. Among the famous visitors who've stayed here are Thoreau, Emerson, Hawthorne, Teddy Roosevelt, and Rudyard Kipling. Today the tradition continues, with many prominent folks staying.

The main building contains 14 guest rooms, all with bath, some with canopied beds. Behind it in what was the livery is a bar with an upstairs gallery, a slate fireplace, and beams and barn siding. The other accommodations are found in beautifully furnished antique-laden cottages—like White Gates, Barrett House, Tuttle House. Most of these rooms contain canopied beds, mahogany chests, comfortable armchairs, candlestand tables, and sitting rooms ideally furnished for quiet reading. They have antique accents like broken-scroll mirrors and demilune tables set with a Staffordshire vase or similar filled with fresh flowers. A couple of the cottages are reserved primarily for families and furnished appropriately. There are no phones or TVs in any of the rooms. The place is filled with authentic antiques (and a few reproductions). A number of really tastefully antique-filled guesthouses sleeping seven to nine, with full kitchens, are also available.

Among the dining rooms are several choices: a formal room, whose oak tables are set with placemats and Mottahedeh china; the pine room, with a beamed ceiling, a fireplace, and Windsor chairs; and the garden room, with a brick floor and potted flowers and plants. The food in each is traditional New England fare—broiled steaks and chops, New England lobster pie, rack of lamb with minted madeira sauce, plus lighter entrees like the salmon with fresh yellow-pepper purée and free-range chicken marinated in white wine and herbs and served with fresh rosemary sauce. To start, try the smoked rainbow trout with horseradish sauce or the classic escargots with garlic butter. To finish, choose from the selection of parfaits, strawberry shortcake, and white-chocolate mousse. Entrees run $15 to $19.

The Old Tavern is not the place to visit if you're looking for nightlife—come in search of peace and quiet, a comfortable chair, a good book, and a brandy in front of a crackling fire. The inn also offers 30km of cross-country ski trails, sleds and toboggans, and a natural swimming pond. Two tennis courts just down the street are free to guests. Platform tennis and a games room with billiards and Ping-Pong complete the facilities.

Rates: Rooms and cottages, $120–$210 double; $480–$520 guesthouse. **Dining Hours:** Mon–Sat noon–2pm and 6–9pm, Sun 11:30am–2pm and 6–9pm. **Closed:** Christmas and Apr.

The **Inn at Long Last,** on the Village Green (P.O. Box 589), Chester, VT 05143 (tel. 802/875-2444), reflects the personality of innkeeper Jack Coleman, who has discovered his dream at last and happily shares it with guests. A former president of Haverford College, Jack has named the 30 rooms after local Vermonters and authors, artists, and musicians he loves—Nathaniel Currier, George Orwell, Robert Frost, and E. B White. All have baths and are furnished differently in singular style. Step onto the front porch and into the lobby and you'll feel the peace and harmony that reigns in the lobby with its stone fireplace and scattering of sofas and armchairs. It's even more obvious in the library, where you can sink into a leather armchair and enjoy a glass of sherry as you read one of the more than 2,500 volumes.

The inn is also known for its dining room, where you can enjoy a candlelit meal in a turn-of-the-century atmosphere. The menu, featuring seven or so entrees, might offer broiled filet of salmon with Thai melon salsa, pan-seared ribeye steak with red zinfandel/juniper demiglaze, or pan-roasted venison medallions with dried-cherry confit and cabernet demiglaze. The appetizers are equally inspiring and may include sautéed crab cakes with capers and sun-dried tomato-basil vinaigrette or flavorsome slices of grilled smoked pork on a corncake with apple-pistachio butter. Facilities include tennis courts, a fishing stream, and a variety of games.

Rates: $120 double B&B; $100 per person MAP or $170 for two MAP.
Dining Hours: Tues–Thurs and Sun 6–8pm, Fri–Sat 6–9pm. **Closed:**
Apr and 10 days in mid-Nov.

What makes the **Inn Victoria,** on the Green (P.O. Box 788), Chester, VT
05143 (tel. 800/732-4288), special is the dedication its innkeepers devote
to afternoon tea. The inn was built in the 1850s and is furnished in Victorian style, boasting parlors with Empire-style couches and Victorian
armchairs. There are seven rooms and suites, all with great deep tubs for
soaking. The beds are high-back carved Victorians with plenty of pillows
and cushions. KC and Tom Lanagan set a lovely table with elegant bone
china and lace placemats for their breakfasts and afternoon teas. They also
operate the Tea Pot Shoppe, and many a guest carries home one of their
handsome teapots, like the Foxy Lady or Farie Glen.

Rates (including breakfast and afternoon tea): $95–$160 double.

At the heart of Saxtons River, you'll find the small and casual **Inn at
Saxtons River,** Main Street, Saxtons River, VT 05154 (tel. 802/869-2110),
a homey idiosyncratically flavored place. It's not your precious perfectly
coiffed New England inn. Built in 1903, it has a character all its own and
is reasonably priced.

Locals gather at the copper-topped bar to sit and chat on the wooden
seats that look as if they came from a local theater or cinema. Many of the
16 rooms exhibit bold floral wallpapers, oak chests with teardrop handles,
clawfoot tubs without showers, and assorted furnishings—couches, lounge
chairs, and pie-crust tables. Room 9 has black-and-white floral wallpaper,
an iron-and-brass bed with a silver-white coverlet, tasseled white swagged
curtains, a chest and mirror, a comfy chair, and a small bath with shower.
Room 6 is a brilliant lime-green coordinated with yellow-green-mauve
floral curtains and comforter, and among the furnishings are a yellow
bamboo chair and a white leather wing chair. On the third floor, the
wallpapers and color schemes seem to get even wilder and the rooms
share baths down the hall. Room 22 sports black-and-rose wallpaper, a
lavender comforter on the bed, a lime carpet on the floor, and pelmeted
pink curtains.

Two of the most popular gathering places for guests are the upstairs
porch, with wicker and hanging flowering plants, and the small TV/VCR
room. Throughout the house are southern pine door frames and woodwork. The dining room continues the colorful flair with its Tiffany
lampshades, floral tablecloths, and rush-seated chairs painted various
shades of pink, yellow, jade, crimson, and orange. The food is traditionally prepared—steak au poivre, chicken marsala, roast duck with
cranberry-nut sauce, and scampi in garlic-butter sauce. Prices range from
$15 to $19. The appetizers are equally popular—try the smoked trout
with horseradish sauce or the steamed littlenecks.

Rates (including breakfast): $88–$98 double. **Dining Hours:** Sun and
Tues–Thurs 5–9pm, Fri–Sat 5–10pm. **Closed:** Mar–Apr for five weeks.

The **Windham Hill Inn,** West Townshend, VT 05359 (tel. 802/874-4080), takes some finding, but it's worth searching out. It's set on 150 secluded woodland-mountain acres overlooking Rattle Snake Mountain and offers a peaceful garden filled with irises, roses, poppies, pansies, and a redolent fringe tree. Ten guest rooms are in the restored 1825 farmhouse and five in the white barn annex, all with bath. Most have beds with candlewick spreads, country maple furnishings, and chintz wallpapers. My favorites are in the barn—a real barn where chamber concerts are performed. Here most rooms have high beamed ceilings and, best of all, decks that have gorgeous views; some are low beamed, like Matilda's Room, furnished with a bed, a rocker, a trunk, and a floor lamp, plus that glorious view and deck.

Guests can choose among three parlors—two comfortably furnished with antiques; the third, which as an outside deck, furnished more casually with wicker pieces. Each one has either a fireplace or wood-burning stove. In the small dining room with oak tables covered with pink cloths and wall niches displaying china, a five-course meal is served that might feature duck with pear, sage, and port-wine sauce or swordfish with jicama-orange relish. A full country breakfast is also served.

In summer guests can hike trails that lead to a brook with a swimming hole; in winter the trails are for cross-country skiing. Innkeepers Ken and Linda Busteed will arrange hiking, biking, canoeing, and fishing trips for you, box lunch included. A pool and a tennis court are planned for the future.

Rates (MAP): Winter, $195–$230 double. Summer, $180–$215 double. Fall, $215–$250 double.

After Dark in the Area

Evening entertainment is largely confined to having a drink in a cozy spot like the **Hermitage Inn** and following it with dinner. During summer, the **Mount Snow Playhouse** (tel. 802/464-3333 or 295-7016) offers summer stock.

You can find plenty of *après-ski* enjoyment at the main base lodge at **Mount Snow** and at the **Snow Barn** on the access road. Other favorite spots include the **Deacon's Den,** the **Dover Bar & Grill,** and **The Pub** in Wilmington.

The Grafton & Chester Area
Special & Recreational Activities

Boating: At Lake Whitingham and in Woodford State Park you can rent a sailboat.

Camping: Four state parks in the area offer camping: Molly Stark in Wilmington, Fort Dummer in Brattleboro, Townshend in

Newfane, and Woodford in Woodford. For information, contact the Department of Forests, Parks and Recreation, Waterbury, VT 05602 (tel. 802/241-3655).

Canoeing: At Lake Whitingham, between Bennington and Wilmington, south of Rte. 9, you can rent a canoe. Also at Harriman Reservoir.

Cycling: For information, contact Bike Vermont, P.O. Box 207, Woodstock, VT 05091 (tel. 802/457-3553). It offers inn-to-inn bicycle touring from May to October on weekends and five-day trips. Rentals are available. Or try Vermont Bicycle Tours, P.O. Box 711, Bristol, VT 05443 (tel. 802/453-4811). They'll also supply bikes.

Fishing: For information, contact the Vermont Fish and Wildlife Department, Waterbury, VT 05676 (tel. 802/241-3700). Licenses are available by mail, but allow plenty of time. A useful guide to fishing and a booklet outlining state laws and regulations are also available.

Golf: There's an 18-hole course at the Sitzmark Lodge, East Dover Road, Wilmington (tel. 802/464-3384), and also at Mount Snow Country Club (tel. 802/464-3333), where the fourth hole was named one of the most beautiful in North America. Haystak Golf Club, Mann Road (R.R. 1, Box 173), Wilmington (tel. 802/464-8301), is an 18-hole, par-72 championship course. Snow Lake Lodge and the Hermitage offer golf packages.

Hiking: Among the legendary mountain trails are the Long Trail, the Molly Stark Trail, and the Appalachian Trail. The Thomson Nature Trail leads from the summit of Mount Snow (follow the signs for the Deer Run ski trail). Long Trail intersects Rte. 9 in Woodford.

For detailed information and maps, contact the Appalachian Trail Conference, P.O. Box 236, Harpers Ferry, WV 25425. Long Trail information can be obtained from the Green Mountain Club, Inc., Rte. 100 (R.R. 1, Box 650), Waterbury Center, VT 05677 (tel. 802/244-7037).

Horseback Riding: Flame Stables, 100 S. Jacksonville Rd., Wilmington (tel. 802/464-8329), has trail rides for $10 per hour. Valley View Horse & Tack Shop, Box 48A, Northwest Hill Road, Pownal, VT 05261 (tel. 802/823-4649), offers trail rides and such specialty rides as Haunted Halloween rides. Take Rte. 346 off Rte. 7.

Ice Skating: There's a public rink in Brattleboro—the Memorial Park Skating Rink (tel. 802/257-2311).

Mountain Biking: Mount Snow is a major mountain-biking facility, with a school and rentals. It also hosts World Cup races. Rentals are about $30 per day and lift tickets are about the same.

Picnicking: Good picnicking is available in the state parks: Molly Stark, Townshend, and Woodford.

Shopping for Crafts: Many craftspeople have settled in the area, and their works are displayed in various locations. At the Marlboro Craft Studios (tel. 802/257-0181), Lucy Gratwick exhibits her hand-weaving; the Applewoods, their furniture and wood pieces (tel. 802/254-2908); and Malcolm Wright (tel. 802/254-2168), his wood-fired pottery. Call any of them to make an appointment.

Skiing: Besides Mount Snow/Haystack, there's also Hogback, Marlboro, VT 05344 (tel. 802/464-3942), which has 12 trails and 4 T-bars.

Mount Snow's cross-country centers are at the Hermitage, P.O. Box 457, Wilmington, VT 05363 (tel. 802/464-3511), with 50km of trails; Sitzmark, East Dover Road, Wilmington, VT 05363 (tel. 802/464-3384), has 40km of trails; and the White House, P.O. Box 757, Wilmington, VT 05363 (tel. 802/464-2135), 45km of trails.

Other centers include the Grafton Ponds Cross Country Ski Center at the Old Tavern (tel. 802/843-2400), with 30km of trails; and Prospect Ski Mountain Touring Center, Woodford, near Bennington (tel. 802/442-2575), with 40km of trails.

State Parks: For information, contact the Department of Forests, Parks, and Recreation, 103 S. Main St., Waterbury, VT 05676 (tel. 802/241-3655).

Swimming: Try Lake Whitingham. There's also a beach at Lake Raponda, north of Rte. 9, between Wilmington and Brattleboro, and a couple of beaches at Harriman Reservoir at Mountain Mills, off Fairview Avenue, and at Ward's Cover, off Rte. 100. In Newfane's Townshend State Park also. Sitzmark Lodge, the White House, and several other accommodations have pools.

Tennis: There are courts at the Snow Lake Lodge (tel. 802/464-3333) and also at Sitzmark (tel. 802/464-3384). There are municipal courts in Wilmington and Brattleboro. Call the chambers of commerce for information.

AN EXCURSION INTO SOUTHERN NEW HAMPSHIRE

Wander across the border from Vermont or Massachusetts into southwestern New Hampshire and you're in the Monadnock region. Dubbed the "Quiet Corner," the Monadnock is indeed that. Solitary 3,165-foot-high **Mount Monadnock,** called "one that stands alone" by Native Americans, dominates the well-forested area and is the major reason for visiting. More than 200 lakes and ponds offer a variety of activities: swimming, fishing, waterskiing, canoeing, and sailing.

In addition, the area possesses several towns and somnolent villages. Among the prettiest are **Fitzwilliam** and **Hancock,** both boasting comfortable inns, and **Peterborough,** model for Thornton Wilder's Grover's Corners in *Our Town*. **Hancock** is a very pretty town where every building on its main street is in the National Register of Historic Places. The old clapboard and brick homes, four-room schoolhouse, town market, and classic steepled church evoke an earlier era. Today Peterborough offers a somewhat unique theater experience at the **New England Marionette Opera** (tel. 603/924-4333), a 135-seat theater with velvet-and-mahogany seats and a state-of-the-art sound system. The **Peterborough Players** (tel. 603/924-7585) perform during summer at the theater on the 125-acre Hadley Farm. Alumni of this venerable company include Avery Brooks, Jean Stapleton, and James Whitmore. Keene is the commercial center.

Traditionally, artists have been drawn to the region—Henry David Thoreau and Ralph Waldo Emerson both climbed Mount Monadnock. The **home and studio of sculptor Augustus Saint-Gaudens** (tel. 603/675-2175) is farther north on Rte. 12A in Cornish, open Memorial Day to October, daily from 9am to 4:30pm. And Willa Cather is buried in Jaffrey. Today the **MacDowell Colony,** west of Peterborough, continues the artistic tradition, while the **Sharon Arts Center** (tel. 603/924-7256), 4 miles south of Peterborough, attracts artists and artisans from throughout the area. It contains two art galleries and a craft shop and offers a variety of lectures and workshops year round.

Area Lodging & Dining

The **Chesterfield Inn,** Rte. 9 (P.O. Box 155), Chesterfield, NH 03443 (tel. 603/256-3211), is an exquisitely decorated lodging that offers 13 rooms with bath, phone, and TV (8 with fireplace). Rooms in the new Johanna Wetherby building have private garden patios. Nine are in the restored 1787 farmhouse/carriage house, and these have great character with their handsome beams and many fine antiques. In Room 14 you'll find a round Empire-style table and on it a ginger jar, a scallop-shell secretary, attractive oak sidetables, and wing chairs, all set against pretty blue-and-rose floral wallpaper. Carved Victorian loveseats, decoratively inlaid desks, and drop-leaf tables are just some of the fetching antiques found throughout. The dining room serves American and continental cuisine— like duck with raspberry sauce, grilled gingered swordfish, and lamb shanks with rosemary and zinfandel. Prices run $16 to $22.

Rates (including full breakfast): Summer, $125–$150 double; $165 suite. Winter, $125–$170 double; $180 suite. Foliage season (MAP), $200–$255 double or suite. **Dining Hours:** Daily 5:30–9pm.

The stately **Monadnock Inn** (ca. 1830), 379 Main St., Jaffrey, NH 03452 (tel. 603/532-7001), offers 14 country-style guest rooms with bath. Some

Three Suggested Driving Routes

First Route

From Peterborough, take Rte. 101 west for 2 miles to Rte. 137. Turn left on Rte. 137, heading south to Jaffrey, in which you can visit the **Amos Fortune Home** and the **Old Red Schoolhouse.**

Then head west on Rte. 124. This road offers 12 miles or so of scenic splendor over hill and dale, skirting the southern edge of **Mount Monadnock** to the town of Marlborough. When you reach Marlborough, turn right on Rte. 101, heading east. Though this is a main highway, it skirts Dublin Lake and bisects **Dublin,** New England's highest town and the town in which *Yankee* magazine and the *Old Farmer's Almanac* are published. Turn left 2 miles east of Dublin onto Rte. 137 and drive to **Hancock,** an old New England village with its Green and meetinghouse with a Paul Revere bell. Continuing through Hancock, Rte. 137 connects with U.S. 202. Turn right on Rte. 202 and ride back to Peterborough.

Second Route

For a much shorter itinerary, start in Jaffrey and take Rte. 124 west. Turn left after about 4 miles and go to **Fitzwilliam.** Then take Rte. 119 east 6 miles toward Rindge. Turn left off Rte. 119 to the **Cathedral of the Pines,** a moving outdoor shrine built 40 or so years ago by Dr. and Mrs. Douglas Sloane in memory of their son who died in World War II. From the Altar of the Nation, a national memorial for all American war dead, are spectacular views of Mount Monadnock. From the cathedral, retrace your tracks to Rte. 119 and turn right to U.S. 202, which proceeds into Jaffrey.

Third Route

From Peterborough, take Rte. 101, skirting **Miller State Park** and **Pack Mountain,** turning left about 7 miles out toward Wilton. From Wilton, travel northeast on Rte. 31 past the **Curtis Dogwood Reservation,** ablaze with white and pink flowers, and travel via Greenfield along Rte. 31 to **Crotched Mountain** and then into Bennington. Return to Peterborough on U.S. 202 south.

are definitely nicer than others: Some have four-posters or brass beds; others have Ethan Allen–style beds matched with painted furniture, as in Room 104. The third-floor rooms are cozy and interesting because of their shapes. On the ground floor, guests enjoy the parlor, complete with a fireplace, a console piano, and assorted comfortable seating. There's also a bar warmed in winter by a woodstove and a dining room decked out in traditional style with Windsor chairs and stenciled walls. The menu is limited, offering six or so entrees like braised quails duxelles, lemon chicken, fettuccine primavera, and veal with artichoke-mushroom cream sauce, priced from $13 to $20.

Rates: $85–$105 double (slightly more in foliage season). **Dining Hours:** Mon–Fri 11:30am–2pm and 5:30–9pm, Sun 10am–1pm and 5:30–9pm.

The **Hancock Inn,** Main Street, Hancock, NH 03449 (tel. 603/525-3318), is a seasoned inn, having operated continuously since 1789. The staircase creaks as you step up to the 11 guest rooms with bath, furnished with antique country pieces against stenciled walls or striking murals. Room 16 has a pastoral scene painted by famous itinerant painter/inventor/journalist Rufus Porter. Its furnishings include a pencil four-poster canopied bed matched with a painted blanket chest, a maple dresser, a rocker, and a wing chair, among other items. Most of the rooms' wide-plank floors are graced with braided area rugs. The ground floor features an inviting tavern room that serves as a common room for guests. The dining room positively glows at night. It's sponge painted in red with Colonial blue trim and lit by tin wall sconces and candles on the tables. The fare is traditional New England: baked Boston scrod; Nantucket seafood casserole with scallops, shrimp, and lobster; filet mignon; chicken amandine; and lamb chop mixed grill. The specialty, though, is Shaker cranberry pot roast that's so tender it just flakes on the fork. Prices range from $16 to $22.

Rates (including breakfast): $108–$160 double. **Dining Hours:** Mon–Sat 6pm–closing, Sun 5pm–closing.

The **Fitzwilliam Inn,** on the Common, Fitzwilliam, NH 03447 (tel. 603/585-9000), dating back to 1796, is almost as venerable as the Hancock Inn and has been operated by the Wallace family for over 30 years. The current proprietor's wife is a professional musician and in winter chamber concerts are often given on Sunday afternoon in the parlor, in which a grand piano shares space with Victorian furnishings.

Old family portraits and wedding certificates hang in the beamed dining room, along with Audubon prints. An adjoining room displays the family's huge basket collection. For summer dining, the Country Dining Room overlooks the pool and garden and exhibits some handsomely painted corner cupboards. The food is traditional—steaks, salmon, trout, stuffed chicken—priced from $9 to $18. Guests also have access to a library room with a TV. In the tap room the fireplace with cooking cradle and pots is original to the building complex.

There are 25 guest rooms (12 with bath), each individually furnished in simple country fashion. Room 5 has chintz wallpaper and stenciling and a sage-green painted chest, while Room 16 sports a pink gingham coverlet and curtains set against rose-colored wallpaper.

Rates: $50–$65 double. **Dining Hours:** Mon–Thurs 8–9:30am, noon–2pm, and 6–9pm; Fri–Sat 8–9:30am, noon–2pm, and 5:30–9pm; Sun 8–9:30am and noon–8pm.

The **Greenfield Inn,** at Rtes. 31 and 136, Greenfield, NH 03047 (tel. 603/547-6327), 10 minutes from Greenfield State Park, is run by friendly Victor and Barbara Mangini. The old Victorian house has a wrap-around veranda leading onto a spacious deck that overlooks Mount Monadnock. Guests have use of a hammock, a TV room, a comfy parlor, and a breakfast room in which a full buffet breakfast is served. The 13 guest rooms, most with bath, are attractively furnished with chintz wallpapers and oak, pine, and other furnishings. In the Samson and Delilah Room a brass bed is covered with a rose-and-cream eider, sharing space with a rocker, a table with a mirror, and a rush-seated stool.

Rates (including breakfast): $59–$109 double.

The **Inn at Crotched Mountain,** Mountain Road (off Rte. 47), Francestown, NH 03043 (tel. 603/588-6840), an ivy-covered brick building, has a magnificent setting on a mountainside overlooking a valley and wooded hills—a surprisingly delightful hideaway. The ceilings are low in parts of the building, as it was built in 1822. There are 14 rooms, 8 with bath. Room 9 is my favorite because it has a door that leads out to the pool and offers a dramatic view. Three rooms have fireplaces, one has a woodstove, and all are nicely furnished with maple pieces, braided rugs, and so on. Guests can use the comfortable living room furnished with wing chairs, a sofa, and two fireplaces. The dining room is crisply turned out with white and red napery and maple Windsor chairs. In the cozy Winslow tavern you can snuggle up by the fireside at tables made from old wagon-wheel hubs. The menu features steaks, chops, or chicken teriyaki, priced from $9 to $13.50. Facilities include a large pool, two clay tennis courts, and 5½ miles of cross-country skiing trails.

Rates: Summer and fall, $70–$80 double MAP weekends, $40–$45 B&B weekdays. Winter weekend package for two nights plus one dinner, $170–$190 MAP, $80–$90 B&B. **Dining Hours:** Fri–Sat 6–8pm. **Closed:** Three weeks in Nov.

Ram in the Thicket, Maple Street, Wilton, NH 03449 (tel. 603/654-6440), reflects the entertaining, fun personality of the Rev. Andrew Tempelman. It's a delightful white clapboard Victorian, set on a little hill in a very quiet area. The rooms are tastefully decorated with wicker, chintz, ruffled curtains, and brass-and-iron beds with country comforters; some have canopied four-posters. The ground floor houses several intimate dining rooms, candlelit at night, that offer fine food with a classical music background. The menu might feature such dishes as chicken breast sautéed and splashed with maple syrup and maple liqueur, shrimp Pondicherry with green and red peppers and onions with spices, and pork glazed with honey, molasses, and mustard and encrusted with chopped roasted pecans and buttered breadcrumbs. Prices range from $16 to $20. For summer dining there's a screened-in porch overlooking the garden. What-ever you do, take a seat at the tiny bar and listen to the philosophy of the ex-Reverend as he serves up a few bons mots along with an ounce or two of alcohol.

Rates (including breakfast): $70 double without bath, $85 double with bath. **Dining Hours:** Wed–Thurs and Sun 5:30–8:30pm, Fri–Sat 5:30–9:30pm.

At the bottom of the hill that leads up to the Inn at Crotched Mountain, **Maître Jacques,** Mountain Road, Crotched Mountain, Francestown (tel. 603/588-6655), operates in a little house. Fresh flowers grace the tables; paintings and prints of France adorn the walls. The chef hails from Brittany and prepares such dishes as roast duckling with chestnut stuffing and green-peppercorn sauce, veal sweetbreads financière (with mush-rooms), and breast of chicken Chesapeake (stuffed with Boursin, leeks, and blended crabmeat, with a white-wine velouté sauce). Prices run $14 to $20.

Hours: Tues–Sat 5–9:30pm, Sun 3–7:30pm.

Southern New Hampshire
Special & Recreational Activities

Fishing: Licenses are available from town clerks and sporting-goods stores. Nonresidents can contact the New Hampshire Fish and Game Department, 34 Bridge St., Concord, NH 03301 (tel. 603/271-3421).

Golf: Bretwood Golf Course, East Surry Road, Keene (tel. 603/352-7626); Keene Country Club, R.R. 2, Box 264, Keene (tel. 603/352-9722).

Hiking: Mount Monadnock is the most climbed mountain in the United States. A round-trip hike to the top will take about three hours. For information, call Monadnock State Park at 603/532-8862. For additional hiking, see "State Parks," below.

At Crotched Mountain there are three trails to the summit. The signposted Bennington Trail starts 3 miles north of Greenfield on Rte. 31 and is probably the easiest to find.

Skiing: Temple Mountain, Peterborough (tel. 603/924-6949), has a quadruple-chair lift, snowmaking, night skiing, and 35 miles of cross-country skiing. For more cross-country, Road's End Farm, Jackson Hill Road, Chesterfield (tel. 603/363-4703), has 32km of trails.

State Parks: Miller State Park, Peterborough, Rte. 101, offers a scenic route to the summit of Pack Monadnock Mountain and opportunities for picnicking and hiking around the summit.

Pisgah State Park, Chesterfield, Hinsdale, Winchester, off Rte. 63 or Rte. 119, affords 13,000 acres of wilderness for hiking, hunting, and fishing, and ski touring and snowmobiling in winter. Greenfield State Park, off Rte. 136, shelters Otter Lake for swimming. Picnicking and camping are also available.

Mid-July is the time to visit Rhododendron State Park, Rte. 119, Fitzwilliam, when 16 acres of wild rhododendron burst into blossom.

Epilogue
And Don't Forget the Big Apple and...

Sometimes all we need to revive our dampened spirits is a break from our daily routine, from the same home surroundings with the same furniture and the same view out the window, and what better way to accomplish this than simply to pack a bag, hop a cab or a subway, and check into a hotel for a new perspective on New York City and its pleasures? Such a weekend could even put a little spice back into your love life.

Never been south of Canal Street or seen Battery Park City, South Street Seaport, the Statue of Liberty, Fraunces Tavern, or Delmonico's? Then why not stay the weekend at the World Trade Center's New York Vista and do it all? And the Vista boasts the largest and best hotel fitness center in New York. Also in the World Trade Center is the magnificent Windows on the World with its staggering views (due to reopen in spring 1996). If you and your significant other need a romantic getaway, spend a weekend at the Inn at Irving Place. Or you can enjoy a weekend at the Waldorf, the Plaza, the Four Seasons, the St. Moritz, the St. Regis, the Pierre—the list goes on and on. Find out about the many weekend packages these hotels offer at low prices by calling them directly or by writing and requesting the tour package directory from the Division of Tourism, New York State Department of Commerce, One Commerce Plaza, Albany, NY 12245 (tel. 518/474-4116). You can also pick one up at the Convention and Visitors Bureau, 2 Columbus Circle (tel. 212/397-8222)—the bureau is scheduled to move sometime in 1996, so check on the address first.

Note: For full coverage of Manhattan's hotels, restaurants, attractions, and so forth, see *Frommer's New York City.*

Or you can go farther afield and fly off to a dream weekend by taking advantage of those accumulated free air miles or the low fares that airlines have offered since deregulation. The possibilities are infinite. Some tour operators even run special weekend packages to London. All it takes to create a wonderful weekend is a little bit of imagination, a phone or fax, you and your loved one, and a lust for life.

Good luck!

Index

FROMMER'S COMPLETE TRAVEL GUIDES

(Comprehensive guides to sightseeing, dining, and accommodations, with selections in all price ranges from deluxe to budget)

Acapulco/Ixtapa/Taxco, 2nd Ed.

Alaska, 4th Ed.

Arizona '96

Australia, 4th Ed.

Austria, 6th Ed.

Bahamas '96

Belgium/Holland/Luxembourg, 4th Ed.

Bermuda '96

Budapest & the Best of Hungary, 1st Ed.

California '96

Canada, 9th Ed.

Caribbean '96

Carolinas/Georgia, 3rd Ed.

Colorado, 3rd Ed.

Costa Rica, 1st Ed.

Cruises '95-'96

Delaware/Maryland, 2nd Ed.

England '96

Florida '96

France '96

Germany '96

Greece, 1st Ed.

Honolulu/Waikiki/Oahu, 4th Ed.

Ireland, 1st Ed.

Italy '96

Jamaica/Barbados, 2nd Ed.

Japan, 3rd Ed.

Maui, 1st Ed.

Mexico '96

Montana/Wyoming, 1st Ed.

Nepal, 3rd Ed.

New England '96

New Mexico, 3rd Ed.

New York State '94-'95

Nova Scotia/New Brunswick/Prince
  Edward Island, 1st Ed.

Portugal, 14th Ed.

Prague & the Best of the Czech Republic,
  1st Ed.

Puerto Rico '95-'96

Puerto Vallarta/Manzanillo/Guadalajara,
  3rd Ed.

Scandinavia, 16th Ed.

Scotland, 3rd Ed.

South Pacific, 5th Ed.

Spain, 16th Ed.

Switzerland, 7th Ed.

Thailand, 2nd Ed.

U.S.A., 4th Ed.

Utah, 1st Ed.

Virgin Islands, 3rd Ed.

Virginia, 3rd Ed.

Washington/Oregon, 6th Ed.

Yucatan '95-'96

FROMMER'S FRUGAL TRAVELER'S GUIDES

(Dream vacations at down-to-earth prices)

Australia on $45 '95-'96

Berlin from $50, 3rd Ed.

Caribbean from $60, 1st Ed.

Costa Rica/Guatemala/Belize on $35, 3rd Ed.

Eastern Europe on $30, 5th Ed.

England from $50, 21st Ed.

Europe from $50 '96

Greece from $45, 6th Ed.

Hawaii from $60, 30th Ed.

Ireland from $45, 16th Ed.

Israel from $45, 16th Ed.

London from $60 '96

Mexico from $35 '96

New York on $70 '94-'95

New Zealand from $45, 6th Ed.

Paris from $65 '96

South America on $40, 16th Ed.

Washington, D.C. from $50 '96

FROMMER'S COMPLETE CITY GUIDES

(Comprehensive guides to sightseeing, dining, and accommodations in all price ranges)

Amsterdam, 8th Ed.

Athens, 10th Ed.

Atlanta & the Summer Olympic Games '96

Bangkok, 2nd Ed.

Berlin, 3rd Ed.

Boston '96

Chicago '96
Denver/Boulder/Colorado Springs, 2nd Ed.
Disney World/Orlando '96
Dublin, 2nd Ed.
Hong Kong, 4th Ed.
Las Vegas '96
London '96
Los Angeles '96
Madrid/Costa del Sol, 2nd Ed.
Mexico City, 1st Ed.
Miami '95-'96
Minneapolis/St. Paul, 4th Ed.
Montreal/Quebec City, 8th Ed.
Nashville/Memphis, 2nd Ed.
New Orleans '96
New York City '96

Paris '96
Philadelphia, 8th Ed.
Rome, 10th Ed.
St. Louis/Kansas City, 2nd Ed.
San Antonio/Austin, 1st Ed.
San Diego, 4th Ed.
San Francisco '96
Santa Fe/Taos/Albuquerque '96
Seattle/Portland, 4th Ed.
Sydney, 4th Ed.
Tampa/St. Petersburg, 3rd Ed.
Tokyo, 4th Ed.
Toronto, 3rd Ed.
Vancouver/Victoria, 3rd Ed.
Washington, D.C. '96

FROMMER'S FAMILY GUIDES

(Guides to family-friendly hotels, restaurants, activities, and attractions)

California with Kids
Los Angeles with Kids
New York City with Kids

San Francisco with Kids
Washington, D.C. with Kids

FROMMER'S WALKING TOURS

(Memorable strolls through colorful and historic neighborhoods, accompanied by detailed directions and maps)

Berlin
Chicago
England's Favorite Cities
London, 2nd Ed.
Montreal/Quebec City
New York, 2nd Ed.

Paris, 2nd Ed.
San Francisco, 2nd Ed.
Spain's Favorite Cities
Tokyo
Venice
Washington, D.C., 2nd Ed.

FROMMER'S AMERICA ON WHEELS

(Guides for travelers who are exploring the USA by car, featuring a brand-new rating system for accommodations and full-color road maps)

Arizona and New Mexico
California and Nevada

Florida
Mid-Atlantic

FROMMER'S SPECIAL-INTEREST TITLES

Arthur Frommer's Branson!
Arthur Frommer's New World of Travel,
  5th Ed.
Frommer's America's 100 Best-Loved
  State Parks
Frommer's Caribbean Hideaways, 7th Ed.
Frommer's Complete Hostel Vacation Guide
  to England, Scotland & Wales

Frommer's National Park Guide, 29th Ed.
USA Sports Traveler's and TV Viewer's
  Golf Tournament Guide
USA Sports Minor League Baseball Book
USA Today Golf Atlas

FROMMER'S BEST BEACH VACATIONS

(The top places to sun, stroll, shop, stay, play, party, and swim, with each beach rated for beauty, swimming, sand, and amenities)

California
Carolinas/Georgia
Florida
Hawaii

Mid-Atlantic from New York to Washington, D.C.
New England

FROMMER'S BED & BREAKFAST GUIDES

(Selective guides with four-color photos and full description of the best inns in each region)

California
Caribbean
Great American Cities
Hawaii
Mid-Atlantic

New England
Pacific Northwest
Rockies
Southeast States
Southwest

FROMMER'S IRREVERENT GUIDES

(Wickedly honest guides for sophisticated travelers and those who want to be)

Amsterdam
Chicago
London

Manhattan
New Orleans
San Francisco

FROMMER'S DRIVING TOURS

(Four-color photos and detailed maps outlining spectacular scenic driving routes)

Australia
Austria
Britain
Florida
France
Germany
Ireland

Italy
Scandinavia
Scotland
Spain
Switzerland
U.S.A.

FROMMER'S BORN TO SHOP

(The ultimate travel guides for discriminating shoppers from cut-rate to couture)

Great Britain
Hong Kong

London
New York

FROMMER'S FOOD LOVER'S COMPANIONS

(Lavishly illustrated guides to regional specialties, restaurants, gourmet shops, markets, local wines, and more)

France
Italy